RECORDS

OF THE

COLONY AND PLANTATION

OF

NEW HAVEN,

FROM 1638 TO 1649.

TRANSCRIBED AND EDITED IN ACCORDANCE WITH A RESOLUTION OF THE GENERAL ASSEMBLY OF CONNECTICUT.

WITH OCCASIONAL NOTES AND AN APPENDIX.

By CHARLES J. HOADLY, M. A.

State Librarian of Conn., Member of the Conn. Hist. Soc., Cor. Memb. N. E. Hist. Gen. Soc.

HARTFORD:
PRINTED BY CASE, TIFFANY AND COMPANY,
FOR THE EDITOR.
1857.

At a General Assembly of the State of Connecticut, holden at New Haven in said State, on the first Wednesday of May, in the year of our Lord one thousand eight hundred and fifty-six:

Resolved, That the secretary be authorized to purchase for the use of the state, two hundred and fifty copies of the proposed publication of the Records of the Colony of New Haven, prior to the union with Connecticut, transcribed and edited by Charles J. Hoadly, Esq. *Provided,* that such publication shall be authenticated by the official certificate of the secretary, as a true copy of the original record; *and provided, also,* that the expense of the same shall not exceed two dollars and fifty cents per volume.

Resolved, That the copies so purchased be distributed as follows; one copy to the town clerk of each town in this state, to be preserved in his office for the use of the town; one copy to the governor, and to each of the state officers of this state; one copy to the governor of each of the several states and territories of the United States, to be deposited in their several state libraries; one copy to the library of congress; one copy to the Smithsonian Institute; one copy to each of the colleges of this state; twenty-five copies to Mr. Alexander Vattemare for international exchange; and the remainder of the said two hundred and fifty copies to be deposited in the office of the secretary, subject to the disposal of the general assembly.

INTRODUCTION.

THE original manuscript, of which the present volume is intended to be, as nearly as practicable, a reproduction, is a large folio of seventeen by eleven inches in size, containing about two hundred and fifty pages. It was evidently written with some care, and the chirography of the whole might be called, for the period, superior, more particularly so that of Thomas Fugill, the first secretary, although it is more abundant in contractions and abbreviations than that of Richard Perry or Francis Newman, his successors.

Many years before the employment of the volume in this country as a Record Book for New Haven Colony, five pages of it had been used, by some great merchant in London, as a Day Book or Journal, and it thus begins,—"Laus Deo, In London, the 6th of January, Anno Dominæ 1608." Who the merchant was to whom it belonged does not appear, and is unknown; it has been a tradition, however, that it was "Governor Eaton's Ledger," but as Eaton was born in 1590, it would hardly seem probable that a youth of eighteen should carry on business, both foreign and domestic, to so great an extent as would appear to be indicated by the entries in this book.

At their first settlement, though within the limits of the old Connecticut Patent, the plantations of New Haven, Guilford and Milford, intended to be, if possible, separate and distinct governments, but finding themselves singly too weak, early in the spring of the year 1643, they confederated with New Haven, which had already by the purchase and settlement of Stamford, Yennycock or Southold, and Totoket or Branford, become the most considerable in size and influence, and thus was formed the Jurisdiction of New Haven.

The present volume contains the records of the Colony of New Haven while it remained distinct, the beginning of the records of the Jurisdiction, and the records of the Town or Plantation up to the year 1650.

From April, 1644, to May, 1653, the records of the Jurisdiction are lost, save that in this volume we have the proceedings of a Court of Magistrates, June 14th, 1646, and a Court of Election, October 27th, 1646. How long these records have been missing we are ignorant, but may conjecture that they have been so for a period of about a century. That Dr. Trumbull did not have access to them, while collecting materials for the history of Connecticut, that is from about 1770 to 1774, is evident upon an examination of that work, and had their disappearance then been recent, we should suppose that there would have been made some reference to the fact, either by him or by the General Assembly in their resolution of May, 1772.

The dates of some meetings of the Jurisdiction Courts for this period, collected from the records of the United Colonies and from those of the town of Guilford, are inserted in their chronological order in the form of notes.

In a note at page 463 is found an account of some of the proceedings of a General Court for the Jurisdiction, May 30th, 1649, which is taken from Thompson's History of Long Island, but I have thus far been unable to learn the source whence the author of that work obtained the citation. The editor has been informed that Mr. Thompson's papers afford no clue, and that it is not found in the records of the town of Southold, L. I. It is to be hoped that the extract may lead to the discovery of the missing volume.

In May, 1772, perhaps at the instance of Governor Trumbull, who, as the venerable historian of Connecticut assures us, had a most thorough acquaintance with the history of the colony, the General Assembly passed the following resolution:

"Whereas the first antient Book of Records of this Colony remaining in the Secretary's office, and the first Records of the Jurisdiction of New Haven, in the office of the Town Clerk of the Town of New Haven, are much worn and decayed, and by constant use in danger of being totally ruined, Resolved by this Assembly, that the Secretary be directed and he is hereby directed to procure the said Records to be fairly transcribed into some proper book or books to be by him procured for that purpose, and laid before this Assembly to be compared and duly authenticated for common use, to the end that the said original ancient Records may be safely preserved and used only upon special and important occasions. The secretary is also directed to receive into his hands and deposit in his office the antient Book of Records of the Jurisdiction of New Haven, now remaining in the office of the clerk of the County Court of New Haven County, who is also hereby requested to deliver the same to him accordingly, that the same may remain for publick use in the publick archives of the Colony."*

The first volume of the Connecticut Records was copied and presented to the Legislature for authentication in May, 1773, but why the New Haven Records were not then also transcribed we are not informed.

The authorities of the town of New Haven have within a few years taken commendable care for the preservation and safe keeping of this first volume of their Records, by causing a copy to be made, and by enclosing the original in a copper box.

In executing the trust of editing these Records, accuracy has been the chief thing aimed at, and to obtain this neither time nor labor have been spared; every page has been carefully compared by the editor with the original; contractions and abbreviations have been followed, but with regard to the use of capital letters and marks of punctuation, it has not been deemed necessary strictly to adhere to the copy; still, however, this liberty has been used with caution, and the editor has not knowingly altered the sense of any passage thereby,

* Colony Records, vol. xi, p. 105.

preferring in all instances where such might be the case, to let the original punctuation prevail.

Changes in the original arrangement of the records have been made in two instances only, one by placing the articles of agreement with the native Indian proprietors at the beginning of the volume, and the other by transferring a list of names recorded on page [138] to page 140 of this volume. The paging of the original has been preserved and will be found in brackets at the side of the page.

Some redundancies in the original have been printed in italics. Where the original has in some places become obliterated or worn away, the missing words, supplied by the editor, are included in brackets. In other cases where words or letters have been omitted or passages of doubtful import occur, the editor feels obliged to charge the fault to those who originally wrote the manuscript.

In citing the records of the United Colonies, it has been found more convenient in general, to cite from the cotemporary manuscript copy preserved in the Secretary's office than to make use of Hazard, since it is known that in the latter many errors occur. In citing Trumbull's history, the edition printed at Hartford in 1797 has been used, and in Savage's Winthrop, though the edition of 1853 has been used, yet the pages of the former edition of 1825–6 are cited.

In conclusion, the editor expresses his thanks and acknowledges his obligations to the General Assembly of Connecticut, by whose liberality the expenses of publication have been in part defrayed; to the Connecticut Historical Society, for their encouragement of the work; to the late Town Clerk, Alfred Terry, Esq., and to the Selectmen of New Haven, for the readiness and courtesy with which they afforded every facility requested for the accomplishment of the same; to Henry White, Esquire, for many valuable suggestions and other important aid, which his very extensive and accurate information regarding the early history of New Haven enabled him to furnish; to Hon. Francis De Witt, Secretary of the Commonwealth of Massachusetts, and to E. B. O'Callaghan, Esq., M. D., of Albany, for copies of documents remaining in the archives of their respective States; to Ralph D. Smith, Esq., of Guilford, Henry Onderdonk, Jr., Esq., of

Jamaica, L. I., and Rev. E. Whitaker, of Southold, L. I., and to others who in various ways have given the publication their countenance or assistance.

To Henry White, Esquire, I am indebted also for the copies and abstracts of wills and inventories found, as notes, in this volume.

Should the present volume meet with sufficient encouragement, the editor proposes to continue it, by the publication of the Records of New Haven Jurisdiction from May, 1653, to the union with Connecticut in 1664–5, together with the New Haven code of 1656.

C. J. H.

State Library, Hartford,
April 14, 1857.

Most of the abbreviations used in this volume require no explanation; the letter m or n with a dash or circumflex over it, m̃ or ñ, was frequently used for the double consonant; a similar mark placed over a vowel indicates the omission of a consonant, generally m or n, thus, com̃ō, for common; the letter c̃ is used for ti, thus, condic̃on, for condition; the letter ꝑ shows the omission of letters, of which r was generally one, thus, ꝑson for person, ꝑꝑ for proper. A caret, ^ , denotes a blank in the original record.

INDIAN DEEDS

OF

THE PLANTATION OF NEW HAVEN.

[These Articles of Agreement were recorded by Secretary Gibbard, at a date subsequent to the records contained in this volume, upon some leaves which had been left blank between pages 50 and 62.]

Articles of agreement betweene Theophilus Eaton & John Davenport & others, English planters att Quinopiocke on the one partye & Momaugin ye Indian Sachem of Quinopiocke & Sugcogisin, Quesaquauch, Caroughood, Wesaucucke & others of his counsell on the other partye, made & concluded the 24th of Novemb^{r} 1638. Thomas Stanton being interpreter.

That hee ye s^{d} sachem, his counsell & company doe jointly profess, affirme & coven^{t}, [th]at he ye s^{d} Momaugin is the sole sachem of Quinopiocke, & hath an absolute and independant power to give, alien, dispose or sell, all or any part of the lands in Quinopiocke, & that though he have a soñ now absent, yet neither his s^{d} soñ, nor any other pson whatsoever hath any right title or interest in any part of the s^{d} lands, soe that whatsoever he, ye forenamed sachem, his counsell & ye rest of ye Indians present doe & conclude, shall stand firme & inviolable against all claimes & psons whatsoever.—

Secondly ye s^{d} sachem, his counsell & company, amongst which there was a squaw sachem called Shampishuh sister to ye sachem, whoe either had or p^{r}tended some interest in some part of ye land, remembring & acknowledging the heavy taxes & eminent dangers wch they lately felt & feared from ye Pequotts, Mohaucks & other Indians, in regard of which they durst not stay in their country, but were forced to flie, & to seeke shelter under the English at Coñecticutt, and observing ye safety & ease y^{t} other Indians enjoy neare ye English, of which benefitt they have had a comfortable tast already since the English began to build & plant at Quinopiocke, which wth all thankfullnes they now acknowledged. They jointly & freely gave & yeilded up all y^{r} right, title & interest to all ye land, rivers & ponds, trees with all ye libertyes & appurtenances belonging unto ye same in Quinopiocke to ye utmost of their bounds East, West, North, South unto Theophilus Eaton, John Davenport & others, the p^{r}sent English planters there, & to their heires & assignes for ever, desiring from y^{m}. ye s^{d} English planters to receive such a portion of ground on the East side of the Harbour towards ye fort at ye mouth of ye river of Coñecticott as might be sufficient for them, being but few in number, to plant in; and yet within these limitts to be hereafter assigned to them, they did coven^{t} & freely yeild up unto ye s^{d} English all the meadow ground lieing therein, with full liberty to chuse & cut downe what timber they please, for any use whatsoever, without any question, licence or consent to be asked from them ye s^{d} Indians, and if, after their portion & place be limited & set out by the English as above, they ye s^{d} Indians shall desire to remove to any other place within Quinopiocke bounds, but without ye limitts assigned them, that they doe it not without leave, neither setting up any wigwam, nor breaking up any ground to plant corne, till first it be sett [ou]t & appointed by ye forenamed English planters for them.

Thirdly ye s^{d} sachem, his counsell & company desireing liberty to hunt & fish [withi]n the bounds of Quinopiocke now given & graunted to the English as before, doe [hereby] jo[in]tly coven^{t} & bind themselves to sett noe traps neare any place where y^{e} [ ] whether horses, [ox]en, kine, calves, sheep, goates, hoggs or any sort [

to take] any fish out of any ware belonging to any English, nor to doe any thing neare any such ware as to di[sturb] or affright away any fish to ye p^{r}judice of such ware or wares; & that upon discovery of any inconveni[en]cy growing to ye English by the Indians disorderly hunting, their hunting shalbe regulated

* A line or two torn off.

and limited for the p^r^venting of any inconvenience, & yet with as litle dam̃age to ye Indians in their hunting as may be.

Fourthly, ye s^d^ sachem, his counsell & company doe hereby covenant and bind themselves y^t^ none of them shall henceforth hanker about any of ye English houses at any time when the English use to meete about the publique worship of God; nor on ye Lords day henceforward bee seene within ye compass of ye English towne, beareing any burdens, or offring to truck with ye English for any com̃odity whatsoever, & y^t^ none of y^m^ henceforward without leave, open any latch belonging to any English mens dore, nor stay in any English house after warneing that he should leave the same, nor doe any violence, wrong, or injury to y^e^ ꝑson of ye English whether man, woman or child, upon any p^r^tence whatsoever, and if the English of this plantation, by y^m^selves or cattle, doe any wrong or damage to ye Indians, upon complaint, just recompence shalbe made by ye English; and y^t^ none of y^m^ henceforward use or take any English mans boate or canoe of what kind soever, from ye place where it was fastened or layd, without leave from the owner first had & obtayned, nor y^t^ they come into ye English towne wth bowes & arrowes, or any other weapons whatsoever in number above 6 Indyans soe armed at a time.

Fiftly ye s^d^ sachem, his counsell & company doe truly covenant & bind y^m^selves y^t^ if any of y^m^ shall hereafter kill or hurt any English cattle of w^t^ sort soever, though casually or negligently, they shall give full satisfaction for the loss or dam̃age as the English shall judge equall, But if any of y^m^ for any respect, wilfully doe kill or hurt any of the English cattle, upon proofe they shall pay ye double valew, And if, at any time, any of them find any of the English cattle straying or lost in the woods, they shall bring them backe to the English plantation, & a moderate price or recompence shalbe allowed for their paynes, provided, if it can be proved y^t^ any of y^m^ drove away any of ye English cattle wheresoever they find them, further from ye English plantation to make an incre[ase] or advantage, or recompence for his paynes finding or bringing y^m^ back, they shall in any such case pay dam̃ages for such dealings.

Sixthly, the number of ye Quinopyocke Indyans, me[n] or youth growne to stature fit for service being forty seven at p^r^sent, they doe covenant and bind y^m^selves not to receive, or admitt any other Indians amongst them without leave first had & obtayned from ye English, & that they will not, at any time hereafter, entertaine or harbo^r^ any that are enemies to ye English, but will p^r^sently ap^r^hend such & deliver y^m^ to y^e^

English, and if they know or heare of any plott by ye Indyans or others against ye English they will forthwith discover & make ye same knowne to y^m^, & in case they doe not, to be accounted as partyes in ye plott, and to be proceeded against as such.

Lastly ye s^d^ sachem, his counsell & company doe hereby promise truly & carefully to observe & keepe all & every one of these articles of agreem^t^, & if any of y^m^ offend in any of ye p^r^misses, they jointly hereby subject & submitt such offendo^r^ or offendo^r^s to ye consideration, censure & punishm^t^ of the English magestrate or officers appointed among them for governem^t^ without expecting y^t^ ye English should first advise with y^m^ about it, yet in any such case of punishm^t^, if the s^d^ sachem shall desire to know the reason & equity of such ꝑceedings, hee shall truly be informed of the same.

The former article being read & interp^r^ted to y^m^, they by way of exposition desired y^t^ in ye sixth article it might be added, that if any of the English cattle be killed or hurt casually, or negligently, & proofe made it was done by some of the Quinopiocke Indyans, they will make satisfaction, or if done by any other Indyans in their sight, if they doe not discover it, & if able to bring ye offendo^r^ to ye English they wilbe accounted & dealt with as guilty.

In consideration of all which, they desire from ye English, that if at any time hereafter they be affrighted in their dwellings assigned by the English unto y^m^ as before, they may repayre to the English plantation for shelter, & that ye English will there in a just cause endeavo^r^ to defend y^m^ from wronge But in any quarrell or warres which they shall undertake, or have wth other Indyans, upon any occasion w^t^soever, they will mañage their affayres by y^m^selves without expecting any ayd from the English.

And the English planters before mentioned accepting and graunting according to ye teño^r^ of the p^r^mises, doe further of their owne accord, by way of free & thankefull retribution, give un[to] ye s^d^ sachem, counsell & company of ye Quinopiocke Indians, twelve coates of English trucking cloath, twelve alcumy spoones, twelve hatchetts, twelve hoes, two dozen of knives, twelve porengers & foure cases of French knives and sizers; All which being thankfully accepted by y^e^ afores^d^ & y^e^ agreements in all points perfected; for rattification & full confirmation of the same, the Sachem, his counsell & sister, to these p^r^sents have sett to their hands or markes y^e^ day & year above written.

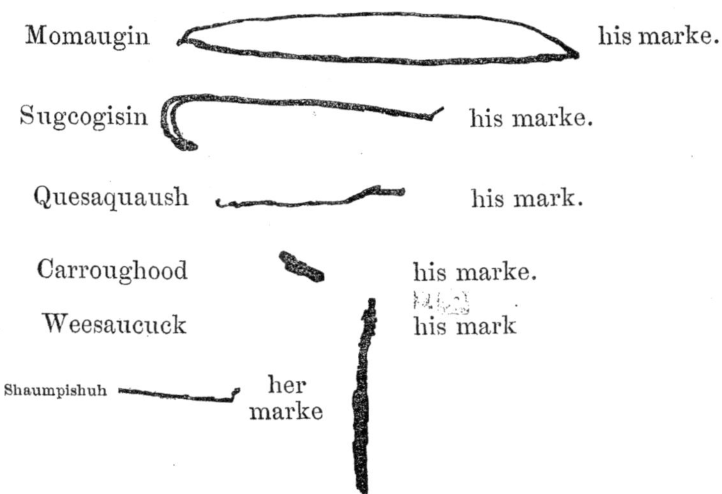

I, Thomas Stanton, being interpreter in this treaty, doe hereby profess in y^{e} p^{r}sence of God, y^{t} I have fully acquainted the Indyans with y^{e} substance of every article, & truly returned their answer & consent to the same, according to ye tenno^{r} of the foregoeing writeing, the truth of which, if lawfully called, I shall readily confirme by my oath at any time.

Thomas Stanton.

Articles of agreem^{t} betwixt Theophilus Eaton, John Davenport, & sundry other English planters at Quinnypiock on ye one part, and Mantowese sonne of an Indyan sachem liveing att Mattabezeck, and nephew to Sequiñ on ye other part, made & concluded the 11th day of Decemb^{r} 1638.

First ye s^{d} Mantowese in p^{r}sence & wth allowance and consent of Sawseunck an Indyan wch came in company wth him, doth profess, affirme and covenant, to & wth ye s^{d} Theophilus Eaton, John Davenport & others above, that ye land on both sides the river of Quinnypiock from ye Northerly bounds ofy^{e} land lately purchased by the s^{d} English of ye Quinnypiock Indyans, namely from ye pond in ye great meadow, about two miles above ye great hill, to ye head of ye river at ye great playne toward ye plantations settled by ye English upon ye river of Quintecutt Southerly, which is about tenn miles in length from north to south, the bounds of which land ruñ alsoe eight miles easterly from ye river of Quinnypiock toward ye river of Quintecutt, and five miles westerly towards Hudsons river, doth truely & solely belong to him ye sd Mantowese in right of his deceased mother, to whom ye sd land did appertaine, & from whom it justly descends upon him as his inheritance, soe yt he hath an absolute & independant power to give, alien, dispose or sell all or any part of ye sd land, as he shall think good; and yt neither his sd father, nor any other pson whatsoever, have any right, title or interest in any part of ye land described and limited as above, whereby he or any other may hereafter justly question what ye sd Mantowese now doth, or lay any clayme to any part of ye sd land now disposed of by him.

Secondly the sd Mantowese being fully acquainted wth ye agreemts lately passed betwixt ye sd English planters & ye sachem of Quinnypiock, his counsell & company, did freely, of his owne accord, upon full & serious deliberation, give, grant & yeild up all his right, title and interest to all ye land mentioned and bounded as above, with all the rivers, ponds, trees, and all liberties & appurtenances whatsoever belonging to ye same, to the sd Theophilus Eaton, John Davenport and other English planters att Quinnypiock, and to their heyres & assignes for ever, desireing from them, the sd English planters, to receive such a small portion of land by the rivers side about two miles beyond ye tree over ye river, in the passage from hence towards ye townes at Quintecutt, as may be sufficient for his small company, being but tenn men in number, besides women and children, wch portion of land they desire may hereafter, upon a view, be assigned, appointed and limited unto them by ye sd English planters, reserveing alsoe to himselfe and his forenamed company, liberty in fitt seasons & due manner without prjudice to ye English, to hunt, & fish, & kill beaver, yet therein alsoe to be regulated by ye sd English upon discovery of any annoyance, as the Quinnypiock Indyans are in that case.

Lastly the said Theophilus Eaton, John Davenport &c accepting from Mantowese this free gift of his hand as above, doe by way of thankfull retribution, give unto him eleven coates made of trucking cloth, and one coate for himselfe of English cloth, made up after the English mañer, wch being thankfully accepted by the sd Mantowese, and the agreements in all points pfected, for ratification, and full confirmation of ye same, Mantowese and Sawseunck have hereunto sett their hands or markes the day and year before written.

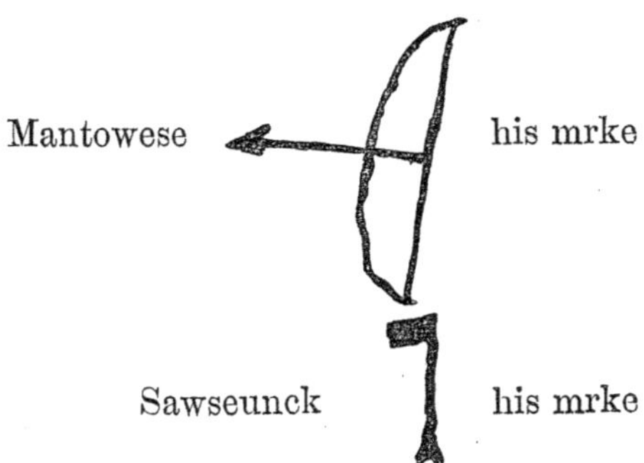

Mantowese his mrke

Sawseunck his mrke

I, John Clarke, being interpreter in this treatie, doe hereby professe in the p^{r}sence of God that I have fully acquainted the Indyans with the substance of every article, to ye wch they have freely agreed, that is to say y^{t} Mantowese have given to Mr. Davenport & Mr. Eaton all his land wch he had by his deceased mother, wch he saith is from ye head of ye great playne to the pond wch he professe to be his, & promise to make it good to o^{r} English, & for this hee is satisfyed with twelve coates, onely reserve a piece of land by the river for his men which are 10 and many squaws, to plant in, & when o^{r} cowes come there what harme their doggs doe to o^{r} cattle, they will satisfye for, and we for what harme o^{r} hoggs doe to them in corne, & as for hunting & fishing, to be free to them as o^{r}selves, provided o^{r} cattle suffer not by them, & with these particulars they are acquainted, & doe freely consent to them, as their marke wittness, the truth of which, if lawfully called, I shall readily confirme by my oath at any time

per me John Clarke

We Robert Coggswell, Roger Knapp and James Love, doe hereby renounce all right to any & every part of the forementioned land.

Wittnes our hands hereunto

Robert Coggswell

James Love

Roger Knapp his mrke.

THE NAMES OF ALL THE FREEMEN

OF THE

COURTE OF NEWHAVEN.

[In the handwriting of Thomas Fugill.]

Mr. Theophilus Eaton.
Mr. John Davenport.
Mr. Robt Newman.
Mr. Math : Gilbert.
Thomas Fugill.
John Ponderson
Jer. Dixon.
Mr. Nath : Turner
Mr. Eze : Cheurs
William Andrewes.
Mr. Sam : Eaton
John Clarke
John Chapman
Robt Seeley
Tho : Geffreyes
Rich Hull
Tho : Kimberley
Mr. Tho : Gregson
John Mosse
Adam Nicholls
Abra : Bell
William Thorpe
Mr. Francis Newman
Andrew Low
Tho : Mounson

Mr. ^ James
Mr. Geo : Lamberton
^ Nash
Mr. Rich : Perry
William Peck
Andrew Hull
Goodm̃ Shirman
Goodm̃ Gibbs
Goodm̃ Liurmoore
Tho Ellsey
Mr. Joshua Attwater
Antony Tompson
Edw Wigglesworth
John Vincent
Mr. John Wakeman
John Benham
Mr. Stephen Goodyear
John Potter
Mr. Jasper Craine
Andrew Warde } Rip :
Francis Bell }
Rich : Miles
Roger Allen
Mr. Richard Malbone
Wiłł Iues

Francis Browne	Bro : Lamson
John Nash	Captaine Underhill
Goodmā Davis	Rich : Gildersleeve
Mr. Gibberd	Math : Moulthrop
Goodman Abbott	Goodm̃ : Preston
Sam: Whitehead	Wiłł Tompson
John Brockett	Hen : Lendall
Richard Law	Wiłł Fowler
Mathew Camfield	Joh : Cowper
Tristram Rayner	Joseph Nash

NEW HAVEN COLONY RECORDS.

[In the handwriting of Thomas Fugill.]

[1] The 4th day of the 4th moneth called June 1639, all the free planters assembled together in a ge[neral] meetinge* to consult about settling ciuill Gouernmt according to God, and about the nominatiō of persons thatt might be founde by consent of all fittest in all respects for the foundacō worke of a church w[hich] was intend to be gathered in Quinipieck. After solemne invocatiō of the name of God in prayer [for] the presence and help of his speritt, and grace in those weighty businesses, they were reminded of t[he] busines whereabout they mett (viz) for the establishmt of such ciuill order as might be most p[leas]ing vnto God, and for the chuseing the fittest men for the foundacō worke of a church to be gather[ed.] For the better inableing them to discerne the minde of God and to agree accordingly concerning the establishmt of ciuill order, Mr. John Davenport propounded diuers quæres to them publiquely praying them to consider seriously in the presence and feare of God the weight of the busines they met about, and nott to be rash or sleight in giue-ing their votes to things they understoode nott, butt to digest fully and throughly whatt should be propounded to them, and without respect to men as they should be satisfied and pswaded in their owne mindes to giue their answers in such sort as they would be willing they should stand upon recorde for posterity.

This being earnestly prssed by Mr. Davenport, Mr. Robt.

* This meeting took place according to tradition, in a large barn belonging to Mr. Newman. Dr. Bacon, Hist. Disc. 20, has shown that it was most probably Robert Newman's, and pointed out its location as being near Temple st., between Elm and Grove streets.

Newman was intreated to write in carracters and to read distinctly and audibly in the hearing of all the people whatt was propounded and accorded on that itt might appeare thatt all consented to matters propounded according to words written by him.

QUÆR. 1. Whether the Scripturs doe holde forth a perfect rule for the directiō and gouernmt of all men in all duet[ies] wch they are to performe to God and men as well in the gourmt of famylyes and com̃onwealths as in matters of the chur.

This was assented vnto by all, no man dissenting as was expressed by holding up of hands. Afterward itt was read our to them thatt they might see in whatt words their vote was expressed: They againe expressed their consent thereto by holdeing up their hands, no man dissenting.

QUÆR. 2. Whereas there was a cout solemnly made by the whole assembly of freeplanters of this plantatiō the first day of extraordenary humiliatiō wch we had after wee came together, thatt as in matters thatt concerne the gathering and ordering of a chur. so likewise in all publique offices wch concerne ciuill order, as choyce of magistrates and officers, makeing and repealing of lawes, devideing allottmts of inheritance and all things of like nature we would all of vs be ordered by those rules wch the scripture holds forth to vs. This couent was called a plantatiō couent to distinguish itt frō [a] chur. couent wch could nott att thatt time be made, a chur. nott being then gathered, butt was deferred till a chur. might be gathered according to God: Itt was demaunded whether all the free planters doe holde themselues bound by thatt couenant in all businesses of thatt nature wch are expressed in the couent to submitt themselves to be ordered by the rules held forth in the scripture.

This also was assented vnto by all, and no man gainesaid itt, and they did testefie the same by holde[ing] vp their hands both when itt was first propounded, and confirmed the same by holdeing vp their hands when itt was read vnto them in publique, John Clarke being absent when the couent w[as] made, doth now manefest his consent to itt, allso Richard

Beach, Andrew Low, Goodm̃ Banister, Ar[thur] Halbidge, John Potter, Robt Hill, John Brockett and John Johnson, these persons being nott [ad]mitted planters when the couen[t] was made doth now express their consent to itt.

QUÆR. 3. Those who have desired to be receiued as free planters, and are settled in the plantatiō wth a purp[ose,] resolutiō and desire thatt they may be admitted into chur. fellow[p] according to Christ as soone [as] God shall fitt them therevnto: were desired to express itt by holdeing vp of hands: Accordingly a[ll] did expresse this to be their desire and purpose by holdeing vp their hands twice, (viz) both att the [pro]posall of itt, and after when these written words were read vnto them.

QUÆR. 4. All the free planters were called vpō to expresse whether they held themselues bound to esta[blish] such ciuill order as might best conduce to the secureing of the purity and peace of the ordina[nces] to themselues and their posterity according to God. In answ. herevnto they expressed by hold[ing] vp their hands twice as before, thatt they held them selues bound to establish such [civil order] as might best conduce to the ends aforesaid.

Then Mr. Davenport declared vnto them by the scripture whatt kinde of persons might best be trusted wth matters of gouerm[t], and by sundry argum[ts] from scripture proued thatt such men as were discrib[ed] in Exod. 18. 2. Deut. 1. 13, wth Deut. 17. 15, and1. Cor. 6: 1 to 7, ought to be intrusted by them, seeing [they] were free to cast themselues into thatt mould and forme of comoñ wealth wch appeareth best for them in referrence to the secureing of the pure and peaceable injoym[t] of all Christ his ordinances [in] the church according to God, wherevnto they have bound themselues as hath beene acknowledged. Having thus said he satt downe, praying the company freely to consider whether they would haue [it] voted att this time or nott: After some space of silence Mr. Theophilus Eaton answered itt mi[ght] be voted, and some others allso spake to the same purpose, none att all opposeing itt. Then itt was propounded to vote.

QUÆR. 5. Whether Free Burgesses shalbe chosen out of chur.

members they thatt are in the foundat[ion] worke of the church being actually free burgesses, and to chuse to themselues out of the li[ke] estate of church fellowp and the power of chuseing magistrates and officers from among themselues and the power off makeing and repealing lawes according to the worde, and the devideing of inheritances and decideing of differences thatt may arise, and all the buisnesses of like nature are to be transacted by those free burgesses.

[2] This was putt to vote and agreed vnto by the lifting vp of hands twice as in the former itt was done. Then one man* stood vp after the vote was past, and expressing his dissenting from the rest in p[t] yett grantinge 1. That magistrates should be men fearing God. 2. Thatt the church is the company whence ordenaryly such men may be expected. 3. Thatt they that chuse them ought to be men fearing God: onely att this he stuck, That free planters ought nott to giue this power out of their hands: Another stood vp and answered that in this case nothing was done but wth their consent. The former answered thatt all the free planters ought to resume this power into their owne hands againe if things were nott orderly carryed. Mr. Theophilus Eaton answered thatt in all places they chuse committyes, in like manner the companyes of London chuse the liueryes by whom the publique magistrates are chosen. In this the rest are not wronged because they expect in time to be of y[e] liu[r]y themselues, and to haue the same power. Some others intreated the form[r] to giue his argum[ts] and reasons wherevpō he dissented. He refused to doe itt and said they might nott rationally demaund itt, seeing he lett the vote passe on freely and did nott speake till after itt was past, because he would nott hinder whatt they agreed upō. Then Mr. Davenport, after a short relatiō of some form[r] passages betweene them two about this quest. prayed the company thatt nothing might be concluded by them in this weighty quest. butt whatt themselues were perswaded to be agreeing wth the minde of God and they had heard whatt had beene said since the voteing, intreated them againe to consider of itt, and putt itt againe to vote as before.—Againe all of them by

---

* Probably Rev. Samuel Eaton, see Mather Mag., B. iii, pt. 4, ch. 1.

holding vp their hands did shew their consent as before, And some of them professed thatt whereas they did wauer before they came to the assembly they were now fully convinced thatt itt is the minde of God. One of them said that in the morning, before he came, reading Deut. 17. 15. he was convinced att home, another said thatt he came doubting to the assembly butt he blessed God by whatt had beene said he was now fully satisfied thatt the choyce of burgesses out of chur. members, and to intrust those w[t]h the power before spoken off is according to the minde of God reuealed in the scriptures. All haveing spoken their apprehensions, itt was agreed vpon, and Mr. Rob[t] Newmā was desired to write itt as an order wherevnto euery one thatt hereafter should be admitted here as planters should submitt and testefie the same by subscribeing their names to the order, namely, that church members onely shall be free burgesses, and thatt they onely shall chuse magistrates & officers among themselues to haue the power of transacting all the publique ciuill affayres of this Plantatiō, of makeing and repealing lawes, devideing of inheritances, decideing of differences thatt may arise and doeing all things or businesses of like nature.

This being thus settled as a foundamentall agreem[t] concerning ciuill gouernm[t]. Mr. Davenport proceeded to propound some things to consideracō aboute the gathering of a chur. And to prevent the blemishing of the first beginnings of the chur. worke, Mr. Davenport aduised thatt the names of such as were to be admitted might be publiquely propounded, to the end thatt they who were most approued might be chosen, for the towne being cast into seuerall priuate meetings wherein they thatt dwelt nearest together gaue their accounts one to another of Gods gracious worke vpon them, and prayed together and conferred to their mutuall edifficatiō, sundry of them had knowledg one of another, and in euery meeting some one was more approued of all then any other, For this reason, and to prevent scandalls, the whole company was intreated to consider whom they found fittest to nominate for this worke.

Quae. 6. Whether are you all willing and doe agree in this

thatt twelue men be chosen thatt their fitnesse for the foundacō worke may be tried, howeu[r] there may be more named yett itt may be in the[r] power who are chosen to reduce them to twelue, and itt be in the power of those twelue to chuse out of themselues seauen that shall be most approved of the major part to begin the church.

This was agreed vpō by consent of all as was expressed by holdeing vp of hands, and thatt so many as should be thought fitt for the foundacō worke of the church shall be propounded by the plantatiō, and written downe and passe w[t]hout exceptiō vnlesse they had giuen publique scandall or offence, yett so as in case of publique scandall or offence, euery one should haue liberty to propound their exceptiō att thatt time publiquely against any man that should be nominated when all their names should be writt downe, butt if the offence were priuate, thatt mens names might be tendered, so many as were offended were intreated to deale w[t]h the offender priuately, and if he gaue nott satisfactiō, to bring the matter to the twelue thatt they might consider of itt impartially and in the feare of God. The names of the persons nominated and agreed vpon were Mr. Theoph. Eaton, Mr. John Davenport, Mr. Rob[t]. Newman, Mr. Math. Gilbert, Mr. Richard Malbon, Mr. Nath: Turner, Eze: Cheu[r]s, Thomas Fugill, John Ponderson, William Andrewes, and Jer. Dixon. Noe exceptiō was brought against any of those in publique, except one about takeing an excessiue rate for meale w[c]h he sould to one of Pequanack in his need, w[c]h he confessed w[t]h griefe and declared thatt haueing beene smitten in heart and troubled in his conscience, he restored such a part of the price back againe w[t]h confessiō of his sin to the party as he thought himselfe bound to doe. And itt being feared thatt the report of the sin was heard farther th[an] the report of his satisfactiō, a course was concluded on to make the satisfactiō known to as many as heard of the sinn. Itt was also agreed vpō att the said meeting thatt if the persons aboue named did finde themselues straitened in the number of fitt men for the seauen, thatt itt should be free for them to take into tryal of fittnes such other as they should thinke meete, prouided thatt itt should be signified to the towne vpon the Lords day who they so take in, thatt eu^{ry} man may be satisfied of them according to the course formerly taken.

[3] Whereas there was a foundamentall agreem^{t} made in a generall meeting of all the free planters of this towne, on the 4th of the fowerth moneth called June, namely thatt church members onely shall be free burgesses, and they onely shall chuse among them selues magistrates and officers to ha[ve] the power of transacting all publique ciuill affayres of this plantatiō, of makeing and repeali[ng] lawes, devideing inherritances, decideing of differences thatt may arise, and doeing all things and businesses of like nature. Itt was therefore ordered by all the said free planters thatt all those thatt hereafter should be receiued as planters into this plantatiō should allso submitt to the said foundamentall agreem^{t}, and testifie the same by subscribeing their names vnder the names of the aforesaid planters as followeth.

Mr Theoph Eaton	John Cooper	John Johnson
Mr John Davenport	Jarvis Boykin	Edward Wiggleworth
Mr Sam: Eaton	John Chapman	John Clarke
Mr Robt Newmā	Tho: Kimberley	Sam. Whitehead
Mr Math Gilbert	John Benham	John Potter
Mr Nath Turner	Mr Wilkes	Arther Halbidge
Mr Rich. Malbon	Tho: Jeffreyes	Edward Banister
Mr Browninge	Robt. Seely	Will Potter
Mr Linge	Nicholas Elsey	John Mosse
Mr William Touttle	John Budd	John Charles
Mr Cheeuers	Rich. Hull	Richard Beach
Mr Perry	Will Preston	Tymothy Forde
Mr Craine	John Brockett	John Reader
Mr Fran: Newm̃	Jer Dixon	John Cogswell
Mr Tho: Yale	Robt. Hill	Mathew Hitchcock
Tho: Fugill	Andrew Low	Francis Hall
William Andrewes	Will Thorpe	Richard Osborne
Richard Beckley	John Ponderson	James Clarke

Andrew Hull	Geo: Smith	Andr. Messenger
Edward Patteson	John Peacock	Geo: Warde
Will Eues	Mathew Moulthrop	Lawrence Warde

[The following are autograph signatures.]

Stephen Goodyeare
Thomas Gregson
Thomas Nash
William Jeanes
Jno Evance
Thomas Munson
John Liuermore
Jeremy Whetnell
Luke Atkinson
Thomas Morris
William Russill
Beniamin Willmott
Thomas Powell
James Russell
Peter Browne
his
John **I** Tompson
marke
Abraham **3** Bell
John **S** Vincent
Tho: |—< Mitchell
John + Walker
Beniamin Pawle
Will **W** Gibbins
John Hall
Richard Merriman
Edw ▭ Chipperfield
Steuen Metcalfe
William Gibbard

Ralph Dayghton
William Peckke
Anthony Tompson
Christ. CT Todd
John Gibbes
John Nash
Adam **A** Nicholls
Tho **8** Beamont
Josua Atwater
Thomas Osborne
John Wakeman
William **W** Davis
Francis **N** Browne
Robert Pigg
Nath Merriman
Roger Alling
Henry **h** Peck
Marke Pierce
Theophilus Higginson
Dauid Atwater
Mathew Camfeld

[In the handwriting of Francis Newman.]

FREE MANS CHARGE

[4] Yow shall neither plott, practise nor consent to any evill or hurt against this Jurisdiction, or any ꝑte of it, or against the civill gouerment here established. And if you shall know any ꝑson, or ꝑsons w^{c}h intend, plott, or conspire any thing w^{c}h tends to the hurt or prejudice of the same, yow shall timely discouer the same to lawfull authority here established, and yow shall assist and bee helpfull in all the affaires of the Jurisdiction, and by all meanes shall promove the publique wellfare of the same, according to yor place, ability, and opꝑtunity, yow shall give due honno^{r} to the lawfull magistrats, and shall be obedient and subject to all the wholesome lawes and orderes, allready made, or w^{c}h shall be hereafter made, by lawfull authority afforesaid. And that both in yor p^{s}on and estate: and when yow shall be duely called to give yor vote or suffrage in any election, or touching any other matter, w^{c}h concerneth this common wealth, yow shall give it as in yor conscience yow shall judg may conduce to the best good of the same.

[In the handwriting of Thomas Fugill.]

[5] OCTOBER 25th 1639.

The Court being settled according to the foundamentall agreem^{t} made the 4th day of June 1639, consisting of those seauen onely who were in the foundacō of the church, namely Mr. Theoph. Eaton, Mr. John Davenport, Mr. Robt. Newman Mr. Math Gibbert,* Tho. Fugi[ll], John Ponderson, and Jerimy Dixon,† after solemne prayer vnto God did ꝑceede as followeth.

First all former power or trust for mannaging any publique affayres in this plantatiō, into whose hands soeu^{r} formerly cōmitted, was now abrogated and from henceforeward vtterly to cease.

Secondly all those thatt have beene receiued into the fellow^{pp} of this church since the gathering of itt, or who being members of other approved church esoffered themselues, were admitted as members of this court. Namely Mr. Nathaniell Turner, Wiłł Andrewes and Mr. Cheeu^{r}s, members of this church, Mr. Sam: Eaton, John Clark, Leiuetennant Seely John Chapman, Thomas Jeffreyes and Rich: Hull, members of other approued churches.

And this charge was giuen and accepted by them. If you shall know any person or persons w^{c}h intend, plott, or conspire any thing w^{c}h tends to the hurt or prejudice of this Jurisdiction, or the ciuill gournment here settled, you shall forthw^{t}h discouer itt to the magistrates, or to one or more of the Deputies who shalbe chosen and intrusted in the publique occasions of the same, you shall assist and be help full therevnto w^{t}h body, minde and goods, in any thing w^{c}h may concerne the safety or promove the peace and welfare thereof, as God shall giue abillity and oppertunity. And you shall be subject

* An error in the recorder for Gilbert.

† "It appears that the churches of New Haven and Milford were gathered to the seven pillars on the 22d of August, 1639. The tradition is that soon after Mr. Davenport was chosen pastor of the church at New Haven, and that Mr. Hooker and Mr. Stone came and assisted in his installation." Trumb. I. 298. Mather, (Mag. B. iii. ch. 6,) says that they were gathered in two days, one following upon the other, Mr. Davenport's and Mr. Pruddens, and alludes to the place as being a mighty barn.

to all lawes and orders wᶜh according to God shall be made by the court, to the vttmost of yoʳ power.

This being done, the court proceeded to the choyce of a magistrate and 4 deputye[s] to assist in the publique affayres of the plantatiō, Mr. Davenport first opening 2 scriptures (viz) Deut. 1. 13. and Exod. 18. 21. wherein a magistrate according to Gods minde is discribed. And Mr. Theoph: Eaton, a member of this church, a man well known and approved by the court as fittly quallified for thatt office according to the said discriptiō, was by full consent chosen magistrate for the tearme of one whole yeare. And Mr. Davenport gaue him his charge grounded vpon Deut. 1. 16, 17. And Mr. Robert Newman, Mr. Mathew Gilbert, Mr. Nathainell Turner and Tho. Fugill was chosen deputyes to assist the magistrate in all courts called by him for the occasions of the plantatiō for the same tearme of one whole yeare a[nd] receiued their charge faithfully to assist according to the trust comitted to th[em.]

Tho. Fugill was chosen publique notary, to attend the court and from time to time to ke[ep] a faithfull recorde of all passages and conclusions of the court, and of whatsoeu[er] else then or att other times shall by the court or magistrate be comitted to him concerning the ciuill publique occasions of the Plantation.

Robt. Seely was chosen marshall, his imploymᵗ and charge from time to time to warne courts according to the directiō of the magistrate, to serue and execute warrants, to attend the court att all times, and to be ready and dilligent in his person or by his deputy to execute the sentences of the court, and in all other occasiōˢ to attend the service of the plantatiō in all things apptaining to his office.

Itt was further agreed thatt there should be a renewing of the choyce of all offi[cers] euery yeare att a Generall Court to be held for this plantatiō the last weeke in October yearely. And thatt the worde of God shall be the onely rule to be attended vnto in ordering the affayres of gouernment in this plantatiō.

[6] OCTOB: 26: 1639.

The ciuill affayres of the plantatiō being settled as before, by the ꝑuidence of God an Indian called Messutunck, alias Nepaupuck, who had beene formerly accused to have murderously shed the bloode of some of the English; of his owne accorde wth a deer's head vpon his back came to Mr. Eatons, where, by warrant the marshall apprehended and pinioned him, yett nottwthstanding by the subtillty and treachery of another Indian his companiō, he had allmost made an escape, butt by the same providence he was againe taken and deliured into the magistrates power, and by his order safely kept in the stocks till he might be brought to a due tryall. And the Indian who had attempted his escape was whipped by the marshall his deputy.

OCTO: 28: 1639.

The Quillipieck Indian Sagamour wth diurs of his Indians wth him were examined before the *the* magistrate and the deputyes for this plantatiō concerning Nepaupuck. They generally accused him to haue murdered one or more of the English, and thatt he had cutt of some of their hands & had presented them to Sassacuse the Pequott sachem, boasting thatt he had killed them wth his owne hands.

Mewhebato a Quillipieck Indian, kinsman to the aforesaid Nepaupuck, comeing att the same time to interceed for him, was examined whatt he knew concerning the murders charged vpon the said Nepaupuck; att first he pretended ignorance, butt wth a distracted countenance, and in a trembling manner; being admonished to speake the truth he did acknowledge him guilty according to the charge the other Indians had before made.

All the other Indians wthdrawing, Nepaupuck was brought in and examined, he confessed that Nepaupuck was guilty according to the tennure of the formr charge, butt denyed thatt he was Nepaupuck. Mewhebato being brought in, after some signes of sorrow, charged him to his face thatt he had assisted the Pequotts in murdering the English, this somewhatt abated his speritt and boldenesse; butt Wattoone the sonne of Carrahoode a councellor[r] to the Quillipieck Indian sagamour comeing in, charged him more perticularly thatt he had killed Abraham Finch an English man att Weathersfield and thatt he himselfe, the said Wattoone, stood vpon the island att Weathersfield and beheld him the said Nepaupuck now present acting the said murder.

Lastly the Quillipieck sagamo[r] and the rest of the Indians being called in, to his face affirmed thatt he was Nepaupuck, and thatt he had murdered one or more of the English as before.

Nepaupuck being by the concurrence of testimony convinced, he confessed he was the man namely Nepaupuck, and boasted he was a great captaine, had murdered Abraham Finch, and had his hands in other English blood, he said he knew he must dye, and was nott afraid of itt, butt layd his neck to the mātletree of the chimney, desireing thatt his head might be cutt of, or thatt he might dye in any other manner the English should appoynt, onely he said fire was God, and God was angry wth him, therefore he would nott fall into his hands. After this he was retourned to the stocks and as before a watch appoynted for his safe custody.

A Generall Court 29: of Octob: 1639:

A Generall Court being assembled to proceed against the said Indian Nepaupuck who was then brought to the barre, and being examined as before, att the first he denyed thatt he was thatt Nepaupuck w[ch] had comitted those murders wherew[th] he was charged, butt when he see that the Quillipeck Sagamour and his Indians did againe accuse him to his face, he confessed thatt he had his hand in the murder of Abraham Finch, butt yett he said there was a Mohauke of thatt name thatt had killed more then hee.

Wattoone affirmed to his face thatt he, the said Nepaupuck, did nott onely kill Abraham Finch, butt was one of them thatt killed the 3 men in the boate or shallop on Connectecutt riuer, and thatt there was but one Nepaupuck and this was he, and the same thatt tooke a childe of Mr. Swaines att Weathersfield. Then the said Nepaupuck being asked if he would nott confess yt he deserved to dye, he answered, it is weregin.

The Court haue had such pregnant proofe, proceeded to pass sentence vpon him according to the nature of the fact and the rule in thatt case, he thatt sheds mans blood, by man shall his blood be shed, accordingly his head was cutt off the next day and pittched vpon a pole in the markett place.

---

[7] A COURT HOLDEN THE 3d OF NOUEMBER 1639.

Thomas Kimberley was admitted member of the court and recived his charge.

Itt is ordered that Mr. Samuell Eaton, Captaine Turner, Robt Newman and Thomas Fugill shall treate wth the Hartfordeshire men about their lotts, to see if they will part wth them and vpon what tearmes.

Itt is ordered thatt gates shalbe made att the end of every streete att the outside of the Towne, wth all the outside fences. Mr. Eaton shall appoynt the men to doe itt.

Itt is ordered thatt Mr. Hopkins shall have two hogsheads of lime for his present vse, and as much more as will finnish his house as he now intends itt, he thinking that two hogsheads more will serve.

Itt is ordered that Mr. Gilbert and Goodman Andrewes shall veiwe the creeke by the landing place, to see if lotts may be layd out there wthout prejudice to ye towne.

Itt is ordered thatt Mr. Eaton, Mr. Sam: Eaton, Captaine Turner, Robt Newmã, Mathew Gilbert, Thomas Fugill and Goodman Andwewes shall advise together about laying out allottments for inherritance.

Itt is ordered thatt Mr. James shall have Francis Parrotts lott.

Thomas Badger being accused vpon suspitiō of stealing mony frō Edward Cox, boatswaine of the Exetor marchant, was referred to further proofe.

A GENrll COURT THE 25 OF NOUEMBER 1639.

Itt is ordered that after this day no man shall cutt any timber downe butt where he shall be assigned by the magistrate, except on his owne ground.

Itt is ordered thatt Leivetennant Seeley and Goodm̃ Andwewes shall walke the woods, and if they finde any timber lyeing in the woods vncroscutt and squared, and acquaint the magistrate therewth, they shall have liberty to seiz vpon it, halfe for themselves, and halfe for the towne, the Yorkshire mens timber onely excepted: that timber wch is squared and crosscutt, time is given till the last of March next to fetch it home.

Itt is ordered that a meeting house shall be built forthwth, fifty foote square, and that the carpenters shall fall timber where they can finde it till allotmts be layd out and men know their owne proprietyes.

Itt is ordered that Mr. Gregson & Mr. Evance shall have fower dayes liberty after this day to square their timber before the former order take holde of them.

Whereas the building of the meeting house will cost 500l wch will require a rate of 30s in every hundred pounds, itt is therefore ordered thatt the said rate shall be estreeted and payd att 3 severall payments (viz.) the first forthwth, the second in March next, and the third in May next after, and wth this every one that are behinde with the formr rate of 25s vpon every hundred l are now to pay itt allso.

Itt is ordered thatt Mr. Eaton, Mr. Davenport, Robt Newman, Mathew Gilbert, Captaine Turner and Thomas Fugill shall from hence forward have the disposeing of all the house lotts yett vndisposed of about this towne, to such persons as they shall judge meete for the good of the plantatiō, and thatt none shall come to dwell as planters here wthout their consent and allowance, whether they come in by purchase or otherwise.

Itt is ordered thatt every one that beares armes shall be compleatly furnished wth armes (viz), a muskett, a sworde, bandaleers, a rest, a pound of powder, 20 bullets fitted to

4

their muskett, or 4 pound of pistoll shott or swan shott att least, and be ready to show them in the markett place vpon Munday the 16th of this Moneth before Captaine Turner and Leivtennant Seely vnder the penalty 20s fine for eu'y default or absen[ce].

---

[8] A Court holden 4th of December 1639.

Itt is ordered that Thomas Saule shall agree wth Goodmā Spinnage before the next court, or else the court will determine the difference betweene them.

Roger Duhurst and James Stewart are injoined to make double restitutiō to John Cockerill for five pound and seaventeene shillings wch they stole out of his chist on the Lords day in the meeting time, and they being servants to the said Cockerell, for wch aggravatiō they were whipped allso.

Thomas Manchester, servant to Mr. Perry being accused by his Mar for being druncke, and for giveing his Mar vncomely language for wch his Mar having given him some correctiō, the court (onely) caused him to be sett in the stocks for a certaine time.

Nicholas Tanner, servant to the said Mr. Perry, for drunkennes and abuseing his Mar in wordes, was whipped.

A Generall Court the 4th of Jan: 1639.

Itt is agreed by the towne and accordingly ordered by the court thatt the Neck shall be planted or sowen for the tearme of seaven yeares, and that John Brockett shall goe about laying it out forthwth, and all differences betwixt pty and pty aboute ground formerly broke vp and planted by English there shall be arbitrated by indifferent men wch shall be chosen to that end.

Itt is ordered thatt Mr. Davenports quarter, Mr. Eatons, Mr. Newmans and Mr Tenches quarters shall have their first divisiō of upland to begin att the sea side after the small lotts are layd out, and so goe on to the cow pasture, and to have their meaddow in the east meaddowes. And Mr. Evance quarter, Mr. Fowlers, Mr. Gregsons, Mr. Lambertons and the subburbs, are to begin wth their lands att the oyster poynt, and so come on to the oxe pasture in order, and to have their meaddow in the west meadowes, in the meadowes called Mr. Malbon meadow, on the Indian side, and in the sollitary cove. Allso that the cow pasture shall begin on the hither side of the Beever ponds, and the oxe pasture on the farre side of the Bever pond, and the way to them both to begin att Mr. Tenches corner.

Itt is ordered thatt no planter or planters shall make purchase of any lands or plantatiō frō the Indians or others for their owne private vse or advantage, butt in the name & for the vse of the whole plantatiō.

Itt is ordered that some speedy course shall be taken to keepe hogs out of the neck.

It is ordered thatt a convenient way to the hay place be left comō for all the towne.

Itt is ordered thatt no cattell belonging to this towne shall goe wthout a keeper after the first of May next.

Itt is ordered thatt those thatt kill wolves and foxes shall have for every wolfe head 15s and for every foxe head 2s 6d, and if any by setting guns or traps shall hap to kill any hogs or other cattell, the towne is to beare the damage till some other course be determined.

Memorand. Itt is agreed that Mr. Evance quarter shall have their meadow in the East meadowes.

Itt was agreed that every planter in the towne shall have a proportiō of land according to the proportiō of estate wch he hath given in, and number of heads in his famyly, (viz) in the first divisiō of upland & meadow 5 acres for every hundred pound, [an]d 5 acres for every two heads, of upland, butt halfe an acre of meadow to a head [and] in the necke an acre to every hundred pound, and halfe an acre to every head.

[9] A COURT HOLDEN THE 5th OF FEBR. 1639.

Itt is ordered by the court, thatt Mr. Malbon and John Reader, and whosoever else hath any thing to doe wth the estate of William Thorpe, late deceased, shall appeare att the next court for the settleing of thatt busines.

Itt is ordered thatt brother Turner shall see a true inventory taken of Mrs Higginsons* goods, thatt itt may be given into the court upon oath.

Itt is ordered thatt Thomas Saule shall pay 5s in the weeke to Mr. Evance, to lye in his hands (for the securing of Goodman Spiñage in respect of his clame to the said Tho: Saule) and thereupon Mr. Evance doth hereby ingage himselfe for the said mony vntill the said Thomas Saule shall neglect to pay the said mony according to ords.

Itt is ordered thatt brother Andrewes, bro: Kimberley, William Eves and Sergeant Beckley shall assist Mr. Ling to ripen Goodman Taps busines against the next court, concerning his demaund of certaine monyes wch he disbursed for bringing cattell from the Bay, appertayning to divers persons.

Itt is ordered that bro: Andrewes shall detaine somuch of Robt Campian his wages in his hands as may secure a debt of 3l wch Mr. Moulenor demaunds of the said Robt.

Itt is ordered thatt Mr. Moulenor shall pay to Mr. Perry 10s wch he owes to him.

Itt is ordered thatt Mr. Wilks shall pay 5 bushells and a halfe of indian corne to Thomas Buckingham for corne destroyed by Mr. Wilks his hogs.

Isaiah, Captaine Turners man, fined 5l for being druncke on the Lords day.

William Bromfield, Mr. Malbons man, was sett in the stocks for prophaining the Lords day and stealing wine from his Mar wch he drunk and gave to others.

Ellice, Mr. Eatons boy, was whipped for stealing a sow and a goate frō his Mar and selling them.

David Anderson was whipped for being drunke.

---

* Widow of Rev. Francis Higginson. For an account of his life see Mather, Mag. iii, p. 12, ch. 1, and Gen. Reg. 6, 105. She may have been a relative, perhaps sister, of Governor Eaton.

John Jenner accused for being drunke wth strong waters was acquitted, itt appearing to be of infirmyty & occasioned by the extremyty of the colde.

Mr. Moulenor, accused of being drunke, butt nott clearely proved, was respited.

Peter Browne licenced to bake to sell, so long as he gives no offence in itt justly.

A Generall Court the 18 of Feb: 1639.

Mr. Gregson and John Mosse were admitted members of the court.

John Charles was forbiden to draw wine because there hath beene much disorder by itt.

Goodman Loue was whipped and sent out of the plantatiō, being nott onely a disorderly person himselfe, butt an incourager of others to disorderly drinking meetings.

George Spencer being prophaine and disorderly in his whole conversatiō and an abettor of others to sin, and drawing on others into a conspericie to carry away the Cock* to Virgenia was whipped and sent out of the plantatiō.

John Proute, Hen: Brasier and Wiłł Bromfield was whipped for joyning in the aforesaid conspericie, and the said Hen: and William were ordered to weare irons dureing the magistrats pleasure.

---

[10] 25th of Feb: 1639.

Mrs. Higgingson, late planter of Quillipieck dyeing wthout makeing her will, & leaveing behinde her eight children, an inventory of her estate being taken, the court disposed of her estate and children as followeth wth the consent and approbatiō of Mr. John Higginson her eldest sonne.†

* The name of a small vessel.

† Rev. John Higginson was born in England Aug. 6, 1616. Some time after the death of his father with whom he came to this country in 1629, he was the instructor of a school at Hartford, his mother with six of her children being somewhat dependent upon his exertions for her support; after this he was chaplain at Saybrook fort

The said John Higginson, the charges of his educatiō considered, is onely to have his fathers books, together wᵗh the value of 5ˡ in bedding for his porcō.

Francis Higginson the second sonne and Tymothy the third sonne, their educatiō allso considered, are to have each of them twenty pounds for their portions.

Theophilus Higginson though well educated, yett in regard of his helpfullnes to his mother and her estate, is to have forty pounds for his portiō.

Samuell Higginson is allso to have 40ˡ for his portiō, and to be wᵗh Mr. Eaton as his servant for the full tearme of 2 yeares from the first of March next ensueing.

Theophilus and Samuell are to have the lott wᵗh all the accommodatiōˢ belonging therevnto, equally to be devided betwixt thē, for fifty pounds of their portiōˢ.

Anne Higginson her daughter, is to have forty pounds for her portiō and her mothers olde clothes, together wᵗh the remainder of the estate when the debts and other portions are payd.

Charles Higginson is to have 40ˡ to his portiō, and to be wᵗh Thomas Fugill as his apprentice vnto the full end and tearme of nine yeares from the first of March next ensueing the date hereof. And the said Tho: Fugill is to finde him what is convenient for him as a servant, and to keepe him att schoole one yeare, or else to advantage him as much in his educatiō as a years learning comes to, and he is to have the benifitt of the vse of his portiō till the said tearme be expired, and att the end thereof to pay itt to the said Charles Higginson, if he live till the said nine years be expired, butt if he dye before, then the said Thomas Fugill is to pay the said portiō to the rest of his brothers thatt are alive att the end of the said nine yeares.

Neophitus Higginson being wᵗh Mr. Hoffe in the Bay of Mattacusetts, is to remaine wᵗh him and to be brought vp by him till he attayne the full age of 21 yeares, and in the meane time, Mr. Hough is to have 40ˡ of the estate, wᶜh he is to pay

several years. In 1641 he went to Guilford and became assistant to Mr. Whitfield whose daughter he married. He was chosen one of the seven pillars there in 1648. He left Guilford in 1659. Allen, etc.

to the said Neofatus att the end of the said tearme as his portiō.

When the farme att Sawgus is sould itt is to be equally devided among the brothers.

ATT A COURT HELD THE 5th OF MARCH 1639:

Whereas a will was made by Nathaniell Axtell the 27th of Jan: 1639*, before his goeing into olde England, and left in the hands of Goodman Miles for the disposeing of his estate wch he left allso in the hands of the said Richard Miles, and he being now departed this life, It is ordered by the court thatt a true inventory of all his goods in this place be taken by Captaine Turner and Goodmā Miles, till further course be taken about them.

Itt was ordered that Mr. Gregson and Mr. Gilbert should prize the goods of George Spencer.

Itt was ordered that Mr. Johnson shall have the cellar that Thomas Welch lived in to make a warehouse off, onely to lay goods in itt while he hath neede of itt for that vse, and then liberty to sell itt (as itt shall be judged), to some planter wth the consent of the court not claymeing any propriety in the ground as inherritance.

Mr. Lambertons man, Hen. Brasier, was freed frō his chaines frō hence forward. Wiłł Bromfield and Tho: Manchestr are to weare theirs a weeke longer.

---

[11] A COURT HOLDEN THE 3d OF APRILL 1640.

Itt is ordered thatt Mr. Fowler, John Cockerill and Leivetenant Seeley shall prize the goods of Tho: Ashby and Tho: Johnson who were lately drowned.

Itt is ordered that John Reader in whose hands William Thorps goods was left, shall have them forth comeing so as to

* The will is not preserved, but Dr. Bacon perhaps overlooked this record when he conjectured Edward Tench's will to have been the first made in New Haven. Hist. Disc. 327.

give a good accoumpt of them att the next court, or when he shall be called, thatt those to whom he was ingaged may be satisfied.

Itt is ordered thatt brother Andrewes and brother Mounson shall veiw the grounds of difference betwixt Mr. Malbon and Thomas Mouleno^r the elder, and acquaint Mr. Turner, Mr. Gilbert, Mr. Lamberton and Thomas Fugill wth the same, who are desired to end the same if they can, or else to certyfye where the impediment lyes.

Itt is ordered thatt Mr. Malbon and Goodman Potter shall equally share in the losse of 24^s due vnto them frō George Spencer, because there is not sufficient to satisfy them both to the full.

Itt is ordered that Arther Halbidge shall pay 40^s fine for falling trees and selling clapboard, contrary to the orders in that case.

Itt is ordered thatt the mony left (in the hands of Mr. Browning) by John Dyer, shall be reserved to secure a debtt and satisfie the demands of bro: Andrewes.

Itt is ordered thatt the gates att the ends of the neck bridge, and the way to itt be made convenient forthw^th.

Itt is ordered thatt John Mosse, Tymothy Forde and Richard Beach shall pay each of them 1^s fine for trees wch they did fall disorderly.

Hen: Akerlye was rebuked for building a cellar and selling itt w^thout leave.

Itt is ordered that all the trained band shalbe in the markett place the 3^d day next weeke by 7 a clock in the morning wth their armes compleat.

A Court holden the 6^t of May 1640.

Itt was ordered thatt Mr. Fowler and John Cockerill shall have the goods of the 2 men thatt was drowned, to satisfie their debt so far as itt will goe; pvided, thatt if any other shall lay just clame to the said goods, then they are to be equally devided among the credetors according to their proportiō.

Itt is ordered thatt a measurer shall be appoynted to measure all the corne thatt comes into the plantatiō to be solde, and for that end a role shall be made to strike the bushell wth.

Liberty granted to Mr. Gregson, bro: Andrewes and Goodm̄ Warde to lett their timber lye in the woods for the space of 2 moneths wthout forfeiture.

An account deliured into the court by Mr. Lamberton betwixt himselfe and Goodm̄ Spencer whom he imployed as his steward att sea in his voyage hither, for wch service he allows him 5l 10s for the whole voyage, butt whereas he dyed before he had served halfe the voyage, he desired that Roger Allen who suc-ceeded him should have the one halfe of the hyer, and promised that if more wages were ordenaryly allowed in that place for thatt voyage, he will allow as much to the said Goodmā Spencer, and wthall that he will be ready att any time to make oath of the truth of that account wch he had given in, wth wch Mr. Fowler, and Goodmā Tapps were satisfied, (who were intrusted for the child of the said Spencer late desceased.)

---

[12] A COURT HOLDEN THE THIRD OF JUNE 1640. GENrll.

All the Mars of the watches received their charge and orders as followeth,

1. The drummr is to beat the drum att the goeing downe of the sunne.

2 The Mar of the watch is to be att the court of guarde wthin halfe an hower after the setting of the sun wth his armes compleate.

3 All the watchmen are to be there wthin an hower after the setting of the sun, wth their armes compleate, and their guns ready charged, and if any of them come after the time appoynted, or be defective in their armes, they are to pay 1s fine, for totall absence 5s fine. And if the Mar of the watch transgresse, either in late comeing, defectivenes in armes or

totall absence, his fine is to be double to the watchmens fine in like case.

4 The Mr of the watch is to sett the watch an hower after sunsett, devideing the night into 3 watches, sending forth two and two together to walke their turnes, as well wthout the towne as wthin the towne and the subvrbs allso, and to bring to the court of guard any person or persons whom they shall finde disorderly or in a suspitious manner wthin dores or wthout, wther English or *or* Indians, or any other straingers whatsoeur and keepe them there safe untill the morning, and then bring them before one of the magistrates.

If the watchmen in any part of their watch see any apparent comoñ danger wch they cannott otherwise prevent or stop, then they are to make an alarũ by discharging their two guns wch are to be answered by him thatt stands att the dore to keepe sentinell, and that allso seconded by beating of the drũ. And if the danger be by fire, then with the alarũ the watchm̃ are to cry fire, fire. And if itt be by the discovery of an enemy, then they are to cry arme, arme, all the towne our, yett so as to leave a guard att the court of guard.

5. The Mar is to take care that one man alwayes stand sentinell in a sentinell posture wthout the watch house to hearken dilligently after the watchmen, and see that no man come neare the watch house or court of guarde; no, not those of the prsent watch who have beene walking the round, but that he require them to stand and call forth the Mar of the watch to questiõ, proceed or receive them as he shall see cause. The Mar of the watch is allso to see that none of the watchmen sleepe att all, and thatt none of their guns remaine vncharged till the watch breake up (and then they may discharge), and allso that no man lay aside his armes while the watch continues.

6. Every Mr of the watch in his course, is to warne both his owne watch and the Mr of the succeeding watch, fower and twenty howers before they are to watch, and not to doe itt sleightly, butt either to warne the psons themselves, or to leave the warning wth some sufficient for such a trust.

Lastly, if any Mar of the watch shall faile either in the

warning or ordering of the watch in any of the forenamed pticulars, or shall breake vp the watch in the morning before itt have beene full halfe an hower day light, or neglect to complaine to one of the magistrates of the neglects or defects of any of the watchmen, he is to be fined by the court according to the quallity of his offence.

Edward Bannister, for his contempt of the court, and therein the ordinance of God, was fined twenty shillings.

Edward Woodcliff for slaundering his Ma[r]s wife was whipped seveerly and sent out of the plantatiō, being a pestilent fellow, and a corrupter of others.

Nathaniell Axtell his will, and inventory of his goods deliuered into the court.

---

[13] A Generall Court helde the 11[th] of June 1640.

Mr. James, Adam Nicholls, Abraham Bell, Francis Newman, Andrew Low and Thomas Mounson was made freemen, and admitted members of the court, and accepted the charge of freemen.

Itt was ordered thatt comodityes well bought in England for ready mony, shall nott be solde here above 3[d] in the shilling for proffitt and adventure above what they cost wth charges, when solde by retayle, when solde by the peece or vessell by wholesaile, lesse proffitt may suffize.

When bought from ships or other vessells here, not above 3[ob]* in the shilling by retale, nor above a peny in the shilling by wholesaile. Butt comodityes of a perishing na[r], subject to waste and damage, fall not vnder the former rates, yet the rates to be so ordered that neither buyer nor seller suffer in the rates.

Comodityes bought and brought frō the Bay, Connectecutt, Virgenia or other places, to be in proportiō moderated in the prises, according to the adventures and nature of the comodityes.

---

* " Obolus is now usually taken to signify our half penny; but in old time it signified the half noble; the noble was then called penny, and its quarter a farthing." Bailey's Dict.

In callings $w^{c}h$ require skill and strength, as carpenters, joyners, plasterers, bricklayers, shipcarpenters, coopers and the like, ma^{r} workemen not to take above 2^{s} 6^{d} a day in sum^{r}, in $w^{c}h$ men may worke 12 howers, butt lesse then 10 howers dilligently improved in worke cannot be accounted nor may be admitted for a full dayes worke, nor in winter above 2^{s} a day, in $w^{c}h$ att least 8 howers to be dilligently improved in worke. And by advice of approved m^{r} workemen the names of others who in their severall trades are to be allowed for m^{r} workemen are to be sett downe. Butt all workemen in the former and like trades, who are not as yet allowed to passe vnder the names of ma^{r} workemen, not to take above 2s a day in sum^{r} and 20^{d} a day in winter, they improveing their time in worke both in sum^{r} and winter as above expressed.

Planters and $labo^{r}ers$, experienced and dilligent in their way, not to take above 2^{s} a day in sum^{r}, and not above 18^{d} in winter improveing their time as above, and others in proportiō, as they may deserve, and boyes to have wages in sum^{r} and winter in $seu^{r}all$ $imploymt^{s}$ according to the service they doe, $w^{c}h$ shall be judged, (when any doubt ariseth), by honest and indifferent men.

For goeing $w^{t}h$ boats of seuerall sorts, the man not above 2^{s} a tyde, the whole tyde being dilligently improved according to the nature of that $imploym^{t}$.

And for boates, according to their quallity and burden. A lighter of 16 tunne $w^{t}h$ a boate or cannow $w^{t}h$ her, not above 3^{s} a tide, and one of 12 tunne, with a boate, not above 2^{s} 6^{d} a tide. A shallop of 4 tunne, not above 1^{s} a tide, and so in respective proportiō. Butt in such raines or stormes that goods cannot be laden without spoyling, nor the boate stirr though the tide serve, no $paym^{t}$ to be made for the boate in such tides, though the man be paid while he attends the service.

Sawing by the hundred not above 4^{s} 6^{d} for boards. 5^{s} for plancks. 5^{s} 6^{d} for slitworke and to be payd for no more than they cutt full and true measure. If by the dayes worke, the top man or he that guides the worke and phaps findes the tooles, not above 2^{s} 6^{d} a day in som^{r}, and the pitt mā, and he whose skill and charge is lesse, not above 2^{s}, and a proportionable in winter as before. If they be equall in skill and charge, then to agree or divide the 4^s 6^d betwixt them.

Falling of timber, that w^{c}h is full 2 foote ou^r or above, one w^{t}h another not above 3^d a foote; lesser timber, being yett full 18 inches ou^r and under 2 foote, not above 2^d a foote; all other trees of lesser size not 18 inches ou^r, either by dayes wages, or as shall be reasonably agreed. Crosscutting, by the day, as other labo^{rs}, or as shall be agreed w^{t}h equity.

Hewing and squaring timber of severall sizes, one w^{t}h another, butt the least 15 inches square, well done that a karfe* or planke of 2 inches thicke being taken off on 2 sides, the rest may be square for boards or for other vse, not above 18^d a tun girt measure. And for timber sleightly hewen a price proportionable, or by day wages. As for sills, beames, plates or such like timber, square hewen to build w^{t}h, not above a peny a foote running measure.

[14] Mowing, when by the acre, not above 3^s salt marsh, nor above 2^s 6^d fresh marsh, when by the day, not above 2^s 6^d, and this to be of skilfull mowers, dilligently improveing their time and skill. A skillfull thatcher, working dilligently, not above 2^s 6^d a day.

Fenceing w^{t}h pales, as houslotts, now are, for felling and cleaveing posts and railes, crosscutting, hewing, mortising, digging holes, setting vp and nailing on the pales, the worke being in all the ꝑts well wrought and finished, not above 2^s a rod, butt in this price pales and carting of the stuffe not included. Fencing w^{t}h 5 railes, substantiall posts, good railes, well wrought, sett vp and ram̃ed, that pigs, swine, goates and other cattell may be kept out, not above 2^s a rod. Fencing w^{t}h 3 railes, good stuff, well wrought and finished, not above 18^d the rod.

Substantiall posts sould in the woods, not above 9^s or 10^s by the hundred, being in length and goodnes answerable to the price. Good railes, 11 foote long, some of them 7, some 6, butt the least in the smallest ꝑt of itt not less then 5 inches

* "Kerf, the way made by the saw or the away slit in a piece of timber or board. The sawn away slit between two pieces of stuff is called a kerf." Bailey's Dict.

broade, one w^t^h another *one w^t^h another* indifferently sorted, not above 7^s^ the hundred.

Inch bords to be sould in the woods nott above 5^s^ 9^d^ ℘ hundred.

halfe inch boards in the woods not above 5—2 ℘ 100.

2 inch planke in the woods not above 7—0 ℘ 100.

inch boards sould in the towne not above 7—9 ℘ 100.

halfe inch boards in the towne, nott above 6—2 ℘ 100.

2 inch planke in the towne not above 11—0 ℘ 100.

Sawen timber 6 inches broad and 3 inches thicke in the woods ruñing measure not above } $\frac{3}{4}$ far^d^ ℘ foote.

in the towne not above 1^d^ ℘ foote.

Sawne timber 8 inches square running measure in the woods not above } 1^d^ $\frac{1}{4}$ ℘ foote.

in the towne not above 2^d^ ℘ foote.

Clapboards in the woods, good stuffe, not above 4^s^ 0 ℘ 100. 6 foote long 3^s^ 6^d^. 5 foote and 4 foote 3^s^ 0 ℘ hundred; hewing and nailing them on roofes and sides of houses, well done not worth above 5^s^ ℘ hundred, butt as most are done, not worth above 2^s^ 6^d^. Shingle, good stuff $\frac{3}{4}$ of an inch, and 6 or 7 or 8 inches broad, sorted in the woods, being 3 foote 2^s^ 6^d^ ℘ hundred. 2 foote 2^s^. 14 inches 1^s^ ℘ hundred, butt if defective, price accordingly.

Lime well burnt vnslaked, and brought by water to the landing place of the towne, by the bushell heaped, not above 9^d^ the bushell, by the hogshead, full gage and so putt in that when carted from the water side to the place where it shall be vsed the hogshead may yet remaine full, not above 5^s^ ℘ hh^d^.

A Court holden the 1^t^ of July 1640.

Daniell Fuller for neglect of his watch was fined three shillings.

Thomas Parsons and John ^ , servants to Elias Parkmore were whipped for their sinfull dalliance and folly w^t^h Lidia Browne.

Andwew Low the sonne of Andrew Low, was whipped for

runing frō his ma^r and stealing fruite out of Goodman Wards lott or garden.

Tho: Chambers being accused for scoffing at religiō, it not being sufficiently proved, he was dismissed onely wth an admonitiō and cautiō.

Arthur Halbidg being charged wth falce measure in lime, was respited till another court for a more full testimony.

---

[15] A Court holden the 5th of August 1640.

Itt was ordered thatt Thomas Games shall pay vnto John Moody or his assigns, 500 weight of good tobacco, wch should have beene payd 14 or 15 moneths agoe. In consideracon whereof, the court doth order the said Thomas Games to pay vnto the said John Moody ½ a hundred weight more of tobacco for the forbearance of itt so long a time.

John Cockerill received in the court 3—8—10 of the mony of Thomas Johnson, vpon condicoñ y^t he shall repay itt into the court in case any others shall lay clame to the same and require satisfactiō.

Itt is ordered that Mr. Craine shall pay the rates due for Mr. Roe* to pay, in consideration of his lott and estate here given in: and thatt if he come not the next yeare, the lott shall be att the towns dispose, and the rates payd for him to be deducted out of his estate here in cattell when they are soulde.

Goodm̃ Osborne fined 5^s for neglecting to warne the watch ma^r next succeding his owne, whereby the watch was neglected 3 nights.

Brother Perry was fined one shilling for warning his watch too late, tho the watch was not neglected.

---

* Owen Rowe was a tradesman in London and of the company designed for New England, and had in 1636 a lot laid out in Boston. Upon the change of times he chose to remain in London, became a colonel in the great civil war and one of the regicide judges. He died in the Tower on Christmas day 1661. Hutch. Coll., 59. Savage Winth. I, 475. (Ed. of 1853.)

ATT A GEN^{rll} COURT HELD THE 1^{t} OF THE 7th MONETH 1640.

Mr. Lamberton and Thomas Nash was admitted members of the court and received the freemans charge.

Itt is ordered that all men thatt have nott yet payd in all the olde rates for the commō charges of the towne, shall pay itt w^{t}hin 14 dayes after the date hereof, or else some other course must be taken to compell them. And allso thatt another rate be forthw^{t}h estreeted of 200^{l}, halfe vpō estates and halfe vpon lands.

Mr. Turner was chosen Captaine to have the comaund and ordering of all martiall affayres of this plantatiō, as setting and ordering of watches, exerciseing and training of souldiers and whatsoeu^{r} of like nature appertaining to his office; all w^{c}h he is to doe w^{t}h all faithfullnes and dilligence, and be ready att all times to doe whatsoeu^{r} service the occasions of the towne requires or may require.

Itt is ordered that eu^{r}y man that is appoynted to watch whether m^{rs} or servants, shall come every Lords day to the meeting compleatly armed, and all others also are to bring their swords, no man exempted save Mr. Eaton, o^{r} pasto^{r}, Mr. James, Mr. Samuell Eaton and the 2 deacons.*

The plantatiō of Totokett is granted to Mr. Samuell Eaton for such friends as he shall bring ouer from olde England, and vpō such tearmes as shall be agreed betwixt himselfe & the comitty chosen to that purpose, (namely) Mr. Eaton and the 4 deputyes.

This towne now named Newhaven.

Itt is ordered that when Mr. Roes lott shalbe fenced in, o^{r} pasto^{r} shall have a way or passage left 8 foote broad betwixt it and Mr. Craines lott, y^{t} he may goe out of his owne garden to the meeting house.

Itt is ordered thatt none in this plantatiō shall either sell or lett a lott to any strainger for yeares w^{t}hout allowance frō the court.

Itt is ordered thatt att this day every yeare all the ram goates in the towne shall either be side stringed or some other

* Matthew Gilbert and Robert Newman.

course taken wth them so as they cannot ram the ewes till the fittest season.

A peece of ground granted to Mr. Lamberton for a yeard to his sellar by the west creeke, butt to be veiwed by the comitty chosen to dispose of all the lotts and lands aboute the towne, and sett out by them to him, vpõ these tearmes, (viz) that he shall give for the ground whatt they shall appoynt, and sell both house and lott at what time and to whom the court shall approve of, and that att a reasonable price.

---

[16] ATT A COURT HELD ATT NEWHAVEN THE 2^{d} OF 7 M; 1640.

Itt is ordered that Leiveten^{t} Seely shall pay vnto John Cockerill 14^{l} 11^{s} either in mony, corne or cattell, as they shall be indifferently prized by indifferent men w^{c}h shall be chosen by them for that end.

Tho: Saule doth acknowledg himselfe bound in the sum̃ of 20^{l}, to be leavied of his goods and chattells for publique vse of this towne, vpon condic̃on thatt he satisfie the just demaunds of Humphra Spinage when soeu^{r} he shall be called to an account aboute a clame w^{c}h the said Spinage doth make in the behalfe of one in London.

Itt is ordered thatt Goodman Chapman shall forthw^{t}h pay vnto Joh. Cockerill the sũ of 5^{l} 10^{s} w^{c}h he is indebted to him.

Robt Cogswell is ordered to pay vnto Mr. Attwater and his bro: David the mony w^{c}h he owes them, before the next court.

A difference betwixt Mr. Craine and Captaine Turner refered to bro: Gilbert and bro: Newm̃ to arbitrate.

Richard Mansfield fined 2^{s} for neglecting his watch.

The men appoynted to veiw the meaddowes, to sett downe before lotts be cast, what allowance is equall to be cast into the acre where the meadowes are bad, Benjamin Linge, William Andrewes, Richard Perry, Will Touttle, Jasper Craine, John Chapman, Mr. Lamberton, Robt Seely, John Wakeman, Rich: Miles, Thomas Welch, Anthony Tompson, John Ponderson, Fran. Newman and Jer: Dixon.

ATT A COURT HELD ATT NEWHAVEN THE 6t OF THE 8th M. 1640.

Goodm̃ Warde fined 2s for neglect of his watch and putt out of his place from being mar of a watch.

Wiłł Gibbons, Francis Browne and Tho: Franckland fined 1s apeece for late comeing to keepe their watch.

Robt Champiō being accused for drinking wine to excesse, was fined 5s.

Thomas Moulenor the elder, and Robt Campiō were fined 5s apeece for affronting the court.

On Wednesday, being the 14th of October, the deputies aforesaid went to veiw the meadowes, and haveing ꝑfected their worke, they gave in an account of their worke, as appeares by the plotts of the meadowes.

---

[17] ATT A GENrll COURT HELD ATT NEWHAVEN THE 23 OF THE 8 M: 1640.

Itt is ordered euery one of the 5 quarters whose proportiō of meadow is vnder 8 acres, shall have itt in the iland in the east riuer, and in the mill meadowes, and their vpland att the vtmost end of the first divisiō of the Yorkeshire quarter wthout the 2 miles beyond the west river.

Itt is ordered thatt Mr. Eaton shall have 50 acres of his meadowes in the meadowes towards Totokett, neare vnto the way that goes to Manunkatucke, wth upland answering that proportiō. And all the rest of his meadow he is to have att his owne choyce in the east meadowes and vpland adjoyning, as itt may best sute his conveniencie wth whatsoeur conveniencies the place will afforde him for a farme.

Itt is ordered thatt or pastor shall have his farme where he shall desire itt wth all the conveniencies of vpland and meadow and creeks wch the place where he pitches will afforde, though above his proportiō, according to his desire.

Itt is ordered that Captaine Turner shall have his lott of meadow and vpland where he shall chuse itt for his owne conveniencie, thatt he may attend the service of the towne w[c]h his place requires.

Itt is ordered thatt all the vpland in the first divisiō w[t]h all the meadowes in the plantatiō shall pay 4[d] an acre yearly, and all the land in the 2[d] divisiō shall pay 2[d] an acre yearely, att 2 severall dayes of paym[t], (viz), the one in Aprill, and the other in October, to raise a comō stock or publique treasury, and thatt a steward or treasurer shall be chosen to receive and dispose of itt according to the occasions of the towne, and give a yearely account of itt to those thatt shalbe appoynted to receive the account.

Itt is ordered thatt in the 2[d] divisiō every planter in the towne shall have for every hundred pound estate given in, twenty acres of vpland, and for every head two acres and a halfe.

Mr. Craine is allowed 300[l] to his estate formerly given in, and Mr. Touttle to add 50[l] to his, provided thatt they pay all rates backward and forwarde, and if they remove, to sell nothing butt improvem[ts].

Itt is ordered thatt all the small lotts about the towne shall have 4 acres of planting ground to every lott, and an acre to every head layd out beyond the east river, betwixt o[r] pasto[rs] farme and the Indians wiggwams.

Itt is ordered thatt Mr. James shall have his meadow att the lower end of the Neck, and bro: Andrewes shall have his meadow among the small lotts as itt shall fall by lott, in the Iland or Mill meadowes.

Itt is granted to the 2 deacons to chuse where they shall have their farms, as neare as may be to the towne, thatt they may the better attend their office.

Itt is ordered that Mr. Gregson shall be Truck ma[r] of this towne for this yeare ensueing, to truck w[t]h the Indians for venison, so as he may afforde to sell to the planters thatt have need att 3[ob] a pound, all together, good and bad, one w[t]h another.

Itt is ordered thatt no English men thatt kills venison shall sell the fattest for above 3[d] a pound, and the leane att 2[d ob].

Itt is ordered thatt the causway to the neck shall be made forthw^{t}h.

Itt is ordered that wampam shall goe in this plantatiō for 6 a peny.

---

[18] A COURT OF ELECTIONS HELD ATT NEWHAVEN THE 29th OF 8 M: 1640.

Bro: Perry, Andrew Hull, Wiłł Peck, Goodm̃ Shirman, Goodm̃ Gibbs and Goodm̃ Livermore were admitted members of the court.

Mr. Eaton chosen magistrate againe.

Mr. Robt Newm̃, Mr. Gregson, Mr. Gilbert, and Captaine Turner chosen deputyes.

Tho: Fugill chosen secretary.

Robt Seely chosen marshall.

Jer. Dixon allowed to add to his estate formerly given in, so much as will make itt 3 hundred pounds, so as he pay all rates for thatt estate backward and forward.

Ben: Linge and Wiłł Touttle are allowed to have their meadow where Mr. Eaton hath his first 500 acres, (viz) in the fresh meadows towards Totokett, and Mr. Craine is to have his allso there.

Allowance is to be given in land to those thatt want of their proportiō in their houslotts, 2 rod for one in the first divisiō, and 3 for one in the 2^{d} divisiō.

Itt is ordered thatt Tymo: Baldwins lott shall have land layd to itt for 6 heads & 500^{l}, and reserved for an elder.

Itt is ordered that nott above 4 moneths shall be accounted for winter in workmens wages, provided thatt they improve 8 howers dilligently in worke every day when they expect to be payd for a dayes worke.

Itt is ordered that if any workem̃ take more then is appoynted for worke and wages, he thatt gives itt and he thatt takes itt shall each of them pay a dayes worke fine, and the inform^{r} shall have the 4th p^{t}.

Itt is ordered thatt every one thatt comes after they beate

the drum̃ ye 2d time, or come defective in armes on trayning dayes, shall pay 1s fine, and for totall absence 5s.

A GENrll COURT HOLDEN ATT NEWH, THE 4 OF THE 9th MONETH 1640.

Whereas Andrew Ward and Robt. Coe of Weathersfield were deputed by Weathersfield men, the 30th of the 8th moneth comonly called October 1640, to treate wth the court att Newhaven about the plantatiō (lately purchased by the said towne*) called Toquams, wch being considered of, itt was agreed vpon by the said court and ꝑtyes aforesaid, that they shall have the said plantatiō vpon these tearmes following. First, thatt they shall repay vnto the said towne of Newhavē all the charges wch they have disbursed about itt, wch comes to 33l as appeares by a note or scedule herevnto annexed. Secondly thatt they reserve a fift ꝑt of the said plantatiō to be disposed off att the appoyntmt of this court to such desireable ꝑsons as may be expected, or as God shall send hither, provided that if wthin one whole yeare such ꝑsons doe not come to fill vp those lotts so reserved, thatt then itt shall be free for the said people to nominate and present to this court some ꝑsons of their owne choyce wch may fill up some of those lotts so reserved, if this court approve of them. Thirdly thatt they joyne in all poynts wth this plantatiō in the forme of govermt here settled, according to the agreemt betwixt this court and Mr. Samuell Eaton about the plantatiō of Totokett.

These articles being read together wth Mr. Sam: Eatons agreemts in the hearing of the said partyes or deputyes, itt was accepted by them, and in witnes thereof they subscribed their names to the articles in the face of the court.

---

* Capt. Turner as agent for the people of New Haven bought of Ponus Sagamore of Toquams, and of Wascussue Sagamore of Shippan, (the other Indians consenting thereto,) all the ground belonging to the said Sagamores, except a piece of ground which Ponus reserved for himself and the other Indians to plant upon, The consideration was 12 coats, 12 hoes, 12 hatchets, 12 glasses, 12 knives, 2 kettles, and four fathoms of white wampum. The liberty of hunting and fishing on the land was reserved by the Indians. This agreement was signed on the first of July, 1640.
Stamford Rec. B. p. 30.

Itt is ordered by the court that Goodm̃ Quick shall give security here for the barke and his account to the owners according to their request to Mr. Eaton, and for thatt end the moneyes thatt are in the hands of Captaine Turner and Mr. Gregson, and should be payd to Weathersley, but layd clame vnto by the saide Quick, are to be detained till things be cleared betwixt them.

Itt was ordered thatt Georg Badcock, servant to Mr. Eaton, shall serve out his time w[t]h his ma[r] to the full end and tearme of six yeares (from his first comeing) according to his ingagem[t] as appeared by the testimony of John Mason and his owne confessiō.

[19] Edward Adams testified vpon oath thatt the note of informacō w[c]h he had form[r]ly delivered into the court (concerning lime w[c]h Arther Halbidg hath delivered to the mill) is true, w[c]h when he had done, Arther Halbidge excepted against itt, thinking to prove the said Edward Adams a ꝑjured ꝑson. Butt Goodman Pigge, Rich: Beach and John Wakefield affirmed the truth of what Edward Adams had testified, (though the said Artur Holbidg did conceive they would have contradicted Edw: Adams his testimony), Itt was therefore ordered thatt the said Arther should pay two folde for all the want of measure thatt is charged vpō him and from hence forth take noe worke by the great, nor burne any lime to sell.

Att the 2[d] of Decemb: 1640.

Thomas Franckland for drinking strong liquors to excess and entertaining disorderly ꝑsons into his cellar to drinking meetings, togeth w[t]h his contempt of the court, was whipped, fined 20[s], and deprived of his cellar and lott, his lott and liberty of staying in the plantatiō being onely granted to him vpoō his good behavio[r].

Andrew Loe jun[r] was whipped for breaking Richard Osborne his cellar and stealing, & y[t] on the Saboth day.

Itt was ordered thatt John Davis, servant to Mr. Wilks, should be whipped for his stuborne carryage to his said ma[r], butt the executiō of the sentence to be suspended for tryall of his future carryage.

Itt was ordered that Mr. Wilks shall abate 2 moneths of the time wch the said Joh: Davis should serve him, for vndue correcting him, strikeing him vpon the head wth a hammer, he being vpō the top of a ladder.

Itt was ordered yt all thatt live in cellars and have famylyes shall have liberty for three moneths to provide for themselves, butt all single psons are to betake themselves forthwth to some famylyes, except the magistrate see cause to respitt them for a time.

Itt was ordered that Mr. Moulenor should give an accoūt to the next court for his pceedings att Totokett.

Att a Court held att Newhaven the 6th of the 11th M: 1640.

Whereas there was a roap lent by Mr. Craine to John Tompson, butt lost by Robt Cogswell who tooke the charge of the boate in wch itt was left, itt is therefore ordered thatt John Tompson shall make itt good to Mr. Craine, and Robt Cogswell shall satisfie John Tompson for itt.

Itt is ordered that Mr. Moulenor shall be comaunded frō the court by the marshall to stay his proceedings att Totokett, inasmuch as whatt he hath done is disorderly and unwarrantably, nott giveing any good account to this court though he have beene required so to doe.

An inventory of Andrew Hulls delivered into the court.

---

[20] A Genrll Court hold att Newhaven the 10th of the 1t moneth [1640]

Itt is ordered thatt all the meadowes belonging to this towne wch vpon pview the *the* deputies for the quarters thought meete thatt 8 acres for 7 should be layde out, (in way of allowance), now itt is to be abated, and thatt allowance wch that, and proportions above that should have had, shall be for makeing thatt allowance w^c^h less proportions are appoynted, and worss meaddow is appoynted to have, in consideracō of the exceeding badnes of the meaddowes. And those that were deputed for the veiw are now to see all the meadowes layde out according to the true intent and meaning of this order; swamps, ponds and creeks nott to be measured.

Itt is ordered thatt all those who by lott shall have their meadow on this side brother Turners fearme, shall have the vpland thatt lyes against itt, or joyning to itt, and if thatt be nott enough to make vp their proportiō for their second devisiō, they shall have itt made up beyond the west river, at the vttmost end of the Yorkshire quarter, among the small lotts.

Itt is ordered thatt after 2 yeares next ensueing be expired, the neck shall be layd for pasture, and thatt all who plant or sow corne therein in the meantime shall secure itt themselves, whether there or elswhere, every one are to secure their owne corne, provided y[t] none doe willfully or negligently trespasse w[t]h their cattell, and it is further ordered thatt after this yeare none shall plant Indian corne in the neck, butt onely sow itt w[t]h English.

Itt is ordered thatt no mans inability or remisnes in fencing his part (in a gen[rll] fence) shall hinder the improvem[t] of land in any of the quarters, the major p̱t consenting.

Itt is ordered thatt those thatt are intrusted in the townes busines shall lay out meadow and vpland for an inne.

Itt is ordered thatt if any mā shoote either bulletts or smaller shott in the towne, or w[t]hin a quarter of a mile of the towne w[t]hout a call, shall pay 5[s] fine for every default.

Itt is ordered thatt if any shall cutt a tree w[t]hout leave where the spruce masts grow, shall pay 20[s] fine for every default.

Itt is ordered thatt if any take either wheele barrow, hand cart or paddles, or oares w[t]hout leave, shall pay five shillings fine.

Itt is ordered thatt if any shall take boate or cannow w[t]hout leave, he shall pay 20[s] fine, and whatt ever damage else may befall the owner for the want thereof.

Itt is ordered thatt fire hooks shall be made for the common vse of the towne, att a commō charge.

ATT A MEETING ABOUT CASTING LOTTS FOR THE EAST MEADOWES AND THE MEADOWES IN THE MILL RIVER 17th 1t MON: 1641

Itt is agreed thatt the small lotts shall begin att the great rock on the farre side of the mill river, and so come downe, towards the sea, and then begin att the lower end of the farre side of the iland in the East river, and so come downe againe on the hither side, and if there shall fall out to be some small pportiō wch will not amount to the quantity of him whose lott falls last in the Mill river, itt shall be in his choyce wther he will have itt, yea or no.

Itt is allso agreed thatt in the East meadowes the first lott shall begin att the neck on the hither side of the river, and so goe on in order to the vper end so farr as there is meadow, and then begin att or pastors farme, and so goe vp againe on the other side so farr as there is meadow, and whosoeur by lott falls next to the farmes thatt are layd out by choyce, if there be not their proportiō there, they must take the rest where itt falls next in order beyond them.

Itt is ordered thatt Thomas Fugill shall have the Iland in the mill river for his pportiō, he being willing to have it when others refused it because itt was bad.

[21] Itt is o[rdered that those] in the neck sha[ll] fence [ ] against [ ] dow tha[ ]ney thatt owe the meadow will fence itt in from the comō.

The name[s of those w]ho are to have their meadow in the East meadow, as their lotts were cast.

1 Mrs. Higginson
2 Mr. Attwater
3 Mr. Pocock
4 Goodmā Nash
5 Mr. Craine
6 Mr. Evance
7 John Ponderson
8 Mr. Lucas
9 Thomas Fugill
10 Edw: Wiglseworth

11 Richard Perry
12 Mr. Constable*
13 Mr. Browning
14 Mr. Marshall
15 David Yale
16 Mr. Brewster
17 Bro: Jer: Dixon
18 John Johnson
19 Mr. Mayers
20 An Elders lott
21 Mr. Roe
22 Mr. Dermer
23 John Chapman
24 Mr. Francis Newman
25 Mr. Malbon
26 Mrs. Eldred
27 Mr. Samuell Eaton
28 Mr. Tench one ye Island.

The names of those who are to have their meadow in Milmeadow and the Iland in the East River, as their lotts were cast in order.

1 John Benham
2 Mr. Cheeuers
3 Tho Powell
4 Abraham Bell
5 Wiłł Andrewes
6 Rich: Beckley
7 Wid: Greene
8 Wid: Williames
9 Tho: Kimberley
10 Robt Hill
11 Jarvis Boykin
12 Andrew Loe
13 Joh: Coop
14 Wiłł Thorpe
15 Mrs. Eaton
16 Mr. Pearce
17 Mr. Yale

The land for the small lotts on ye banke side and by ye west creeke was appoynted to be layd out, as their lotts were drawne in order as followeth.†

1 Steven Metcalfe
2 Adam Nicolls
3 Nath: Merryman
4 John Tompson
5 Bro: Kimberleys bro:
6 John Nash
7 Mrs. Swiñrton
8 Goodmā Davis
9 Rich: Newm̃
Tho: Mitchell
Tho: Morris
Goodm̃ Peck
Another lott
Goodm̃ Hames
Goodm̃ Dighton
Good Pigge
17 Francis Browne
George Larrymor
Tho: Beamt
Tho: Leaver
John Vincent
Joh: Hall
Wiłł Russells
Christopher Tod

* Was this Sir William Constable who as Mather B. iii, chap. xiii, 6, informs us proposed to come to New England with Rev. Ezekiel Rogers? We learn from Winthrop i, 294, that the New Haven gentlemen labored by all means to draw Mr. Rogers and his company to them.

† In the margin. "The order for it is in fo: 17 and in 27."

25 Thomas Mounson	A brickmaker
Ben: Willmott	Obadiah Barnes
Joh: Walker	Eliz: the washer
Ben: Pauling	Will Gibbons

ATT A COURT HELDE ATT NEWHAVEN THE 7th OF THE 2d MON: 1640*.

John Reader was fined 40s for breakeing the order of the Court in exacting greater wages (then the Court had determined,) for 20 dayes worke wch he confessed he had received mony for.

John Thomas was fined 1s for neglecting his watch.

Susanna Man, servant to Mr. Goodyeare, haveing accused John Thomas for stealing a peece of stuff, valued att 3l 6s. she now confessed thatt she had slaundered him, and said thatt God had given her ouer to the Devill to make her lye, wherevpon it was ordered thatt she should pay to her mar double the price of the stuff as the said Joh: Thomas should have done if he had beene guilty, according to the law of God in thatt case.

---

[22] A GENrll COURT HOLDEN ATT NEWHA[VEN] 3d MON 164[1]

Mr. Goodyeare, Mr. Gregson, Mr. Newm̃ and Mr. Gilbert chosen deputyes for the halfe yeare next ensueing.

Mr. Gregson was chosen Treasurer to receive the yearely rates and keep accounts of all disbursemts vpon all necessary occasions for the comō affayres of the towne.

Bro: Pecke chosen measurer for the towne to fill and strike all the corne thatt comes into the plantatiō from other places, for wch he is to have 6d for every score bushells wch he measureth, an a halfe peny for every bushell vnder tenne bushells, the one halfe to be payd by the buyer, and the other halfe by the seller.

---

* I presume this should be 1641.

Itt is ordered thatt all those thatt have hoggs shall drive them from the plantatiō about 5 miles frō the towne, and haunt them forth abroade, neuerthelesse every one is to endeuo[r] to secure their corne by sufficient fences.

Itt is ordered thatt the clay pitts shalbe layd out as comō, as itt was first intended, and what charge of fencing Goodman Mansfield or others shalbe att extraordinary by thatt meanes, the towne is to beare itt in gen[rll].

Itt is ordered thatt Mr. Goodyeare shall have his vpland (w[c]h he is to have in the 2[d] divisiō,) in a place w[c]h he hath chosen beyond the west rocks.

Itt is ordered thatt those who should have a ꝑt of their vpland on the right hand of the mill way (betwixt itt and the river where the land fall narrow,) butt leave itt, shall have their ꝑportiō made up beyond the rocks w[t]hout the 2 miles compasse.

Itt is ordered thatt every house in the towne shall have a ladder (in length to sute the height of their chimney,) w[t]hin 5 weeks, to stand ready by their houses, vnder the penallty of 5[s] fine.

An inventory and will of olde father Shirmañs was delivered into the Court.

Itt is ordered thatt every quarter thatt would fence their land in the Neck, they may have liberty so to doe, provided thatt they doe itt att their owne charge, and leave out the springs for the cattle to drinke att wheresoever any fall w[t]hin the bounds of the neck.

Itt is ordered thatt the rates of wares and worke as they were p[r]sented to the Court by the magistrate shall be settled and be in force in this plantatiō as followeth,

[23] RATES

Itt is ordered thatt seaven howers shall be accounted a dayes worke for a teame, if thatt whole time be dilligently improved in worke according to the nature of thatt imploym[t], and the hyer for a steere by the day 9[d], for a growne oxe or bull 12[d], for a horse or mare 16[d], for cart furniture and man 6[d].

For ma[r] carpenters, joyners, plasterers, bricklayers, mowers, cowpers, thatchers, ryvers of clapboards, pailes, shingles, lathes and the like callings which require skill and strength, nott above 2^s in sõmer and 20^d in winter.

Butt others of the same trades or callings, nott allowed ma^r workemen, nott above 20^d in sommer and 16^d in winter.

Plaisterers, haymakers, fellers of timber, those thatt crosscutt timber, and all sorts of $labo^r$ers experienced and dilligent in their way, improveing time as above, in som^r nott above 18^d, in winter nott above 14^d.

Vnskillfull negligent $labo^r$ers, and boyes, both in som^r and winter in severall $imploym^{ts}$, according to the service they doe, wch when any doubt ariseth shalbe judged by able and indifferent.

Boates of severall sorts, the whole tyde being dilligently improved, according to the na^r of that $imploym^t$. The man by the tyde nott above 16^d. A lighter of 16 tunne wth sale boate or cannow, nott above 2^s. A lighter of 12 tunne 20^d. A shallop of 4 tunne 8^d, and so in respective proportiō, butt in such raines or stormes that goods cannott be laden or vnladen w^thout spoyling, nor the boate stirre though the tyde serve, no payment to be required for the boate in such tydes, though the man be payd while he attends the service.

Worke taken by the greate, sawing by the hundred to be payd for no more then is cutt full & true measure, boards nott above 3^s 8^d, planks 4^s, slit worke 4^s 6^d.

When men saw by the day, the top man or he whose skill guides the worke, and phaps findes the tooles, in som^r and winter respectively as ma^r workmen, and the pitt man as vnskillfull or nott approved ma^r workmen, and if they be equall in skill and charg, then to devide the wages, wch shall be 22^d a peece in sõmer and 18^d in winter.

Felling of timber, thatt wch is full 2 foote over and one wth another nott above 2 pence halfe peny, lesser sorts of timber full 18 inches over, and vnder 2 foote, three halfe pence p foote, all other trees of lesser size then 18 inches over, either by dayes wages as $labo^r$ers or as shall be reasonably agreed.

Hewing and squareing timber of several sizes one wth another, butt the least 15 inches square, well done thatt a kerfe or planke of 2 inches thick being taken off on 2 sides the rest may remaine square for boards or other vse, by the tunne, girt measure 15^d, and for timber more sleightly hewen a lesse price in proportiō. Sills, beames, plates or such like timber hewen square to build w^{t}h, running measure, by the foote nott above 3 farthings.

Mowing well done, w^{c}h vpon quest. is to be judged by other skillfull mowers, salt marsh by the acre nott above 3^s 6^d, fresh by the acre nott above 3^s.

Fencing w^{t}h pales, as house lotts are now done, for felling & cleaveing posts and rales, cross cutting, hewing, mortising, digging holes, setting vp, well raming the posts and nailing on the pailes, by the rod, all the worke being well and sufficiently done in every ꝑt appertaining to itt, 18^d, butt if the worke in any ꝑt be defective, the price to be abated answerably, and thatt to be judged by indifferent men and honest workmen, and so in all other fencing w^{t}h posts and rales as below.

Fencing w^{t}h 5 rales, strong and substantiall posts and rales att least of sizes expressed below, the posts sett two foote and a halfe in the ground, well wrought, sett up, and well rammed so thatt pigs, goates and all other cattell may be kept out, by the rod nott above 18^d.

[24] Fencing w^{t}h 3 rales, such stuff, workmanship as w^{t}h 5 rales, nott above 14^d, substantiall and strong posts, 7 foote and a halfe long, 12 inches broade and 4 inches thick att least where they are felled and cloven, by the hundred 7^s. Substantiall and strong rales 11 foote long, some of them 9 inches broade, some 7, some 9 inches, butt the least, in the smallest ꝑt nott lesse then 5 inches broad, and all of such a thicknes as thatt they may be strong and lasting, proportionably sorted of all the forenamed sizes, by the hundred, nott above 5^s 6^d.

Inch boards solde in the woods by the hundred nott above 4^s 8^d, halfe inch board 4^s 2^d, and 2 inch planke 5^s 6^d ꝑ hundred.

Inch board solde in the towne 6^s, halfe inch boards 5^s, planke 8^s 6^d ꝑ hundred.

Sawen timber 6 inches broade 3 inches thick, in the towne by the foote runing measure nott above 3 farthiñgs, 8 inches square soulde as before nott above 1^d ^{ob} a foote.

Clapboards solde in the woods, good stuff 6 foote long 3s 4d 5 foote long 2s 10d.

Pales 6 foote long 3s, |5 foote 2—8,| 5 foote 2s 4d.

Hewing and naleing clapboards on roofes and sides of houses well done, nott above 4s p hundred, butt as most are done nott worth above 2s or 2s 6d, therefore if any questiō arise, the worke to be rated and judged by indifferent men.

Shingle, good stuff $\frac{4}{3}$ inches thick, some six, some seaven, some eight inches broad, sorted in the woods, being 3 foote long 2s p hundred; 2 foote long 18d, 14, 15 or 16 inches long 9d, butt if defective, price accordingly. Hewing and shooting shingle, well done 3 foote nott above ∧ —, 2 foote nott above 9d p 100, 14, 15 or 16 inches nott above 7d p hundred. Lathing and laying shingle, squar worke wth sawen laths 3 foote ∧ 2 foote 14, 15 or 16 inches long, 10d p hundred—If hewed shingle 11d p hundred. If there be diurs gutters to be laid, then together 13d p hundred. Lime well burnt, vnslaked, brought by water to the landing place for the towne, by the bushell heaped, nott above 7d, by the hogshead full gaged contayning 8 bushells 4s, and the lyme so putt in thatt when the hhd is carted frō the water to the place where itt shall be vsed itt may remaine full.

Plastering, for drawing and carrying water, scaffolding, lathing, laying and finishing the plastering, provideing and paying his laborer, haveing the lime, clay, sand, hayre, hay wth materialls for scaffolding layd neare the place.

By the yeard for seeling 4—ob, for side walls, being whole or in great paines 4d, betwixt the studs, the studs not measured, 5d—ob. rendring betwixt the studs 2d.

Dyett for a laboring man wth lodging and washing 4s—6d by the weeke Venison sould by the English, if fatt, not above 2d—ob p pound, if leane 2d p pound, fowle a pportionable abatemt to whatt was sett last yeare.

All comodityes bought and sould among the planters, and all worke wages and labor (hence forward, till some other course be settled by order,) to be payd for either in corne, as the price goeth in the plantatiō, or in worke as the rates settled by the Court, or in cattell of any sort as they shall be indifferently prized, or in good marchtable bever according to its goodnes; and paymt to be made att the times wch shall be agreed vpon.

---

[25] A COURT HOLDEN THE 7th OF THE 5th MONETH 1641. ATT NEWHAVEN.

Nicholas Tanner haveing ingaged himselfe to pay vnto Mr. Bryan three pounds about three moneth agoe wch he hath nott yett pformed, wherevpon Mr. Bryan desired the justice of the Court. And the said Nicholas did pmise to the said Mr. Bryan thatt he would give him good security before the next Court, wch Mr. Bryan accepted.

Arther Halbidg was allowed to take worke by the great vpõ good behavior.

Mr. Browning being mar of a watch, and neclecting to warne the watch, so as itt was neclected, was fined 10s.

An inventory of Goodman Luckings deliured into the Court.

ATT A COURT HELD ATT NEWHAVEN THE 4th OF THE 6t M: 1641.

John Seckett servant to Mrs. Stolyõ for goeing about to slaunder and reproach his said Mrs, was admonished to tender to his Mrs such satisfactiõ as she might accept, wch was referred to Mr. Goodyeare to determine.

George Warde ingaged his house to satisfie Mr. Huitt for a bill of debt and to satisfie Thomas Laude for a debt of 4l allso.

Andrew Low junr for Saboth breaking, lying and stealing was severely whipped, and ordered to weare a lock.

A GENrll COURT HELD ATT NEWHAVEN THE 30th OF THE 6t MON: 1641.

Whereas there was a purchase made by some pticular psons of sundry plantatiõs in Delaware Bay, att their owne charge, for the advancmt of publique good as in a way of trade, so allso for the settling of churches and plantations in those pts, in combinatiõ w^t h this. And therevpon itt was propounded to the Gen^{rll} Court w^t her plantations should be settled in Delaware Bay, in combinatiõ w^t h this towne, yea or nay, and vpon consideratiõ and debate itt was assented vnto by the Court, and exp^r ssed by holding vp of hands.

So far as Captaine Turner hath refference to the civill state and imployed therein, ꝑvided thatt his place be supplyed in his absence, the Court hath given free liberty to him to goe to Delaware Bay for his owne advantage and the publique good in settling the affayres thereof.

Itt is ordered thatt those to whome the affaires of the towne is comitted shall dispose of all the affayres of Delaware Bay, according to the intent of the agreem^t for combinatiõ w^t h this towne in settleing plantations and admitting planters to sitt down there.

Mr. Goodyeare propounded his purchase of Mr. Farretts Iland* to the towne, butt itt was nott accepted.

Itt is ordered thatt the survayers shalbe payed for all the meadowes, creekes, and ponds w^c h they survay, though itt be cast in for or above allowance w^t hout measure.

Mr. Craine resigned Mr. Hickocks lott into the townes hands.

ATT A COURT HELD THE 1^t OF THE 7th MONETH 1641. ATT NEWHAVEN.

Francis Hall being complained against by Luke Attkinson for w^t hholding frõ him some mony justly due to him, he was injoyned by the Court to make satisfactiõ to the said Luke forthw^t h.

---

* Now called Shelter Island. Mr. Goodyeare purchased it of Mr. Farrett May 18, 1641, and sold it June 9, 1651 to Thomas Middleton, Thomas Rouse, Constant Sylvester and Nathaniel Sylvester, for 1600 lbs of good, merchantable *Muscovado Sugar*. Thompson's L. I., 2d ed., vol. I., 118, 364.

[26] Att a Court holden the 6t of October 1641, att Newhaven.

Itt is ordered that Edward Harwoode shall pay to Leivten^{t} Seely (for takeing his cannow w^{t}hout leave,) twenty shillings.

Mr. Wilks being accused by his man John Davis for forceing him to be bound after he came on shipboard halfe a yeare longer then his father had consented to before, and agreed w^{t}h the said Mr. Wilks for, butt the said John Davis being defective in the proofe of his accusatiõ, and Mr. Wilks wanting his witnesses to prove his innocencie, itt is ordered thatt if the said Mr. Wilks doe nott make it appeare by witnes (thatt his agreem^{t} was for 4 yeares and a halfe) betwixt and the last of September come 12 moneth after the date hereof, he shall pay vnto the said John Davis 20^{s} for every moneth so long as he stayes w^{t}h him above 4 yeares.

Att the Gen^{rll} Court of Elections held att Newhaven the 27th of Octo: 1641.

Mr. Craine of this church, and Andrew Warde and Francis Bell of Rippowams, admitted members of this court and received the charge of freemen.

Mr. Eaton and Mr. Goodyeare chosen magistrates of this towne.

Thurston Rayner chosen constable for Rippowams to order such busines as may fall in thatt towne according to God, for the next ensueing year, butt is nott to be established in his office till he have received his charge frõ this Court and testified his acceptance thereof to this Court.

Mr. Gregson, Mr. Robt Newman, Mr. Gilbert and Mr. Wakeman chosen deputyes for this plantation.

Tho: Fugill chosen secretary.

Robt Seely chosen marshall.

A Court held att Newhaven the 3^{d} of Novem: 1641.

Whereas Robt Johnson maketh clame to the house and lott of his brother John Johnson, late planter of this towne deceased, by vertue of a contract betwixt them, the Court haveing debated itt and nott findeing itt ripe for issue, itt was ordered thatt those thatt can give best light about itt should ripen their app^{r}hensions so as they may be able to make oath of whatt they can testifie concerīng itt, w^{c}h may stand vpon record for posterity.

David Anderson for his contempt of authority in carrying away a delinquent contrary to order and his owne ꝑmise, was fined 20^{s}.

Itt is ordered thatt an attachm^{t} be sent forth to distraine the goods of Mr. Trobridge, to pay the townes rates, and to satisfie the demaunds of those ꝑsons to whom he is indebted, as Mr. Gregson 20^{l}, Mr. Whitfield 20^{l}, w^{t}h divers others of this town.

Itt is ordered thatt every one thatt have beene in the watchs shall pay to Steven* the drum^{r} and Jarvis Boykin nine pence a peece for a yeare and a halfe ending the first of Decem: next ensueing.

---

[27] A Gen^{rll} Court held att Newhaven the 29° of Novem: 1641.

Richard Miles and Roger Allen admitted members of the Court.

Itt is ordered thatt so many of those (who have the small lotts by the sea side) as will resign their land beyond the East River shall have 6 acres for every single ꝑson, 8 acres for man and wife, and one acre for every childe, att the farre end of the Great Plaine in lew thereof, provided thatt vpon veiw itt be layde out so as the townes occasions may be accomodated w^{t}hout p^{r}judice to the towne, and if any remove, they shall onely sell improvem^{ts}.

---

* Stephen Metcalfe.

Itt is ordered thatt Wequash shall have a sute of cloths made att the townes charge.*

Itt is ordered thatt the townes rates shall be payd in corne att 2s 4d a bushell by all those who chuse to pay their rates in Indian corne.

Itt is ordered thatt if any shall furnish the Indians, whether directly or indirectly, wth any amunitiō whatsoever, shall pay for the first default 5l fine, and afterward att the discretion of the Court.

Tho: Fugill is allowed his 2d divisiō att the foote of the West Rock of the cleare ground wch is there, or so much of itt as he desires, according to his proportion.†

Itt is ordered thatt all the voyd lotts, belonging to absent ꝑsons shalbe fenced att the townes charge untill the ꝑsons come thatt shall possesse them, and then all the charges to be retourned by the owners, and bro: Andrewes and bro: Mounson are to see thatt the fences be done well according to the order of the Court.

A Court held att Newhaven the 1t of Decem: 1641.

Itt is ordered thatt the firkin of butter wch Mr. Wilks tooke vp shall be left in the hands of bro: Ponderson, (or the vallue thereof) and remaine there till some cann challeng itt by the marke.

Itt is ordered that Goodm̄ Hall shall have liberty to dispose of the children wch he brought our till the Court have light to dispose otherwise of them, provided thatt they be well looked vnto and well vsed. And Goodmā Hitchcock who is to have one of them is to pay to the Treasurer what is due for the boy, and Goodm̄ Hall is to be payd out of itt whatt is due to him.

---

* "One Wequash Cook, an Indian living about Connecticut river's mouth, and keeping much at Saybrook with Mr. Fenwick, attained to good knowledge of the things of God and salvation by Christ, so as he became a preacher to other Indians, and labored much to convert them, but without any effect, for within a short time he fell sick, not without suspicion of poison from them, and died very comfortably."
Sav. Winth. II. 74 *sub anno* 1642.

† See page [133.] It was for falsifying this order by omitting the words "according to his proportion," that Fugill was excommunicated and deprived of his place, in 1645.

A COURT HELD ATT NEWHAVEN THE 5th OF JAN: 1641.

Itt is ordered thatt all the goods of Mr. Trobridg wch remaine shall be attached to satisfy the demaunds of the psons to whom he is indebted, namely Mr. Perry, Mr. Craine 10l and damages, Hen: Gibbons and Mr. Caine of Boston.

Tho: Badger being accused and convicted for defileing himselfe by divers vncleane passages wth one of his mars children not above 6 yeares of age, was whipped att a carts arce about the towne to make his punishment examplary.

---

[28] A GENrll COURT THE 25th OF 12th MON: 1641.

Mr. Malbon and Goodman Ives admitted members of the Court and received the charge of freemen.

Francis Browne, Thomas Morris, Abraham Smyth, Will Russells, Thomas Beamont, John Wilforde and Goodmã Pigge are allowed to have their land in the Plaine, amongst the rest of their neighbors.

Itt is ordered thatt Mr. Robt Newman, Mr. Francis Newmã Thomas Mounson and Adam Nicholls shall veiw the comõ way to the Plaines, and afterward itt is to be ordered so as may be most comodious for the publique good.

Itt is ordered thatt the Neck bridge shall be repaired forthwth, and thatt as speedyly as may bee a cart bridge be made ouer the West River and another over the Mill river.

Itt is ordered thatt a cart bridge be made over the East River allso, as soone as conveniently may be after the other two bridges are fully finished, onely itt is referred to consideracõ wther the towne will beare the whole charge, or disburse a hundred pounds towards itt and lett the rest be borne by those thatt have their lands on the east side, and in consideracõ thereof, allow them the liberty and proffitt of fishing and the towne to stand to the repair of the said bridge.

Itt is ordered thatt the lawes formrly made conceriñg wares and works shall frõ hence forwarde be voyd and of no force till the Court see cause to the contrary.

Itt is ordered thatt all the voyde lotts in the towne shall be reserved for those for whom they were intended till the comeing of the first ships, and if then ye persons come nott for whom they are so reserved, the towne may dispose of them as they see cause, and itt is to be considered by the Court what is equall to be allowed for the improvem^{ts} vpon them.

Itt is ordered thatt a free schoole shall be sett vp in this towne, and o^{r} pasto^{r} Mr. Davenport, together w^{t}h the magistrates shall consider whatt yearly allowance is meete to be given to itt out of the comō stock of the towne, and allso whatt rules and orders are meet to be observed in and about the same.

Itt is ordered thatt the comō feild called the oyster shell feild shall be lett to such ꝑsons whose ꝑ^{r}sent need requires itt, the ordering and disposeing of w^{c}h is referred to the magistrates and deputyes.

Bro: Tompson, bro: Clarke, bro: Miles, bro: Wakem̃, bro: Atwater, bro: Francis Newmā, bro: Robt Newmā, bro: Perry and bro: Craine are desired to know the mindes of their severall quarters, how many are contented to exchang their land in the neck for land in the oxe pasture.

Brother Davis sute for a little additiō of land to be added to his proportiō in the plaines, to save him some charge in fencing was granted by the Court.

Itt is ordered that none shall hant their hoggs thatt way where their land lyes nott, butt to endevo^{r} as much as may be to haunt them thatt way where their 2^{d} divisiō lyes.

---

[29] A GEN^{rll} COURT HELD AT NEWHAVEN THE 2^{d} OF THE 1^{t} MONETH, 1641, ABOUT GEOR: SPENCER.

Francis Browne admitted member of the Court and received the charge.

The 14th of February, 1641, John Wakeman a planter and member of this church acquainted the magistrates thatt a sow of his w^{c}h he had lately bought of Hen: Browning, then w^{t}h pigge, had now brought among divers liveing and rightly shaped pigs, one ꝑdigious monster, w^{c}h he then brought w^{t}h him to be veiwed and considered. The monster was come to the full growth as the other piggs for ought could be discerned, butt brought forth dead. Itt had no haire on the whole body, the skin was very tender, and of a reddish white collour like a childs; the head most straing, itt had butt one eye in the midle of the face, and thatt large and open, like some blemished eye of a man; over the eye, in the bottome of the foreheade wch was like a childes, a thing of flesh grew forth and hung downe, itt was hollow, and like a mans instrumt of genration. A nose, mouth and chinne deformed, butt nott much vnlike a childs, the neck and eares had allso such resemblance. This monster being after opened and compared wth a pig of the same farrow, there was an aparant difference in all the inwards. Some hand of God appeared in an imprssion upon Goodwife Wakemans speritt, sadly expecting, though she knew nott why, some strange accedent in thatt sows pigging, and a strange imprssion was allso upon many thatt saw the monster, (therein guided by the neare resemblance of the eye,) that one George Spencer, late servant to the said Henry Browning, had beene actor in unnatureall and abominable filthynes wth the sow, thus divers upon the first sight, expressed their apprehensions wthout any knowledge whatt conjecture others had made. The foremenconed George Spencer so suspected hath butt one eye for vse, the other hath (as itt is called) a pearle in itt, is whitish & deformed, and his deformed eye being beheld and compard together wth the eye of the monster, seamed to be as like as the eye in the glass to the eye in the face; the man had beene formrly notorious in the plantatiō for a prophane, lying, scoffing and lewd speritt, as was testfyed to his face, butt being examined concerning this abominatiō, att first he said he had nott done itt thatt he knew off, then denyed itt, butt being comitted to prison, partly on strong probabilities of this fact, and ptly for other miscarriages, the same evening, being the 24th of February as above, Mr. Goodyeare, one of the magistrates, went to the prison, found Sam: Martin and another yong man talking wth the said Georg Spencer, he asked him if he had nott comitted thatt abominable filthynes wth the sow, the prisonr att first denyed itt. Mr. Goodyeare asked him whatt he thought of the monster wch had beene shewed him, whether he did not take notice of something in itt like him, the prisonr after a little pause asked the magistrate whose sow itt was, who replyed, he knew best himselfe, att wch the prisonr was againe silent, the magistrate apprehending in the prisoner some relenting, as a preparatiō to confession, remembred him of thatt place of scripture, he thatt hideth his sin shall not prosper, butt he yt confesseth and forsaketh his sins shall finde mercie, and asked him if he were nott sory he had denyed the fact wch seemed to be witnessed frō heaven agst him. The prsonr answered he was sory and confessed he had done itt, butt as Mr. Goodyeare was going away, the prsonr tolde Sam: Martin what he had confessed to Mr. Goodyeare was for fauor, thereupon Sam: Martin called Mr. Goodyeare back. Mr. Goodyeare retourning, asked the prisonr if he said soe, who said no, affirīng yt Sam: Martin mistook him, Mr. Goodyeare demaunded of him whether had comitted the fact yea or no, he answered he had done itt, and so Mr. Goodyeare departed.

The 25th of Febr. 1641, both the magistrates wth divers others went to the prison to speake wth the prisoner, wished him to give glory to God, in a free confessiō of his sin, he againe confest the bestiality before meñconed, said he had comitted itt while he was in Mr. Brownings service, and in a hogstie of his; yett Mr. Goodyeare after going to him, he att first denyed the fact, but Robt Seely the marshall thereupon minding him of wt he had confest to him, he againe freely confessed the fact, butt said he had nott done itt in the stye wch Mr. Goodyeare spake off, butt in a stye wthin a stable belonging to Mr. Browning. And thatt he, the said Geo: Spencer being there att worke, the sow came into the stable, and then the temptatiō and his corruptiō did worke, and he drove the sow into the stye, and then comitted thatt filthynes.

The 26th of Feb: Mr. Eaton and Mr. Davenport going to speake wth the prisoner, Mr. Goodyeare came to them and in the presence of Goodman Mansfield, Wiłł Newmā, Tho: Yale, Theophilus Higginson, Joh: Brocktt and others, questioned him more perticularly concerīng the beastiality, namely how long the temptatiō had beene upon his speritt before he comit-

ted itt; he answered itt had beene upon his speritt 2 or 3 dayes before; being asked w^{t} workings he had w^{t}hin him att thatt time, he said he found some workings against itt, both frō the haynousnes of the sin and the loathsomenes of the creature; being asked whether he did nott in thatt time seeke help frō God against the temptatiō, he said no, if he had he thought God would have helped him; being asked whether he did nott vse to pray to God, he answered he had not since he came to New England w^{c}h was betweene 4 or 5 yeares agoe, in Engl[and] he did vse to pray, butt itt was onely in his bed; being asked in w^{t} manner, he answered [he] said (Our Father &c); being asked whether he did nott read the scriptures he answere[d] his ma^{r} putt him upon itt else nott, being asked whether he
[30] found nott some workinge [*upon him*] || in the publique ministry, he answered sometimes he had some workings, butt they did nott abide w^{t}h him, being asked how long he was in the stye w^{t}h the sow, he said about 2 howers; being asked about w^{t} time, he said about 6 a clock in the evenīg, when the sun was sett, and the day light almost shutt in; being asked w^{t} itt was in the monster thatt did affect him, he answered the whit[illegible]es in the eye; being charged frō the testimony w^{c}h had beene given by sundry person who had conversed w^{t}h him, w^{t}h a prophaiñe, atheisticall carryag, in unfaithfullnes and stubornes to his ma^{r}, a course of notorious lying, filthnes, scoffing att the ordinances, wayes and people of God, he confest miscarryages to his ma^{r}, and lying, and thatt he had scoffed att the Lords day, calling itt the Ladyes day, butt denyed other scoffing, wicked and bitter speeches witnessed against him, and other form^{r} acts of filthynes, either with Indians or English, w^{c}h out of his owne mouth were charged upon him. On the Lords day, being the 27th of Feb: he caused a bill to be putt up, intreating the prayers of the church to God on his behalfe, for the pardon of the sinns he had committed, and confessed, professing he was sory he had greived the magistrates in denying itt, acknowledging thatt Satan had hardened his hart both comitt and denye it.

ATT A GENrll COURT HELD ATT NEWHAVEN THE 2d OF MARCH 1641.

George Spencer being brought to the Barr and charged as wth other crimes so wth the foremenconed beastiality, and the monster shewed, upon wch God from heaven seamed both to stamp out the sin, and as wth his finger to single out the actor; being wisht therefore, as he had done before many witt-nesses formerly, so againe, by confessiō to give glory to God; butt he impudently and wth desperate imprecatiōs against himselfe denyed all thatt he had formerly confessed, whereupon the formr perticulars were fully testified in open Court to the prisonrs face by the persons before mencōned respectively, and other testimonyes was added, namely, Robt Seely the Marshall affirmed thatt the prisonr did dictate to him the foremencōoned bill by wch he desired the prayers of the church for the pardon of thatt beastiality, professing therein thatt Satan had sometimes hardened his hart to deny itt, and yt on the Lords day att night after he had heard himselfe prayed for in the congregatiō, he againe confessed the fact to him, and seamed to be greived for the sinne, and some teares fell from the prisonrs eyes greiving as he said thatt he had denyed itt.

Ezechiell Cheevers affirmeth thatt the next morning after the aforesaid Saboth, being the 28 of Feb: the said Georg Spencer tolde him thatt he founde his hart more softned then itt had beene, and thatt the Lord had given him a sight of his sinne, and he hoped he would lett him see itt more.

Richard Malbon affirmed thatt the prisonr confessed the fact to him in the prsence of Tho: Yale and Wiłł Newmā, and added thatt if he had nott confessed itt, yett itt was true, and God knew itt though he should denye itt, and the said Richard Malbon att another time turned him to thatt scripture Livit 20. 15. ad bid him make applycatiō of itt to the marshall whom he left wth him, the marshall affirmeth thatt when the said Rich: Malbon was gone, the prisoner tolde him thatt thatt scripture stroke like a dagger to his hart.

Wiłł Harding, a sawyer, and one thatt was suspected by some in Court to have given the prisoner evill councell, testifyed to the prisoners face in Court, thatt the prison[r] had said to him the said Harding thatt Thomas Badgers sin was worse then his, for Badger lay w[th] a Christian, butt himselfe the prisoner, lay butt w[th] a rotten sow, and the p[r]son[r] being then asked by him the said Harding, how he could make the sow stand, he answered well enough, & being asked when he did comitt the sin, he answ[d] he did itt since he came from Connectecutt.

Wiłł Aspenall affirmeth thatt he confessed the sinne to him, and being asked att whatt time he did itt, he said after he came from Connectecutt, in Mr. Brownings stable. Wiłł Aspenall objected how could thatt be, seeing he was nott then in Mr. Brownings service, he said he had busines there; being asked whatt busines, he was silent.

Wiłł Bladen testified thatt the prisoner confessed the sinne to him, being asked if he did itt butt once, the prisoner answered he had done itt butt once; to this testimony the prisoner replyed in Court, Itt is true Wiłł, thou hast cleared thyselfe.

Rob[t] Newman and Mathew Gilbert testified thatt the prisoner did confess itt to them, they asked how his conscience wrought while he was acting itt, and whatt pleasure he founde, and how long he was acting itt, he answered about halfe an hower, and itt was the most terrible halfe hower thatt ever he had, they asked how he could doe itt if he had no pleasure in itt, he answered he was driven by the power of the devill and the strength of his [corr]uptiō to doe the thing.

[31] ‖ John Clarke testified thatt he had beene wth the said Georg Spencer in prison, and asked him whether he did comitt thatt sin of beastiality charged upon him, the prisoner answ[d] yea; he the said John Clarke asked him againe, butt did you doe itt, he answered I did doe itt; againe John Clarke asked him, butt did you doe itt, he answered the third time, he did doe itt. John Clarke replyed, though there were none thatt knew of it butt yo[r] owne selfe, and thatt yo[r] confessiō might prove dangerous to you, yett would you confess itt, he answered thatt he did doe itt. John Clarke asked him, if he were not drawne to confess itt in hope of favo[r], and said did

you doe itt, he answered he did doe itt; then John Clarke asked him, why he had denyed itt to the magistrates, the prisoner answered thatt he had nott denyed itt to the magistrates, butt onely said he did nott know thatt he did itt. John Clarke asked him why he did now confess itt, he answered because he did doe itt.

Roger Alen testified thatt he was p[r]sent when the former discourse passed betwixt John Clarke and the prisoner, and thatt he the said Roger Alen asked the prisoner why he confessed the fact, he answered because he did doe itt, and the monster was like him. Roger Alen further testified thatt the prisoner sent for him, as one he knew in olde England and thatt knew his friends, and, as the prison[r] said, w[t]h a purpose to deny the fact, yett when the said Roger Allen came, the prisoner reconed up many sins of w[c]h he was guilty, against his parents and against his maister, and att last named this abominable fact w[c]h he wondered att, having sent for him w[t]h a contrary purpose.

Rob[t] Ceely the Marshall added to his former testimony, thatt having in prison heard the said George Spencer deny the fact after so many confessions, and after he had intreated the prayers of the church for the pardon of thatt perticular sinne, the said Robert Seely asked him, how he durst mock God in putting up a bill desiring the congregatiō to pray for the pardon of thatt sinne w[c]h now he denyeth. The prisoner, after some pause, confessed to him thatt he did comitt the fact, and desired him to looke upon him as one acted by the devill in denying itt.

This cleare and plentifull testimony and evidence being given in Court to the prisoners face, out of his owne mouth, thatt he had freely and often confest the *the* fact w[t]h the scircumstances and his confession concurring w[t]h the worke of God, as itt were poynting him out in the monster, the prison[r] was asked whatt he had to say against the wittnesses, or against their testimony, he answered thatt the witnesses did him wrong, and charged things upon him w[c]h he had nott spoken. Whereupon the Court, (though aboundantly satisfied in the evidence, and the prisoner having att sundry times upon examinatiō confest the fact to the magistrates,) yett began to examine the witnesses upon oath. Whereupon Robert Newman, Mathew Gilbert, John Clarke and Roger Alen upon oath did confirme the evidence they had before given, and others were ready to doe the like, butt the prisoner stopped the course, confessing what they had testified was true, and by him had beene spoken to them, yett obstinately and impudently persisted to deny the fact.

The Court, weighing the premises did finde and conclude the prisoner to be guilty of this unnatureall and abominable fact of beastiality, and thatt he was acted by a lying speritt in his denyalls. And according to the fundamentall agreem[t], made and published by full and gen[rll] consent, when the plantatiō began and government was settled, that the judiciall law of God given by Moses and expounded in other parts of scripture, so far as itt is a hedg and a fence to the morrall law, and neither ceremoniall nor tipicall, nor had any referrence to Canaan, hath an everlasting equity in itt, and should be the rule of their proceedings. They judged the crime cappitall, and thatt the prisoner and the sow, according to Levit. 20 and 15, should be put to death,* butt the time of executiō, and the kinde of death were respited till the next Gen[rll] Court.

[Page 32 of the original is blank.]

---

[33] A Gen[rll] Court the 6th of the 2[d] Moneth, 1642.

Brother Davis and bro: John Nash admitted members of the Court and accepted the charge of freemen.

Mr. Mitchell and John Whitmore of Rippowams was allso admitted members of this Co[rt], and accepted the charge of freemen.

Mr. Malbon, Mr. Gregson, Mr. Gilbert and Mr. Wakeman chosen deputyes for the halfe yeare next ensueing.

The plantatiō of Rippowams is named Stamforde.

Whereas the Deputyes for Stamforde complaine thatt their plantatiō are att some difference wth the Indians, and there-

* It would appear from Winthrop, II. 61, that he was not condemned to death without advice from Massachusetts, and some other places.

fore require help of advice frō this Court how to carry towards them, Itt is therefore ordered, thatt the magistrates and deputyes for this plantatiō shall advise w^t^h the aforesaid deputyes of Stamforde whatt course may best conduce to their peace and safety.

John Touttle of Yennycok, deputed by the Court to be constable to order the affayres of thatt plantatiō, the time being, till some further course be taken by this Court, for the settling a magistracie there according to God.

Itt is ordered thatt every planter shall pay the drumer his last yeares wages forthw^t^h (viz) 6^d^ a peece for every one thatt is in the watches, and his wages due to him for this yeare to be payd in October next ensueing.

Itt is ordered that Mr. Malbon shall order the watches and all the martiall affayres of this plantatiō dureing Captaine Turners absence.

Itt is ordered thatt every first Wednesday in Aprill and every Wednesday in the last whole weeke in October shall be a Gen^rll^ Court held att Newhaven for the plantations in combination w^t^h this towne.

Itt is ordered that from hence forwarde the woods and meadowes shall be burned the tenth of March every yeare, and therefore every man is to take care to secure any thing thatt is his, w^c^h may be in danger of burning, either in the woods or meadowes.

Itt is ordered thatt no yong men shall live by themselves in cellars, butt betake themselves to such famylyes as the ma^rs^ thereof may nott onely watch over them, butt be able to give and account of or concerning them or their conversatiō when they shall be required.

George Spencer, the prisoner, being brought forth, was demaunded whether he would yett give glory to God in owning his guilt in thatt loathsome sin of beastiality wherein God from heaven had seemed to single him out, and himselfe so often, and before so many witnesses had made acknowledgm^t^, butt he retayning his form^r^ obstinacie, peremtorily denyed itt, whereupon Robt Newman and John Clarke gave in evidence in Court to his face, thatt since he was sentenced to dye, he had fully confessed the fact to them. Att first he denyed thatt he had so done, butt they minding him of the passages betwixt him and them, he said thatt if he had confessed itt he knew nott whatt he said, butt after a while, he acknowledged thatt he had confessed itt to them, being asked in Court, why he did now deny itt, he answered, because he neither knew heaven nor hell.

Ezechiell Cheevers testified thatt the prisoner had confessed the fact to him since he was condemned to dye, and did allso professe to him att the same time thatt he would neu^{r} denye it againe while he lived. The said Ezekiell asked him, what people might thinke of him if he should deny itt againe, if they might nott justly thinke he was led by the devill, he answered, they could thinke no lesse, and added, the Lord might justly have strucken him dead form^{r}ly, or might have caused the earth to have swallowed him upp quick for denying the fact in Court, and taking the name of God in vaine, in kneeling downe and calling God to witness his innocencie, when he himselfe knew his guiltiness, all w^{c}h the prisoner acknowledged he had spoken to Ezekiell Cheevers.

[34] || Francis Church testified thatt the prisoner had confessed the fact to him since he was condemned, and tolde him thatt he wondred thatt the people of God did nott come to him, and thatt he feared there was no hope of him, because the people of God did not speake to him as form^{r}ly they had done.

The prisoner acknowledged in Court thatt he had confessed the fact to Francis Church, though he had formerly oft denyed itt, and further confesseth, that Will Harding, a sawyer, had given him evill councell to denye itt.

Being hereupon demaunded in Court whether he would yett give glory to God in a free acknowledgm^{t} of his sinfull and abominable filthynes in the beastiality before named, he answered he would leave itt to God, adding thatt he had condemned himselfe by his former confessions.

The Court seriously considering the clearnes of the testimonyes together w^{t}h his answers, were aboundantly satisfied and confirmed, both concerning his guilt, and their form^{r} sentence against him, and now proceeded to determine whatt time, and what kinde of death he should dye. Itt was therefore by gen^{rll} consent concluded and adjudged, thatt on the 6th day next, being the 8 of Aprill, he the said Georg Spencer shall be hanged upon a gallows till he be dead, the place to be the farthest part of the feild called the Oyster-shell field, by the sea side, butt thatt first, the foremencõned sow att the said place of executiõ shall be slaine in his sight, being run through w^{t}h a sworde.

THE 8th OF APRILL, 1642.

The day of executiõ being come, Georg Spencer the prisoner was brought to the place apoynted by the Court for executiõ, in a cart; upon sight of the gallowes he seemed to be much amazed and trembled, after some pause he began to speake to the youths about him, exorting them all to take warning by his example how they neglect and dispise the meanes of Grace, and their soules good as he had done, in the educatiõ he had from his parents, the goverm^{t} of his religious ma^{r}, and the publique ministry he had lived vnder, by all w^{c}h he might have gott much sperituall good, butt thatt his hart was hardened. In perticular he directed and pressed his exhort. upon Anthony Stevens, servant to Mr. Malbon, then present, who being discontented w^{t}h his condicõ, as the prisoner had heard, purposed to be gone from this place. He tolde him if he went from the ordinances he went from Christ, as he had heard itt delivered in publique, and many other wordes he vsed to the same purpose; w^{c}h being finished, he was advised to improve the small remainder of his time in the acknowledgm^{t} of his owne form^{r} sinfull miscarriages, together w^{t}h the abominable lewdnes he had committed w^{t}h the sow there present, and his desperate obstinacie in such fearefull denyalls after such cleare and full confession as he had oft made before sundry witnesses. Att first w^{t}h the acknowledgment of sundry evills, both in his yonger yeares, and in his late service, he joyned a denyall of his fact, butt the halter being fastened to the gallowes, and fitted to his neck, and being tolde it was an ill time now to ꝓvoke God when he was falling into his hands, as a righteous and seveere judge who had vengeanc att hand for all his other sins, so for his impudency and atheisme, he justified the sentence as righteous, and fully confessed the beastiality in all the scircumstances, according to the evidence in Court, and called for one Wiłł Harding, a sawyer there present, who coming neare, the prisoner charged upon him the murder of his soule, affirming thatt the said William Harding coming into the prison to him, had given him councell to deny the fact, and had tolde him thatt the Court could nott proceed against him, butt by his owne confession, wch pernicious councell had stopped his eare against all wholsome councell and advice thatt had, from time to time, beene given him, both by Mr. Davenport and others, for his speritualL good, and had hardened his hart to such a peremtory denyall in Court, though he had so often confessed the fact more privately, and though executiō had beene respited betwixt 5 and 6 weeks [35] after the || first sentence, and his life so long spared, yett the councell of the said Harding had beene a meanes to hinder his repentance, and now he was ready to dye, and knew no other butt he must goe presently to hell. Harding denyed whatt the prisoner charged him wth, butt the prisoner wth earnestnes confirmed whatt he had spoken, and said he would beare witness of itt to the death, and wished Harding to thinke of itt, for he was a cause of his souls damnatiō. Being desired to express somthing what apprehensions he had of the haynousnes of his sin, as against God, and whatt impressions of sorrow were wrought in him for itt, and whatt desires of pardon and mercie in Jesus Christ, he could not, though much pressed, be drawne to speake a word to any of those purposes, and in this frame for ought could be discerned, the sow being first slaine in his sight, he ended his course here, God opening his mouth before his death, to give him the glory of his rightousnes, to the full satisfactiō of all then prsent, butt in other respects leaving him a terrible example of divine justice and wrath.

[36] ATT A COURT HELD ATT NEWHAVEN THE 4th OF THE 3d MONETH, 1642:

Itt is ordered thatt the watches shall be settled forthwth, consisting of 31 watches, 7 men to each watch, the mars whereof received their charge given by the magistrates.

Itt is ordered thatt Mr. Evance shall have the 2 trees wch stands before his house, in lew of 2 peeces of timber thatt brother Andrews had of his about the meeting house.

Two of bro: Wakemans men is excused frō watching for the present, because of their imploymt att Pawgasett.

ATT A COURT HELD ATT NEWHAVEN THE 1t. OF JUNE 1642.

Itt was propounded by the owners of the mill to the Courts consideratiō whether the towne will take itt into their hands, or establish itt in the place and ꝑsons hands where it is.

Mr. Pearce, being mar of a watch and neglecting to order his watch according to his charge, was onely admonished, because itt was the first time that he hath transgressed the order in that kinde.

A COURT HELD THE 5t DAY OF THE 6t. MONETH 1642.

Whereas some goods of Mr. Broadstreets and Mr. Saltingstons were left here by Goodman Quick, Mr. Loudlow desired to have an attachmt entred agst the said goods for one debt of three pounds and another debt of twenty & two pounds, of wch the Court tooke notice, butt demurred in granting the attachmt.

Itt is ordered thatt if att any time one of the watches be broake, and the watchmen devided into severall watches, the captaine shall give warning (to those mars whome itt concernes) of the alteratiō, least there be mistaks as formrly.

Itt is ordered that if any souldier come late on trayning dayes, he shall show himselfe to the clarke of the company, who is to take notice of his comeing, or else his late comeing shall be counted as totall absence.

Josuah Attwater, by reason of his weaknes, is excused from trayĩng, yett to serve as clarke to the company; he is contented on trayning dayes to take the names of the souldiers, and to observe who is absent or defective and p^r^sent them to the Court, and for that end, he is to call the company att 7 a clock every trayĩng day.

Itt is ordered that frõ hence forwarde none of the watchmen shall have liberty to sleep dureing the watch.

Itt is ordered thatt on trayning dayes, one man shall stay at home in every farme house, to prevent such danger as may happen or fall out at the farms if none should be left to keepe them.

Richard Beach for nott perforĩng covenant in the worke w^c^h he undertooke to doe att the mill, w^c^h he was to doe strongly and substantially, butt did itt weakely and sleightly as was *was* proved by the testimony of John Wakefield the miller, himselfe allso nott denying itt; Itt was ordered that he should make good the damage, butt because the damage is not justly known what itt is, Mr. Goodyeare and Mr. Gregson are to [ve]iw the worke, and consider off and sett downe the damage by his [defec]tive workmanship.

[37] ||Goodman Barker, for neglecting to watch, was fined five shillings, and his man for comeing to watch w^t^hout pouder fined 1^s^.

Samuell, servant to Edward Chipperfield, for comeing to watch w^t^h his armes defective, was fined 2^s^.

Mr. Evance is spared frõ personall trayning, provided thatt he finde a man in his roome, or else pay to the company a man's hyre every trayning day.

A difference betweene Mr. Evance and Goodm̃ Mead is referred to Mr. Gilbert and Mr. Gregson w^t^h the consent of both ptyes.

Samuell Hoskings and Elizabeth,* for their filthy dalliance together, w^c^h was confessed by them both, they were both severely whipped.

* In the margin, "Hoskins and his wife."

A GEN^{rll} COURT HELD ATT NEWHAVEN THE 6th OF THE 6 MONETH 1642.

Brother Abbott and brother Whitehead admitted members of the Court and received the charge of freemen.

Robt Ceely chosen leweten^{t} of the trayned band, & Fran: Newmā ancient. Bro: Andrewes, bro: Mounson, bro: Clarke and Goodman Jeffreyes was chosen sergeants.

Brother Kimberly, bro: Mosse, bro: John Nash, and bro: Whitehead chosen corporalls.

Itt is ordered that the gen^{ll}: trayning dayes shall be observed once every month: for the whole company, and thatt whosoever shall not appeare when he is called, his fine is 1^{s}. If totally absent, or dept w^{t}hout leave before the company breake up, his fine is 5^{s}.

Itt is ordered thatt all those thatt have musketts or guns shall keepe them still, and the pikes thatt are made shall be att the townes charge, and kept for the townes vse and service.

Itt is ordered that their shall no other mill be built for this towne, provided thatt the mill thatt now is be so fitted as thatt itt may serve the townes occasiō^{s} to grinde both Indian and English corne well.

Memōrd. The Court declared their app^{r}hensions thatt itt was form^{r}ly ordered thatt a cart bridge should be made over the East River att the towns charge next spring.

Goodmā Moulthrop is allowed to have 6 acres of land added to his lott in the first divisiō, and 12 acres in the 2^{d}.

Itt was ordered thatt one of the squadrons in course, shall trayne every last day, except onely thatt weeke in w^{c}h the gen^{rll} trayning is (w^{c}h is to be every fift weeke,) and whosoever shall come late to those weekly traynings, his fine is 6^{d}. If totally absent, his fine is 2^{s}-6^{d}. He y^{t} shall come after the second drum hath left beating, shall be accounted a late commer.

[38] A COURT HELD ATT NEWHAVEN THE 3d OF THE 7th MON: 1642.

Mathew Wilson, for killing a dog of Mr. Perryes willfully and disorderly, finde 20s. for his disorder, and ordered to pay 20s. damage to Mr. Perry, wch 40s. Edward Chipperfield vndertooke to see payd by the last of September next.

John Lovell, the miller, for sinfull dalliance wth a little wench of Goodm̃ Halls, was whipped.

A COURT THE 7th OF SEPT. 1642, HELD ATT NEWHAVEN.

Tho: Pell and attournay for the executor of Richard Jewell, demaunded the remainder of the tearme of nine yeares wch Thomas Toby late servant to Jerymy Whitnell, wch bound by covenant to serve wth the said Richard Jewell as appeared by his indenture, wherevpon the Court wth the consent of the ptyes, referred to Captaine Turner and Mr. Evance to consider of and sett downe what damage the said Richard Jewell might have in his disbursmts and adventures about the said Thomas Toby, thatt what appeares to be equall may be retourned to the executors of the said Rich: Jewell out of the wages of the said Tho: Toby.

Thomas Dickinson, being convicted of stealing divers things from severall psons, as Mr. Goodyeare, Mr. Evance and others (who had imployed and intrusted him wth many things and businesses) and for diverse other notorious crimes, as lyeing and counterfeating, and denying his name &c, his sentence was to be severely whipped, and to make two folde restitutiō for all thatt is proved against him or confest by him to be stolen by him, and to work in irons vntill he have done the same, and given satisfactiō for other debts wch he owes in the towne.

Samuell Hoskins and Elizbeth Cleverley, being desireous to joyne together in the state of marryage, and nott being able to make prooffe of their parents consent, butt seeing they both affirme they have the consent of their parents, and wth all haveing entred into contract, sinfully and wickedly defiled each other wth filthy dalliance and vncleane passages, by wch they have both made themselves vnfitt for any other, and for wch they have both received publique correctiõ, vpon these considerations, granted them liberty to marry.

---

[39] A Genrll Court held att Newhaven the 17th of Sept. 1642.

Itt is ordered thatt when any allarum is made upon the approach of any enemy, every souldier in the towne is to repaire to the meeting house forth with, and nott to loose time in attend-ing his owne private concernments, except onely in case of some present assault in or neare the place where he is, or at least some discovery of Indians comeing in a hostile manner.

Itt is ordered thatt in case of any expiditiõ against the Indians, whosoever the captaine or leivetennant shall thinke meete to send forth vpon service (wth approbatiõ of the magistrates) shall forthwth goe wthout any further dispute, and judge themselves called to goe, though itt should be to the extreame hazard of their lives, and if any man shall refuse to goe upon such a call, the magistrates is to presse him to goe, whether he will or no.

A Genrll Court of Elections the 26th of the 8th Moneth, 1642, att Newhaven.

Mr. Eaton and Mr. Goodyeare are chosen magistrates for this towne this ensueing yeare.

Goodman Warde of Stamforde, is chosen constable for Stamforde this ensueing yeare.

Mr. Malbon, Mr. Gregson, Mr. Gilbert and Mr. Wakemã are chosen deputyes for this ensueing yeare to assist in the Courts by way of advice, butt nott to have any power by way of sentence.

Mr. Gregson is chosen Treasurer.

Thomas Fugill is chosen Secretary.

Robert Ceely chosen Marshall.

Itt is ordered thatt the magistrates and deputyes w^t^h Capatane Turn^r and Leivetennant Seely, shall advise w^t^h the deputyes of Stamforde, how they may carry towards the Indians about them, who have comitted divers insolencies and injuries to the people there.

Itt is ordered thatt whosoever findes any things thatt are lost shall deliver them to the marshall to be kept safe till the owners challeng them.

---

[40] A Court held att Newhaven the 2^d^ of Nouem: 1642.

Whereas there hath beene two attatchments out, in the hands of Mr. Gregson, the one in the behalfe of Mr. Pocock, and the other on the behalfe of Mr. John Evance of Newhaven, concerning some goods left here by Mr. Owen, Itt is therefore ordered thatt those attatchments shall nott take away the said goods from this place, untill this Court have seene and determined the equity of those attatchments.

Att the request of Mr. Malbon, Itt is ordered that an attachmente be sent forth to detaine all the goods left in the hands of Captaine Turner by Mr. Owen, vntill the Court have ordered concerning them.

Forasmuch as the causway to the west side beyond the bridge is damaged by the cowes goeing thatt way, before the workemen had fully finished the same, Itt is therefore ordered, that John Wakeman, Josuah Attwater, John Clarke and Anthony Tompson shall veiw the damage, and sett downe whatt in their judgm^ts^ they conceive is for the workemen to have in way of satisfactiō.

Itt is ordered thatt if their be any goods due to John Woollen in the marchants hands in reference to Delaware Bay, there shall be 3^l^ detained to secure a debt to Mr. Bryant of Milforde till things be cleared betwixt John Woollen and him.

Itt is ordered thatt Mathew Hitchcock shall either pay 20^s^ to Mr. Perry w^c^h he vndertooke in the behalfe of his brother, or else sell so much of his brother's goods as will satisfie the said debt.

Itt is ordered thatt John Mason, Sam: Higginson and George Badcoke shall pay to Thomas French the sū of 20ˢ for takeing his cannow wᵗhout leave, according to an order in thatt case.

By a letter from Mr. Marshall to Mr. Hill of Winsor, bearing date the 7th of Aprill 1636, and a letter to Goodmā Mansfield, dated the 13 of October 1641, itt is evidenced to this Court thatt some of the cattell goeing under the name of Mr. Trobridge doth belong to Mr. Marshall as his pp goods, namely a white cow, red sparkled, a heifer, white and red sparkled, and one white and blacke sparkled; Henry Gibbons testimony allso concuring wᵗh the aforesaid letters.

Jervas Boykin is ordered to pay vnto George Badcocke the sū of 20ˢ for taking his cannow wᵗhout leave.

Mr. Gregson affirmed thatt he hath nott received paymᵗ for the passage of Thomas Toby, wherevpon Mr. Pell as attournay for Richard Jewells executours undertooke to see him satisfied.

The difference betweene Mrs. Stolyō and Mr. Eliz: Goodmā wᵗh their owne consents is refered to Mr. Goodyeere and Mr. Gregson to determine.

---

[41] A Genʳˡˡ Court held att Newhaven the 7th of Nouem: 1642.

Brother Brockett admitted member of this court, and received the charg of freemen.

Bro: Kimberley chosen Marshall in stead of bro: Ceely.

Itt is ordered thatt if any member of the Court, being warned to the Genʳˡˡ Courts, shall not come and make their appearance in the Court before all the names of the members be read ouer by the Secretary, his fine is 1ˢ 6ᵈ, and if any of the rest of the planters shall be absent after their names allso be read, his fine is 1ˢ.

Itt is ordered thatt those who have their farmes att the river called Stony River shall have liberty to make a sluce in the river for their owne conveniencie.

A Court held att Newhaven the 7th of December 1642.

Forasmuch as John Owen hath had some damage done in his corne by hogs, occasioned through the neglect of Mr. Lamberton, John Bud and Wiłł. Preston in nott makeing vp their fence in season, itt is therefore ordered thatt the said Mr. Lamberton, John Bud and Wiłł. Preston shall make satisfactiō to the said John Owen for the damage done, (viz) eight dayes worke and two pecks of corne, wch is to be payd according to the severall ꝑportiōs of fence vnsett vp respectively.

Mr. Evance delivered into the Court an awarde betweene Goodmā Whitnell and Tho: Toby on the one ꝑt, and Mr. Pell, attournay for the executor of Richard Jewell on the other ꝑt, wherein Thomas Toby is awarded to pay vnto Mr. Pell three pounds six shillings and fower pence, wch Goodman Andrewes and Goodmā Whitnell vndertooke to pay in his behalfe. And itt is ordered thatt the said Thomas Toby shall be bound apprentice for three yeares, (from the end of his formr tearme wth Goodman Whitnell) to them, the said Goodmā Andrewes and Goodman Whitnell, who are to finde him foode and rayment convenient, till the said three yeares be expyred.

A Court held att Newhaven the 4th of the 11th Moneth 1642.

Wiłł Harding being convicted of a great deale of base carryage and filthy dalliances wth divers yong girles, together wth his inticeing and corrupting divers servants in this plantatiō, haunting wth them in night meetings and junckctting, &c, was sentenced to be seveerly whipped and fined five pounds to Mr. Malbon, and five pounds to Wiłł Andrewes, (whose famylyes and daughters he hath so much dishonored and wronged in attempting to defile them,) and presently to depart the plantatiō, and not to retourne vnder the penalty of seveer punishment.

[42] A Gen^rll Court the 16th of 11th Moneth 1642. Att Newhaven.

Brother Lamson admitted member of the Court and accepted the charge.

Itt is ordered thatt two pounds shall be made forthw^th, one att brother Whiteheads corner, wch brother Peck is to keepe, and another by the creeke, (where brother Nash his shopp did stand) wch brother Kimberley is to keepe. Thatt cattell trespassing may be putt in and kept vntill itt appeare who shall pay the fine and beare the damage, either the owners, if they have putt them in, or if their keepers have beene negligent or the cattell beene unruly have gott in when the fences have beene sufficient, or they whose fences have beene defective or who have left open or broken downe gates or fences or by any other meanes have occasioned the damage, in all such cases the gouenors to answer for those vnder them, butt they againe to satisfy their gou^rno^rs as shall be judged meet, and the keeper of the pound, for impounding every mans cattell to have of the trespasser 2^d a head for hogs and all greater cattell, and a peny a head for goates and kids, halfe to the bringer in of the cattell & halfe to the pound, or if the pinder take all the paines he is to have all.

Itt is ordered thatt the Neck shall be a stinted cōmō for cattell, and fenced & fitted wth gates to keep in and out according to order, and then he thatt breaks or leaves open gates or putts in any cattell contrary to the order (the gou^rno^r to answer for those vnder him as above) to pay for every beast by the weeke (any lesse time then a weeke reconed a weeke,) 3^d. Note thatt—12 acres to a horse, 6 acres to an oxe, 3 acres for a yong steere nott above 2 yeares olde, and 2 acres for a calfe, and none are to putt cattell into the neck above this proportiō.

Itt is ordered thatt all those thatt have their meadowes in the west meadowes shall heard their cowes on the west side onely, and all the rest of the towne are to keepe their cowes on this side, and nott att all to heard them beyond the West river for this yeare, and no dry cattell are to goe wth the heards of cowes vnder the penalty of 3^d a weeke for every head, the one halfe to be payd by the owners, and the other halfe by the heard.

Itt is ordered thatt a booke shall be kept by the Secretary, of all the alienations whether houses or lands belonging to this plantation, butt no entry to be made w^t^hout order of the Court, and every such entry to be accounted good, according to the nature and intent of itt, against any form^r^ promise, covenaunt, bargaine or morgage nott so entered, though such deeds or promise shall have their just force against such person or persons thatt made them, and against any other part of his estate, and for every such entry the secretary to be payde 2^s^.

Itt is ordered thatt the magistrate shall keep a booke of every warrant and attatchment given out by him, and direct them to the marshall, and thatt the marshall for serveing them receive of the plaintiff, till itt be ordered who shall pay, 4^d^ for a warrant, and 6^d^ for an attatchment. For every tryall in the Court, the plaintiff or deffendant, or both (if there be cause) pay to the Treasurer ouer and above the warrant or attachm^t^ 2^s^.

Itt is ordered thatt every one warned to the Court for transgressing any Gen^rll^ Courts order, and found an offendo^r^, or being warned for fines or rates due and the same haveing beene first pryvately demaunded by the Treasurer or Marshall, shall pay to the Marshall 4^d^.

Itt is ordered thatt every one comitted to prison, besides after charges and attendance as the Court shall judge, shall pay the Marshall for turning the key—1^s^.

Itt is ordered thatt a whole yeares rate be forthw^t^h payd w^t^hin 6 weekes att the most, [a]nd the constant yearely rates to goe on in their halfe yeares course, according [to the] form^r^ order, notw^t^hstanding.

[43] Itt is ordered thatt whosoever cutteth or causeth any tree to be cutt downe vpon any comoñ w^t^hin 2 miles of any ꝑt of the towne, w^t^hout leave, contrary to order, shall leave the tree to the towne, lose all his labo^r^, and pay 1^s^ fine. If he carry away the tree or any ꝑt of itt he shall pay further damage as the Court shall judg meete.

A Court holden att Newhaven the 1t of the 1t Mon: 1643.

John Laurence and Valentine, servants to Mr. Malbon, for imbezilling their mars goods, and keeping disorderly night meetings wth Wiłł Harding, a lewd and disorderly person, plotting wth him to carry their mars daughter to the farmes in the night, concealing divers vncleane filthy dalliances, all wch they confessed and was whipped.

Ruth Acie, a covenant servant to Mr. Malbon, for stubornes, lyeing, stealing frō her Mrs, and yeilding to filthy dalliance wth Wiłł Harding. was whipped.

Martha Malbon for, consenting to goe in the night to the farmes wth Wiłł Harding to a venison feast, for stealing things frō her parents, and yeilding to filthy dalliance wth the said Harding, was whipped.

Jane Andrewes, for yielding to filthy dalliance wth the said Harding, was whipped.

Goodm̄ Hunt and his wife for keepeing the councells of the said William Harding, bakeing him a pasty and plum cakes, and keeping company wth him on the Lords day, and she suffering Harding to kisse her, they being onely admitted to sojourne in this plantatiō vpon their good behavior, was ordered to be sent out of this towne wthin one moneth after the date hereof, yea in a shorter time, if any miscaryage be found in them.

Mr. Moulenor, for his disorder att Totokett in building, fencing, planting and the like, contrary to order, after he had againe and againe beene warned frō this Court to the contrary, he haveing no right so to doe, haveing sould all thatt plantatiō to this towne, onely reserving liberty for a lott for himselfe when a peo: should settle there, as is expressed in his owne convayances, since wch time as he passed away his whole right, he purchased a peece of a neck discribed in a writeing bearing date the 27th of ^ 1639, writ by Mr. Gregson, butt in itt hath forged a discriptiō differing frō thatt made in Mr. Gregsons presence, and thereby layd clame to the whole necke, whereas the other was lymitted by a line and marked wth three strokes, butt his sentence respited.

[44] A GEN^rll HELD ATT NEWHAVEN THE 5th OF THE 2^d MONETH, 1643.

A letter from Andrew Ward constable att Stamforde, bearing date the 3^d of this p^rsent, written in the name and by the consent of the free burgesses there, was read, wherein they appoynt Captaine John Vnderhill and Richard Geldersleeve for their deputyes att this Gen^rll Court, and desire a magistrate may be chosen for the better carrying on of their affayres in thatt place, and doe nominate Mr. Mitchell and Thirton Rayner for thatt place. Captaine Vnderhill and Richard Geldersleeve haveing accepted the charge given here to members of this Court, the Court proceeded to electiō, and Thirston Rayner was chosen magistrate, to execute thatt office att Stamforde vntill the next Gen^rll Court of Elections att Newhaven wch will be in October next.

Allso vpon a motiō made by the afforesaid deputyes for Stamforde, Itt is ordered by this Court y^t those fower men allready imployed in the townes occasions there, namely, Captaine John Vnderhill, Mr. Mitchell, Andrew Warde and Robt Coe shall, (till the aforesaid next Gen^rll Court for elections) assist as the deputyes att Newhaven in councell and advice for the more comely carrying on of publique affayres, the being annexed to and p^rserved in the magistrate or magistracie.

Mr. Malbon, Mr. Gregson, Mr. Gilbert and Mr. Wakeman chosen deputyes for the next halfe yeare.

Mr. Malbon chosen Treasurer for this yeare.

Itt is ordered thatt leivetenaunt, the antient, an the fower sergeants, out of respect to their places, and for their incouragement, shall be henceforth exempted frō watching, yett so as thatt they must take their turnes by course to see thatt the watches be duely observed.

Itt was further ordered vpō the desire of the aforesaid deputyes for Stamforde, thatt the trayned band may, (till the aforesaid next Gen^rll Court for elections,) chuse or confirme inferio^r officers, namely a sergeant or a corporall, or both, to exercise them in the millitary way, provided thatt such officers be both members of the church, and p^{r}sented to and approved off by the magistrate and deputyes for Stamforde, the fundamentall agreement for votes and elections being still p^{r}served intyre and inviolable.

The Court being informed thatt peeces of eight, both in the Matachusetts Bay and some other places, doe by order passe currantly att five shillings, itt was ordered thatt they shall pass att the same rate both here and att Stamforde among the planters till the Gen^{rll} Court see cause to alter itt.

Itt was ordered thatt in case any publique occasiō require the helpe of labourers or workmen on trayning dayes, the magistrate may send to the Captaine for so many as the case requires, or if itt fall out att other times when there is no trayning, and thatt men cannott otherwayes be had or procured for the carrying on of some necessary worke w^{c}h is of publique concernment, the magistrate may putt forth an act of authority and p^{r}sse men for the said service and the effecting thereof.

Itt is ordered thatt brother Abbott and brother Hull shall be freed frō trayning, by reason of their bodyly infirmityes.

[45] Itt is ordered thatt brother Attwater and Robt Hill shall be exempted frō watch in their owne persons, by reason of their bodyly infirmityes, yett so as to finde each of them a man to watch in their roome.

Itt is ordered thatt sister Preston shall sweep and dresse the meeting house every weeke, and have 1^{s} a weeke for her paines.

Whereas Goodmã Osborne hath heretofore spoyled divers hides in the tañing w^{c}h he aleadgeth was for want of skill or experience in the tanne of this country, he promiseth for the time to come to make good whatt is spoyled in the tañing, for now he knowes the nature of the tanne, and therefore, if any hides be now spoyled itt is through his default.

A GEN[rll] COURT THE 6[t] OF THE 2[d] MONETH 1643.

Itt was ordered thatt Mr. Eaton and Mr. Gregson as comissioners for this jurisdictiō of Newhaven shall goe w[t]h other comissioners for other plantatiōs into the Bay of Massacusetts tò treate about a Gen[rll] combinatiō for all the plantations in New England, and to conclude and determine the same, as in their wisdome they shall see cause, for the exalting of Christs ends and advanceing the publique good in all the plantations.

And allso thatt Mr. Goodyeare, o[r] pasto[r], the fower deputyes, together w[t]h Georg Lamberton, Rob[t] Newman and Tho: Fugill shall meete and advise w[t]h them before they goe, the better to p[r]pare them for thatt greate and weighty busines. And more ouer thatt if any of the members of the Court, or of the plantatiō have any thing of weight to suggest for consideratiō, they are desired to repaire to the comittee, or any one of them to cast in whatt light they can.

A GEN[rll] COURT THE 26th OF THE 2[d] MONETH, 1643.

The comissioners aforesaid desired the Court now to propound any thing to them thatt they would have considered of in reference to the foremencōned combinatiō, and thatt if any of them had any light to cast in to them, thatt they would att this time impart itt, because the time of their goeing drew neare; butt the whole Court seemed to rest satisfied in the wisdome and faithfullnes of those w[c]h they had chosen and intrusted for thatt great busines, and therefore had nott thought of any thing butt whatt they thought had beene considered off, and would be provided for by those intrusted.

Itt is ordered thatt Goodm̄ Osborne shall have liberty to cutt downe some trees in the com̄on to gett bark fōr his tanning, and the trees to remaine to the townes vse, either for posts, railes or other vses as the Court shall see cause to dispose of them.

[46] A Court held att Newhaven the 3d of the 3d Moneth.

Nicholas Gennings for com̄itting fornicatiō wth Magerett Bedforde was seveerely whipped, butt his punishmt for other misdemeanors respited vntill another Court.

A Court held att Newhaven the 7th of the 4th moneth, 1643.

James Stewart, the last trayning day, for runing att Robt Campiō wth his pike, whereby he tore his doublett, and might have hurt him, was fined 5s for the disorder, wch might have beene of evill consequence.

Bro: Brockett, for late coming to traine fined 1s.

Joh. Beach, haveing killed a cow of George Smyths wth the falling of a tree, the said George required satisfactiō, forasmuch as he conceiveth thatt the said John did itt through negligence, butt he the said John Beach alleadged for himselfe, thatt he did nott doe itt negligently, for he being falling a tree, there came some cowes about him, and the tree in the falling did rest vpon the bowes of another tree thatt stoode neare, and then he left the tree, and drave away the cowes as he did conceive wthout the reach of the tree, and in the meane time some goates com̄ing vnder the tree he retourned to drive them away allso, and then came in haste to give 3 or 4 chops att the tree to hasten the falling of itt before the cattell could come againe.

Butt itt was testifyed by brother Andrewes and brother Tompson (who were intreated to veiw the cow and the place,) thatt he had nott done whatt in reason he might, and ought to have done to prserve the cattell, and thatt if he had beene as carefull as he might, no hurt need have be done, for the place was so hemmed in wth fallen trees as thatt there was little way open, (on thatt side wch he said he drave the cowes) for them to come in att againe, so thatt he might have kept them from danger if he had beene as carefull as he ought to have beene, besides, they affirme thatt the cow was killed about a rod or 20 foote wthin the reach of the tree, moreouer itt was testifyed by brother Andrewes and Robt Campion, thatt he the said John Beach did affirme thatt when he was cutting the tree the last time, he saw the cowes comeing againe, and he did throw sticks att them, butt confessed he did not goe to drive them as before, wch was noted to be a great neglect of him, and allthough he did alleadge in the Court thatt he did drive the cowes wthout the compasse of the fallen trees aforesaid, brother Tompson observed itt to be an vntruth, for he had tolde them att the first, when they went to veiw the cow, thatt he drave them to such a place, wch both he and brother Andrewes affirme was wthin the aforesaid compasse. Vpon all wch testimony i[t] was ordered thatt the said John Beach shall make good the damage to the vallue of 5l wch price Georg Smyth sett vpon his cow wth much moderatiõ, though she was really worth more.

Margerett Bedforde, being convicted of fornicatiõ and stealing wth divers other miscarryages, was severely whipped, and ordered to be marryed to Nicholas Gennings wth whome she hath beene naught.

---

[47] A Court held att Newhaven the 5th: 5th moneth, 1643.

Wiłł Fancie his wife, being charged wth stealing divers things from sondry ꝑsons, she confessed thatt she did steale about 5000 of pins frõ Mrs. Lamberton wth divers ꝑcells of lynning, and a jugge to the vallue of 17s as they were prized. She confessed allso thatt she stole from Mrs. Gilbert, two pillow beares and a shift, all wch she tooke forth of a tub of water in the colde of winter when the famyly was att prayer. And att Conectecutt, being kindely entertained as a strainger by a friend there, she stole a table napkin att her goeing away.

Now forasmuch as itt appeares to have beene her trade, she haveing beene twice whipped att Connectecutt, and thatt still she continues a notorious theefe and a lyer, itt was ordered thatt she should be seveerly whipped, and restore whatt is found wth her in specie, and make double restitutiõ for the rest.

Andrew Low, Junr for breaking into Mr. Lings house, where

he brake open a cup[board] and tooke frō thence some strong water, and 6[d] in mony, and ransackt all the house frō roome to roome, and left open the dores, for w[c]h fact he being comitted to prison brake forth and so escaped, and still remaines horrible obstinate and rebellious against his parents, and incorrigable vnder all the meanes thatt have beene vsed to reclame him, wherevpon itt was ordered, thatt he should be as seveerly whipped as the rule will beare, and to worke with his father as a prisoner w[t]h a lock vpon his leg, so as he may nott escape.

Itt was ordered thatt Luke Atkinson shall be payd 18[s] and 7[d] out of Lawrence Watts estate, in consideratiō of vse of his bedding and houshold stuffe when he lived w[t]h him, w[c]h was for the space of a yeare and a quarter thatt he sojourned in his house: and Goodman Hitchcock is allso to have 4[s] out of the said estate w[c]h the said Lawrence Watts did owe him.

Theophilus Higginson testified thatt Lawrence Watts did borrow a gun of John Dillingham w[c]h he was to restore againe, butt dyed before itt was restored.

[48]

Names of the Planters.	Persons nubered.	Estates.	Land in the first divisio.	In the neck.	Meadow.	Land in the 2d divisio.	Rates yearely payd for land.
Mr. Theoph: Eaton	6	3000	165	33	153	612	10-13-00
Mr. Sam: Eaton	2	800	45	9	41	164	2-19-00
Mrs. Eaton	1	150	10	2	8	32	00-12-00
David Yale	1	300	17½	3½	15½	62	01-02-06
Will Touttle	7	450	37½	7½	26	107	02-01-06
Eze: Cheevers	3	20	8½	1½ 32	2½	10	00-05-11
Captaine Turner	7	800	57½	11½	43½	174	03-06-06
Rich: Pery	3	260	20½	4½-16	14½	58	01-02-08
Mr. Davenport	3	1000	57½	11½	51½	206	
Rich: Malbon	7	500	42½	8½	28½	114	02-05-06
Tho: Nash	7	110	23	4½ 16	09	36	00-18-02
John Benham	5	070	16	3-32	6	24	00-12-04ob
Tho: Kimberley	7	012	18-16	3½-19	4-16	16½-24	00-11-02
Joh: Chapmā	2	300	20	4	16	64	01-04-00
Math: Gilbert	2	600	35	7	031	124	02-05-00
Jasper Craine	3	480	16½	3¼-8	25½	120	01-15-01
Mr. Roe	6	1000	65	13	53	212	
An elder	4	500	35	7	27	108	02:01:00
Geo Lamberton	6	1000	65	13	53	212	03-19-00
Will Wilks	2	150	12½	2½	8½	34	00-13-06
Tho: Jeffrey	2	100	10	2	6	24	00-10-00
Robt. Ceely	4	179	18¾-32	3¾-8	10¾-32	43	00-18-05
Nich: Elsey	2	30	6½	1¼-8	2½	10	00-05-01
Joh: Budd	6	450	31½	7½	25½	102	02-00-06
Rich: Hull	4	19	11	2-30	3	11¾ 4	00-07-04
Will: Preston	10	40	27	5¼-24	7	28	00-17-09
Ben: Fenne	2	80	9	1¾-8	5	20	00-08-07
Will Jeanes	5	150	20	4	10	40	00-18-00
Joh: Brockett	1	15	3¼	½-24	1¼	5	00-02-06ob
Roger Allen	1	40	4½	¾-24	2½	10	00-04-03ob
Mr. Hickocks	6	1000	65	13	53	212	03-19-00
Mr. Mansfeild	4	400	30	6	22	88	
Tho: Gregson	6	600	45	9	33	133	
Steph: Goodyear	9	1000	72½	14½	54½	218	09-19-02
Will Hawkins	2	1000	55	11	51	204	
Jer: Whitnell	2	0050	7½	1½	3½	14	00-06-06
Sam: Bayley	1	250	15	3	13	52	00-19-00
Tho: Buckingham	4	60	13	2½ 16	5	20	00-10-02
Rich: Miles	7	400	37½	7½	23½	94	01-18-06
Tho: Welch	1	250	15	3	13	25	00-19-00
Nath: Axtell	1	500	27½	6	25½	101	01-16-07

Hen: Stonell	1	300	17½	3½	15½	62	01-02-06
Will Fowler	3	800	47	9½	41½	166	03-06-06
Peter Preden	4	500	35	7	27	108	02-01-00
James Preden	3	10	8	1½-16	2	8	00-05-02
Edmond Tapp	7	800	52½	11½	43½	174	03-06-06
Wid: Baldwin	5	800	52½	10½	42½	170	03-03-06
An elder	6	500	40	8	28	112	0-0-0
Rich: Platt	4	200	20	4	12	48	01-00-00
Zack: Whitmā	2	800	45	9	41	164	02-19-00
Tho: Osborne	6	300	30	6	18	72	01-10-00
Hen: Rudderforde	2	100	10	2	6	24	00-10-00
Tho: Trobridge	5	500	37½	7½	27½	110	02-02-06
Wid: Potter	2	30	6½	1¼	2½	10	00-05-01
Joh: Potter	4	25	11¼	2¼	3¼	13	00-07-09
Sam: Whitehead	2	60	8	1½ 16	4	16	00-06-06
Joh: Clark	3	240	19½	3¾ 24	13½	54	01-11-00ob
Luke Atkinson	4	50	10	2 16	4½	18	00-09-06
Arther Halbidge	4	20	11	2 32	3	12	00-07-04
Edward Banister	3	10	8	1½ 16	2	8	00-05-02
Will Peck	4	12	10½ 16	2 16	1½-16	10¼	00-06-10
Joh: Mosse	3	10	8	1½-16	2	8	00-05-02
Joh: Charles	4	50	12½	2½	4½	18	00-09-06
Rich: Beach	1	20	3½	½ 32	1½	6	00-02-10
Timothy Forde	2	10	5½	1-16	1½	6	00-03-08
Peter Browne	3	30	9	1¾-8	3	12	00-06-07
Daniel Paule	1	100	7½	1½	5½	22	00-08-06
Joh: Livermoore	4	100	15	3	7	28	00-13-00
Antho: Tompson	4	150	17½	3½	9½	38	00-16-06
Joh: Reeder	2	140	12	2¼ 24	8	32	00-12-10
Robt. Cogswell	4	60	13	1½-16	5	20	00-10-02
Mathi: Hitchcock	3	50	10	2	4	16	00-08-00
Fra: Hall	3	10	8	1½-16	2	8	00-05-02
Rich: Osborne	3	10	8	1½ 16	2	8	00-05-02
Will Potter	4	40	12	2¼ 24	4	16	00-08-09ob
James Clark	4	50	12½	2½	4½	18	00-09-06
Edward Patteson	1	40	4½	¾ 24	2½	10	00-04-03ob
Andr. Hull	4	40	12	2¼ 24	4	16	00-08-09ob
Will Ives	2	25	6¼	1¼	2¼	09	00-04-09
Geo: Smyth	1	50	5	1	3	12	00-05-00
Widd: Shirman	2	50	7½	1½	3½	14	00-06-06
Math Moulthrop							
Tho: James sen.	5	200	22½	4½	12½	50	
Wid: Greene	3	80	11½	2¼ 24	5½	22	00-10-02
Tho: Yale	1	100	7½	1½	5½	22	00-08-06
Tho: Fugill	2	100	10	2	6	24	00-10-08

Joh: Ponderson	2	180	14	2½ 32	10	40	00-15-06
Joh: Johnson	5	150	20	4	10	40	00-18-00
Abra: Bell	1	10	3	½ 16	1	4½	00-02-02ob
Joh: Evance	1	500	27½	5½	25½	102	01-16-06
Mr. Mayres	2	800	45	9	41	164	02-19-00
Mrs. Constable	3	150	15	3	9	36	00-15-00
Josuah Attwater	2	300	20	4	16	64	01-11-06
Tho: Fugill	1	400	22½	4½	20½	82	01-09-06
Edward Wigglsw:	3	300	22½	4½	16½	66	01-05-06
Tho: Powell	1	100	7½	4½	5½	22	00-08-06
Hen: Browing	8	340	37	7½ 24	21	84	01-15-09
Mrs. Higison	8	250	32½	6½	16½	66	01-08-06
Edw: Tench	3	400	27½	5½	21½	86	01-12-10
Jer: Dixon	1	300	11	2½	15½	62	01-01-04
Will Thorp	3	10	8	1½ 16	2	8	00-05-02
Robt. Hill	1	10	3	½ 16	1	4	00-02-02
Wid: Williams	2	60	8	1½ 16	4	16	00-07-02
Andr. Low	3	10	8	1½ 16	2	8	00-05-02
Fr. Newman	2	160	13	2½ 16	9	36	00-14-02
Joh: Caffins	2	500	67½	13½	29¼	73	02-08-6
David Attwater	1	500	- - -	- - -	24¼	141	1-11.4
Lucas	6	400	35	7	23	92	
Dearmer*	1	300	17½	3½	15½	62	
Ben Ling	2	320	21	4-32	17	68	01-05-04
Robt. Newman	2	700	40	8	36	144	02-12-00
Will Andrews	8	150	27½	5½	11½	46	01-02-06
Joh: Cowp	3	30	9	1¾ 8	3	12	00-06-07
Rich: Beckley	4	20	11	2-32	3	12	00-07-04
Mr. Marshall	5	1000	62½	12½	52½	210	03-17-06
Mrs. Eldred	5	1000	62½	12½	52½	210	03-17-06
Fran: Brewster	9	1000	35	7	54½	263	03-15-10
Mark Pearce	2	150	12½	2½	8½	34	00-13-06
Jarvis Boykin	2	40	7	1¼ 24	3	12	00-05-09
James Russell	2	20	6	1-32	2	8	00-04-04
Geo: Warde	6	10	15	3-16	3½	14	00-09-08
Lawrence Ward	2	30	6½	1½-8	2½	10	00-04-09
Moses Wheeler	2	50	7½	1½	3½	14	00-06-06

* In the margin, Thom Lord, ½. Robert Tamadg, ½.

[The following is in the handwriting of Francis Newman.]

[ ]

The names of ye Tennants of oystershell field, beginning 1648. Mrch 10th.

Francis Browne 3 acrs *for ye ferrey: rent free.*

	Accrs
Thom Moris	4
William Paine	2
Widdow Knowles	2
Jno Coopr	4
Mr Malbon	7
Henry Morell	2
Mr Gilbert	4
Robert Pig	2
Francis Browne	2
John Walker	2
John Hall	2
Thom: Munson	2
Robert Martin	2
William Holt	2
William Pecke for a shooting place.	1
	43
Phillip Leeke yt is his owne	1

Mr. Lucas home lott. Joseph Pecke, William Johnson, Thomas Beamond } each an equall ꝑ portion.

Mr. Lucas out lotts. William Thorpe 4: acrs of ye first devizion next his owne.

Joseph Pecke, Henry Pecke, Tho Beamond, William Johnson } each of them 5¾ acrs in 3: pts, wthin the two mile: 3 acrs of meddow and 12 acrs of vpland in ye second divission.

Jeremiah Whitnel 4: acr in ye 3d devission wthin ye 2 mile. three acrs of meddowe & 12 acr of ye second division.

John Ponderson 5 acr of meddow: 20 acr of ye sec devission.

George Laremore 3, ac meddowe: 12 ac of ye sec devission.

Richard Hull, 4 acr of ye sec devis wthin ye 2 mile.

Mris Eldreds out lotts. Thomas Wheeler senior, Thomas Wheeler junior, Henry Glouer, William Holt, Joseph Alsop, Ephrahim Penington, Phillip Leeke } Each of these are to haue: 6: acrs wthin ye two mile in 3 ptes.

Jno Vincon, Joseph Nash } each 3 acr: wthin the two mile in 3: pts.

Andrew Low, Christopher Todd, Henry Morell } Each of these to haue 4 [acrs] wthin ye 2: mile in 3: pts.

The Meddow and second divission to be devided equ[ally] betwixt Nathaniel Merriman, Mathias Hitchcocke and Isacke Whitehead if he accept it.

Mr. Roes out lotts. William Gibbons, John Hall, Jeremiah How, Robert Martin, William Russell, William Paine, Jonathan Marsh, John Walker, Francis Browne, Abraham Dowlitle } Each of these are to haue 1½ acr in ye first devission wthin ye two mile & 1¾ acrs in each of ye other two devissions wthin ye two mile.

Thom. Munson $4\frac{1}{6}$ ac[r] in y[e] 2[d] devisiō w[t]hin y[e] 2 mile next Mr. Malbons.

Phillip Leeke two ac[r] in y[e] first devis. 2 : in y[e] 3[d] w[t]hin y[e] two mile.

Joseph Nash two ac[r] $\frac{3}{4}$ out of Mr. Roes first devis & y[e] Elders and two ac[rs] on a sixt pt of Mr. Roes third devis. w[t]hin y[e] two mile.

The meddow and second devission of vpland is granted to John Brocket and Thomas Barnes.

A lott reserved for an Elder } Mr. Auger the home lott and halfe y[e] accomodations.
Thom. Moris 1 quarter of y[e] accomodations.

William Andrewes 3 : ac[r]s of meddow, 12 ac[rs] of y[e] sec deviss.

Andrew Low 2 ac[r] $\frac{1}{4}$ of meddow : 9 : ac[rs] of y[e] sec deviss.

Joseph Nash $1\frac{1}{2}$ ac[r] meddow in y[e] mill meddow : 6 : ac[r] sec d[eviss]

John Vincon, Joseph Nash } aboute 5 ac[r] $\frac{3}{4}$ of y[e] sec & third deviss.

At a Court 8[th] Nouemb[r] 1652, the land in the neck belonging to Mr. Roes lott, M[ris] Eldreds, and Mr. Lucas was giuen to y[e] Gouerno[r].

Aprill the 20[th] 1[ ]*

The cōmittee appointed to dispose of the absent lott mett & vpon the request of Mathew Camfeild, granted to him the home lott w[c]h was laide out and reserved for M[ris] Eldred, vpon the conditions following viz[d]

That he plant it all w[t]h fruit trees, except aboute one ac[r] next the front, and that he p[r]sently paye for the fenc belonging to it, as it is now worth, being vallewed by indifferent men, & so maintayne and keepe it, and if in y[e] terme of five yeeres, the towne shall see cause to dispose of it to any man w[c]h may be of publique vse and benefit to the towne, it is to be at the townes dispose, payeing him for his trees and his fenc aboute y[e] lott, as they shall be then worth, being equally vallewed by indifferent men, but if the towne shall not dispose of it to some such man w[t]hin y[e] terme of 5 yeeres, that then the said Mathew Camfeild shall haue the lott, paying to the towne for y[e] ground as it is worth, being vallewed by indifferent men, and that then he shall build a dwelling house vpon it, comely and fitt for habitation, that so it may not lye as a vacant lott :

And vpon the same termes, at the same time the cōmittee granted Mr. Roes home lott, to Mr. Davenport, Mr. Gilbert and Mr. Crane.

---

* The date of this entry is probably 1648.

[Next after are recorded in the handwriting of Mr. Gibbard, the Indian deeds which have been transferred to the beginning of this volume.

There appears to have been no pages numbered from 51 to 62.]

[In the handwriting of Thomas Fugill.]

[62] ATT A GEN^rll^ COURT HELD ATT NEWHAVEN FOR THE PLANTATIONS W^t^HIN THIS JURISDICTIŌ, THE 6^t^ OF JULY, 1643.

Mr. Leete and Mr. Disbourough of Manunkatuck were admitted members and received the charge of freem̃ for this Court. Brother Preston allso admitted member of this Court and accepted his charge.

Mr. Eaton and Mr. Gregson, lately sent from this Court as comissioners w^t^h full power to treate, and, if itt might be, to conclude a combination or confœderation w^t^h the Gen^rll^ Court for the Massachusetts, and w^t^h the comissioners for New Plymouth and Connectecutt, did this day acquaint the Court w^t^h the issue and successe of thatt treaty. The articles agreed and concluded att Boston, the 19th of May, 1643, were now read and by this whole Court approved and confirmed. And itt was ordered thatt the Secretary enter them as a recorde. A letter allso from Mr. Wintropp, Governo^r^ of the Massachusetts, dated the 19th of June last past was read, wherein from Mr. Winslow he signifies the cheerefull concurrence of the Court att Plymouth in the said confœderatiō, according to the forenamed articles.

Itt was further ordered by this Court, thatt all the males in or belonging to every of the plantatiō^s^ in this jurisdictiō, frō sixteene yeare olde to sixty, be duely numbred according to the said articles. And thatt a true and particular account of them be brought in, betwixt this and the midle of August next, to be sent to the next meeting of the comissioners at Boston. Lastly, the said Mr. Eaton and Mr. Gregson were by this Court chosen and invested w^t^h full power, (according to the tenno^r^ and true meaning of the said Articles,) as com̃issoners for this jurisdictiō in the meeting for this confœderatiō, to be held att Boston, the 7th of September next.

Manunkatuck named Guilforde.

Itt is ordered thatt every male, frō 16 yeares olde to sixty, w^t^hin this jurisdictō, shall be forthw^t^h furnished of a good gun or muskett, a pound of good pouder, 4 fathom of match for a match-lock, and 5 or 6 good flints, fitted for every fyre lock, and 4 pound of pistoll bulletts, or 24 bulletts fitted to their guns, and so continue furnished from time to time, vnder the penalty of 10ˢ fine vpon every defect in any of the fore-named perticulars. And itt was further ordered thatt the Captaine shall give order to the officers thatt they take a strict veiw of all the defects or neglects of the trayned band, once every quarter, vnder the penalty of 40ˢ, and if the officers shall neglect to do itt, att his appoyntment, their fine is 40ˢ allso, to be leivyed att the discretiō of the Court, and thatt a retourne of the said veiw be made to the Court by the Captaine or the clark of the company at his appoyntment, vnder the penalty aforesaid.

Itt was ordered thatt 5ˡ frō Stamforde, and 5ˡ frō Guilforde, and 2ˡ frō Yenycott shall be forthwᵗh raised and payd into the treasury of Newhaven towards the charges about the combinatiō.

Mr. Goodyeere was desired by the Court to write to the inhabitants of Yenycott, to lett them know the equity of the proceedings of this Court in rateing all men imptially according to their accom̄odations wᵗhin the libertyes of this plantation, & thatt it will be expected thatt the same rule be attended vnto by them there allso.

[63] ||Itt was ordered thatt each plantatiō wᵗhin this jurisdictiō shall have a coppy of the Articles of Confœderatiō, for wᶜh they are to pay the Secretary.

A letter from Mr. Wintropp was read, wherein he layd downe divers reasons why the Massachusetts gave liberty to the Frenchmen, late arrived there, to gett whatt help they coulde in thatt jurisdictiō to assist them in their enterprize att the French plantatiō.

[The remainder of this page is blank.]

[64] Articles of Confœderatiō betwixt the Platations vnder the Gouermt of the Massacusetts, the Plantations vnder the Gou'nt of Newplymouth, the Plantations vnder the Gou'mt of Conecticutt, and the Gou'mt of Newhaven wth the Plantatiōs in combinatiō wth itt.

Whereas we all came into these pts of America wth one and the same end and ayme, namely to advance the kingdome of or Lord Jesus Christ, and to enjoy the libertyes of the Gospell in purity wth peace, and whereas in or settling, (by a wise pvidence of God,) we are further dispersed vpon the sea coasts and rivers then was at first intended, so thatt wee cannott (according to our desire) wth conveniencie comunicate in one governmt and jurisdictiō, & whereas we live incompassed wth people of severall nations and strange languages, wch hereafter may prove injurious to vs or our posterity, and forasmuch as the natives have formrly comitted sundry insolencies and outrages vpon severall plantations of the English, and have of late combined themselves against vs, & seeing, by reason of the sad distractions in England wch they have heard of, and by wch they know we are hindred both from thatt humble way of seeking advice, and reaping those comfortable frutes of protectiō wch att other times we might well expect, We therefore doe conceive itt our bounden dutye wthout delay to enter into a prsent consociation amongst ourselves for mutuall help and strength in all our future concermts, thatt as in natiō and religiō, so in other respects, we bee and continue one, according to the tennure and true meaning of the ensueing articles.

1 Wherefore itt is fully agreed and concluded by and betweene the ptyes or jurisdictions above named, and they joyntly and severally doe by these presents agree and conclude thatt they all be, and henceforth be called by the name of the United Collonyes of New England.

2 The said United Colonyes, for themselves and their posterityes, doe joyntly and severally, hereby enter into a firme and perpetuall leage of frendship and amyty, for offence and defence, mutuall advice and succour, vpon all just occasions,

both for prserving and ppagateing the truth and libertyes of the Gospell and of their owne mutuall safety and wellfare.

3 Itt is further agreed thatt the plantatiōs wch att present are or hereafter shall be settled wthin the lymitts of the Massacusetts shall be for ever vnder the govermt of the Massacusetts, and shall have peculiar jurisdictiō amongst themselves in all cases as a entire body, & thatt Plymouth, Conectecut and Newhaven shall each of them in all respects have the like peculiar jurisdictiō and govermt wthin their lim̃itts, and in refferrence to the plantations wch allready are settled or shall hereafter be erected, and shall settle wthin any of their lym̃its, respectively; provided, thatt no other jurisdictiō shall hereafter be taken in as a distinct head or member of this confœderatiō, nor shall any other, either plantatiō or jurisdictiō in prsent being, and nott already in combinatiō or vnder the jurisdictiō of any of these confœderates, be received by any of them, nor shall any two of these confœderates joyne in one jurisdictiō wthout consent of the rest, wch consent to be interpreted as in the sixt ensueing article is expressed.

4 Itt is allso by these confœderates agreed thatt the charge of all just warres, whether offensive or defensive, vpon whatt pt or member of this confœderatiō soever they fall, shall both in men, provisions and all other disbursmts be borne by all the pts of this confœderatiō in different proportions, according to their different abilityes in manr following, Thatt the comisionrs for each jurisdictiō from time to time, as there shalbe occasiō, bring a true account and number of all the males in each plantatiō, or any way belonging to or vnder their severall jurisdictions, of whatt quality or conditiō soeur they be, from sixteene yeares olde to three score, being inhabitants there, and thatt according to the different numbers wch from time to time shall be found in each jurisdictiō, vpō a true and just account, ye service of men & all charges of the warre be borne by the pole, each plantatiō or jurisdictiō being left to their owne just course & custome of rateing themselves and people, according to their different estates, wth due respect to their quallityes and exemptions among themselves, though the confœderatiō take no notice of any such prveledg, and thatt

according to the differ^{t} charge of each jurisdictiō & plantatiō the whole advantage of the warre, (if it please God so to blesse their endeavo^{rs}) whether itt be in lands, goods or ꝑsons, shall be ꝑportionably devided among the said confœderates.

[65] 5 Itt is further agreed thatt if any of these jurisdictions, or any plantation vnder or in combinatiō w^{t}h them, be invaded by any enemy whomsoever, vpon notice and request of any three magistrates of thatt jurisdictiō so invaded, the rest of the confœderates, w^{t}hout any further meeting or expostulatiō, shall forthw^{t}h send ayde to the confœderate in danger, but in different proportions, namely, the Massacusetts one hundred men, sufficiently armed and ꝑvided for such a service and journay, and each of the rest forty five men, so armed & ꝑvided, or any lesse number, if lesse be required according to this ꝑportiō. Butt if such a confœderate in danger may be supplyed by their next confœderate, nott exceeding the numb^{r} hereby agreed, they may crave help there, and seeke no further for the p^{r}sent, the charge to be borne as in this article is expressed and att their retourne to be victualled and supplyed w^{t}h powder and shott (if there be need,) for their journay, by thatt jurisdictiō w^{c}h imployed or sent for them, butt none of the jurisdictions to exceed these numbers, till by a meeting of the comissioners for this confœderatiō, a greater ayde appeare necessary, and this proportiō to continue till vpon knowledge of the numbers in each jurisdictiō (w^{c}h shall be brought to the next meeting,) some other proportiō be ordered, but in any such case of sending men for p^{r}sent ayde whether before or after such alteracō, it is agreed thatt att the meeting of the comision^{r}s for this confœderatiō, the cause of such warre or invasiō be duely considered, and if itt appeare thatt the fault lay in the ꝑty so invaded, thatt then thatt jurisdictiō or plantatiō make just satisfactiō both to the invaders whome they have injured, and beare all the charges of the warre themselves, w^{t}hout requireing any allowance from the rest of the confœderats towards the same. And further, if any jurisdictiō see any danger of an invasiō approaching, & there be time for a meeting, thatt in such case three magistrates of thatt jurisdictiō may sum̄on a meeting att such

convenient place as themselves shall thinke meete, to consider and pvide against the threatned danger. Pvided, when they are mett they may remove to whatt place they please, onely while any of these fower confœderates have butt 3 magistrates in their jurisdictiō, a request or sum̃ons from any two of them shall be acounted of equall force wth the three mentioned in both the clauses of this article, till there be an increase of magistrates there.

6 Itt is allso agreed thatt for the managing and concluding of all affayres pp to, & concerning the whole confœderatiō, two comissioners shall be chosen by and out of each of these 4 jurisdictiōs, namely, two for the Massacusetts, two for Plymouth, two for Conectecutt, and two for Newhaven, being all in church fellowship wth vs, wch shall bring full power from their severall Genrll Courts respectively, to heare, examine, weigh & determine all affaires of warre or peace, leags, aydes, charges and numbers of men for warre, devisiō of spoyles, or whatsoever is gotten by conquest, receiveing of more confœderates or plantations into combinatiō wth any of these confœderates, and all things of like nature wch are the pp concom̃itants or consequents of such a confœderatiō, for amyty, offence and deffence, nott intermedling wth the gourmt of any of the jurisdictions, wch, by the third article, is prserved intirely to themselves.

Butt if these eight comissionrs, when they meete shall nott all agree, yett it is concluded thatt any six of the eight agreeing shall have power to settle and determine the busines in question. Butt if six doe not agree, thatt then such propositions wth their reasons, so farre as they have beene debated, be sent and referred to the fower Generall Courts, (viz) the Massacusetts, Plymouth, Conectecutt and Newhaven, and if at all the said Generall Courts the busines so referred be concluded, then to be psecuted by the confœderates, and all their members. Itt is further agreed thatt these eight comissioners shall meete once every yeare, besides extraordinary meetings, according to the fifth article, to consider, treate and conclude of all affayres belonging to this confœderatiō, wch meeting shall ever be the first Thursday in September, and thatt the next meeting after the date of these p^{r}sents, w^{c}h shall be accounted the second meeting, shall be att Boston in the Massacusetts, the third att Hartforde, the fowerth att Newhaven, the fifth att Plymouth, the sixt and seaventh att Boston, and then att Hartforde, Newhaven and Plymouth and so in course successively, if in the meane time some middle place be nott found out and agreed on, w^{c}h may be comodious for all the jurisdictions.

[66] 7 Itt is further agreed thatt att each meeting of these eight comission^{r}s, whether ordinary or extraordinary, they all, or any six of them agreeing as before, may chuse their president, out of themselves, whose office & worke shalbe to direct for order and comely carrying on of all proceedings in the p^{r}sent meeting, butt he shalbe invested w^{t}h no such power or respect as by w^{c}h he shall hinder the propounding or progresse of any busines, or any way cast the skales, otherwise then in the p^{r}sedent article is agreed.

8 Itt is allso agreed thatt the comission^{r}s for this confœderatiō hereafter att their meetings, whether ordinary or extraordinary, as they may have comissiō or oportunity, doe endeavour to frame and establish agreem^{ts} and orders in gen^{rll} cases of a civill nature wherein all the plantations are interessed, for p^{r}serving peace amongst themselves, and p^{r}venting, (as much as may be) all occasions of warre or differences w^{t}h others, as about the free and speedy passage of justice in each jurisdictiō to all the confœderates equally as to their owne, not receiving those thatt remove frō one plantatiō to another w^{t}hout due certifficates, how all the jurisdictiōs may carry itt towards the Indians, thatt they neither grow insolent, nor be injured w^{t}hout due satisfactiō, least warre breake in vpon the confœderates through such miscarryages. Itt is allso agreed, thatt if any servant run away from his ma^{r} into any other of these confœderated jurisdictions, thatt in such case, vpon the certifficate of one magistrate in the jurisdictiō out of which the said servant fled, or vpon other due proofe, the said servant shall be deliu^{r}ed to his said ma^{r}, or to any other thatt ꝑsues and brings such certifficate or proofe, and thatt vpon the escape of any prisoner whatsoever or figitive for any criminall

cause, w^t^her breaking prison, or getting frō the officer, or otherwise escapeing, vpon the certifficate of two magistrates of the jurisdictiō out of w[c]h the escape is made, thatt he was a prisoner, or such an offendo[r] att the time of the escape, the magistrates, or some of them, of thatt jurisdictiō where, for the p[r]sent the said prisoner or fugitive abideth, shall forthw[t]h grant such a warrant as the case will beare for the apprehending of any such ꝑson, and the delivery of him into the hand of the officer or other ꝑson who ꝑsueth him, and if there be help required for the safe retourning of any such offender, then itt shall be granted vnto him thatt craves itt, he paying the charges thereof.

9 And for thatt the justest warres may be of dangerous consequence, especially to the smaller plantatiōs in these vnited collonyes, itt is agreed thatt neither the Massacusetts, Plymouth, Conectecutt, nor Newhaven, nor any of the members of any of them, shall, att any time hereafter begin, vndertake or ingage themselves, or this confœderatiō, or any ꝑt thereof, in any warre whatsoever, (sudden exegents w[t]h the necessary consequences thereof excepted, w[c]h are allso to be moderated as much as the case will ꝑmitt,) w[t]hout the consent and agreem[t] of the forenamed eight comission[r]s, or att least six of them, as in the sixt article is provided, and thatt no charge be required of any of the confœderates in case of a defensive warre, till the said comission[r]s have mett and approved the justice of the warre, and have agreed vpon the sum̃ of mony to be leivied, w[c]h sū is then to be payd by the severall confœderates, in proportion, according to the fowerth article.

10 Thatt in extraordinary occasions, when meetings are sum̃oned by three magistrates of any jurisdictiō, or two, as in the fift article, if any of the comissioners come not, due warning being given or sent, itt is agreed thatt fower of the comissioners shall have power to direct a warre w[c]h cannot be delayed, & to send for due proportions of men out of each jurisdictiō, as well as six might doe if all mett, but nott less then six shall determine the justice of the warre, or allow the

demaunds or bills of charges or cause any levies to be made for the same.

11 Itt is further agreed thatt if any of the confœderates shall hereafter breake any of these p^r^sent articles, or be any other way injurious to any one of the other jurisdictiōs, such breach of agreem^t^ or injury shall be duely considered and ordered by the comiss^rs^ for the other jurisdictions, thatt both peace and this p^r^sent confœderation may be intyrely p^r^served w^t^hout violatiō.

[67] 12 Lastly, this ꝑpetuall confœderatiō and the severall articles and agreem^ts^ thereof, being read and seriously considered, both by the Generall Court for the Massacusetts, and by the comission^rs^ for Plymouth, Conectecutt and Newhaven, were fully allowed and confirmed by three of the forenamed confœderates, namely, the Massacusetts, Conectecut and Newhaven, onely the comissioners from Plymouth, haveing noe comission to conclude, desired respite till they might advise w^t^h their Generall Court, Wherevpō itt was agreed and concluded by the said Court of the Massacusetts, and the comissioners for the other two confœderates, thatt, if Plymoth consent, then the whole treaty, as it stands in these p^r^sent articles, is and shall continue firme and stable, w^t^hout alteratiō. Butt, if Plymouth come nott in, yett the other three confœderates doe, by these p^r^sents, conclude the whole confœderatiō and all the articles thereof, onely in Septem̃. next, when the second meeting of the comission^rs^ is to be att Boston, new consideratiō may be taken of the sixt article, w^c^h concerns number of comissioners for meeting and concluding the affayres of this confœderatiō, to the satisfactiō of the court of the Massacusetts, and the comission^r^s for the other two confœderates, butt the rest to stand vnquestioned. In testimony whereof, the Gen^rll^ Court of the Massacusetts, by their Secretary, and the comission^r^s for Conectecutt and Newhaven have subscribed these p^r^sent articles, this 19th day of the 3^d^ moneth, comonly called May, 1643.

A Court held att Newhaven the 2d of August 1643.

Whereas there is a difference depending betweene Robert Ceely, and Daniell Paule, about a note of agreement betweene them vnder both their hands, wth both their consents, itt was referred to Mr. Malbone and Mr. Wakeman to arbitrate and determine as they shall see cause.

A difference allso betweene Wiłł. Fowler and Steven Medcalfe about a trespasse, wth both their consents, was referred to Mr. Malbon and Mr. Wakeman to arbitrate and determine as they shall see cause.

Forasmuch as itt appeareth by the testimony of Lawrence Warde thatt Margerett Poore, alias Bedforde, now wife to Nicholas Gennings, was to be servant to Captayne Turner, vnto the full end and terme of 4 yeares from the time of her first coming to him, butt she runing away wth the said Nicholas, before the saide tearme was expired, itt was ordered, thatt the said Nicholas, her said husband, shall make satisfactiō to Captaine Turner (her said mar,) for thatt losse of time, according as itt shall be arbitrated by Mr. Gregson and Mr. Wakeman, who are desired by the Court to doe the same. And the said Nicholas is to make 2 folde restitutiō for those things wch are confessed by them to be stolen from the said Captaine Turner.

[68] A COURT HELD ATT NEWHAVEN
2 AUGUST 1643.

John Thickpeny, about the age of 25 yeares, marrianer, in the Cock wth George Lamberton in his last voyage to Delaware Bay, being duely sworne and examined, deposeth,

Thatt he was present in the pinace called the Cock whereof Georg Lamberton was ma^r, rideing at ancre about 3 miles above the Sweeds fort in Delaware River, when a letter was brought the Sweeds $governo^r$ by Tim. the barber and Godfrey the marchants man coming wth him; they tolde him, this deponent in Dutch, a language wch he vnderstoode, thatt the contents of the letter was thatt the Indians, being att the fort the day before, had stolen a golde chaine from the $governo^{rs}$ wife, and thatt the $governo^r$ did intreat Mr. Lamberton to vse meanes to gett itt againe of the Indians who were then come to trade with the said Mr. Lamberton, desireing thatt they might stay aboarde till the next morning, thatt he might discover the Indian to him, affirming thatt he could know the Indian thatt had stolen itt, by a marke wch he had in his face, butt, though many Indians came aboard while he was there, yett he went away and never made more words of itt. This deponent further saith, thatt he was aboard when a second letter was brought aboard the Cock to Mr. Lamberton from the Sweeds governor the contents whereof he knows nott, butt a while after, the same day, he wth Isaac goeing to carry Mr. Lamberton ashoare to the Sweeds fort, into wch being entred, before they spoke wth the $governo^r$, the said Mr. Lamberton, this deponent, and the said Isaack were all cast into prison together, (butt a while the said Mr. Lamberton was taken forth of thatt roome, butt as he vnderstood was kept in another prison,) where he, this deponent, continued 3 dayes, in wch time John Woollen, servant to Mr. Lamberton, (and his interpreter betweene him and the Indians,) was cōmitted to the same prison in irons, w^ch, he himselfe said, the $governo^r$ had putt vpon him wth his owne hands.

And further this deponent saith thatt the said John Woolen tolde him thatt att his, the said John Woollens first coming into the Sweeds fort, he was brought into a roome in wch the governours wife, Tymothy the barber, and the watch maister came to him and brought wine and strong beere and gave him, wth a purpose, as he conceived to have made him drunck, and after he had largly drunk there, the Govr sent for him into his owne chamber and gave him more strong beer and wine, and drunk freely wth him, entertayning of him wth much respect seemingly, and wth profession of a great del of love to him, [69] ||makeing many large promises to doe very much good for him if he would butt say thatt Georg Lamberton had hyred the Indians to cutt off the Sweeds, butt the said John Woollen denyed itt, then the $governo^{r}$ drunke to him againe, and said he would make him a man, give him a plantatiō, and build him a house, and he should not want for golde nor silver, if he would butt say as is said before; he would doe more for him then the Eng: could, for he loved him as his owne child, butt the said John answered, thatt there was no such thing, and if he would give him his house full of golde, he would nott say so, and then the $governo^{r}$ seamed to be exceeding angry, and threatned him very much, and after thatt drunke to him againe, and prest him to confess as before, wch the said John Woollen refusing, the $governo^{r}$ was much enraged, and stamped wth his feete, (wch this deponent himselfe heard, being in the roome vnder him,) and calling for irons, he putt them vpon the said John Woollen wth his owne hands, and sent him downe to prison as before is expressed. And this deponent saith, thatt the aforesaid Sweeds $watchm\bar{a}^{r}$ came into the prison, and brought strong beere, and drunke wth them about 2 howers in the night, and pressed the said John Woollen to say thatt the said George Lamberton had hyred the Indians to cutt off the Sweeds, and he should be loosed from his irons presently, butt John Woollen said he would not say itt if he should be hanged, drawne and quartered, because he would nott take away the life of a man thatt was innocent, then he prest him further, thatt he would speake any thing to thatt purpose, be itt never so little, and he should be free presently, butt John Woolen said he could nott say itt nor he would nott say itt. And he further saith thatt the said watchma[r] prest him, this deponent, to the same purpose, and he should have his liberty, w[c]h he allso refused, knowing no such thing.

This deponent, thatt att another time while he was in prison, Gregory, the marchants man, came to him and tolde him they were sent by the governo[r] to charge him w[t]h treason w[c]h he had spoken against the Queene and Lords of Sweden, namely, thatt he had wished them burnt and hanged, w[c]h he this depon[t] vtterly denyed, and then the said fetched a flagon of strong beere and drunke itt w[t]h him, and after thatt fetched the said flagon full of sack and drunke thatt w[t]h him allso, and bid him call for wine and stronge beere whatt he listed, and questioned w[t]h him about Georg Lambertons hyring the Indians as aforesaid, his answer was, he knew no such thing. Then the watchma[r] affirmed thatt itt was so, and thatt George Lamberton had given cloth, wampom, hattchetts and knives for thatt purpose, pressing him to say so and he should be free, and he would take vp, and cleare him of the treason thatt was charged vpon him, and if he feared to say so because of Mr. Lamberton, he should not need to feare him, for he should pay him his wages before the vessell went, and he should chuse whether he would goe back, or stay w[t]h them, butt he answered, lett them *them* doe whatt they pleased w[t]h him, for he could nott say any such thing, and further he saith nott.*

---

* At the meeting of the commissioners for the United Colonies, at Boston, in September, 1643, Mr. Eaton and Mr. Gregson complained of the injuries the people of New Haven had received from the Dutch and Sweeds both at Delaware Bay and elsewhere, and the commissioners instructed Winthrop to write Printz concerning the foul injuries offered by him to Mr. Lamberton and his company. They gave also a commission to Mr. Lamberton to go treat with the Sweedish governor about satisfaction, and to agree with him about settling their trade and plantation. Hazard, II., 11. Winthrop, II., 140. Brodheads N. Y., I., 382.

[70] A COURT HELD ATT NEWHAVĒ THE 6t OF SEPTEMBER 1643.

Marke Pearce, Will Holt, Edward Camp, brother Potter, Hen. Lendall, Hen : Line, Theophilus Higginson and Mathew Row, for coming late the last trayning day, were fined each man one shilling.

A COURT HELD ATT NEWHAVEN THE 4th OF OCTOBER 1643.

Robt Hill, for neglect of his watch, was fined 5 shillings.

Robt. Lea, for want of armes, was fined 5s.

Mighell Palmer, for the same, was fined 5s.

Ricc. Edwards, for the same, was fined 5s.

Luke Attkinson and John Vincent fined each 1s for late comeing.

Itt is ordered thatt there shall be a genrll muster, the next second day, wth an exact veiw of all the armes, to see thatt none be defective in armes, shott and pouder, according to the order in thatt case.

Nathan Burchall confessed, thatt he haveing lived some time in Mr. Newmans house, and thereby haveing acquantance wth the house and the wayes of itt, had divers temptations to steale something out of itt, and though he prayed against the temptatiō, yett he was att last overcome by itt, and the last Lords day, in the time of the publique ordinances, he went into the house and so into the chamber and closett, where he found and tooke from thence to the vallue of 13l in mony, and to the value of 34s in other things. The processe respited till the next Court, and in the meane time he is to be kept in prison, or else lye in baile for his appearance att the next court.

A Genrll Court held att Newhaven the 14th of October 1643.

Itt was ordered thatt 6 men shall forthwth be sent from hence (to joyne wth 8 of Connectecutt, to assist Vnkas against the Narragansett Indians, whom he expects shortly to warr vpon him,) and accordingly to be fitted and furnished wth all necessaryes for such a voyage and enterprize.*

---

[71] A Genrll Court held att Newhaven the 23th of October 1643:

Whereas this plantation att first wth genrll and full consent laid their foundations thatt none butt members of aproved churches should be accounted free burgesses, nor should any else have any vote in any election, or power, or trust in ordering of civill affayres, in wch way we have constantly proceeded hitherto in our whole court, wth much comfortable fruite through Gods blessing. And whereas Stamforde, Guilforde, Yennicock, have vpon the same foundations and ingagements entred into combination wth vs, this Court was now informed, thatt of late there have beene some meetings and treatyes betweene some of Milforde† and Mr. Eaton, about a combinatiō, by wch it appeareth, thatt Milforde hath formerly taken in as free burgesses, six planters who are nott in church fellowshipp, wch hath bred some difficulty in the passages of this

* The Commissioners of the United Colonies having, at their session at Boston, in September, decided upon delivering up Miantonimo to be put to death by Uncas, were apprehensive that the Narragansetts would seek to revenge his death.

† "Vpon a motion made by the comissioners for New Haven jurisdiction, it was graunted and ordered that the towne of Mylford may be received into combinacon & as a member of the jurisdiction of New Haven, if New Haven & Mylford agree vpon the tearmes and condicons among themselves." Rec. U. Col. Sept. 1643. Up to this time then, Milford seems to have remained a separate and independent colony. Hubbard, Hist. N. E. p. 277, speaking of the settlement of Guilford and Milford, says that "every one stood so much for their liberty that every plantation almost intended a peculiar government of themselves, if they could have brought it about, but those designs tended to the weakening of the country and hinderance of the general good of the whole." See also Sav. Winth. i, 306. Lambert, Hist. Col. N. H. 62.

treaty, butt, att present, itt stands thus, the deputies for Milforde have offered, in the name both of the church and towne, first, thatt the p^{r}sent six free burgesses who are nott church members, shall nott att any time hereafter be chosen, either deputyes, or into any publique trust for the combinatiō. Secondly, thatt they shall neither personaly, nor by proxi, vote att any time in the electiō of magistrates. And, thirdly, thatt none shall be admitted freemen or free burgesses hereafter att Milforde, butt church members according to the practice of Newhaven. Thus farr they granted, butt in two perticulars they and their said six freemen desire liberty, first, y^{t} the said six freemen being already admitted by them, may continue to act in all proper perticular towne busines wherein the combinatiō is nott interressed. And, secondly, thatt they may vote in the electiō of deputyes to be sent to the Generall Courts for the combinatiō or jurisdictiō, wch deputyes so to be chosen & sent, shall allwayes be church members.

The premises being seriously considered by the whole Court, the brethren did express themselves as one man, clearely and fully, thatt in the foundations layde for civill governm^{t} they have attended their light, and should have failed in their dutye had they done otherwise, and professed themselves carefull and resolved nott to shake the said groundworks by any
[72] change for any respect, and ordered, ||thatt this their vnderstanding of their way, and resolution to maintaine itt should be entred wth their vote in this busines, as a lasting recorde. Butt nott foreseeing any danger in yeilding to Milforde wth the forementioned cautions, itt was, by gen^{rll} consent and vote, ordered thatt the consociation proceed in all things according to the p^{r}mises.

A Gen^{rll} Court of Elections held att Newhaven for this Jurisdictiō the 26th of October 1643.

Captaine Turner and Mr. Lamberton were chosen Deputyes for the Court of combinatiō.

Mr. Eaton was chosen Governo^r for this yeare ensuing.

Mr. Goodyeare was chosen Deputy Governo^r.

Mr. Gregson chosen Magistrate for this towne.

Mr. Fowler and Goodman Tapp were chosen Magistrates for Milforde for this ensueing yeare, & Mr. Rayner for Stamforde.

Mr. Leete and Mr. Disbrough were chosen Deputyes for Guilforde this yeare ensueing.

Thomas Fugill was chosen Secretary for the whole combinatiō or jurisdictiō for this ensueing yeare.

Thomas Kimberley was chosen Marshall for this whole jurisdictiō, for this ensueing yeare.

---

[73] A GEN^rll COURT HELD ATT NEWHAVEN FOR THE JURISDICTIŌ THE 27th OF OCTOBER 1643.

Present.

Magistrates.	*Deputyes.*	
Theophilus Eaton, Gouerno^r,	George Lamberton	℘ Newhaven
Stephen Goodyear, Deputy,	John Astwood	℘ Milforde.
Thomas Gregson,	John Shirman	
William Fowler,	Will Leete	℘ Guilforde.
Edward Tapp,	Sam: Disbrough	
	Rich: Gildersleeve	℘ Stamforde.
	John Whitmore	

Itt was agreed and concluded as a foundamentall order nott to be disputed or questioned hereafter, thatt none shall be admitted to be free burgesses in any of the plantations w^thin this jurisdictiō for the future, butt such planters as are members of some or other of the approved churches in New England, nor shall any butt such free burgesses have any vote in any electiō, (the six present freemen att Milforde enjoying the liberty wth the cautions agreed,) nor shall any power or trust in the ordering of any civill affayres, be att any time putt into the hands of any other then such church members, though as free planters, all have right to their inherritance & to comerce, according to such grants, orders and lawes as shall be made concerning the same.

2 All such free burgesses shall have power in each towne or plantation wthin this jurisdictiō to chuse fitt and able men, from amongst themselves, being church members as before, to be the ordinary judges, to heare and determine all inferior causes, wther civill or criminall, provided thatt no civill cause to be tryed in any of these plantatiō Courts in value exceed 20l, and thatt the punishment in such criminalls, according to the minde of God, revealed in his word, touching such offences, doe nott exceed stocking and whipping, or if the fine be pecuniary, thatt itt exceed nott five pounds. In wch Court the magistrate or magistrates, if any be chosen by the free burgesses of the jurisdictiō for thatt plantatiō, shall sitt and assist wth due respect to their place, and sentence shall pass according to the vote of the major part of each such Court, onely if the partyes, or any of them, be nott satisfyed wth the justice of such sentences or executions, appeales or complaints may be made from and against these Courts to the Court of Magistrates for the whole jurisdictiō.

[74] || 3. All such free burgesses through the whole jurisdictiō, shall have vote in the electiō of all magistrates, whether Governor, Deputy Governor, or other magistrates, wth a Treasurer, a Secretary and a Marshall, &c. for the jurisdictiō. And for the ease of those free burgesses, especially in the more remote plantatiōs, they may by proxi vote in these elections, though absent, their votes being sealed vp in the prsence of the free burgesses themselves, thatt their severall libertyes may be preserved, and their votes directed according to their owne perticular light, and these free burgesses may, att every electiō, chuse so many magistrates for each plantatiō, as the weight of affayres may require, and as they shall finde fitt men for thatt trust. Butt it is provided and agreed, thatt no plantatiō shall att any electiō be left destitute of a magistrate if they desire one to be chosen out of those in church fellowshipp wth them.

4. All the magistrates for the whole jurisdiction shall meete twice a yeare att Newhaven, namely, the Munday im̃ediately before the sitting of the two fixed Generall Courts hereafter menc̃oned, to keep a Court called the Court of Magistrates,

for the tryall of weighty and capitall cases, whether civill or criminall, above those lymitted to the ordinary judges in the perticular plantations, and to receive and try all appeales brought vnto them from the aforesaid Plantation Courts, and to call all the inhabitants, whether free burgesses, free planters or others, to account for the breach of any lawes established, and for other misdemeanours, and to censure them according to the quallity of the offence, in wch meetings of magistrates, less then fower shall nott be accounted a Court, nor shall they carry on any busines as a Court, butt itt is expected and required, thatt all the magistrates in this jurisdictiō doe constantly attend the publique service att the times before menc̃oned, & if any of them be absent att one of the clock in the afternoone on Munday aforesaid, when the court shall sitt, or if any of them depart ye towne w^{t}hout leave, while the court sitts, he or they shall pay for any such default, twenty shillings fine, vnless some providence of God occasiō the same, wch the Court of Magistrates shall judge off from time to time, and all sentences in this court shall pass by the vote of the major part of magistrates therein, butt from this Court of Magistrates, appeales and complaints may be made and brought to the Gen^{rll} Court as the last and highest for this jurisdictiō; butt in all appeales or complants from, or to, what court soever, due costs and damages shall be payd by him or them thatt make appeale or complaint w^{t}hout just cause.

5. Besides the Plantatiō Courts and Court of Magistrates, their shall be a Gen^{rll} Co^{rt} for the Jurisdictiō, wch shall consist of the Governo^{r}, Deputy Governo^{r} and all the Magistrates w^{t}hin the Jurisdictiō, and two Deputyes for every plantatiō in the Jurisdictiō, wch Deputyes shall from time to time be chosen against the approach of any such Gen^{rll} Court, by the aforesaid free burgesses, and sent w^{t}h due certifficate to assist in the same, all w^{ch}, both Governo^{r} and Deputy Governo^{r}, Magis-
[75] trates and Deputyes, shall have their vote || in the said Court. This Gen^{rll} Court shall alwayes sitt att Newhaven, (vnless vpon weighty occasions the Gen^{rll} Court see cause for a time to sitt elsewhere,) and shall assemble twice every yeare, namely, the first Wednesday in Aprill, & the last Wednesday

in October, in the later of wch Courts, the Governo^r, the Deputy Governo^r and all the magistrates for the whole jurisdictiō wth a Treasurer, a Secretary and Marshall, shall yearely be chosen by all the free burgesses before mencōned, besides wch two fixed courts, the Governo^r, or in his absence, the Deputy Governo^r, shall have power to summon a Gen^rll Court att any other time, as the vrgent and extraordinary occasions of the jurisdictiō may require, and att all Gen^rll Courts, whether ordinary or extraordinary, the Governo^r and Deputy Governo^r, and all the rest of the magistrates for the jurisdictiō, wth the Deputyes for the severall plantatio^s, shall sitt together, till the affayres of the jurisdiction be dispatched or may safely be respited, and if any of the said magistrates or Deputyes shall either be absent att the first sitting of the said Gen^rll Court, (vnless some providence of God hinder, wch the said Court shall judge of,) or depart, or absent themselves disorderly before the Court be finished, he or they shall each of them pay twenty shillings fine, wth due consideratiō^s of further aggravations if there shall be cause; wch Gen^rll Court shall, wth all care and dilligence provide for the maintenance of the purity of religion, and shall suppress the contrary, according to their best light from the worde of God, and all wholsome and sovnd advice wch shall be given by the elders and churches in the jurisdictiō, so farr as may concerne their civill power to deale therein.

Seconly, they shall have power to mak and repeale lawes, and, while they are in force, to require execution of them in all the severall plantations.

Thirdly, to impose an oath vpon all the magistrates, for the faithfull discharge of the trust comitted to them, according to their best abilityes, and to call them to account for the breach of any lawes established, or for other misdemeano^rs, and to censure them, as the quallity of the offence shall require.

Fowerthly, to impose and oath of fidelity and due subjectiō to the lawes vpon all the free burgesses, free planters, and other inhabitants w^thin the whole jurisdictiō.

5ly to settle and leivie rates and contributions vpon all the severall plantations, for the publique service of the jurisdictiō.

6ly, to heare and determine all causes, whether civill or criminall, w^{c}h by appeale or complaint shall be orderly brought vnto them from any of the other Courts, or from any of the other plantatiō^{s}, In all w^{c}h, w^{t}h whatsoever else shall fall w^{t}hin their cognisance or judicature, they shall proceed according to the scriptures, w^{c}h is the rule of all rightous lawes and sentences, and nothing shall pass as an act of the Gen^{rll} Court butt by the consent of the majo^{r} part of magistrates, and the greater part of Deputyes.

These gen^{rlls} being thus layd and settled, though w^{t}h purpose thatt the scircumstantialls, such as the vallue of causes to be tryed in the Plantation Courts, the ordinary and fixed times of meetings, both for the Gen^{rll} Courts, and courts of magistrates, how oft and when they shall sitt, w^{t}h the fines for absence or default, be hereafter considered off, continued or altered, as may best and most advance the course of justice, and best sute the occasions of the plantations, the Court proceeded to p^{r}sent perticular busines of the jurisdiction.

[76] || Vpon a proposition and request made by Captaine Vnderhill and Mr. Allerton by instructions from the Dutch Governour and some of the freemen of thatt jurisdictiō, for the raising of one hundred souldiers out of these plantations of the English, and armed and victualled, to be led forth by Captaine Vnderhill against the Indians now in hostility against the Dutch, to be payd by bills of exchaing into Holland.

The Court seriously considerd the propositions w^{t}h the consquences thereof, and though they were affected w^{t}h a due sence of so much Christian blood, both Dutch and English vnder the Dutch governm^{t}, lately shed by the Indians, yett nott clearely vnderstanding the rise and cause of the warr, and well remembring the articles of confœderatiō betwixt themselves and ye rest of the vnited collonyes in New England in the case of warr, they did nott see att present how they might afforde the ayd propounded w^{t}hout a meeting and consent of the comissioners for the rest of the jurisdictions. Butt if peace be nott settled this winter, so soone as the comission^{r}s may meet in the spring, both the ground of the warr, and the ayd or assistance desired, may be taken into due consideratiō, and if, in the meane time, there be want of corne for men and foode for cattell in supply of what the Indians have distroyed, these plantations will afforde whatt help they may.

The Court nott thinking itt meete to afforde thatt ayd of souldiers to the Dutch, nor to send Captaine Vnderhill to lead their men against the Indians w[t]hout the consent of y[e] comissioners for the collonyes as is before expressed, a motion and request was made by Captaine Vnderhill thatt twenty pounds might be lent him to supply his present occasions, w[c]h 20[l] shall be repayed by the towne of Stamforde out of the sallary they have ingaged themselves to allow him yearely, the one halfe in March come twelve moneths, the other halfe the next ensueing March, w[c]h will be An[o] 1645. W[c]h being duely considered, itt was ordered, thatt if the lending of this 20[l] may be a meanes to settle the captaine, and if they conceive his settlem[t] may tend to their comfort and security, and if the towne of Stamforde will see the said sū duely repayd att the times above menc̄oned, the jurisdictiō is willing to lend the said sum̄ to prevent the snares of larger offers for his remove.

The court considering thatt by the articles of confœderatiō the com̄ission[r]s for the severall jurisdictions may be called to meete extraordinarily vpon the vrgent affayres of the collonyes, and thatt perhaps, w[t]h such short warning thatt there may nott be time to call a Gen[rll] Court from the remote plantations, they did thinke itt needfull now to puide accordingly, and by gen[rll] consent and vote, Mr. Eaton, Governo[r], and Mr. Gregson, Magistrate, were chosen comission[r]s for this jurisdiction for the meeting at Hartforde in September next, w[t]h full power to treate and determine, according to the forme ordered by the comissioners att their last meeting. And in case either of them should be sick, or by any other providence of God hindred from the journay and service, Mr. Malbon is by full consent and vote chosen and ordered to supply in thatt case. Butt if a meeting should be sum̄oned before thatt time w[c]h might occasion a farther journay, Mr. Goodyeare, Deputy Gouerno[r], and Mr. Gregson were chosen com̄ission[r]s, w[t]h like full power for the service of this jurisdictiō. And if either of them, by any providence, be disabled or hindred from the said journay, Mr. Malbon was chosen com̃ission^{r} wth full power to supply thatt place.

[77] || The Court considering thatt some charges have beene already expended for the jurisdictiō in the journayes made for the settling a combinatiō and service of the jurisdictiō, and thatt 6 souldiers being now sent forth to joyne wth 8 from Hartforde for Vncus defence against the assults wch may be made vpon him by the Narragansett Indians for Meantonimoes death, w^{ch}, wth the shallop attending them, will be a further charge to the jurisdictiō, And lastly, considering the loane of this twenty pounds to Captaine Vnderhill, if Stamforde imbrace the proposition, as is before exprest, they thought, and by gen^{rll} consent and vote itt was ordered, thatt a farther stock be raised, and forthwth payd into the treasurer att Newhaven by the severall plantations in this jurisdiction, namely, five pounds for Guilforde, and five pounds by Stamforde, and thatt Milforde pay ten pounds to equall Guilforde or Stamforde who have allready beene assessed each of them five pounds towards the foremenc̃oned charges, besides the present leavy, and thatt Newhaven beare their proportionable share, itt being by gen^{rll} consent and vote of this Court ordered and concluded, thatt all the charges for this jurisdictiō, both for the p^{r}sent and hereafter, be borne by the ${}^{\text{different}}_{\text{severall}}$ proportions of males wch from time to time shall be found in them from 16 to sixty yeares olde, as in the articles of combinatiō is agreed for the jurisdictiō^{s}, of wch stock, both received and expended, the treasurer shall from yeare to yeare give account to this Gen^{rll} Court vpon demaund, thatt itt may appeare thatt all disbursements are for the publique service of this jurisdictiō, and thatt no plantation be charged above their just proportiō.

Two letters being now read in court from the magistrate* of Stamforde, the former being dated the 18th, the latter the 23th p^{r}sent. Itt appeared by the form^{r} thatt the justice of the Court of Stamforde hath beene charged by the ma^{r}† of an Indian captive, for thatt the said captive was sensured to be publiquely whipped for publique misdemeanours, the ma^{r} telling the magistrate before witnesse, itt was neither honesty nor justice so to proceed, he haveing corrected the boy att home,

* In the margin, "2 letters fro Mr. Rayner." † Richard Crab, *post* [83.]

wherevpon the Court did neither think famyly correctiō sufficient for such publique offences, nor thatt such affronts to magistracie should either be evaded by sleight interpretations, nor passed by wth some private acknowledgment, Ordered, that the ma^r^ of the said captive boy be bound ouer to the Court of magistrates wch will be held att Newhaven on Munday the first of Aprill next, to answer his miscarryage.

In the second letter from Stamforde, the magistrate supposing, in respect of the many in-juries from the Indians received, they have cause to begin a warr vpon them, and they sitt still for want of a concurrence of the rest of the jurisdictiō, expreseth their apprehensiō, thatt if their houses should be fired, &c. the jurisdictiō should beare the burden, wch the whole Court marvilled att, conceiving thatt the councell given Stamforde in the case was most safe for themselves to take, and considering the ingagem^t^ wherein this jurisdictiō standeth to the rest of the collonyes, absolutely necessary for vs to give, and thatt no man would be forewarde to give advice if therefore he must beare the afflicting providences of God wch may follow.

---

[78] A GEN^rll^ COURT HELDE ATT NEWHAVEN THE 30th OF OCTOBER, 1643, FOR THIS PLANTATIŌ.

Mr. Malbon, Mr. Lamberton, Mr. Evance and Mr. Wakeman were chosen deputyes of this plantatiō, and Mr. Malbon continued Treasurer for this yeare.

Tho: Fugill chosen Secretary, and Tho: Kimberley chosen Marshall.

Itt was ordered thatt one of the squadrons in their course shall come to the meetings every Saboth compleatly armed, fitt for service, wth att the least 6 charges of shott and pouder, and be ready att the meeting house, w^thin^ halfe an hower after the first beating of the drum̄, then and there to be att the comaund of the officers in such service as they are appoynted to attend vnto on those dayes, vnder such penalty as the court shall judge meet, according to the nature of their offence; allso the sentinell and those thatt walke the round shall have their matches lighted dureing the time of the meeting, if they have match locks.

A Court held att Newhaven the 1t of November, 1643.

Robert Lea, for comeing to trayĩng wth his gun̄ charged wth shott, contrary to order, and carelessly discharging itt against Mr. Gregsō his house, to the great danger of the lives of divers persons, who were in the chamber when the shott came through the window, was fined 20s to the towne, and to repaire the window wch was broken by the said shott.

The difference about the neck bridg was respited to another Court, onely itt was ordered, thatt those who did the worke are to repair itt for the prsent, and to have three pounds for the doeing of itt, provided thatt they doe itt well and substantially, and for that end brother Andrewes is to oversee and direct the work while itt is a doeing, and when itt is finished the comittee formerly appoynted to veiw, are to veiw itt againe, to see thatt itt be done according to the intent of this order.

Itt was ordered thatt brother Andrewes shall take care thatt three or fower lighter loades of stones be layd by the bridge, to breake the force of the water from itt.

Whereas Nathan Burchall hath beene formerly convicted in this Court, for stealing out of Mr. Robt Newmans house on the Lord's day, in mony the sum̄ of thirteene pounds, and other things to the vallue of 1l 14s, itt was ordered thatt he should make double restitutiō for the said severall sum̄s, and have some corporall punishment for the aggravations of his fact.

Allen Ball is ordered to have 2s 2d of the goods of Lawrence Watts.

---

[79] A Genrll Court held att Newhaven the 13th of November, 1643.

Itt was ordered thatt all those thatt will pay their rates in Indian corne shall pay itt att 2s 4d ℘ bushell, good marchantable corne, and thatt every man pay his rates, (wch are now due,) forthwth, either in Indian corne as itt is now ordered, or in wampom, or in cattell as they shall be justly prized by indifferent men, to such persons as the treasurer shall assigne to receive the same w^{t}hout any delay, or putting the treasurer to further trouble.

Itt was ordered thatt every famyly w^{t}hin this plantatiō shall have a coate of cotton woole, well and substantially made, so as itt may be fitt for service, and that in convenient time the taylours see itt be done.

Itt is ordered thatt the great guns shall be forthw^{t}h fitted for service, and Mr. Lamberton and Mr. Rudderforde are desired to see itt done.

Itt was ordered thatt every chimney in the towne in w^{c}h fire is constantly kept, shall be swept once every moneth from Septm̃ber till March, and once every 2 moneths in sum̃^{r}, w^{c}h worke Goodman Cooper hath vndertaken to doe, and is to have 4^{d} a peece for every chimney thatt is two storyes high and vpward, and 2^{d} a peece for all thatt are vnder 2 storyes high, to be duely payd him by all those thatt agree w^{t}h him, butt if any will doe itt themselves, and Goodman Cooper come after the time lymitted and finde them not done or not well done, he is to doe itt well, and to have double pay of those whose neglect itt is, and if he shall neglect to doe those, according to the intent of this order, w^{c}h he vndertakes, he is to pay double pay for his neglect.

Att a Court held att Newhaven the 6th of December, 1643.

Goodmā Chapman, brother Davis, John Thomas, Sam: Hoskins, brother Nicholls, Joh Charles, Thomas Barnes and Thomas Wheeler were fined 5^{s} apeece for want of ladders.

Brother Thorpe, for comeing late to sett his watch, and neglecting to order itt aright when he did come, was fined 10^{s}.

Jerimy Whitnell for nott keeping a sentinell forth, and suffering att least some of his watchmen to sleepe, was fined 5^{s}.

Whereas John Tompson required satisfactiō for some damage done to his corne by the hoggs of Mr. Eaton, Mr. Malbon and Mr. Lamberton, itt was ordered, that he should have satisfactiō made by those (whose fence vpon veiw shall be found defective) according to every mans proportiō, wch shall be judged by indifferent men. John Chapman, Thomas Kimberley & Will Preston are desired to goe wth John Tompsō to veiw and judge accordingly.

Whereas Tho: Moulenor desired thatt some other should have the hearing of the difference betweene himselfe and this plantatiō for his disorderly proceedings at Totokett, itt was ordered, thatt he shall have 6 moneths time to bring his arbitrators whom he shall chuse, (provided they be godly wise) wch if he shall not doe wthin the said tearme, he shall submitt to the judgment of this Court, wch condicō he accepted.

---

[80] ATT A COURT HELD ATT NEWHAVEN THE 4th OF JANUARY, 1643.

Isaack Whitehead, Will Mecar, Thomas Powell, Tymothy Forde, Goodmā Hitchcock, Rich: Webb, Pillipp Leake, bro: Elsey, Jonathan Marsh, Ricd Beach, John Lawrenson, Robt Emery, Will Iles, Hen: Gibbons, Tho Robinsō, Nicholas Gennings, Tho: Yale, John Hill, bro Lamson, fined each 1s for late com̃ing to trayne. And Rich: Newman, John Beach, and James Stewart fined each man 2s for twice late com̃ing.

Richard Newman, Peter Browne, Will Potter, John Beach, Goodmā Ward, John Benham, Isaack Whitehead, Robt Leay, Tho Blakeley, John Medcalfe, bro Lamson, fined each man 2s for defect. guns. Will Bladen, Rich: Spery, Hen: Glover and John Thomas for defect in their cocks fined each man, 1s.

Richard Newman and Will Potter & Isaack Whitehead fined 6 pence a peece for want of shott. Will Mecar fined 1s for want of shott and pouder, & Edward Chipperfield allso.

John Hunter, Will Mecar and Will Blayden fined each man 1s for defect. sworde.

John Hill, Edward Hitchcock and Amrose Sutton, fined each man 6d for want of flints, & Rich: Lowell 6d for want of match.

John Hill & Edward Chipperfield, for want of worme and skourer, each 6d.

John Wolforde, defect. rest, fined 6d.

Joh: Griffin, Jonathan Rud, Wiłł Wooden, Tho: Toby, Roger Knap, Sam: Hoskins, Edward Parker and Lanclott Fuller, fined each mā 3s 4d for totall defect in armes.

Johnathan Marsh, Edmond Towly, fined each man 2-6 for totall absence, & James Stewart and Math: Crowder, each man 5s for twice totall absence.

Mathew Hitchcock, fined 3s 4d for a disorder in his watch.

Whereas Thomas Blakeley suffered a sack wth 3 bushells of meale of Mr. Lings, and a sack wth one bushell of meale of Mr. Francis Newmans, wch he had the charge off, to be carryed to Long Iland, itt was ordered thatt he shall make good the said sacks and meale to the owners forthwth, and he himselfe seeke satisfactiō frō those who tooke the said sacks.

And forasmuch as vpon this sentence of the Court, he went forth in discontente, and, in the hearing of divers, he reproached the Court, charging the Court wth injustice, wch vpon examinatiō appeared to be most falce, therevpon the Court ordered thatt the said Blakley shall pay 20s fine and be comitted dureing the magistrates pleasure.

Att a Court held att Newhaven the 8o of February, 1643.

Whereas an attatchmet hath beene granted against Francis Smyth to Thomas Blackley, for a debt of 17s wch the said Francis Smyth received of the said Blackley, as appeares by the testimony of Lawrence Warde, and forasmuch as the sum̃ of 13s rests in the hands of Sam: Whitehead wch belongs to the said Francis Smyth, itt was therefore ordered thatt the said 13s shall be detained on the behalfe of the said Blackley.

Francis Church desired the justice of the Court agst Thomas Moulenor (for a debt of 2l 2s wth damages for 3 yeares forbeareance,) on the behalfe of Thomas Whiteway, wch debt the said Moulenor did confess to be due to the said

Thomas, and *did* referred himselfe to judgm[t] of the Court, and therevpõ it was ordered thatt the principall, w[t]h 12[s] damages, shall be forthw[t]h payd to the said Church by the said Moulenoʳ.

[81] ||Itt was ordered, thatt 1[l] 2[s] of James Nortons in the hands of Thomas Blackley shall be attatched on the behalfe of the Dellaware Company.

Itt was ordered, thatt Thomas French beare halfe of all the losse w[c]h was layd vpon Thomas Blackley, the last Court, concerning the 2 sacks of meale w[c]h was carryed to Long Iland, because he was a cause of the mistake in the sacks.

Mr. Cheevers desired 4—3—6 out of the estate of Mr. Trobridge, w[c]h is justly due to him for teaching y[e] children.

Richard Beach hath ingaged his house and lott to secure a former agreem[t] in reference to the children of Andrew Hull, late deceased.

A difference betweene Rob[t] Ceeley and John Mason was referred to Mr. Gregson and Mr Malbon to determine.

A Court held the 7th of March, 1643.

Mr. Stiles of Conectecutt desired the justice of the Court against Geo. Larrymoʳ concerning a debt of 10[l], the remainder of a debt of 25[l] w[c]h the said George was to pay for a servant, (by name Geo: Chappell,) w[c]h he bought of the said Mr. Styles, w[c]h was testifyed on his behalfe by the said Geo: Chappell vpon oath as apeares vnder the hand of Mr. Swaine, a magistrate att Connectecut, before whome he was sworne, and confessed by the said Geo: Larrymoʳ himselfe, onely he aleadged thatt he was nott to pay the said 10[l] vnlesse the said Georg Chappell did serve out his time, butt the said Geo: Larrymoʳ did sell his time; therefore the Court ordered, thatt the said Geo: should pay the said 10[l] to the said Mr. Stiles w[t]hout delay.

Rich: Mansfield demaunded a debt of 40[s] of Hen: Gibbons, w[c]h the said Hen: promised to pay w[t]hin a moneth, onely desired to have 20s of itt abated for lodging and fire wood for a whole winter in his cellar, wch was thought reasonable, and Rich: Mansfield ordered to allow itt.

Math: Hitchcock, for a willfull neglect to walke the round when the officers called him, was fined 5s.

James Haward, Joh: Tompson, Will Bassett, Anthony Tompson, David Evance, Samuell Willson and Sam: Hoskins, fined each mā 6d for foole guns.

Tho: Yale and Jonathan Marsh for the same, 6d a peece.

Rich: Perry and his 2 men, Will Gibbard, and James Stewart & Will Ball, for late comeing fined each mā 1s.

Roger Knap, defect. all except a gun, fined 5s.

Bro. Lamson defect. gun fined 4s.

Theo: Higginson, James Stewart and James Haward defect. belt, fined 6d.

Itt was ordered, thatt the treasurer shall pay 1s to bro: Mosse wch he layd downe for Goodmā Paull.

Mr. Eatons 3 men, Theo: Higingson and his man, for coming wthout armes on the Lords day, fined each mā 2s.

Math Crowder, Thomas Caffins, Theo: Higginson, James Stewart, Tho: Meaks, Isaack Whitehead, Math: Row, Rich Mansfield, Tho: Iles, Lawrence Warde, Joh: Hill, John Cooper, Jarvice Boykin, & Mr. Eatons 3 men, fined each man 6d, for late comming to the meeting wth their armes Feb: 18, 1643.

---

[82] Att a Genrll Court held att Newhaven the 25th of March, 1644.

Mr. Malbon & Captaine Turner chosen Deputyes for this towne agst the Genrll Court for the jurisdictiō.

Mr. Malbon, Mr. Evance, Mr. Lamberton and Mr. Wakemā chosen Deputyes for this halfe yeare next ensueing.

A comittee was appoynted to consider of the springs, highwayes and fences in questiō about the neck, thatt itt might be fenced in for a pasture, wherevpon a questiō was raised by bro: Gibbard, wther they might not fence in their quarter w^t^h the spring w^c^h is w^t^hin the bounds for their land there, w^c^h, after some debate, itt was resolved they might nott, because their was an order y^t^ none should fence the springs in the neck frō the comō when it is layd for a pasture, and so they rested satisfied.

Mr. Malbon, Mr. Gilbert, Mr. Francis Newmā and Joshuah Attwater were chosen comittee for the premises.

Mr. Malbon vndertooke to see the neck fenced forthw^t^h, and those who have land their are to pay the charg, according to their proportiō, w^t^hin 20 dayes after the account is given to them, or else they shall loose the feed of their land for 2 yeares next ensueing the date hereof.

Itt was ordered thatt every quarter shall appoynt comittees for their quarters to veiw the outside fences, and where they finde defects to lett the owners know; and if they doe nott see itt mended vpon notice so given, if cattell breake in, though it cañott certainely be found where they gott in, yett they must beare the damage whose fence was found defective and nott mended.

Itt was ordered thatt they to whome the affayres of the towne is intrusted shall dispose of Totokett according as in their wisdome they see cause.

Itt was ordered thatt the 2^d^ drum̃e shall be the period of the souldiers coming on the Lords day.

Itt was ordered thatt Stephen the drm̃^r^ shall have 5^l^ payd yearely out of the treasury while he continues drum̃^r^.

Vpon a propositiō made by those who have the small lotts, thatt they may have the Bever meadowes granted to them by the Gen^rll^ Court, itt was ordered, thatt Mr. Wakeman, Mr. Gibbard, Goodmā Gibbs and Mr. Pearce shall veiw the said meadowes and certifie the Court if they conceive it may nott be inconvenient for the towne to part w^t^h itt.

[83] [*Att a Court of Magistrates held att Newhaven*] THE FIRST OF APRILL, 1644.

Present, { Theophilus Eaton Gou^r^no^r^, Stephen Goodyeare, Dep^t^y Gou^r^no^r^, & Thomas Gregson, Magistrate for New Haven.
Wiłł Fowler & Edmond Tappe for Milforde.
Thirston Rayner for Stamforde.

Thomas Stevenson and Georg Slowson of Stamforde, being appoynted in their course to watch the Dutchman who murdered Captaine Pattricke,* (he being kept prison^r^ in the house of Captaine Vnderhill from whence he made an escape through their negligence,) were charged w^t^h the said escape.

Tho: Stevenson said thatt they were carefull to discharge the trust comitted to them, according to the best of their vnderstandimg, butt Captaine Vnderhill perswaded them to lett him goe to bed in a chamber and tolde them thatt if they did butt lock the dore of the chamber wherein the prisoner lay, they might sitt by the fire in the lower roome att the foote of the staires, w^c^h the did and had no company butt the captaine and his wife who stayed nott long w^t^h them before they departed to their lodging, and about 2 or 3 howers after, they missed the prison^r^, and then the called vp the magistrate.

George Slowson saith, thatt he questioning about the safety of the window of the chamber where the prisoner lay, the captaines wife† showed some dislike of itt, and said what adoe is here, yet the said Geo: rested not there, butt spake to the Captaine himselfe, who said thatt he had spoken w^t^h the pris-

* Capt. Daniel Patrick had been a common soldier of the Prince's guard in Holland, was admitted freeman in Watertown, Mass., May 18, 1631, and chosen captain March 9, 1636-7. He grew, says Winthrop, proud and vicious, and perceiving that his evil courses would not be endured in the Bay, he removed to within twenty miles of the Dutch and put himself under their protection, and when the Indians arose in those parts he fled to Stamford. He was killed in Capt. Underhill's house, on a Sunday afternoon during the time of afternoon exercise. "The Dutchman had charged him with treachery for causing 120 men to come to him upon his promise to direct them to the Indians, etc., but deluded them. Whereupon the captain gave him ill language and spit in his face, and turning to go out, the Dutchman shot him behind in the head, so he fell down dead, and never spake."—Mass. Records i., Sav. Winth. ii., 151.

† It will be remembered that Captain Underhill's wife was a Dutch woman.

oner to know if he had no temptatiō to escape, who answered yea, butt alas, said he, whither can I goe, I had rather dye vnder the hands of a christian magistrate then vnder the hands of the Indians, and therevpon the said George rested more secure, he further saith, thatt when the messengers came from Newhaven, the captaine said to them, now looke to the prisoner yor selves for I will take charge of him no longer now that Newhaven men are come.

They both alleadge and stedfastly affirme, thatt they had no perticular directiō how to order their watch, butt onely a gen^rll charge wch was given att first to the watchmen, namely, watch the prisoner, and thatt itt was meere ignorance wch was the cause of this miscarryage. Butt because the magistrate affirmeth thatt he gave a new and more strict charge thatt night (vpon the cōming of the messengers frō Newhaven,) then he had done formerly, and the watchmen deny thatt ever they heard of any other, so y^t the case seemes darke, and because the Governo^r intends to go to Stamforde shortly, the Court referred itt to him to examine and determine their, if he see cause, or else to referre itt to the next Court of magistrates and binde the partyes whom it concernes to answer the same then and there.

Richard Crab of Stamforde was called to answer his miscarryage in chargeing the Court at Stamforde wth injustice and dishonesty, he said he did nott charge the court, butt said itt was his apprehensiō, and thatt he had studdyed the case, butt professed he could not yett see light thatt itt is just to punish the boy twice for one fact, he said thatt the occasiō of the boys fact was because he was wont to borrow a gun of the man frō whom he tooke itt, and therefore thought he might make the more bolde to take itt att this time, butt att last seeing so cleare an evidence against him, he confessed he had failed in speakeing such words, and said he was vnder a temptatiō, fearing thatt if his boy were publiquely whipped, itt would cause him to run away, wch would be a great losse to him and a greefe to his wife. The Court haveing heard all thatt he could say for himselfe, sensured him to pay 5^l fine to Mr. Rayner the magistrate att Stamforde before the next court of magistrates, and allso to acknowledge his miscarriage.

THE 2d OF APRILL 1644.

Whereas some cattell of the goods of Owen Row of London, marchant, have beene form'ly attatched att the suite of Rich: Bellingham of Boston Esqr. (for a debt of 62l 10s,) who hath ordained Rich: Malbon of Newhaven his attournay to psecute the said attatchmt, and the said Mr. Malbon hath now desired the judgmt of this Court concerīng the saide debt, wch he cleared to the court to be due to the said Rich: Bellingham. And therevpon the court gave judgment for the said Mr. Bellingham, he haveing vndertaken, by a bill vnder his hand, to save this Court harmless frō all just molestations for the same.

---

[84] A GEN[rll] COURT HELD ATT NEWHAVEN [*for the jurisdictiō*] THE 3d OF APRILL 1644.

Present.

Magistrates.		*Deputyes.*	
Theoph: Eaton, Governor, Stephen Goodyeare, Depty, Thomas Gregson,	pro Newh	Captaine Turner, Rich: Malbon	pro Newh:
Will Fowler, Edmond Tapp	for Milforde	Zack: Whitman, John Astwood	pro Milford
Thirston Rayner for Stamforde		Will Leete & Jacob Sheath	ꝑ Guilford
		Andrew Ward & Robt Coe	pro Stamforde

Itt was ordered thatt the fundamentall orders concerning the fixed Genrll Courts and Courts of Magistrates shall be a sufficient sum̄ons to all the plantations wthin this jurisdictiō, and thatt they shall expect no other warning to prepare them for the same, and for thatt end the magistrate or magts of every plantatiō shall call a meeting some convenient time before the said Genrll Courts to chuse their deputyes who are to be sent wth due certifficates, and not to come w^thout as some now did, though the Court passed itt over att this time.

This day a forme of an oath for the Governo^r and magistrats to take, and another forme of an oath to be imposed upon all the inhabitants w^thin this jurisdiction was propounded to the consideratiō of the court, who, after some serious debate and consideratiō, rested satisfyed wth the said formes. And therevpon ordered, thatt itt should be forthw^th putt in executiō, and whereas the Governo^r doth shortly intend a journay to Stamforde on other occasions, the Court desired him to improve thatt opportunity, both att Stamforde and att Milford, for the giveing of the oath, and the like att Guilforde in time convenient. Itt was further ordered thatt no person or persons shall hereafter be admitted as an inhabitant in this jurisdictiō or any of the plantations therein butt he or they shall take the said oath vpon his or their admittance.

Itt was ordered, thatt there shall be two marketts or fayrs for cattell and other goods every yeare att Newhaven, (viz) one on the third Wednesday in May, the other the third Wednesday in September.

Itt was ordered, thatt the Court att Stamford shall proceed in all their conclusions and determinations as the rest of the plantations in this jurisdictiō doe, and as is ordered in the fundamentall orders of the last Gen^rll Court for the jurisdictiō, (viz) thatt the sentence of the Court be carryed by the vote of the majo^r part of the Court.

Itt was ordered, thatt whensoever any capitall offendo^r shall be apprehended w^thin this jurisdictiō, he shall be sent wth all convenient speed to Newhaven, there to be kept in safe custody till he be brought to due tryall.

Itt was ordered thatt the judiciall lawes of God, as they were delivered by Moses, and as they are a fence to the morrall law, being neither typicall nor ceremoniall, nor had any referrence to Canaan, shall be accounted of morrall equity, and gen^rlly binde all offendo^rs, and be a rule to all the courts in this jurisdictiō in their proceeding against offendo^rs, till they be branched out into perticulars hereafter.

Itt was ordered thatt in case any of the magistrates in the

smaller plantatiōs see need of help in some weighty causes or difficult knotty cases, vpon due notice and request to the Governo^r, provisiō shall be made accordingly.

[85] ||Itt was ordered thatt for the more comfortable carrying on of the affayres att Guilforde till they have a magistrate their, the free burgesses may chuse among themselves fower deputyes and forme a court.

Itt is ordered thatt every male from 16 to 60 yeares olde w^thin this jurisdictiō be furnished forthw^th, wth a good gun, a sword, a pound of good pouder, 4 fathom of match for a matchlock, 5 or 6 good flints fitted for every fyre lock, and 4 pound of pistoll bulletts, or 24 bulletts fitted for every gun, and so continue furnished from time to time, vnder the penalty of 10^s fine for every person found faulty or defective.

Itt was further ordered, thatt the Captaine shall give order to the officers, that they take a strict veiw once every quarter of a yeare, thatt all the males from 16 to 60 be furnished as above, vnder the penalty of 40^s fine, and if the officers shall neglect to doe itt att his appoyntment, their fine is 40^s allso, to be leivyed att the discretion of the Court, and thatt a retourn of the said veiw be made vnto the magistrate or Court, by the captaine or his clarke att his appoyntm^t, vnder the penalty of the fine aforesaid. Moreover, itt was ordered, thatt there shall be att least 6 traynings every yeare in every plantation, & never above one of those 6 in a moneth, vnder the penalty of 5^l fine, to be leivyed of the military officers for every default. Note thatt in such plantations where there is no captaine for the present, there the cheefe officer is in stead of the captaine, and is to veiw vnder the penalty of the captaines fine.

Itt is allso ordered, thatt throughout this jurisdictiō, there shall be a comon stock of pouder and shott, according to the orders of ye comissioners for the collonyes,* (viz) a hundred

* "The comissioners do think it fitt to aduise every general court that they would see thatt every man may keepe by him a good gun and sword, one pound of pouder with foure pounds of shott, with match or flints sutable, to be ready vpon all ocations, and to be carefully viewed foure tymes a yeare at least. And that over and aboue this, euery generall court do see that they keep a stock of pouder, shott and match ever by them. And it is conceived by the comissioners that one hundred pounds of

pound of pouder and 400[l] of shott, (layde vp in every plantatiō,) for every hundred men or males as aforesd, and so in proportiō differently, vnder the penalty of 1[s] fine for every pound of pouder, and 20[s] for every hundred weight of shott w[c]h shall be found wanting after 3 moneths next ensueing be expyred; the fines for these defects are to be payd into the comō wealths treasury.

Itt was ordered, thatt a 4[th] part of the trayned band in every plantatiō shall come to the publique wor[ps] of God att the beating of the 2[d] drum att furthest, w[t]h their armes compleat, their guns ready charged, w[t]h their match for their matchlocks and flints ready fitted in their firelocks, & shott & pouder for att least 5 or 6 charges, (besides their charge in their guns,) vnder the penalty of 2[s] fine for neglect or defect in furniture, and 1[s] for late comeing, allso the sentinell, and they who walke the rounde, shall have their matches lighted dureing the time of the meeting, if they vse match locks.

Itt was ordered, thatt a strict watch shall be kept in all the plantatiō[s] in this jurisdictiō, from the first of March to the last of October every yeare ordinaryly, leaveing extraordinary cases to the Governo[r] or Magists, to order as occasion may require, and in the ordinary course to be observed as followeth; The drum̃ is to beate att the goeing downe of the sū, all the watchmen to be there w[t]hin an hower after the setting of the suñ, w[t]h their armes compleate and guns charged, and att least 5 or 6 shotts of shott and pouder besides, for each of them, and if any of them come late, or be defective in their armes, they are to pay 1[s] fine. If totally absent, 5[s] fine. The watch is to be sett w[t]hin an hower after the sunsett, and so is to continue vntill itt be halfe an hower day light in the morning, in all w[c]h time none are to sleepe. These fines are to be payd into the severall plantions treasury.

---

pouder and foure hundred pounds of shott, with match sutable, at the least, be provided for every hundred men thorow all the vnited Colonies of New England, and that the comissioners at each meeting report how the seuerall jurisdiccons are furnished. * * * It is judged meete by the comissioners that there be trayneings at least six tymes euery yeare in each plantacon within the confederacon."—Rec. U. Col. Sept. 1643. Hazard ii, 9.

Itt was ordered, thatt the Deputy Governo^r shall give the Governo^r his oath.

Itt was ordered thatt the Secretary shall have sallary, and the marshall 3^l p anū.

---

[86] A COURT HELD ATT NEWHAVEN THE 5th OF APRILL 1644.

John Dillingham, Jonathan Rudd, Edmond Tooly, John Massam, John Hurndell, Mr. Auger, Lanclott Fuller, Wiłł Wooden, Dauid Evance, for a drunken disorderly meeting at the prison on a Lords day att night, where they drunke 3 bottles of sack containing 3 quarts, and 2 quarts of strong water besides; were fined every man, according to the quallity and aggravatiō of his offence, as followeth, John Dillingham and Jonathan Rud were fined 20^s apeece, being the authers principally, Edmond Toly 10^s for fetching the wine, and John Massam for fetching the strong liquor, fined 10^s, John Hurndell, Mr. Auger, and Wiłł Wooden, fined each man five ^{s}, and Lanclott Fuller and David Evance fined each 3^s 4^d apeece, because they were butt occasionally present w^{t}h the rest.

Itt was ordered thatt Sergeant Beckley according to his desire, shall have liberty for this yeare to make a ware in the East River and thatt none shall take liberty to doe the like w^{t}hout license of ye court.

Forasmuch as the whole estate of Thomas Trobridge of Newhaven is to be sequestred for the paym^t of his debts, (he absenting himselfe, and takeing no course concerñg the same,) and his famyly to be disolved, Sergeant Geffrey and his wife being willing to take the children of the said Thomas Trobridge vpon tearmes as followeth, thatt he may have 20 bushells of corne, a brass pott, and a bed for the children to lye vpon, the Court ordered thatt the children should be putt to the said Sergeant Jeffrey vpon the said tearmes; provided thatt in case their father shall come over, or send to take order concerning them, thatt then he will referr himselfe to the Court to judg and determine whatt is equall for him to have for the keeping of them, & in the meane time he will take care thatt they be well educated and nurtured in the feare of God.

ATT A COURT HOLDEN THE 1t OF MAY 1644.

Bro: Pery, being mar of a watch and willfully neglecting itt, was fined 40s.

Math Row, for sitting downe to sleep when he should have stood sentinell, was fined 5s.

Bro: Nicholls, bro: Gibbert, Rich: Web, Tho: Wheeler, Hen Lendall and Witt Bassett, fined each man 1s for late coming on the Lords day wth their armes.

---

[87] A GENrll COURT HELD ATT NEWHAVEN THE 25 OF MAY 1644, ABOUT THE INDIANS.

A letter from Mr. Ludlow was read in Court wherein he intimated thatt whereas an Englishman hath been cruely murdered of late by the Indians, (as he was travilling betwixt Stamforde and Vnkaway,) he had caused 7 Indians to be apprehended, hopeing thereby to procure the murderers, butt the Indians riseing in great companyes about theire towne doe putt the inhabitants thereoff in feare, and therefore he desired advice whatt *to* he should doe in the case. Wherevpon itt was ordered yt advice should be given him to detaine the Indians prisoners, wth intematiō thatt if there be cause of help and they desire itt, men shall be sent vnto them vpon the retourne of the messengers, and for thatt end thatt 20 men shall be putt in readynes forthwth, and fitt to send if need be upon a short warning.

A GEN^rll COURT HELD ATT NEWHAVEN THE 3 OF JUNE, 1644.

A letter from Thirston Rayner, magistrate of Stamforde, being read in the court, itt appeares, thatt a womã of thatt towne hath of late beene cruelly wounded if nott murdered by an Indian,* so thatt itt is thought thatt the Indians being so bolde and insolent are misceivously bent to begin a warr against the English, therefore, itt was ordered, thatt a speedy course be taken to finde out the murderer, and thatt the Governo^r, magistrates and deputyes, wth the captaine and leivetennant as a councell of warr, shall order all the martiall affayres in this jurisdiction vntill the next court of electiō.

ATT A COURT HELD ATT NEWHAVEN 5th OF JUNE, 1644.

John Chapman being ma^r of a watch and neglecting itt, was fined 10^s.

Mr. Gilberts man, being absent att his watch, was fined 5^s.

George Larrymo^r, for neglecting his watch, fined 2^s 6^d.

Theophilus Higginson was complained off for keeping a dog wch hath trespassed divers of his neighbours, and he hath beene tolde of itt.

A will and inventory of John Owens delivered into the court by John Hall, his executo^r.

Itt was ordered thatt George Pardy shall dwell wth Francis Broone as his apprentice, for the tearme of 5 yeares from henceforwarde, dureing wch time the said Francis is to doe his endeuo^r to teach him the trade of a taylo^r.

---

* "At Stamford an Indian came into a poor man's house, none being at home but the wife, and a child in the cradle, and taking up a lathing hammer as if he would have bought it, the woman stooping down to take her child out of the cradle, he struck her with the sharp edge upon the side of her head, wherewith she fell down, and then he gave her two cuts more which pierced into her brains, and so left her for dead, carrying away some clothes which lay at hand. This woman after a short time came to herself, and got out to a neighbours house, and told what had been done to her, and described the Indian by his person and clothes, etc. Whereupon many Indians of those parts were brought before her, and she charged one of them confidently to be the man, whereupon he was put in prison with intent to have him put to death, but he escaped, and the woman recovered, but lost her senses. Sav. Winth. II. 188.

[88] ATT A GEN^rll COURT HELD ATT NEWHAVEN THE 23 OF JUNE, 1644.

Bro: Will Tompson and Henry Lendall were admitted members of the court.

The formes of two oathes were propounded to the Court to be taken the next second day in the morning, by all the inhabitants in this plantatiō, one of them is to be taken by all, and the other by the governo^r onely.

A motiō made on the behalfe of Goodmā Smyth for a lott by the sea side, beyond the West River, was taken into consideratiō and referred to bro: Gibs, bro: Miles, bro: Ceely, bro: Clarke and bro: Peck, to see if itt may stand wth the conveniencie of the towne to grant itt.

Itt was ordered thatt the night watches be carefully attended, and the warde of the Saboth dayes be dilligently observed, and y^t every one of the trayned band bring their armes to the meeting every Lords day; allso y^t the great guns be putt in readynes for service; allso y^t the drū be beaten every morning by breake of the day, and att the setting of the sunne.

Itt was ordered y^t every Lords day 2 men shall goe wth every heard of cattell wth their armes fitted for service vntill these dangers be ouer.

Itt was ordered thatt the fearmes shall be freed frō watching att the towne while there is need of watch att the farmes, provided thatt they keepe a dilligent watch there.

ATT A GEN^rll COURT HELD ATT NEWHAVEN THE 1^t OF JULY, 1644.

The Governo^r tooke this oath as followeth,

I Theophilus Eaton, being att a Gen^rll Co^rt in October last, chosen Governo^r w^thin Newhaven Jurisdictiō for a yeare then to ensue, and vntill a new Governo^r be chosen, do sweare by the great and dreadfull name of the ever living God, to promove the publique good and peace of the same, according to the best of my skill, and will allso maintaine all the lawfull priviledges of this comō wealth, according to the fundamentall order and agreem^{t} made for governm^{t} in this jurisdictiō, and in like manner will endeuo^{r} thatt all wholsome lawes thatt are or shall be made by lawfull authority here established be duely executed, and will further the executiō of justice according to the righteous rules of Gods worde, so help me God in o^{r} Lord Jesus Christ.

The Governo^{r} haveing allso received the oath of fidelity as followeth, I Theophilus Eaton, being by the providence of God an inhabitant w^{t}hin Newhaven Jurisdictiō, doe acknowledge myselfe to be subject to the goverm^{t} thereof, and doe sweare be the great and dreadfull name of the ever living God, to be true and faithfull vnto the same, and doe submitt both my person and my whole estate therevnto, according to all the wholsome lawes and orders thatt for present are or hereafter shall be there made and established by lawfull authority, and thatt I will neither plott nor practise any evill agst the same, nor consent to any thatt shall so doe, butt will timely discover the same to lawfull authority here established, and thatt I will as I am in duety bounde, maintaine the hono^{r} of the same and off
[89] the lawfull magistrates thereoff, promoting the || publique good of the same whilest I shall continue an inhabitant there. And whensoever I shall be duely called as a free burgesse, according to the fundamentall order and agreem^{t} for governm^{t} in this jurisdictiō to give my vote or suffrage touching any matter w^{c}h concerneth this comō wealth, I will give itt as in my conscience I shall judge may conduce to the best good of the same w^{t}hout respect of persons, so help me God, &c.

Then he gave itt to all those whose names are herevnder written,

Stephen Goodyeare	Thomas Fugill	Rich: Hull
Thomas Gregson	Ezech: Cheevers	John Mosse
Richard Malbon	John Ponderson	Adam Nicholls
John Evance	Wiłł Andrewes	Abraham Bell
John Wakeman	John Chapman	Joshuah Attwater
Nath: Turner	John Clarke	Tho: Kimberley
Math: Gilbert	Robt Ceely	Tho: Jeffreyes

Wiłł Thorpe
Francis Newmā
Andrew Low
Tho: Mounson
Tho: Nash
Rich: Pery
Wiłł Peck
John Gibbs
John Livermoore
Nicho: Elsey
Antho: Tompson
John Vincent
Wiłł Potter
Jasper Craine
Rich Miles
Roger Allen
Wiłł Ives
Francis Browne
John Nash
Will Davis
Sam: Whitehead
John Brockett
Math Camfield
Tho: Lamson
Math: Moulthrop
Wiłł Preston
Tho: Beamont
Marke Pearce
James Russell
Wiłł Tompson
Henry Lendall
Robt Abbott
Wiłł Gibbard
Wiłł Bassett
Thomas Wheeler
Henry Browning
Benjamin Linge
Tho: Yale

Rich: Beckley
John Cowp
Jarvis Boykin
Robt Hill
Robt Johnson
Arther Halbidge
Edward Banister
Tymo: Forde
Mathias Hitchcok
James Clarke
Rich: Osborne
Edward Patteson
Geo: Smyth
Wiłł Janes
Jerr: Whitnell
Tho: Morris
Benjamin Willmott
Tho: Powell
Peter Browne
John Tompson
John Tomas
Tho: Mitchell
Wiłł Gibbons
John Hall
Luke Hitchcock
Rich: Newman
Tho: Knowles
Edward Chippfield
Steph: Medcalfe
Christo: Todd
Tho: Osborne
Robt Pig
Nath: Merrymā
Sam: Higginson
Theoph: Higison
David Atwater
Rich: Mansfielde
Hen: Glover

Daniell Paule
John Wilforde
Hen: Peck
Wiłł Russells
Wiłł Fowler
Geo Larrymore
Robt Allen
John Caffins
Tho: Wheeler
Luke Atkinson
Thomas Lupton
Ephraim Penington
Allen Ball
Edward Parker
Lawrence Warde
Tho: Coefield
Johnath: Rudd
John Griffin
James Hewarde
Rich: Beach
David Evance
Robt Campion
Edward Watson
John Dillingham
Wiłł Slow
Robt Martin
John Hill
Ambrose Sutton
John Walker
Thomas Blakeley
Thomas Clark
Rich: Spery
Henry Morrill
Tho: Iles
Edmond Tooly
Johnathan Sergant
Tho: North
Robt Persons

Will White
Raiph Lines
Robt Bassett
Roger Knap
Robt Mecar
Will Mecar
John Beach
John Hutchison
Joseph Peck
Tho: Robinson
Will Fancie
Rice: Edwards
Tho: Robinson juñ
Mighell Palmer
Robt Lee
Will Holt
Tho: Barnes
Robt Emery
Robt Vsher
James Guillam
Ed: Campe
Phillip Leake
Abra: Doolittle
Will Ball
Nich: Baly
Rich: Harrison jur

James Bell
John Linley
Isaack Mould
Joseph Alsop
Rich: Lambert
Edward Preston
Edward Newton
Will Bladen
Rich: Webb
John Mors
John Kimber
Joh: Seckett
Fran: Church
Hen: Gibbons
Will Paine
John Hurnde[ll]
Tho: Caffins
Isaak Beache[r]
Edward Hitch[cock]
John Massam
Geo: Duning

August 5th
1644

Fran: Brewst[er]
Geo: Lamberton

Joh: Benham
Edw: Wiglsewor[th]
Johnath: Marsh
Raiph Dightō
Mr. Bracie
Joh: Wakefi[eld]
Hen: Bish:p
Will Bradley
Abra: Stolyon
Geo: Warde
Roger Betts
Nath: Burchall
Fran: Hall
Joh: Herrima[n]
Sam: Hoskins
Rich: Harrison [sen]
Nich: Auger
Sam: Willson
Peter Mallery
Joh: Hunter
Martin Titchin
Sam: Caffins
Will Toutle
Hen Ruderford
Joh: Bassett
Joh: Megs

[The following names in the handwriting of Francis Newman.]

March the 7th 1647
Samuell Ceffinch
Thomas Johnson
Mathew Rowe
Isacke Whithead
Richard Mordan
Joseph Gernsye
Edward Keylye
Richard Hubball
Job Halle

Henery Loynes
William Judson
James Bishope
Daniel Turner
Thomas Meekes
Henery Carter
John Chidsye
Beniamen Hill
Joseph Nash
Thomas Beech

Henery Bristowe
John Winston
Robert Preston
Thomas Marshall
Thomas Dun
Joshua Griffen
Samuell Goodanhouse
John Tompson
Edward Watters
John Jones

The 2th of Maye 1647

———

old Willmott
Samuell Marsh

———

the 18th of October 1648 at a court of Magistrats.

Mr. Westerhouse

———

Aprill 4th 1654

———

Mr. Samuell Eaton
Robert Talmage
Thomas Harrison
John Downe
Timothy Nash
Jeremiah How
Sam: Farres
Ephraim How
John Knight
John Johnson
Geo: Pardy
James Eaton
John Jackson
Jeremiah Osborn
Robert Clarke his man
Edward Perkins
Andrew Hallaway
John Brookes
John Hudson
Thomas Trobridge
Jeremia Hull
John Potter
Richard Johnson
John Allen
John Baile
William Pringle
William Gibbs, Hatter
John Benham jun^{r}
Joseph Benham

———

May 2^{d} 1654

———

Hen: Boutle
Sam Andrewes
Thom Hogg
Math: Molthrop jun
Joseph Potter
Anthony Tompson
Ellis Mecs
Hen Hummerston

———

22th *May* 1654.

Will Willmott
Will Wooden
Richard Miles jun^{r}
Daniell Hopper
[J]ohn Tuttill
see 138

[Transferred from page 138. In the handwriting of Francis Newman.]

The names of persons that haue taken the oath of fidellitie are entered in fo: 89, and follow as hereafter, ye 7th 2^{d} mo: 1657.

Mr. Bower
Mr. John Dauenpo^{rt} jun
Samuell Wakeman
Geo: Constable
Jonathan Tuttill
Jeremiah Johnson
John Lambert
John Dauis
Anthony Ellcott
Willm: Chatterton
Tho: Tomlinson
Tho: Addams
John Walker
Sam: Ford
Benja: Bunill
Edmund Dormer
Sam Myles
John Browne
John Hull
Thom Weeden
Isack Hall
Daniell Bradley
Joseph Mansfeild
John Tompson
Humphery Spenning
Willm Tyler
Mr. Melyen
Jacob Melyen
Willm. Anderson
Richard Anderson
Stephen Daniell

[The following in the handwriting of Mr. Gibbard.]

The first of May 1660	Joseph Pecke	Stephen Bradely
Thomas Huckly	Nathaniel Boykin	Zackariah How
Daniel Shearman	Nathan Andrewes	Nathaniel How
Moses Mansfeild	Thomas Tuttle	John Hichcock
Richard Bowten	Hackeliah Preston	Mathias Hithfeild
George Rawse	Isaac Turner	Cornelius Offhening
James Clarke junio[r]	Nathaniel Thorp	
Jehiell Prestõ	Eliazer Browne	

[In the handwriting of Thomas Fugill.]

[90] Itt was ordered thatt the weekely traynings of the squadrons shall be renewed as before, every last day of the weeke, (except thatt weeke wherein the gen[rll] trayning is, w[c]h is to be every fift weeke, and that the olde orders be observed, w[c]h was made the 6[t] of August 1642, concerning the trayning of y[e] squadrons.

Liberty was given by the Court to begin an Artillary company, and to ad to themselves such as out of the trayned band or others being free, doe offer thẽselves to be of the Artillary, and to chuse their owne officers and settle their owne orders, so as they use the said liberty moderatly, nott intrenching upon the fundamentall agreem[t] of this Court, provided allso thatt they so order their traynings, thatt if any of the officers of the trayned band be of the Artillary, they may attend the squadrons traynings and yett not loose the opportunity of the Artillary meetings, and thatt all such as are accepted of the Artillary shall be freed from the squadrons traynings if they be nott officers of the trayned band.

Itt was ordered, thatt if a trayning day prove rayny, the next second day after shall be for a gen[rll] trayning in stead thereof.

John Clarke desired to lay downe his sergeants place, whereupon John Nash was chosen sergeant.

Abraham Bell was chosen corporall in stead of John Nash.

Joshuah Atwater desired to lay downe his clarks place, and thereupon Rich: Perry was chosen clarke of the trained band in his stead, and he freed from trayning in respect of his weakenes.

Mr. Gregson and Mr. Wakemã propounded, thatt the land towards Mr. Goodyears farme and the plaine by the pine rock may be veiwed, to see if it will accomodate their quarters for their 2[d] divisiõ and sute the townes occasions allso.

Mr. Gregson desired thatt he might have his 2[d] divisiõ by the Sollitary Cove,* and Mr. Hawkins by the sea towards Milforde.

Captaine Turner, Mr. Malbon, Rob[t] Ceely and Francis Newman were desired to veiw the said lands in question.

Itt was ordered thatt whatsoever pigs under 3 quarters of a yeare olde shall be found in the corne unyoaked, no fence being downe, the owners of them shall pay 6[d] apeece. This order to be in force no longer then till Indian harvest be inned.

Itt was ordered, thatt Rich: Miles, Wiłł Davis and Nicholas Elsey, shall see thatt all the measures in the towne be made according to the stander sent from the Bay.†

A Court the 3[d] of July, 1644.

Wiłł Andrews was warned to the Court about some defects in the meeting house, butt the prosecutiõ of itt respited.

Joh: Hall demand 3[l] due to him from Roger Knap in the right of his wife w[c]h he did acknowledge, whereupon it was ordered, thatt he should paye the said 3[l], only abateing 14[s] w[c]h he hath done in worke for John Woollen, brother to the said John Halls wife.

Edward Banister demaunded 4[l] of Goodmã Bishop on the behalfe of Joh: Burrows, whereupon it was ordered, that the said Goodmã Bishop shall putt in security to pay the mony into the Court the next Court, excep he can show cause to the contrary.

---

* Mr. Gregson was the first white settler of East Haven. Dodd, E. H. Mem. 11.

† "It is thought fit and ordered that there be one and the same measure throughout all the plantations within these vnited Colonies, which is agreed to be Winchester measure, *viz:* eight gallons to the bushell." Rec. U. Coll. Sept., 1643. Hazard, ii. 10.

[91] ATT A GEN^{rll} COURT HELD THE 5th OF AUGUST, 1644.

Forasmuch as there are certaine percells of meadow adjoyning to the skirts of ye upland in severall parts of the neck, w^{c}h belongs to sundry planters in the towne and thatt meadow cannott be improved to the best advantage of the owners w^{t}hout being inclosed, the neck being now layd for a pasture of cattell, itt was therefore ordered, thatt in the towns behalfe the treasurer shall pay for one halfe of the fence thatt is or shall be made betwixt the said meadowes and the upland, w^{c}h fences being once made, they who owe the meadowes are to maintaine them ever after at their owne proper charge. And in case any ꝑticular quarter or ꝑson shall desire to fence their land in ꝑꝑ, before they begin they shall pay to the treasurer their proportiō of the aforesaid gen^{rll} charge, as itt shall be then judged worth.

Mr. Malbon, Mr. Lamberton, and Mr. Evance, having seriously considered the great damage w^{c}h this towne doth suffer many wayes, by reason of the flatts w^{c}h hinders vessells and boates from coming neare the towne when the tyde is anything low, did propound to the Court thatt if they will grant them 4 dayes worke for every man in the towne frō 16 to 60 yeares olde, towards the digging of a channell, and lett them have the benifitt of a wharfe and warehouse, (w^{c}h they will build) upon such tearmes as shall be agreed betwixt themselves and a comittee, (whom they desired the Court then to chuse to treat w^{t}h thē about itt,) they will digg a channell w^{c}h shall bring boates, (att least) to the end of the streete besides Wiłł Prestons house, att any time of the tyde, except they meete w^{t}h some invincible difficulty w^{c}h may hinder their digging the channell so deepe—Whereupon itt was ordered, thatt they shall have the help propounded by them, (viz:) 4 dayes worke of every male in the towne from 16 yeares old to 60, those thatt cannott worke, to hyre others to worke in their stead, and those thatt can, to worke in their owne persons. And thatt Mr. Robt Newman, Mathew Gilbert, John Wakman, Wiłł Gibbard, Jasp Craine, Wiłł Andrewes, Anthony Tompson, and Robt Ceely as a com̃ittee, w^{t}h the advice of the governo^r and magistrates to treate wth the said vndertakers, and agree upon such tearmes as may be equall and for the publique good, setting downe in writing whatt is done and expected on either pt.

Wiłł Peck having butt halfe of a small lott to his houslott, whereby he is much straitened, desired 20 rod of ground over agst his house by the creeke, wch was granted wth this proviso, thatt, if the towne see cause to take itt frō him for any publique vse, he shall relinquish itt, they paying him such charges as shall be judged just.

Mr. Gregson desired thatt he might have his 2^d divisiō by the place called the solitary cove, wch was granted him.

Itt was ordered thatt all the measures in the towne shall be fitted according to the new measure wch is brought from the Bay and appoynted to be the standard for all the collonyes, and marked wth a new marke NH, and those who are to doe itt are to have 4^d for every bushell wch they so fitt and marke, 2^d a peece for every halfe bushell, peck and halfe peck, and 2^d allso for every bushell wch the onely marke and doe nott cutt. The day appoynted for the said service is the 19th day of this moneth, att wch day every one thatt have measures to fitt are desired to bring them to the meeting house.

Those who were desired to veiw the Beauer meadowes made retourn thatt they conceive itt will not be convenient for the towne to part wth itt.

---

[92] ATT A COURT HELD THE 7th OF AUGUST, 1644.

Whereas complaynt was made by Thomas Nash of damage done in his corne to ye value of 9 bushells by hoggs in their quarter, itt was ordered, that the co͞mittee form^rly appoynted, (viz:) Thomas Kimberly, John Chapmā, Thomas Mounson and John Tompsō, naylo^r, shall veiw the fences of the said quarter, and so farr as damage hath come by defective fences, they are to lay the charge of the said 9 bushells upon the severall fences they finde defective, and if all cannott meete about the said veiw, then 3 of them may determine itt.

Theophilus Higginson desired the Court to forbeare him till the next springe, aleadging thatt he is nott able to pay his fines till then, whereupon the Court granted his desire.

Itt was ordered thatt all the fines shall be demaunded forthwth, and if any refuse to pay, the marshall is to warne them to the Court.

Richard Newmā, being warned to the Court for neglect of his watch, he nott appearing, itt was ordered, thatt if he come nott before the Court rise, he shall pay 1s fine for not appearing, and 1s to him thatt watched in his steade.

Richard Perry having beene formerly fined 40s for neglect of his watch, att his humble request for some moderatiō, the Court ordered thatt he should pay onely 15s.

Will Andrewes, haveing undertaken to build and finish the meeting house, did lett out some part of the worke to Thomas Mounson, and Jervas Boykin, who putt itt off to Thomas Saule and Will Gibbons, wth the said Will Andrewes consent and approbatiō, provided they did itt well, butt in the issue itt was defectively done by the said Thomas Saule and Will Gibbons, and Thomas Mounson and Jarvas Boykin conceive they are discharged of their bargaine, butt Will Andrewes alleadged thatt he never discharged them of their covenant whereby they were bound to doe itt well and substantially, butt wth condicō, thatt they should see the said Thomas Saule and Will Gibbons pforme their bargaine wch was to make the roofe of the tower and turrett thite to keep out wett, butt because there was a defect of testimony on all sides, the Court advised them to consult together and doe itt amongst them so as the meeting house may be kept dry wthout delay.

ATT A GENrll COURT HELD THE 19th OF AUGUST 1644.

Captaine Turner and Mr. Malbon were chosen Deputyes for the Genrll Court to be held for this jurisdictiō about the tryall of an Indian, (called Busheage,) who is to be arrayned for murder.*

Itt was ordered, thatt whosoever doth pass through a comō gate or a gate into a comō field and leavs itt nott well shutt, shall pay 5s fine and beare all damage wch shall come by such their neglect. If children or servants shall doe itt, their parents or governors shall pay itt for them, butt the servants to beare itt out of their wages.

Itt was ordered, thatt they of the watch who walk the last round shall call up the drumr an hower before day every morning to beate the drum̄.

Itt was desired, thatt seeing Mr. Malbon is to be frō home, thatt the other 3, (viz:) Captaine Turner, Leivtenant Seely and Antient Newmā would perfect the veiw intrusted wth them the 1t of July last.

The marshall is to cry all lost things wch are brought to him to keep, on the lecture dayes and faire dayes, and to have 1d for evry cry, of the partys who shall challeng the things cryed.

Itt was ordered, thatt the next 5th day shall be a genrll trayīng, and the next genrll trayning to hold notwthstanding.

---

* For the murder of the woman at Stamford, *ante* p. 135. He was arrested and delivered to the English by Wuchebrough a Potatuck Indian. The record of the trial is lost, but Winthrop informs us that "the magistrates of New Haven, taking advice of the elders in those parts, and some here, did put him to death. The executioner would strike off his head with a falchion, but he had eight blows at it before he could effect it, and the Indian sat upright and stirred not all the time." Sav. Winth. ii. 189. Rec. U. C. Sept. 1646.

[93] ATT A COURT HELD ATT NEWHAVEN THE 2d OF OCTOBER 1644.

Roger Knap was discharged of his fine wch was sett upon his head for want of armes, because the Court was informed thatt his armes was burnt in Delaware Bay, and after he came hither he was afflicted wth sicknes and so poore thatt he was nott able to buy armes in due time, butt now he is furnished wth armes.

Mrs. Stolyon demaund a debt of 3l–8–6 of Goodman Chapmā, butt Robt Seely testified thatt Mrs. Stolyō had given him a note of thatt debt among others, to be payd into the ship on her behalfe, and accordingly he accepted itt, and thatt the said John Chapmā from thatt time became debttor to the shipp, butt Mrs. Stolyō affirmed yt afterward she having payd all her part into the ship, and John Chapmans debt being yett unpayd, she desired Mr. Attwater, (who was then to receive the ships pay,) to lett John Chapmā know thatt now she expected the 3l–8–6, should be payd into her owne hands, and to strike out his name out of the aforesaid note, wch Mr. Atwater affirmed upon oath he had done, and thatt John Chapmā said to him then that he cared nott, for he had as leave pay itt to Mrs. Stolyon herselfe, whereupon itt was ordered, thatt John Chapmā shall pay the 3l–8–6 to Mrs. Stolyō.

ATT A GENrll COURT HELD THE 21th OF OCTOBER 1644.

Thomas Lupton, Wiłł Russells and Henry Glover were admitted members of the Court.

Itt was ordered thatt the Secretary shall write to all the plantations in this jurisdictiō to lett them know thatt att the Court of Elections consideratiō will be had of chuseing the comissionrs for the collonyes att the said Court by the vote of all the freemen, thatt accordingly their deputyes may come prepared.

Mr. Malbon and Captaine Turner were chosen Deputyes for the Genrll Court next ensuing.

Mr. Malbon, Mr. Lamberton, Mr. Evance and Mr. Wakemā were chosen Deputyes for the next ensuing halfe yeare.

Mr. Malbon was chosen Treasurer for this ensuing yeare.

Tho: Fugill was chosen Secretary for this ensuing yeare.

Tho: Kimberly was chosen Marshall for this ensuing yeare.

After some serious debate about the turning of the Mill River, Mr. Goodyeare, Mr. Turner, Mr. Malbon and Mr. Wakemā were chosen comittees and desired by the Co^rt to take unto them such workmen as have skill and veiw the said River, exactly to see whatt advantages or disadvantages they can discerne wch may either incourage or discourage the worke, and allso to veiw the bridge ouer the Mill River and report to the Court whatt they discerne or conceive is most meet to be done concerning the p^rmises.

The Treasurer desired, thatt every one to whom the towne is indebted would bring in their accounts, and thatt all those thatt have alienated any land would enter itt, thatt the treasurers booke may be perfected.

Goodmā Smyth of Stratforde desired thatt he may have 30 or 40 acres of upland and 10 acres of meadow granted him for the comfortable keeping of sheepe about the Oyster River, whereupon itt was ordered that those who are intrusted in the townes occasions for disposeing of lotts, shall consider of the said ppositiō, and order itt as they see cause.

Richard Miles, Jasper Craine, Anthony Tompson and Francis Newman were chosen to be constant survayers, (untill others be chosen instead of them,) of all the comon high wayes aboute the towne and the bridges allso, and if need be, to press men & carts for the repair of all such defects as they shall finde from time to time, and the charge to be borne by the towne.

[94] || Whereas divers trespasses have beene comitted by those of the suburbs in Mr. Lambertons quarter, by the driving of hoggs to the Oyster poynt and haunting them there. Mr. Lamberton desired to know the judgm^t of the Court, whether itt be meete for them to haunt their hoggs there, seeing for want of foode they will unavoydably trespass, whereupon a comittee was chosen to veiw the matter in questiō, and to report to the Court how they finde itt. Mr. Malbon and Mr.

Gilbert for the suburbs, and Mr. Gibbard and Richard Miles for Mr. Lambertons quarter.

[A General Court for the jurisdiction was held Oct. 30, 1644, as appears from the date of the appointment of Commissioners, and probably at the same time the jurisdiction resolved upon taking measures to procure a patent from the Parliament.]

ATT A COURT HELD THE 6t OF NOVEMB.
1644.

Henry Humerston, for creeping into Captaine Turnrs house att a window in a felonious manner in the time of the publique meeting on the Lords day, was sentenced to be whipped.

Mathew Camfield, for neglect of his watch, was fined 10s.

Thomas Nash desired satisfactiō for 12 bushells of corne damage done in his corne, by reason of defective fences ptly, and partly the nott setting up of the fence in due time according to agreemt; whereupon itt was ordered thatt the quarter shall beare the damage of ^ bushells, because the fence belonging to the towne was nott sett up in time, and the other ^ bushells to be borne by those perticular fences wch upon veiw was found defective.

ATT A GENrll COURT HELD THE 11th OF
NOVEMB: 1644.

The propositiō for the releife of poore schollars att the colledge att Cambridg was fully approved off, and thereupon itt was ordered, thatt Josuah Attwater and William Davis shall receive of every one in this plantatiō whose hart is willing to contribute thereunto, a peck of wheat or the vallue of itt

Whereas the Genrll Court for this jurisdictiō did see cause to putt forth their best endeuors to procure a Pattent frō the Parliament, as judging itt a fitt season now for thatt end, and therefore desired Mr. Gregson to undertake the voyage and busines and agreed to furnish him wth 200l in this jurisdictiō, of wch, in proportiō to the other plantations, Newhaven is to pay 110l in good marchantable beaver, itt was thereupon ordered, thatt the said 110l shalbe procured at the charge of the towns treasury, vpon such tearmes as itt may, and the towne to stand to the tearmes and beare the damage thatt may come thereby.

The comittee thatt were appoynted to veiw the land for Mr. Gregsons and Mr. Wakemans quarters, reported, thatt they found much land wch they conceive is good, butt what quantity they cannot judge, and therefore desired thatt a comittee may be now appoynted to veiw and survay the land y^t yett is unlayd out, to see if it be such land for quallity as hath beene layd out to other quarters for their 2^d divisiō, and allso w^t quantity there is of it. Mr. Malbon, Mr. Francis Newmā, Anthony Tompson and Leivtenant Seely were appoynted for the said veiw.

Vpon complaint made by some of the planters of Totokett, thatt the Mohegin Indians have done much damage to them by setting their traps in the walke of their cattell, itt was ordered, that the marshall shall goe wth Thomas Whitway to warne Vncus or his brother or else Foxen to come and speake wth the Governo^r and the magistrates.

[95] || Itt was propounded thatt, (because many men thatt come and appeare att the Genr^ll Courts when their names are called over, goe away before the Court rise,) the order for appearance att Gen^rll Courts under a penalty be read att the next Gen^rll Court, thatt itt may be altered if there be cause.

Itt was propound thatt att the next Gen^rll Court, survayers may be chosen for every quarter to veiw the fences belong to their severall quarters, and where they finde any defective, to acquaint the owners, and if the defect be nott mended by a day appoynted, the survayers to gett itt done and the owners to beare the charge wth some fine.

Itt was allso propounded thatt a comittee may be appoynted to veiw all the orders thatt are of a lasting nature, thatt such as are defective may be mended and presented to the Court to be confirmed.

A Court held att Newhaven the 4th of December, 1644.

John Gibs and William Gibbard were fined each of them 10s for neglecting their watch, they being mars of the watch.

A Court held att Newhaven the 2d of January, 1644.

Whereas some goods belonging to Mr. Pike of Vncaway, in the hands of Tho: Robinson of this towne have beene attatched by warrant from Mr. Gregson att the sute of John Livermore of this towne allso, who desired the judgmt of the Court, whereupon itt was ordered, thatt Thomas Robinson shall keep somuch of the said goods in his hands as will satisfie the just demaunds of the said John Livermore.

John Dillingham and Thomas North, for totall absence att trayĩng, fined each man 2s 6d.

Whereas there was a difference betweene Mr. Evance and John Tompson, nayler, about the price of 2 heifers wch the said John Tompson bought of Mr. Evans, itt was agreed betweene them in the Courtt, thatt Mr. Evans should have his heifers againe.

Forasmuch as itt appeared to the Court, thatt Mr. Leach hath brought some bricks from the brickills in the plains wch did belong to Mr. Gregson, itt was ordered thatt Mr. Leach shall pay Mr. Gregson for them.

Mr. Evance desired the judgmt of the Court concerning a debt of 6l 15s, wch he demaund of Edward Chipperfield who had put him of wth excuses, and did alledge it should have beene payd out of a kill of bricks wch was to be devided betwixt Steven Medcalfe, John Medcalfe and himselfe, butt upon examinatiō, itt appeared thatt there were not so many bricks due to him of the said kill full as would satisfie Mr. Evance his debt.

Wiłł Andrewes allso desired a debt of 5l due to Wiłł Harding frō the said Chipperfield, who having nothing wherewth to pay either the one or the other, said he would referr himselfe to the Court.

Tho Blacksley, because of his poverty, had part of his fine remitted, (viz) 6^s 8^d.

Nathan Burchell his fines for defects remitted hitherto, provided thatt he gett armes and attend trayīngs duely for time to come.

All y^t have beene fined for not bringing their armes to the publique wor^{ps} remitted hitherto.

Bro: Abbott demaunded satisfactiō of Mr. Lamberton for damage done by his hogs in the Oyster shell field, butt respited.

Robt Parsons desired his fine might be remitted, but the Court see no cause why.

---

[96] ATT A COURT HELD ATT NEWHAVEN THE 5th OF FEB: 1644.

Whereas certaine goods belonging to Mr. Lewis of London have beene attatched in the hands of William Andrewes att the sute of Thomas Stevenson of Yenicott, Mr. Priden as his attournay required $judgm^t$ upon the said goods. The Court understanding that the said Stevenson solde and delivered to Mr. Lewis aforesaid a boat att Virgenia valued att 8^l. Thatt the said Lewis did promiss in lew thereof thatt the said Stevenson should have a mare of his wch was then in the hands of Mr. Russells of Charlestowne in the Massacusetts, butt when the said mare was demaunded, the said Mr. Russells said he had sould her for fower pounds, whereupon itt was ordered, thatt the said Wiłł Andrewes shall pay unto the said Mr. Priden the sū of 4^l wch was the price of the mare when shee was solde, and the remainder of the said goods in the hands of Wiłł Andrewes belonging to Mr. Lewis shall rest there as attatched till the Court dispose otherwise of or concerning them.

William Tompson demaunded satisfactiō of Mr. Gregson for damage done in his corne by his hoggs, itt being evidenced in the Court thatt the fences of Goodman Banister, Edward Patteson and John Charles were defective att the same time when his hogs did the damage, itt was ordered, thatt they should beare the damage according to their different just ꝑportiōs, (viz) Edward Banister 3 bushells, and the other 2 each of them one bushell and a halfe.

Thomas Mouleno[r] sen[r], and Thomas Mouleno[r] his son, being charged wth sundry miscarryages and breach of peace but nott issued, itt was referred to another Court and in the meane time itt was ordered, thatt they shall both enter into *into* a recognisance of each man 100[l] to keep the publique peace and be of the good behavio[r] towards all people and especially towards the inhabitants of Totokett.

Arthur Halbidge, having beene formerly charged by Mr. Browning for stealing frō him a bushell of corne to the vallue of 4[s], and a shirt or frock to the value of 1[s], w[ch] he att first denyed w[th] cursing himselfe butt now confessed the fact, and was sentenced to be whipped and to make two fould restitutiō to Mr. Browning, and to beare all the charges w[ch] have beene caused by him.

Richard Lambert, having beene form[r]ly convicted and sensured for sundry miscarriages in was of unrightousnes, now made an acknowledgm[t] of his guilt in the court, thinking thereby to give satisfactiō, who showed themselves willing to take satisfactiō, butt yett advised him to be carefull to make his peace w[th] God, and seeke to gett that bitter roote, (whence such evill frutes did spring,) that a reformatiō of those evills may appeare in his conversatiō.

A Court held the 6th of March 1644.

Mathew Crowders fine remitted upon Mr. Brownings testimony thatt his was sick att thatt training frō w[ch] he was absent.

John Walkers fine was *was* remitted bec: he was lame.

Rob[t] Parsons fine respited till May or June.

[97] Att a Gen[rll] Court held att Newhaven the 24 of Feb. 1644.

Jer. Whitnell, Thomas James, Rob[t] Martin, John Gregory and John Meggs were admitted members of the Court.

Itt was ordered thatt if any members of the Court shall depart from the Gen[rll] Courts w[t]hout licence after their names be called, they shall pay each man 1[s] 6[d] fine, and if any planter shall depart w[t]hout licence while the Court sitts, he shall pay one shilling fine.

Whereas the plantatiō hath beene much exercised w[t]h hoggs distroying of corne, the Court tooke itt into serious consideratiō how they might prevent the like damage for time to come, and after much debate itt was ordered, thatt a comitte shall be chosen in every quarter to veiw the comon fences and fences belonging to every quarter, some one day in the first weeke in every moneth, from the first of March next unto y[t] day 12 moneths, and observe diligently whose fences are defective and acquant the owners therew[t]h, calling upon them to gett them mended, and to lett them know thatt they are to make good all the damage w[c]h shall be done w[t]hin thatt fence till theirs be mended if none other be found defective besides; and they whose fences are defective shall pay the said veiwers for their expence of time about the said veiw, butt if no fences be defective, then the whole quarter shall pay them. And the said veiwers are to acquaint every famyly in their said severall quarters, or every pson that hath any part in the fences w[c]h they are to veiw, what day they intend their first veiw that every said owner may go or send one w[t]h them to marke their owne fences att both ends, that the veiwers may afterwards exactly know w[c]h is every mans fence, and if any man upon notice so given shall neglect to goe or send as aforesaid, he shall pay 2[s] fine. And if the veiwers shall neglect to veiw att the times appoynted, or shall neglect to observe exactly the defects, or shall neglect to give due notice as aforesaid, each mā shall pay 5[s] fine for every default as aforesaid. Moreover if any fences belonging to the towne, (and once accepted as good by the treasurer,) be found defective, the veiwers shall gett them mended, and if they cannott otherwise gett workmen they shall have power to press men to mend them, and the treasurer shall pay them.

Itt was allso ordered, thatt if any mans corne be damaged by cattell or hoggs, he may pound them if he finde the beasts y[t] have done the damage and cannott finde where they gott in or at whose fence, he may goe to the veiwers appoynted for thatt quarter where the damage was done, and gett them to veiw the fences, and he or they whose fences they finde defective shall beare the damage and pay the veiwers for their expence of time if they be called to veiw extraordinaryly.

Jasper Craine and William Touttle for Mr. Davenports quarter, John Caffins and Jarvas Boykin for Mr. Newmans quarter and Mr. Brownings, Robt Johnson and Thomas Powell for the Yorkshire quarter, Wiłł Fowler and Henry Glover for Mr. Wakem̃[s] quarter, Rich: Miles and Williã Davis for Mr. Gregsons quarter, Rich: Hull and Nicholas Elsey for Mr. Lambertons quarter, Wiłł Ives and Edward Banister for the suburbs, Thomas Mounson and Robt Pigge for the Oystershell field, Rich: Mansfield and David Atwater for the farmes, and Francis Browne and John Vincent for the plaines.

The Court desired the magistrates together wth the deputies to veiw all those orders w[ch] are of a lasting nature, and where they are defective, to mend them and then lett them be read in the Court thatt the Court may confirme or alter them as they see cause.

Whereas much disorder hath beene done by some in cutting downe trees in the comõ w[t]hin the 2 miles contrary to order, the Court required Anthony Tompson and John Clarke to enquire who they are that have transgressed thatt order, and to take notice who doe hereafter transgress in like kinde vntill some other be chosen in their stead.

Itt was ordered, thatt all men shall duely pay their rates to the treasurer, or to those whome he shall appoynt to receive them w[t]hout putting him of to others, and that all those who have alienated land shall pay the rates for itt themselves untill it be entered in the Court booke according to order.

Itt was ordered, thatt all those of the squadrons w[ch] in their course doe bring their armes on the Lords dayes to the meeting, shall bring them to the meeting the lecture day imediatly before, so many of them as doe come to the lecture.

[98] ||The Governo[r] desired thatt all meanes might be vsed to pfect souldiers in the military art, and thatt the gen[rll] trainings and squadrons wth an artillary allso may be incouraged and improved to thatt end, and wished thatt all those thatt are free and willing, would goe to the leivtennant and sergeants and enter their names to be of an artillary, who, when they are approved, shall be exempted frō the squadron traynings.

Mr. Pearc desired the plantatiō to take notice, thatt if any will send their childr. to him, he will instruckt them in writing or arethmatick.

Rob[t] Abbott and Wiłł Paine desired that their land might be layd out on the East side, in such a forme as may be convenient for them to fence itt and improve itt. Jasper Craine and Wiłł Touttle were desired to veiw it and consider how itt may be layd out to sute the townes occasions and their conveniences.

Jasper Craine was freed from watching and trayning in his owne person, because of his weaknes, butt to finde one to watch in his stead whē his turne comes.

Goodmā Goldam freed from watching and trayning in his owne person in like manner in regard of his weaknes, onely he is to finde a man to watch for him when his turne comes if his estate will beare itt.

Att a Gen[rll] Court held att Newhaven the last of March 1645.

Wiłł Fowler, Tho: Mitchell and Phillipp Leake were admitted members of the Court.

Mr. Malbon was chosen Treasurer.

Mr. Malbon, Mr. Evance, Mr. Gibbard and Mr. Francis Newman were chosen deputies for the halfe yeare next ensuing.

Captaine Turner and Mr. Malbone were chosen Deputies for the Jurisdictiō Court.

Elder Newman exempted frō attending att the Gen^{rll} Courts by reason of his many occasions.

Itt was ordered thatt Jasper Craine and Robt Ceely before the next second day, shall veiw all the cannows belonging to the English about this towne, and marke ỹ w^{t}h the townes marke all such w^{c}h they shall approve as fitt for the English to vse, and thatt no person or persons in this plantatiō or belonging to itt shall lend or vse any cannow thatt is nott so marked by the ꝑsons aforesaid, under the penalty of 20^{s} fine for every default.

Itt was ordered thatt no ꝑson or ꝑsons shall kindle a fire to burne leaves, straw, cornestalks or any kinde of rubbish either in gardens or houslotts in or about this towne vnder the penalty of 2^{l} fine.

Itt was ordered thatt no man shall putt any cattell into the neck frō this day foreward above his ꝑportiō, under the penalty of 6^{d} a weeke for every head, according to the intent of a form^{r} order in that case mad 16th of Jan: 1642. And thatt before any man putt any cattell into the neck, he shall give notice to the governo^{r} whom the Court desired to take the paines to cast up whatt every mans proportiō is, when he knows in whose right they come.

Elder Newman and Captaine Turn^{r} are desired to see the fence belonging to the neck well done and a gate towards the farmes, old Bassett and his son were desired to doe itt.

Itt was ordered thatt no cattell shall be putt into the neck att the spring, untill the first of May.

Itt was ordered thatt the drūs belonging to the towne shall be putt in good repaire att the townes charge, and Steven Medcalfe and Robt Bassett shall have 8^{l} betwixt them, for w^{c}h they shall attend all the townes occasions as comoñ drūm^{rs} for the towne till this time 12 moneths, and maintaine the drūs att their owne charge in good plight, and leave them so att the end of the tearme.

Itt was ordered thatt the treasurer shall pay Steven Medcalfe 20^{s} for the service he did the last winter extraordinary.

[99] ||These following officers and orders of the Artillary company were p^{r}sented to the court and confirmed by the

court, leaving the sett time of trayings to the company themselves to order as they shall see cause.

Mr. Malbon Captaine, Leivten^t^ Ceely, Leiveten^t^ Francis Newmā, Standard bearer Wiłł Andrews, Tho: Mounson, Tho: Jeffrey and John Nash Sergeants.

Orders for the Artillary Company att Newhaven.

1 Thatt the company from time to time chuse their officers from among themselves, as captaine, leivtennant, ensigne, sergeants and others necessary for service, and thatt upon such choyce they yearly p^r^sent them to the Gen^rll^ Court for Newhaven for approbatiō & confirmation.

Thatt every man offering himselfe to this company be either free and att his owne disposeing for such a service, or if a servant and ingaged to any other, thatt he bring a certifficate or other satisfying testimony of his ma^rs^ consent thatt his way may be cleared before he be admitted to exercise.

Thatt every member of this company att his first entrance pay the sum̃ of 18^d^ for and towards the raising of a small stock for the necessary vses of the company, to be payd in to the treasurer or clarke appoynted by the company for thatt purpose.

Thatt once a ^ upon the 4th day of the weeke after the lecture is ended, this company exercise themselves in a military way for increase of their skill and activity against times of service. And for this exercise the first drum̃ to beate att the going out from the lecture, and the second drum̃ one hower after, and thatt att every such exercise every one of the company be present upon the markett place and answere att the call of his name and bring w^t^h him his muskett and all other armes appoynted for the said exercise.

Thatt whosoever of them cometh late or nott compleatly armed, on any of these dayes of exercise, shall pay 6^d^ for a fine, and for totall absence 12^d^, and thatt the offendors being first demaunded, duely pay these fines before or att the 2^d^ exercise next after the forfeiture.

Thatt every one of this company purposely coming to any

Gen^rll^ or perticular Court, or to the ordinances att any publique meeting, whether on the Lords dayes, lecture dayes, dayes of solleme fasting or thanksgiving, shall carry and weare his sword by his side, under the penalty of 6^d^ for every such omission and default if he give not a sufficient reason to the satisfactiō of the company.

Thatt if any member of this body fined by the majo^r^ pt of this company for any default before mentioned be not satisfied concerning the same, he may offer the consideratiō of his offence and fine to the company, to the next perticular court, (upon due notice by him given to the company,) who shall heare and determine betwixt the company and him according to their light in referrence to the forgoing orders.

Thatt the stock of this company whether arising from entrance mony, fines, mony given, or any other way, shall from time to time be disposed off by the consent of the major part of the company att some meeting, and nott other wise.

Thatt every member of this company, (according to his place and estate,) come to these exercises in decent apparrell, thatt all excess, all contentious, provoking, sinfull carryage in speech, gestures and actions be avoyded, butt if any offend, upon complante, the perticular court to examine, censure and reforme as they shall judge meete.

Lastly for their further incouragm^t^, itt is granted and ordered thatt all the members of this company duely attending the gen^rll^ traynings be freed from the perticular squadron meetings and traynings wherein the rest of the towne are exercised by the sergeants.

Whereas, by reason of the artilary, the squadrons will be small, itt was ordered thatt 2 companyes shall be joyned into one, of the sergeants in their course shall exercise them one in every 2 weekes.

Itt was ordered thatt the markett place shall be cleared forthw^th^, and the wood to be carryed to the watch house there to be piled, and thatt the busines may be effected, the care of itt is comitted to the 4 sergants.

Itt was ordered thatt if any mans goates shall be found out

of his owne ground wthout a keeper after this weeke, he shall pay 6d a head.

James Russells, by reason of his lame thumb, was excused frō bringing his muskett on the Lords dayes and other dayes of publique sollemn worps.

[100] ||Mr. Davenport having a desire to remove his fence from thatt side of his lott towards the clay pitts way to the other side of his lott towards the mill highway, requested thatt he might have liberty to fence up the way to the clay pitts and he will make a gate, sett a lock upon itt and leave the key att John Coopers house, wch being considered by the court they granted his request.

Itt was ordered thatt from hence forward the monthly court shall be kept on the 3d day of the weeke.

Phillip Leake was chosen corporall instead of Abraham Bell.

Itt was ordered thatt a chist shall be made forthwth to putt the pikes in, to keepe them from warping, wch Thomas Mounson and the rest of the officers undertooke to see done.

Itt was ordered thatt those thatt live att the farmes shall bring or send their armes to be veiwed on such dayes as are appoynted, and they all attend the genrll traynings except one man att every farme.

Itt was left to the Governor and Captaine Turner to order and appoynt the genrll trainings so as may be most for the common good of the plantatiō in respect of hay time and harvest.

A Court held att Newhaven the 8th of Aprill 1645.

Mr. Malbon required satisfactiō of Mr. Caffins for damage done in his corne att seurall times, once by his swine, and another time by his cattell, wch was valued att 8 bush:s each time, butt Mr. Caffins aleadged thatt the damage came by defect of their owne fence wch was nott made up betweene the clay pitts and their corne. The case being something darke, wth consent of both parties, it was referred to John Wakemā,

Rich: Miles and Jasper Craine to veiw and arbitrate & determine, or else to report to the court how they finde itt.

Robt Ceely was desired to advise wth some thatt have skill in leather to gett whatt light they can agst the next court, thatt some course may be taken if itt may be to moderate the price of leather and shooes.

John Meggs accused Captaine Turner, Tho: Pell and Tho: Robinson of extortiō or vnrighteousnes in the prices of leather wch they sould to him, butt being nott prepared to make proofe of whatt he had charged them wth, the proceeding was respited vntill the next court.

Captaine Turner having received eighteene pounds and eighteene shillings of Mrs. Higginsons estate, and John Wakemā fifteene pounds allso of the said estate, have both severally ingaged their *their* houses and lands att Newhaven unto the court of Newhaven for the true paymt thereof in current country pay att the full end and tearme of 5 yeares from October last past, together wth 3s att every pound for consideratiō of the said mony.

John Walker desired satisfactiō for damage done in his corne by hoggs wch Thomas Morris testified was 12 bushells, whereupon it was ordered that the defective fences shall make itt good.

The marshall was required to warne their quarter to gett the defective fences mended, and the treasurer is to pay for thatt wch belongs to the towne.

Mr. Leach having cutt shingles in the woodes contrary to order, desired to know the minde of the court, whether or noe he may have them, itt was ordered thatt he shall, if he will make vse of them referring himselfe to the court for the price of the shingles and his disorder in getting them wthout license.

[101] A Court held the 6^{t} of May 1645.

Obadiah Southwood being apprentice to Goodman Tainter for runing away from his said ma^{r}, and being convicted for a notorious lyar, was sentenced to be seveerly whipped.

Concerning the defference betweene Mr. Browning and John Moss, they were desired to cleare mistakes betweene them about the diffective fences in the oyster shell field w^{c}h concernes them, w^{c}h the veiwers have given them warning of 3 times, and yett the are nott mended.

Itt was ordered thatt they whose fences in the oyster shell field are defective, or were found to be so upon veiw, shall pay the veiwers for their loss of time as well in attending the court as in veiwing, because the did nott gett their fences mended according as they were advised, (viz) Mr. Browning, ^ Abbott, Mathew Moulthrop, Goodmā Pigg and John Moss.

Thomas Barnes required satisfactiō of Raiph Dighton for a cow of his w^{c}h perished as he conceives through his sons neglect who kept the heard thatt day, butt Raiph Dighton alleadged thatt a cow of thatt heard being swamped, his son came home to the towne to gett help, and left his partner w^{t}h the cow in the interim, and before they had gott the cow out of the swamp itt was night and the heard was coming home, and they nott knowing of any dangerous place betwixt the bridge and the place where the cattell vsed to come over, did nott conceive itt necessary to follow the cattell, butt came over the bridge, and though they came on the other side of the river over against the place where his cow was afterwards found perished w^{t}h her foote in a hole betwixt the banck and the roote of a tree, yett they did neither heare nor see her. Itt was testified by others that there was noe knowen place of danger in thatt place before mencõned. The judgm^{t} of the Court was thatt itt was an afflicting providence of God w^{c}h the said Barnes was to beare himselfe, and that the boy was innocent in the case.

Robt Johnson for a defective gunstock was fined 1s and charged to gett itt mended.

A COURT HELD THE 3d OF JUNE
1645.

The difference betwixt Captaine Turner and John Hill concerning a Bull wch the Captaine conceived did dye by the default of the said John Hill in working him contrary to his mars express comaund, was referred by consent of both ptyes to John Wakeman and Mr. Robert Newmā to arbitrate and determine if it may be, or else to report to the Court how they finde itt.

John Meggs having formrly charged Captaine Turner, Thomas Pell and Tho: Robinson wth extortiō or sinfull vnrightousnes, and nott being able to make good the said charge agst them, did now acknowledg his error, wch acknowledgmt was accepted as satisfactiō, onely he was sentensed to pay 1s fine for nott appearing att the last court, and to pay the charges of those who had attended 3 courts together by his meanes.

James Till for stealing 2 fadd: of black wampom, and one fadd: of white from Laurence Turner, into whose company he intruded himselfe under pretence of frendship, was sentenced to be whipped and to make 2 folde restitutiō to the said Laurence for what he hath stolen.

The difference betweene Mr. Goodyeare and John England, by consent of both ptyes, was referred to Mr. Robt Newmā and Mr. Gilbert to arbitrate and determine if it may be, or to make report to the Court how they finde it.

Edward ^ Mr. Gilberts man, desired the judgmt of the court whether his mar can force him to serve any longer, he having nothing to show in writing, itt was answered that he must stay wth his mar one yeare more, and in the meane time, both he and his mar may write to his friends for both their satisfactiō, and if he doe serve a yeare longer thē he should have done, then his mar is to pay him for his last yeares service.

An account was delivered into the court by Mr. Craine conceri̅ng Mr. Roe and ordered in case itt be questioned it is to be tryed in a Court of Magistrates.

Andrew Low, for late coming to watch, fined 2s, and Geo. Larrimor and Goodmā Harrison fined each of them 1s for the same.

Tho: Caffins fined 6d apeece for his goates pounding.

Rich: Webb promised to pay vnto Josuah Attwater 33s wch he demaunded of him as due to the shipp.

Fifty shillings of Steven Medcalfe's in the hands of Peter Browne is attatched by Mr. Gregson for a debt of the said Stevens.

---

[102] Att a Gentll Court held att Newhaven the 16th of June, 1645.

Those who have the small lotts propounded their want of meadow to the serious consideratiō of the court, desireing that the court would grant them the meadowes called the Beaver meadowes and they will endevor to improve them, and if they can so improve them as to make them comodious for their vse they will be content to pay rates backward and forward in a moderate way as shall be judged equall, butt if nott they will retourne the said meadows into the hands of the towne.

Leivtenant Seely and Jer Witnell complained thatt their meadowes are so bad as that they are alltogether unserviceable to them and cannott be improved, and therefore desired the court to take their case allso into serious consideratiō.

The Court seriously considering and debateing the said propositions, declared themselves willing to attend the necessityes of the partyes aforesaid and others whose meadowes by charge cannott be improved, and therefore ordered that Jasper Craine, Marke Pearce, John Clarke and Henry Lendall shall veiw the said meadowes in referrence to the aforesaid ꝑpositions and make report to the Governor and the rest of the Court, (whatt they conceive concerning them,) who shall have *have* power upon the retourne of the said veiw to dispose of the said meadowes, to lay out proportions and to settle rates according to each mans different and severall considerations interessed in the aforesaid propositions as they in their wisdome shall see cause.

Francis Browne moved in the court thatt if he may have a little house or shade made att the water side to worke in and competent allowance for his paines, and if itt may be, some land in the Oyster-shell field to plant, he will keep a ferry boate to carry people over the East River, and thatt he will attend itt every day from the rising of the sun to the going downe of the same in an ordenary course till 12 moneths be expired from the date here-of, exceptinge Saboth dayes and other times of solemne publique worp of God. Whereupon itt was ordered that he shall 2d apeece if there be nott above 3. If there be above 3 and not above 6 he shall have 3ob a peece, and if above 6 he shall have butt 1d a head for their fare. Itt was allso ordered thatt if any English man shall transport any person or persons in any other boate or cannow in the ferryes way, he shall pay to the ferryman 1d a head for every person so transported by him, provided notwthstanding, that if any planter in this towne have a boate or cannow of his owne he may make vse thereof to transport himselfe, famyly or worke folkes to and againe, (as their busines or occasions require) wthout offence. Note allso that the farmers on the East side are left free either to vse their owne cannowes or boates, or to agree wth the ferryman as they can when they have need. The Court desired the Governor wth the magistrates and deputies to take care thatt a shade or little house be made as aforesaid, and that the ferryman may be accomodated wth 2 or 3 acres of land convenient for him in the Oyster shell field if it may be.

Whereas much damage hath beene done to timber in the comon by getting barke for dying and tanning, itt was therefore ordered thatt Sergeant Andrewes, Sergeant Jeffreyes & Sergeant Mounson, wth Corporall Whitehead shall consider where the dyers and tanners may gett their barke for time to come wth least damage to the publique and that from henceforward if any shall gett barke in the comons wthout their allowance, or contrary to their appoyntment, they shall be punished att the discretiō of the Court.

Whereas the court did desire the Governo[r] and the captaine to consider and order the traynings so as may sute best wth the townes occasions, w[ch] accordingly they have ordered as followeth; the first Munday in March to traine and veiw armes, the last Munday in Aprill & the last Munday in May to traine, the third Munday in June to trayne and veiw armes, the last Munday in September to traine and veiw armes, the first and last Mundayes in October to trayne, the second Munday in November to traine and veiw armes, w[ch] dayes were approved and confirmed by the court.

Itt was ordered that if any person or persons, whether directly or indirectly, in this towne shall sell wine by retayle of quarts or pintes or the like, after 14 dayes next ensueing be expired, w[t]hout license, he or they shall be punished att the discretiō of the court.

Wiłł Andrewes licensed to draw wine and to sell by retayle.

Vpon a motiō made by William Andrewes for some convenient place to putt straingers horses in, itt was ordered thatt the said William Andrewes shall have liberty to fence in 20 acres of land att the hither end of the plaines joyning unto Francis Newmans lott, and if dye or leave the ordinary, the land shall goe to the ordinary still for the vse aforesaide, onely his charges are to be allowed by him thatt shall succeede, thatt he *or* be no looser when he leaves itt if the hyre he receives doe nott pay him in the interim.

[103] || Itt was ordered thatt a standard of weights and measures shall be made forthw[th], and thatt every one in the towne who have weights and measures w[ch] they intend to buy or sell by, shall bring them to the meeting house this day fortnight att 8 a clock, and Rich: Miles, Josuah Attwater and Nicholas Elsey shall fitt and marke them by the standard and goe to the houses of those who have great weights w[ch] cannott wth conveniencie be brought to the meeting, and what time the spend in the aforesaid service, the treasurer is to pay them. And if any person or persons shall after the aforesaid,

shall sell by any weight or measure not so marked as aforesaid, he or they shall be punished att the discretiō of the Court.

Whereas some have taken offence att the shepheards keeping his sheep and making a penne for them towards the Oyster river thinking they were wronged by itt, butt the order of Court the 21 of October 1644 being read, itt appeared thatt nothing was done butt by order of Court.

Itt was ꝑpounded thatt another ordinary might be sett up towards the water side, butt none was found fitt for the present, onely itt was left w^t^h John Livermore to consider off if he can be free & fitt to undertake itt.

Itt was propounded thatt every souldier in the band may have a yeard of canvis for such vse as the captaine shall appoynt. Itt was allso propounded thatt a marke may be sett up in some convenient place for the company to shout att for some priz.

Whereas the place where John Benham now makes bricks is w^t^hin the compass of Mr. Eatons farme, and noe way to itt butt *butt* by water except through his ground, w^c^h nevertheless hitherto he hath nott beene debarred of, but of late brother Benham having a purpose to inclose some ground there, the Governo^r^ Mr. Eaton lett him know itt would nott be convenient for him to have a farme w^t^hin his farme, whereupon the said John Benham propounded to the Court where he shall make bricks, butt nothing was determined concerning.

Itt was ordered thatt a chist be made for the pikes and the great guns putt in readynes for w^t^h, according to a former order.

A Gen^rll^ Court held the 20th of June, 1645.

Whereas itt doth appeare there is need of sending forth some souldiers to strengthen Vncus agst the Narragansett Indians, for the present and y^t^ some thing may fall out w^c^h may occasiō the sending of more men, itt was therefore ordered thatt the Governo^r^ w^t^h the rest of the Court w^t^h the Captaine and Leivtenant as a councell of warr shall dispose and order all the military affayres untill the Gen[rll] Court for the jurisdictiō shall settle some course concerning the same.

A Court held the 1[t] of June, 1645.

Wiłł Russells being ma[r] of a watch, for suffering his watch to sleepe was fined 10[s].

The sentinell fined 5[s] and all the rest 1[s] a peece.

John Hunter fined 5[s] for neglecting his watch.

Sam Dighton and Anthony Stevens respited.

A Court held the 5 of August, 1645.

Rob[t] Abbott having his goates driven forth towards the keeper, butt were found in the quarter yett had done no damage, desired the judgm[t] of the Court whether he were lyable to pay 6[d] a head by vertue of the order agst goates.

[Here the records cease to be in the handwriting of Thomas Fugill, and what follows, as far as page 194, is in that of Richard Perry.]

[104] At a Gen[ll] Court held at Newhauen the 18th of August, 1645.

Vppon a letter from the Governour* it was desired that some course may be taken for the common saftie in these rumours & tumults of the Indians.

The gunne smithes were desired to lay aside all other buissines & gett those gunnes repayred that are defective.

Henry Pecke and old Bassett were desired to sett the great gunnes vppon good strong carryadges.

The farmers that have butter and cheese were desired to keepe it in their hands, that in case the publicque service require it, they may be furnished.

All those that goe abroad in the woods or meddowes were

---

* From Boston, where he was attending a meeting of the Commissioners of the United Colonies.

desired to carry their armes wth them, & to worke as neare together as may bee.

It was desired that those that goe forth with the heards and flocks would carry their gunnes wth them & it was advised that 2 might goe wth euery heard onn the Lords dayes.

At a Gennerall Court held at Newhauen the 25th of August, 1645.

The court tooke it into serious consideration what should be done wth farmes, but nothing was concluded about them but left to further consideration, only those that live at the farmes were desired to keepe good watch & be carefull of their owne saftie, till there be more apparent danger and some further order concerninge them.

It was debated whether the dischardging of a gunne in the towne, woods or meddowes, shalbe taken as an allarum dureing these times of danger, but it was left.

It was propownded that those that have gunnes most fit for service abroad, shall lend them to the souldiers that are to goe abroad, Also that those that have shoes & stockeings to spare, would furnish the souldiers wth them, and Mr. Gregson vndertooke to see them satisfied for them.

A Court held the 2d of September, 1645.

Richard Catchman desired the justice of the court agaynst Thomas Hart and complayned that the said Hart carryed away his negroe servant from Virginia w^thout his licence, wherby he was damnified to the vallew of 2000 waight of tobacco in the price of her, besides what was dew to him from the said Thomas Hart for the service of the said servant for sundry monthes.

Thomas Hart pleaded that the said Catchman did owe him a debt, & delivered a noat of severall accompts into the court.

But because they wanted clearnes of evidence onn both sides, the court advised them to refferre it to arbitration, accord-

22

ingly they chose Mr. Gregson and Mr. Malbon to arbitrate it, & if they cannot end it they desired Mr. Eaton the governour to vmpire it.

Richard Catchman as aturney for Florence Payne in Virginia demanded a debt of Mr. Hart wch hee the said Thomas Hart did acknowledge, but conceived that part of it was paied, if not all, but had not his proofe readdy, whereuppon it was respited that he may have time to make proofe; in the meane time to lay in security to the court for the said debt till hee make proofe of the payment of it in Virginia.

John Thomas for absence at a gennerall trayninge was fined 5s.

---

[105] A COURT HELD AT NEWHAVEN THE 6th OF OCTOBER, 1645.

Michaell Palmer complayned that Richard Beech did promise to pay him a debt of 35s in beaver but had fayled.

Richard Beech acknowledged the debt & his promise to pay beaver, but professed he could not gett beaver.

The court ordered that Richard Beech should pay the debt in some other pay soe as it may equall beaver, to the said Palmers satisfaction (wth damadges for forbearance,) before the next court, or elce an execution shall goe forth agaynst him.

Arthur Holbridg hath sould to Mr. Malbon all his land in the necke conteyninge two acres and thirty two rodds.

Jeames Russell desired satisfaction of John Walker for damadge done in his corne by his hoggs.

John Walker pleaded that the fences were defective, whereuppon he was advised to warne those whose fences were defectiue.

Anthony Stevens for comming too late to watch, and wthout bullets was fined 2s.

Joseph Brewster and Joseph Cox were accused for drinkeing to excesse; Joseph Brewster confest that they had drunck sacke in his fathers cellar out of the bung wth a tobacco pipe, & in the chamber out of a bottle, and that they went after that to the ordynary, and there drank a quart of beare. Sister Linge testified that she saw them as they came from the ordynary & Joseph Brewster did lead Joseph Cox by the arme, & she speakeing to them asked whether Joseph Cox were drunk, wherevppon Joseph Brewster let him goe and then she saw him stagger & reele, & as she conceived, being not able to goe nor stand as a man, he sit him downe vppon a blocke or logge by the pales, but could not sit as one sober, wherevppon she agayne said he was drunke, because he could not goe nor stand, and then Joseph Brewster called him to come to him wch he did, but yet in a reeling mainer. Mrs. Evance and her mayd testified that when they first saw Joseph Cox after this they could perceive nothinge that hee ayled.

The Court being fully satisfied in the evidence given by sister Linge, and the Governour testifing that vppon examination he had taken, they tould aboundance of lyes, espetially Joseph Brewster, the premises considered, the Court conceyved they deserved to be sevearly whipped, but referred it to Mr. Evance & Mr. Brewster to give them correction in their famylyes.

At a Gennerall Court held att Newhauen the 22th of Octo: 1645.

John Cooper & Joseph Nash were admited members of the Court.

Captayne Malbon & Captayne Turner were chosen deputies for the gennerall court for the jurisdiction.

Mr. Malbon, Mr. Evance, Mr. Gibbard, Mr. Francis Newman were chosen deputies for the towne.

Mr. Atwatter chosen treasurer.

Mr. Goodyeare, Mr. Evance, Mr. Gibbard, Mr. Wackman, Mr. Francis Newman, & Mr. Atwatter were chosen to audit the accompts of the former treasurers.

Thomas Fugill chosen secretarie. Thom Kimberly chosen m^rshall.

The surveyours of the causwayes & bridges wth their consent are to be continued another yeare.

[106] ||Mr. Lamberton propownded that he might have a peece of grownd neare his howse to sett a warehowse by the creeke and for a wharfe also, & he will give the towne soe much as it is worth, or if the towne be not willinge to sell it, if he may have it for the present, when there shalbe cause he will part w^t^h it vppon such tearmes as shalbe thought by indifferent men.

Jaspar Crayne & Robert Seely are desired to joyne w^t^h the Court to view the said grownd, & (if they see cause) to dispose of it to Mr. Lamberton, vppon such tearmes as shalbe thought meet by them for the publique good.

The Governour complayned that he could not gett workmen to mend the mill, wherevppon it was ordred that the governour shall have power to presse men for that worke, & if any man be preingadged they shall goe onn w^t^h their ingadgments after the presse is satisfied or the work done for w^c^h they are pressed.

It was debated what order the miller should observe in grinding mens corne, but left to the millers discretion & the rule of equitye.

The Governour wished the towne to take notice that if any send baggs vnmarked, the miller will take noe chardge of them.

Goodman Smith desired the court to take some order that his land may be layd out. The Governour wished the Court to consider whether they would confirme their former grant to the said Smith or revoake or alter it, but it was respited to further consideration, because for the present he hath put of his sheepe.

It was ordered that Goodman Deighton should burne the playnes w^t^h all convenient speede, takeing the fittest season, and therfore every one should take warninge & secure their fences or what elce may be in danger.

It was propownded to the court in case damadge be done in corne who shall beare the damadge, it was resolved they whose fences are defective, if the defective fences bee fownd.

The Governour called vppon those who were defective though appoynted to veiw the Beaver Meddowes, & bro. Seely to know what was done in it, but their answere was they had done notheing in it.

The marshall was desired to see the hooks and hinges of the towne gates least they be lost.

At a Gennerall Court held the 30th of Octob: 1645.

Mr. Lamberton was chosen deputy in Mr. Malbons stead for the jurisdiction court, and Mr. Crayne deputy for this towne.

[A General Court for the Jurisdiction was also held on the 30th of October, 1645, at which the magistrates and commissioners were chosen for the year ensuing, as appears from the date of the commissions of the latter in the Records of the United Colonies.]

A Court held the 4th of November 1645.

Bamfeild Bell being reproued by Wm Paine for singinge profane songs, answered & said, you are one of the holy bretheren that will lye for advàntadge. It was testified by the said Wm Payne & Joseph Brewster. Mr. Evance testified that it was his constant frame to reproach those that walke in the wayes of God. The premisses considered the centence of the court was that he should be seveerly whipped.

Mrs. Brewster intreated the Court that the execution of the sentence may be respited till her husband côme home, because he is her husbands kinsman.

John Beech & Ambrosse Sutton being sent forth by the mr of the watch to walke the rownd went into a howse & layed them downe to sleepe, & soe neglected their trust, for wch they were fined 5s apeece.

Mr. Leech beinge complayned of for not bringing his armes on the Lords days, his answere was that his man brings his armes for him, wch was satisfyinge.

Thomas Clarke for totall neglect of his watch was fined 5s.

Mr. Evance hath sould vnto Mr. Robert Newman & to Mr. Gilbert 67 ac: of vpland, lying betweene Captayne Turners farme and *and* the said Mr. Newmans farme.

[107] AT A COURT HELD THE 3d OF DECEMBER 1645.

Thomas Robinson was chardged for remoueing some land marks in Mr. Hooks & setting new stacks in Wm Fowlers meddowe haveing hired in the meddow adjoyninge some grasse for this yeare.

He pleaded that he vsed the best meanes he could to find the range. Richard Miles testified that he gave such exact directions that he could not misse the bowndes of Mr. Hooks meddowe, if he observed the range of Mr. Gregsons fence on both sides of the meddowes.

Thomas Barnes also testified that Thomas Robinson did remove a stacke though he advised not to doe it. Wm White testified that when he went to mowe in Mr. Bracyes meddow there was new staks sett, and that bro: Iues tould him if hee did mow by those staks he should cutt crosse brother Fowlers meddow. George Smith testified that after Thomas Robinson had bin sicke, haveing some meddow to cutt, he said if he had bin well he would have made them goe nearer together, meaning he would have cutt more then was left him or was dew as was concejued, for wch vnrighteousnes in disturbing the publicque peace, he was fined 40s to the publicque & ordered to set the staks right at his chardge.

Captayne Turner informed the court that Mrs. Stolion hath complayned to sundry persons that he made a bargaine wth her for cloth for wch shee accepted cowes, but was disapoynted to her great damadge, & therfore he desired she might shew what cause he had given her soe to doe.

Mrs. Stolion pleaded that the captayne came to her howse to buy some cloth, chose a peece of 20s a yard, and said he would have sixe yards of it, and Mrs. Stolion should have a cow, and both aggreed to have her prized by some indifferent men; the captayne said alsoe that he had neede of more cloth & commodityes to the vallew of 12l & told her she should have 2 cowes, and she said when her son came home he should come & chuse them; accordingly when her son came home he went to the captayne, chose 2 cowes, and when he came home he tould her the captayne would come the next day & speake wth her, but came not according to his pmise, and though she sent to him yet he came not.

The captayne said he did really intend to have had some cloth and that she should have a cowe, and when Mr. Stolion came to chuse one of the best cowes he had, and Mr. Stollion told him he might as well let his mother have 2 cowes, for she had neede of cowes and the captayne had need of cloth and commodities, wherevppon the captayne let him chuse another cow & set him a prise, namely 12l. Mr. Stolion said he would give but 10l, the captayne told him he would abate 10s. Mr. Stolion said he would give noe more but 10l, they parted and the captayne promised he would come and speake wth his mother, but because he could not well goe to Mrs. Stolion, & haveing heard of the dearnes of her commodities, the excessive gaynes she tooke, was discouradged from proceedinge, & accordingly bid his man tel her he would have none of her cloth, and nameing sundry perticuler instances of commodities sold by her at an excessive rate, left it to the consideracon of the court whether she had not done him wronge in complayning of him, and if she might not be dealt wth as an oppressor of the commonweale.

The court conceyved the captayne was to blame that he did not goe to her according to his promisse, espetially that after he heard she was vnsatisfied he did not attend her satisfaction, but wthall that the captayne might justly offer it to the consideration of the court whether such selleinge be not extortion and not to be sufferred in the commonweath.

[108] || 1 The captayne complayned that she sold some cloth to Wm Bradly at 20s ℘ yard that cost her about 12s, for wch she received wheate at 3s 6d ℘ bushell, and sold it presently to the baker at 5s ℘ bushell who received it of Wm Bradly, only she forbaring her monny 6 monthes.

2 That the cloth wch Leiut Seely bought of her for 20s ℘ yard last yeare, she hath sould this yeare for 7 bushells of wheate a yard, to be delivered in her chamber, wch she confest.

3 That she would not take wompom for commodityes at 6

a penny though it were the same she had paid to others at 6, but she would have 7 a penny, as Thomas Robinson testified.

4 That she sold primmers at 9^d apeece w^{c}h cost but 4^d here in New England. Thomas Robinson testified that his wife gave her 8^d in wompom at 7 a penny, though she had but newly received the same wompom of Mrs. Stolion at 6.

5 That she would not take beaver w^{c}h was m^{r}chantable w^{t}h others at 8^s a pownd, but she said she would have it at 7^s and well dryed in the sun or in an oven. Leiut. Seely, the m^{r}shall & Isaacke Mould testified it. John Dellingham by that meanes lost 5^s in a skinne (that cost him 20^s of Mr. Evance and sold to her,) viz^d 2^s 6^d in the waight and 2^s 6^d in the price.

6 She sold a peece of cloth to the 2 Mecars at 23^s 4^d p yard in wompom, the cloth cost her about 12^s ℘ yard & sold when wompom was in great request.

7 That she sold a yard of the same cloth to a man of Connecticott at 22^s p yard, to be delivered in Indian corne at 2^s p bushell at home.

8 She sold English mohejre at 6^s ℘ yard in silver, w^{c}h Mr. Goodyeare and Mr. Atwater affirmed might be bought in England for 3^s 2^d ℘ yard at the vtmost.

9 She sold thridd after the rate of 12^s ℘ pownd w^{c}h cost not above 2^s 2^d in old England.

10 That she sold needles at one a penny w^{c}h might be bought in old England at 12^d or 18^d ℘ hundred, as Mr. Francis Newman affirmeth.

The Court seriously weighing all the perticulers chardged agaynst Mrs. Stolion, conceived that the nature and aggravations of the aforesaid chardges was proper for a court of magistrates to consider off, and therfore respited and refferred it to the Court of magistrates to be held at Newhaven the last Munday in March next.

Stephen Medcalfe complayned that he going into the howse of John Linley, Francis Linley, his brother, being in the howse told him he would sell him a gunne, the said Stephen asked him if it were a good one, he answered yea, as any was in the towne, wherevppon they bargajned, and Stephen was to give him 17s. As Stephen was going out of dores he questioned the sufficiency of *of* the locke, Francis told him indeed John Nash told him she was not wo'th 3d, but for his part he did not vallew it worse for that, for smithes doe not affect olde gunnes, for he knew one gunne wch John Nash disprajsed wch is a good one for all that, soe Stephen went home & afterward dischardging the said gunne the brich flew out & struck into his eye and wounded him deepe and dangerously into the head.

Francis Linley pleaded that he told Stephen that John Nash told him that the gunne was naught, that it was not worth 3d, that the barrell was thinne and would not beare a new britch, and advized Stephen to scoure her well and if he tryed her to put but a little chardge in her.

Mr. Gregson and John Nash testified that when he was examjned before Mr. Gregson, Francis Linley denyed he had told Stephen that the barrell was thinne and would not beare a new britch, that it was crackt on one side from the britch to the touch-hole.

[109] || John Nash testified that he tould Francis it was a very naughty peece, not worth the mendinge, & yet he prest him to mend it as well as he could & let it be as it will, he told him moreover that the barrell at the britch was as thin as a shilling, crackt from the britch to the touch-hole, and would not beare a britch, and after he had mended it, he tould him he would not give 3d for it, and to his best remembrance, he saith, he tould him he would not dischardge it for all New-haven, for it would doe some mischeife.

Richard Myles also testified that he heard John Nash speake much of her badnes & vnserviceablenes to Francis Linley.

John Linley being demmanded why he was taken wth such a quakeinge and trembling when Stephen was going to shoote, he said he did not quack nor tremble.

Thomas Clarke testified vppon oath, that John Linley tould him when he heard Stephen dischardge the gunne that he was affraid he had hurt himselfe.

Goodwife Fancy testified, that John Linley came oft times to speake wth Stephen, when he thought he lay vppon his death bedd, to know if he would cleare his brother, for he said he feared he had hard thoughts of his brother concerning the gun. Mr. Pell confirmed her testimonny. Richard Beech affirmed that Francis offered him that gun to sell & demanded 20^{s}, telling him to his best remmembrance that it had a new britch.

The court considering the premises, the great damadge Stephen Medcalfe had susteyned in the losse of his eye, w^{t}h the losse of his time & the great chardge of the cure, Mr. Pell affirming it was worth 10^{l}, ordered Francis Linley to pay to Stephen Medcalfe 20^{l} damadges.

Brother Thomas Nash for his sons absence at a gen^{ll} trayning pleaded his necessity of buisines in fetching home his hay by watter & that he could gett noe other helpe at that time, but the court judged his plea common to others & ordered him to pay his fine.

Mr. John Evance pleaded that wheras he had hired John Basset & his wife to be servants to Mr. Goodyeare in New England, vppon condition that if Mr. Goodyeare did not accept of him he should be at liberty, only pay to the said Mr. Evance the monnyes w^{c}h he hath disboursed for him & his wife both for their transportation & other occasions, Mr. Goodyeare did not accept of their service, & yet the said Basset refuseth to pay him the said monnyes.

John Bassett pleaded that their was noe such covenant. Mr. Evance produced a noat vnder his owne hand w^{c}h implyed such a covenant, Basset acknowledged his marke but said he never heard the note read though he set his hand to it, yet he said if Mr. Evance would take his oath of it he would submit. Mr. Evance answered he made sufficient proofe of it by 2 witnesses, and one of them vppon oath, (& deliuered an affedavit into the court,) of John Ogden, taken before Mr. Eaton Governo^{r}, in which John Ogden relateing the aggreement betwixt Mr. Evance & the said Basset sweres expresly, that if Mr. Goodyeare doth not accept of him and his wife they were to pay Mr. Evance what he had layd out for them, & so be free to dispose of themselves, yet was willing if the court pleased, to make oath of it, but the court tould John Basset that Mr.

Evance needed not to doe it haveing proved by 2 witnesses, and one of them vppon oath; at last the said Basset said he would reffer it to the Court, let them doe as they pleased.

[110] ||It was aggreed but vppon further discourse betweene the parties themselves that John Bassett should pay vnto Mr. Evance 11^{l} 7^{s} wch is the debt demanded & sume disbursed, (Mr. Evance being willing to take notheing for consideration,) wch sume the said Basset promised to pay at 2 certayne dayes vizt, the one halfe at midsommer next ensewing, and the other halfe w^{t}hin 6 monthes after that.

Brother Wackman & bro: Miles reported to the court that they had (as the court desired them) viewed the clay pits way and the fences adjoyninge, in refference to the difference betwixt Mr. Malbon & Mr. Caffinch, and fownd that the way to the clay pitts was to lye open, but the quarter that lay on the one side could not accomplish their part of the fence, and therfore haveing planted, were forced for safeguard of their corne to make a fence crosse the said way w^{t}h rayles, w^{c}h way the other quarter driveing their cattle, & somtimes leaveinge oppen the rayles & somtime breakeing them, much damadge hath bin done by cattle and hoggs, whereuppon the court determined that the quarter that should have fenced & did not, must beare the damadge, and those that have trespassed in breakeing & leaveing open gates or rayles shall contribute, and desired the afforesaid committee to take some more paynes for the setling of it.

Brother Crayne desired the judgment of the court concerning damadge done in his corne by Mr. Caffinch's hogs w^{c}h he fownd in the corne and brought home to his howse requiring satisfaction of him & he refussed to give him any. The court ordered that Mr. Caffinch pay the damadge till he pay the defective fences.

Jarvis Boykin complayned that sundry fences about their quarter are defective, and he hath told the owners of some of them, & some they know not to whome they doe belonge.

The court advissed they should get the fences measured and cast vp euery mans proportion, and then they may know whose it is, that it may be mended to prevent future damadge;

and to put an end to the wrangles about the fences belonging to the vacant lotts, it was ordered, that brother Andrewes and brother Munson shall veiw them all, and allow those that made them soe much as they were worth when they were sett upp, and the quarters to gett the said fences well & substantially made as speedily as may bee, and in the meane time they shalbeare all damadges themselues wch come by the badnes of the said fences.

Hannah Marsh complayned that Mr. Brewster called Billingsgate slutt, and that she was sent for on shipboard to play the slutt.

Mr. Brewster confest he being much provoaked and disquieted by her frowardnes and brawling on shipboard, did call her slut & Billingsgate slutt, and said he hoped she would dance about the whipping post, and affirmed that Mrs. Norton at Charlstowne told him that a seaman was speakeing filthy words to her the said Hannah, and would have had her goe on shipboard, being asked what to doe, he said to play the slutt, George Walker testified he heard Mrs. Norton speake what Mr. Brewster hath affirmed.

Mr. Brewsters mayd and Mr. Lambertons maid testified that the said Hannah Marsh was very froward and contentious & a cause of much contention and vnquietnes amongst them as they came from the Bay.

When the governour had showne what was the ordynary acceptation of Billingsgate slutt, namely that some that were soe called were convicted scolds and punished at the cuckeing stoole for it, & some of them chardged wth incontinency, [111] || Mr. Brewster said he had sufficiently proued the one true, & he would not acquit her in the other, being asked what grownd he had to lay such an implicit chardge vppon her, he said he had notheing at all agaynst her but what he gathered from Mrs. Nortons words. The court told he ought to acknowledge his fayleing & soe repaire her reputation as much as he may. At length he did acknowledge he was too blame & said he was sorry he had spoke soe rashly, and that he intended noe such chardge agaynst her. The court also according to the evidence reproued Hannah Marsh for her froward disposition, remembring her that meeknes is a chojse ornament for weomen, and wished her to take it as a rebucke from God, and to keepe a better watch over her sperit hereafter, least the Lord proceede to manifest his displeasure further agaynst her.

Hannah Marsh did acknowledge it had bin some trouble to her that she had bin soe froward and contentious to the disquieting of others, & hoped it should be a warninge to her for time to come.

A GENNERALL COURT HELD THE 8th OF DECEMBER, 1645.

Brother Fowler & Thomas Knowles vppon some vrgent occasions were dismissed wth the leave of the court.

Mr. Malbon late treasurer, vppon the casting vp of his accompts acquaynted the court that the towne was much indebted to himselfe & others & propownded that some course might be taken by the court for the payment of the said debts. The court considered how heavy the publique chardges grew, that most of them have bin expended for the publique safty and about things of common public vse, wherin all that live in the plantation have a like benifit in their proportions, and yet many live in the plantation & have manny priveledges in it have hitherto borne noe part of those publicque chardges, wherevppon it was debated whether or noe in equity such should not be rated some way or other for time to come, so as those that have borne the whole burden hitherto may be eased; but because it was not ripe for an issue, the court refferred it to the Governor, magistrates, deputies wth elder Newman, the 2 deacons, Mr. Cheevers, bro: Miles, bro: Clarke, bro: Anthony Thompson & bro: Munson as a committee, to consider & digest the said case and report to the court rates they conceive such persons ought to pay towards the former & future publique chardges.

And forasmuch as the publique occasions require that a rate should be levied forthwth, it was ordered that all the rates alreddy due and the rates due in Aprill next shalbe paid into the treasurer at his owne howse wthin one month after the date hereof, in monny, beaver, wampom or corne, in good wheate at 4^s ℘ bushell, in rye & pease at 3^s 4^d ℘ bushell, and if any pay in Indian corne at 2^s 8^d ℘ bushell w^{t}hout assignements.

Whereas by an order formerly made for the incouradgment of those that kill woolues & foxes 15^s was allowed for a woolfe, & 2^s 6^d for every fox they killed, the court considering that none make it their buisines to attend it, thought that allowance to much, and ordered that the treasurer shall pay 2 pownd of powder & 4 pownds of shott or bullets for euery woolfe, and 1^s for euery old foxe & sixe pence for every yonge one, to those that shall kill them.

The court declared their apprehensions that the 2^s to be paid to the secretarye for alyenations should be accompted as part of his 10^l salery, but reffered it to the afforesaid commitee to consider what is meet to be allowed to the secretary and marshall themselues out of the said alyenations, and of the warrants.

[112] ‖ It was ordered that every one that comes to enter an action or an allienation in the court pay to the secrettary (before any such entry) the fees ordred by the court, and that euery one that shall bring a warrant or attatchm^t to the marshall shall pay to him the fees due for the same before he execute the same.

The Governour propownded to the court whether they would confirme their former grant to Goodman Smith in refference to his sheepe, or such part of it as might bee conveynient for him & his famyly, w^{c}h occasioned a lardg debate, and sundry questions were put to Goodman Smith, both about the quantitye of grownd he desired and keepeing sheep for the townes benifit.

Goodman Smith declared that he would not be content w^{t}h 5 acres of meddow, nor would he be tyed to keep any sheepe but his owne, at w^{c}h the court was offended, because his promise to keepe other mens sheepe was the grownd of their former grant. In conclusion, the former conditional grant being voted, was by this Court revoaked.

Mr. Gibbard desired to know where their quarter may have

their 2d devission. It was, they must let the survay goe on for all the quarters, & that then the Court would consider where they, and others that want grownd, may be accomodated.

It was ordered that wompom shall goe for currant pay in this plantation in any payment vnder 20s, if halfe be blacke & halfe be white, & in case any question shall arise about the badnes of any wompom, Mr. Goodyeare shall judge, if they repaire to him.

It was ordered the miller shall grinde all the grists that is brought to the mill by course as it comes in order.

Brother Potter made an offer to carry every mans grist from their howses to the mill & bring it home againe to their howses for 2d ℘ bushell, but that was respited.

It was propownded by Mr. Malbon that our pastors lott may be fenced at a common chardge, & for his part he would cart all the stuffe; it was gennerally approued, the governour desired all those that could and were willing to helpe, that they would repaire to Mr. Malbon & he would direct and order the worke.

It was ordred that Mr. Pearce in respect of some weaknes of boddy & some service he is appoynted to doe in giveing out and laying vpp the pyks from time to time, shal be freed from trayning & watching also in his owne person, only he is to find a man to watch for him at his owne chardge.

The comitee that viewed brother Seelys meddow reported that for the present some of it is vnvsefull, but conceive wth chardg it may bee improved.

It was ordered that Phillip Leake shall have land layd out according to his proportion, on the east side among the small lotts and that then the land shalbe layd out in such a forme as may be vsefull for them and may also suite the townes conveyniencye.

Brother Browne desired he might have 3 acres of land out of Mr. Brownings proportion in the Oystershell feild, Mr. Browning beinge willing, it was reffered to the commitee to order as they shall se cause.

It was ordered that bro: Preston shall keepe the pownd instead of bro: Kimberly.

Because the court could not now determine any thing concerning fences, & Capt Turner may probably be gone before another court, he desired the court to take notice that he hath had much damadge done both in his corne & meddowes by reason of those that drive hoggs that way & have noe land there & the leaveing open a gate wch Dauid Atwater should mayntayne, he complayned also that some drive their oxen & dry catle towards his farme soe that his cowes want food.

---

[113] A [ ]

Richard Beech hath sould his owne howse to bro: Wm Pecke & whereas the said howse was sugadged for the securitye of the portions of the children of Andrew Hull, (whose widdow he marryed,) in liew thereof he hath now ingadged his howse, barne, cellar & well, vallewed at 40l wth the 7 acres of land on wch it stands, the howse, barne & celler being compleatly finished being built wth bricke & stonne as he promiseth & so kept in repaire & the land in hart for securitye of the portions of the said children.

The difference betwixt Wm Burret of Copeage & Henry Whelpley of the same, (because they were deffective in poynt of proofe on both parts,) was refferred by consent of both partyes to Goodmn Groues, John Hurd, Goodman Judson and Goodmn Shirman to arbitrate & end if they can, if they cannot Alexander Knowles was chosen by them both to umpire it.

Georg Warde haveing bin twice warned to the court but appeared not, now appearing, for his contempt was fined 10s, and was chardged wth slandering Mr. Davenport, saying that Mr. Davenport told him that he had not any hand in the trade of Delaware, wheras Mr. Davenport said he did not medle wth the mannadging of any trade, as was testified by some of the court that heard him.

He pleaded that he apprehended Mr. Dauenport had denyed that he had any thing to doe in the trade, being asked why he would not goe to Mr. Davenport or some other that could satisfie him before he did slander him in other plantations, he answered he did not intend to slander him. The slander being of soe high a nature considering the person slandered that the court thought it meete to reffer it to the court of magistrats to be held in Aprill next & therfore let him know that he must appeare at that court and answere the said slander.

Mr. Rotherford to Mr. Malbon all his land in the necke.

Mrs. Eaton hath sould to Mr. Pery all her land & propriety in this towne wth all accomodations whatsoever therevnto belonginge.

Wheras the estate of Thomas Trowbridge hath bin attatched to satisfie his creditors, Mr. Evance offered 100^l for the howse and howselott wth al the accomodations therevnto belonginge, it was debated but not issued.

A Generall Court held the 23^d of February, 1645.

The governour declared to the court that the commitee had now audited all the towēs accompts, (from the begining til October last,) and find them right, only they are not satisfied about the chardge of the seates in the meeting howse, soe that if that worke bee not cleared to the audito^rs some other workmen must judge what the worke is worth, and that the towne is yet indebted soe that probably there wilbe neede of a new rate, but that's respited.

Alsoe that the orders have bin veiwed & they conceive that the fees of the court had neede to be increased, viz^d, that the marshall receive for every warrant 8^d, and for every atatchm^t 1^s before he execute them, and to have $\frac{1}{3}$ part thereof for his paynes therin & for gathering the fines due to the court, and the rest to be accompted vppon his wages to the treasurer, also that 3^s 4^d be hereafter payd for every action that is entred, and 2^s for every alienation, both to the treasurer for the ease of publicque chardge.

It was ordered that those who are admitted freely as planters into howselotts shall have planting land sixe acres for a single person, eight acres for a man and his wife & one acre added for each child at present, & shall pay 2^d an acre from October last for all their lands in the playnes & beyond the east river, and that such as are admited planters in the towne, but either desire noe land, or accept not what is allotted shall pay 1s a yeare a peece towards publicque chardges. The land which shalbe layd out to them to be either at the further end of the great playnes, soe farr as the land wth in the fence wil reach, & the rest onn the east side, so as may be most conveynient for them & not prejudiciall to [the ^ & they,]

[114]*

[ ]e towne and enjoy [ ] Mr. Godfrey, and Stolion, it was ordered that Mr. Leach shall pay 40s ℘ ann, Mr. Godfrey 20s ℘ an, and Mrs. Stolion 20s ℘ an, from the latter end of October last past towards publique chardges.

It was propownded to be considered whether those that have bought howses & have noe land should not have some land layd to them as the rest of the small lotts have, but it was respited.

It was desired that men would be moderate in keepeing cowes & hoggs least the court be constrayned to lay some restraynt vppon them.

It was ordered that if any man (after this day month) shall find any hoggs vnyoaked & vnringed, either in any corne feilds or meddowes belonging to the towne and designed for mens proprietyes though not layd out, he shall vppon due proofe in court receive of the owner 6d a peece, & the keeper of the pownd is to have 1d a head more if they be brought to the pownd, & the owner is besides to make good all the damadge done by them.

It was ordered that the old orders shall stand in force concerninge fences, and the veiwers be continued as before.

It was ordered that brother Wackman and brother Gibbard shall goe wth brother Brocket to se the lott belonging to Thomas Fugill at the West rocks measured & surveyed & report to the court what distance it is from the center & what quantitye of land there is.

It was ordered that bro. Atwater, the treasurer, bro: Andrewes & brother Munson shall prize the frame that was provided for an inne, (& wth the approbation of the governr,) sell

* About two lines are torn from the top of this page.

it or dispose of it as they can for the townes best advantadge to bro: Francis Newman or others wch may have occasion to vse the whole or part of it.

It was ordered that if any goats shalbe fownd in any street, way or lott, in or about the towne w^thout a keeper, the owner shall pay 6^d a head to him that pownds them, halfe whereof he is to have for his paynes & a 1^d a head to the keeper of the pownd; if he himselfe pownd them he is to have 4^d apeece, the other 3^d a peece is to bee paid to the treasurer.

It was by the $Governo^r$ propownded alsoe, whether the deputies may be chosen once a yeare as the magistrates and other officers are, and that the treasurer may allwayes be a deputy to sit in court to see to the gathering of fines and fees, wch was respited.

Also whether the millitary affayres of the towne may be comfortably carryed on w^thout a captayne, or whether it were not conveynient to chuse a captayne instead of Captayne Turner, not knowing when he will returne; after some debate, Mr. Malbon was chosen captayne wth liberty to resign his place to captayne Turner at his returne.

It was ordered that dayes of gennerall traynings shalbe the first 2^d day in March, Aprill, May, June, August, September, October & November, wth proviso if there be cause in respect of harvest or vnseasonable weather the magistrates wth the cheife military officers may alter or change a day as they judge meete for the publicque good, and if any second day appoynted for trayñings prove wett & soe hinder the service, the next second day being faire shalbe a trayning day.

It was ordered that the squadron traynings shalbe as neare as may be about the midle betwixt the 2 gennerall traynings every month.

It was ordered that the next 2^d day shalbe a gennerall view of armes, and soe once a quarter as was formerly ordered.

It was ordered that the artillery shall goe on according to their owne orders formerly read in court & approued.

It was propownded that all the fines for absence & late comminge to the $genn^{ll}$ traynings and squadrons &c shalbe allowed the military company to bee disposed of by the officers in powder or otherwise for the incouradgement & helpe of military service & discipline.

It was propownded that those of the trayned band who are growne to some good measure of skill and dexterity in the military art might have some incouradgement by ease or liberty, but respited.

It was ordered that brother Browne shalbe left to his liberty to come to the gennerall traynings as the occassions of the ferry (his man being lame & not able to carry on that service at all times) will permit.

[115] || It was ordered that 3 acres of land in the Oystershell feild, out of Mr. Brownings part shalbe layd to the ferry w^t^hout rent dureing the courts pleasure & that Mr. Browning shall have just considerac̄on allowed for it out of his rent dew to the towne for the rest.

It was propownded that a bridge may be made over the east river in the way to Connecticott.

Bro: Andrewes, brother Munson, brother Bradley, Richard Mansfeild w^t^h John Thomas are appoynted to view the said river & consider in what place & how w^t^h the least chardge it may be most conveynient & commodious to suite the end propownded & report to the governour & magistrates what their apprehensions are concerninge it

Forasmuch as much damadge hath come to the quarters adjoyninge to the Oystershelfeild by some mens lots being vnfenced, as namely Wm Payne & Wm Blayden, the courts called vppon them to gett their lotts fenced & gave them leaue to take some of the trees on the common w^c^h the tann^r^s have felled for barke, but in the meane time they are to pay for all damadge w^c^h comes by their default.

It was propownded whether the towne or those that live by the seaside shall mayntayne the high-way before their lotts. The surveyors of high-wayes were desired to view it & also the wattercourse in the streat by Mr. Gilberts, & report to the court how they find them.

It was ordered that brother Brockett shall survey the meddow betwixt the two rocks onn the farr side of the harbour to see if it will accomodate brother Seely & brother Whitnell, both whose meddow is soe bad as not to be improved w^t^h any toller-able chardg for their advantadge, and report what quantity there is of it that the court may consider & order therein.

Joseph Pecke & Goodman Hitchcocke propownded that they might have each of them a small lott by the creeke neare brother Pecks yard. Bro: Crayne & bro: Myles are desired to view and report to the court if it may accomodate them & suite the townes conveyniency.

Mr. Evance haveing aggreed w^t^h refference to the creditors for Mr. Trowbridg his howse, desired the court to grant him the cellar belonginge to it to build a warehowse vppō it, it was granted, provided that the ware howse exceede not 20 foot square.

It was propownded that Mr. Davenports may be fenced as speedily as may be, & for that end it was desired the next trayning day every quarter may be spoken w^t^h to know what euery man will doe, and that they would appoynt a time for the speedy carrying on of the worke.

The court w^t^h elder Newman & the two deacons are desired to place men in the méeting howse.

It was ordered that the last yeares orders concerning the Necke shall still stand in force vnder the penaltie as then appoynted.

Brother Livermore hath liberty granted to cut wood in the necke, but was desired to advise w^t^h such as can informe him how he may so cut it as to cause it to dye.

The treasurer acquaynted the court that the last rates are disposed of, & yet the treasury is emptie and indebted, desire-ing the court to consider how it might bee supplyed to suite the present occassions of the towne, wherevppon those that are indebted were desired to make payment forthwith, least they be warned to the court & soe bring further dammadge vppon themselues.

The peece of grownd brother Mitchell propownded for, is refferred to bro: Miles and brother Davis to view, and informe the court whether such an addition to him may not hinder some other planter who might have his proportion there.

Goodman Plat desired that his second devission may be layd out & if it might be he would have it beyond Mr. Malbons meddow by the sea side, it was ordered that the survay may goe on that he w^t^h others may have their land as it fals.

[Here follows the revision of such orders as were designed to be of a more permanent nature, which the General Court, Feb. 24, 1644-5, beginning to lose confidence in Fugill's integrity, appointed a committee to see effected.]

[116] In the layinge of the first fowndations of this plantation and jurisdiction, vpon a full debate wth due & serious consideration, it was aggreed, concluded & setled as a fundamentall law, not to bee disputed or questioned hereafter, that the judiciall lawes of God, as they were deliuered by Moses, & expownded in other parts of scripture, so farr as they are a fence to the morrall law, & neither tipicall, nor ceremoniall, nor had refference to Canaan shalbe accounted of morrall & binding equity and force, and as God shall helpe shalbe a constant direction for all proceedings here, & a gennerall rule in all courts of Justice how to judge betwixt partie and partie, & how to punish offenders, till the same may be branched out into perticulers hereafter.

And for the due carrying on of all affaires according to God, it is also agreed, concluded & setled for a fundamentall law as aforesaid, that noe man of what degree or quality soever shall at any time be admitted to be a free burgess $w^{t}hin$ this plantation, but such planters as are members of some or other of the aproved churches of New-England, nor shall any but such free burgesses have any vote in any election, nor shall any power or trust in & for the ordering of any publicque civill affaires, be at any time put into the hands of any other then such members, though as free planters all have right to their inheritances & to com̃erce, according to such grants, orders & lawes as shalbe made concerning the same.

All free burgesses $w^{t}hin$ this plantation, admitted as before is expressed shall have vote in every gennerall election court for this jurisdiction, in the choyce of all magistrates for the jurisdiction, whether governour, deputy governour or other magistrates, $w^{t}h$ a treasurer, secretarie & marshall, who shalbe yearly chosen on the last Wenseday in October; they shall also have vote in the chojse of deputies for the jurisdiction generall court so oft as it shall assemble, whether in an ordynary course or vppon extraordynary occassions, & in the election of other officers, for the plantation, as in the choise of fit and able men from among themselues, being church members, who shalbe called deputies, & shall asist $w^{t}h$ the magistrates of this plantation in a monthly plantation court, $w^{c}h$ is to sit every first Tewsday each month at nine of the clocke in the forenoone, to heare & determine all causes brought before them, whether civill or criminall, according to the light of scripture as before exprest, but this plantation court to bee regulated in the vallew of causes & nature of the punishm^{ts} to the orders w^{c}h are or shall be made by the generall jurisdiction court, & in all these plantation courts, sentence shall passe according to the vote of the major part of magistrats & deputies present, but if the parties or either of them be not satisfied w^{t}h the justice of any such sentences or executions, appeales or complaynts may be made from or agajnst these monthly perticuler courts to the court of magistrates for the jurisdiction, according to the generall courts order in October 1643. They shall also from among themselves choose all military officers for this plantation, as captayne, leiutenant, ensigne, serjeants, corporalls &c. and make lawes & orders for generall traynings, artillery exercises, squadron traynings, veiw of armes, watchings, comming armed to publicque meeteings, deviding of inheritances in this plantation, purchaseing lands of the Indians, ordering of fences, stinteing of comons, ordering and keepeing of cattle, preventinge dangers by fire or water, & gennerally in althings w^{c}h only concerne this plantation, & are not contrary vnto either to the fowndation beforesaid, or to some artickles in the confœderation w^{t}h the collonjes, or law or orders of the jurisdiction generall court.

It is ordered that every planter give in the names or number of the heads or persons in his famylye (wherin his wife together w^{t}h himselfe & children only are to be reckoned,) w^{t}h an estimate of his estate, according to w^{c}h he will both pay his proportion in all rates & publique chardges, from time to time to be assessed for civill vses, & expect lands in all devissions w^{c}h shalbe generally made to the planters, w^{c}h was accordingly don.

Vppon due & serious consideration how the severall planters, according to their different estats and famylies, at present might be accomodated w^{t}h grownd, both vpland and meddow, it is ordered that in the first devission, w^{c}h is to be made of vpland w^{t}hin two miles of the towne (a place called the Necke being all or the greatest part w^{t}hin 2 mile not reckoned,) euery planter shall have, after the rate of five acres of land for euery hundred pownds in estate & for euery person or head in his famylye reckonned as before, two acres & a halfe of land & further that every planter shall have in the necke afforesaid after the rate of one 100^{l} in estate, & halfe an acre for every person, & the meddow belonging to the towne being duely considered & estimated it is ordered that euery planter shall have after the rate of five acres for every 100^{l} in estate, & halfe an acre

of meddow for every person, & in the second devission of vpland lying w^t^hout & beyond the two miles from the towne, it is ordered that [*every planter shall have*] after the rate of twenty acres for every 100^l^ in estate and [*for every head two acres and a halfe*]
[ ] expended in the first veiw of this towne [ ] lands from the Indians [*
[117] || for euery 100^l^ w^c^h yet falling short to defray necessarie & publique chardges, a rate of 200^l^ was granted & levied vppon the planters, halfe vppon estates, w^c^h came vnto 5^s^ 10^d^ ½ ℔ 100^l^, & halfe vppon land in the first devission in the necke & meddow, w^c^h came vnto about 4⅝^d^ ℔ acre.

For that publique occassions require a publique stocke or treasurie, for the rajseing & majntayning of such a stocke, vppon serious consideration & debate, it is agreed & ordered that every planter, who as before receiveth & holdeth land from the towne, shall pay a yearely rate to the towne towards publique chardges, namely for every acre w^t^hin the first devission & in the necke, & for all meddow 4^d^ an acre, and for all land w^t^hin the second devission, 2^d^ an acre; w^c^h rates are to be paid in equall portions, the one halfe at or before the last day of Aprill, and the other halfe at or before the last day of October yearly, (besides what may be assessed vppon extraordjnary occasions,) to the treasurer in such manner & vnder such penaltyes as this court shall appojnt, which treasurer shall also pay out all due & necessary publique chardges as shalbe ordered, & of all his receipts & payments he shall give a true & just account to this court, or to such audito^r^s as they shall appoynt yearly, or oftner if it be required, & shall also pay & deliver vpp vnto the suceeding treasurer, or vnto whomsoever this court shall appoynt, all such writtings, books of accounts, monny, goods or estate of what kind soever, due to the towne vppon such reasonable warning as this court shall judge meete.

Heere should have bin inserted the planters names, estates, numbers in their famjljes, w^t^h their severall proportions of vpland & meddow in each devission, w^t^h the rates they are to pay, but the treasurer having it, it was here omitted & thither reffered.†

---

* A line or two worn off.

† The book to which reference is here made is still extant in very good preservation, and in the hands of Henry White, Esq. It is a parchment covered volume, in size 7¾ by 6¼ inches, of originally about ninety leaves; a few have been subsequently added. Upon its cover it bears the following title, now nearly illegible; "A Booke of all the landes w^c^h Planters at first or by allienations since possesse w^t^hin New Haven

It is agreed & ordered, that Mr. Davenports quarter, Mr. Eatons, Mr. Robert Newmans & Mr. Tenches quarters shall have their first devissions of vpland to begin at the east side of the towne towards the sea, (after that certayne small lotts are layd out, & a feild about 40 acres called the Oystershelfeild, left to the townes dispose,) & so goe on by the Mill river, takeing in all the land as it fals, (highwayes exepted) to the 2 miles end, till compassing about they come vnto a common w^c^h is to be left for a cow pasture onn the east side of a certayne fresh medows called the Beaver ponds, & that the said 4 quarters, w^t^h Mr. Evance his quarter shall have their meddow by lott, (some ꝑticular ꝑsons hereafter named excepted,) on both sides the river called Quillipiocke or the great river, *begining* with meddow *next the great rock & soe on to seaward* are called the east meddowes, only some of the smaller lotts w^t^hin the said 5 quart^r^s, by their owne consent, are to have their proportions on the east side of the Mill river, begiñing at the meddow next the great rocke & so on to seaward, & on an island in the great river before named, by lott as they shall fall in order; only in the Mill river, he that should fall last, not haveing his full proportion, may leave it to the towne & take his ful share in the said island. And island is also to be layd out by lott from the south end vp the east side & so rownd downe the west side in order, & the lotts being cast, the names & order followeth,

1. John Benham,
2. Mr. Cheevers,
3. Thom Powell,
4. Abrahm Bell,
5. William Andrewes,
6. Richard Beckley,
7. Widdow Greene,
8. Widdow Williams,
9. Thomas Kimberley,
10. Robert Hill,
11. Jarvis Boykin,
12. Andrew Low,
13. John Cooper,
14. Wm Tharpe,
15. Mrs. Eaton,
16. Mr. Peirce,
17. Thom Yale.

Thomas Fugill who hath one of the foresaid smaller lotts, by consent & order is to have the island in the Mill river below the bridg for his ꝑportion of meddow, w^c^h is 6 acres, & to have his vpland for his second devission of that cleare land by the West rocke, provided it be neither w^t^hin the 2 mile nor granted by the court to any other.

Towne. Began by R. P. Secretarie, 1645—Also it conteyneth the somes due from men to ye Treasurer, according to ye rate of 4d per acre first devision and meddow, and 2d per acre for the second devission throughout the Towne—Anno Dom. 1646." Very few entries appear to have been made in it after 1652. Each man is made debtor to the number of acres held by him in each division at the rate he was to pay for it per annum, and credited on the other side for what he sold.

It is ordered that Mr. Lambertons quarter, the subburbs, Mr. Gregsons quarter, Mr. Fowlers quarter & Mr. Evance quarter, begin to take their first devission of vpland at a place called Oyster poynte, on the south part of the towne & west part of the harbour, and so goe rownd in order, takeing in all the land as it falls, (highwayes excepted) to the 2 mile end, till compasseing about they have their full proportion, leaveing the rest on the west side of the Beaver pownds as a common for an oxe pasture, and the way to both these to lye, both for ox pasture & cow pasture, at the norwest part of the towne, from the streat where Mr. Evance his howse is. And Mr. Lambertons quarter, ye subburbs, and Mr. Gregsons quarter, wth Mr. Fowlers, shall have their meddow in the west meddow, in a meddow called Mr. Malbons meddow, and on the Indian side below, or to the seaward of those meddowes appoynted for the 5 quarters as before, and yet more to the seaward in the meddow called the solitary cove.

It is granted & ordered that Mr. Eaton shall have 50 acres of his meddow on the east side of the harbour neere the way to Totoket, wth a proportion of vpland for a farme, and the rest of his meddow at his owne choyse in the east meddowes, wth the remajnder of his vpland for the second devission allong the river by the brick kils, adjoyninge to such part of his meddow as he will improve for another farme wth the best convejniencye the place can afford, only whereas a small peece of meddow on the west side of the Mill river adjoyneth to the vpland of his first devission, it is to be lajd [as part] of [his] proportion & so the m[ed]dow
[118] || that adjoyneth to any mans vpland vppon the west side of the said river.

It is ordered that Mr. Davenport, pastour of the church, shall have his meddow & the vpland for his second devission both together, on the east side of the great river, where himselfe shall choose, wth all the conveniency the place can afford for a farme, though by the naturall bownds of the place, whether by creeks or otherwise, the vpland or meddow prove more then his proportion.

It is ordred that Captayne Turner shall have his meddow & vpland of his second devission vpon the west side of the great river, where himselfe shall choose for his best convejniencye, that he may the better atend the publique service in his military office.

It is ordered that Mr. Robert Newman and Mr. Mathew Gilbert the present deacons shall have their meddow and their vpland for their second devission, vpon the west side of the great river where themselues shall judg most convejnient for farmes neere the towne, that they may the better atend their office.

It is ordered that the small lotts in those 5 quarters before named, who have their meddow on the east side of the mill river, shall have their second devission of vpland at the vtmost end of the first devission of Mr. Evances quarter, by some called the Yorkshire quarter, w^t^hout the 2 miles, beyond the west river, by lott. And that the rest of the plant^rs^ in the said 5 quarters shall have their meddow by lott, begining at the east side of the necke, on the west side of the great river, and so goe on in order to Mr. Eatons farme at the brick kills, and then to beginne at the north side of Mr. Davenports farme on the east side of the river, and goe on to the vpper end, only whosoever by lott falls next any of the farmes before granted & setled, if he want any part of his due pportion when he cometh to such a farme or grant, he is to take the rest where it next falls, though on the other side of the river. And such as by lott shall have their meddow to the seaward of Captayne Turn^rs^ farm̄e, shall have the vpland adjoyninge, towards their second devission, but if it fall short of their proportion they shall have the rest by lott among the small lotts, w^t^hout the 2 mile beyond the west river at the end of Mr. Evances quarter. And the rest, whose meddowes falls to the northwards of Captayne Turners farme, shall have the vpland for their second devission betwixt the great river and the Mill River, lying as neare their meddow as may bee, w^t^h refference to the former grants, and their neighbours convejniencye.

Here followes the order wherin the planters fell by lott in the east meddowes.

1. Mrs. Higginson,
2. Mr. Atwater,
3. Mr. Pococke,
4. Thomas Nash,
5. Jasper Crayne,
6. Mr. Evance,
7. John Ponderson,
8. Mr. Lucas,
9. Thomas Fugill,
10. Edw. Wigglesworth,
11. Richard Pery,
12. Mrs. Constable,
13. Mr. Brunwin,
14. Mr. Marshall,
15. David Yale,
16. Mr. Fr. Brewster,
17. Jeremy Dixon,
18. John Johnson,
19. Mr. Mayers,
20. An elders lott,
21. Mr. Owen Roe,
22. Mr. Dermer,
23. John Chapman,
24. Mr. Fr. Newman,
25. Mr. Malbon,
26. Mrs. Eldred,
27. Mr. Sam: Eaton,
28. Mr. Tench.

It is ordered that the other 4 quarters, namely, Mr. Lambertons, the subburbs, Mr. Gregsons & Mr. Fowlers, shalhave the vpland for their second devission beyond the 2 mile from the towne, on the west side of the harbour, takeing in all the land to the seaward, wthin Newhaven bownds towards Milford, and soe come rownd towards or vnto the land granted to the small lotts of the other 5 quarters, till they have their due proportion, only Mr. Goodyeare shall have the vpland for his second devission in a place wch he hath chosen for a farme beyond the west rocks, and Mr. Gregson shall have the vpland for his second devission on the east side of the harbour by the meddow called the solitary cove.

Libertie is granted Mr. Crayne & Mr. Tuttle to inlardge their somes they had formerly put in for their estates, namely Mr. Crayne to 480l, Mr. Tuttle to 450l, & they agreed to pay rates to the towne accordingly, both for time past & time to come, & if they should remove, to sell only improvements, & what vpland they want in their first devission & in the necke, by consent & order it is to be supplyed vnto them in the second devission, acre for acre. It is also granted to Mr. Crayne, Mr. Tuttle & Mr. Linge, vppon their request, that they should have their meddowes & the vpland for their second devission in the way to Totokett, after Mr. Eatons farme is layd out, only Mr. Crayne is to have meddow & vpland for 180l, the estate he first put in, betwixt the great river & the Mill river, among the 5 quarters as his lott falleth.

Jeremy Dixon had also libertie to inlardg his some put in for estate to 300l, payeing rates & receiveing land for any want in the first devission & necke as Mr. Crayne and Mr. Tuttle.

[119] || It was ordered that Mr. James sometime & elder in the Bay, shall have Francis Parrotts lott in the quarter called Mr. Evance quarter, and for his greater conveyniencye shall have his meddow at the bottome of the necke.

It is ordred that Timothy Baldwins lott in Mr. Fowlers quarter shalbe bought in by the towne & shall have land layd to it for 500l estate and for 6 heads or psons, & reserved for an elder, but the necke being layd out, what wants there, to be supplyed in the second devission.

To prevent offence as much as may bee, & that all mens sperits be the better satisfied wth their allotments, it is ordered, that where the planters doe not fully agree among themselues in deviding their lands, all devissions gennerally, (the former grants excepted,) shalbe made by lott through the towne, both in vpland & meddow.

Whereas part of the Neck hath bin formerly planted by severall men for prsent necessitye or convejniencye, it is agreed & ordered, that henceforward it be wholy laid & vsed for pasture & dry cattle, and stinted according to each mans interest & propriety, wherein 12 acres is to be reckoned for a horse, 6 acres for an oxe, 3 for a stere under 3 yeares old or not aboue 2 yeares old, and 2 acres for a calfe. And that noe man put in any catle yearly before the time ordered for the yeare, nor before he hath given notice to the governo^r what cattle, & in what right he puts in, vnder the penaltye of 6^d a head each weeke, any time lesse then a weeke reckoned & paid for as a weeke. It is also ordered that the necke be fenced from the farmes above, and a strong gate made for carts & cattle to passe through, and sufficient gates at the bridge, that so cattle allowed may be kept in from straying, & others may be kept out, & that noe man breake any part of the said fence, or any gate, or leave any gate open, vnder such penalty as the monthly court shall judge meete for each time.

Yet if any of the quarters will fence in their owne proportion, & soe relinquish all right to the common pasture in the necke, they may at their propper chardge doe it, leaveing out all springs, though w^thin their proprietye, for the cattle to drinke at, and wheras there are certayne parcells of meddow adjoyning to the vpland in some parts of the necke, wch meddow belongeth to some of the planters, and cannot be secured from the cattle w^thout a fence betwixt the vpland & the said meddow, it is ordered, that the treasurer out of the townes stock shall pay for halfe the said fence wch alredy is or shalbe made betwixt the vpland & such meddow, but the fence being once made & paid for, according to this order, the severall owners of the meddow agreed, & it is ordered, that themselues, severally, shall ever after mayntayne the said fences, or beare what damadg befalls them in their meddow, & if any perticuler quarter or person shall resolue to fence in their proportions in the necke, they shall first pay to the treasurer their proportion of the foresaid generall chardge as it shalbe judged worth, before they beginne to fence.

It is ordered that all such who are admitted planters into howselotts freely, but have had noe outland formerly allotted to them, they shall each of them have 6 acres of vpland to plant in for every single person, 8 acres for a man & his wife, wth an acre added for euery child they have at present, wch land is alreddy layd out for some of them at the further end of the great playne, in proportion as before, only a small adition was granted to William Davis to save him some chardge in fenceing, and more is to bee layd out for others there so farr as the land w^thin the fence will serve, & for the rest, their proportions shalbe layd out on the east side of the great river, betwixt Mr. Davenports farme & the Indian wigwams, in such forme as may be convejnient for them to fence & improve, and not prejudiciall to the towne, and Mr. Crayne & Mr. Tuttle were desired & appojnted to veiw & settle it, and it is ordered that all planters so admitted and holding land from the towne, shall pay yearely towards publique chardges 2[d] for each acre, as other planters doe for the 2[d] devission, & that the rates shal-beginne from the last of October, 1645, & so goe on by halfe yearly payments, and if any of them, satisfyed wth their trades, or not likeing the place or their allotment, shall refusse or neglect to take vpp the land, yet every on admitted to be a planter as before, shall pay 12[d] a yeare to the treasurer towards publique chardges.

Here followeth the names of those planters wth their proportions whether at the further end of the great playne or on the east side of the great river or harbour.

[Page 120 is blank.]

[121] || For that some of considerable estates & tradeing doe live in the towne & have hitherto injoyed comfortable fruite of civill administrations & chardges, themselues in the meane time haveing small or noe rates, it is ordered that hence forward all such shalbe rated from time to time as this court shall judge meete. And for the present Mrs. Stolion is ordred to pay after the rate of 20[s] a yeare to the treasurer, Mr. Godfrey 20[s] a yeare, & Mr. Leech 40[s] a yeare, all w[ch] are to beginne & to be reckoned from October, 1645.

Wheras a certayne quantity of land, fit for a small plantation, hath bin purchased of the Indians at the chardge of Newhaven, about 40 miles to the westward, towards Hudsons River, vppon a motion made of some of Wethersfeild, it is granted to them & their companny for a plantation, they repaying what chardges have bin expended, w[ch] amount vnto about 33[l], & joyning in one jurisdiction in Newhaven, vppon certayne considerations then propownded, but since perfected, in a fundamental agreement setled for this jurisdiction in Octob[r], 1643, as by that record more perticulerly may appeare, & vppon their desire that plantation is called Stamford.

Monunkatuck, formerly purchased & planted by Mr. Whitfeild & his company, was also admitted into this jurisdiction, vppon the same fundamentall agreement as Stamford, & vppon their desire that plantation called Guilford.

Milford, a neighbour plantation to the westward, was also admitted into this jurisdiction vppon the same fundamentall agreement in Octob[r], 1643.

Totoket, a place fit for a small plantation, betwixt Newhauen & Guilford, & purchased from the Indians, was granted to Mr. Swayne & some others of Weathersfeild, they repaying the chardge, wch is betwixt 12 & 13l, & joyning in one jurisdiction wth Newhaven & the forenamed plantations, vppon the same fundamentall agreement setled in Octobr, 1643, wch they, duely considering, readjlye accepted.

Whereas severall yeares since a tryall was made of setling a confœderation or consociation betwixt the Massachusets & Connecticott, but at time wthout successe, vppon a late overture wth hopes of a more comfortable issue, Mr. Eaton & Mr. Gregson were deputed & fully authorised to treate wth the commissioners of the Massachusetts, New Plimouth & Connecticut, to settle a generall combination, (if it shall please God to blesse their indeavours,) that the civill peace wthin these 4 collonyes may be the better secured, wthout any impeachment of speritual priveledges. At their returne they acquaynted both this court & the deputies for the jurisdiction wth the successe of the treatye, and the articles of confœderation, agreed & concluded vppon at Boston the 19th of May, 1643, and after aproued & ratified by the generall court of New Plimouth were read, & by generall consent confirmed, and the Secretary was ordered to enter them as a recorde, vppon all occassions & in all perticulers to be duely observed in future times, & vppon serjous consideration of the nature of this trust it was ordered that the commissionrs for this jurisdiction be yearly chosen by the vote of all the free burgesses, at the election court, and that they be furnished wth a comission in the name of the gennerall jurisdiction court yearly, for manadging all affajres belonging to the collonyes thus combined, in phrase or words agreed by the commissionors.

It is ordered that noe planter, inhabitant or sojourner, wthin or belonging to this towne, nor any vnder or for them, shall either directly or indirectly, purchase any plantation or land, more or lesse, of any Indian, Indians or others, or receive it by way of gift, or vppon any other termes, for their owne private vse or advantadge, wthout expresse allowance or liberty, to be granted & entred in & at some one of the monthly courts, vnder the penalty of the losse & forfeiture of his & their so acquired right, title & interest, to the towne, and such further fine as the monthly court, vpon cōsideration of the offence, shall see cause to impose.

It is ordered that none lopp, fell, cutt downe, or cause to be lopped, felled or cut downe, any tree, vppon any occassion, for any vse, vppon any common wthin 2 miles of any part of the towne, wthout speciall lisence from the governour or magistrates of Newhaven (of wch lisence the governour or magistrates to keepe a booke or memoriall, to prevent mistaks,) vnder the penalty of looseing all his labour, about euery such tree, leaveing it wholy to the towne, & paying besides on shilling as a fine for each tree so cutt, but if he carry away the tree or any part of itt w^{t}hout leave, he shall pay such further fine as the court shall judge meete.

And that none vnder the same penalties barke or cause to be barked any trees whether for tanning, dying or other vse, w^{t}hout order & appojntment of Serjeant Andrewes, Serjeant Jeffrejes, Sarjent Munson & Corporall Whithead, who are to consider where the tann^{rs}, dyers or others, may conveyniently gett barke wth least damadge to the publique. And if any man cutt, bark, lopp or fell any tree w^{t}hin the proprjety or allotment of any planter w^{t}hout leave, he shall pay damadg to the owner, according to the course of justice.

[122] || It is ordered that the magistrates, elders & deacons, shall henceforward have the disposeing of all howselotts not yet granted, w^{t}h the outward accomodations therevnto appertayning, to such person or persons as they shall judge meete for the good of the plantation, & that none be received as a planter, either by admission or purchase, w^{t}hout their consent or allowance, & that noe planter or proprietor sell or let any howse or land to any stranger or other not before a planter, either by lease or otherwise, w^{t}hout the approbation & consent of those before mentioned & intrusted, & all bargaynes, &c. not agreeing w^{t}h this order to be voide.

It is ordered that every male from 16 to 60 yeares of age who shall dwell or sojourne w^{t}hin this plantation, or any part of the bownds & limitts of it for a month together, shalbe & continew at all times compleatly furnished w^{t}h armes, viz^{d} a good serviceable gunne, a good sword, bandeleeres, a rest, all to be allowed by the military officers, one pownd of good gun powder, fower pownd of bullets, either fitted for his gunne or pistoll bulletts, w^{t}h fower faddome of match fit for service w^{t}h every match locke, & 4 or 5 good flints fitted for every firelock peece, all in good order & ready for any suddayne occassion, service or veiw, vnder the penaltie of 10^{s} fine, to be paid by or for euery person, so oft as he shalbe fownd defective & faulty; each master or governour paying not only for himselfe, but for all such as are vnder his chardge, for whome he should provide, & others to pay for themselues. It is further ordered that the captayne, (besides occassionall & extraordynary veiwes,) give order once every quarter of a yeare at least to the millitary oficers, that they take a stryckt veiw of all the armes belonging to the towne, that they may see & report that every male from 16 to 60 be furnished as before mentioned, vnder the penalty of 40^{s} fine if he neglect to give order, & that the military officers doe accordingly take the said veiw vnder the penalty of 40[s], to be levyed of them as the court vppon examjnation shall find cause, & that a due returne of all defects be made to the captayne & by him or the clarke at his appoyntment, vnder the penalty afforesaid, to the court, that the fines may be duely gathered & that each of those veiw dayes be so published & made knowne, that euery one may bring his compleate armes, powder, shott, &c. as before exprest, to the place & at the time appoynted, vnder the penaltye of 10[s] fine as if not furnished, the monthly court to judge of the difference of defects.

It is ordered that there be henceforward six generall traynings every yeare, viz[d], the first Munday in Aprill, the first Munday in May, the first Munday in June, September, October and November. But if any of these dayes proue raynye, so that the service cannot be carrjed on to satisfaction, it shalbe supplyed the next following second day w[ch] proues fayre, or if the governour & magistrates vppon any publique respects see cause to put of the trayning on any of the dayes before named, though proueing faire, adviseing w[th] the cheife military officers, it shalbe carryed on in some other fit season as they shall appoynte; on every of wch trayning dayes before expressed, all & every of the males w[t]hin, or belonging to this plantation, from 16 to 60 yeares of age, not exempted by the place or office they hold, or vppon some other respect dispensed w[t]h by the generall court, shall diligently atend the military nurture & exercises, that they may learne the better to handle & vse their armes, reddyly vnderstand & obey the words of command, & be generally fitted for all military service as occassion may require. And whosoever shall totally absent on any of those appoynted trayning dayes, ŏr shall dept w[t]hout leave befor the company breake vpp, or shall not be furnished w[t]h compleat armes for traynings shall pay 5[s] fine. And whosoever shall come late after the second drume hath left beating, his name being so returned, he shall pay one shilling fine, But if any man come late, & shew not himselfe to the clarke that he may enter his appearance such as it is, it shalbe chardged as totall absence, and he shall pay accordingly.

And for the incouradgment of military officers and company, it is ordered and granted that all the fines for absence & late comming, whether on the generall trayninge dayes or on the squadron dayes of trayning hereafter mentioned shall wholy goe to them, to be disposed by the military officers in powder & shott, &c, that they may set vpp marks to shoote at, or may furnish themselues for their military exercises, that the service may be more comfortably carryed on, & yet, if there be cause, the court will give all just assistance in the levying of them, and for other miscarrjadges as stubornes, contempt or neglect of the officers in their directions or due commands, quarrelling, fighting, disorderly talkeing, bringing & shooting of peeces wth bullets or shott, & all other misdemeanours, a fine to be paid to the towne by each offendor according to the nature of his fault, as the court vppon chardge & proofe shall judge meete. But in all publique traynings, liberty is granted [123] that at every || farme howse one man may stay at home to atend occasions & prevent dangers, but all the rest shall trayne, shew armes, and be subject to all the former orders & penalties.

Wheras there are 4 serjents & 4 corporalls chosen & appoynted for the millitary service & accordingly the plantation is devided into 4 squadrons, it is ordred that one of the squadrons in their course come constantly to the meeting howse to the publique worshipps of God, both every Lords day & on other dayes ordynary & extraordjnary, & be there at or before the second drume hath left beatinge wth there armes compleate, there guns ready chardged wth a fit proportion of match for match locks & flints ready fitted in their firelock peeces & shott & powder for 5 or 6 chardges at least, there to attend the publique service and safty as the officers shall appoynt, vnder the penaltie of five shillings fine for neglect, or defect of furniture, & one shilling fine for late comminge. The sentinells also, & they that walke the rownd in their course, shall dilligently atend their trust & duty, & shall have their matches lighted dureing the time of meeteing, if the serve wth matchlock peeces, vnder the penalty of 4s fine; and the serjeants duely to returne the names of all such as fayle & transgresse this order, vnder such penalty as the court shall se cause. And according to the course already begunne, that squadron wch is to bring armes the following Saboth shalbring armes the lecture day or any other extraordynary day of sollemne worshipp immediatly before, if they come to the lecture, &c.

All the former fines to be moderated as the court se cause.

The court considering how necessary it is in times of peace to prepare for warre, & accordingly to fit & trayne vp men by degrees to all military service & skill, besides the generall traynings & certayne squadron traynings hereafter mentioned, gave liberty and incouradgment to beginne an artilery company, & to add to it from time to time, such as out of the trayned bands, or others being free & fit, shall offer themselues therevnto. And it was granted to the said company that they may chuse their owne officers yearly & setle their owne orders, presenting both officers & orders from time to time to the generall court for approbation & confirmation, provided that they order their times of meeting & exercise wth due respect to the occassions & convejniency of the towne, and perticulerly that the traynings be not hindered. And it is further granted that all such who are admitted into the artillery company, while they atend & improve those meeteings shalbe freed from the squadron traynings (hereafter ordered,) if they be not officers who are to exersise others, & accordingly an artilery company was begune, the officers & orders were presented to, & approued & confirmed by the generall court M^rch 31, 1645.

The orders allowed for the artilery company are inserted page 99, therfore here omitted.

And whereas, by reason of the artilery company, the number for the squadrons wilbe lessned, it is ordered that henceforward, two squadrons joyne in one boddy, & that the 4 serjeants wth their respective corporalls exercise them thus joyned in their course, about a fortnight before each generall trayninge, but on the last day of the weeke in the afternoone, & whosoever shall come late to any of these squadron traynings, namely after the second drume hath left beating, he shall pay 6^d fine. And whosoever shalbe totally absent, 2^s 6^d to the company, as in the gennerall traynings. And for all other miscarriadges in this service, the fine to be judged in the monthly court.

It is ordered that a constant & strickt watch shalbe kept every night in this plantation, from the first of M^rch to the last of October every yeare ordynaryly, leaveing extraordynary cases, either of mildnes or sharpnes of weather or times of danger to the governour & magistrates, who may remit or continew the watch longer, or increase & order them as seasons & occassions may require. But in the ordynary course, the watch is every night to consist of one intrusted as ma^r of the watch, (who is diligently to attend & observe all the orders made by this court for the watch while they stand in force,) & of six other watchmen. This watchm^r is to be appojnted yearly, & the six watchmen to be sorted as may be most convejnient in respect of their dwellings, by the captayne wth approbation of the magistrates. But if by death, remove or any other occassion, after the watches are setled in their course for the yeare, a breach be made, & so cause of an alteration, the captayne shall wth all conveinient speede, order & setle them agayne, so as may *may* be most convejnient for the towne, and shall give seasonable warning to all the watchmasters whom it concerneth, that the service may goe on

[124] w^t^hout interruption || or disorder, & in times of danger, whether from Indians or others, as the townes watch may be increased, soe to prevent mischeife there may be cause to watch abroad, it is therfore ordered, that in such times, the farmes be free from watchings in the towne, provided they keep a dilligent watch at ye farmes.

The present orders & penalties are as followeth.

It is ordered that when vppon any occassion an allarum shal hereafter be made w^t^hin this plantation, both the millitary officers & every trayned souldier shall forthw^t^h repaire to the meeting howse w^t^h their compleate armes & all furniture for present service, & shall not spend time & hazard the publique safty by attending their owne private respects and affections, vnder the penalty of ^ , except only in the case of some present assault made vppon or neere the place where he or they were, or at least some discouery of Indians, or others knowne or suspected to be enjmies, & cōminge thitherward in a hostile manner. And when there shalbe cause to send out any company of souldiers, either to keepe of danger or enemjes, repaire or recover any losse, or in any just warre, whether offensive or defensive, whosoever shalbe appoynted & called to such service, whether officer or trayned souldiers, by the governour, magistrates, or others to whome trust and power is committed in such cases, he & they shall forthwith attend the call, & goe vppon the service according to direction, w^t^hout dispute or gaynsayinge. And whosoever shall refusse, or by questions & scruples delay & hinder the service, or discouradge others, shalbee proceeded agajnst by imprisonment & such further punishment as the nature of his contempt and miscarriadg shall require. And whosoever shall refusse his boate or vessell, his teame or horse, his armes or any part of it, offensive or deffensive, or any provission for the publique service, vppon just consideration & allowance to be afte^r^wards made for the same, (w^c^h in like manner shalbe observed to the men sent forth,) shalbe so proceeded agajnst by the authority settled in & for the plantac̄on as that the contempt & miscarriadge bee duely punished in the offendor, & the like disorder prevented or supprest in others for the future, that the publike receive no damadge by the folly and stubbornnes of perticuler men.

To prevent much inconveniencie & danger w^c^h may grow, it is ordered that whosoever shall shoote any bullet, bulletts, or small shott in the towne, or w^t^hin a quarter of a mile of the towne w^t^hout a sufficient & just call, w^c^h the monthly court will judge, shall pay 5^s^ fine for every such default, besides due satisfaction for what hurt or damadge may arise thereby.

It is ordered that whosoever shall furnish any Indian directly or indirectly either wth any gunne, greate or small, by what name soever called or wth any sword, dagger, rapier or the blade of any of them, arrow head, or other weapon or instrument for warr, or wth any powder or shott of what name or seize soever, or shall mend any gunne for an Indian, w^thout expresse order from the governour or comissioners for the collonye in wrightinge, shall pay either 5^l fine, or twenty for one, according to the nature and importance of the offence as the court shall judge meete.

The court serjously consideringe how husbandry may be carrjed on wth due incouradgm^t in this plantation, thought it meete that the quarters severally or two or more of them joyntly as they shall agree, should fence in such parcells of arable or plantinge land as might best suite their occassions, & ordered that in any such case, every planter, or whosoever holds land w^thin such a compasse soe to be fenced, doe attend the publique good in carrying on his part & proportion of such fenceinge in due time, that his neighbo^rs receive noe damadge through his default, nor may the innability, negligence or stubbornenes of any one or more perticuler men hinder a generall advantadge in improvement of land in any quarter or quarters, howselotts or abroad, when the major ꝑte agree to fence. But vppon complaynte, the monthly court to settle the best course & order they can, soe tendreing each perticuler planter that the publique receive noe damadge, & because in some of the quarters there are lotts vacant, not yet disposed, it is ordered that till they be filled, the quarters themselues fence them or procure workmen to doe it, and the chardges shalbe payed by the treasurer out of the townes stocke, both for the present in setting vpp the just ꝑportion of fence for each such lott, & hereafter in repairing the same when there shalbe cause, provided that the quarters in the wch such lotts are, beare all damadge if the said fences or any of them be not either made or repajred in due season, and that henceforw^rd before the treasurer pay for any such fence makeinge or repajreing, the quarter give notice for what perticuler lott it is, that soe the treasurer may keepe account of the chardges.

[125] || Each quarter in wch any such lott is shall also see that the fence in strength & goodnes answer that order of court made May the 5th, 1641, and for their helpe herein, brother Andrewes and brother Munson are appoynted veiwers for the towne, to see & certifie the treasurer how they find such fences, whether sufficient or not. If defective they are to judge of the worth wth respect to that order, and the quar-

ters or workmen to receive payment or to make abatement accordingly.

And for that in such common inclosures, severall workmen for their present ease are apt to make slight fences, & fences well made at first in time decay, wch may bring much damadge vppon them that plant, it is ordered that each quarter or quarters so joyning in a common feild, shall yearly appoynt 2 committees or veiwers from among themselues, who some one day in the first full weeke of every month shall dilligently veiw & observe, & shall set marks vppon all such fences or parts of fences as are defective, & acquajnt the owners, (or the quarters if it belong to some absent lott,) therew^th, calling vppon them to get them forthw^th mended, remmembring them that what damadge befalls the quarter or any planter till such fence or fences be sufficiently mended, they are to make it good, vnlesse they cann clearly prove that the damadge, or part of it, came some other way, wch wilbe justly considered. And the perticuler planters whose fences are fownd defective, shall from time to time pay the veiwers for their paynes in this service; but if noe fences be fownd defective, or none but for absent lotts, then the quarter or quarters to pay them according to their different proportion of fence about each such inclosure, the towne for the absent lotts to be wholy freed from all chardg towards these veiwers. But in any of them, the fence being well made at first, & so reported to the treasurer by the townes veiwers appoynted for that service, or an abatem^t made to the treasurer according to the defect, if the quarter cannot get them otherwise mended, their veiwers afforesaid may presse men to doe it, and the treasurer, out of the townes stocke shall pay for the worke. And for that some of the veiwers yearly appoynted may not know each mans fence at first, in such case they are to acquajnt the quarters, famjlies, or persons to whom any part of the said fence belongeth, what day they intend their first veiw, that euery one whome it concerneth may goe or send to shew their fences, and to marke them at both ends, that the veiwers may know what belongeth to each absent lott, and what to each present planter, and if any vppon due warning shall neglect to goe or send, he shall pay 2^s fine; and if the veiwers shall neglect to veiw at the times appoynted, or duely to observe & marke the defects, or seasonably to call vppon them whom it concerneth to amend them, they shall pay each of them five shillings every month for any such default.

And whosoever shall put any cattle w^thout a keeper, whether by day or by night, into any such inclosure, w^thout a joynt consent & expresse agreement made by the quarter or quarters interessed, he shall pay 6d a head, one halfe to the towne, and the other halfe to the informer vppon due proofe, & shall besides pay the ful damadge where it shalbe due. If he put them in wth a keeper, he shall pay all due damadge to the partie, wch growes either by the vnrulynes of cattle, or through the keepers neglect, only he may abate out of the wages of any servant or hired man, or by other just meanes require reparation for what he payeth through their default & miscarriadge; and whosoever passeth through a gate, whether a common gate or other gate leading into a common feild where corne is planted or sowen, & leaveth it open, or not well & sufficiently shutt, he shall pay 5s fine, the one halfe to the towne, the other halfe to the informer vppon due proofe & shall besides pay all damadge to the quarter or partie wch shall come by such miscariadge, parents or governours answering for children & servants, though it be after abated out of servants wages, or otherwise as before expressed.

And for that the fences belonging to the towne are generally weake & decaying more & more, & by the best & joynt care of the owners & veiwers hardly now to be repaired & majntajned strong & sufficient to keepe out swine of all sorts, and these small rivers are fownd noe fences agaynst swinne wch swimme over daylye, and by them much damadg is don every yeare, both in corne feilds & meddowes, manny complajnts are made & much contention ariseth, to prevent all wch inconveiniencyes, (if it may bee,) it is thought commodious & necessarie that the quarters or planters consider & joyne as they may to haunt, heard & keepe, their swine abroad at sufficient distances from all corne feilds & meddowes belong-
[126] inge || to any planter, whether in the towne or at the farmes. And it is concluded & ordered that what swine soever, greater or smaller, shall after the 23th March, 1645, be fownd either vnyoaked or vnrunge or both in any corne feild or meddow as before, the owners of them shall pay 6d a head to the informer vppon proofe, & if they be brought to the pownd, he shall pay a peny a head more to the pownder for impownding them, and the owner of them besides, pay the full damadge, whether in corne or meddow to him agajnst whom the trespasse is comitted, as it shalbe prised by indifferent men, wch course & care to keepe swine at a distance may also prevent much damadg & offence betwixt the English & the Indians, wch ariseth oft by our trespassinge vppon their corne, & their killing our swinne.

And for that it is fownd by experience that goates being left carlesly either by the owners or keepers in the mrket place, streates or high-wayes in or about the towne, climb over, or some way get into mens howse lotts, orchards or gardens, & in a short time by barkeing of trees or otherwise doe much damadge note easily repayred, it is ordered, that whatever goates are hereafter fownd w^t^hout a keeper in any place in or neare about the towne, save w^t^hin the owners howses or howse lotts, the owner shall pay 6^d^ a head for each such default, halfe to the towne & halfe to the informer vppon due proofe. And if they or any of them be brought to the pownd, the owner shall pay a penny a head more for impownding them, and if the pownder drive any of them to *to* the pownd, he is to have 4^d^ a head for the service, & the towne 3^d^ a head for the disorder. Besides w^c^h the owner shall pay full damages for whateuer hurt they doe in any mans propriety whether to trees or otherwise, as it shalbe prized by indifferent men; But in all the former cases the owner may recover from the keeper, as his chardge & damadge growes through his default.

The court being informed that the com̄ons are over burdened, & that the plantation in generall suffers by over great quantities both of greater cattell & swine, kept by such as have least right, as by noats from most of the quarters now brought in appeareth, desired that men would seasonably regulate & moderate themselues, otherwise the court, according to rules of righteousnesse & prudence must provide for the publique good.

It is ordered that the clay-pitts on the north side of the towne, w^c^h lye w^t^hin the first devission of vpland to Mr. Newmans quarter, be reserved from being any mans propriety, & kept as a common for the vse of the towne, and a conveinient high way left to it for carts to passe to & froe. Only it is granted to Mr. Davenport, that if he shall thinke fit to remove his fence from that side of his lott, lying by the way to the clay-pitts, to the other side by the Mill highway, he may fence crosse the way to the clay-pitts, makeing a gate & hanging a lock vppon it, the key to be still left at Goodman Coopers howse, that vppon all occassions it may be ready for them that fetch clay. And it is further granted to Mr. Davenport, that when the lott at first reserved for Mr. Roe comes to be fenced in, if he desire it, he shall have a way or passadge of 8 foot broad left betwixt that lott & Mr. Craynes, that he may goe out of his owne garden to the meeting howse.

It is ordered that those intrusted for the townes affaires, when they se cause may lay out both vpland and meddow for the conveiniency & incouradgment of him that shall keepe an inne or ordynary for strangers, in the meane time, it is granted to Wm Andrewes who at present carrieth on that imployement, that hee may fence in twenty acres of vpland at the hither end of the plaines, adjoyning to Mr. Francis Newmans lott, to put in strangers horses as there shalbe occassion, provided that if he either dye or give over keepeing the inne the said land shall immedjatly goe to him that succeeds in that imployment for the vse afforesaid, he makeing just allowance towards the chardg in fenceing, if by the hire & benifit of strangers horses, the said Wm Andrewes have not bin duely satisfied in the interim.

A foote bridge formerly made over the Mill River into the Necke being much decayed was for the present repajred, but wthall it is ordered that a cart bridge over that river, & another over the West River, wth sufficient causeies to them both, be forthwth made & kept in repaire from time to time at the publique chardge, when private ingadgements are out.

[127] || And it is further ordered that after those two bridges are finished wth the first conveniencye a cart bridge be also made over the East River, only it is refferred to further considerac̃on whether the towne will beare the whole chardge of such a bridg, or only disburse 100l towards the building of it for the present, and repaire & majntayne it when its built, and let the rest of the present chardges in building be borne by them that have lands onn the east side, & in consideration thereof grant them the full & sole liberty & proffit of all fish wch by weares or otherwise may be taken at the said bridge.

For the better trayning vpp of youth in this towne, that through Gods blessinge they may be fitted for publique service hereafter, either in church or com̃onweale, it is ordered, that a free schoole be sett vpp, & the magistrates wth the teaching elders are intreated to consider what rules & orders are meete to be observed & what allowance may be convenient for the schoolemars care & pajnes, wch shalbe paid out of the townes stocke. According to wch order, 20l a yeare was paid to Mr. Ezekiell Cheevers, the present schoolemar for 2 or 3 yeares at first, but that not proueing a competent majntenance, in August, 1644, it was inlardged to 30l a yeare & soe contineweth.

A proposition made to the commissionrs at Hartford, Ao 1644, by Mr. Sheppard, pastour of the church at Cambridge in the Bay, for a free contribution out of these parts of a pecke of wheate or the vallew of it of every person whose hart is willing for an increase of majntenance to the colledg there begunne, that children, (to what collony soeuer they belong,) being fit for learning, but their parents not able to beare the whole chardge, might the better be trayned vpp for publique service, was considered and fully approued, and Mr. Atwater

& Goodman Davies were intreated for that first yeare to receive and collect it, that it may be sent accordingly.

Whereas the gennerall court for this jurisdiction judging the season now fit, did see cause to joyne w^t^h Connecticott* in sending to procure a pattent from the Parliment for these parts, and for that purposse desired Mr. Gregson to vndertake the voiadge & buisines, & agreed to furnish him w^t^h 200^l^ out of this jurisdictiō in good marchantable beaver, of w^c^h in proportion this towne should furnish about 110^l^, it is ordred that Mr. Gregson, if there be cause, take vpp soe much, vppon such termes as he may, & it shalbe repaid out of the townes treasurie, w^t^h what allowance or consideration he shall agree for.

That commerce may the better be carryed on betwixt man & man in these pts where monny is scarce, it is ordered that Spanish monny, called peeces of eight shall passe here as they doe in some other parts of the country, at 5^s^ apeece. And that Indian wompom shall passe, the white at 6 a penny, and the blacke at 3 a penny. And some men being at present loath to receive the blacke, it is ordered that in any payment vnder 20^s^, halfe white & halfe blacke shall be accounted currant pay, only if any question arise about the goodnes of the wampō, whether white or blacke, Mr. Goodyeare, if the parties repaire vnto him, is intreated to judge therin.

That righteousnes & peace may be preserved, it is ordered that whosoever shall take any mans boate or cannow w^t^hout due leave shall pay 20^s^ fine, & whosoever shall take any mans oares or padle, hand cart, wheele barrow, or any thing of like nature w^t^hout due leave, shall pay 5^s^ fine, w^t^h what further damadge in any of the cases the owner may susteyne by such an injurious practisse.

And for that divers cannowes, some made by the English, some bought of the Indians, are altogether vnfit for the service to w^c^h they are vsually putt, & may prove dangerous to the lives of men, Mr. Crayne & Leiutennant Seely are by this court appoynted viewers, & are intreated forthwith, & soe from time to time hereafter, to veiw & seriously to cōsider of all the cannoes belonging to the English about this towne, (the owners bringing all & *and* every of the said cannowes to

---

* This was in 1644, however in the records of Connecticut there is no mention made about joining with New Haven to procure a Patent, but May 13, 1645, the governor, the deputy governor, Mr. Fenwick, Mr. Whiting and Mr. Welles were desired to "agitate the busines concerning the enlardgment of the liberties of the patent for this jurisdiction," and July 9, 1645, Mr. Fenwick was desired to go to England to endeavor the enlargement of patent and to further other advantages for the country. Trumb. Col. Rec. Conn. I. 126, 128. Mr. Fenwick did not go, and Mr. Gregson was lost on the voyage, in the famous phantom ship.

such place as the said viewers shall appoynte, giveing them notice that they are there ready to be veiwed,) who are to marke all and every cannowe wch they shall approve & judg meete for service, and whosoever shall henceforward hire out, lend or vse any cannowe not soe marked, for or in any passadg by watter, shall pay 20s fine for every such default, besides what further damadge may grow thereby.

[128] || Whereas much damadge & wast often growes by fire, & among other causes, the neglect of keeping chimneyes cleane may bring forth sadd effects, not only to the howse so neglected, but sometime to neighbours, it is ordered that every chimney in the towne in wch fire is dayly kept shalbe well & duely swept once every month from September to March, & once every two monthes after, through the whole summer, & all other chimneyes lesse vsed, in due pportion, wch worke & service, Goodman Cooper vndertooke in court, & by order is to have 4d a time for sweeping every chimney that is two storyes highor vpward, & 2d a time for sweepeing every chimney vnder two storyes high, to be duely paid by all them that consent & agree that he shall sweepe their chimnejes, but if any will doe it themselues or vse any other in that service, he or they are to take care the thing be duely performed, according to the true and full scope & intent of this order; And if Goodman Cooper come at any time after the month in winter or 2 monthes in summer, and find any chimney vnswept or ill swept & so not kept cleane according to this order, he is appoynted to sweepe every such chimney well & to have double pay for his worke, & if any refusse, vppon complajnte, the monthly court to proceede as they judge meete for a contempt. And if Goodmn Cooper neglect duely to sweepe the chimnejs he vndertaks or any of them, he is to pay double for what he should receive for each chimney, as a fine for his default.

It is ordered further that every howse wthin this plantation shall have & contjnually keepe & mayntaine a ladder of a conveinient height answering his howse, standing ready vpon all occassions to prevent or stop the hurt wch may growe by fire either kindling or breaking out in any chimney or other vpper pt of the howse vnder the penalty of 5s fine to be paid to the towne vpon euery view or due complainte of his neglect & default therin.

It is further ordred that fire hooks shalbe made at the chardg of the towne, *in such*, to hang in some convenient place where they may bee kept drye & ready for the vse of the towne in such times of danger, & lastly it is ordered, that whosoever shall kindle any fire in his garden or any part of his howselott in or about this towne, whether to burne leaues, straw, stalks of corne, or any kind of rubbish whatsoever, he shall pay 40s fine to the towne for euery such default, notwthstanding any excuse he can make of his care & attendance, the standing of the winde, or calmnes of the season.

Whereas the frameing & setling of orders for regulating the affaires of the plantation is of weighty concernment & every member & planter hath liberty eithr to vote or to offer light in any buisines propownded, & that noe man may prtend ignorance in any order that concerns him, it is ordered that when a generall court, vpon any occassion shalbe summoned, whosoever makes not his due apearance, when his name is called, or befor the secretary hath done reading their names, he shall pay, every member of the court, 18d, & every other planter, 12d fine. And after the names are read, whosoever shall depart wthout leave, while the court sits, shall pay the same fine, whether member of the court or other planter, as for late comming or totall absence.

It is ordered that whosoever shall cut any tree where the spruce masts grow, wthout leave from the governour or magistrates, he shall pay 20s fine for every such default.

It is ordered that soe oft as any publique occassion shall require, whether for the mill or any bridge, cawsey, building, fence, highwayes, or other worke wch is of publique concernement, or to be done vpon the publique chardge, in every or any such case, the governor or magistrates may on a trayning day send to the captayne for soe many fit men as the worke requires, or if the service fall, or may be well respited to another time when their is noe trayning, and that fit men on reasonable tearmes cannot be had otherwise, the governour or magistrates may put forth an act of authority, & for the publique good presse men for the worke vppon just pay, & in every such case all private contracts & ingadgemts shalbe suspended till the publique service be pformed, & yn return to yr full force as if ye presse had not bin.

[129] || Whereas a considerable part of righteousnes betwixt buyer & seller consisteth in knowne, certayne & just weights & measures, and whereas a halfe bushell measure for a standart, (according to the agreement of the commissioners for the vnited collonyes,) is pcured & brought from the Bay, it is ordered that all corne measures be exactly fitted & conformed therevnto, and Richard Miles, Wm Davies & Nicholas Elsy are intrusted & appojnted to veiw & try all measures vsed in buying & selling corne by any of the planters, farmers, sojourners, or others belonging to this towne & to fit them to the forementioned standart, & then to marke them wth the townes burnt marke NH. And for every bushell wch they so fit &

marke, they are to have 4d of him to whome it belongs, & 2d apeece, for every halfe bushell, pecke & halfe pecke, & 2d for every bushell wch they only marke & finding it fit doe not cut it.

It is ordred also that a standart be fitted for all waights & other measures as ell, yard, quart, pinte & halfe pinte. And Richard Miles, Joshua Atwater & Nicholas Elsy are appoynted to inquire for just standarts, agreeing as neare as may be wth London waights & measures, and then to fit & marke as they may all the waights and measures vsed in the towne for buying & sellinge to those standarts. And the treasurer is to allow them for their time in this service out of the townes stocke, & if any planter, farmer, sojourner or other, wthin the limits of this plantation shall buy or sell by any other then such tryed & allowed measures & weights, he or they shalbe punished as the monthly court, wth respect to the nature & extent of the offence, shall judge meete.

It is ordered that a convenient company & number of pyks be provided at the townes chardge, that the military & artillery companyes may be trayned & exersised in the vse of them, but no man herby to be freed from providing & at all times continueing furnished wth all other armes, powder & shott, as before expressed, & that a chest be made in some conveinient place in the meeting howse, to keepe the said piks from warping or other hurt or decayes, And Thomas Munson and the rest of the serjeants vndertooke to have it done wthout delay, and Mr. Peirce was appoynted to give out and lay vpp the piks from time to time, that they receive noe damadge betwixt times of service, & in consideration hereof & of some bodjly weaknes, he is at present freed from traynings and allowed to provide a man to watch for him.

It is ordered that when canvas & cotten woole may conveniently be had, due notice & warninge shalbe given, & then every famyly wthin the plantation shall accordingly provide, & after continew furnished wth a coate well made & soe quilted wth cotten woole as may be fit for service, & a comfortable defence agajnst Indian arrowes, and the taylors about the towne shall consider & advise how to make them, & take care that they be done wthout vnnecessary delay. And whosoever shall transgresse this order shalbe fined to the towne as the monthly court shall judge meete.

It is ordered that the markett place be forthwith cleared & the wood carryed to the watch-howse & their pyled for the vse & succour of the watch in cold weather, and the care of this buisines is committed to the fower serjeants.

It is ordered that whosoever findeth any thing lost wch is of vallew & fit to be restored to the owner, shall w^t^hin 3 dayes deliver it to the marshall who shall safly keepe the thing, but w^t^hall shall write it downe in some paper booke w^t^h the name of the person from whom & the time when it came to his hands, & shall cry it twice onn the lecture dayes followinge. And, if their because, a third time on a faire day, when the greatest concourse of people may be present & heare it. And the marshall shall have & receive from the owner, a penny a time for soe cryĩng it. And he shall also write downe who challengeth & receiveth it. If it be a liveing creature of any kinde, the marshall shall have notice & shall cry & be paid as before, but he that findes it or w^t^h whose cattle of any kinde it falls in may keepe & feede it, that it be preserved, & the owner shall pay all just chardges for it. But if any man omit, neglect or refuse the scope & intent of this order, the monthly court shall proceede agaynst him as the fault requireth.

[130] || Whereas divers hides have bin spoyled or much hurt by ill tanninge to the prejudice both of the owner & of him that shall weare or vse them, at first, (as hath bin alleadged,) for want of knowledge & experience of the nature of the barke or tanne of this country, but that beinge now so sufficiently knowen that every man that vndertakes or setts vp that imployment may seasonably informe himselfe, & therby prevent damadge both to himselfe & others. It is ordered that each tanner shall hereafter justly & fully allow & pay for all defects & miscarriadges in his tanneing, according to the damadge proved, as in other trespasses w^t^h all due chardges if it come to publique tryall.

It is ordered that Mr. Craine, Mr. Peirce, John Clarke & Henry Lindoll shall veiwe the meddowes called the Beaver ponds, & make report to the governour & the rest of the monthly court what they conceive concerning them, who vpon returne & reporte, shall have power to dispose & proportion the said meddow as they judge meete, to such planters as being freely remitted into small lotts have hitherto had noe meddow granted by the towne, & to setle rates for them to pay according to each mans different proportion of meddow, & that w^t^h respect to time past & time to come, w^c^h grant & order the planters afforesaid accepted, promiseing to pay rates accordingly, only if vppon tryall they find they cannot conveniently improve the said meddowes, they would forthwith returne them backe to be otherwise disposed by the towne.

To prevent contention & much inconvenience w^c^h may grow by secret promises, covẽnts, deeds of bargaine & sale, mortgages & other alienations of land, it is ordred that a booke of entryes shalbe duely & fairly kept by the secretary, of all alienations, conveyances & assurances of what kind soever, whether of howses or lands belonging to this plantation, wth such limits, extents & descriptions as may conveniently be done, and may vppon any question after, serve to cleare the agreement & bargaine, but noe entry to be made but by expresse order of court, & every such entry to bee accounted good *agaynst* according to the intent & nature of it, agajnst any former promise, covennant, bargaine, mortgage, deed of gift, or any convejance whatsoever not so entred, though all & every such promise or deede shall have its just force against every person or persons that made them, and against any other part of his or their estates. And before any such entry passe, the parties equally betwixt them, or one of them as they have agreed, shall pay downe to the treasurer for the townes account, two shillings for the same.

To suppresse vnnecessary contentions partly, & partly to ease publique chardges, it is ordered that each magistrate w[t]hin this plantation shall keepe a book of every warrant & attatchment given out by him, & direct them all to the marshall, & that the marshall shall receive of the plaintiffe before he serve them, eight pence for each warrant & 1[s] for each attatchment, of wch fees one third part shalbe for his paines in serveing them, over & aboue his sallery, the rest he shalbe accountable for as pte of his wages, & it is further ordered, that before any tryall in court betwixt pty & partie, the plaintiffe pay to the treasurer for the townes vse, three shillings & fower pence, over & aboue the warrant or attatchment, all w[c]h chardges shalbe finally borne by the plaintiffe or defendant, or both of them, as the court shall judge meete.

It is ordred that every one warned to the monthly court for transgressing any order of the generall court, & fownd an offendor, or being warned for fines or rates after they should have bin payd by the generall courts order, the same haveing bin first privatly demanded by the treasurer, m[r]shall, or any other officer o[r] psons appojnted for that purpose, shall pay to the m[r]shall 4[d], and that every one vppon any occassion committed to prison, besides other fees, chardges & attendance, (wch the court will order & judge) as the cause requireth, shall pay to the marshall for turninge the key one shillinge.

[131] || It is ordered that a certayne quantity of planting land by the small lotts, on the east or southeast side of the towne, called the Oyster-shell feild, shall by the magistrates & deputyes be let out to such planters as neede & desire the same, for seaven yeares from a[o] 1641, at a moderate & due rent to be yearly paid to the treasurer, for the ease of publique

chardges, wch was accordingly done, the rent from severall psons amounting to about tenn pownds a yeare.

Uppon a due consideration of the trouble & hinderance wch sundry, both of this towne & other plantations find & vndergoe in getting over the East River, over wch as yet there *there* is noe bridge, it is thought meete & ordered that a ferry be forthwith setled, and as it may be continued for the ease of such as have occassion to passe that river to or from the towne, and that a shedd be made at the townes chardge, by the watter side, & 3 acres of planting land in the Oyster shell feild, wth as much conveniency as may bee, be lajd out for the ferryman rent free, so long as this court shall judge meete, wth an abatement of rent, or some further allowance, (as the magistrates and deputies shall see cause,) to Mr. Brunwing, who from the towne according to the former order, rents that part of the Oystershell feild. And it is ordered that the ferryman, providing & maintayninge a lardg & serviceable cannow or boate fit for that service as the court shall appojnt, & giveing due & constant attendance about it every day frō sun riseing to sun setting, (Saboth dayes & times of solemne & publique worshipps excepted,) may demand & receive of every one he carrjeth or recarieth over the said river at the ferry place, two pence a time, if there be not aboue 3 passengers, If aboue 3: & not aboue 6, he may take three half pence a person, If aboue 6 to 8 or 9, the fare to be 9 pence, and for any greater number, a penny a person. And for the further incouradgment of the ferryman in this service, it is ordered, that if any belonging to this plantation shall transport any person or persons in any other boate or cannow in the ferry way, (his owne famyly or workfolks as their buisines & occassions require excepted,) he shall pay to the ferryman a penny a pson for every one so transported, but the farmers on the east side are left free, either to vse their owne cannowes or boats, or to agree wth the ferryman as they can when they have neede. And Francis Browne vppon the considerations before expressed, accepted the service vppon tryall, and became ferryman for a yeare from the 16th of June, 1645. And after that either to continew or desist as the court and he shall see cause, and his man being lame & so not able to carry on the service at all times, he is left to his liberty to come to the generall traynings as the occassions of the ferry will permitt.

Vppon the consideration of the hurt & mischeife wch is like to arise & increase by woolues & foxes seizeing vppon sheepe, goates, swine and the smaller & weaker sort of great cattle, it was formerly ordered that 15s should be paid by the treasurer to every one that brings a woolfes head & 2s 6d for every fox head, but vppon a further debate, December the 8th, 1645, the court being informed that noe man attends this service as his imployment & busines, but improves oppertunitie as he findes it occassionally, ordered that the treasurer henceforward pay only two pownd of powder & 4l of bullets or shott, or the vallew thereof for every wolues head & one shilling for every old fox head, & sixe pence for every younge one, to such of this plantation as wthin Newhaven limits kill & soe bring them.

It was granted to Mr. Lamberton that he might take in a peice of grownd for a yard to his cellar by the west creeke, but the quantity & limits to be ordered by those that are intrusted to admitt planters & dispose of lotts, provided that he pay for the said grownd as they shall set the rate, and shall hereafter sell both that cellar & this yard thus granted to whom & when the court shall appoynte, and at reasonable price & vppon a [132] further proposition & request made since by || Mr. Lamberton, the magistrates & deputies wth Mr. Craine & Leiutennant Seely were desired to veiw a peece of grownd neare Mr. Lambertons howse, vppon the side of the East creeke for a wharfe & warehowse, & if they judge it convenient, they may dispose of it to Mr. Lamberton, he either paying the worth of it, or enjoying it for the present & hereafter parting with it to the towne at such rate as indifferent men shall judge meete, or vppon such other tearmes as they shall conceive tend to the publique good.

Wm Pecke, haveing but halfe a small lott for a howselott, & therby much streightned, desired an addition of twenty rodd of grownd over against his howse by the creeke for their further conveniency, wch on this condition was granted, that if the towne se cause at any time hereafter, for publique vse or respects to reasume it vppon allowance of such chardges as shall then bee judged meete, he shall resigne it.

To prevent much sin & inconveniencie wch may grow by disorderly meeteings & drinkeings, it is ordered that none of or belonging to this plantation shall either directly or indirectly wthin their howses, cellers or other places, sell or deliver out any sort of wine or strong licquors by retayle, namely by pottles, quarts, pintes or the like, wthout expresse lisence from this court, vnder such penalty & fine as the monthly court, vppon due consideration of the miscarriadge or contempt shall see cause to impose. And at present, Wm Andrewes and Georg Walker are allowed to drawe & sell by retayle, but wth advice & order that they be carfull & circumspect to whom & what quantities they either deliver out or suffer to be drunck in their howses, or any place where they draw or have command, that disorder may be either prevented or observed & punished.

Mr. Trowbridge his howse for want of due & timely repaire falling more & more into decay, the court thought fit, for the advantadge of the creditors as shalbe hereafter ordered by the court of magistrates, to sell it to Mr. Evance vppon such considerations as are expressed in a wrighteing & agreement about it, but herevppon Mr. Evance propownded and desired the court to grant him the cellar formerly belonginge to Mr. Trowbridge before his howse lott, but not wthin the compass of it, wth some small inlardgement to build a ware howse vppon, which was granted, provided that in the whole it exceede not twenty foote square. . . F . . . .

F: 1645.

[133] AT A GENERALL COURT HELD ATT NEWHAVEN THE 16° MARCH 1645.

The last generall court held February 23th was now read & confirmed, only in that order about Thomas Fugills second devission, it was neither granted nor propownded that Mr. Gibbard should consider of any exchange of land or other course for such overplus as should be fownd taken in by him vnrighteously; this was looked vpon as a miscarriadge & vnfaithfulnes in his place, that wthout warrant he should frame & pen an order for his owne advantadge, & he therevpon in court presently blotted out those lynes.

John Brocket haveing, according to the last courts order, surveyed the land fenced in by Thomas Fugill for his second devission & measured how farr it lyeth from the towne, a report was made to the court that it is about 2 miles from the center of the towne, yet so that $\frac{3}{8}$ parts of an acre, or 60 rods of the land inclosed, is wthin that distance, wch is expresely contrary to order, as it was granted and should have bin entred; but by survey it appears that instead of 24 acres, his full proportion for that second devission, he hath taken in 52 acres & 13 rodd. Being asked what warrant or grownd he had so don, he confest his fault in fenceing it in without a surveyor, & his sinfull miscarriadge in takeing in a quantity soe farr above his proportion, but by way of excusse alleadged, that his grant being for cleare land, it would have bin very chardgable had he not carryed his fence to the rocke. He was told he had taken in aboue 28 acres of cleare land, hath gon over the river for part of it, wch he should not have done, & hath taken in neare 24 acres of wooddy & hilly land; wch if it had eased him in fenceing, wthout a grant from the court he ought not to have don; but by the plott it appeareth he might have taken in 24 acres wth lesse fenceing then these 52 acres require, though the rocks, soe farre as they reach, serve for a fence, and if the place would not have afforded 24 acres of land fully cleare, he must have taken it as it falls, his proportion & grant being noe more, and though he vnderstood that some of the church and probably some of the towne, were offended at this his vnjust course, yet in some yeares he had neither procured a survey nor advized w^t^h the court about it though from time to time he had sufficient oppertunitie.

This being considered was fownd and judged a publique vnrighteousnes, & so a publique offence & scandall, wch may not passe w^t^hout due censure, It was *remem-* remembred that when Thomas Robinson, one that is noe planter, for removeing some land marks in an vnrighteous way for his present advantadge in the grass then to be cutt, though he could not hold nor get the inherritance, had bin latly fined 40^s^ in court, Mr. Wackman & Leiutennant Seely were therfore desired to advize w^t^h the magistrates and deputies whether this offence be not more proper for the court of magistrates then for Newhaven monthly court, and onn the townes behalfe they were ordered to prosecute accordinglie.

But the court was further informed, that besides the former vnrighteousnes in the quantity of land, a small part lying w^t^hin 2 miles, he had severall wayes offended & falsified orders; in entring this order made November the 29th 1641, the grant in the substance was this, that he should have his second devission of the cleare grownd by the west rocke, provided it were not w^t^hin the 2 mile nor granted to any other, & by sundry in court it was remmembred that he was bownded & limitted w^t^hin 2 rivers; but in his booke of noates then taken in court, he hath left out the 2 mile, hath mentioned nothing of the rivers and hath added (or so much as he desires), of w^c^h clause he can give noe satisfying reason; it was neither by him so propownded, nor was it any part of the courts order. And as whereas besides his booke of noats, before mentioned, he keepes two other books, wherof the latter is to be a faire and lasting recorde, besides the former materyall defects they differ from his booke of noates in other respects. In both of them that clause (if not granted to any other) is left out, & a clause is added in such manner, & w^t^h such circumstances as gives much offence.

[134] ||For Mr. Cheevers & Mr. Wackman heareinge of his vnrighteous inclosure desired to se how the grant was penned,

Mr. Cheevers read it in Mr. Wackmans & Thomas Fugills hearing; he is assured & knoweth that at that time the order ended wth these words, or as much of it as he desires. Mr. Wackman conceiveth that clause, (according to his pportion,) was not then in the booke, they both affirme that vpon that grownd, Mr. Cheevrs tould Thomas Fugill that the order was vnlimitted & not easily transgressed & seemed to marvayle men should speake of his takeing in too much land, but added, you meane according to yor proportion, Thomas Fugill closed, both that that was his meaninge, (yet said not it was soe entred or written,) and that men would be talkeinge. Mr. Cheevers, when they were gon from Thomas Fugills howse, repeated the order to Mr. Wackman, & presently after wrott it downe, according to wch he reported to Leiutennant Seely how it was entred, who confidentlye replyed that the entry soe made was a falce entry. This soone came vnto Thom Fugills knowledge, but when the book came after to be veiwed, the line affording roome, these words were added, (according to his proportion,) but wth other pen & inke, a lesse character & crooked, as wth a trembling hand. The booke vppon occassion being brought & left wth the governor, Mr. Cheevers observed & was offended at this alteration, and at a meeteing wth Thomas Fugill before the governour & elders, questioned him about it; Thomas Fugill begininge to justifie himselfe, the governour, to prevent further rashnesse and sinfull expressions, by way of caution told him the book was wthin, & he had veiwed it, and if he could judge of writing, these words were added & written after the former part of the order wth other pen & incke, & wth a different character, notwthstanding wch, Thomas Fugill boldly replied, that if the govenor would give it, he would presently take oath they were written at one & the same time wth the rest, but the booke being brought out, the difference was so apparent that Thomas Fugill was forced to chang his expressions & said he would take oath it was not written since Mr. Cheevers saw & read the order, herevpon his second booke was sent for, out of wch this record was coppied, and therein also, (the line affording roome,) the same words seemed to be added, the difference in writinge, (though not soe much as in the great booke,) was cleare & evident, wch miscarriadge of his gave offence to all present; but this second booke, being by the governour & elders since veiwed, they severally, but each of them stronly, apprehended that a pen & blacker incke hath bine drawne over it, their being now either none or a difference so small as is scarce discernable, yet Thomas Fugill being questioned, againe & againe denieth it.

The governour informed the court, that, being offended at the former recited passadges, the next time Thomas Fugill came vnto him he warned him in private of his bold & sinfull way of protestations & offering to take oath, as if by confident contradictions he would drive men from the truth they knew, and besides the former passadge, instanced in a case betweene Thomas Fugill & old Goodman Wilmott, minding them of that rule, let your communication be yea, yea, nay, nay, oathes even in certayne truthes are not lawfull till they be necessary and duely called for. Profane men indead in other places who litle attend truth, thinke they must swere that they may be beleived, and in his case, it would be noe other then a high breach of the 3^{d} commandement. Thomas Fugill justified his offereing to take oath to Goodman Wilmott in regard of the truth in question betwixt them; and for the former passadge about addeing the words in the great booke, at first said he offered to take oath it was not done since Mr. Cheevers read the order, but being minded of the former perticulers, he
[135] seemed convinced & acknowledged ||it was his sinfull rashnesse, yet in court began againe to turne & winde, & so to evade the governo^{r}s testimony, but gave noe satisfaction.

The premises being duely considered, some of the members of the court & towne propownded whether it were not requisite & necessary to choose another secretarie, who might more faithfully enter & keepe the townes records. The secretarie confessed his vnfitnesse for the place by reason of a low voyce, a dull eare & slow apprehensions. He was answered the *the* court had longe taken notice of sundry miscarriadges through weaknesse o^{r} neglect, yet in tender respect to himselfe & his famylie, they had continued him in the place, (though wth trouble to others,) a review of orders, before these offenses brake out, being vppon that consideration thought necessarie & ordred. But vppon this discouery of vnfaithfulnesse & falsyfying of orders & records, they were called to lay aside those private respects, for the publik saftie. By the court therfore he was presently put out of his office of secretarie for this plantation, but the court not being prepared to make a new choyse so suddenly, Mr. Francis Newman, Mr. Richard Pery & brother John Clarke were intreated to take noats of what should be propownded & ordred in the remayning part of this court, & so of the next monthly court Aprill the 7th, & severally to draw vpp each court, fit for a record, that this court may have a tryall of their severall abilities, & in due season may, wth better satisfaction to themselues, proceede to a new elexion.

But notwithstanding all the former discoveries & proceedings, Thomas Fugill in the close of the day being called to read his noats about those first passadges, his entry about the secretaries office runs thus, (It was propownded whether the court will chuse another secretarie, because Thomas Fugill hath bin defective in his place, it was agreed that a new one be chosen,) wch being so directly contrary to the expressions, carriadge & conclussion of the court, gave further offence.

It was ordered that the old deputies shall continew this halfe yeare to come, & then in October next at the new choyse deputies are to be chosen for a whole yeare as the magistrats are.

Mr. Browning, Mr. Ling, Wm Payne, Thomas Knowels, Jno Hall & Mr. James, vppon their request & their occassions being knowne to the court, had leave for to depart the court.

It was propownded that the free gift of corne to the colledge might be continued as it was the last yeare & it was granted.

Mr. Atwater, the present treasurer, informed the court that he had sent from Connecticott fortie bushells of wheat for the colledge by Goodmn Codman for the last yeares gift of Newhaven, although he had not received soe much.

Brother Abraham Bell & brother Mathew Camfeild were chosen collectors for this present yeare for the gift of corne to the colledge, and wompom was allowed to be paid by those that had not corne to pay in, each pecke of corne being vallued 12d & 2 or 3 monthes time was allowed for men to bring it in to the collectors in.

It was propownded that Edw: Chipfeild might have libertie to make bricks in the playnes vnder the West Rocke to wch their is a good highway, which was allowed off.

[136] ||The court was informed that sundry swine had bin killed by the Indians doggs, and vppon the demand of damadges they promised to kill their doggs, & have brought the heads of 7 or 8, & hervppon desired that if the English swine doe trespasse them they may also be satisfied for the same, or rather prvent their swine from trespassing them. Leiut Seely herevppon informed the court that the Sagamore told him he durst not acquaynt him who had mischeivous dogs yet alive, because they would poyson him. Leiut Seely was herevppon requested to learne the names of such as the Sagamore feared & had doggs left & returne ym to the governour.

It was propownded (that seing we have a miller that gives content to the towne,) that we might have a loader alsoe. 20l a yeare was offred by Capt. Malbon to any that would vndertake it, & he would find them wth two horses & keepe them wth meate, only he should tend them, or els he would allow 40l a yeare & ye loader should find 2 horses wth meate all the yeare, & he further said if any man would vndertake the former worke, he would carrie the towne corne to mill for 1d½ ℘ bushell. This was refferred to consideration.

Whereas at the last gennerall court it was propownded that a bridge might be made over Newhaven River going to Connecticott, viewers were chosn, & vppon view have fownd a conveynient place, aboue a mile & halfe above the old passadge. Bro. Andrewes & bro. Munson require 4l 10s for the carpenters worke & carriadge, & they thought 20s might serve for to fit the banks for passadge. John Thomas promised to helpe doe that, & as soone as possibly may bee.

It was ordered it should be don, & that a surveyor looke onn it & lay out a way from the place, that the farmes might not be damadged by passengers that goe & come that way.

It was propownded that sister Lampson should be provided for at the townes chardge, so farr forth as her husband is not able to doe it.

It was ordred the last gennerall court that men & weomen should be seated in the meetinghowse, therfore it was propownded that all the seats be finished for feare of want of roome & to avoyd offence.

It was formerly ordred & now againe spoken to, that euery one turne their swine & other cattle the same way their land lyeth.

It was ordred that euery man throughout the towne repaire and mayntayne the highwayes before their homelotts the breadth of two rodds.

It was propownded that noe calues goe in the cowes walke, namely the cowes & ox pasture, not intending the farmes on y[e] east side.

It was ordred vppon Goodman Dightons information of the court of a good place for the feede of calves vnder the West Rocke or beyond it, that it should be viewed, & himselfe was intreated to goe & shew the place he intended, that it might be knowne whether it will answere the end or noe.

Complaynts being made of some mens putting their calves in the spring & fall into the meddowes to the prejudice of them, it was thought to be a transgression, but refferred to private consideration.

[137] ||Bro: W[m] Thompson complayninge of damadge don to his [*meddowes*] for want of his neighbours fenceinge, & a peece of wast grownd lying w[t]hout him of ½ an acre, he desired it might be granted him: bro: Myles & bro: Hen: Lyndoll were desired to view it & to returne their thoughts to the court concerninge it, so that if the land exceede not the quantity mentiond, he might have it if it prove not to the damadge of the towne or the prejudice of the highway.

Bro: Wackman & bro: Cheevers were chosen deputies for the jurisdiction court in Aprill next.

It was ordred that Leiut. Seely should have 6 acrs of meddow added to his pportion & next to the sea by the black rocke.

It was ordred that those persons whose names are vnder written shalbe viewers of the fences about the town ye next yeare.

Thom Nash & Rich Pery, for Mr. Eatons & Mr. Davenports quarter; Jno. Cooper & Christopher Todd for Mr. Newman & Mr. Brownings quarte; Jno Ponderson & Thom James for Mr. Evance quarter; Jerimy Whitnell & serjt Jno Nash for Mr. Gregsons quarter; Hen: Lindoll & Roger Allen for Mr. Lambertons quarter; Jno Mosse & Jno Walker for the Oyster shell feild; Jno Clarke & Corpl Whithead for the suburbs qurter; William Bradley & John Thompson for the farmes.

It was ordered that the perticuler court & cheife military officers should consider whether it be meete for watchmen to sleepe that are on the guard or noe, also whether lesse then seaven may not be sufficient to watch in one night.

It was propownded by captayne Malbon, that if a conveynient companny of the trayne band would of themselues be willinge to bring their armes and attend the service on the Lords dayes & Lecture dayes, & the lik vnder a penaltie, appoynting sentinells in their course from amongst thmselues, might not be freed from walking the rownds, & have libertie and conveyniencye of seats made & appoynted in the meeting howse for that service & the walking the rownds to be supplyed by them of the towne that bring not their armes constantly.

It was ordered that the way to the oxe pasture be where it is now layd out, although not formerly soe intended.

It was desired that a view might be made of the land behind Mr. Wackman & Mr. Goodyears quarters, in the reare of their devizions. Alsoe what land lyeth behind the Yorkshire quarter for ye small lotts.

It was propownded whether any should watch in the towne whose dwellings were a mile out of the towne, also whether those that had noe howses nor estats in the towne should serve therin. This was refferred to the perticuler court & the cheife military officers consideration.

It was propownded by brother Thomas James that his second devizion might be laid out, this was referred to consideration.

[Next on page 138 follow the names of sundry persons who at different times took the oath of fidelity, which have been already printed on pages 140 and 141 of this volume, and then succeeds an entire blank page.]

[138, *bis.*] [*A Court holden April* 7th, 1646.]

A difference betwixt some of Guilford, for whom Mr. John Caffinch stood plaintiffe, & Elias Parkman of Windsor, for whom bro: Jno Benham stood defendant, was prsented to the court, but testimony not being prsent for either side it was respited.

Bro: Thom Beamont hath sold his homelott lyeing next vnto Robert Pigg by allowance of the court vnto the said Robert Pigg.

Samuell Marsh being complayned of for absence & late comming to traynings, Mr. Crayne gave some answere for him, but it was respited till he doe appeare to answere for himselfe.

Thomas Tobie, Robert Vsher, Wm Andrewes, Wm Fancye & Theophilus Higginson were complayned off for disorderly drinking strong licquors to the abuse of some of them, so farr as that they lost the vse of their senses.

Thom Tobie said that it was true he fasting & watching ye day & night afore & not being acquaynted wth the nature of the licquoir, drinking thrice of the bottle, was overcom by it, so that he had not the vse of those abilities that elce he might have improved, but was carryed vp to bedd by two, wch he desireth to owne as his sinne & shame.

Robert Vsher acknowledged he dranke soe much as that going into the ayre it wrought soe on him that he had not the ordring of his tongue nor feete.

Wm Fancy owned it as his sin his oft drinking, being that at the first he felt it hott in his throate, but he was not distempred, howeur submits to ye court.

Wm Andrewes junior confessed he was as a meanes & occassion of this, wch he desireth to owne as his sin, but he intended only refreshing them.

Theophilus Higginson said he dranck three times, but he not loveing of it tooke but litle.

For wch disorder of all & distemper of some, they were all fined, viz^d Tho^m Tobie, Robert Vsher & Wm Andrewes junio^r 20^s each of them, Wm Fancy 10^s & Theophilus Higginson 5^s.

Corporall Leavermore being complayned of for his mans defect in want of a rest, sword, worme & scourer, but haveing procured som & p^romising to provide the rest as soone as possibly he can, was fined but 1^s.

Serjeant Munson being complayned of for taking away 3 hands fro^m traynings to goe fetch hay, he alleadging a promise to have had it don while he was gonn to Moheigin, & after he came home, but being putt of & in hazard whether he should gett cannowes or the like to doe it, & if he had not imbraced that oppertunjty he could not have had hands to helpe him & considering it was don on a shewing day after they had shewed their armes he was fyned 2^s each person.

---

[139] [ ]

Richard Pery chosen secretarie for the court of Newhauen vntill October next.

Francis Browne had liberty to depart the court, to helpe some cattle over the river.

Brother John Herryman received the chardge of a freeman.

Consideringe the state of the jurisdiction & the righteousnesse the towne is bownd to attend in payment of severall debts, which for the p^rsent were due, it was thought meete that a new rate be assessed, and that it be paid w^thin a month, & that the halfe yeare rate due in October be paid into the treasurer in June & July next ensueing at farthest, in monny, beaver, corne or wompom, in butter or cheese & great cattle moderatly p^rised.

It was propownded by the governo^r that each person that hath land or doth rent any this yeare in the necke doe bring in their quantities to the govern^r, & how he will improve it this yeare, before the first of May next or before he put in any cattle into the necke, vnder the penaltie formerly setled, and that bro: Cooper drive the necke the 17th of this instant Aprill & afterwrds whose cattle soeuer be fownd there they being pownded shall pay ℘ the owner 6d a head as ℘ a former order.

It was desired that those that desire right in the Beaver Ponds should issue their thoughts about it wthin a month, & if they doe not, nor give in their mynds to the governor, it is to be left to the courts dispose.

It was granted that brother Wm Thompson might fence in his meddow & the small parcell of land straight from the quarter to the causey with it.

Brother Wackman & brother Seely were desired to view that meddow Mr. Goodyeare desireth at his farme, & to returne their thoughts of it to the court.

Brother Wm Tharpe was spared from future traynings, with respect to the weaknesse of his boddy.

Brother Francis Newman & bro: Crayne were desired to view a peece of grownd which brother Leeke desireth to build a shopp onn agaynst his howse.

It was ordered that the surveyours of the highwayes doe view them, & returne the names of those that are defective either for cart or foote.

It was ordered that each man mayntayne a good way before his howse lott throughout the towne, whether it be for cart or foote.

---

[140] [ ]

Mr. Brownings son wanting a gune & sword, his case being such as his armes were sold before winter, his intents being to have gon for England, & pmising to provide agaynst the next trayning day, his fine for prsent was remitted.

Ambrosse Sutton being defective in his armes, ye mayne spring of his gune being naught, was fyned 12d.

Goodmn Whitnell, defective in worme & scourer, was fyned 1s.

Goodman Lampson, for a defect in ye length of his rest was fyned 6d.

The townes fence being complayned off as defective wthin Mr. Davenports quarter, towards ye Mill River, wch was don by Jno Mosse & Timothy Ford, they submit to the prising their fence, & yeald it vpp to the towne, wch was vallued at ^ d ꝑ rodd & was in all ^ rodds, as ꝑ the viewrs noat appears.

Brother Crayne haveing sett vpp some fence before any court order was made for the sises of posts & rayles, it being now fownd defective, it was appoynted that his accompt be viewed & so to see the ꝑportion betweene the fence & the prise paid for it.

Timothy Ford was complayned of for his powder being short in waight & dusty & soe not serviceable as it ought to bee, was fyned 2s 6d.

Robert Emery for his defective fence of his gune, fyned 1s.

Jno Cooper wanting a rest was fyned 6d.

John Gibbs defective in his gun fyned 6d.

Robert Vsher defective in ye sockett of his peece fyned 1s.

Benjamin Hill defective in scourer, but being warned to ye court he neithr acquainting his master wth it nor appearing, it was counted a contempt.

Samuell Wilson wanting worme & scourer & rest was fyned 5s, considring he had notice given him of providing & he doing it not.

Thom James, his scabbord being too short fyned 6d.

Natha: Seely defective in scourer fyned 6d.

Bro. Davis for 3 men of his being defective in bulletts & one in match, for wch he was fyned 20s.

Wm Wooden defective in powder fyned 12d.

Bro. Iues wanting a scourer,
Bro. Mitchel wating a gun sticke, } each fyned 6d.

Goodman Osborne defective bulletts, scourer, worme & rest, but being now supplyed was fyned but 5s.

Samuell Daighton wanting all armes, but he being latly come to towne & at prsent provided, it was passed by.

James Bishopp defective in his rest fyned 6d.

Thom Beech defective in his rest fyned 6d.

Thom Knowles defective in his rest was fyned 6d, & he not

haveing paid a former fine was ordred to cleare it before the next court.

Samuell Marsh being seeking cowes during his absence from traynings, it was accepted of the court as a sufficient excuse.

Goodman Plat hath sold 6 accres of meddow on the west side vnto Roger Allen, wch meddow lyeth next above Mr. Gibbard, in a peece of meddow called an island, & the West River runeth vpp on the other side thereof.

[141] || Goodman Platt hath sold about 11 acr. ½ of vpland to Mr. Jno Wackman & John Gibbs wch fronteth against Mr. Evance quarter & is bownded on the reare by Jno Gibbs & Hen: Glovers lotts, & lyeth betweene Mr. Wackman & Mr. Bracys lotts.

Goodm^n^ Platt hath sold all his land in the Necke to Wm Thompson.

Goodman Platt hath sold 2 acr: of meddow to Tho^m^ Fugill.

Richard Hull hath sold 6 acr of vpland vnto Wm Thompson, which fronteth towards the subburbs quarter, & lyeth at that end of his lott, & is betweene Wm Preston & Henry Lindoll lotts.

The Governour being informed of severall leawd passadges, ordered Wm Fancy to appeare wth his wife at the Court, to answere for them. The examjnations of Goodm^n^ Fancy & his wife following were read in court, viz^d^.

Goodwife Fancye examined the 14th Aprill (46) said that, 1. About two yeares since working for Goodwife Robinson, being alone in the cellar with Tho^m^ Robinson her husband, he tooke hold of her, put downe his owne breeches, put his hand vnder her coates, & wth strength & force labored to satisfie his lust, & to defile her, indeavoring to throwe her downe, & when shee began to cry out, he stopt her mouth, but some of the shipmen occassionally calling him away he left her for that time.

2. When they lived in Leiut. Seely's cellar shee going into the planted lott to fetch in a barrow full of wood, Indian corne being then & there growne man high, hearing a noyse amongst the stalks of corne & lookeing about shee saw Tho^m^ Robinson

& said vnto him, goe & be hanged, what doe you here, but he fastened vppon her, strove to have kissed her, but vppon her hallowing or crying out, (though the winde being high she conceiveth she was not heard,) he left her.

3. Another time being at worke there, Goodwife Robinson desired her to goe into the lott to gather pompions, & there he agayne attempted the like, but she resisted & told him these practises of his would not long be hidd.

4. After this againe she going forth to catch a hen, he came & put down his breeches, strove to stop her mouth, but she makeing a noyse, her husband came forth of the cellar, & Robinson seing him left her.

After this Wm Fancy lived at Thom Clarks howse, Thom Robinson came thither, this examinate saith she seing him comminge, & fearinge his filthy lustfull attempts, gott & stayed out of the howse. Robinson prayed her to come in, proffessing he came with noe evill intent, but to make peace wth God & her, she told him her husband knew of his filthy leawd carryadges, he must therfore make peace with him; this was about 12 monthes since.

Notwthstanding all former passadges, Thom Robinsons wife wanting help in her childbed state, he impudently desireth Goodie Fancy to keepe her, she sends him vnto her husband, & he, considring the weomans neede, consents. After she had bin there a weeke, her husband asked her how Robinson carryed himselfe, she answered she thought he was become a new man; but the second weeke he returned to his former filthy course. Goodwife Fancy going forth with him into the cow howse in the evening to hold the lanthorne while he cought a hen for his wife, he suddenly darkned the lanthorne, fownd & tooke hold of her in the darke, she crying out, (fearing he would kill her,) what shall I doe; but he put downe his breeches, put his hands vnder her coats, & gott them vpp, thrust her to the wall or pale & indeavored with his boddy to committ adulterie with her, but she resisted & hindered him

[142] & told him that if || he went onn thus, he would come to the gallowes; he pished at that, but told her he would never medle wth her more. This was about 10 weeks since.

6. Yet againe during that attendance onn his wife, this examinate going forth to fetch wood to make a fier, itt being her night to watch, Robinson followed her, put downe his breeches & indeavored to satisfie his lust as before, but she cryed out, threatned to awake his wife & to acquaynt her wth his course, wherevppō he gave over & this was his last attempt vppon her.

This examjnate saith that she hath from time to time acquainted her husband wth Robinsons leawd lustfull attempts vppon her, (except that 5th passadge in the cowhowse, wch yet she after told him off,) & prest him to complayne to the govr, but Wm Fancy refussed & desired it might be concealed, fearing, (as hee then & now professeth,) that his wife haveing bin publicquely punished for theevery, should not be beleived; & by way of excusse, he now further added, that being ignorant of the mynd of God in the Scriptures, he knew not but that it might be concealed.

By examynation & confession it appeareth that the former leawd & outragious attempts came thus to light, Thom Robinson, at Mr. Evance his howse hearing Hannah Marsh say she delivered a paire of sizars to Stephen Medcalfe before he went for England, Robinson in the hearing of Jno Thomas and others replyed, there is another cutler in towne for a neede who could spare a paire of sizars or a knife, & added he thought he saw the sizars spoken of att Goodwife Fancyes, & that she was a theife & other words to that purpose. Goodwife Thomas sometime imployinge Goodwife Fancye in her occassions, either told her or sent her word what Robinson had said. Fancy his wife passionatly & in way of revendge tooke vp this proverbiall speech, save one from the gallowes & he will hang you or cutt your throate if he can. Goodwife Thomas, by the words supposing some great guilt was concealed & lay hidd, inquired the meaning, & Fancyes wife discouered Robinsons filthynesse & villeny.

After this Fancyes wife going home from Jno Thomas his howse fownd Robinson staying for her in Stephen the cutlers shopp, & weeping he spake passionatly, is this come forth & added he would rather that his life & all goods were gone then that his wife should have knowne of it.

Goodwife Robinson hearing these things was exceedingly troubled & desired they might be taken vpp in a private way if it might bee, and Thom Robinson and his wife pressed Goodwife Thomas to that purposse; Goodwife Thomas replyed that he might see a hand of God in this busjnesse, for his other vnrighteous dealings, yet told him if she might saflye, she could be content to conceale it if she might see a generall reformation in his course, but Robert Vsher knew of it & must by a due acknowledgmt be satisfied. Robinson meeting wth Vsher that night, insteede of satisfying him, provoaked him by telling him it was but a word in jest, & that Fancy his wife wronged him, herevppon it was resolved that counsell should be asked & proceeding ordred accordingly.

Wm Fancy & his wife both affirme that about a fornight since Thom Robinson offred them 10s in silver for their satisfaction that there might bee noe further prosecution.

John Thomas & his wife say that Robinson did before them acknowledge some miscarriadges & did but weakly if at all deny the rest that Fancyes wife chardged him with; he knew, (as he said,) that a weomans word would passe before a mans in this case, espetially seing Fancy his wife said she would take her oath for the truth of her chardge.

[143] ||Goodwife Robinson confessed she had heard her husband confesse he had spoke some words to try Fancys wife but he could not owne all she had chardged him with, being asked where her husband is, she saith that yesterday in the afternoone he went forth in a sadd discontented frame, and as she since heareth, passed over the ferry, but since she hath not heard of him.

Wm Fancyes wife saith further that about 3 monthes since Marke Meggs came to their howse & asked for her husband, saying he was ordred by Mr. Francis Newman to receive 8s of him, she replyed her husband should gett it for him so soone as he could, but it since appeareth Mr. Newman sent him nott. As Fancys wife then passed by him he caught hold of her, strove with her, put his hands vnder her coats, shewed her a string of wompom & told her he would give her that & 5s more if she would teach him to gett a boy, but she resisting he went away. When her husband came in she told him Marke Megs was a roague, & acquainted him what he had done, wherevppon her husband & the cutler went & spake wth him; he presently acknowledged his fault to them, & severall times since hath acknowledged it to Fancys wife.

Concerning Stephen Medcalfe the cutler she saith, that her husband & she lying in his howse soone after the hand of God was vppon Stephen in the losse of his eye, he came, (as she was sifting meale,) in a basse lustfull way to kisse her by force, she said it were better he never touched any while he lived, yet after this while he was vnder cure when her husband was abroad, it being his watch night, Stephen went to bedd but left his candle burninge, she called to him to put it out, he bad her come put it out or take it for her vse if she would, she refusing, he after put it out & she went to bedd, but first tyed downe the latch of the dore soe as she thought it could not be opened from wthout; yet, as she conceyveth about midnight, the dore was opened, & by the creeking awackned & frightned soe that she cryed out with much feare, who is there, then Stephen spake & went to his cubbard, dranke some strong watter & went away. Fancys wife arose, went out & came in againe, walking vp and downe. After the day brake the weauer & her husband came home, she told her husband Stephen was a rogue, & said she would complayne to the magistrate but her husband diswaded her. Stephen lay long in bedd that morning. After he was vpp he went to Mr. Pells, her husband met him & told him of his miscarriadge. Stephen came home and asked Fancys wife what she had told her husband, she answered nothing but what Stephen knew was true, yet at his request, her husband promised to passe it by.

Marke Meggs being called to answer Goodwife Fancyes chardge did at the first wholy denny it, wherevppon Wm Fancy informed the court that so soone as he came to the knowledge of his forementioned action, he called to hm to speake wth him, who was then killing a pigg at Goodmn Mosses & there told him of it, & that since Marke had sought to make his peace, & at that time Robert Vsher, that he might not come to the knowledge of it, was sent out of the way, & he the said Marke Meggs told them if it came to light he should be vndone.

[144] ||Corporall Mosse informed the court that James Heywood told him that Marke Meggs came into Goody Fancys howse & downe with his breeches.

Goodman Banister informed the court that Daniell Paule & himselfe being at worke wth Wm Fancy, he upp & told them that Robinson was run away & feared his wife would be a cause of his being whipped and so Marke Megs.

John Meggs informed the court that Wm Fancy being at his shopp told him what his bro: had done, & that he thought he would be fyned, & if that it were soe he would take nothing of him.

John Thomas informed the court that Marke Megs told him that the $Govern^r$ said that Jno Thomas needed not come to court if he could say nothing for him, the wch words the gov^r said not, but Marke Meggs exprest to have hidd his sinne & guilt.

Robert Vsher informed the court that one night Marke Meggs came and called Wm Fancy & his wife to speake wth them, & Goodie Fancy desired him the said Robert to goe vpp into the chamber, then he asked the matter, she said nay, neither shall Stephen tell you what Marke came about.

Goodwife Fancy vppon oath affirmed that Marke Meggs comminge for 8^s or 10^s vppon a last day at night, she told him she thought her husband had it not, but he should gett it, & thought Mr. Newman would not be soe deare, then went out into the lott & comminge in agayne he caught hold of her, put his hands vnder her coats, offred her a string of wompom he then had & 5^s more if she would teach him gett a boy— & y^e next day save one, being the second day of the weeke, he went to him.

$Goodm^n$ Fancy vppon oath affirmed that he spake wth Marke Meggs in $Goodm^n$ Mosses yard & said to him he was a basse fellow for to goe to abuse his wife, offring some wompom & 5^s more & that he going to acquajnt Mr. Gregson wth it, Marke mett him, acknowledged his fault & said if hee should goe &

tell of it he should be vndone, & intreated him to consider his case, for he had dranke a cupp of sacke & Stephen desiring him, he granted to passe it by.

Capt. How, being then in court, told Marke Meggs it was not his way to deny it before God & a court of justice, for though the court might, God would not cleare him if guiltie, for God may have left him to the act, although there may want evidence, as he may remember a defect of evidence in a case of this nature formerly. Therfore desired him not to leave God & himselfe in this act.

For wch sinful & lustfull attempt, although denyed at prsent by himselfe yet sufficiently proved to the satisfaction of the court, he was centenced to be severely whipped.

Goodie Fancy for herselfe in concealmt of the forementioned vylenous & lustfull attempts by severall as appeareth by her own confessions, & Wm Fancy for his being as it were a pander to his wife & neglecting the timely revealing of these forementioned attempts to have defyled his wife, who should have bin her ptector, & although he was told of them, neither did discover them himselfe, nor would he suffer his wife to doe it. Both were centenced to bee sevearly whipped.

Joseph Guernsy for his wilfull neglects of obedience to his mr his commands & rysing vp & abusing his mr & his bro., as appeared by the testimony of bro: Joshua Atwater, bro. Cheevers, Mr. Francis Newman and Eliza Downinge, was centenced to be sevearly whipped.

---

[145] [A *Gennerall*] Court held the 25th May 1646.

In regard of severall occassions & worke to be done agaynst trayning day, bro: Nash is spared & bro: Leavermore also, because that if hee attend this court it will hinder his burning of potts this whole weeke.

It was remmembred that the last Genll court it was ordred that men should have payd their rates, but it being 6 weeks since & yet all not brought into the treasurer, men were advized to take some speedy course, or elce the marshall shall have order to warne them into the court the next weeke.

It was likwise considered that whereas there was an order made to p^r^serve meddow & cornefeilds, & swine ordred to be kept abroad, but for p^r^sent it not being attended, it was desired men would attend it better for ye future.

It was ordred that whatever swine were fownd w^t^hin the necke or any fenced vpland w^t^hin two myles of the towne vnyoaked & vnrunge shall pay 6^d^ a head besides a penny powndage, & that this order take place the next day following at night.

Bro: Cooper was desired to drive the necke, & he ꝓmised to doe it.

It was ordred that every man bring in the eare marke of his swine that so if they should be pownded, they might be knowne therby, but if the swine e. c. be not knowne therby they shalbe duely cryed & somtime after they shalbe prised, & a new & publique marke sett vppon them, wherby the pownder may know them, & yet euery one may see his owne marke also, & that before any new marke be added or the creature prized, the approbation of the magistrate is to be required.

It was ordred that bro: Cooper be cryer in the marshalls stead, in regard that he cannot attend it manny times because of prison^r^s.

It was ordred that henceforward all dry cattle be kept by a keeper, (a ꝑticul^r^ agreement by them at the farmes on the east side excepted,) although this order passe w^t^hout a fine.

It was ordred that noe man put any oxen in the oxe pasture, Mr. Evance only excepted who hath liberty granted vppon his indeavour to keepe them from the cowes.

Bro: Phill: Leeke was desired to keepe an ordynary or inne, & to ꝓvide for the refreshing of seamen, w^c^h he tooke into consideration.

Libertie was granted bro: Phill: Leeke to draw wine for Mr. Malbon, he attending a court order formerly made for sobryety.

Bro: Peter Browne had liberty to depart the court for the remaynder of this day.

Jerymy How had libertie also to draw strong watters for

Mr. Evance & Mr. Gilbert, he attending a former order made for sobryety.

It was ordred that if they that live at the farmes come vppon trayning dayes by that time the company is in ranke & file, & before they have moued, it shall not be accompted late comminge.

The choyce of the Artylery company officers was allowed of.

Bro: Francis Browne, Mr. Caffinch & Goodman Bassett were dismissed from attending the court, occassions wch were vrgent calling them away.

[146] ||Mr. Malbons meddow so called, belonging to Mr. [*Gregsons & M*]r. Wackmans quarters I[*t was moved*] they might have a way to their land, and the subburbs desired the like. Mr. Gilbert, Mr. Francis Newman were chosen as committees to looke on the way, & one of each quarter was ordred to goe with them, to propownd their objections to them.

Bro: Phillip Leeke, vppon some pressant occassions, had leave to dept the court this day, & liberty was given him also to make vse of a peece of grownd before his dore, provided that if it so fall out that the townes occassions require it, he then surrender it & remove his howseing from it.

It was moved that some place might be fenced in wherein strang^{rs} horses might be kept, but at present respited.

Mr. Goodyeare & Mr. Robert Newman being desired to goe to Mrs. Stollion who lyeth very weake & thought her change draweth nigh, they had leave to depart the court.

It was ordred that whosoeuer fetcheth fire, or sends for it & not in a covered vessell, though the fire be denyed them, or vppon any other occassions they come w^{t}hout it, they shall pay 6^{d} fine; but if they carry any fire away, they shall pay 12^{d}, because great damadg may growe to the towne by slightnesse & carlessnesse this way.

It was ordred that whosoever shalbe fownd takeing tobacco in an vncovered place, as in the streate of the towne, or in mens yards, shall pay 6^{d} fine each time, also if onn trayning dayes, either in the company or the meetinghowse at any time.

It was ordred that the waights & measures of this towne bee viewed once a yeare, somtime in September, it being at their liberty that are to doe it in what part of the month, vnder the penalty formerly mentioned.

Bro. Jn° Mosse, Natha: Merryman, Richard Webb & Wm Payne were freed from attending the court, to helpe Mr. Malbon get goods ashore.

It was ordered that brother Seely & brother Gregory doe looke that noe hydes come out of the tanners hands but those that are well tanned, & that they seale them if they doe allowe them, & that they have 4d ℘ hyde for veweing & sealing of them.

The remaynder of the former court orders reviewed were now read in court.

The order for a corne measurer in this towne was repealed.

---

[147] AT A COURT HELD AT NEWHAUEN THIS 2d JUNE, 1646.

Mrs. Brewster, Mrs. Moore & Mrs. Leach being warned about severall miscarriadges of a publique nature, appeared and were chardged severally as followeth,

Elizabeth Smith late servant to Mrs. Leach, saith that hearinge Mrs. Brewster loud in conference wth Mrs. Eaton, Mrs. Moore & her Mrs. as she sate at worke in the next roome, shee called Job Hall, her fellow servant to heare also, who could better remember the perticulers of such a conference then herselfe.

Imprmis, Job & Elizabeth both affirme that Mrs. Brewster repeating somthinge of Mr. Davenports prayer to this purposse, Lord add to the church such as shalbe saved & build vpp to perfection those whom thou hast added; and speakeing of his sermon said, Mr. Davenport maks the people beleive that to come into the church is as much as the receiveing of Christ. Job saith she added, Mr. Davenport carryeth it as if they could not have salvation wthout comming into the church. What concerneth Job in this part of his testimony he gave in wrighteing, & affirmed before the magistrates, yet now in court was somewhat doubtfull whether he heard the words from Mrs. Brewster herselfe, or only heard Elizabeth repeate them from Mrs. Brewster. His best light, (he said,) serveth for the former, yet he was loath to give oath therein. The court blamed him that he had not better considred this before, yet wished him to deliver nothing vppon oath but what he was cleare in.

Mrs. Brewster as before the Governo[r] & Mr. Goodyeare form[r]ly, so now in court denyed the chardge.

2[dly]. Job & Elizabeth affirme that Mrs. Brewster speaking of somthing Mr. Davenport had deliuered vppon Ephes. 4, 12, concerning personall faith, that if a man lived where he might joyne to the church & did not, it would prove a deluzion to him. Job affirmeth that Mrs. Brewster said, when she heard it her stomacke wombled as when she bredd child, & spake it twise or thrice if not oftner in refference to the sermon. Elizabeth saith, that twise or thrice she spake to that purpose, that she was sermon sicke, & that proceeding in conference she presently said that when she came home she badd her son mak wast pap of it, w[c]h she the said Elizabeth conceiveth was spoken in refference to the noats of Mr. Davenports sermon.

Mrs. Brewster denyed these words, sermon sick, or that it was in refference to the sermon, & those words of making wast paper &c. but confesseth she said her stomack wrought, smelling an ill savo[r] in the seate, wherin she gave noe satisfaction to the court.

3[dly]. Job & Elizabeth affirme that Mrs. Brewster (in conference speaking of scandelous persons,) asked Mrs. Moore whether she had not heard for what Mrs. Eaton was cast out of the church.* Mrs. Moore asked Mrs. Eaton why she did not confesse her sinne, Mrs. Eaton answered she had don it, but not to the churches satisfaction. Mrs. Brewster said if Mrs. Eaton had seene her light before she came into the church she had not come in.

Mrs. Brewster confesseing the former part, saith she remembers not that she spake those words, if Mrs. Eaton had seene

* The reader can learn some of the reasons for which Mrs. Eaton was cast out of the church, (in May, 1645,) by consulting Bacon's Hist. Disc., 296-306.

her light &c; she hath heard that Mrs. Eaton came into the church in a hurrey, and went out in a hurrey.

[148] || 4thly. Job & Elizabeth affirme that Mrs. Brewster speakeing of the contributions said, it was as going to masse or going vp to the high alter, & being asked by Mrs. Moore why she then went to them, she answered, because her husband had comanded her.

Mrs. Brewster denyeth that euer she spake of masse, or high alter in refference to the contributions, the first time she heard of the word alter, applyed that way, was in the seate, Mrs. Lamberton speaking of that text, when thou bringest thy gift to the alter, but she saith Mrs. Moore asked what rule there was for going to the high alter in the contributions, but Mrs. Eaton defended the practise of the church.

5thly. Job saith he heard Mrs. Brewster say that Mr. Fugill being at her howse proffessed vnto her that Mr. Eaton laid one thing to him wch if God should take him away that night, he did not know it to be soe, Mrs. Brewster added they goe two and two together, & writt down what scandelous persons say & soe hurrey them & compare their writeings, & if they find any contradictions they are chardged for lyes. She concluded, I pray God keepe mee from them.

Elizabeth remmembreth that Mrs. Brewster said, Mr. Fugill was chardged by Mr. Eaton wth that he could not remmember nor owne if he should dye, & that shee concluded, God keepe mee out of their hands.

Mrs. Brewster denyeth that euer Mr. Fugill told her, or she to any spake of any thing chardged vppon him by Mr. Eaton wch he could not owne, but in generall, that something was chardged wch he could not owne, & she denyeth all the latter part, going 2 & 2 together, wrighting, comparing, chardging lyes, & her conclussion from thence.

6thly. Job affirmeth that Mrs. Brewster asked Mrs. Leach whether she had any mynd to joyne wth the church, Mrs. Leach answered, noe, Mrs. Brewster asked whether she had not formerly had a mynd, Mrs. Leach answered, yes. Mrs. Brewster replyed, yor mother is a weoman of wisdom, this she doubled, yor mother is a weoman of wisdome, adding. she can teach you well enough at home. Elizabeth remembreth the question put to Mrs. Leach wth her answere as before, & that Mrs. Brewster replyed, her mother could teach her, or tutor her well enough at home, or words to that purpose.

Mrs. Brewster saith she told Mrs. Leach she had heard she was about to joyne wth the church but now declyned it. Mrs. Leach answered, (as formerly to Mrs. Wackman or some other of the church,) it was because she fownd soe manny vntruthes among them, but Mrs. Brewster denyeth that shee said her mother was a weoman of wisdom & could teach her at home.

7thly. Elizabeth saith that Mrs. Brewster being asked by Mrs. Moore whether she saw the persons whipped for their vnnaturall filthjnesse about a month since, she answered noe, but they were cruelly whipped & that her son said he had rather fall into the hands of Turks, & hath rather be hanged then fall into their hands.

Mrs. Brewster denyeth that euer she spake of cruelty in their punishment, she rather thought they deserved more, & that the censure was mercyfull, nor euer did she heare her son speake of falling into the hands of Turks, though he spake somthinge pytying them that were first corrected & that if he were fit for death, he would rather be hanged then soe whipped.

[149] || 8thly. Elizabeth saith that onn the fowerth day of the weeke, before Wm Preston was cast out of the church, Mrs. Brewster mett wth some sister of the church betwixt her owne howse & Mr. Leaches, & seing her look sadd, Mrs. Brewster asked her what was the cause. The sister told her some passadges of Wm Prestons miscariadges for which the church was like to proceede against him, Elizabeth sath Mrs. Brewster related this to Mrs. Moore in a scoffing manner, adding in her speech to Mrs. Moore, I looked pittyfully when I spake wth the sister, as if I had bin one of them, which Elizabeth conceiveth she did, to draw from the sister what shee could.

Mrs. Brewster confessed she mett wth Goodie Charles & spake with her, to the purpose the chardge, (in the first part,) importeth, but denyeth the latter part, concerninge scoffeing & lookeing pittyfully, as if she had bin one of them.

Job & Eliz[a] both say, that Mrs. Brewster vsed to laugh & scoffe at all the former passadges they have respectively testified.

9thly. Elizabeth Smith saith, that haveing bin forth & comming in to her Mrs. howse, she heard Mrs. Brewster, speaking lowd to Mrs. Eaton concerninge banishment, say, they could not banish her but by a Gennerall Court, & if it came to that shee wished Mrs. Eaton to come to her & acquaynt her wth her judgment & grownds about baptizing, & she would by them seduce some other weoman, & then she, the said Mrs. Brewster would complayne to the court of Mrs. Eaton & the other weoman should complayne of her as being thus seduced, and soe they would be banished together & she spake of going tõ Road Island.

Mrs. Brewster confesseth the chardge, but saith she spake it in jest & laughing, she was told, foolish & vncomely jesting are sinfull, but to harden one agaynst the truth who already lyeth vnder guilt, may not passe vnder a prtence of jesting.

10thly. Job saith, that the last day of the weeke, being May the 9th, he was called vpp before Mrs. Brewster, Mrs. Moore & Mrs. Leach, at Mr. Leaches howse. Mrs. Brewster told him shee had bin where she had justified herselfe agaynst a great manny of his lyes & added, she would have him & his slutt, you & yor harlott, to the whipping post. Elizabeth saith that she being below in the howse at this time, heard the former words. Mrs. Brewster spake them soe lowd that, (as she conceiveth,) they might be heard into the midst of the streate.

Mrs. Brewster denyed those words, you & yor slutt, you & yor harlott, to the whipping post, in refference to Job Hall. Mrs. Moore & Mrs. Leach being questioned about them, acknowledged such words were spoken, but conceive, yor slutt, yor harlott, were not reffered to Job Hall, but to them the said Mrs. Moore & Mrs. Leach, Elizabeth standing in relation to Mrs. Leach as her servant.

The court thought it scarce probable, the whole speech being continued to Job Hall, that yor slutt, yor harlott should be reffered to others, nor is it likly that Mrs. Brewster should cast any appearance of blame vppon Mrs. Moore and Mrs.

Leach for Elizabeths miscarriadges, as yor slutt, yor harlott seeme to import.

11^{thly}. Elizabeth saith that onn the same day, May the ninth, Mrs. Brewster told her that she went about carrying lyes, to currey fauo^{r} to keepe her whores back from whipping, adding, she would call her nothing but whore and harlott till she had bin whipped and was marryed, then she must call her so noe more, & if the fellow did not come home he must take
[150] his monney || if he can gett it, or els he must take it out in whippinge. Mrs. Brewster further said that Elizabeth told halfe truthes & halfe lyes. Eliz^{a} answered, her halfe truthes will prove whole truthes. Mrs. Brewster replyed, will they so, you brasen facd whore. Elizabeth answered she was greived for her sinne, & desired to be soe all her dayes. Mrs. Brewster said, she had gotten a few of the fine words.

Mrs. Brewster denyed the word whore, she said she called her only harlott, she was told such rayling landguadge was vncomely & sinfull, Micaell the Archangell durst not carry it soe wth the Divell, though he had matter enough against him.

12^{thly}. Job affirmeth that Mrs. Brewster, speaking at Mr. Leaches howse of a conference she had with widdow Potter said, she asked her why she was not received into the church agayne, widdow Potter answered, because she could not leave Edw: Parker, yet if they could shew her a rule for it, she would. Mrs. Brewster added, Parker is not vnder scandall, yet because he gave not satisfaction to the elder, they will not lett y^{m} marry.

Mrs. Brewster acknowledging the substance of this chardge, saith that widdow Potter thought the rule they would hold forth would be against the marrying of him, & she conceiveth she heard either widdow Potter or Edw. Parker say he had bin with the elder, but had not given satisfaction in his account, & therfore thought they would not let him marry her.

Edward Parker & widdow Potter being herevppon demanded, before the Governour, magistrates & eld^{r}s, how they vnderstood the churches proceedings, whether the widdow were kept out because she would not part wth Edward Parker, what reports they had made & to whom.

They both acknowledged severall conferences betwixt Mrs. Brewster and them. Edw. Parker saith he told Mrs. Brewster he did not know whether the church were against the marryadge or not, they did not make the match, nor did they goe about to break it off, but advized them to walke according to rule. Mrs. Brewster wished him to take 2 or 3 witnesses & goe to the magistrates & desire them to marry them, and if they reffussed it, then before witnesses to take one another & goe together. Edw: Parker saith he told her he would not doe soe, yet she pressed the former advize vppon him 2 or 3 tymes. That she also said the widdow should doe well to confesse in a publik meeting that she had done him the said Edward Parker wronge in what she had said of him, when to hold forth repentance she confessed her sinne intreating marryadge with him. He further saith that Mrs. Brewster shewed her dislike of the churches proceedings, & 2 or 3 times wished him to bidd widdow Potter come to her before she came.

Widdow Potter saith that Edw. Parker told her that Mrs. Brewster disliked the churches proceedings & desired to speake with her, after wch widdow Potter going for some anyseeds, & Mrs. Brewster vnderstanding who she was, she bad her sit downe, gave her a cupp of sacke & dranke with her, and as she remembreth, the first question Mrs. Brewster asked was whj she was not received into the church, her answer, (being sometime in a hurrey of sperit & apt to lay blame on the church,) might probably bee, she was kept out of the church because she could not leave Edward Parker, though now she se cause to judge herselfe for it.
[151] || The elders severally and severall times haveing clearly expressed themselues in such manner as might wholy have freed her from such apprehensions, pressing they concluded nothinge in the case, but advized her to attend and submitt to rule when it should be held forth, she saith further that Mrs. Brewster hath often advized her to make an end of the buisinesse with Edw: Parker in the way she had propownded to him, & told her of 2 partyes in the Bay who had don soe, Widdow Potter also acknowledged her fault in tellinge Mrs. Brewster the latter part of a speech of Mr. Malbons,

that if Edw: Parker should hange himselfe at her dore she might have peace in it, but not telling the former speech wh[r]in Mr. Malbon put the weight, the whole speech running thus, that she should keepe close to the rule, and in soe doing she might have peace though he should hange himselfe at her dore; she saith she concealed Mr. Malbons name, but Mrs. Brewster wondrd at her speech as she reported it.

Mrs. Brewster said, Edw: Parker & widdow Potter were hipocrits & she would prove them soe, what they spake was to currey favo[r] that she might get into the church againe. She chardged Edward Parker that comminge from the foresaid meetinge, he told her the govern[r], (when he was examjned,) looked wissly vppon him, as if by Mrs. Brewsters confession he had knowne all before, and so drew things out of him, and her mayde being called, spake to the same purpose. Edw: Parker denyed the chardge as it was layd, & the magistrats and ruling elder then p[r]sent cleared the govern[r]. Mrs. Brewster proceeding to perticulers concerning her famylyarity w[th] widdow Potter an excommunicate person, she at first seemed to justifie it, saying her pastour in England admired that none of the sisters went to one Mrs. Bennett, cast out of a neighbour church for obstynacy in erro[r], to reclayme her in a way of love. The Govern[r] answered her pastour was absent, the court knew not what hee had spoken in the case, nor on what grownds, but for her to eate, drinke, & to shew such respect to excomunjcate persons did expressly crosse y[e] rule. Herevpon she denyed she had dranke w[th] widdow Potter. Widdow Potter in court affirmed it, & added Mrs. Brewster drank to her. Mrs. Brewster said she dranke not though she put the cupp to her mouth, she asked whether any of the sacke went downe, widdow Potter said, from her carryadge & outward appearance she app[r]hended she drunke, but could not say what quantity went downe. Mrs. Brewster herein gave much offence to the court, but she proceeding said, she disliked not the churches proceedings, but had wished Parker & widdow Potter to attend rule, and for the councell she gave them that they should goe to the magistrates, & before witnesse desire to be marryed, & if the magistrats refussed, then before witnesses to take one another & goe together, she said she spake it in jest & laughed when she spake. Edward Parker confessed she laughed, but said she pressed it vppon him two or three times. Widdow Potter affirmed the same & that she gave instance in a couple in the Bay who had don soe. The court could not allow her answer in poynt of truth, the evidence was stronge agaynst her that notwithstanding any laughing or smyling contenanc, the advize was seriouslie given & pressed vppon the partyes severally & uppon each of them severall times, & sett onn from an instance in the Bay.

[152] ||Mrs. Brewster was also chardged that contrary to an expresse & knowne order made by Newhaven Gennerall Court, she had retayled wyne both out of dores by forbidden small parcells, & had suffred workmen & others to sit drinking wyne by pyntes and quarts within her howse. She answered it was when there was noe other wyne in towne, & divers were either sicke or hadd neede of it. She was answered, she might have sold a butt or lesse quantity to Goodman Andrewes who was intrusted to retayle & must be accomptable had there bin any disorder, she replyed he could not make pay to her content. She added that Mr. Goodyeare, Mr. Malbon & Mr. Evance, who are of the court, sent to her for small parcells, she hoped they would not lay snares for her. Mr. Goodyeare denyed that he had sent for small parcells. Mrs. Brewster said his wife had don it. Mr. Malbon & Mr. Evance answered, they had broken noe order in sending & were not willing to send for more then they must needs, on her termes. It was chardged that she had vsed her howse as a taverne, suffringe company to come in & spend their money in drinking wine by quarts & pints, she said she had suffred none so but her workmen, she was answered, she might not suffer workmen so to drincke, but her answere was not true, as would bee proued if there were cause, but she seemed to fall vnder it.

Mr. Malbon informed the court that Mrs. Brewster had said she would prove him a lyar, which he hoped she could not doe.

Mrs. Brewster said what she spake was because Mr. Malbon came to her howse and chardged her with things he could not prove, Mr. Malbon affirmed the matter was true, if there were any mistake in circumstances, it was not cleare whether the mistake were in him or Jonathan Rudd.

Edw: Parker said he could take oath Mrs. Brewster said she would prove Mr. Malbon a lyar, w[c]h being spoken against a magistrate, without a call, in a whisping way, besides the refference to the ninth commandement, is an offensive, sinfull miscariadge, against the fift commandement, but Parkers oath was not required.

Mrs. Brewster being asked what further she had to say either for herselfe or against the witnesses, shee was full of speech, offered to take hold of the witnesses & to draw them to her, as if she would have over-ruled their testimony; she was told meeknesse & modesty would better become her in such a place. In anythinge she doubted or denyed, the court would tak noe evidence but vppon oath, she seemed to chardge the court as if she could not be heard, but being reprooued for such boldnesse contrary to truth, she fell to justifie herselfe that she approved Mr. Davenports ministry. If some one tyme he had not expressed himselfe so clearly and fully as at others she propownded questions for his information, and at last, going to Mr. Davenports, she was fully satisfied. She denyed that euer she vsed the words sermon sicke, or masse, or high alter, in refference to the contributions. She confessed she had rather have given twice as much in a private way to pastour or teacher, she went because her husband commanded her, yet afterwards she expresly denyed that her husband had commanded her.

[153] ||Dyvers witnessing against her therein, she would have wound herselfe out of the contradiction by saying her husband allowed her to goe, then that her husband wished her to goe, but she gave noe satisfaction.

Then she laded the witnesses with reproach that she might disable their testimony, all of them were lyars, Job by his lying had bin the death of Mrs. Leach her child, w[c]h, (she not being able to prove,) was accounted a rash or false chardge. She saith he was taken in two lyes about her beinge sermon sicke, wch he had after denyed, and that Mrs. Malbon had bin the occassion of his sinne in telling lyes out of dores. Job denyed the chardge of lying. Mr. Godfrey being called to it, vppon oath testified, that Job had said he had sinned in reporting things out of the famyly, but Mrs. Malbon had sinned more in drawing them from him. Job answered that looking on himselfe as the accuser, he was one while discouradged from complayninge to the magistrate, but being at Mr. Malbons howse & Mrs. Malbon questioning with him about the meeting at Mr. Leeches howse, his owne sperit being then burdened, he then accounted it a call to speak what he had heard, though some doubts after returned.

Arthur Holbridge testified he had heard Mr. Leech speake well of Job, as satisfied wth his service & carryadge. Mrs. Brewster said Elizabeth was a harlott. She accused her also of lyinge, for proofe wherof she brought in Goodwife Elsie, who testified that Elizabeth had said, that would be the last weeke in Mr. Leeches service, Phillip fearing she might hurt herselfe therin, whereas Phillip had spoken nothinge to Mr. Leach or to her. Elizabeth replyed that she spake her owne app^rhensions herin. Mr. Leach witnessed that Elizabeth from the first entrance into his service, was of a crooked disposition, & apt to speake vntruthes, & when himselfe or his wife had called her to account for miscarriadges she would seeme to be affected and promise amendement, but they could never see much amendement in her.

To all wch the Governo^r replyed, that the court would duely proceede against any of the witnesses according to allegation & proofe in due season. In the meane time he propownded to the court whether any thing objected & proved by Mrs. Brewster were of weight against them or any of them in the cause, or whether they would notwithstanding take their testimonyes vppon oath.

W^ch being duely considred, the magistrats & deputjes severally expressed themselves that Mrs. Brewster had proved nothing to disable any of the witnesses, they were therfore to give in evidence severally vppon oath, that the cause might come to a due issue. And accordingly Job Hall & Elizabeth

Smith, Edward Parker & widdow Potter, vppon oath testified all the perticulers they had respectively chardged, in mannr as is before expressed. Only Edward Parker & widdow Potter, though they conceived Mrs. Brewster in her course & carriadge disliked the churches proceedings, yet not remembring she had in soe many words expressed it, gave it not in vpon oath.

[154] Mrs. Moore appearinge was chardged as followeth, vizdt.

Mrs. Brewster before the governor & Mr. Goodyeare, first in a more private way & now in court, in Mrs. Moors presence witnessed, that Mrs. Moore in confference about the churches course in contributions asked what rule there was for going to the high alter.

Mrs. Moore at first denyed that ever she spake such words, yet afterwards seemed to fall vnder the chardge.

Job Hall, servt to Mr. Leach saith, that Mrs. Moore in prayer wth Mr. Leaches famyly saith, Lord thou hast brought vs indeede, indeade into a wildernesse, the wildernesse of Sinaj, where they are in bondadge wth Hagar & her children, but let never a soule of vs, (speaking of the famyly at prayer wth her,) have any fellowshipp with them. She further saith, when Christ assended, he gave gifts to men, some to be apostles, some prophets, some evangelists, some pastors, some teachers, but they are gon through the world & are now assended into heaun. That in opposition, as he conceiveth to Mr. Davenports sermon vpon Ephesians 4, 11 verse, she added that night in prayer, that now pastours & teachers are but the invention of men. That in conference with Mrs. Brewster she said, a vayle is before the eyes of mjnsters and people in this place, & till that be taken away, they cannot be turned to the Lord. He saith further, that Mrs. Moore vseth to expresse content & satisfaction when Mr. Davenport holdeth forth the exellency of Christ in his ministry, but she saith she loveth not to heare him presse for practise.

Elizabeth Smith late servant to Mr. Leach saith, she remembreth the substance of what Job saith & affirmeth, but not all the perticulers. She witnesseth that in prayer Mrs. Moore saith, this people are lik the people at Sinaj vnder bondadge, & prayeth that the Lord would take the vayle from their eyes, (in conference w^{t}h Mrs. Brewster she hath spoken of a vayle before their eyes.) That Christ gave some to be apostles, some profets, some evangelists, some pasto^{r}s, some teachers, & that when he ascended he gave gifts to men. But now pasto^{r}s & teachers are but the inventions of men. It is impossible they should have gifts. & that in the famyly they observe that Mrs. Moore is pleased when Mr. Davenport in his ministry sets forth the exellency of Christ, but she loveth not to heare him presse for practise.

Mrs. Moore denyed the chardge.

Thomas Kimberly saith that he being in conference with Mrs. Moore, she asked him what rule they had for church officers now, he answered from Ephesians 4, 11 v. that pastors & teachers are appoynted for the work of the ministry, & that Christ hath promised his presence & blessing to them therin, Math: 28. 20. v. Mrs. Moore replyed Christ was with the apostles to the end of the world, his promise is fulfilled & ceaseth, she told him he did depend on the interp^{r}tac̄on of men. Tho^{m} Kimberly asked her whether she tooke the end of the world in that promise to refferre only to the places through w^{c}h they should travayle, she answered yes, or to that purpose. Thomas Kimberlye sayinge he vnderstood it to be an incouradgement to the apostles & to those that should succeede them in the teaching offices till Christ should come, she agayne told him he did depend on mens interp^{r}tations, adding, I warr^{t} you take the angells to be men & church officers, he answered he did take those angells mentioned Revel-
[155] lation, chapt. 2^{d} & chapt. 3^{d} to be men ||and officers to the seaven churches of Asia; she a third time told him he tooke the interp^{r}tation of men. She quoted that scripture, He hath made his angells ministring sperits, & for exposition & confirmation, alleadged that of Christ, a sperit hath not flesh & bones; it could not therfore, (she said,) be spoken of men as officers to those churches, and added, if he could shew her owne place of scripture for it she would beleive. Tho^{m}

Kimberly advized that if, out of tendernesse of conscience, she scrupiled these things, she should attend the best light; the priests lipps should preserve knowledge &c. She answered in a great rage, she would goe to none of them all for any truth of her salvačon, she was as cleare as the sunne in the firmament, & if he were not soe, she would speake noe more with him. After this Thom Kimberly went agayne to deale with her about her error in the poynt of church officers, but she drew backe & would not heare him, giveinge only this answer, if she were in an error it was to herselfe, he had noe authoritye to examine her about it.

Mrs. Moore denyed that euer she said, pastors & teachers are the inventions of men, she told Thom Kimberly she would conceale her judgmt. She acknowledged Christ was present with the apostles in their travayls to the end of the world, according to Mathew 28. 20. v. but for any other meaninge she dependeth not on mens interpretations, and she conceived those angells of the 7 churches to bee sperits, & not teaching officers. She alleadged Psalme 104. 4. & Hebrewes 1. 7. 14. v. Thom Kimberly said, he had told her there were 2 sorts of angells, some sperits, some in flesh, Mrs. Moore, said he, pished at it.

The Governor told Mrs. Moore she was full of error notwithstanding ye scripturs, Angell is a name of office, signyfies messengrs, & may be applyed either to those glorious sperits his messengrs. Psalm 104. 4. or to men whom God imployes in such service, as in the Revellation. Christ was indead with his apostles in their worke through all their travells, & they travelled farr, yet could not goe into euery part or country of the world, probably they were never in this lardge tract & part of the world, called America. The promise is therfore of a lardger extent, that he would bee with them & their successors, such as in all ages & places he should imploy & send vppon the great messadge & buisjnesse of mans salvatiō to the end of the world; had she kept her error to herselfe, herselfe only had bin hurt, but it is not to be suffered that she should blaspheame & revyle the holy ordynanses of Christ & the church & people of God, that she should, as much as in her lyeth, by spreadinge her erro'^rs corrupt others & disturb the peace of the place.

Mrs. Moore againe denyed the chardge, & perticulerly that euer she said, pasto'^rs & teachers were the inventions of men. She affirmed herselfe to be a member of a church, she was asked of what church, but made noe reply. She was told that by three witnesses it is affirmed she had vppon severall tymes, & vppon severall occassions said, that pastours & teachers are the inventions of men, & against one of the witnesses [156] ||she could have noe just exception, he is of approued fidelity, she said Thom Kimberly had revyled her, but though demanded, shewed not wherein. Thom Kimberly denyed it, & Mrs. Leach, daughter to Mrs. Moore, who had bin present at their conference, beinge asked, said, she knew noe such thinge. Herevppon Leiut Godfry who had lodged & dyeted at Mr. Leaches, & was brought in (this court) as a witnesse concerning Job Hall, was asked what he heard Mrs. Moore say about pastors & teachers. He affirmed that in opposition to Mr. Davenport, Mrs. Moore, in his hearinge, had said, that all those to whom Christ gave gifts are dead, & that now pastours & teachers are the inventions of men. Mrs. Moore asked him where she spake it, he answered, she spake it in Mr. Leaches parlour.

Mrs. Moore was told that the evydence was full & perticuler, & suffitient to convince her, yet since she seemeth not satisfyed, the court, (as in such cases,) would require oath, & accordingly Leiut. Joseph Godfrey, Thom Kimberly, Job Hall & Eliza Smith, vppon oath testified what they had severally affirmed.

Mrs. Moores daughter Mrs. Leach, being chardged, that vppon a question or conference about joyning with this church, she had said to Mrs. Brewster, (as formerly to Mrs. Wackman or some others of the church,) that she somtime had a mynd to joyne, but now declyned it, because she fownd so manny vntruthes amonge them.

The Governr asked what she said to the chardge, she readyly owned it, confessing she had said soe. Being demanded what moued her to lay such a slanderous reproach vppon a church of Christ desiring to walke vprightly, & to goe from one to another with such a slaunder, she boldlye answered. She was told it was a cleare evidence of the churches integryty, that they could not beare with them that are evill, that as they are able they keepe their watch, exhort & censure according to rule, that vppon such a grownd any might have declyned Christs famyly, because there was a theife, a divell in it, & might have reproached that primitive pure church at Jerusalem, because Ananias & Saphira were fownd out & punished for lyinge. Such discoverys & censures did & ought to restrayne the presumption of hipocrites, but beleivers were the more added, and the people saw cause to magnifye such a church, Acts 5, 13, 14.

Mrs. Leach neither excussed nor replyed, but as guilty seemed to take the weight of the chardge vppon herselfe, & continueing in Court, spake vncomly for her sex & age, and once falsly chardged the witnesses with contradiction, when there was noe appearance or disagreement betweene them, soe that her carryadge offended the whole court.

These 3 causes being thus opened, & proofe thus made, were all ready for censure, but vpon consideration of the nature & weight of the offences, the magistrates & deputyes conceived they were all proper for a higher court. By order therfore sentence was respited & refferred to the court of magistrates for the jurisdiction.

[157] || Edward Parker was complayned of for going vp & downe spreading false reports to the defamation of Mr. Richard Malbon, Magistrate, in saying that greater then Wm Preston lately cast out of the church for lyeing, should shortly be called in question for neglecting to take knowledge of the drunckenesse of the boatswayne of the Adventure, and saying vnto him the next day after, that he would not for tenn pownds any had seene him as he did the last night. And this he reported vnto Robert Emery & Mary Emery his wife, who lived at Mr. Malbons farme & now testified the same in court. Wheras in truth, as was testified by Mr. Malbon, he seeing him the night spoken of runne in hast & it being darke, did

not thinke whom it was till he was past h^m^, & to his observation he reeled as he went, but soe soone as he saw h^m^ the next day, he asked him whether he mett him not, & in what case was he in, the boatswayne answered, in good case. Mr. Malbon replyed that if he did miscary in this place he would feele the smart of it. But the former report being spread by Edw. Parker who said he was told so by Jonathan Rudd, who was told so by the boatswayne & he told Samuell Daighton. Mr. Malbon going to cleare it to Jonathan Rudd, Jonathan Rudd afterward told Edw: Parker Mr. Malbon went to cleare h^m^selfe, but to abase h^m^. But Mrs. Brewster hearing of it, Edw. Parker said, I had rather be questioned by any boddy then her, for she hath a notable patte.

Furth^r^, Edw. Parker going to Mrs. Turn^r^s from Mr. Malbons where he had killed a very fatt oxe, tells Mrs. Turner that Mr. Gregson was playne downright, but Mr. Malbon kept the best & gave the seamen the worst of his oxe, Mrs. Turner questioning him about it the day following, he told her she was a cunning weoman. But Mr. Goodyeare testified, the worst bit of that was better then the best of most. Mr. Malbon testified the oxe had bin two yeares a fatting, and haveing filled his tubbs, he was contented to spare the seamen of that wch was left, & after the boatswayne had seene it he said he would have it, but he never did as Edw. Parker reported, by his faire tongue prevayled wth them to take it. Goodm^n^ Walker testified that he went into the cellar wth the boatswayne to shew him the meate, & did shew himselfe willing in his hearing to have it.

Mary Pery testified that they were told that if they liked it not they should leave it, & that she had had some of the shoulder & it was very good meate.

Edw. Parker fell vnder that speech of his wherin he had said Mr. Malbon by his faire tongue had prevayled with them to take the beefe, & for his defam̄ing of him, & by his false reports seekeing to take away his good name, as the breach of the 5th and ninth commandem^ts^, submitted himselfe to the court. The centence of the court was that he should pay five pownds as a fine to Mr. Malbon for his defameing of him, &

be imprisoned the courts pleasure. Mr. Malbon informed the court, vppon Edw. Parkers petition to the court for release from imprisonm[t] and further acknowledgm[t] of his evill w[t]h more answerable affection, that he would not inrich h[m]selfe in this way, but remitted freely the fine, & the court freely released him from his imprisonment, vpon hopes of this being a warning to him how he transgresse in the lik kind, for if he did, it would not passe so easylje.

Phillip Galpin and Elizabeth Smith,* standing guilty of fornication and defyling themselues, w[c]h was the breach of the 7[th] commandement, both fully acknowledged it & their sinne in it, & expressed their sorrow for it. The centence of the court was, that both of them should be publiquely whipped, Phillip at present, & Elizabeth being now w[t]h child, the execution of the centence was respited vntill she was deliuered.

[158] || Samuell Swayne complayned of Mr. Mullyner for neglecting of traynings, watchings & bringing of his armes when it was his turne one the Lords days.

Mr. Mullyner acknowledged he had neglected it & pleaded he had not done it in Newhaven nor in the Bay, but for what has bin done by him he submitts to the court & promiseth amendement. Samuell Swayne desired the jugment of the court for the time that is past, & that he be ordred for the time to come. The court agreed that he doe the service for the time to come, & for what is past the court will further consid[r] of it. Samuell Swayne desired to know whether all from 16 to 60 should trayne, if they had bine magistrats elswhere. The Courts answer was that it was meete to be respited vntill the next Gennerall Court for the jurisdiction, provided they be all furnished with armes.

Ric[d] Pery, Plant.
Luce Brewster def.

[The remainder of this page and also pages 159 and 160 are blank.]

* In the margin, "Phillip Galpine and his wife."

[161] AT A COURT OF MAGISTRATS HELD FOR NEWHAUEN JURISDICTION JUNE 4th 1646.

Wheras Thomas Fugill vpon complaynts from the genll Court at Newhaven, was two monthes since summoned to this Court of Magistrats to answere severall miscariadges & offenses chardged onn him, but then through indisposition of boddy, (as was proffessed,) he could neither appeare nor give an answere as the case required, and since, the said Thom Fugill hath bin selling off part of his goods & hath expressed some purpose of a voiadge or remove; vpon a motion made this day by Mr. Wackman, the court sent Mr. Francis Newman and Mr. Gibbard to the said Thom Fugill requiring him, either by himselfe or by his deputy, to make his defence, & had this returne from him, that being still payned in his head, he could neither appeare personally, nor was he prepared to answere by any other, if the court would proceede he should submitt, but wished them to looke to their evidence; wch answer was thought overbold & vncomly for a man vnder such apparent guilt. It is therfore ordered, and by this Court hee is required, that he neither proceede further in sale of his goods or estate, nor remove from the plantation, till (as before) he either answere the court of magistrats, or Newhaven court, wth such magistrats as they shall call in to asist them, for his severall miscarriadges, if hee doe otherwise, the court shall take it as a contempt and proceede accordinglie.

AT A COURT HELD AT NEWHAUEN THIS 7th JULY, 1646.

James Steward for a defective worme & scourer was fined 5s, he haveing deluded the officers wth another mans armes when his owne were defective.

Mathew Row for haveing a foule gunne was fyned 1s. Mr. Peirce wanting a rest fined 1s.

Roger Knap for wanting bullets, scourer, belt & rest, fined 5s.

Edw. Parker defective gun & touchole fined 1s. Robert Preston defective guñe & wanteing a scourer fined 2s.

Jn° Benham for a foule locke fined 1s. Edw. Chipfeild haveing a foule lock, wanting a pownd of bulletts, haveing often vsed meanes to have bin better provided was fined 1s.

Jn° Kimber wanting bullets fined 1s. Wm Pert haveing a foule gune & wanteing a new touch-hole was fyned 1s.

Ricd Newman, Fran: Browne, Robert Vsher, Wm Bassett & Thom Beech for their defects in their guns, fyned 1s a peice.

Geo. Banks fined 1s for want of a belt.

Sam. Wilson defective cock of his peece, & his bandeliers wanteing covers was fined 5s.

Benjamin Wilmott defective sockett & bullets, fined 1s.

Jam. Heywood wanting match, fined 1s. Mihill Palmer wanting worme & scourer, fined 1s.

John Morse beinge bidd to walke the rownds on a Lords day, came into the meeting howse & stayed there, so that the service was neglected, fined 10s.

James Steward was complayned of for severall disorderly expressions and contempt of the magistracye in this place.

James Steward haveing bin prest by Mr. Malbon for to help mend some of the towne highwayes, vpon the intreaty of Mr. Newman & Mr. Crayne, hee at first grumbled at it, at length said he would chuse his time if he went, however vnwilling he was to goe, although others had expressed themselues willing as much strejtned as himselfe, but being told that if he went not it would bee accomted a contempt, then he said he had noe tooles. Mr. Tuttle tendred the lending of him tooles, provided he would make them good, his answere, as Mr. Tuttle testified, was that he would not come into their claues or pawes.

James Stewards answere was that he being charged by Mr. Malbon to attend the service, he wondred whj himselfe more then other freemen should bee pressed, but howsoever, he sought for Luk Atkinson to have gon in his roome, but he would not mak good tooles, but he intended seing he could not get Luk, to have gon, but it rayned.

John Coop being wth Mr. Tuttle one morning at the gate, James Steward came along wth his cattle, & said what must I help you work? then Jn° Coop said, you must help the towne.

James answered he was vnsetled & wanted tooles, Mr. Tuttle offred h^{m} tooles, but if he brak them he should mak them good, he said noe he would not nor come in their pawes or clawes, wherevpon Mr. Tuttle told him he must make good the tooles. Jno Coop added, wh^{n} it left rayning oth^{r}s came, as Jno Kimber & others, but not himeself, & next day would not, could not, if had not 6^{s} p day, & he told Roger Knap he was a foole to goe so easylie.

[162] || The centence of the court was, that for his contempt of the surveyo^{r}s, magistrate & magistracy, he should pay five pownd as a fine, & be imprisoned the courts pleasure.

Edw. Parker & his wife p^{r}sented their desires to the court to invest Jno Potters two sons in the right of their fathers land & howse, & declared themselues willing to bestow a hejfer of a yeare old on Hannah, & deliuer it presently for her vse, & so to be improved as a stock for her, &c. as ꝑ a perticuler writting in the hand of the secrettarie, made & signed by both of them before the governour, deputy governour, & magistrate.

Pawquash a Quillipiock Indian was first complayned of for leaveing open the Oystershelfeild gate, & damadge being done therby refussed to give any satisfaction.

Secondly, he about 4 years since came into Mr. Craynes howse when they were blessing God in the name of Jesus Christ; and that he then did blaspheamously say that Jesus Christ was mattamoy & naught, & his bones rotten, & spake of an Indian in Mantoises plantation assended into heaven, w^{c}h was witnessed by Mr. Crayne, Mrs. Crayne, Mrs. Ling, Wm Holt, Goodie Camp. The centence of the court was the he should be searverly whipt for thus scorning at o^{r} worshipping God & blaspheame the name of our Lord Jesus, & informed h^{m} that if he should doe soe hereafter or now, it had bin against the light he now has, it would hazzard his life. And for the damadge by meanes of the gats being left open, he was to pay 5^{s} to Tho^{m} Knowels.

Thomas Fugill appearing now before the court, was first desired to give answere to the court whj he had soe long held them vnder delayes; his answer was, that it was true he had bin sent for oft, but although it might be conceived he was able to come, yet his boddyly weaknesse was such & soe great that it hindred him, & that once he attempted to put forth nature to the vtmost & he had smarted for it.

Secondly, he being sent for the last court of magistrats sitting, & he returned this answer by Mr. Fran: Newman & Mr. Gibbard, that if they pleased to pceede, he was not prepared but wisht them look to their evidence, wch was thought too bould an answer; he denyed it, wherevpon Mr. Fran: Newman & Mr. Gibbard informed the court it was truth, & that they were far from making the most of it, for they told not wth what frame of sperit he expressed himselfe.

Thirdly, that after an order left wth you, made by the court of magistrates, wherin hee was ordred to sell nothing vntil he had attended the court, yet he had gon about to sell somthing since, wch he acknowledged true, he had treated wth old Goodman Wilmott about some swyne.

Fourthly that this day he sends a noate to the court, & cometh not himselfe nor sends a deputy. Thomas Fugill answered he was vnder two heavye sensurs. First, the losse of his place, 2dly, the centence of excom̄unjcation. And for the vnrighteousnesse he stands chardged wth, in taking in & detayning of land vnder the West Rocke wch was not his owne, but the townes, he said he did it not wth any intent to deceive the towne, & that land was not judged worth more then 12d an acre. Secondly for the chardge of falsifyinge orders, he expected not to have bin questioned about it, therfore he is not provided for it. He being asked by Capt. Astwood, why he was not prpared to give answer to the 2d thing, he answered he vnderstood not; and added, he did not add those words in the great book chardged to be don by hm, since Mr. Cheevers read the order, however he fayled in putting in, wthin the 2 myles, & said he neur said to any, it was a bowndlesse ordr, because it is said, as much as he desires.

The plantifs desired the court the overplus of land might returne to the towne, & his proportion kept wthin the two rivers & wthout the two myles.

[163] The centence of the court was, ||that for his vnwrighteousnesse in taking in & detayning of the townes land, and

falsifyeing of orders, & his contempt of the court, Thomas Fugill should pay 20^{l} fine to the towne, and that the land be reduced to its dew bownds, according to the first grant, namely, betweene the two rivers and w^{t}hout the two myles.

It was ordred vpon Edward Hitchcocks informing of the court that the time was out that he was to enjoy Goodman Budds meddow, Mr. Francis $Newm^{n}$ & John Cooper be vallued what the grasse is worth & that it be accounted for in rates.

AT A COURT HELD ATT NEWHAVEN THE 4th AUG. 1646.

Henry Lindoll informed the court that Wm Ball had told him that his peice was chardged, & he blowing through it, went & knoct it, & out came 4 bulletts, but he fownd noe powder. Jerymy & Thomas Osborne affirmed that there was noe powder seene to come out of the peice. Richard Fydo informed the court that Wm Ball told him laughingly, that he knew there was noe powder in his gune.

For w^{c}h guilfull carriadge of his & vntruth vnto the m^{r} of the watch, Wm Ball was fined 40^{s} & to pay the chardges of them that have attended vpon the court.

Whereas Benja: Hill, $form^{r}$ly warned to the court & appearing not, was entred a contempt, the m^{r}shall not being cleare he gave him meete warning, the contempt was taken of, & he fined for his defective scourer 6^{d}.

Ric^{h} Perys action w^{t}h $Goodm^{n}$ Bishopp was refferred vntil next court.

Joseph Brewster absent on a trayning day, was fyned 5^{s}, & for want of a worme & scourer 12^{d}.

Jno Thomas, gun being defective, was fined 1^{s}.

Wm Blayden complayned of by the m^{r}shall for nonepayment of his fines, it was ordred that he pay them by the next court, & if he did not a stresse should be made.

Mr. Joshuah Atwatter desired the justice of the court about some nayles that Tho^{m} Robinson had stole from the shipp, viz^{d} $16^{lb}\ \frac{1}{2}$ at 8^{d} ℘ ^{lb}. Ordred by y^{e} court that 11^{s} more then the nayles bee stopt in the treasurers hands vntil hee shew cause to the contrary.

The mrshall informed the court that he had sent vnto Geo. Ward for his fyne & his answere was, that for the present he knew not or could not tell what answere to send. It was ordred he should be warned to attend the next court.

AT A GENll COURT HELD AT NEWHAVEN THIS 16th AUG. 1646.

Brother Benham & bro. Glover had liberty to dept the court.

The former order about swine was confirmed.

A protest from the Dutch Governour* was read in court, &

---

*" The protest came in Lattyn, the contents in English are as followeth,

Wee Willyam Kieft, Genrall Director, & the Senate of New Netherland, for the high & mighty Lords the States of the United Belgicke Provinces for his excellency the Prince of Orange & for the most noble Lords the Administratrs of the West India Company, To thee, Theophilus Eaton, Gournor of the place by us called the Red Hills in New Netherland, (but by the English called New Haven,) we give notice, That some yeares past, yours, without any occasion given by us, & without any necessity imposed upon them, but wth an unsatiable desire of possessing that wch is ours, against our ptestacons, against the lawe of nations, & against the antient league betwixt the kings matie of Great Brittaine & our Superiors, have indirectly entred the lymits of New Netherland, usurped diurs places in them & have beene very injurious unto us, neither have they given satisfaction though oft required. And because you & yours have of late determined to fasten your foote neere Mauritius Ryver in this Province, & there not onely to disturbe our trade of noe man hitherto questioned, & to drawe it to yrselves but utterly to destroy it, we are compelled againe to ptest & by these prsents we doe ptest against yu as aginst breakers of the peace & disturbers of the publique quyet, that if yu doe not restore the places yu have usurped & repaire the losse we have suffered, we shall by such meanes as God affoards, manfully recour them, neyther doe we thinck this crosseth the publique peace, but shall cast the cause of the ensuing evill upon you. Given in Amsterdam Fort Aug. 3. 1646. new stile.

WILLYAM KIEFT.

" The answer was returned in Lattin to the sayd ptest, the contents as followeth,

To the Right Worll Wm Kieft, Gournor of the Dutch in New Netherland,

Sr. By some of yrs I have lately receaved a ptest under yr hand dated August the 3d 1646, wherein yu ptend we have indirectly entred the lymitts of New Netherland, usurped diurs places in them, & have offered you many inuries; thus in genrall & in reference to some yeares past, more particularly to the disturbance, nay to the utter destruction of yr trade, we have lately set foote neere Mauritius Ryur in that Province.

We doe truly pfesse we know noe such Ryur, neither can we conceave what Ryur yu intend by that name, unlesse it be that wch the English have long & still doe call Hudsons Ryur. Nor have we at any time formrly or lately entred upon any place to wch yu had or have any knowen tytle, nor in any other respect beene inurious to yu. It is true we have lately upon Paugaset Riur, wch falls into the sea in the midst of an answere to the same sent, and directions given to them that keep the trading howse. And it was fully & satisfyeingly voted, that the court would mak good their titles here, & at the trading howse, & leave the issue of things to God, whateuer they may bee.

Nehemiah Smith's request was read, viz[d].

These are the propositions I thought meete in wrighting to propownd to yo[r] worp[s], vpon w[ch] I desire land,

First, that I might have for myne owne propryety 20 acr. of vpland & 10 acr. of meddow.

2[dly], that I might have it vpon that hill where I have made a sheeps penne, of the south side of the hill of Mr. Malbons cove, because the sheepe may have the ayre of the sea in the summer time, lyeing 4 square by reason lesse chardge will fence it.

3[dly], also I desire when the sheepe doe returne, I may have 20 acr. more of vpland, & 10 acr. of meddow, for w[t]hout 20 acr. of meddow I can doe noe good w[th] keepeing the sheepe.

---

these English plantacons, built a small house within o[r] owne lymitts, many miles, nay leagues from the Monhattoes, from yo[r] trading house & from any part of Hudsons Ryu[r], at which we expect little trade, but can compell none. The Indians being free to trade wth y[u], us, Conecticaut, Massachusets or wth any other, nor did we build there till we had first purchased a due tytle from the true proprietors. What inuries & outrages in our psons & estates, at the Manhattoes, in Deleware Ryu[r], &c. we have receaved from y[u], o[r] form[r] letters & protest doe both declare & pve, to all w[ch] y[u] have hitherto given very unsatisfying answers, but whateu[r] o[r] losses & sufferings have beene, we conceave we have neither done or returned any thing, even to this very day, but what doth agree wth the lawe of God, the lawe of nations, & wth that antient confederacon & amity betwixt o[r] superiors at home. Soe that we shall readily refer all questions & differences betwixt y[u] & us, even from first to last, to any due hearing, examination & iudgemt, either heere or in England, & by these psents we doe refer them, being well assured that his Ma[tie], o[r] Sou[r]aigne Lord Charles, King of Great Brittayne & the Parlyament of England now assembled will mayntaine their owne right & our iust lyberties against any whoe by uniust incrochemt shall wrong them or theirs, and that yo[r] owne principles, upon a due and mature consideracon, will alsoe see & approve of the righteousnes of o[r] pceedings.

New Haven in Newe England T. EATON.
Aug. 12th 1646. ould stile."

Records of the United Colonies, Sept. 1646.

Van der Donck, as cited by O'Callaghan, Hist. N. Netherland, i. 375, says in allusion to this post, "The English of New Haven have a trading post on the east or southeast side of Magdalen Island, not more than six (Dutch) miles from the North River; for this island lies towards the upper part of the North River, twenty-three (Dutch) miles and a half higher up than Fort Amsterdam, on the east bank." Magdalen Island is on the east side of Hudsons River a little below Redhook, upper landing, Dutchess county, N. Y.

Also that it may be the hithermost of the Oyster River, & y[t] I may cutt timber for fenceinge vpon the common, by reason there is litle timber besides walnut vpon that land.

[164] ||This being granted, I shall doe what I am able for the keepeing the townes sheepe & the good of them. This I desire may be granted as speedyly as may bee, that I may provide for them against they come.

Nehemiah Smith.

The abovesaid request of Nehemiah Smith was granted to him according to his propositions in the close of his wrighteing if it be accepted.

It was ordred that the surveyour should runne the lyne on this side Mr. Davenports farme, from the stone, east & by south 120 gr. parrallell to the other.

Mr. Davenport propownded that men would sow one & the same grayne in their quarters, w[c]h was respited.

Mr. Gibbard & Mr. Francis Newman informed the court, that for Mr. Gregson's & Mr. Wackmans quarters highway to their meddowe, w[c]h is in that place called Mr. Malbons meddow, the way vnder the rocke they apprehend is best & meetest, although not without inconveyniency to the subburbs quarter, & deviding their lands, w[c]h was respited to further consideration.

At a Court held at Newhaven the 1 Sept. 1646.

Bro: Edw: Wigglesworth hath sould his howse & home lott vnto Samuell Wilson.

Mr. Francis Newman hath sold his howse & home lott, 13 acr. vpland w[t]hin two myle, & 4 acr. meddow vnto John Herryman.

Bro: W[m] Fowler informed the court that his bro. John Caffinch had taken vpp a horse of his & did denny to deliuer him vnto him, but said it was his. W[m] Fowler brought Mr. Pell, bro. Myles, Rich[d] Marden & Mr. Gilbert, who informed the court they tooke that horse to bee W[m] Fowlers, vppon severall grownds.

Mr. Caffinch affirmed the horse was his, and brought Mr. Newman, Ric[d] Smolt, John Guernsie and Jn[o] Downe to informe the court that the horse was Mr. Caffinches vppon severall grownds, w^t^h much confidence ; at length it was respited vntill further light, none of either syde being cleare enough to make oath.

Richard Marden being fownd asleepe at the watch-howse dore fyned 5^s^.

Hen. Bishop haveing in court chardged Ric^d^ Pery with takeing a false wrighteing from Goody Ball & presented it in court, w^c^h Ric^d^ Pery apprehended a slander.

Richard Pery said that at his first goeing, he writt the wrighteing mixed w^t^h some characters, & writt it as his owne words, but his father* desiring him to wright it out playne & considering that she related the story as Susans, he then write it as Susans, & then he went againe & desired Goody Ball to set her hand to it; he pulled out the wrighteing & began to read, & desired her to deale truly, for somthinge shee told him concerning her bro. Russell, he fownd was not soe. Goody Ball propownded a question, is such a thing in; what it was he had forgott, but he told her it was nott. Saith Henry Bishop, is it not? then I will say the wrighteing is not true.

Goody Ball saith that that w^c^h was left out of the wrighteing was, that Mrs. Eaton denyed, & he writ she had not done it.

Further Ric^d^ Pery said he did not present the wrighteing to the court, but left it at ho^m^, as he told his wife he would, & that because he would not lay himselfe vnder a temptacon, & he said, indeed last court he had it in his pockett, but it was his erro^r^ & mistake.

The Go^r^ said, Hen: Bishopp, the theing is whether you made a right chardge in saying he presented a false wrighteing to the court.

Hen. Bishop said he should prove that he said he had a pap in his hand & said, here is her testimony. Goody Ball testified that when she was speakeing Mr. Pery had a pap in his hand & said here is her testimony, I took from her mouth.

---

*i. e. Mr. Malbon.

Mrs. Brewster said when Goody Ball was about to speak, Mr. Pery said, (haveing a pap in his hand,) here is her testimony. Mrs. Russell saith to the best of her remembrance, when her sister was speaking, Mr. Pery said, here is her testimony, holding vp a pap in his hand. Mr. Cheevers said there were such passadges of Mr. Pery in court. John Nash said he was in the court & neare Mr. Pery, & I saw not nor heard such words of Mr. Pery. But the Go[r] said thus to Goodm[n] Bishop vpon his speech, why doe you say soe, seing there is noe pap p[r]sented *presented* to the court. And there was noe reply made.

[165] ||The second part of the chardge was, Goody Ball saith that Mr. Pery writ that Mrs. Eaton had not lyen w[th] the Governour, when he should have writ that she denyed as she said. Allen Ball saith that at Mr. Pery's second cōming he said that he had said it to severall that Mrs. Eaton denyed to lye w[th] the Gov[r]n[r], but that would nothing advantadg Mrs. Brewster. Dorithy Ball saith that Mr. Pery said, he would not denny that he said she denyed to lye, but if any said that he said she denyed conjugall fellow[p], he must have put y[m] to prove it.

A wrighteing taken by Mr. Malbon from Allen Ball was read in court.

Before they took oath the Governour told them the waight of an oath & wished them to be wary in it. Vpon some speech of Mr. Pery's, the elder & Mr. Cheevers were sent to Mrs. Malbon* & Mrs. Malbon, to know if they had anything to except against the witnesses. They returned this answere. Mrs. Pery gives two reasons why her oath may [not be tak[n], first because she did not deliuer it so in court, 2[dly] because she hath heard she will affirme a thing & deny it againe presently.

The court declared that they saw not that in what had binne said w[ch] should hinder their testimonys, although Mrs. Malbon hath jealouzyes that she will speak vntruth, yet can prove nothing to disable her testimony.

---

* A slip of the recorder's pen for "Mrs. Pery," as the context shews.

Allen Ball testified vppon oath, that his wife & Susan & Mr. Pery, being in the pynace, they were speakeing they m^r^velled such reports were in the Bay about Mrs. Eaton, his wife answered she thought they were false; saith Susan, Mrs. Eaton would not lye w^t^h her husband since she was admonished, but caused her bedd to be removed to another roome. but Mr. Pery writ, they lay apt, & left out, she refused, as his wife had said. And this he acknowledged afterward.

Dorithy Ball testified vpon oath, that Susan said that Mrs. Eaton would not lye with the governour since she was admonished, but caused her bedd to be removed into another roome; so she told Mr. Pery, & he write they lay apart & left out she denyed, & acknowledged when she came afterward that he had left out refuse, & writ lay apart.

The centence of the court was that the cause must goe against Mr. Pery, & he must pay the chardge of the court & the damadge of Hen: Bishop's attendance & his witnesses, w^c^h the court conceives from Henry Bishopps owne words to be 10^s^. Allen Ball saith that the first time Mr. Pery was not chardged w^t^h the thing in refference to Susan, but to himselfe, but the second time hee writt it in refference to himselfe.

AT A COURT HELD AT NEWHAVEN THE 6th OF OCTOBER, 1646.

Mr. Wm Tutle & Jeremy Watts complayned off for sleeping at the watch-howse. Mr. Tuttle said he was overcome, & Jeremy being centinell, sat downe onn the threshold & slept, but confesseth his fault & hopes it shalbe the last. Mr. Tutle was fined 2^s^ 6^d^ & Jeremy Watts was fined 5^s^, ye court desiring it may be a warning to them both.

Richard Marden wanting all armes save a sword, was fined 5^s^, he neglecting to vse due care to bee provided.

Samuell Marsh was complayned of for absence two trayning dayes, but he being seeking cowes, it being in the spring, y^n^ catle being lyable to be swampt, it was satisfyeingly passed by.

Allen Ball complayned of for a defective tricker, but it haveing passed so for three years together, & he promjseing to mend it, was passed by. Also he was late on trayning day in the afternoone, he being wth his sister Fugill vpon her depture it was passed by.

Hen. Gibbons, late in the afternoone one trayning day, his answere was his head aked, & he went into the meeting howse, but suddenly came & treyned that afternoone. It was passed by, first because he was not well, 2 because Goodm^{n} Banister & Corp^{ll} Leavermore were intreated by him to wak h^{m}.

Corp^{ll} Leavermore being late one trayning day in the afternoone was fyned 1^{s}. Also totaly absent on a squadron day, w^{c}h was respited.

[166] || Caleb Seaman wanteing armes was fined 10^{s}.

John Sackett & Henry Morrell for wanting rests were fined 6^{d} apeice.

John Speede wanteing worm & scourer, fined 1^{s}.

Henry Gibbons two squadron trayning dayes absent, once fier in the lotts hindred him, for the fier had caught hold onn the fence; the last day he was at Mr. Goodyears farme, for wch he was fined 5^{s}.

Samuell Marsh absent one squadron trayning day, fined 2^{s} 6^{d}.

Ralph Loynes came late to trayning in Aprill, was fined 1^{s}; for the want of a rest he was fined 6^{d}.

Samuell Cabell, Adam Nichols, being warned to the court & not coming themselus nor gave notice of their submission, ordred to be warned against the next court, & then to answere for their contempts.

Edmund Tooly was absent 3 trayning dayes, of w^{c}h 2 of y^{m} he was not well & fined 5^{s} for not comming the third.

Vincent Meggs, absent the 14th of June, was fined 2^{s} 6^{d}, but if he bring proofe that he trayned twice in one fortnight, the fine is to be remitted.

Wm Blayden complayned of for nonpaym^{t} of his fines, he intreating forbearance one month longer, it was given him.

Thomas Blatchley haveing formerly given the court some offence, & neglecting the imadge of God in magistrats, & goeing away soe irreverently and sayeing he would have justice in another place if he had it not here, w^{c}h now lyeing on his conscience, desirs to cleare himselfe, wherewth the court was satisfied.

Samuell Marsh was warned by Mr. Crayne, who had an estat in his hand, & finding him defective in ordring it for either of their comforts desired a hearing of the court; at length when much debate had bin, both did agree to put it vnto arbitration. Samuell Marsh declaring himselfe willing to leave the farme, Mr. Crayne accepted it, & Mr. Crayne chose Anthony Thompson, & Samuell Marsh chose Goodman Myles, wth liberty that if they did not agree, they should chuse an vmpire.

Samuell Daighton, absent one squadron day & one Lords day, fined 3^{s} 6^{d}, if he cannot give satisfyeing answere.

Samuell Cabells lock of his peice being defective, was fined 1^{s}.

Georg Banks, for wanteing a worme & scourer, 1^{s}, absent 3 squadron traynings fined 7^{s} 6^{d} & absent one Lords day fyned 2^{s}, 10^{s} 6^{d} in all.

Goodm^{n} Johnson haveing a lott that was his brothers desired to cleare to the court his proofe for what he possesseth.

John Punderson said he had almost forgott, but Samuell Whithead & he heard Thomas Fugill expresse as ℘ the noate vnder his hand appeareth, viz^{d}.

When Jno Johnson was p^{r}paring to goe to the Bay, he told mee he had sould his howse & accomodations belonging to it, vnto his brother (viz^{d}) Robert Johnson for the 40^{l} he said I knew he received in Old England, vpon condic̃on, that if he should see it his way to come back & live here, then he might have it, paying to his brother the said 40^{l}, & what chardges he should lay out about it, or if hs brother should sell it to come & live in the Bay, 40^{l} of the price he should keepe to himselfe & pay the overplus to him, only deducting his chardges. But if the said John should not returne, & the said Robert his brother should resolve to setle here, then the said Robert Johnson should have it forever, for the said 40^{l}; this is the substance of the agreement as the said John related it to mee, witnesse my hand.

Tho: Fugill.

Bro. Tharpe said his m^{r} said to h^{m} his bro: was to have his howse & lott, but if he returned he was to have it againe, returning to his bro. what he had of him. By all wch, finding as yet the proofe defective, the court determine nothing in the case, wanting further light.

Thom Fugill hath sold 6 acr½ of land in the Necke vnto Robert Johnson, he paying 30s to Geo: Downing & the rest in cartadge, as Allen Ball witnessed and a noat vnder Thom Fugils hand prsented in court by Robert Johnson appeared.

---

[167] AT A GENl COURT HELD THE 7th OF OCTOBER, 1646.

The Governor acquaynted the court that sundry miscariadges by drinke hath bin of late, by whom he cannot come to the true knowledge off & where it hath bin hadd.

Bro. Andrewes propownded that he might lay downe the ordynary.

It was ordred to prevent that excesse of drinkeing, that God may not be dishonered nor religion reproached, that wine & strong watters, *that wyne & strong waters* bee drawne only at the ordynary.

The neglect of finishing the pewes was remembred, & them that should doe them & the chest for the pyks were desired forthwith to dispatch them, that the seating of people may goe forward.

It was propownded that helpe might be affoarded to launch the shipp, for Goodman Paule informed the Governor that the keele would rott if it were not launched before winter. Bro. Leeke had liberty to draw wine for them that work at the shipp.

It was propownded that the marke of swine be brought into the pownder.

It was propownded that Wm Meaker might be loader to mill, & it was ordred that for a 12 month he bind himselfe to goe in all seasons except vnseasonable weather, & further it was ordred that if any cary their owne corne, yet that they carry not for others.

And that before any give over that are chosen to any service of the towne, as to view measures & weights, and sealing leather, others are to be chosen, but vntil then they that are in those imployments are to continew.

Bro. Richard Mansfeild had libertye to dept the court.

Goodman Bassett, Henry & Joseph Peck desired to cutt woods on the common, wch was granted, provided it be according to the approbation of the viewers.

Those that desire land to be layd out to them amongst the small lotts were desired to bring in their names to the secretary.

Edw. Hitchcocke propownded to the court for a dispensation of bringing his armes on the Lords dayes, bec he bringing his children was therby disabled of comming so soone as he ought if at all with them. But it was respited.

It was propownded to the court whether it were their mynds that men should come to traynings or watchings without powder and shott. It was therevpon ordred that every time men come to either, they bring 4 chardges at least of powd^r^ & shott.

Bro. Whitnell & bro. Russell promised to help about the seats in Thom Morris hs roome.

AT A GEN^l^ COURT HELD AT NEWHAVEN THE 26th OCTO. 1646.

Thom Wheeler had leave to dept the court because of some ingadgem^ts^ against ye 4th day next.

Mr. Francis Newman, Mr. Gibbard, Mr. Crayne & Goodm^n^ Gibbs were chosen deputjes for Newhaven monthly courts this yeare ensewinge.

Mr. Jno Wackman, Mr. Ezekiell Cheev^r^s wer chos^n^ deputyes for the jurisdic̃on gen̄erall court.

Mr. Joshua Atwater was chosen treasurer for Newhaven the yeare enseweing.

Richard Pery was chosen secretary for Newhaven the yeare enseweing.

Thom Kimberly was chosen m^r^shall for the yeare enseweing.

The pticuler court of Newhaven, w^t^h Mr. Evance & Mr. Wackman were chosen auditours for the treasurers accompts.

Bro. Davis & bro. Fowler were chosen surveyo^rs of the high-wayes on that side the towne.

Bro. Cooper & bro. Mansfeild chosen survey^rs for the other side of the towne.

Bro. Andrewes & bro. Abrah^m Bell were chosen viewers, that noe spoyle of wood bee made in the commons, also that they look to the tann^rs, that wast be not made of timber by barkeing it which may prejudice the towne.

Bro. Davis & bro Phillip Leek chosen view^rs of measurs, as bushels, &c.

Bro. Francis Newman & Mr. Gibbard chose to look to the waights & licquid measures and yards and ells.

Leiut Robert Seely had liberty of the court to goe for England although a publick officer.

---

[168] AT A COURT OF ELEXION HELD AT NEWHAVEN FOR THE JURISDICTION THE 27th OF OCTOBER, 1646.

The worp^l Theophilus Eaton Esqr. chosen Governo^r for the yeare ensewinge.

Mr. Stephen Goodyeare chosen Deputy Governo^r for the yeare enseweinge.

Mr. Gregson & Mr. Malbon chosen magistrats for Newhaven ye yeare enseweinge.

Mr. Fowler & Capt. Astwood chosen magistrats for Milford the yeare enseweinge.

Mr. Samuell Desbrow chosen magistrat for Guilford for the yeare enseweinge.

Mr. Andrew Warde chosen magistrate for Stamford for the yeare enseweinge.

The worp^l Theophilus Eaton Esq. & Mr. Stephen Goodyeare chosen commissioners for this yeare enseweinge.

Mr. Atwater chosen treasurer for this yeare enseweinge.

Mr. Leete of Guilford chosen secretary for the jurisdic̃on for ye yeare enseweinge.*

* Whether Fugill was deposed from his office of Secretary of the Jurisdiction, as well as from that of the Plantation of New Haven, we are not informed. It may be

Thom Kimberly chosen mrshall for the jurisdiction for the yeare enseweinge.

AT A PERTICULER COURT HELD THE 3d OF NOVEM: 1646.

Leiut. Robert Seely hath sold his howse & howse lott in towne vnto Jno Basset wth 2 acres of vpland out of his first devizion; wch 2 acr. is 8 rodd in breadth & in length runneth crosse from the high-way betweene the suburbs quarter & Mr. Lambertons quarter, to Mr. Mansfeilds lott that was, & betweene Wm Iues and

Caleb Seaman desired his fine might be remitted for defect of armes, he going shortly for England, & vpon his request it was remitted, pvided he goe for England.

Edw: Chipfeild promised to pay 3l or 4l the next week in pt of about 5l he was ordred to pay to the towne for Wm Hardy, & promised paymt for the rest in the spring, wch the court accepted. Also a fine for absence one trayninge he was excused from payment of, he being a burning bricks, wch if that time had not bin improved, it would have inforced him to have attended it on the Saboth followeing.

AT A COURT HELD AT NEWHAVEN THE 1 JAN. 1646.

Bro. John Leavermore, brother Adam Nicholes, bro Wm Fowler and Mr. Thom Pell, being warned to the court & appearing not themselues nor by deputys, were layd vnder contempt of the court.

AT A GENll COURT HELD THE 4. JAN. 1646.

The Governour propownded that considring rates had bin made & levied on each plantation in this jurisdiction & sallerys

---

presumed that at this time he had left the town, from the excuse made by Allen Ball for late coming on a training day, page 271.

It is probable, however, that Richard Pery was appointed to succeed in that office also until the next Election Court, for his signature as 'Secretarie' is affixed to the certificate of the choice of Commissioners for the United Colonies at this time, the original of which is preserved among the archives of Massachusetts.

being yet vnpaid, besides severall debts, it was desired that April rates might be now forthwith paid, & it was ordred that they be forthwith paid into the treasurer.

It was appoynted that bro. Anthony Thompson & bro. Camfeild, & the 2 deacons doe speake with brother Lampson & see what his estate is, & to consider what proportion he is able to beare of the charge of maynteyninge his wife.

Bro: Robert Hill recd the chardge of a freeman.

It was ordred that the perticuler court wth the 2 deacons, takeing in the advice of the ruling elder, should place people in the seats in the meeting-howse, and it was alsoe ordred that the governor be spared herein.

It was now ordred that the former orders made for swyne & fences remayne of force, & that if swine be vnyoaked & vnrunge & goe into any feild, the fence lyeinge downe, that the damadge should be borne at halves, & that the fine of 6d a head be still payed to him that finds the swyne & brings them to the pownd.

It was ordred that the viewers of the fences finding fences defective & warninge those that owne them to mend them, if they doe it not & their names be not returned to the court, the viewers shall pay their fynes.

It was ordred that bro Peirce, bro. Coop & Jarvis Boykin & Mr. Caffinch shall look to the layeing out of the fence in their quarters to the absent lotts, according to their proportions.

The contribution for the colledge was renewed & bro. John Nash & bro. Phillip Leek chosen collectors for the same.

Bro. Andrewes had for his incouradgement liberty granted him to put strangers horses in the Neck.

It was ordred that they that already have or desire land among the small lotts bring in their names & quantitjes wthin a month to ye secretary, or els they are to loose their lands.

[169] AT A COURT HELD AT NEWHAVEN THE 5th OF JANUARY, 1646.

Mr. Edward Tench his will* was presented to the court by Elder Newman & Mr. Gilbert, & it was ordered that the estate bee improved for the good of the child.

Bro: John Leavermore confessed that he was warned to the court, 2 courts since, but some fence being downe he went to set it vpp & thought to have bin time enough, but comming about Mr. Grigsons howse he saw the court was broken vpp. Bro. Adam Nichols said he forgott it vntill it was too late. Both for their contempts were fyned 10s apeice.

Bro. Adam Nichols was fined for want of worme & scourer 1s.

Mr. Caffinch alleadged that he had bin brought into court about a horse formerly owned by his bro. Wm Fowler, but now bro. Fowler hath fownd his owne & seeth he was mistaken, but as he suffred therby in the court, so now he sought right.

Bro. Wm Fowler answered that he did not intend his bro.

---

* Mr. Edward Tench's will, Planter in Quinypiock and his dear wife Sarah Tench lying in the house with him dangerously sick and much wasted by a consumption—confirms certain small legacies, part given by his wife and part added by himself and all contained in a schedule annexed—He gives to his wife one half of the remainder of his whole estate, whether here or in Old England, and the other half to his only son Nathaniel Tench, now about five years of age—If his wife dies before himself, his son to have his whole escate, and makes his said son Nathaniel executor—If his wife should die before himself he entrusts his son both for his education and the ordering and improving his estate till he becomes 21 years of age, to the wisdom and care of the church of Christ gathered and settled at Quinnypiocke, whereunto Mr. Davenport is pastor, upon whose love and faithfulness in accepting and managing this his desire he quietly rests with assurance and satisfaction to his spirit.—If his wife die, and her sister come over into these parts and should desire to take his son back to Old England, his express will is that his son return not, but continue with, and be brought up by the forenamed church of Christ—If his son die before he is 21 years of age, he gives one half of his estate to the treasury of the forenamed church, and the other half to his brother Francis Tench and to his children. Witnesses, Henry Brunwin, Willm. Jeanes, Tho. Fugill, 13th February, 1639.—Inventory taken by Thom. Gregson, Robert Newman and Mathew Gilbert the 19th Feb. 1639, amount £409, 3, 6.

Debts oweing to Mr. Tench when he dyed, The mayds tyme £6, 2, the mans time £10. Mr. Alcok owed £5. Thom. Marshfeilds Connt. £9.

Debts owing by Mr. Tench when he dyed as followeth, To Goodie Pigg's wages £2, to the bricklayer £1, 4, 9, to Mr. Pell £0, 16, to Mr. Higginson £0, 19, 6, to Goodman Whitnell £0, 14, to Mr. Watters £1, 4, 6, to Mr. Grigson £3, 12, to a Conecticott man £4, 17, 6, to Mr. Langham of London £4, to John Brocket for mesuring land £0, 6, 9, to Mr. Delingham, London, £27.

Caffinch any wronge, but he refuseing to end it privatly caused him to doe it, but now acknowledged he had done his bro. Caffinch wronge. The Governo[r] demanded of Mr. Caffinch whether he looked for any more the reperation in his name, Mr. Caffinch said 10[s] damadge for witnesses, w[c]h the court ordred bro. W[m] Fowler to pay & his damadge 10[s] more, 20[s] in all.

Mr. Pell was warned to answere Mr. Caffinch for defaming him in sayeing he had gott his brothers horse, & said he would lay 5[s] of it. Roger Allen said he rememb[r]s Mr. Pell going by asked whether Mr. Caffinch was showeing his bro. Fowlers horse, but Mr. Caffinch not being able to prove his chardge because of want of proofe, hee was nonsuited.

It was ordred, w[t]h the consent of Edward Parker & his wife, that Jn[o] Potter should be put an apprentice for 8 years from the first of August past, vnto Roger Allen, for to learne him his trade & to give sutable apparell & 5[s] at the end of his time.

Luk Atkinson was chardged w[t]h defameing Mr. John Davenport, viz[d].

First to Ric[d] Osborne Luk Atkinson questioned whether this church is rightly constituted, and this ariseth from some pticulers falling out, not in respect of the members of it, for he judged them faithfull, but somthing in respect of h[m]selfe and others, as one thinge Mr. Davenport should speak & Mr. Davenport denyed it, although Luk Atkinson affirmed it & two more with him.

2[dly] to Richard Osborne he said that if things were carryed soe as he conceived them to bee, & as takeing vp things of others that he had spoken with, he conceives in all probabjlity this church cannot stand long without some breach.

3[dly], to John Speede he said that Mr. Davenport had said that w[c]h afterward he denyed, w[c]h two more with himselfe could witnesse.

To Richard Osborne he said, Mr. Davenports name had bin very pretious, but now it was darkned. That when Mr. Davenport spoke of the high-preist, out of the 21[th] Levit. on the Lords day, Mr. Davenport spake against himselfe. Richard

Osborne demanded wherein, Luke Atkinson answered that as he is a pastour of a *of a* church, he ought not to lay any vnder vnjust scandle as Mr. Davenport had done him, layeing his name vnder blame vnjustly.

To Richard Osborne he further said, that Mr. Davenport said he had noe ꝑt in the trade at Delaware & therevpon could make noe promise, & yet after, Mr. Davenport said that he had part in the trade. All these perticulers as concerne Mr. Davenport, Luk Atkinson related vnto John Speede. Also all the above written Luck Atkinson acknowledged himselfe to have spoken vnto Richard Osborne and to John Speede, & now againe repeated them vnto Anthony Thompson, John Clark, Richard Osborne & John Speede.

Before these ꝑsons spoke vnto Luke, they advized him to be very wary what he expressed, for he must look to be called to answere it. He answered hee expected it. In conclussion in reading all the ꝑticulers manny tymes over & wishing John Speede to take a copie of them, we asked him whether he owned all or would wave any, he owned them & thought he should answere them.

Mihill Palmer saith Luke Atkinson chardged Mr. Davenport wth vntruth.

[170] ||Luke Atkinson acknowledged what he stood chardged with was true, he had sinned & had slandered Mr. Davenport. This being done against much light and often convinced of his folly & had made acknowledgments of it, for his slandering the church and Mr. Davenport, he was fyned 40^l vnto Mr. Davenport.

Mrs. Turner & John Meggs haveing a difference betweene them, did in court agree to put it vnto arbitration, & Jno Meggs chose Mr. Goodyeare, & Mrs. Turner Mr. Malbon.

Mr. Pell pl.
Mr. Caffinch def. } For 50^l he should pay Mr. Atwater ℘ order of his bro. Samuel Caffinch, the wch bill was turned over vnto Mrs. Luce Brewster. Mr. Caffinch not tendring sutable pay, he was warned to court. But in fine, both were intreated by the court to put it vnto arbitration, & Mr. Pell chose Anthony Thompson, & Mr. Caffinch chose Mr. Tutle, who wer added vnto Mr. Francis Newman & Mr. Crayne to issue it.

The court see cause to judge the debt dew from Mr. Caffinch, but leave the prise of corne unto the arbitrato^rs, as also the prise of cattle, thinking it meet they be not vallued to the worth of them at present, but somwhat vnder. And Mr. Caffinch is to present that wherby it may bee issued w^thin this weeke.

Richard Marden requested the court to remit his fine, of 5^s, he haveing vsed his indeuo^r to gett armes, & haveing ill somtime since he has bin free, halfe his fine was abated.

It was ordred that if bro. Wigglesworth call for an execution against Mr. Mullyner because he attends not the courts order.

Goodman Walker released from a squadron fine, because his wife being ill & in very great payne, she was forced to send him seeke for Mr. Pell.

John Evance informed the court that he had cōmitted the chardge of a shallopp, on a voiadge to Guilford & Seabrooke, & backe againe to Newhaven, to Jno Charles as m^r of her, two others not fit for such a trust being vnder him in the vessell, & at his cōmand & appoyntm^t. That through the grosse, if not wilfull, negligence & default of h^m the said Jno Charles, the said vessell was cast away or broken, & a quantitje of pease belonging to h^mselfe, wth certayne pipes of Madera wyne belonging to h^mselfe & others were lost, all w^ch, wth the shallopp, a boate, &c. & other chardges occassioned therby, he vallued at 100^l, & desired he might be repayred according to right and justice. He further acquaynted the court that at the first hearing of the said losse, he app^rhended it as an afflicting providence of God immediatlye sent for his exersise, but being since fully informed of the forementioned negligence, he questioned Jno Charls about it, & by their mutuall consent ye matter was refferred vnto 4 arbitrators indifferently chosen by y^m the said ꝑties, being men y^t have long bred the sea & are well experienced in such cases. That they bownd themselves by assumpsit in 100^l to stand to ye award they should make in ye case, & if they agreed not, then to the award of any other man whom ye said arbitrators should choose as vmpire therin.

The said arbitrators not agreeing, Robert Martin, marryner, was by their joynt consent chosen vmpire, & vppon a full hearing of the parties wth their allegations & proofes, had in wrighting vnder his hand, given h^s judgment & award that the shallopp, boate & goods were lost by negligence & ought to be made good to the owners, but the s^d Jno Charles refusseing to stand to the award, he the said playntiffe was constreyned to crave ye help & justice of this court.

Herevpon a wrighteing made by the said 4 arbitrators, wherein they choose Robert Martin vmpier, & another writting made by ye sd Robt. Martin, as his awarde & vmpieradge in the cause, were read in court, the contents being as followeth,

These are to certifie those whom it may any wayes concerne, that we whose names are vnder written, being chosen arbitrators betweene Mr. Jno Evance on the one side & Jno Charles on the other, to end a difference betweene the foresaid parties, & not able to end the same by reason of some difference in our app^rhensions, did thinke it meete to make chojse of Robt Martin to be vmpiere in the case, to end that wch we for want of light could not agree to end, and what end the foresaid Robt. Martin shall make in the aforsaid case, wee assent therevnto, as vmpiere chosen by our mutuall consent, to wch agreem^t the afforesaid Mr. Jno Evance & Jno Charls did bind themselues in an assumpsit of 100^l sterling to stand to the agrem^t of the foresaid arbitrators or the afforesaid vmpiere chosen by vs. In witnesse whereof wee have h^rvnto set our hands the 24th of November 1646.

Daniell Paule Tobias Dimocke
George Frost Daniel How.

As concerning the looseing of their boate Jno Charles saith their boate roape was rotten, Ralph Loynes speaks to Jno Charles to make fast another roape vpon the boate. It was not don, the boate was lost through neglect. As concerning their lyeing ashore w^thout an anchour lyeing off, to haule off by when they saw occassion, was a neglect. As concerning their lyeing ashore when they had all their goods aboard, haveing 3 tyds before the storme began to haule off, was a great neglect. As concerning the leaveing the boate when they had hawled off, was very unsafe, soe that I cannot vnderstand nor see, but both boate & goods were lost through neglect of what might have bin done, & they must stand to their courtoysie that oweth both boate and goods.

Robert Martin.

John Charls being demaunded whj he did not submitt (according to h^s ingadgem^t) to the awarde & vmpieradge of the said Robert Martin, affirmed he had noe chardge of the said vessell, nor was any of the companny; that he went volluntaryly in her to Guilford, haveing some occassions of his owne there; that the shallop was lost for want of due provizions, haveing but one anchour and cable, & ye boate (by ye failing [171] of ye boate roape) was lost || before, so that in the storme they could not carry out their anchour so farr as was meete, & till the cable broake, the vessell roade safely. Being dem̃anded whether he would yet stand to the arbitration, or refferre the whole cause to the heareing & judgement of the court, at length by mutuall consent the arbitration was waved, both parties submitted, & the playntiffe was required to make proofe both that the said Jno Charles was m^r & that the losse came through his neglect or default. But the governo^r, & deputye governour, being both interressed in part of the wine lost, and leaveing their interresse to be pleaded by & issued wth that of Mr. Evance, desired liberty to rise, that they might neither judge, speake, nor sit in court, while a cause wherein themselues were concerned was in hand, wch was granted.

The plaintiffe affirmed that he at first intended & appoynted S^rjt Jefferies to goe ma^r of the sd vessell or shallopp for this voiadge to Guilford, Seabrook, & back to Newhaven, but Mr. Crayne, Mr. Wackman & Mr. Atwater, intrusted as feoffees for the building of a ship at Newhaven, desired y^t S^rjt Jefferies might be spared to goe to the Massachusetts about rigginge & other occassions concerninge the said shipp. The plaintiffe answered he could not spare him, unlesse som other man were ꝓcured to goe ma^r in S^rjt Jeffrejs roome, & mentioned the defend^t to them as fit for that service. Hervppō they the said foefees, spake to Jno Charles about it, he tooke time to consider of it & at last yealded & went, though S^rjt Jeffreis (not sent to the Massachusetts,) was after free & willing to returne to his former chardge, & to goe ma[r] of the said shallopp, & so told the said Jn[o] Charles. Herevppon Mr. Jasp Crayne & others were called to give in their testimony, & vpon oath they severally declared as followeth,

Jasper Crayne vpon oath testified that h[m]selfe & some other of the feoffes asked Mr. Evance whether he would let S[r]jt Jefferjs (who was ma[r] of the foresaid vessell,) goe a journey into the Mattachusetts Bay for them, Mr. Evance answered hee could not spare him vnlesse they could gett Jn[o] Charles, herevpon the said feofees spake w[t]h Jn[o] Charles to goe in Mr. Evance his boate, in S[r]jt Jefferies roome, because of some occassions they had to send S[r]jt Jefferies to the Bay, who could not be spared vnlesse he (the said Jn[o] Charles) would goe in his roome, but at that time Jn[o] Charles gave them noe direct answere, but said he would consider of it.

John Wackman vpon oath testified that h[m]selfe & other of the feofees haveing had speech w[t]h S[r]jt Jeffrejs about goeing to the Bay, they asked Mr. Evance whether he could spare h[m], Mr. Evance told them he could not carry on his designe w[t]hout him, he knoweth not whether Mr. Evance named Jn[o] Charles, but they meeting with Jn[o] Charles, asked him whether he could goe the voiadge w[c]h S[r]jt Jeffrejs was to goe & mentioned to h[m] the takeing off of S[r]jt Jefferies vpon another imploym[t]. Jn[o] Charles took time to consider of it; after, they the feofees meeteinge w[t]h Mr. Evance asked h[m] if he would let S[r]jt Jeffres goe, he then said he would, for he had spoken w[t]h John Charles.

Joshuah Atwater not remembreing he was w[t]h the other feofees at their first conference w[t]h Mr. Evance, vpon oath testified, that after meeteing w[t]h Mr. Evance, they asked h[m] whether he was willing to release S[r]jt Jeffrejs, Mr. Evance then answered he was willing, for he had spok[n] w[t]h John Charles.

Henry Brunwin vpon oath testified, that goeing along in comp[a] w[t]h Mr. Evance, they mett w[t]h Mr. Wackman & Mr. Crayne, who desired Mr. Evance to release S[r]jt Jefferies that he might goe to the Bay for them, Mr. Evance was not then willinge, but comming to Corporall Leeks howse, and finding

Goodm^{n} Charls there, Mr. Evance made a motion to him, wch to the best of the deponents remembrance was, to goe in the roome of S^{r}jt Jeffrejs to Guilford & to the Rivers mouth (called Seabrooke,) Goodm^{n} Charles told him the feofees had spoken w^{t}h h^{m} about it, & hee would consider of it, whereupon Mr. Evance after meeteing w^{t}h the feofees, seemed willing to let Serjeant Jefferies goe.

Phillipp Leeke vpon oath testified, that at his howse Mr. Evance spake to Goodm^{n} Charles to goe in his vessell in the roome or stead of Searjeant Jeffreis. Goodm^{n} Charles answered, the feofees had spoken to h^{m} about it, but what further answere Goodm^{n} Charles made he remembers not.

Serjeant Thomas Jeffreis vpon oath testified, that the morninge the boat was to goe, he went vp to Mr. Evance his howse, & asked him whether the boate was ready to goe, he remembers not Mr. Evance his answere, but he the said Tho^{m} Jeffreis went downe to the watter-side, purposeing to goe the voiadge, but finding Goodm^{n} Charles there, he asked him whether he went the voiadge in Mr. Evance his boate, Jno Charls told him he did goe, they had spoken to h^{m} to goe & he was to goe, & this deponant further testified, that he, before Jno Charls was spoken to, vnderstood h^{m}selfe to be ma^{r} of the said vessell, & that the chardge of the boate was to lje on him, & the rest of the comp^{a} to be at his cōmand, otherwajs he should not have gon in the boate.

John Griffin, one of the seamen in the said boate, vpō oath testified, that h^{m}selfe & Ralph Loynes the other seaman goeing to Mr. Evance his howse, asked h^{m} who should goe w^{t}h them as m^{r} to take chardge of the said vessell, for they knew not the place & would not take chardge. Mr. Evance answered, take you noe care, Jno Charls or Serj^{t} Jeffrejs shall goe along w^{t}h you; & this depon^{t} further testified that Jno Charles did helpe to stow the salt; that in the voiadge he accounted h^{m} as master; & y^{t} h^{m}selfe & Ralph Loynes did what he the said Jno Charles commanded them, & that Mr. Evance, being at the boate-side when the boate was goeing off, said Ralph Loynes had the wrighteing wherin was the order for ye deliu-
[172] ery of salt, lading aboard & taking of pease ||at Guil-

ford & other businesse to be done at the Rivers mouth, & Goodm[n] Charles was in the boate, but he cannot say Mr. Evance therein only directed his speech to John Charles.

Testimony being thus farr given in to prove Jn[o] Charles ma[r], he pleaded for himselfe that he went in the said boate as a freeman, takeing noe chardge vpon him, & that the said Jn[o] Evance made noe agreement w[t]h him for voiadges. Mr. Evance answered that he had imployed the said Jn[o] Charles 2 yeares together, in w[c]h he made severall voiadges as m[r]; that he only agreed w[t]h him for wages the first time, & had ever after allowed him the same wages vpon account, where-w[t]h the said Jn[o] Charles was content, & the same wages might now justly have bin demanded & must have bin allowed, but there had never passed any speech of Jn[o] Charles his goe-ing in the boat as a freeman w[t]hout wages, nor could it in reason either have suited the occassions of the plaintiffe, or the calling & course of the defendant, being a seaman. Jn[o] Charles only answered that the former voiadges were in a ves-sell wherein h[m]selfe had a fourth part, but that altered not the case for wages, and the court told Jn[o] Charles that hee was a man well knowne not to be so free of his sea labour, as to goe forth vpon a voiadge as a freeman w[t]hout wages in a vessell wherein himselfe was cheife seaman, & noe man elce fit to take chardge. To this he made noe replye, but affirmed noe seaman could prove him master by the evidence given in.

Mr. Tobias Dimocke & Rob[t] Martin, marryners, & both now or lately ma[r]s of shipps, being present were desired to expresse what they apprehended in the case.

Mr. Dymock testified that when he came from Pequott, he mett w[t]h Ralph Loynes, who was one of the seamen of the said vessell when it was cast away, but now absent, & y[e] said Ralph Loynes related to h[m] the manner of their comminge to the Rivers mouth, & how the vessell was cast away; namly, that they came in the sixth day of the weeke & tooke in 3 pipes of wine, & the next day tooke in the rest, and on the second day of the weeke, called Munday, they fetched aboard an anchour they were by order to receive there, & they lay agrownd at the wharfe from the second day till the fowrth day at noone, all wch time her ladeing was in her, and when the storme came, they carryed out an anchour as farr as they could from the shore, but the storme being then great, they could not carry it farr enough, and Mr. Dymock thought the boate did not ride above a quoyts cast from the shore, & they haveing rowsed vp vpon the roade, could not gett her further off, & both Jno Charles and the other two seamen went on shore & left the boate, & somtime after, the road bracke & the vessell drove onn shore.

The court for Jno Charles his better satisfaction desired Mr. Dymocke to declare his opinion, whether one shipt in the roome or stead of a mar of a vessell bee not really the mar of the said vessell & so to be accounted. Mr. Dimock answered, that if any one were shipt in the roome of a master of a shipp, & had his power, that then he conceived he was master.

Robert Martin testified that by the evidence given in, he could not conceive but that Jno Charles, so shipt in Srjt Jeffreis roome, was master, & he thought Jno Charles in his owne conscience thought hmselfe mar, & would have required masters wages if he had returned safe.

The court wished Mr. Evance to proceede & make proofe that the boate & goods were cast away & lost through negligence. Wherevpō Jno Griffin one of ye seamen in the said vessell was required. Vpon his oath taken to declare and testifie what he knew in the case, he affirmed that they went hence on the 3d day of the weeke in the afternoone, the winde then westerly, that he thought the skiffe roape stronge enough, yet against Thimble Islands she brake away, & they came to an anchour til the boat came vp to them, then they went to weigh their anchour, but it was 2 howers before they could efect it & then the flood was made, & the skiffe gon they knew not whether. The next day they got to Guilford & Goodmn Charles brought the vessell into the place where they should lye, and this depont to the best of his remembrance asked Goodmn Charles whether he would goe into the towne, & he said no, yn Mr. Evance his directions were given to this deponent by Ralph Loynes, whether it were because Goodmn Charles could not read he knoweth not, the next day some of their salt being deliuered and their pease taken in, they set sayle. The next day by noone they came to the Rivers mouth, came to the wharfe, vnloaded the rest of their salt & tooke in 3 pipes of wine, & the last day of the weeke tooke in 4 pipes more. Vpon the second day of the weeke they gott aboard an anchour they were by order to receive there & to bring to Newhaven; at night they heard of a skiffe was cast ashore at the corne feild poynt, told Goodm^{n} Charles of it, asked h^{m} if it were not best to goe & see it, if it were not theirs, & goeing fownd it to be theirs, the next day they brought ockham & caulked her. While they were at worke about her, the winde on a sudden fell calme, then Goodm^{n} Charles said we wilbe gon, we shall have an easterlie winde, but after, their arose a storme w^{c}h increased, but they returned before the vessell was afloate; they did what they could, but had neither cannow nor boate of their owne to helpe them. At length the Dutchmen there did helpe them, & Goodm^{n} Charles went w^{t}h them, & they carried out their anchour as farr as they could for the storme, then they rowsed vpon the boate roape and sett off w^{t}h their oares, and gott her afloate, & laid her offe as farr as they could, then they came all on shoare & left her, and in the night the road brake.

Jno Griffin being farther questioned about the losse of the skiff & other passadges, vpon his oath affirmed, that ther was an old cable & a tacle aboard, w^{c}h might have binne made fast to the skiffe to have saued her. Secondly that the vessell lay agrownd & noe anchour off, three tydes after she was loaden, before the storme began, & that the reason of their leaveing the vessell was because they were wett, & ye Dutchmen said, what will you doe starveing here, it were better for you to goe on shoare.

John Charles alleadged that the said Dutchmen had testified before the governour that the vessel might have bin saved had she had another anchour & cable, the governour confirming the same withall informed the court, that he had advized Jno Charles that Mr. Evance might be present to heare what they could testifie vpon oath, but they came noe more.

[173] || Leiut. Joseph Godfrey vpon oath testified, that the

Dutchmen in his hearing told Mr. Evance, they apprehended Jn° Charles his neglect lay in letteing the boate lye so longe loaden ashoare, til the storme was so great that they could not carry her off so farr as she should have bin for her preservation.

Serjeant Jeffreis vpon oath informed the court, that seamen vse there to dropp or let fall an anchor in the channell, for it is a dangerous place to ride at the wharfe; that if there had bin an anchour dropt at their comming in, 20 or 30 faddom off, that the cable might have had scope, it is like it would have held; that if the vessell had layne 20 or 30 faddome farther from the shoare, though the cable had broak, as the winde in the storme was, they might have gon cleare of the poynt vpp the river, and as she lay, had the seamen bin aboard, much might have bin done for the boats safety, to have cast her by flatting her foresayle.

Herevpon the court asked Jn° Charles whether hmselfe, (if proved mar of the vessell,) must not conclude there was a greate neglect in him. He answered that if he were mar, he must confesse their was a great neglect, but he still pleaded that if the vessell had bin provided wth 2 cables & anchours, they would have held her, & it is lik she would have ridd safe where she was laid.

After much time spent in examjninge witnesses, & debateing the cause, the plaintiff & defendant vpon demand acknowledgeing that they had notheing further to say, the court inquired after the damadge, & fownd by dew proofe that 5 pipes of Madera wine were wholy lost, which cost first penny 10l a pipe, that 50 bush. of pease were laden, that of them one hogshead was only saved, the rest were lost, wch cost at least 7l, that the damadge in the boate lost, by anchour & cable, wth other chardges necessaryly followeing, being rated wth all moderation, came at last to 10l more.

The premjses being dewly considered the court proceeded to sentence, and first finding the evidence full yt serjt Jeffrejs was shipped mar of the sd vessell, for the voiadge to & froe, that Mr. Evance would not have spared hm if Jn° Charles had not bin pcured in his roome, that the treaty wth Jn° Charls in this buisnes, the time he tooke for consideration, & hs consent at last, all tended to that purpose, that the other seamen that went in the boate ꝑfessed they knew not the place, & therevpon could not take chardge, that Serj^{t} Jeffrejs not goeing to the Massachusetts would have returned to his place of ma^{r} for the voiadge, but Jno Charles said thej had spoken to h^{m} to goe & he was to goe, y^{t} ye other seamen in ye voiadge tooke h^{m} to be ma^{r} & were at his cōmand, & considering w^{t}hall, y^{t} what Jno Charls p^{r}tended about hs going as a freeman in the said voiadge, & about wages, is in itselfe vnreasonable & w^{t}hout any proofe at all, the court, in refference to the sentence followeing, concluded him to be master.

Secondly by the evidence given in concerninge the neglect, ye court did find that Jno Charls had not improved his owne skill, nor exersised the ordynary care of a man takeing chardge, for p^{r}servation of ye vessell & goods.

For first, haveing lost the skiffe, he did not as reason requires, & as the practise *is* of seamen in such cases is, to let fall an anchour at a reasonable distance in the channell, by w^{c}h means he might have hauled off, as occassion should require, & the vessell might have ridd more safely, & the cable w^{t}h more scoape might have held better, & if it had broke, they might have set sayle, &, as the wynd stood, might have runne vpp the river w^{t}hout difficultye.

Secondly, he suffred the vessell to lye agrownd at the wharfe, though all her lading were aboard, from ye second day to the fowrth day at noone, & though the weather were faire, carryed out noe anchour to secure her.

Thirdly, after the storme beganne, & that they had hawled the vessell a litle off from shoare, the storme contineweing, & the vessell in danger, haveing but one anchour out, & that litle scoape, yet himselfe & the other seamen did all forsack her, leaveing noe man to prevent, or prevent in time of danger; but as the said Jno Charles himselfe confest, there went somtimes one, somtimes another, from ye ordynary, being a quarter of a mile from the watter-side, to see how she ridd; whereas, probably had they binne in the vessell, they might have vsed means either to have saved her, or some pt of the goods now lost.

Fourthly, John Charles in court confest, that if he were proved mar, there was a great neglect.

The court asked John Charles whether he could chardge the seamen, or either of them, wth any miscariadge in their places, that part of the damadge might be layd onn them, but he objecting notheing against them, the court adjudged John Charles, for his grosse negligence, & vnworthj carryadge in such a place of trust, to pay Mr. Jno Evance, for hmselfe & the other interessents, threescore & seaven pownds, besids the ordynary court chardges, in refference to the pticulers before mentioned.

Mr. Evance vpon the sentence thus given, moved the court that he might have an execution granted, because Jno Charles is shortly to goe to Virginia & thence to England. But the court being slow to grant execution so suddenly, John Charles of himselfe told Mr. Evance in court, he had 36l or 38l in his owne hands already towards it, & he would tak order wth Mr. Gilbert to pay the rest, wherewth Mr. Evance was satisfied.

---

[174] AT A GENl COURT HELD THE FIRST FEBR. 1646.

Mr. John Evance & Theophilus Higinson had liberty to dept the court.

The orders of the last Jurisdiction Gennerall Court were now read.

It was propownded that those planters, howseholders & sojourners, would give in their names, who desire to have their seats in the souldiers seats, ingadging themselues to bring their armes constantly, to all publicque meeteings for the worps of God.

It was ordred that the military officers should meete forthwith, & chuse 32 psons fit for the forementioned service, & send for them & speake wth them, & see whether that they be willinge to attend the service, or elce it is to continew in the same order as at present it is.

It was propownded to the court that they would expownd

themselues in a former order, about corporals assisting the serjeants in the exersise of their squadrons. And it was ordred that the corporals doe assist the srjts in that exersise.

It was ordered that the Neck this yeare be imployed as formerly.

It was ordred that bro. Myles, bro: Coop & bro. Benham, or Edward Chipfeild, as a committee from this court, speake wth Goodman Wilmott about the land he holdeth of the townes, (in refference to the clay fownd there,) to let him still injoye it, or leave it.

Bro: Andrewes propownded that some of them that held the small lotts behind Mr. Evance quarter, might have some land granted them in liew thereof, on the east side Mr. Malbons farme. Mr. Malbon, Lieft. Seely and Mr. Francis Newman, wth some of them, were chosen to view it, and to make report to the court concerning it.

It was ordred, that another view be made by bro. Wackman & bro. Myles their quarters, & that those of the quarters goe along wth the viewers.

It was ordred that the court wth Leiut. Seely, consider what prrivelidges may be meete to allow seamen, wth refference to watchings & traynings.

Bro. Beamont had liberty to exchang 2 acr. of land at the playnes.

It was ordred that the rest of those deputed to seate people in the meeting-howse shall seate the deputyes.

Liberty was further given them that have or desire land wth the small lotts to give in their names wthin 8 dayes.

Liberty was given Mr. Stephen Goodyeare to brew beare for this towne, all others excluded wthout the lik liberty & consent of the towne.

Vpon view of some meddow at Mr. Goodyears farme, it was granted hee might take it for the lik vallew of vpland.

Bro: Lampson was fownd able, & exprest himselfe willing, to pay 3 shill. ℘ weeke, from first to last, towards the mayntenance of his wife, till the court see cause to alter it, but whatever work his wife doth, it is to bee reckoned in part of what her husband is to allow.

At a Court held at Newhaven the 2d Febr. 1646.

Wm Meaker informed the court that 7 pecks of meale he hath received of Sam: Daighton, & that yet he doth want a sack & one peck, & he had order from the court to dispose of 6 pecks of meale, vntill the court se cause to order it to the partyes that did loose by Samuell Daighton.

Geo: King chardged wth blaspheaming the name of God by curseing, James Heywood said he heard him swere by the name of God, & told him the danger of such a course, & since, he hath heard him sweare.

Thomas Morris affirmed he had bin told of swearing aboard the ship, & since, *& since*, swore by the name of God, aboard a Dutchman, & he told him of it. The oath was a by God. Geo. King confessed he spak the words.

[175] || The Governor told him that when the son of an Egiptian blaspheamed the name of God it was not borne. Its the peirceing through the name of God in passion, wch is a high provokation of God, whereas the rule is, let yor words be yea, yea, & nay, nay, & by a mans words he may loose his life.

It was hoped it was only a rash & sinful oath, some have bin boared through the tongue, other have bin in the stocks & their tongues in a cloven stick. But hopeing this was not dispitfully don, the centence of the court was, that he should be whipped, and in the interim be kept in the marshals hands.

John Meggs informed the court, he had received much damadge in a parcell of hay by Mrs. Turnrs cattle, about 4 load.

Mr. Gilbert witnessed that he saw Mrs. Turnrs cattle 3 times at G. Meggs hay.

Wm Wooden informed the court that 3 times he fetched cattle thence.

Mrs. Turner replyed, the cattle gott in at som fence being downe, & dry catle had bin in the meddo, 100 at a time.

James Till said, he has seene 3 yonge catle 2 or 3 dayes together, & 3 cowes at once from morning till night, at the hay.

Goodman Andrewes and Goodman Cooper, being at Mr. Gilberts farme, were desired by Goodman Meggs to goe see the hay, & by others relation of what it had bin, they judged that 4 load was stroyd, Goodman Cooper had form^r^ly seene it when there was litle losse, &c. The centence of the court was that Mrs. Turn^r^ pay Jno Meggs 3 load of hay, or 30^s^ equivalent vnto it.

Ric^d^ Beech informed the court that his coz^n^ Wm Iles had done some work for Mr. Mullyner, & severall times he had desired to have had it issued but he hindred it, & now latly he refusseing to make payment for what was don, he had him warned to the court to answere it.

Mr. Mullyner told Ric^d^ Beech, if he would prove the bargaine & ꝑformance of it, he would pay him.

John England said he was to vnderpin his howse, make a backe to a chimney, stone a well & get the stons, for three pownds; but to his knowledge he had noe time set him for the doeing of it; he being at work at Mr. Shirmans, whose necesjtj was very great, he desired Wm Iles to get some boddy els to help h^m^, but in fiue severall times they came & things were not ready, & when they had don his howse & almost finished the well, insomuch that there was 20 inches water, 7 weeks after Michaelmas; after that, Jno England would have put a caske in the bottom, & dugg it deeper, but Mr. Mullyner would have ꝑswaded him the spring were risen 2 foote in the well, when it was otherwayes in Goodm^n^ Wards well, as was tryed, & he hath held them of wth delayes, that it is yet vnfinished.

Edward Tredwell informed the court, that he has heard it said it was well don, so far as it was donne, but in the issue the sand lyeing one the side of it, it being made in a banke side, filled.

The centence of the court was, that Mr. Mullyner pay 55^s^ vnto John England and Ric^h^ Beech, (and that he pay 5^s^) besids the chardges vnto them, Jno England finishing it.

Theophilus Higinson hath sold 3 acr ½ of vpland vnto John Punderson, lying w^t^hin the first devizion.

Theophilus Higinson hath sold vnto Goodm^n^ Johnson seaven acr. of vpland lyinge w^t^hin the first devizion, lying next Goodman Todd.

John Nash hath sold 5 acr ½ of meddow on the Indian side, vnto Jn° Vincent.

John Nash hath sold 7 acr ½ vpland vnto Roger Allen, w[c]h lyeth in Mr. Lambertons quarter.

[176] ||Thomas Hogg haveing bin imprisoned vpon suspition of bestyality w[t]h a sow of his mistreses, for about 2 or 3 monthes agoe, there was a discovery of that w[c]h is conceived bestyalitye, a sow of Mrs. Lambertons pigging two monsters, one of them had a faire & white skinne & head, as Thomas Hoggs is. It being considred of, Mr. Pell was sent for, and afterward was fownd another w[t]h a head lik a childs & one eye lik his, the bigger on the right side, as if God would discrib the party, w[t]h the discription of the instrument of bestyalytie. This examinant being sent for & examjned about it, he fetched a deepe sight, fell in his countenance, but denyed it; but information was made of sundry loathsome passadges concerning him, as discovereing his nakednesse in more places then one, seemeing therby to indeauo[r] the corrupting others, and being told of it, he said his breeches were rent, when indead his sperit was rent.

Thomas Hogg said his belly was broake, & his breeches were streight, & he wore a steele trusse, & soe it might happen his members might be seene.

Goodie Camp informed the court, that for all she could say to him, yet he did goe so as his filthy nakednesse did appeare; she has given him a needle & thridd to mend his breeches, but soone it was out againe, & he would tell her his breeches were tore & burnt.

The faults for w[c]h he was imprisoned were two. For that of bestyalytie, guilt did appeare in his carryadge, although he denyed he was at farme when the sow took bore, & would not have gon to fetch home the swyne about their pigging time, & being sent once & agayne, he went, but brought them not home, but one of bro. Thompsons famyly fownd them in lesse then halfe a day.

Afterward the governo[r] & deputy, intending to examyne him, caused him to be hadd downe vnto his M[rs] yard, where the swyne were, & they bid him scratt the sow that had the monsters, & immedyatly there appeared a working of lust in the sow, insomuch that she powred out seede before them, & then, being asked what he thought of it, he said he saw a hand of God in it. Afterwards hee was bid to scratt another sow as he did the former, but that was not moved at all, which Thomas Hogg acknowledged to be true, but said he never had to doe wth the other sow. The court was informed that he seeing his mrs swyne, & this sow that had the monsters, yet he would not bring them home.

Nicholas Elsie said he knoweth that Thomas Hogg did question whether that sow was his mistrises or noe, & shewed an vnwillingnesse to have them home.

Mary, servant vnto Mrs. Lamberton, informed the court that the neagar was the first in the famyly that observed his discovereing his nakednesse, & told him she would flying fier in his breeches if he continued thus; and divers times herself saw it, & told him of it, but he would deny it.

He had discovered himselfe to be an impudent lyar, and forward in stealing. Lucretia, the governors neagar weoman, informed the court that while she was in the famyly wth hm, she saw him act filthjnesse wth his hands by the fier side, & the next day the child & Hannah told her of it, & she asked whether hee was not ashamed. And she hath seene him take his hand out of the pott & a dumpling with it. Mary, aforementioned, added she saw him take cheese out of the buttrey, & speaking to him about it he denyed it presently.

The centence of the court was, (leaveing that about beastyalytye to be further considred on,) that for his filthynesse, lyeing & pilfering, he should be sevearly whipped, & for the future time during his imprisonement, that he be kept wth a meane dyet & hard labour, that his lusts may not bee fedd.

[177] ||John Charles was required to answere for his contempt of the court, that they sitteing & sending a warrant for him, yet he goes away wthout any leave, contem̄ing the authority of the place therein.

John Charls answered, it was true he went away, it being vpon a pinch of time and skipper Zeaker stayed for him, & he was told that warninge should have bine given before that time, & so not lawfull warninge. Espetyally speakeing to his bro. of Totokett that he should informe the court how it stood wth him, he thought it noe contempt.

Thomas Wheeler, Thomas Lawrence and Timothy Alsopp vpõn oath affirmed, that when the said Thom Wheeler had told John Charles he must goe to Newhaven, John Charles asked him what he should doe there, Thomas Wheeler said he must answere to such things as were brought against him. John Charles answered, that they had more neede answere him for threescore pownds they tooke away from him. Thomas Wheeler saith further that John Charls said, that to take away his mony & to deale so wth him, was the Judasest trick that either he or ever man was served. Thomas Wheeler told him he must take heede, it was against authority, but John Charles answered he ment Mr. Evance. Thomas Wheeler replied that Mr. Evance could not take away his monny & that it must be meant of the court, for what Mr. Evance had of him, it was by order of court.

Thomas Wheeler further affirmed, that haveing the warrant he went to the vessell & told them his businesse, John Charles replyed he had noe power over him and that he could not doe ought wthout a water-bayly. Skipper Zeakar comming ashore, was vnwilling & refussed to set them aboard or John Charles ashore, although he told him he had a warrant for him. Then he told him that if he carryed him away, he must give an account for it; the he told the said Thomas Wheeler that if he went aboard he would carry him away. Then gott they an Indian to helpe them aboard, & then they brought John Charles away with them. All wch John Charls sought to evade & fell to say he had bin wronged by Mr. Evance, however now he must lye at the mercy of the court, but he intended noe contempt of the court, although told at Connecticott they give three dayes warninge.

Goodman Banister informed the court, that on the second day at night, George Smith & himselfe were at Goodman Brownes the bakers, where John Charls was & said the shipp was goeing forth but might not returne, then said he why?

John Charles answered they had gott sixty pownds from him, but if any wise man were in the plantation, it had not bin soe.

George Smith informed the court that he heard John Charls say, if it had binne in any part of Newhaven he had not bin cast, but he remembers noe more.

The centence of the court was that (for his contemptuous cariadges and vile expressions, tending to the deffameing the court for doing justice according to their light,) he should pay twenty pownds to the jurisdict'.

Mr. John Evance informed the court that John Charls had gone vp and downe in a slanderous way reproachi[ng] him and sayeing he had cheated him, and said he was as vnmercyfull as a dogg &c. Although he had the next day after the court, bin downe w^{t}h him w^{t}h anoth^{r} & told him he perceived his sperit was troubled, but mynded him how he had sate downe satisfied till he heard such reports that made it necessary for him to move, & told him further if yet it should appeare that it was not his dew w^{c}h the court ordred him, he desired not to possesse it.

[178] ||Brother John Mose informed the court that his brother John Charles sayd Mr. Evance had broken his promise once or twice in monney or beauer lent him, the w^{c}h Jno Charles acknowledged. Jno Charles said he had bin out of his wages these two yeares and has had promise of beaver, and 60^{l} in beaver he paid Long Islandmen, & yet h^{m}selfe was vnpaid. Againe he helped Mr. Evance w^{t}h some beaver w^{c}h he heard, together w^{t}h that he should have, goeing for England, but it was sent to Connecticott, Mr. Evance telling him he should have it w^{t}h him for England. Captayne Smith commeing in received it & carryed it into the Bay, when his expectation was to have it w^{t}h him ⅌ way of Virginia to carry for England.

Mr. Evance replyed that Goodman Charles haveing sayled longe in the bark, at length, makeing vp accounts the companny were fownd his debto^{rs}, and hee was ordred to pay it, then John Charls said, you oweing mee already 20^{l} or 30^{l}, pray let me have it altogether when I shall goe for England, & I promised to pay it him in beaver or by a bill of exchange to Mr. Eldred. And in September or October last Jno Charles came to Mr. Evance & told him he would then for England, so that till then noe monney was due so as to call for damadge vpon nonpayment.

In September Mr. Evance sending to John Charles by Mr. Dymocke to keepe that coat beau^r in his hands wch he had, for his purpose was it should goe with him to England. But John Charles afterward hearing that Ralph Worry had some coate beauer of Mr. Evance, he thought that was it, but it was some other as appeared by Wm Andrewes oath, servant to Mr. Jno Evance, wch was as followeth,

That Wm Andrewes maketh oath that by the order of his m^r Mr. Jno Evance he, the said William Andrewes, packed vp 107^lb of coate beaver & one otter skine in a cask, wch he received of the Dutchmen for the vse of his m^r Mr. John Evance, wch was directed to Mr. Lacke of Boston to be sent to Mr. Eldred of London, out of wch he was innordred to pay Goodm^n Charles his bill of exchange. Mr. Evance informed the court that he paid Mr. Woory wth beau^r that he received from the fort of D'Aurange. Leiut. Joseph Godfrey informed the court that he heard Mr. Evance give order to Wm Andrewes, and also the promise that passed to John Charles.

Mr. Evance said he dealt faithfully wth John Charles, for he intended to have sent it by way of the Bay, hearing he went that way, til afterw^rd, wch made him take that care. Although he seeth himselfe short in that he gave not due notice thereof, seing he might have gonne ℘ the way of the Rivers mouth.

Jno Charles said this was all he had to say for damadge, if it did amount to anything or noe. Bro. Mosse required of Mr. Evance a reason whj he demanded execution so suddenly, he answered, because of Jno Charles speedy purpose to dept.

Thomas Newton of Fairfeild maketh oath, that John Charles, being at Mr. Pells howse, affirmed that Jno Evance, for the goodwill of the said John Charles in len[ding] him coate beau^r for some time, for wch the said John Evance had promised him a bill of exchange, hee had mearly cheated h^m.

Joseph Alsop of Newhaven affirmed that he had sayled for John Evance two years, & it was longe erre he could get him to acc^{t}, & that being come to accompt, & he was to have his monny, he sd hee was mearly cheated by him as at last.

[179] ||Leiut. Seely witnessed that before the court John Charles said that there was noe more mercy in Mr. Evance then a dogg, & when he had any advantadge he would vse it, and that thus he spake at Phillip Leeks.

John Charles acknowledged the grownd of all these words was the boate.

The centence of the court was, that seing this way of slandereing not only reached to the defaming Mr. Evance, but the wounding him in his credit & faithfulnesse, w^{c}h is to vndoe him so fare as lay in his power, he was fyned 50^{lb} to Mr. Evance.

AT A COURT HELD MARCH THE 2^{d} 1646.

John Sackett demanded a debt dew from Stephen Medcalfe of 18^{s}.

Wm Fancy informed the court that Stephen Medcalfe said vnto Jno Sackett in his hearing that he had forgott to reckon the 15^{s} he owed him, w^{c}h he said he would pay him the said John before he went, of w^{c}h he was ready to make oath.

Bro: Myles & bro. Whitnell are desired to view Stephens howse & judge what it is worth ℘ weeke.

Wm Illes his inventory* was presented to the court, whereupon the Go^{r} propownded that Ric^{h} Beech give in securyty to the content of this court, or els pay into the treasurers hands the vallew of the inventory. Bro. Anthony Thompson and bro. Clarke are desired to view the land Ric^{h} Beech presents for securyty at home. Also ordred that the secretary wright a

---

* "An inventory of Willm. Iles his goods with the prizes."

Sum £9. 19. 10. prized by John Clarke, Antho: Tompson.

Wm. Iles Dr. To Mrs Shearman £0. 10. to Goodman Charles £0. 10. 3. to Goodman Ives £0. 10. to Goodman Pecke £0. 0. 6. to Goodman Larramore £0. 0. 3. to Peter Mallorie £0. 6. to Rich Booth £0. 4. to Serjeant Andrewes £0. 0. 7. to Wm. Bassett £0. 0. 6.

Wm Iles Creditor. For work done at mill £2. 7. from Mr. Godfrey £2. 1. from Goodman Heards £0. 15. from Mr. Mullyner £1. 1. 6. from Arthur Halbidge £0. 0. 10. from Wm Peck £0. 1. 10. for 9^{s} which was in a purse of womp^{m} brought from the trading house £0. 9. from Isaac Beecher £0. 2. from John Mosse £0. 0. 6. for a howe valued by Roger Allen £0. 2. 6.

letter to the towne where Wm Iles lyved, vnto his brother, and that Richard Beech should bring into the court what chardges he hath bin at in gathering the inventory.

Thomas Yale hath sold vnto Robert Johnson 62 acr. of vpland in the 2d devizion, 15 acr $\frac{1}{2}$ of meddow, & 5 acr. $\frac{5}{6}$ in 2 pcells, wch is $\frac{2}{3}$ of the first devizion of David Yale, & 3 acr. $\frac{1}{2}$ in ye neck.

It was ordred that the proportions of John Meggs, John Gregory and Robert Preston be setled vpon them severally, they buying the proportions of 300l from Mr. Evance.

Samuel Hodkejs was called before the court for theft.

Sarah Rutherford informed the court that Samuell Hodkejs had taken from her 20lb of lead wch he had brought agayne. But she haveing promised some lead looked for it & fownd it wanteing, wondred at it what was become of it. At length Goodman Walker had some suspition of Samuell Hodkeyes, & speakeing vnto one of it, he telling Sam. Hodkeys of it, he then layd it wth Edw: Preston & Wm White, & said he had it of them, informing that vpon the ships coming back unexpectedly & these yong men in her, they were called lead marchants, & so he slandred them.

But now he acknowledgeth his sinne, & he judgeth in hmselfe that the court cannot passe too heavy a centence vpon him, for he had sinned against his light & conscience, and confesseth he hath formerly bin given to this way of theft. It is now the greife of his hart that he cannot bee suffitiently affected wth it. And further acquaynted the court that the axe he formerly tooke from Mr. Evances gate, he did in his conscience feare now it was his, although then hee wthstood it.

The centence of the court was that Samuell Hodkejs make double restitution, and that for his slanders & lyes that hee be whipped publicquely, and that he pay the chardgs of the court.

[180] At a Generall Court held the 10th of March, 1646.

The names of people as they were seated in the meeting-howse were read in court & it was ordred they should be recorded, wch was as followeth,

First for the mens seats, vizd.

The midle seates have to sit in them,

1 Seate, the Governour and Deputye Governor.

2 Seate, Mr. Malbon, Magistrate.

3 Seate, Mr. Evance, Mr. Bracey, Mr. Fra: Newman, Mr. Gibbard.

4 Seate, Goodmn Wigglesworth, Bro. Atwatter, Bro. Seely, Bro. Myles.

5 Seate, Bro. Craine, Bro. Gibbs, Mr. Caffinch, Mr. Linge, Bro. Andrewes.

6 Seate, Bro. Davis, Goodman Osborne, Antho: Thompson, Mr. Browning, Mr. Rothrford, Mr. Higginson.

7 Seate, Bro. Camfeild, Mr. James, Bro. Benham, Wm Thompson, Bro. Lindoll, Bro. Martin.

8 Seate, Jno Meggs, Jno Cooper, Peter Browne, Wm Peck, Jno Gregory, Nich Elsie.

9 Seate, Edw. Banister, John Herryman, Benja: Wilmott, Jarvis Boykin, Arthur Holbridge.

In the crosse seats at the end.

1 Seate, Mr. Pell, Mr. Tutle, Bro. Fowler.

2 Seate, Thom Nash, Mr. Allerton, Bro. Pery.

3 Seate, Jno Nash, David Atwater, Thom Yale.

4 Seate, Robert Johnson, Thom Jeffery, John Punderson.

5 Seate, Thom Munson, Jno Leavermore, Rogr Alln, Jos: Nash, Sam Whithead, Thom James.

In the other litle seate, John Clarke, Marke Peirce.

In the seates on the side for men.

1. Jeremy Whitnell, Wm Preston, Thom Kimberley, Thom Powell.

2. Daniell Paul, Rich Beckly, Richard Mansfeild, James Russell.

3. Wm Potter, Tho^m Lampson, Christopher Todd, Willm Ives.

4. Hen. Glover, Wm Tharpe, Mathias Hitchcocke, Andrew Loe.

On the other side of the dore.

1. John Mosse, Lucke Atkinson, Jno Thomas, Abraham Bell.

2. George Smith, John Wackfeild, Edw. Pattison, Richard Beech.

3. John Basset, Timothj Ford, Tho^m Knowles, Robert Preston.

4. Rich Osborne, Robert Hill, Jno Wilford, Henry Gibbons.

5. Francis Browne, Adam Nicholes, Goodman Leeke, Goodman Daighton.

6. Wm Gibbons, John Vincent, Thomas Wheeler, John Brockett.

Secondly for the weomens seates. In the midle,

1 Seate, Old Mrs. Eaton.*

2 Seate, Mrs. Malbon, Mrs. Grigson, Mrs. Davenport, Mrs. Hooke.

3 Seate, Elder Newmans wife, Mrs. Lamberton, Mrs. Turner, Mrs. Brewster.

4 Seate, Sister Wackman, Sister Gibbard, Sister Gilbert, Sister Myles.

5 Seate, Mr. Fr: Newmans wife, Sister Gibbs, Sister Crayne, Sister Tuttil, S. Atwat^r.

6 Seate, Sister Seely, Mrs. Caffinch, Mrs. Pery, S. Davis, S. Cheev^rs, Jno Nash's wife.

7 Seate, David Atwat^rs wife, S. Clarke, Mrs. Yale, S. Osborne, Sister Thompson.

8 Seate, S. Wigglesworth, Goody Johnson, G. Camfeild, S. Pond^rson, G. Meggs, S. Gregory.

9 Seate, Sister Todd, S. Boykin, Wm Pott^rs wife, Mathias Hitchcoks wife, Sister Cooper.

---

* The following passage, from Lechfords Plaine dealing, explains why no seat is assigned for Mrs. Eaton, the Governor's wife. "At *New-haven, alias Quinapeag*, where Master *Davenport* is Pastor, the excommunicate is held out of the meeting, at the doore, if he will heare." Mass. Hist. Coll. 3d series, iii. 73. Reference has already been made to Mrs. Eaton's excommunication.

In the crosse seats at the end.

1. Mrs. Bracey, Mrs. Evance.
2. Sister Fowler, Sister Ling, Sister Allerton.
3. Sister Jeffery, Sister Rotherford, Sister Leavermore.
4. Sister Preston, Sister Benham, Sister Mansfeild.
5. S: Allen, G: Banister, S. Kimberley, G. Wilmott, Sister Whitnell, Mrs. Higinson.

In the litle crosse seate.

Sister Potter ye midwife, and old Sister Nash.

[181] || In the seates on the sides.

1 Seate, Sister Powell, Goodye Lindoll, Mrs. James.

2 Seate, Sister Whithead, Sister Munson, Sister Beckly, Sister Martin.

3 Seate, Sister Pecke, Joseph Nash his wife, Peter Brownes wife, Sister Russell.

4 Seate, Sister Iues, Sister Bassett, Sister Pattizon, Sister Elsie.

In the seates on the other side the dore.

1 Seate, Jno Thomas his wife, Goody Knowles, Goody Beech, Goody Hull.

2 Seate, Sister Wackfeild, Sister Smith, Goody Mosse, James Clarks wife.

3 Seate, Sister Brockett, Sister Hill, Sister Clarke, Goody Ford.

4 Seat, Goody Osborne, Goody Wheeler, Sister Nichols, Sister Browne.

Brother Andrewes, bro. Munson & Goodman Basset were desired to view the posts of the meeting-howse, & to see if the girts fly not out & to doe whats necessary for the preservation of the whole, lest insensibly they should decay.

Mr. Evance had liberty to depart the court.

Richard Pery secretarie had liberty to goe a voiadge for the comfort of his famylye, and Mr. Francis Newman was dissired &* declared himselfe willing to attend the service in his absence.

* These words [was dissired &] interlined by Mr. Newman.

It was ordred that the former men chosen to view Goodman Wilmotts land should set a rate vpon it, that so the towne may be paid Thomas Fugills fine.

Mr. Malbon informed the court that himselfe & those chose wth him to view the land that bro: Andrewes, bro. Cooper & Serjt Beckly desired onn the east side, & thought it might be noe way prejuditiall to the towne, wherevpon it was ordred that a survey be taken of the quantytye of the land.

Brother Crayne, brother Myles and Leiutenant Seely were deputed to view a cart-way betweene Milford and Newhaven, and to make report to the court how they find it.

It was ordred that ^ d a head be layd on the cattle (im̄edyatly, but finally on the fences that are defective,) brought to the pownd, report being made of some fences that are downe. It was also ordered that the fences be viewed after stormes, and that the viewers be paid for their paynes therein by those whose fences are defective.

It was ordred that the view be made euery last whole weeke in euery month by the viewers of the fences, that so defects may be returned to the next court, wch may be a means to prevent damadge.

It was ordred that every cow-keep burne his owne walk & that he be paid by them whose heard he tendeth.

Whereas there hath bin a question about a highway to those lotts at the Oysterpoynt, it is ordred that Mr. John Wackman & bro. Anthony Thompson shall issue it by order of this court and consent of the qurter.

It was ordred that noe man put any cattle in the Necke before May day. And if any be fownd there, they are powndable, & that noe man drive his cattle any other way then as his land lyeth in the towne, eastward or els northward.

Brother Wackman, brother Myles and brother Davis vpon request of bro: Mitchell were to view some land desired by him at the playnes.

[182] AT A COURT HELD AT NEWHAVEN THIS SIXT OF APRILL, 1647.

Thomas Nash informed the court that there is some fence downe in that quarter w[c]h they call Mr. Malbons quarter that they find noe owner for, therfore the court ordred that the owners of the land w[t]hin that quarter shall meete vpon the fift day of this weeke, at 4 a clocke in the afternoone to setle the fenceinge vpon the partyes it properly belongeth to. And for euery partye that fayles to meete according to this order, they haveing lawfull warninge, shall pay 12[d].

James Heywood was called forth to answere for the sinne of drunkennesse, the chardge against him standing thus, that being called to went aboard a Dutchmans vessell, and did there drinke stronge watters in such excesse that he made himselfe drunk by it, so as that he had not the vse of his reason, nor of his tongue, hands or feete; so that there is all the caracters of a drunken man, as was most fully proved when he was cast out of the church. The Governour further declared to him how greatly his sinne was agravated w[t]h manny circumstances, but espetially that he, being a member of the church w[t]h whom the Lord had dealt so kindly with, and he so to requite the Lord was a sinfull foolish thinge, oh foolish people & vnwise, doe you thus requite the Lord.

He haveing liberty to speake for himselfe answered, I owne my sinne and take the shame, and doe confesse the name of God hath bin dishonered and blaspheamed through mee, for my sinne hath manny circumstances w[c]h maks it greivious, for w[c]h the hand of the Lord is justly out against mee, so that I have nothing to say, but doe justifie the proceedings of the court in what God shall guide their harts to.

This answere being given, the Governour opened the case thus, Drunkenesse is among the fruits of the flesh, both to be witnessed against, both in the church and civill court, and its a brutish sinne, and so to be witnessed against. A whip for the horse, a bridle for the asse, & a rodd for the fooles backe, & his sinne is more heynous as he was a member of the church. But it hath not bin brought to mee that this man hath bin given to drunkennesse, nor is it fownd that it was an appoynted meetinge for drinking, but he being called, drank an excessive quantitye wch caused these efects. I leave it therfore to the courts judgement whether they shall find it a dispositiō to drunkennesse or an act onlye.

The court considering what had bin said, thought it not a disposition to drunkennesse in him, nor a match appoynted for drinking, therfore thought not to punish it wth corporall punishement, but by a fine. Therfore the centence of the court was, that James Heywood pay fivety shillings to the towne for this act of drunkeñesse.

An atatchmt being layd vpon the goods of Mrs. Stallion by Richard Platt of Milford for a debt of 57s, it was ordered, that Mr. Goodyeare & Mr. Newman, who were intrusted by Mrs. Stallion wth her estate, doe pay *doe pay* the aforesaid Ricd Platt the 57s wch is due to him for rent of the howse wch Mrs. Stallion did live in, & the said Ricd Platt doth promise, that for any thing done to the howse by Mrs. Stallion, when the covenant is out he shall stand vnto such just considerations as is fitt.

AT A COURT HELD AT NEWHAVEN THE 4th MAY, 1647.

An entry of 5 acr. ¼, 12 rodd of land lyeing on the west side abutting eastward vpon a highway by the west meddow, westward vpon the second devizion of land on the west side, allyenated from Richard Beech to Anthony Thompson.

Richard Myles & Jeremy Whitnell haveing bin apoynted to view Stephen Medcalfes howse, returned to the court that the fence stands, and John Sackett hath put vp some pales & spent some nayles; the said John gave in a noate to the court, of chardges wch had bin spent about the howse, to the vallew of about 17s 8d, & what the howse & lott was worth by the yeare to defray this chardge, or what it is worth to be sold, was refferred to Richard Myles & Anthony Thompson, and to take in the helpe of some workmen with them.

[183] || Brother Leavermore desired his fine wch he was

fined for contempt of the court might be remitted, but it was respitted.

Brother Leavermore is also charged wth late comming wth his armes one Lords day, but because the serjeant was not there wch accused him it was respitted.

Richard Smoolt, servant to Mrs. Turner, was chardged by his Mrs. for sundry grosse miscariadges, as for scoffing at the word of God wch was preached by Mr. Cheevers, for other rebellious carriadges in the famylye, as when his mistrisse sent him for any necessaryes he hath thow^n^ part of it into the fire, & part into the watter, & said it should never doe here more good. When he hath asked for a pott in the howse, & it was told him his Mrs. had it, he bid the Divell goe with it, and when his Mrs. came to correct him for a lye, he turned againe and did wringe her by the arme & if the other servant had not taken him of, it was thought he would have beaten her. He asked her daughter Rebecca if she were not w^t^h child and therin slaundered her, he haveing noe grownd soe to doe. These things being cleared to the court by witnesse and his owne confession, besids other miscarriadges charged vpon him, the centence of the court was that he should bee seuearly whipped.

Edward Banister complayneth that Tho^m^ Osborne being cow-keeper for the cowes on their side, and his among the rest, did one day loose one of his cowes neglegently by leaveinge her in the feild swamped, and saith that the said Tho^m^ kept in howse that day to keepe himselfe drye because it did rayne & saith Mr. Hooks man can say something to it.

Mr. Hooks man sath that he mett w^t^h Nathanjell Seely as he came home, who kept cowes w^t^h Tho^m^ Osborne that day, & told him that it was a wett day to keepe cowes in. I, saith hee, but I was the most part of the day in a wigwam or some shelter.

Tho^m^ Osborne, answered for h^m^selfe, that day he kept the cowes & Nathanjell Seely with him, and carfully turned the cattle from the swamps, & when they were to come home, Nathaniell Seely he sent throughout the playnes w^t^h the cattle & went to search the swamps himselfe, least any cattle should be there, but fownd none, and thought there had not bin a cow behind, but at night Goodman Banister demaunded his cow, & he would have gon that night though it rayned to seeke her, but they agreed to goe in the morning & did so, but fownd her not. It was demanded of Nathaniell Seely how long they were in the howse, he answered, not aboue $\frac{3}{4}$ of an hower. And Tho^{m} Osborne said the day was exceeding wett & they went in there to shelter themselues a litle, the cowes being hard by the howse, & staid not, & for what shelter els they had vnder some bowing or hollow tree. The next day after they went againe to seek her, and Georg Smith and Ric^{h} Osborne went with them. George Smith said they went downe that swamp where afterward the cow was fownd and on that side of the swampe, but saw noe cow but a black thing in the swampe w^{c}h they tooke for a stumpe of a tree, yet they sought dilligentlye as if the cow had bin their owne.

Richard Osborne said they went rownd the swampe as well as wee were able, we searched & went through the swampe twise, and if it had bin my owne cow I could have looked noe otherwayes, & for my part if it had not bin a thing hidd, I cannot tell how wee could misse her.

The court considring things as they have bin held forth by the severall witnesses, doe not see grownd to charge Thomas Osborne w^{t}h any grosse neglect in this matter, either in looseing first the cow, or after in seekeing her vpp. Therfore the centence of the court was, that Thomas Osborne be freed from the losse, & Goodm^{n} Banister must beare it as an afflicting providence of God cast vpon him.

John Bishopp, serv^{t} to Mr. Allerton, was complayned of for want of armes, & though hee made sundry apologies, yet the court saw cause to fine h^{m}, but because his M^{r} is much absent & y^{t} it did also appeare y^{t} wh^{n} his M^{r} heard of it he tooke care to pvide, ye court did inclyne to favour & did abate halfe of the fine for want of armes, so y^{t} the fine to be paid*
[ ]

[184] ||Wm Payne for neglectinge to bring his armes one lecture day, was fined 6^{d}.

* Half a line worn away.

Further Wm Payne was complayned off for not comminge time enough one Lords day morning & eveninge, but seing it appeared he was very neare before the drume had don beating, and consideringe the distance at wch he lives & he saith he could not heare the first drū, the court saw cause to moderate the fine, & was fined for both but 1s.

Roger Knapp was complayned of for not bringing his armes one Lords day, & for not cōming to the squadron meeteinge, but being absent it was respited.

Wm Gibbons was complayned of for late comminge one Lords day, but it apearing he was not well, nor in case to come, it was passed by.

Mr. Caffinch was complayned of for late comming one Lords day, but respitted.

John Lawrenson was complayned of for late comminge 2 Lords dayes & one night to watch, but respited.

Rich: Beech propownded to the court for helpe, Mr. Mullyner not paying to hm what the court ordred hm to pay for his cozn, Wm Iles. The court propownded that hee would stay till another court, wch he inclyned to doe.

Further, whereas Anthony Thompson & John Clarke were to view some land of Rich Beeches for securjtie of Wm Iles his estate, they thinke the land is not securytye, therfore the court gave him time till the next court to provide sufficient securytye, or els to pay it into the treasurer.

At a Genll Court at Newhaven 17th May 1647.

The Governor propownded & acquaynted the court that those that were apoynted to audite the treasurers accompts had done it & fownd that the towne was indebt, and sundry things were to be paid to severall men & the treasurer had it not in hand to pay, therfore there is cause for a new rate to be levyed, that righteousnesse may be attended. After much debate, it was voted that one halfe years rate be forthwith paid into the treasurer, ouer & aboue the yearly rates in their ordynary course.

The Governo[r] propownded to the court about the monney paid for imprisonements, whether it should wholly goe to the m[r]shall over & above his yearly sallery, and it was voted that it should.

It was propownded by Leiut. Seely that the planters in the towne whose mynds were industrious that way, might have libertye to set vp wares to catch fish for the releife of their famyljes and good of the towne, and it was granted they should, provided that there be noe stopping of lighters, nor damming vpp of rivers or harbour to bring further inconveynyence to the towne, & that they be not p[r]juditiall to the wares the Indians have already set vpp, nor shall any man set vp any ware to the hinderance of another w[c]h is already set vp before.

Serjeant Nash propownded whether it was the courts mynd that m[r]s of watches should be freed from walking the rownds & standing sentinell on the Lords dayes, but after some debate, the thing was respitted till another court.

W[m] Preston, who was intrusted to looke to the shutting the meeting-howse dores, was desired to keep them constantly shutt, & that they be opened vpon the Lords dayes & lecture dayes before the first drum̃e is to beate, and W[m] Andrewes was desired so to repayre & order the dores that they may be opened on the outside when vnlocked & vnbarred, & at other times to shutt fast & secure.

Robert Bassett was desired to beat both the first & second drum̃e, vpon Lords dayes and lecture dayes, vpon the meeting-howse, that soe those who live farr off may heare them the more distinkly, & he promised so to doe.

Capt. Malbon propownded to the court, that seing the towne had noe cull[r]s for the trayne band, that therfore the towne would pay for part of them or wholly, & let the artillery have the vse of them, & the drummer might be paid by the towne for drumming for the artillerie, but it was respitted.

[185] ||The Governour propownded that the colledge corne might be forthwith paid, & that considering the worke is a service to Christ, to bring vp yonge plants for his service, and

besides, it wilbe a reproach that it shalbe said Newhaven is falne off from this service.

It was propownded that they wch want hay, would speake in time to the treasurer, that the meddow in the townes hand may be disposed off.

It was propownded that seing it doth apeare that both yonge cattle & hoggs doe goe vpp the neck way, and finding the gate shutt doe swime over & doe damadge, whether it was not necessarie therfore that a fence and gate be made crosse the way at Mr. Tutls corner, for preventing the same, & it was voted, that a strong fence & gate be made & kept at the townes chardge.

Brother Andrewes acquajnted the court that he is now goeing to fence in his meddowe in the necke wherin the springs is, that therfore the towne would appoynt some to view what may be for the townes conveyniency, that it may be left out & he have allowance for it elswhere, & bro: Cooper was appoynted to doe it.

It was ordered that the Necke be driven this afternoone by bro: Cooper, and what cattle are fownd more then belonginge to them who have given in their names & quantitjes of land to the governo^r, shalbe pownded for breach of order.

The Governo^r acquaynted the court that bro: Andrewes had bin wth him & told him that hee thought it not conveynient for him to keepe the ordynary any longer, then August next he cannot keepe it; & therefore declares it now, that the towne might thinke how to provide for another to doe it.

Bro. Andrewes & Goodm^n Meggs both came late to the court, but they made such excuses as the court accepted, & they were freed from the fine.

Henry Morrall & bro. Lampson vpon their request had liberty to dept the court.

Captayne Malbon propownded that the towne had bin ill provided of serjeants, in regard that Serjeant Jefferys is abroad much by reason of hs occassions at sea, therfore whether the towne will not see cause to chuse another serjeant in his roome, and the rather seing Serj^t Jeffreys hath earnestly desired it, as Leiut. Seely & Serj^t Munson did testifie in court.

The captayne also affirmed the same & that he was vnwilling to move for a change till that now he vnderstandeth Serj^{t} Jefferys purposeth to imploy himselfe more fully in sea affayres. W^{c}h being considered, bro: Wm Fowler was chosen serjt for the towne.

Corporall Leavermore desired the court that he might be freed from the place of a corp^{ll}, because he thought his necesary occassions would call him to goe for England, his desire was granted & bro. Joseph Nash was chosen corp^{ll} to the towne companny.

Goodman Wilmott propownded to the court that he might have the 24 acres of land w^{c}h was Tho^{m} Fugils, at the foote of the West Rock, granted to him as land is given to other planters as inheritance, and he will give to the towne 3^{l} a yeare till the 20^{l} be paid for the fine due from Tho^{m} Fugill, w^{c}h fine the said Thomas ord^{r}d to be paid out of this lands; and the said Goodman Wilmott will fence it at his chardge. After much debate about it, the court saw cause to grant it to Goodman Wilmott vpon his desire, and so it was ordered. But seing it did appeare in court that the said Tho^{m} Fugill had made over this land to one in the Bay for monny he owed, & that before he left it to the towne for their fine, therfore it is ordered, that if any one come & lay clayme of the land & recover it, that then what rent the said Goodm^{n} Wilmott hath paid to the towne, they shall pay back agayne to h^{m}.

[186] ||And further it was ordred that the said 24 acres of land shalbe soe laid out as Goodm^{n} Wilmotts howse shall not stand vpon it, but neare to the side thereof, for the more conveynient improvement of the said land, and what land he hath broken vpp without the 24 acres, he is to have the vse of it for this yeare.

It is ordered that the measures and waights of greater or lesser quantity, w^{c}h men buy & sell by, shalbe brought into the meeting howse to be tryed, vpon the fift day come seaventh night, w^{c}h wilbe the 27th of this instant month, & whosoever shall faile hereof is to pay 12^{d} fine & yet to fall vnder the gen^{l} courts order for any vnrighteousnesse.

Viewers chosen for the severall quart[rs] for this yeare ensewinge.

For Mr. Eaton & Mr. Malbons quarter, Mr. Francis Newman & Tho[m] Kimberly.

For Mr. Newmans & Mr. Brownings q[r]tr : Rich[h] Becklye and Andrew Loe.

For Mr. Evance quarter, John Meggs and Thomas Wheeler.

For Mr. Wackmans quarter, Mr. Wackman & Tho[m] Osborne.

For Mr. Grigsons quarter, Henry Lindoll and Thomas Barnes, but Tho[m] Welch is to satisfie Tho[m] Barnes for his paynes, or els to pvide another.

For Mr. Lambertons quarter, Mr. Jannes and W[m] Preston.

For the suburbs onn both sides the creeks, Mathew Camfeild & W[m] Thompson.

For the Oystershelfeild, Francis Browne & Mathew Moulthropp.

For the playnes, W[m] Davis and Adam Nicholls.

For the farmes on this side the East River, Joshua Atwatter & W[m] Potter.

It was ordered by the consent of the planters of Mr. Wackmans quarter & Mr. Evance qu[r]ter, that Jasp Crayne and Francis Newman shall consider of the fence in difference betwixt them, & so end it if it may bee, if not, to report back to the court againe. They are also to consider of a like difference betwixt Mr. Lambertons quarter and the suburbs.

It was propownded whether all the towne but magistrats & church officers should not watch and trayne, but after much debate it was respited vntill another court.

W[m] Andrewes propownded that himselfe, Jn[o] Cooper & Rich[h] Beckly might have a neck of land lyeing one the east side, beyond the pine river, conteyning 113 acres, which was formerly refferred to the view of Mr. Malbon and Mr. Francis Newman, and that they might have this 113 acres instead of 70 acres w[c]h they were to have in their second devizion at the end of Mr. Evance quarter.

The court considring the distance of this land from the towne & the difficultjes w[c]h would attend the improvement of land so farr off, & on the other side of the river, granted it to them, provided that a place be left next the great river and a conveynient way to it, that there may be liberty to bring any thing to or from the land beyond, if it shall come to bee improved, and further it is agreed y[t] they shall pay rates for their 70 acres w[c]h was there first prop alottment, the 43 acres added being rate free. The bownds & lymitts of this necke of land is as following, viz[d].

[The remainder of this page is blank.]

---

[187] AT A COURT HELD AT NEWHAVEN THE FIRST JUNE 1647.

Tho[m] Kimberly alyenated one acre of meddow vnto Francis Browne, w[c]h meddow lyeth on the island in the East River, & on the side next Mr. Davenports farme.

Mr. Caffinch for late comminge one Lords day was fined 1[s].

Ric[h] Osborne haveing in a gen[l] court chardged the watchmasters of this towne w[t]h sleeping all the night, & said he had rather watch for a watchm[r] for 6[d] a night then for a watchm[n] for 12[d] a night, w[c]h expressions were to the great offence of the watch-masters, and the case was then commended to the perticuler court to consider of Ric[h] Osborns chardge, by the gen[l] court then mett. The Go[r] informed Ric[h] Osborne that he had, by his rash words, layd the watchmasters vnder vnfaithfulnesse in their trust.

Ric[h] Osborne said in his defence, that his answere was in the gen[l] court, that he could not clearly prove they slept all the night, & so desired to fall vnder his rash words.

Ric[h] Osborne added that in a perticuler his witnesse is absent wherby he should have proved a m[r] to have slept, & in answere to a question put to him he said, hee did know of this case before he spake in court, w[c]h was Mathew Camfeild, who being watchm[r], finding fault w[t]h some one of his watchmen, said he would not burden his conscience for any of them, but himselfe, after the watch was set forth, fell asleep, and then one of the watchmen said to him, doe you not burden yo[r] conscience w[t]h that, viz[d], sleepinge.

Againe Richard Osborne complayned of Anthony Thompson, that the last night hee watched he fell asleep before the watch was sett forth, & he spake to Georg Smith of it, & he touched him w[t]h his sword & waked him, & that Luke Atkinson told him, alas, poore man, he was asleepe. Ric[h] Osborne was informed this was not his way, but that he should labour to see his owne evill & acknowledge it, and not indeavour to lessen his evill in this way of searching out somthing to hide his sine, as this of Antho: Thompson, if it should be true, would prove, espetially it being don since the last generall court, wherein he spake so slanderouslie of the watchmasters.

The centence of the court was, that Ric[h] Osborne should pay 40[s] fine to the towne, for his slanderous reproach layd on the watchmasters, w[c]h he was not able to make out or prove, and also that in a generall court he make a full acknowledgem[t] of his sinne.

Ric[h] Osborne complayned of Antho. Thompson, that the last time he did watch he fell asleep before the watch was sett forth, and that he did speake to Geo. Smith of it & then he, the said George Smith, did touch him w[t]h his sword to wake him. Also he saith Luke Atkinson told h[m], as they walked the rownds together, alas, poore man, he was asleepe, & his hat did lye vpon the grownd.

Luke Atkinson informed the court that Ric[h] Osborne poynted vnto him to bee an eye witnesse of the thinge, but it was before the watch was sett he thinks.

Ric[h] Osborne herevpon said that Luke Atkinson in regard of the absence of one watchm[n] (standing somtime sentinell in his behalfe) standing long & not being releived, went into the fier to warme him & fownd him asleepe, & that after he had stood sentinell awhile & come in, Antho. Thompson desired him to stand sentinell againe, w[c]h shewed he had bin asleepe.

The Go[r] asked Ric[h] Osborne whether he could prove a sleepe in an vndue manner.

Ric[h] Osborne answered he thought he might take oath he was asleepe so long as a man might goe from the watch-howse to the meeting-howse, although neither of the other two chardge him w^{t}h it, adding he had told Luke Atkinson that hee was disord^{r}ly sleepinge. But Luk Atkinson saith he remembreth noe such thinge. But this case was thus left w^{t}h the aprobation of the court & Richard Osborns consent.

[188] || Roger Knapp absent from squadron trayning ye 7th Aprill & late vpon the Lords day 18th Aprill, he answered that for the squadron trayninge he had forgott it, & his wife being forth he stayed with the children; & for that Lordsday, his wife *his wife* had bin sicke the Lordsday before, & she desiring now to goe to meeting, he stayed at home. He was fined 1^{s} towards the squadron trayninge neglect & the other was passed by.

John Nash hath sold his second devision of vpland w^{c}h he had w^{t}h Mr. Mansfeilds lott, viz^{d} 11 acres, to Mathew Moulthropp & 11 acres to George Smith.

Peter Browne hath sold 2 acres 32 rodd of meddow to George Smith w^{c}h is all the p̱portion of meddow in the west meddow, & 5 acr. $\frac{1}{4}$ of vpland lyeing in the first devision of the suburbs quarter.

George Smith aljenats 1 acre 16 pole of the forementioned meddow vnto Mathew Moulthropp.

Peter Browne hath sold all his land in the Neck to Mr. Malbon.

Geo: Smith hath sold all his land in the Necke to Mr. Malbon.

Vincent Meggs was complayned off for not bringing his armes one shewing day and was late one Lords day, & was fined 6^{s}.

John Lawrenson complayned off for comminge late to watch one night, for com̄inge late 2 Lords days. Mr. Malbon answered for h^{m} & said that one Lords day the cattle brake out of ye yard & he followeing them to prevent damadge, because it was in the spring & then cattle were apt to be swampt, but he came & mett y^{m} that walked the rownds in the m^{r}ket place, and at another time fell asleepe & outslept himselfe, fined for 2 defects, 2^{s}.

Thomas Lampson absent from one squadron trayninge, hs

answere was that it fell a rayning & thundring when he was at lott & he thought that would put by the trayninge, but the comp^{a} exersised. He was fined 2^{s} 6^{d}.

Jno Leavermore desired that his fine for contempt might be taken off, but the court, *but ye court* as yet see noe reason to move y^{m} to it.

Samuell Hodkejs totally absent one trayning day answered he did want bread & went to mill; this answer not satisfying the court, it was ordred that hee pay 5^{s}, the fine for totall absence.

At a Genl Court held at Newhaven 5 July, 1647.

It was desired that as men had formerly ingadged themselues to contribut a portion of corne to the colledge, that the would not now be slacke in carrying it to the collecto^{r}s, but that w^{t}hin 7 or 8 dayes at farthest, these that are behind would pay, for its a service to Christ & may yeald pretious frut to ye collonyes herafter, being that the commission^{r}s have taken order that none should have the benifit of it but those that shall remayne in the country for the service of the same, the bringing in of w^{c}h corne was ingadged by vote.

It was now remembred that form^{r} orders were made for the incouradgement of the sheapheard, but lately it is fownd that vppon some speeches that he hadd mett w^{t}hall from some, he has entertayned thoughts to remove. Therfore it was desired that things might be so considered off, that the sheepe with himselfe might bee kept in this towne, for thereby much good may redound to the publicque.

Herevpon it was ordred that the Necke, or so much of it as may be improved by the sheep, should from time to time be made vse of as a sheep pasture, & to that purpose it was further ordered that euery one who hath grownd in the neck should cleare his land, according to order from the committee to be chosen to treate w^{t}h Goodman Smith, & consederation was had also about a penn to keepe sheepe in, all w^{c}h w^{t}h sundry other questions was com̃itted by this gen^{ll} court vnto those of the perticuler court, joyning to them elder Newman,

bro. Myles, Mr. Tuttle, Mr. Caffinch, Mr. Gilbert, Mr. Wack-
[189] man, || Wm Preston, bro: Camfeild and Goodman Johnson, as a committee vnto whom all questions concerninge the sheep buisinese is refferred.

In regard of a former order made concerninge the leaveing of some questions about a highway in Mr. Lambertons quarter, vnto bro. Wackman & bro. Antho. Thompson to issue, & their thoughts beinge that it will best, as they conceive, answere all the quarter if the highway runne through the midle of their lands. Goodm^{n} Hitchcocke thinking his right too much to be intrenched vpon therby, besides some extreame inconveyniencjes to follow on him besides, the consideration & full determynation of all questions in that poynt was recommended vnto Mr. Malbon & Mr. Francis Newman, bro: Wackman & bro. Thompson, and the quarters meetinge, and the said committee are to give notice when & where they will meete, & if any fayle of comminge, he shall pay 12^{d} fine for his defect in none appearance, & also shalbe bownd to stand vnto what those that meete doe conclude of in the case.

Bro: Andrewes was desired that himselfe & some others formerly deputed, would againe view the west bridge, that all further damadge may be seasonably prevented and the worke as soone as may bee (thats to be don,) finished.

It was ordred that in the orders about watching, theise words be added, (that euery watchm^{r} must see & view the armes of every watchman that they be compleat,) w^{c}h is but the exposition of the former order.

It was propownded that men would cleare wood & stones from their pale sides, that the watchmen in darke nights might the more safely walke the rownds w^{t}hout hurt thereby, & the orders about watching were read in court.

Richard Osborne who had formerly given publicque offence by chardgeing the watchm^{r}s generally w^{t}h disorderly sleepeinge, neglect of their dutie in their trust committed to them, now made acknowledgement of his sinne in so chardgeing them, whereas he is not able to prove any such miscarriadge, & perticulerly, to justifie himselfe had called Antho: Thompson into the court, & had chardged Mathew Camfeild & Mr.

Tutle wth neglects or sleepeing dureing the time they should have bin wakeing & attending their trust, wch he was not able to prove against any of them, wch did satisfie.

Bro: Mitchell & Goodmn Daighton request the court to bestow a peice of spare grownd vpon them which lay betweene their howse lotts, with promise to mayntayne the highway before their dores or howselotts & stopp the currant that now spoyleth the way. And the grant of the land wth a view of the conveyniency of it to the towne & them with the inconveyniences that may attend Goodman Buckingham was refferred vnto brother Rich Myles & bro: Wm Davis, & what they should doe therein the towne would allow of. The land to be devided in proportion to each as the committee see cause.

It was ordred that the captayne wth the rest of the mjlitary officers should see one Jno Jackson, servant to Mr. John Wackman, & judge whether he be meete for exersise and watchings, considering that he is purblynd.

At a Court held at Newhaven this 6th July, 1647.

The Governor informed the court that it had bin above a twelue month since Mr. Thomas Trowbridges howse & land had bin sould vnto Mr. Evance, & that therfore he had desired Mr. Evance to come to the court, none of the monneyes being yet paid.

Mr. Evance answered that he received the land for country pay & also he bought in it refference to debts dew to him from some of the creditors, who owed hm monnyes.

The Gor told Mr. Evance that monnyes were due to the towne for the rates of ye land 10l or vpwards, wch must bee paid. Mr. Evance promised to see that dischardged, only said if the debt were demaunded, he would hope the court would doe hm the lik right, that he may have whats dew to him from others, wch the court told him he should not fayle of. Wherevpon Rich Pery & Henry Gibbence were desired against the next court, to cleare the debts dew to them by good testimony.

[190] || John Hall informed the court that Mr. Wilks formerly of this towne had promised to give his wife tenn pownds if she should serve out her time w^{t}h him w^{c}h she did. And to prove that promise brought first Wm Payne, who vpon oath affirmed, that the first time that he heard his Mr Wilks speake this was at Boston, on what grownds he knoweth not, that if his mayd would stay out her time, he would give her tenn pownds, & this hee heard him say often here before the servants in the howse.

Brigett Wilks vpon oath affirmed that she heard her vncle promise to give Goodye Hall ten pownds if shee served out her time.

Sister Hall informed the court that she demaunded nothing of her mistris because her mistris told her her master would give her a portion.

A difference betweene Mr. Francis Newman, Tho^{m} Mitchell and Goodman Dayton was presented to the court. Vpon the courts advize that 2 men might be chosen to end it, by consent Mr. Crayne & Goodman Myles wer chosen.

Mr. Tho^{m} Pell haveing attatched about 200^{l} of Mr. Zellicks goods, Mr. Pell & Mr. John Evance entred themselues as security to the court for ye damadges.

Ambrosse Sutton for comminge too late at watch was complayned off. But Mr. Crayne affirming day light was not in, & armes not viewed, nor the watch sett, it was passed by.

Richard Osborne haveing satisfied the court & the watchm^{r}s concerning his wronging them, desired his fine might be taken off, but it was respitted.

Wm Blayden being warned to the court and not appearing, it was accounted a contempt.

Brother David Atwater being absent from the watch one night was ordred to pay his fine. Also defective another time, but he layeing the fault on the m^{r} of the watch it was respitted.

Mr. Henry Brunwin hath sould to Goodm^{n} Wm Judson, his dwelling howse, howse-lott, w h the orchard in it, & the barne that now is standing onn it, 37 acr of vpland w^{c}h is his first devizion w^{t}hin 2 myle, w^{t}h 7 acr. $\frac{1}{4}$. 24 rodd in the Necke, 21 acr. of meddow, and 84 acres of vpland wch is his second devision, all his right in comons & oxe pasture & whateuer hereafter shalbee a privelidge to his lott, together wth a bedstead and trundlebedd, a paire of vallance & a peice of blew darnix, a malt-mill, a well buckett & chayne, two loads of clay brought hom, & the fence about the lott repayred, as ℘ a bill of sayle appeard p^r^sented in court.

AT A COURT HELD AT NEWHAVEN AUG. 3^d^, 1647.

Wm Blayden warned for a contempt the last court, his answere was the could not *not* come because of the extreame payne he was vnder wch satisfied.

Also he was complayned of for late comming 2 Lords dayes, one day he heard not the drume, and thother day he haveing wett the day before in the evening it rayninge, & he not able to mak a fier to dry his clothes, was forced to lye abedd the Lords day. For these defects his answere was vnsatisfying, & he fyned 2^s^. It was ordered that the next court he appeare to hold forth the sight of his sine in profanely neglecting to co^m^ to the ordynanses.

Bro. Benham for his neglect in warninge David Atwater to watch was fined 5^s^.

Mrs. Turners man absent from the watch one night was complayned onn, Mrs. Turner did answere that she had 2 oxen tooke hurt & were in danger to dye, & in attendance on them it proved the neglect of the watch, wch satisfyed the court.

Mihill Palmer was complayned of for absence one night from the watch, he answered he had provided & agreed Ric^h^ Osborne to watch all the yeare for him. Ric^h^ Osborne denyed any such agreem^t^ absolutlje made w^t^hout condicon, but he being ill could not attended as in former seasons he had, & when he gave Mihil Palmer notice he was ill, did his indeauor to have gotten one to have watched but could not, wherevpon it was passed by.

[191] || Mr. Whitman, elder at Milford, alyenated his

howseing, lands, & what right he either hath or may have hereafter in Newhaven, vnto Mr. John Bracey.

Richard Osborne acknowledged that he had in a gennerall court chardged the m[rs] of the watches wth that he could not prove, nor was true in itselfe, & by what was said in court he was convinsed of his sinne, & haveing satisfied the masters of the watches in a gennerall court his fine vppon his intreaty was remitted.

Mr. Jn[o] Bracey doth alyenat to Mr. Wackm[n] 21 acr. ½ & 20 rodd of meddow w[ch] lyeth in the west meddow, 10 acr½ beyond the river, w[t]hin the lynes of the quarter, & 11 ac. & 20 rodd to be layd out in Solitary Cove or Mr. Malbons meddow as its cast.

Also 19 ac. ½ of vpland, lyeing beyond the West River in the first devizion.

And 164 ac. w[ch] is all his second devizion, w[th] all the allotem[t]s & privelidges which shalbelong thereto.

At a Court held at Newhaven the 7[th] Sept. 1647.

Sister Preston presented her husbands will & the inventory of his estate to the court to be entred.*

---

* "The will of William Preston, made July 9, 1647.

"I William Preston, a member of the church of New Haven, being upon my death bed as I conceave, through the blessing of God have my understanding and memory perfect as in tymes past, doe make and ordayne this my last will and testament, in manner and forme followinge.

"To Joseph Alsops wife, my daughter, I give 20[s], or if her husband be willing to take 3 acres of land, lying in first devision by the sea side, and build and dwell there, he may. But if hee intend not to dwell there, the 20[s] is all she can demande. My sonn Edward, I give him in the same lott before mentioned three acres of ground, if my wife see it may be a benefit to him to further him his way according to God, or els 20[s] is all he can demand. To my sonne Danyell I give 20[s], and John is to have 20[s] when he comes to bee twenty yeares of adge; and I give to my daughter Mary, 20[s], to be paid when she is nineteene years of age, and for the rest, where the time of payment is not mentioned, I leave it to my wife when she can conveniently pay it. As for Wm. Meakars wife, in that upon her marriadge and since I have given her is more than I can give to any of her brothers or sisters, yet I give her five shillings. As for the rest of my estate, which consists in house, lands and cattles, moveable goods which I have here in New Haven, in New England, I give all to my wife for the bringing up of my children that God hath given mee by her, in consideration she was a means to bring mee and the rest to New England. I have an estate in Old Eng-

Wm Blayden contemptuously neglecting to bring his armes one Lordsday, made it his excuse, that being wett the last day of the week, & his clothes being wett & not haveing means to dry them as he said, came not to the exersise that Lordsday. The truth appeareing to be noe other then a profaine neglecting, yea dispising the ordynances of Christ through sloathfulnesse, wherevpon the judgment of the court was that he be publicquely whipped, as he is the first profanely breaking the Saboth, worshipping not God nor wayting for a blessing from him onn himselfe.

Edward Parker being warned to the court for rates dew to the treasurer, some pt before he marryed the widdow, & some part since, Edw. Parker promjsed pay for what is dew since he marryed the widdow, in corne shortlye, & for that before John Potters death dew, it was respitted.

Wm Pert was warned to the court for taking water-myllions one Lords day out of Mr. Hooks lott, & Mr. Hooke complayneth that he hath often bin abused this way, & since that time his orchard hath bin robd.

Wm Perts answere was that his Mr sent him into the quarter & to see whether there were any hoggs wthin the fence, & he was bidd by his Mr to bring hom a watter-milion wth him, he being bidd to goe that way through Mr. Hooks lott, after the Saboth, he tooke 2 wattermilions, he said it was the first

---

land, and for part of my house and land and other goods given by my father to my elder brother and myself, wherein a foefment of law calling to councell and left in the hands of two foefees, namely, Mr. William Lawson and Mr. William Banke, to be kept in trust on our behalfe when wee should demand it, ourselves, heires, executors, administrators or assignes, lying in Yorkeshire in a town called Giglesweke in Craven. This land and goods, what is of it, is to be devided into fouer parts, to be equally devided amongst the children I had by my former wife, as Daniell, Edward and John Preston, and my daughter Elizabeth, Sarah and Mary, and the fourth part I give to my wife, and for my son John, I leave him in the hands of Brother Roger Allen and Brother Thomas Munson, to place where they two shall thinke good to dispose of him, to such a calling, either by land or sea, as he shall like his calling and master.

"To these former I set my hand, William Preston, as my owne act. Witnesse Roger Allen, Thom. Munson."

Wm. Preston Dr. to Zachry Whitman £10, to Mr. Malbon £0, 7, 8, to Joseph Alsop £0, 18, to Roger Allen £1, 5, to Bro: Wheeler £0, 6, to Isaac Whitehead £0, 5, 8, to Wm. Russell £0, 1, 6, to Mrs. Lamberton £0, 3, 9, to John Chidsey £0, 9.

Wm. Preston is Cr. dew from Mr. Allerton £0, 6, 9, from John Clarke £0, 4, 10. Inventory taken 30th day of the 6th month 1647, by Mathew Gilbert, Joshuah Atwatter, sum £65, 15.

act of his in this kind & hoped it should be the last. For his vnrighteousnesse & profannesse of his sperit & way, so soone thus to doe after the Saboth, he was to be publiquely corrected, although moderatly because his repentance did appeare.

Mr. Francis Newman & Goodman Myles were desired by the court to vallew Mr. Turners estate.

Thom Ceffinch his will was presented to the court, wherin Mr. John Ceffinch was made executor, but at the present he declared himselfe not free to accept of it.

AT A COURT HELD AT NEWHAVEN THIS 5th OCTOBER, 1647.

Mr. John Bracy allyenats vnto Mr. Kitchell his house and* homelott, conteyning 2 acr. & halfe, and 25 ac. of vpland, lyeing in Mr. Wackmans quarter next Mr. Wackmans land, and 5 ac. of meddow, be it more or lesse, lyeing at the end of Mr. Wackmans quarter in the west meddowes, & 9 acr. of vpland, be it more or lesse, lyeing in the neck wth what comonag remained yn vnsold.†

Mr. Bracey alienats to Mr. John Evance 5 ac. of meddow lyeing at the end of the Yorkshire quarter, in the west meddowes.

Mr. Bracey alyenats to Goodman Boykin 9 acr. 20 rodd of meddow, lyeing next Goodman Gibbs & Goodman Fowler in the west meddowes.

[192] || Mr. Evance hath sold to Wm Potter 27 acr$\frac{1}{2}$ of meddow as it commeth to him in the townes books, and it lyeth in the east meddow betweene Mr. Crayne & bro. Punderson, and 32 acr. of vpland belonging to it next to Mr. Gilberts farme.

Mr. Evance hath sold to Henry Gibbons 20 acr. $\frac{3}{4}$, 17 pole of the land formerly belonging to Mr. Trowbridge, wch is part of the first devizion of land lyeing one this side the West River; and 2 acr. of meddow in the west meddow lyeing next Mr. Allertons meddow.

---

* These words [house and] interlined by Mr. Newman.

† The last six words added by Mr. Newman.

Mr. Evance hath sold to Antho: Thompson 4 acr. 26 rodd of Mr. Trowbridges first devizion, lyeing on the west side.

Mr. Evance hath sold to Wm Gibbons 2 ac. of Mr. Trowbridges meddow next Mr. Allerton.

Mr. Evance hath sold to Mr. Rotherford 3 acr. of meddow.

Mr. Evance hath sold to Jno Walker 3 acr. of the same meddow.

Mr. Evance hath sold to Ric^{h} Osborne 3 acr. of the same meddow.

Mr. Ceffinch chardged Hen. Whelply w^{t}h driveing away a bullock of his long since, by w^{c}h means its lost.

Henry Lions testimony vpon oath was read, wherin he testifieth that though they had indeauored to have driven back a beast of Mr. Ceffinches towards Newhaven, from Mr. Crayns penn onn the west side, they could not, but went w^{t}h the cattle driven to Milford, & neere Mr. Tapps they parted Mr. Tapps cattle, & testifieth that Henry Whelply w^{t}h the rest of hs cattle drove away a stray beast of Mr. Ceffinches, &c.

Goodm^{n} Daighton saith that hee looking w^{t}h others for Mr. Bernards cattle, & finding them with strange cattle, mett Mr. Crayne who told them they had neede looke to it what they did to drive away strañg cattle, for he had smarted for it, but being at Mr. Crayns penn on the west side, some Milford cattle went away & Mr. Ceffinches bullocke w^{t}h them, then he told Henry Whelply, he would not have any hand in driveinge away strang cattle & so came away. But he further affirmeth that about 3 weeks after he saw the same bullocke vnder the West Rocke.

Mr. Knell informed the court that at the waterside at Poquanock ferry they did indeavour to have driven ouer their cattle, and then one ranne away but afterwards was fownd, and Mr. Caffinch doubting it had bin his bullocke had the sight of it & liked it not, and indead all of them proved Mr. Bernards. Goodm^{n} Daighton testfied vpon oath what he had respectively testified.

The centence of the court was that the damadges must fall vpon the playntiffe, he being defective in proofe of hs chardge, and ordred to allow 5^{s} to Henry Whelply besids the chardges of the court.

Roger Knapp complayned of wronge don him by Mr. Ceffinches swine & monney dew to him, but could not get it, but by consent of both partjes. G. Judson & Mr. Wackman were chosen to arbitrate and end the difference.

Goodm[n] Johnson alienated 5 ac $\frac{5}{6}$ of vpland to Rich[h] Pery, w[c]h was the 2[d] pt of the first devizion belonging form[r]ly to Dauid Yale.

Phillip Galpin appeared on behalfe of his wife who should have bin corrected for her sinfull folly in fornication, but now seing a barre was put in by God in her affrightm[t] so as her miscariadge would be hazarded, she being w[t]h child, if she were brought forth, as appeared vpon testimony from the midwife, she was fined 20[s], the court respecting m[r]cy in her case.

Ambrosse Sutton was warned to the court for giveing out a false report concerninge Margaret Cadwell, that she should goe out of her M[r] howse vnto Mr. Jn[o] Ceffinches when they were abedd, & that Joseph Guernsie & Eliz[a] Downinge went forth w[t]h her into the quarter to eate wattermjllions, about one aclock at night, & were fownd by the watch. But he added to her wronge, that they sent away Elizabeth Downinge least that Mr. Caffinch should wake, and they two went together, & that Joseph Guernsie should say he could doe what he would with her.

Ambrosse Sutton confesseth the thing is true,but feare hindred him at the Go[r] and hearinge it would be denyed, he also denyed it against hs present light. Joseph Guernsie told him part of this, and Richard Lovell the other part.

[193] || Rich[h] Lovell said that Joseph Guernsie told him he had bin gathering watermjllions w[t]h Margeret, & sitting downe he fownd her plyable, he might have done what he would, but said nothing to h[m] of the girles being there or sent away.

Joseph Guernsie denyed that he had told them soe as before exprest, but true he had told them somthinge, but he could not say soe of her.

Rich[h] Lovell and Ambrosse Sutton both testified that he had told them he could have don what he listed with her.

Eliz[a] Downinge said she was by all the while & not sent away as its reported.

Thom[m] Dum̃e, who lived in the famyly wth Margeret, informed the court he had never seene any light carryadge in her.

John Lawrenson told Mr. Malbon he was sorry he had spoken at all of it, seing that them that had said it did denny it.

Joseph Guernsie for his raysing a reproach vpon Margarett Cadwell & afterward lying in the thinge when he was questioned, for wch he was fined 40s to the mayd & 20s to the towne.

Ambrosse Sutton hearing this report spreads it to strangers, & hearing he is lik to be questioned about, saith he will & doth denny it before the magistrates, although it was witnessed by two to his face. He was fined 40s to the maid he wronged and 20s to the towne.

Richard Lovell was fined for his hearinge this false report & resolution to conceale it from the cogniscance of the magistrate, 10s to the maide.

Mr. John Ceffinch refussed to accept of the executorship to hs bro. Thom estate.

R. P. 1647.

[The remainder of this volume is in the handwriting of Francis Newman.]

[For the record of the General Court October 18, 1647, see *post* p. 354.]

[We learn from the Guilford Records that there was a Court of Magistrates held at New Haven, October 24, 1647.]

[194] AT A COURTE HELD AT NEWHAVEN THE 2th DAY OF NOUEMBER, 1647.

Samuell Hogkines dissired that he might have his fine, or p̱t of it, taken of, wch he was fined for goeing awaye from trayning in the afternoone wthoute leave, but the courte sawe no cause to abate any p̱t therofe.

Richard Myles being warned to bringe in an inventorie of Thomas Clarkes estate, informed the courte that Thomas Clarke only gave hime order to receive of Robert Emry 11l for a house and lott sould to the saide Robert, wch 11l hee, the said Richrd Myles hath received, but he knoweth of nothing *of nothing* elc left heare as any part of Thomas Clarkes estate.

George Ward and Lawranc Warde plantiffs, declare against the company of marchants of Newhauen, vizd, Mr. Theophilus Eaton, now gouerner, Mr. Stephen Goodyeare, Mr. Richard Malbon, Mr. Thomas Gregson. First, that the said company spake to them to make a suit of blockes for the great shipp. 2dly, that they spake to Mr. Lamberton to give them the demensions. 3dly, that Mr. Lamberton did it. 4tly, that these blockes were made by them the said Geo: and Lawranc Warde and deliuered in and received by Mr. Hart as the companyes agent. 5tly, that for these blockes the marchants promised paye. 6dly, for these blockes they the said Geo: and Lawranc Warde haue received p̱t of ther paye.

First Lawranc Warde saith that, meetting Mr. Gregson and Mr. Lamberton together in Mr. Dauenports streete, Mr. Gregson said to hime the said Lawranc, are yow aboute those blockes, (for Mr. Gregson had formerly bespoke the blockes,) Lawranc answered, I have spoke with my brother and wee are willing to goe on if wee agree, but wee must haue the demensions from yow. Mr. Gregson said, brother Lamberton will yow doe that, hee answered yea, Lawranc tould Mr. Gregson that Goodman Myles had spake somewhat to hime aboute them; then Mr. Gregson said, what hath Goodman Myles to doe w^t^h them, the belonge to ye rigging, doe they not brother Lamberton, he answered yea; but Liftenant Seely can saye somewhat to this matter.

Liutennant Seely affeirmed that he could testifye nothing that Mr. Gregson did bespeake these blockes for the shipp, but Lawranc Warde asked hime, the said Leiutenant, on time to goe along w^t^h hime to Mr. Lambertons, accordingly he did goe w^t^h hime; hee spake to Mr. Lamberton aboute paye for these blockes, Mr. Lamberton said he bespake them not for himeselfe, butt was sett on by the company and was their agent to give direction to haue them done.

The Governer answered that they the saide marchants were no company to any such purpose that what on did all did, but euery on acted for himeselfe and must answer for his owne doeings, but for himselfe in perticuler hee knew nothing of it, so saith Mr. Goodyere and Mr. Malbon, and Mr. Gregson being absent could not answer for himselfe.

Further Lawranc Warde saith that Mr. Lamberton came a second time and bespake the blockes for the company as his brothers wife can testifye. Goodey Warde saith she remembred when Mr. Lamberton came downe he wished her husband and brother to goe on, for the marchants were willing to suit them w^t^h paye. She was asked if she knew wheither it were for these blockes or no, she answered she knew not.

Lawranc Warde saith that Mr. Lamberton spake to them to make some moldes w^c^h they did and brought them to hime, and hee wrotte vpon them how many ther should be of a sort. That the marchants did receive them, hee, the said Lawranc Warde, proues by his owne testimony and Mr. Harts hand, for he saith y^t^ Mr. Malbon wished hime to deliuer them to Mr. Hart for them, and they did so, as Mr. Harts bill vnder his owne hand will showe. Mr. Malbon saith he remembers it not, but if hee did it was to doe them a kindnesse, because they were to goe out of the towne and might not knowe where to laye them.

Further Lawranc Warde saith that the feoffees, viz^d^, Mr.

Wakeman, Mr. Attwatter, Mr. Crane and Goodman Myles can saye something in this matter.

Mr. Wakeman saith for the bargaine he can saye nothing, but a litle before Mr. Gregson went, some mottion was made to them the said feoffees to paye, wch was verey strange to them, and thervpon they mett at the gouerners wth the marchants, Goodman Warde was there and aleadged his want of paye, the marchants conceived it belonged to the feoffees to paye, but they thought it belonged to the rigging and could not consent to paye any thing towards them. In that meetting many speeches pased betwixt Mr. Lamberton and Goodman Warde, and as the said Mr. Wakeman remembreth, Goodman Warde said Mr. Lamberton and Mr. Gregson acted wth hime, and minded Mr. Gregson of that speech wth hime in Mr. Dauenports streette. Mr. Gregson seemed not to remember it, thoughe hee denyed it not, but said w^{t}hall that hee did it as a servic to ye feoffees, these feoffees denyed y^{t}, thervpon Mr. Gregson seemed somewhat moved and said to the gouerner, if they will not paye then I shall leaue my share, but then I will haue them in my or our custody and will bee payde before they passe.

Richard Myles saith that Mr. Gregson said as hee vnderstood hime that hee should leaue inoughe heare to paye for the blockes and would take them into his owne custody and would bee satisfyed w^{t}houte losse before they went, it was asked wheither it was vpon this ground that hee bespoke them, he said he could not tell.

Mr. Attwatter saith hee can add nothing to what hath bine expressed.

[195] || Mr. Crane said he tooke it vp that Mr. Gregson intended they should be payde for out of his owne estate, rather then the men should bee vnpayde. It was demaunded wheither Mr. Gregson in all these debates did saye or carye it as the companys agent, but they could not affeirm that, but Mr. Evanc said that Mr. Gregson ever denyed it.

Lawranc Warde saith that his wife went to the gouerner for some cloth vpon this account, Goodey Myles being wth her; the gouerners answer was that hee had payde a some allreadie for her brother, wch was as much, for any thing hee knew, as his pt came to. Goodey Myles saith she went wth Goodey Ward to ye gouerners, she dissiered some cloth, he said hee had not but for his owne vse, but for his pt hee had payde as much as his p^t^ came to, it was asked if she knew vpon what account, she said no. Goodey Warde saith that the gouerner said he had payde as much as his share, but cannot saye that is was as a debt to her husband.

The Gouerner answered, it is true Goodey Warde came to hime for some cloth, he tould her then, that for the blockes he had nothing to doe wth them, nor did hee bespeake any, but if the feoffees would joyne, rather then they should bee vnpayde, hee would paye his pt; and for that he said hee had payde as much as his share, it was thus, Goodman Whelply threatening to put George Warde into ye courte for a debte of 3^l^: 10^s^:, the governer wished hime first to gett a meeting of the feoffees to consider further of the blockes, others of them being from home, Mr. Crane only came, and wth his consent the gouerner gave a note to Goodman Whelply for the 3^l^: 10^s^, and tooke the accquittanc in his owne and Mr. Cranes name, refusing vtterly to paye a penny but in a joynt way wth the feoffees. This both Mr. Crane acknowledged and the acquittanc cleared.

Further, Lawranc Warde saith that Mr. Goodyere sent for pt of these blockes & made vse of them. Mr. Goodyere saith that Mr. Fowler sent to hime to gett him on blocke wch he wantted for his vessell; he, the said Mr. Goodyere, tould them that came, he had no right more then another to them, yett the case being a case of necessitie, he acknowledgeth he sent for on blocke, and Mr. Fowler promised to deliuer such another for it, for he had spoke to Goodman Ward for some.

Captaine Astwood propounded that seing the case was difficulte, ther wanting full evidenc on the plantiffs pt to cast the cause against the defendants, and yett it was fitt the poore men should bee payde for ther labour, that therfore the m^r^chn^tt^s and the feoffees, by consent, would joyntly put the whole case to a referenc wth the plantiffs. The marchants expressed themselues willing, and the feoffees answered, that as feoffes they knew not wheither they had power to doe it, but being searched into and it appearing they had, they expressed themselues willing allso, and bothe the Wards expressed themselues very willing. The matter being thus muttually agreed they chose ther men, the marchants chose Captaine Astwood, the Wards Mr. Disbrowe, the feoffees Mr. Davenport; so the suit being stoped, the cause was reffered to these 3, or any 2 of them to isue, by the consent of all ꝑties.

Mr. William Westerhouse dissires of the courte, (Mr. John Evanc being his interpreter,) that the three Duch men wch are prissoners at this time, maye haue ther libbertie, and he and Mr. Samuell Goodanhouse will bee bound in a bond of a thousand Holland gilderes for ther appearanc.

Answer was returned them from the court, that if the said Mr. William and Mr. Samuell would enter a recognesanc of a thousand gilderes, that these three men wch are prissoners, all and every on of them shall be forthcoming att the courts call, they shall haue ther libbertie, and the said Mr. William and Mr. Samuell being both present, said they would bee so bound, whervpon the marshall had order from the courte, that before Mr. Evanc he should deliuer the three prissoners to them.

Further, Mr. William Westerhouse, (Mr. Evanc interpreter,) dissiered the courte to grant him an arest vpon that money wch is in Mr. Goodyeres hand, to be payde to ye Duch gouerner*, vpon the consideration of his shipp being taken awaye; the courte answered that ther was a fixed estate stoode ingadged for that money, and vnless a fixed estate can be put in for securetie to such a vallew as maye beare all damadge wch maye arise by such an arest, it cannot be granted.

Mr. Pery passeth over 35 acrs of vpland to John Clarke and Samuell Whithead, lying on end butting vpon the necke highway, the other end butting vpon the mill highwaye, be-

* For the ship called the Zwoll, which the authorities of Fort Amsterdam had sold, Sept. 21, to Mr. Goodyear, and contracted to deliver at New Haven. Under pretext of conveying the craft in safety, they put soldiers on board, and by their means seized Mr. Westerhuyzens ship, the St. Beninio, and carried it to New Amsterdam. O'Callaghan, N. N. ii. 48.

twixt the land of William Tuttill and the land of Fra: Newmã.

Mr. Pery paseth over to Richard Hull, 10 acrs and halfe of vpland, wch lyes neare the mill, wthin the two myle.

[196] ||Mr. Pery passeth ouer to Mris Turner 14 acrs and a halfe of meddow, lying in the east meddowe, wch is all that proportion wch did belonge to his owne proper lott.

Mr. Pery passeth ouer to Thomas Munson, 16 acrs of vpland, wch is on halfe of the second devission of land wch belonged to that lott wch was old Mris Eattons, lying on the other sid of the West River, behind the Yorkesheir quarter.

Hee passeth over 16 acrs more of the same land, lying in the same place, to Thomas Moris.

Mr. Pell being warned to the courte to answer for some ill returnes he sent to the generall courte when they sent to hime for his wives fine, wch, as the gouerner tould hime, rather held forth a contempt of the courte then otherwise, hee said he thought it not his debte, but it was tould him his wiues debts were his; he said, the court cannot take what is mine. The gouerner said ye courte must consider that, he said it was a new thing to hime, he heard not of it, it was tould hime that was not likely, but hee must know of it, seing it was done in open courte, but if he had come to the court and given a faire answer, something might have bine considered, but he said he dissiered to consider of it. The court gave hime a moneths time, and if he dissiered a copie of the proceedings of the courte, he might have it, payeing the secretarie for wrighting of it.

The 16th of the 9th moneth, William Andrewes junr was called before the gouerner, magistrats and deputies for the towne, and then was charged for the sinn of drunkennese the last weeke, wch thing he did not deney but confessed as hee needes must, ther being severall wittnesses wch sawe it; as John Clarke, John Walker, his master Mr. Evanc; this fact was considered. The gouerner tould hime he was sorey he was come before the courte againe for this miscariadge, seing he had bine fined onc allreadie, either for drunkennese or drinking and the cause of others being drunke, that now the courte must thinke of some other waye of punishment, seing it seemes to bee a sinn rooted in him.

The court considering these things sawe cause to agree that he should receive corporall punishment by whipping, for that was the proper punishment for such brutish sinns, but because he was to goe awaye suddenly in his masters shipp, (maye be this night,) therfore the courte agreed that 5l. be depossitted as a fine laide vpon hime, for wch 5l his master Mr. Evanc did vndertake, that hee at his returne *he* maye be brought forth to the courte againe, and vpon good testimony of his good cariage and behauiour the courte will consider of it.

ATT A COURTE THE 7th DAY OF DECEMBER 1647.

The will of Nathaniel Draper* was deliuered into the courte by William Russill, for Phillip Galpin, and being read was deliuered to the secretarie to be recorded, wth the testimony of Arthur Branuch and a bill from Mr. Leach of the wages due to the deceased Nathaniel Drapr, wch is to be pd by Mr. Pell.

The gouerner acquainted the court that he heard that Anthony, the neager, his servant, gott some stronge watter, and hee heard that hee was drunke, therfore, because it was openly knowne, he thought it necessarie the matter should bee heard in the courte, whereas, had it bine keept wthin the compase of his owne family, he might have given him family correction for it.

Anthony saith he did goe to Mr. Evanc his house for some suger, and Mathew, his neager, asked hime to drinke, he did not refuse it, Mr. Evanc his neager pouered somewhat out of a

---

* "Will of Nathaniel Draper made the 25th of the 2d month 1467."

Gives to Phillip Galpine; all of the tobacco I have aboard of the barke Faulcon. Said Phillip to receive all his wages due to him from Thomas Pell for his service in this barke.—Acquits Elias Parkman of a bill of £3. 6. 4. except 20s that he gives to Henry Rotherford. Witness, Arthur Branch.

Affidavit of Arthur Branch before Mr. Edward Hopkins at Seabrooke the 1st of November 1647, that he witnessed the above will aboard the barke Faulcon, of New Haven, then riding near Rikatan in Virginia.

runlett and gaue it hime and went awaye, and he drunke, not knowing what it was, and after hee had drunke hee was light in his head after hee came abroade.

Mr. Evanc his neager saith, Anthony coming to their house he asked hime to drinke and poured out some strong watter w^c^h was in the bottome of a runlett into a pint pott and drunke to hime. It was asked hime, how many times Anthony drunke, hee said but onc, but as hee conceiveth, at onc hee dranke aboute the quantetie of 2 wine glasses. It was asked hime wheither he gaue it hime for beare, or tould him what it was, or wheither Anthony knew it was stronge watter, he said he could not tell.

The courte considering that it is the first time they haue heard any thing of Anthony this waye, and possibelly he might not know what he drunke till afterwardes, it being given him in such a vessell as is vsed to drinke beare out of, and hopeing it will bee a warning to hime for time to come, thought it fitt and agreed not to inflict any publique corporall punishment for this time, but as the gouerners zeale and faithfullnes hath appeared, (not conniving at sinn in his owne family,) so they leaue it to hime to give that correction w^c^h hee in his wisdome shall judge meete.

[197] ||M^ris^ Turner deliuered into the courte an inventorie of the estate left by her deceased husband, Mr. Nathaniel Turner*, w^c^h was read and deliuered to the secretarie to bee recorded.

M^ris^ Turner and Mr. Pery chose Mr. Gibbard and Francis Newman to heare and end some differenc betwixt them aboute the payeing in of some pease, w^c^h Mrs. Turner was to paye in to Mr. Pery for some meddowe she bought of hime.

---

* "An inventorie of the estate of Mr. Nathaniel Turner." Amount, £457. 7. 3. prised the 3^d^ day of the 10th month, 1647, by Francis Newman and Richard Miles.

Debtors, Thomas Meekes, £14. Samuel Hodgkins £5. Thomas Knowles £0. 18. Mrs. Gregson £1. 2. John Benham £0., 2. Benjamin Willmot £0. 9. Thomas Pell, William Andrewes for 3 hides.

The estate of Mr. Nathaniel Turner is debtor

To Mrs. Higginsons estate £28. 7. to Mr. Malbon £7. 9. to Mr. Gilbert £1. 10. to Roger Allen £1. 7. to Mr. Pery £7. 13. 6. to Mr. Allerton——for wages to servants £2. to Mrs. Stollion £0. 12.

M^{ris} Turner declared to the courte that she conceives her husband made a will and left all hee had to her dispose, as two of her daughters can testifye the same. Rebecka Turner saith, that when her father was to goe awaye, her mother dissiered hime to make a will, but hee answered that hee would make no will, but hee judged her faithfull and had found her faithfull, therfore left all to her and wished her to bee good to the chilldren, and wished the chilldren to beare wittness. Abigaile Turner testifyeth the same.

Mr. Evanc declared to the courte that he had taken out an attachment for some goodes of Mr. Godfereyes, to the vallew of 4^{l}, but because he was to goe awaye and he was lothe to put hime to trouble, it was by his order only serued vpon on hogshead of pease, he, the said Mr. Evanc, being content to take some debtes of his hear for the rest, if it might be made goode, but now some of those debtes seeme not to bee good, and the hogshead of pease is required by his order to carye to the Barbadoes. The court tould hime that Mr. Godfery is not heare to answer for himselfe, nor can any in the court answer for hime, but the attachment being for the hogshead of pease, if Mr. Evanc put in securetie to answer the damadge, he maye dispose of them, and Mr. Evanc promised to put in securetie.

Steven Reekes, master of a vessell that came from the Barbadoes, was called before the court to answer for some miscariadges of his on the Saboth daye, viz^{d} :—that he, the said Steven, did, contrary to the law of God and of this place, halle vp his shipp to or towardes the necke bridge vpon the Sabothe, which is a laboure proper for the six dayes, and not to be vndertaken on the Lords day. Mr. Reekes answered that their shipp laye on ground and had not flotted some dayes before, but that day the winde coming vp at the southeast, brought in a great tide, and then she flotted, and that all ye company did was but to keepe her of frōm runing on the banke or driving vpon her ancor, the shipp hauing neuer a boate to carie another ancor forth. Hee was toold they should have provided for that before, for it is ye duty of all men to remember the Saboth, and to provide so beforehand that nothing maye disturbe them vpon the Saboth, vnlesse it bee in cases of mercy or workes of such necessitie as could not be provided for the day before nor staye till the day after.

Mr. Larebe, a seaman belonging to the Phenix, was called before the courte, to answer to some miscariadges of his vpon the same Saboth, viz[d], that he, w[t]h some other company, went aboard the Phenix, and did worke not proper for that day, as halling of the vessell, and emptying some stones out of a cannow to help them in that servic. Mr. Larebe replied, that hee conceived the worke was a worke of charitie, to preserve the vessell that it might not perish, for their was some danger of her ouer-setting; besid, Mr. Pery came to hime himeselfe, and saide it was fitt some bodye should goe downe. Mr. Malbon saith that Mr. Pery was at his house, and he was speakeing of some danger the vessell might bee in, whervpon he wished his sonne Pery to goe to Mr. Davenport and aske his advise. Hee did, and Mr. Davenport tould hime hee should leave it to Gods providence, the Saboth was a day of rest, and therfore hee ought to rest. Then Mr. Malbon wished hime to give order that nothinge should bee done, w[c]h hee did, only on might goe downe and see what state the vessell was in, but that nothing, w[t]hout apparent necessitie, be done to her, yett Mr. Larebe, w[t]h diueres others, went and wrought, contrary to the lawe for the Saboth.

The courte considered bothe these cases and finde them to be much alike, and considering the persons, that they are strangers, and thinking they did not doe it out of contempt, but ignorantly, they agreed for this time, (that they acknowledging ther failings, and promising amendment for time to come,) to passe it by, but if any of our owne take libbertie heareby, the sentenc will bee heavier on them.

Abraham Bell paseth ouer to Jobe Halle his wholle lott w[c]h was given hime by the towne.

Mr. Rudderforde passeth ouer to William Ives 4 ac[rs] 1 quarter and 30 rode of vpland, of the first devission, w[t]hin the 2 myle, lying on the further side of the West River, on both sides of a pec of lande called the club, on end abutting vpon the west meddowe.

[196 *bis*] Theophilus Higenson passeth ouer to Christopher

Todd his house and home lott in Newhaven, containing ^ lying betwixt the lott now William Judsons, and Mr. Tenches; wth 8 acrs and a halfe lying in the third devisson of that quarter, wthin the 2 myle, on end abutting vpon the plaines, wch is the cow pastuer, betwixt the land of ^

And 24 acrs of land, if he haue so much, lying in the Necke, by the fenc side wch goes downe to the meddow. On pec of meddowe lying next the 24 acers of land, lying for 5 acrs and a halfe, bee it more or lesse, wch is all the meddowe Mr. Higenson hath remaining to himselfe at present; and 20 acrs of land on the other side the West River, wch is to lye amounge the smalle lotts.

Mr. Gibbard and Francis Newman were chossen in courte by Mr. Caffinch and his brother Samuell, to heare, and if they can, isue some differenc betwixt them, aboute some land wch is to bee devided betwixt them.

James Hayward entreth againest William Wooden an action of defamation, & declareth that the saide William Wooden, hauinge bine in the Baye and returned home heither to Newhaven, hath reportted diveres things of hime, of his cariadge in the Baye, wch are not true, but scandalous, and to his great wronge. As that he, the saide James, went aboute wth many lyes and vntruethes, and goeing aboute to cleare matteres concerninge a maide there, hee made them much worse. He saide hee had discovered himselfe to bee very false harted, and was perswaded he should neuer be received into the church againe, but if all was known yt he knew, they coulde not but banish hime oute of the cuntrye, and that hee had discovered a base frame of spirit when they liued at Captaine Turners together, wch things hee dissiered the saide William might bee called to answer for.

William Wooden, being called to answer, saith, the things hee spake he heard Goodey Pery, mother of the maide whome James should have had, speake, onely hee denyeth that hee saide if all were knowne that hee knewe, hee deserved banish ment, but his wordes were, if all were true that he had heard.

Richard Sparkes testifyeth vpon oath, that he heard William Wooden saye, that James Haywarde was hollowe harted, and dealt basely wth hime at Captaine Turners, and that he went downe into the Baye to cleare matters and made them worse, and if all knew that he knew, he would bee banished. And aboute Mr. Noris, that James gott a letter written, makeing Mr. Noris beleiue he gaue the woman and maide satisfaction, when hee did beleive ther was no such thing; and that James saide a man could not haue a pare of shooes at Newhauen vnder 6s, readie siluer; and that he caried lyes from henc to the Baye, and brought lyes from thenc heither, and that this was on of the basest places he euer came in.

Beniamen Hill saith, he heard William Wooden saye James was hollowe harted, and if the church knew that hee heard, he would not bee received againe, and that he would bee banished if all was true he heard, (or they knew as much as hee,) and that he dealt basely wth hime at Captaine Turners, as in the margent.

John Mascalle saith, that hee goeing into the Baye, went to Goodey Perys, the maids mother James should haue had, she asked hime howe James did, he said he thought bad inoughe, for he was cast out of the church, she said for what, he said for being drunke, she and her daughter said he was much given that waye when hee was there. They said they thought to come heither, but James discouradged them, and this pasadge she read in a letter, that they could not haue a pare of showes hear vnder 6s, readie silver, nor diett vnder 5s 6d a weeke, and that there was hardly any imployment for men. Aboute her daughter she saide, he gaue her no satisfaction, but went to Mr. Noris and wth colouging wordes gott a letter.

The court considering the premises, and seing ther is a letter spoken of wch Goodey Pery hath of James his wrighting, in wch, wheither ther be any thing to discover further guile in James, or any thing further to cleare the matter in hand, they are not yett cleare; therfore, the courte thinkes fitt to respitte it, only this they judge, that William Wooden hath spread these things in a defaming waye, and therfore must bee bound to attende the courte when they call for hime. Therfore it was propounded to James, if he was willing to respite it, he saide yea, so William putt in securetie; therfore the courte ordered that William putt in securetie. After a small space of time, James Hayward sertifyed the courte that he had receiued securetie of William Wooden for his appearanc, till the first of March next.

The inventorie of the estate of Mr. Thomas Gregson deceased, was deliuered into the courte, and being viewed, was deliuered to the secretarie to be recorded.*

Vpon a request from M[ris] Lamberton, ther is a monethes time given her to bring into the courte an inventorie of the estate her husband left.

[197 *bis*] || Harvie declareth, that aboute a yeare agoe he propounded some termes to Mr. Pell aboute some beavor, that is to saye, if Mr. Pell would procure hime beavor, he would deliuer hime 20 or 30[l] worthe of goodes into his hand, and it should remaine till shipps returned againe from England the next yeare, whervpon they came to some termes of agreement, first they bargained for a cowe, then for hoggs. For the cowe he promised beavor w[t]hout exception, her pric was 6[l]. For the hoggs hee would not absolutly ingadge himselfe for beavor, but if the bargaine went on, if hee payde not in beavor heare, he would paye in England, but if beavor came in, he should bee payde in that heare. And sinc that time, Mr. Pell tould the saide Goodman Harvie, he had beavor for hime, and he being at Mr. Pells house, when his barke came from Delaware Baye, the beavor then coming into his house, he said he had not sent his barke theither but for beavor for hime, and he said he thought he had gott so much as would paye hime; but not longe after he, the said Goodman Harvie, came to receive it, Mr. Pell said hee had it not, nor was hee ingadged to

---

* "An inventorie of the estate of Mr. Thomas Gregson, taken the 2nd of the 9th month, 1647." Real estate £246. Personal estate £225, 19, 6. Debts £18, 7. Total £490, 6, 6, signed Mathew Gilbert, Richard Miles.

The estate is Cr. to Phillip Leeke £1, 7, to Burwood of Stratford £1, 5, to Adam Nicolls £1, 5, to an adventure in the Susan to Barbadoes £14, 2, to John Gregory £0, 8.

The estate is Dr. to Mr. Stephen Goodyeare £6, to Mr. John Evance £3, 6, to Henry Lindolle £6, 5, 2¼, to the towne for rates £0, 7, 8, to the partable acco. of Mr. Stephen Goodyere and Mr. William Hawkines £40, 7, 2¼, to Mr. Davenport, £3, 4, to Mrs. Lamberton £3, 2, 11, to Mr. Malbon £2, 7, to Edward Wigglesworthe £10, 6, to Thomas Wheeler £1, 16, 5, to Mr. Butler £36, 4, 9, to Mr. Ling £10, to Mrs. Turner £1, 6, to several in smaller sums £1, 10, total £126, 3, 2.

paye beavor, and bide hime, the said plantiffe, prove that he was to give a bill for England. The plantiffe asked hime what paye he was to have, he said if he had gon to England, he would have given hime a bill. Mr. Attwatter saith, he heard Mr. Pell saye, if Goodman Harvie had gone himeselfe for England, he would haue given hime a bill out of curtesye.

Mr. Evanc saith, he heard Mr. Pell saye, he was to provide beavor for Goodman Harvie, but in refferenc to the bargaine he can saye nothinge.

Mr. Pell answered, that for the cowe he did acknowledg beavor, but for the hoggs the trueth is, Goodman Harvie vrged hime to take them, he denyed it many times, but when hee brought them and they were killed, he then demaunded beavor or bills for England, at w^{c}h Mr. Pell saith he wondered, and denyed it, but, as a frend in curtesy, promised to doe what hee could, but no pertickular paye was expressed in the bargaine.

Goodman Harvie saith he first made a punctiall bargaine before he brought his hoggs, that is to saye, 6^{l} in beavor for a cowe, and porke at 3^{d} the pound, to the vallew of twenty pounds in beavor, or a bill for England, for some wampome he left at his house. Mr. Pell said it laye by as he brought it, and so he should haue it againe.

Mr. Pell obiected against on of the hoggs w^{c}h was miselled, w^{c}h Goodman Harvie was willing to let goe at 2^{d} a pound, w^{c}h hogge waide about ^

Mr. Pell was asked wheither he had any more to saye, he said no, then the court proceeded to censure, but being devided in ther apprehensions, would not isue it at that time, but after by an appeale by Goodman Harvie it was brought before the generall courte for the jurisdiction which then was sitting at Newhauen, and they, hauing heard the case, did incline to perswade the plantiffe and defendant to isue it themselues, so Goodman Harvie propounded to Mr. Pell, that if he would paye for the cowe presently in beavor, and for the hoggs in good marchantable beavor at 8^{s} the pound in June next, he would be content to staye, Mr. Pell giveing hime good securetie for it. This offer Mr. Pell accepted, so that the case isued thus; what is in Mr. Pells booke, as a just debte due to hime by Goodman Harvie, is to be deducted out of the debte for the cowe and porke; 2^{d} ꝑ ^{l} is to be allowed for the miselled hogge, for the rest of the porke 3^{d}, ꝑ ^{l}, and what remaines vpon this debte, the cowe being payde for in beavor presently, he is to haue in June next, in good marchantable beavor, at 8^{s} ꝑ ^{l}.

The Gouerner tould Mr. Pell he was warned to bringe in the inventorie of his wives estate, left by her former husband; he said he could not, because accounts was not nor coulde not yett be made vp, but he was tould he must bring it in as farr as it can goe; he dissiered time till the next court and he would doe it, and it was granted hime.

Mr. Pell was asked for his wiues fine, he dissiered more libertie to consider of it, the courte tould hime they conceived ther was forbearanc inoughe allreadie, but yett they granted hime libbertie till the next monthly courte.

Mr. Evanc, for M^{ris} Lamberton, declareth, that Mr. Pell, possesing the estate of Mr. Francis Brewster, by mariage of his wife, is debto^{r} to M^{ris} Lamberton, 46^{l}: 06^{s}: 02^{d}, as appeares vpon account in M^{ris} Lambertons booke.

Mr. Pell said Mr. Brewster left behinde hime a bill of his debts, in wch is Mr. Lamberton 3^{l} in his debte, beside they wear ꝑtners in some goodes they bought together, but those accounts for ought he knowes are lost.

Mr. Evanc saith it is true that ther was a ꝑtable account betwixt them, w^{ch}, as is conceived, was isued betwixt them before they went henc, beside this proper acc^{o} now demaunded, and for that he offered proofe, first by Rogger Allen, whoe had ꝑt of those goodes wch were ꝑtable betwixt them.

Rogger Allen testifyeth vpon oathe, that he bought some iorn and coales of Mr. Lamberton, in wch he conceiveth Mr. Brewster had part, and thinkes he had some of them before they were emptyed. Mr. Lamberton sent for hime, and tould hime if he would take them together, he would gaine but a litle by them, he bought about 20^{l} worth of them, and was to paye in wheat. A little before the shipp went, Mr. Lamberton and Mr. Brewster demanded it, and Mr. Brewster thought much it was not payde, but this deponent could not gitt it in time, and therfore tould hime he would allowe whateuer damadge hee susteined for want of due payement, so they had [198] a meeting aboute the acc° at Mr. Lambertons, || and they appointed this deponent to come, whoe was ther as he coceives, more then onc or twic, at last the reckoning was agreed, and they together demaunded damadge for 10l, not payde in time, and they had it, so wee isued. After this time, Mr. Brewster spake no more for the wheat, thoughe he had bine very earnest for it before, nor did he, after this, offer the remaining pt of the coales, thoughe before he had, but this deponent conceiveth that that day they went awaye, he was at Mr. Lambertons, and vpon speech of the debte, Mr. Lamberton tould hime he must paye it to his wife, for so it is agreed, saide hee, in makeing vp our accounts, and for the rest of the coales, saide hee, I would faine haue the take them, and I will take paye for them in England, of yo[r] father.

M[ris] Linge testifyeth that they being to by some things of Mr. Brewster, they dissiered Mr. Lamberton to paye hime, w[c]h he sayd he would doe, but they hearing Mr. Brewster complaining of the badness of the paye of this place, fearing least it should be offencive to hime, they went and payd hime themselues in mault, and after, told Mr. Lamberton they had satisfyed hime for those things he was to paye for for them, Mr. Lamberton said he was sorie, for he had accounted w[t]h Mr. Brewster, and Mr. Brewster was in his debte.

Mr. Evanc further, to proue the proper debte, (beside the booke vnder Mr. Lambertons hand produced in courte,) offered the testimony of Phillip Leake, and of Mary ^ , w[c]h was Mr. Lambertons servant.

Phillip Leeke testifyeth vpon oath, that Mr. Lamberton and Mr. Brewster being at his house, as he takes it that day captaine Turner went aboard to goe awaye, he heard Mr. Lamberton saye Mr. Brewster owed hime 45l, and he heard Mr. Brewster make no replie against it.

Mary ^ , saith that the Lords day at night, before her master went awaye, hauing sate vp late to cast vp the accounts, she heard hime saye that Mr. Brewster owed hime 45l, beside the cordadge.

Mr. Pell obiected against some coate beavor at 12s ꝑ l, wch was brought to 10s, and against some turtle shells at 8s, wch was allso brought to 7s: 6d ꝑ l, and ther was halfe a quarter of beefe, ye waight not knowne, wch was rated at 10s, so that the debte is brought to 44l, 17s, 08d.

Mr. Evanc was asked if he had any more to saye, he answered, for the cordadge and stufe, he conceived it is cleared to the courte, for the stufe was returned and the cordadge entered vpon acco. The ꝑtable acco he conceiveth is cleared by Rogger Allen and Mris Linge, and the proper acco by Phillip Leeke and Mary ^ . And by the booke wch is produced.

Mr. Pell was asked if he had any more to saye, he spake of the cordadge, and passadg of a maid, and some wine; he was told that what appeared to be justly due to hime must be allowed.

Bothe ꝑties hauing had libbertie to saye as much as the would to the case, the courte proceeded to judgment, wch is this; that they judge that the ꝑtable acco was cleared, and for the debte demaunded of Mr. Pell by Mris Lamberton, 44l: 17s: 08d, hath bine proved, and must be payde to Mris Lamberton by Mr. Pell, provided, that what debtes Mr. Pell makes appeare to be oweing to hime, must be deducted.

Richard Beech dissiered of the courte that he might, till further order, retaine in his hands the estate of William Iles, deceased; but he being not fitted to give in sufficient securetie, it was respited till another courte.

John Meges declareth that at two severall times or agreements, he bargained with Henery Gregory of Stratford to make 14 dosson of shooes, and was to give hime 12d a pare for makeing them, carying them to hime readie cutt out. That he payde 48s of this before hand, and 6l more he was to haue when he had done halfe the worke. He was to doe it well and sufficiently. That Goodman Gregory hath made 13 dosson of them, but they are all naught and fall in peces, some in a weeke, some in 14 dayes time, so that the plantiffe is damadged both in his name and estate. In his name, bothe at Connecticote, Long Island, Totoket, Guilford, Stratford, Farefeild, they

all cry out, and some thinke the plantiffe worthy to be putt in prisson. And by reasson of it he further saith, he hathe bine forced to breake ingadgments w^{t}h Mr. Evanc, whoe should haue received 30^{l} worth of this ware, and he turned it backe as vnmarchantable, and what damadge will come further, he knoweth not. Beside it hath hindered hime in his trade to his great damadge, he being on that deales w^{t}h many people, they haue shuned to by any ware of hime. The plantiffe further saith that Goodman Gregory hath not onely made the ware badely, but hath spoyled the leather by layeing them
[199] in the sand || that some of them are rotten, they were ꝑtly couered w^{t}hin and w^{t}hout, and the ꝑttye that fetched them was faine to washe them to make them cleane. Further he hath altered the propertie of the ware, for whereas he should haue made some wooden heeles, and had wherw^{t}hall to doe it, he made them plaine, and by that is Mr. Evanc disapointed allso; and some of them he hath made a size shorter then he should, and some of the 9, marked them w^{t}h the 10. He complained for a last I sent hime onc, yett he made them as he did before. Lastly the plantiffe saith, it is to his hindranc that he hath laide out this money so longe before hand.

Henery Gregory, the deffendant, saith, that he received a hide from John Meges at 48^{s} pric, for which hide he was to make hime 4 dosson of shooes w^{c}h came to 48^{s}; ꝑt of this he did before the other bargaine, and he sawe the ware and accepted it, and Mr. Evanc tooke it as currant and good, but it proved not so. The plantiffe seing this ware, agreed for the rest, but hee, this deffendant, before the agreement, told the plantiffe he would make no more of such leather. The plantiffe promised bothe better leather, and to procure hempe from Connecticote to sow the showes w^{t}h, but did not performe accordingly, so that the deffendant was forced to buy flax at 18^{d} ꝑ ^{l}, and sowed them w^{t}h flax. The plantiffe bringing more worke, the deffendant saith he told hime the bargaine was to carye away that was done, he said it laye better then he could laye it, so left some of it till the 3th or 4th of Nouember. The deffendant minded hime of his promise to bringe better leather, & told hime, this is as bad or worse then the first, that if he had not better leather he would doe no more, and added, it is pittie but the tanner should be hanged wch tanned it, for he cossens the cuntrye, but he said it was not the tanners fault alltogether, he the plantiffe was faine because of Mr. Evanc his hast, to take it out when neither the tanner nor himselfe could tell wheither it was tanned inoughe or no. The deffendant dissiered to haue hemp, the plantiffe said that thred would last as longe as the leather; so this deffendant went on and did the worke, all but on dosson, but he neglected to fetch them awaye. Some leather the plantiffe, or some for hime, left at Moses Wheelers, wch his wife tooke vp & rent the graine from the flesh, and some of the leather is to be seene in the towne at Mr. Evanc his house. The defendant saith further yt he tooke out ye best pare of shooes he could picke out of the first 4 dosson; Mr. Blackmans sonn had them, and in a short time they tare out in the whole leather. For makeing the showes lesse then they were cutt out, it was because they were marked by hime more then they would reach, for some wch was to be made vp of ye tens, would not reach a nynes last, but would teare, they were so little and the leather so bad. And for markeing them longer then they were made, it was because he sent me word that I should marke them as he had marked them; and secondly, he sent me a last of the tenns, wch was not of ye tenns. The deffendant further saith, that he lost 15 weekes time by the negligenc of John Meges, for want of worke, contrary to agreement, as appeares in the wrighting. And for makeing the wooden heeles shooes otherwise then hee appointed, it was because the deffendant was faine to take those rands to make welts for the plaine shooes. For this the court blamed hime, telling hime he should have forborne makeing them till he had bine supplyed wth matterialls, but Goodman Meges saith he sent welts wth all the shooes he sent.

The plantiffe and deffendant hauing spooken, wittneses were called and examined.

Jonathan Sargant testifyeth vpon oath, taken before the gouerner, the 22th of October 1647, that he buying a pare of russitt shooes, clossed in the inside at the side seames, of Goodman Megs, he wore them at the first 2 or 3 times to a neighbours house, but did not, that he knowes, then wett the soales of them; secondly he wore them onc at the meeting, being aboute 40 rode; 3[dly] he wore them onc more to the meeting; that night he walked downe to y[e] watter side, aboute 60 rod from his house, and then he brought home y[e] soales of on of his shooes in his hand, and the other lose, readie to fall of; then he gott them sowed againe, and wore them now and then, but not constantly, for a weeke or a fortnight, then the insoales and outsoales and all fell from the vper leather; he cannot remember that he wore them any more then this.

Thomas Whitewaye dothe testifye vpon oath, that he bought a pare of russit shooes of Goodman Meges of Newhauen, clossed in the inside at the side seames; he wore them 3 or 4 dayes and then the out soales ripped, then he sowed them againe and wore them 3 or 4 dayes more, and the insoales, welts and all came of, then he sowed them together againe, and shortly after the vpper leather, seames, heeles and sides ripped, so as that they would not hange vpon his feete, the vper leathers being not broken, nor the out soales so much as broken at the toes, insomuch that this deponent said, he thought it was fitt Goodman Megs should be putt in prisson for so coussining the cuntery, and he doth expect sattisfaction from Goodman Meges.

[200] ||John Parmele of Guilford testifyeth vpon oath, taken before Mr. Disbrowe, the first of Nouember, 1647, that he bought a pare of shooes w[c]h came from Goodman Meges of Newhauen, russet, clossed in the insides at the side seames, and that wearing them but 6 dayes, or 7 dayes at the moste, the soales ripped from the vper leathers.

Samuell Netelton of Totokett doth testifye vpon oathe, taken before the gouerner, the 4[th] day of Nouember 1647, that he bought a pare of shooes of Goodman Meges of Newhaven, russed, clossed in the inside at the side seames, for his wife, she put them on on the Lords day, and the next third day morning they weare ripped, the soales being good, neither shranke nor hornie that I could perceive. And he allso testifyed that for and in consideration of satisfaction from Goodman Megs, he expecteth a new pare.

Marke Meges testifyeth vpon oath, taken before the gouerner, the 16th of Nouember 1647, that he being at Stratford to fetch home the shooes that were made by Henry Gregory for Jno Meges, he found the shooes lying in the sand, many of them being ptly couered wth the sand, bothe wthin and wthoute, so that he was forced to take awaye the sand with his hands to come at them, and handed them to Ralphe Loines, whoe handed them to old Gregory, whoe washed them in watter to wash awaye the sand and filthe from them. Allso he testifyeth that he seing the old man worke wth a very great aule and a small thred, wth very litle wax, blamed hime for it. That at that time they left some behinde that were not made.

Other testimonies were deliuered in wrighting to the courte to the same purpose, but not vpon oathe.

Goodman Gregory pleaded that it was the badnese of the leather wch was the cause of the shooes ripping and falling apeces, for the leather was hornie and not tanned. The court bad Goodman Gregory prove that.

Mr. Evanc saith that being at Mr. Blackemans, they had speech of these shooes. Mris Blackman said that after 2 or 3 dayes wereing, the leather was like flaps of a shoulder of mutton; and Mr. Evanc further saith that he sold shooes of these to a ptie himselfe, and the leather was so bad that the ptie would not have them.

Mr. Blackman saith that his sonn had a pare of shooes of these, wch he thinkes lasted not aboue 3 weekes, then they broke in the whole leather, and another pare of shooes mended for another of his sonns wth some of that leather, wch in on dayes wereing, being wett, was spoyled.

Juda Gregory testifyeth vpon oath, that he looked vpon pt of the leather wch his father was to worke of Goodman Meges, and some of it was so hornie that according to his judgment, no man could make shooes to pase his word on them to hold. Allso shooes so tainted, thoughe they might seeme to be tanned, yet they would not hold that a man was able to justifye himselfe or the leather in it. Allso that his father complained to hime, this deponent, and himselfe sawe shooes of the tenns marked for eleuens, that by a size he could not sowe them either for credite to himselfe or proffitt to the cuntery. Allso that Goodman Royes showed hime shooes he made for Goodman Meges and he could not last them, but was faine to sett them on a last a size shorter then Goodman Meges would haue them made. Allso that Goodman Meges would have had this deponent wrought, but he sawe the lether so bad that if he neuer wrought more he would not worke it, in regard of the vncomfortablnese to worke, because it was hornie, and so litle that it would not come together, and because it would be a wronge to the cuntery. Further he saith that Goodman Royes told hime that he complained to Goodman Meges of cutting his shooes so litle, he stranged at it, but Royes told hime he lost by cutting his soales so bige and his vper leather so litle, but Goodman Meges said he did not vse to doe so. For the lying of the shooes in the sand, this deponent saith he tooke a pcell, pare by pare, from the place where those laye that Marke Meges fetched away, and they laye, in his aprehension, w^t^hout any damadge, w^t^hout any sand in any pare that he coulde discerne, thoughe he cannot saye they were the same pcell that Marke Meges fetched awaye, thoughe it was aboute that time.

[201] ||Moses Wheeler testifyeth vpon oath, taken before Captaine Astwoode, the 30th of Nouember 1647, that Goodman Meges his man left some leather at his house for Goodman Gregory, and the next day his wife tooke vp some of it in her hand and said she thought it was tainted, and pulling it betweene her hands it did teare w^t^h ease, and this he heard & sawe. Further he saith he heard Goodman Gregory saye at on time, (but wheither at ye time before mentioned he cannot tell,) that he was sicke of that leather, and that he should neuer have credit of it for his worke, nor they profitt that should weare it, and further he saith, that he speaking w^t^h Goodman Gregory aboute a pare of shooes, he answered it was not fitt to were in this cuntery, for it was to be caryed out of the cuntery, and that he durst not pase his word vpon it.

The wife of William Crooker testifyeth vpon oathe, taken before Captaine Astwoode, the 30th of Nouember 1647, that when Goodman Meges came for the shooes, he sawe them lye vpon a sandye bench in the sellar, and he said he liked the lying of them very well, saying to her father he could not laye them better. And her father finding fault with the hornynesse of the leather, that the flax would not hold it, Goodman Meges answered that the next weeke he would goe to Connecticote and gett hime hempe, but he said he thought the flax would last as longe as that leather, but after Goodman Meges was gon, and delaied to fetch awaye the shooes, her father wiped them wth a cloth, and tooke some clapbords and other things, and laide vnder them. And further she saith, her father blamed the tanner for the leather not being well tanned, Goodman Meges answered he could not blame the tanner so much, for he was faine to take it oute before it was tanned. She saith further, she sawe it teare in peces when her father put it vpon the last, and on shooe her father was faine to pece on the side.

The court having heard these things on bothe sides did thinke there was a fault in bothe, and that the cuntery was much wronged in this waye, therfore they were willing to call in some workemen, bothe shoemakers and tanners, that they might see it and judge whose the fault was, and so give into the courte what light they coulde. To this ꝑpose, some of the shooes thus made was brought from Mr. Evanc, wch were some of the best of them, and the court called and dissiered Leivtenant Seely, Goodman Dayton, Goodman Groue of Millford, shoemakers, and Goodman Osborn and Seriant Jeffery, tanners, to take those shooes aside and veiwe them well, and if ther be cause, ripe some of them, that they maye give into the courte according to ther best light, the cause of this damadge. They did so, and returned this answer, Leivtenant speaking in the name of the rest. Wee aprehend this, that the leather is very bad, not tanned, nor fitt to be sold for servicable leather, but it wrongs the cuntry, nor can a man make good worke of a great deale of it. And wee find the workemanship bad allso, first ther is not sufficient stufe put in the thred, and instead of hemp it is flax, and the stiches are two longe, and the threds not drawne home, and ther wants wax on the thred, the aule is to bige for the thred. We ordinarily put in 7 threds, and hear is but 5; so that according to our best light wee laye the cause bothe vpon the workemanship and the badnesse of the leather.

Goodman Gregory, vpo this testimony, seemed to be convinced that he had not done his pt, but then laide the fault on Goodman Meges, that he was the more slight in it thourough his incouradgment, whoe said to hime flap them vp, they are to goe farr inoughe.

William Hooke jun^r testifyeth vpon oath, that he clearly remembreth Goodman Gregory was makeing 2 pare of shooes in their shopp, Goodman Meges came in in the meane time, and he said to Goodman Gregory, flapp them vp together, they are to goe farr inoughe.

John Gregorie testifyeth vpon oathe, that Goodman Meges said, flapp them vp together, they are to goe farr inoughe, this was aboute the beginng of the last bargaine, w^{c}h was for the 10 dosson.

Concerning the 15 weekes time, w^{c}h Goodman Gregory demaunds damadge for, that is to saye, from July to Nouember, it did appeare by Goodwife Meges her testimony in court, that she, from her husband, told Goodman Gregory at the faire in September, that her husband was discouradged to send hime any more worke because his worke was naught, thoughe hee had more worke readie cutt out.

John Gregory saith, that aboute the time of the bargaine he gaue Goodman Meges some cautions, because his father was old and his eyesight failed hime, and he durst not imploye hime himeselfe, for he could not doe as he had done.

Mr. Evanc was asked the cause why he turned the shooes vpon Goodman Meges his hand, he said the maine reasson was the badnesse of the leather, thoughe he allso excepted against the workemanship.

Goodman Meges was called to propound his damadge, he instanced first in his name, 2dly damadge to Mr. Evanc, 3dly

his ware being turned vpon his hand, 4dly hindranc in his trade, 5dly money payde severall men for satisfaction.

[202] || The plantiffe and deffendant professing, vpon the courts demaund, that they had no more to saye, and the courte considering the case as it had bine presented, debated and proved, found them bothe faultie. Goodman Gregory had transgresed rules of righteousnes, both in refferenc to the cuntery and to Goodman Meges, thoughe his fault to Goodman Meges is the more excuseable, because of that incouragement Goodman Meges gaue hime to be slight in his workemanshipp, thoughe he should not have taken any incouragement to doe evill, should haue complained to some magistrate, and not have wrought such leather in such a manner into shooes, by wch the cuntery, or whosoeuer weares them, must be deceived. But the greater fault and guilt lyes vpon John Meges for putting such vntanned, horny, vnservicable leather into shooes, & for incourageing Goodman Gregory to slight workemanshipp, vpon a motive that the shooes were to goe farr inoughe, as if rules of righteousnes reached not other places & cuntryes.

The Court proceeded to sentenc, and ordred Goodman Meges to paye 10^{l} as a fine to the jurisdiction, wth satisfaction to every perticuler person, as damadge shall be required and proved. And further the court ordered that none of the faultie shooes be caryed out of the jurisdiction, to deceive men, the shooes deserving rather to be burnt then sould if ther had bine a lawe to that purpose; yett in the jurisdiction they maye be sould, but then only as deceitfull ware, and the buyer maye knowe them to be such. They ordered allso Goodman Gregory, for his slight, faultie workmanshipp and fellowshipp in the deceipt, to paye 5^{l} as a fine to the jurisdiction, and to paye the charges of the courte, and that he require nothing of Goodman Meges for his lose of time in this worke, wheither it were more or lesse; and the court thought themselues speedily called and seriously to consider how these deceipts maye be, for time to come, prevented or duely punished.

A Generall Court the 18th of October 1647.

Mr. Wakeman, Francis Newman were chossen deputies fo the jurisdiction generall courte.

Mr. Gibbard, Mr. Crane, Jn° Gibbs, Francis Newman chossen deputies for the plantation courte of Newhaven.

Francis Newman chossen secretarie for Newhaven for ye next yeare.

Thomas Kimberlie chossen marshall for the next year for the towne of Newhaven.

Brother Pery had libbertie to depart the courte, to goe aboate the Phenix.

The Gouerner onc againe dissiered that the colledg corne, wch is yett behinde of the last yeare, might be caryed in to the collectors; hee allso propounded that seing corne is now more plentifull then in the sumer, that therfore now collectors might be chossen to gather it for the next yeare, but it was respited to another courte, that so the former collectors might finish their worke.

The Gouerner, magistrats and deputies, wth Mr. Evanc and Mr. Wakeman, were chossen to audite the treasurers accounts for the year past.

John Brockett was chossen veiwer for the fenc of Mr. Lambertons quartr, wth Henery Lendall for this pt of the yeare ensuing, in the roome of William Preston deceased.

Mr. Evanc made a propossition to the courte that seamen might be freed from watching and trayning, and gaue in the names of sundry into the courte, but seing it is now neare winter, wherin watchings and traynings cease in their ordinarie course, the courte thought fitt therfore to respite it for this time.

Mr. Evanc had libertie to depart the courte.

The Gouerner acquainted the courte that vpon notice of the generall courts order to staye the Duch shipp* wch was

* This was the St. Beninio, which the Dutch, claiming to be a smuggler, by a stratagem seized and cut out of the harbour, on a Sunday, and carried to New Amsterdam, where the vessell and cargo were confiscated. O'Callaghan, N. Netherlands, ii, 45. Brodhead, i, 479. Rec. U. Col. *sub anno* 1648.

seized and caryed out of this harboure by the Duch, the Duch gouerner hath sent a letter and a protest against Newhaven for it, professing he will have controversie only wth Newhauen, and requiers us to send the three prissoners and the Duch marchants and their goods, to them to the Mannatoes, wth some threatening speeches if wee doe not. He acquainted the courte allso wth the answer* he had sent, as allso wth another letter since received by the fiscalle, more milde in phrase, but still continewing his title to the place, and sending for the prissoners; but seing he wrights so that if the sending of them maye be interpreted as done in a waye of subordination, it was not thought fitt to send them. The gouerner therfore dissiered the courte to consider what shall be done. Further, the 3 Duchmen w[ch] dissier to be planters, viz[d], Mr. William Westerhouse, Mr. Sam: Goodanhouse, Mr. Henery ^ dissire to knowe wheither the towne will protect them or no, that they maye knowe howe to dispose of themselues. Further, he propounded to the courts consideration, how safe it maye be for vessells to pase by the Mannatoes till these questions be cleared, and wheither wee be not called to make some slight workes, and plant some gunns for the townes present defenc against small vessells, w[ch] wth ther gunns maye possiblely hurt the towne if no provission be made to keepe them of.

[203] ||The things being many, the courte agreed that a committe be chossen to consider & proceed therin as they see cause, and by the generall consent and vote, the pticulr courte for Newhaven, calling to them Mr. Evanc, Mr. Wakeman and Leivtenant Seely, had full power granted to them to consult, consider and conclude, bothe concerning receiving and protecting the Duchmen, wth all matters aboute fortifycation, the place and manner, wth all other things therto belonging.

It is ordered that this October rate bee forthw[th] payde.

*Appendix, B. C. D.

A COURTE THE 4th DAY OF JANUARY 1647.

Mr. Pell, Mrs. Lamberton, Francis Hall, John Tompson, Mathias Hitchcocke, Richard Beech, being all warned seasonably, made no appearanc, thoughe the court satt a good space of time. The court gave order that they should be warned to the next courte, to answer for this neglecte.

A GENERALL COURTE THE 31th OF JANUARY 1647.

The orders of the Jurisdiction Generall Courte were published and vpon the gouerners proposition the courte chose Leivtenant Seely and Robert Preston to veiwe and seale leather according to the tennour of that order, to whom an oath was given that they should, according to the best light they haue, discharge the trust committed to them in sealing leather, according to the jurisdiction generall courts order. And further, this courte ordered that calues skines, deares skines, goats skines, wch are fully tanned, should be sealed, (seing they maye serve well for vper leather for some shooes,) and that the rate of sealing be 4d a hide, and 2d a skine, and that the seale for the best, wch is fully tanned, be **N : G** : and for that wch is faultie, **N F** : and, if the sealers be both in towne, they are to be together when they seale, but in case on of them is out of towne, or otherwayes justly hindred, then on of them maye seale notwthstanding, and the sealers, for the better informing themselues wheither the hides or skines be fully tanned or no, haue libertie to cutt them in such places as they see meete, provided they make not spoyle of ye leather.

And seing the shooemakers haue libertie to make shooes, not onely of neats leather, but the vper leathers of some of calues leather, or deares, or goates, being fully tanned and sealed, and seing ther is great differenc in the goodnesse of these shooes, that the buyer be not deceived, the court ordered that every shoemaker in this towne marke all those shooes he makes of neats leather, before he sell them, wth an

N: vpon the lap w^thinside, belowe the place where they be tyed, and for failing hearin, they shall suffer such punishment as the perticuler courte shall judge meete.

It was propounded to the shooemakers, that seing hides are now neare as cheape as ordinarily they are in England, that shooes might be sould more reasonable then they have bine, and the shooemakers promised they would consider of it.

The gouerner acquainted the courte that those whome they appointed to audite the treasurers accounts have done it, and see cause to propound to the court that a new rate be now granted, for defraying necessisary charges for the towne, and to paye the rate levied vpon the towne for the jurisdiction; and after some debate the courte ordered that next Aprill rate and on halfe yeares rate extraordinarie be forthw^th payde.

The 4 deputies were chosen by the court to joyne wth the treasurer in setting out publique workes to be done for the towne, to see that they maye be don substantially, and wth as litle charge to the towne as maye be, and they are to call in what workemen they please for advise.

The bridge above the brickills in the way to Connecticote is to be caryed on wth as much speed as maye be.

It was propounded to consideration wheither it be fitt for the towne to allowe 8^l a yeare to the drumer; the court and the military officers were dissiered to speake wth the drumer, and see if his sollarie might not be lesse.

William Andrewes was dissiered to take care that the meeting-house dores maye be made safe, in hanging them wth such irones and such lockes and bolts as they may be stronge and secure, and that the floure above might be laid forthw^th.

It was propounded to the court, that seeing William Andrewes, whoe hath kept the ordinarie, is aboute, or hath laide it downe, that therfore some other might be found to doe it, that so strangers might knowe wheither to goe to be refreshed, but the court againe propounded it to William Andrewes to see if he would not still keepe it, he answered he would consider of it and in a short time give in his answer to the magistrats.

Those that were behinde in payement of their colledge corne

were dissiered to carie it in to the severall collecto^rs^. Collecto^rs^ chossen to gather the colledge corne for this yeare, are Anthony Tompson and Rogger Allen.

John Gregory propounded to the courte, that a good while sinc their was a pare of shooes spake of in courte wch he sould William Paine, of the tenns, French falls, at 5^s^ 10^d^, at wch their was some offenc taken, and he condemes himselfe that he hath lett it lye so longe vncleared, but now he presented a noat in courte wch showed the perticulers howe they did amount to so much, vnder two shooemakers hands, but the court professed they could not see cause shooes should be sould at this rate.

[204] ||It was propounded to the courte to consider wheither it were not meete to make a lawe for restraining of persons from their ordinarie outward imployments vpon any ꝑt of the Saboth, and the rather because some have of late taken two much libertie that way, and have bine called to answer for it in the perticuler courte. The courte considering that it is their duty to doe the best they can that the lawe of God maye be strictly observed, did therfore order that whoesoeuer shall, w^t^hin this plantation, breake the Saboth by doeing any of their ordinarie outward occaisons, from sun sett to sunn sett, either vpon the land or vpon the watter, extraordinarie cases, workes of mercy and necessetie being exceptted, he shall bee counted an offender, and shall suffer such punishment as the perticuler courte shall judge meete, according to the nature of his offenc.

It is ordered that no man shall fall any tree or trees w^t^hin the boundes of the common of this towne, w^t^hout leaue from some magistrate, and then he shall haue but for his perticuler trade or necessarie vse, and haueing cut it downe, iff he doe not make vse of it w^t^hin the compase of 14 dayes it shall be forfeite to hime that shall come to the magistrate and aske & have leaue for it.

It was propounded that a causwaye might be made from Mr. Perys corner to the meeting-house, but it was respited.

A Courte the first day of Feburarie 1647.

Richard Chadwell haveing had an attachment vpon three hogsheads of suger of Robrt Persons, and claimes a right in his house and other estate, to make good the transportation of what goods Richard Chadwell is to haue from Sandwich and some other demaundes, in w^c^h things he craved the help of the courte.

The courte tould hime they maye not trye and issue a cause of such valew, it must be reffered to the courte of magistrats, but they will see that the goodes attached maye be secured and preserved from damadge as much as maye be; and therfore gave order, that the suger bee veiwed and put into the tresurers hand and sould to ye best advantage, and the proceed so kept safe for the best proofe Mr. Chadwell can bringe, and what goodes elc ther is of Robert Persons, it is to be brought to the treasurer, that so the estate maye be preserved from losse as much as maye be.

Mr. Pell, atturnye for Mr. Edmund Leach, entereth an action against the estate of Robert Persons for a debte of 18^l 4^s 0^d, w^c^h ariseth thus, 15^l 14^s, he conceaveth due vpon a pcell of goodes the said Robert received of Mr. Leach, and 2^l 10^s due for fraight, w^c^h makes 18^l 4^s, w^c^h he thus indeavoured to prove. Robert Person received of Mr. Leach goods, to the vallew of 61^l, as they were rated by Mr. Leach, w^c^h he was to carye to the Barbadoes and sell, the said Robert to have halfe the proffitt and to paye halfe the fraight till the returne be made, w^c^h the said Robert was to make either to England or elc to Newhaven; now of this 61^l worth of goods, he sould to the valew of 34^l 10^s, and for this deliucred 752^l of cotton woole, w^c^h the plantiffe conceives cannot arise to so much, as cotton woole is worth and paseth in the Barbados. And that this was the agreement he produced Mr. Leach his letter to Mr. Pell, and Mr. Pell tooke oathe that Robert Persons acknowledged that this in the letter was the agreement. The clause of the letter runes thus: I have sent by Robert Persons, to the Barbadoes, 61^l worth of goodes, he to allowe me halfe the proffitt of them, and to beare halfe the adventure and halfe the charge of the said goods, vntill the returne be made to me or my assignes, when the proffitt is to be shared; his order is to send either to England or to Newhaven the returne, and if he come or send to Newhauen, yow will heare of hime, and he will and is to give yow accounte of the goodes. Mr. Pell testifyed vpon oath that Robert Persons acknowledged to hime that this was the agreement. John Thomas saith that Robert Persons tould hime the goods would not of, but at his coming awaye he sould the goods for 800^{l} of cotton woole. Now of this 800^{l} of cotton woole, the said Robert deliuered 752^{l} to Mr. Pell, and 48^{l} was disposed of for necesarie charges.

The court considering that the deffendant is dead, and none present that can clearly answer for hime, and that the plantiffe can make no cleare proofe for what, nor how the goods was sould, could not see cause to cast damadge vpon the estate of Robert Persons, leauing the plantiffe to make what further proofe he can hearafter, either for the fraight or for the principalle.

John Thomas acquainted the courte that Robert Persons haueing lett halfe his house & halfe his lott for 40^{s} a yeare, before he went agreed to make them a well, wch they that are in it dissire maye be done. The courte tould hime that now the ceason of the yeare is past, but he might provide stones readie that it maye bee done so soone as the ceason serves.

It was propounded to the court that Goodman Bud dissiered some allowanc out of the estate of Robret Persons, for some suger wch fell short in a hogshead of suger Goodman Budd had of Robert Persons for his house and lott he sould hime, wch hogshead he expected to be 500^{l}, but it fell not out so much, but John Thomas saith that Robrt Persons said he payd hime all, and Mr. Chadwell saith that Robert Persons did not warrant hime 500^{l} in the hogshead, but did bide hime chuse wch he would & that should satisfye hime. And further he saith he saw 1 hogshead of them waid at Roade Island wch waid above 500^{l}.

[205] ||A noat of some debtes owing to Robert Persons was presented in courte.

John the Duchman dissiered libertie for himselfe and the other two wch were prissoners wth hime, to goe to the Duch gouerner; it was tould hime that if he had dissiered it at first they might haue bine sent, but then they were alltogether vnwilling; that the court are still free to send them, onely as they were put vnder that bayle, vnder wch they stand, by the courte of magistrats, so the bayle must bee released by the same power, wch should be done as speedily as the court of magistrats could meete.

Mrs. Lamberton presented the inventorie of the estate of Mr. George Lamberton, her late husband, in courte, wch was veiwed and deliuered to the secretarie to be recorded.*

The will of M^{ris} Wilkes was likewise deliuered into the courte by Mr. Ro: Newman, and deliuered to the secretarie to be recorded.†

---

* "An inventorie of the estate of Mr. George Lamberton."

The estate is creditor, to the worpll Theophilus Eaton, pr bill, £28. 17. 1½. more to him for the negars clothes, £3. to Mr. Stephen Goodyeare, pr bill, £65. 4. 9. to Isacke Allerton, pr bill, £22. 2. 6. to John Chapman, pr booke, £6. 6. to Mr. Pell, for Mrs. Brewster, £30. 14. 2. to Rogger Allen £7. to John Clarke £1. to Mr. Hooke £3. 12. 8. to Mrs. Gregson £3. 14. to Geo. and Lawrance Warde £6. 10. 8. to ship Fellowshipp, put in £50, £25. to Goodman Stone 8^s. to Jonathan Sarjant 15^s. to Adam Nicolls £1. 2. 5. to Roger Knap 10^s. to John Thomas 7^s. to Capt. Turner £1. to Mr. William Tinge £1. to land at Stamford £4. to Moses Wheeler £1. 9. 10. to Brother Nash £1. to John Nash £0. 17. 9. to Richard Everit £0. 10. to Serjant Jeffery £1. to William Andrewes, senior, £4. to John Chidsey £0. 15. to 8 oxe hides £4. 8. to William Davis £0. 8. 5. to John Tompson £1. 8. to Michaell Taintor £6. 6. to Mr. Gregson, Mr. Hawkines and Mr. Goodyeare £3. 17. 6. to the 24th part in the Susan £16. 11. 8. to Mr. Pery £20. to goods in the Susan and Phenix £29. 5. to Phillip Leake £1. to John Rider £1. to Mr. Gilbert £34.

The whole estate is	£1218. 12. 4.
owing,	16
rest good estate,	1202. 12. 4.

The estate is debtor to Mr. Malbon £13. to John Willford £3.

Prised the 4th of January 1647. Mathew Gilbert, Richard Miles.

† "The will of Joane Wilkes made the 12th day of January 1645.

"I Joane Wilkes being called to goe to my husband, but not knowing whether he be living or not, and not knowing whether I may live to come to England or to returne heither, doe desire, so farr as I have or maye have power in my hands, to dispose of that estate that God hath given me in this place. First I will and bequeath to our deare pastor tenn pounds. To our teacher five pounds. To the church of Christ in this place five pounds. To my neece Bridget Wilkes thirty pounds. To my nephew Joseph Dalman, in London, twenty markes. To my nephew Nathaniel Warner, of Bristoll, twenty markes, and to Susanna Gregson twenty markes, and to our beloved elder, Mr. Robert Newman, five pounds, whom I nominate and appoint the sole execu-

Robert Hill deliuered into the court an inventorie of his brother John Hills estate*, wch was likewise deliuered to the secretarie to be recorded.

Mr. Pell brought in and deliuered to the courte an inventorie of his wives estate, left by her late husband, Mr. Francis Brewster†, wch was read and deliuered to the secretarie to be recorded.

Mr. Pell was tould he was warned to the courte aboute his wives fine, that he might either paye it, or show a sufficient reason why he did not; he dissiered to know by wt lawe it was demaunded, it was tould hime, by the lawe of his marrying the widdow, wch owed it before he marryed her; he said he knew not howe it comes to be her debte or his either, the gouerner tould hime he had a copie of the courte order, and if he could obiect any thing against the justic of the courtes proceedings, hee might; he said ther is that charged in the order that is not proved, he was told it was a reproachfull slander cast vpon the courte to saye they had laide a fine for any offenc not proved, and he was called to make proofe; he instanced in a passage wherin excese in drinking wth other

---

tor of this my last will and testament, intreating him to take upon him this care and trust and to see it performed accordingly. And if my house, lands and goods left hear should not amount to so much, then my mind is that the abatement shall be upon the three legacyes of twenty markes equally, and if it shall arise to more, that it be added equally to those three legacyes of twenty markes a peece. In witnes whereof I have hereunto put my hand this 12th day of the eleventh moneth 1645.

Jone Wilkes.

"Joane Wilkes declared this to be her will and testament before mee.

Tho: Gregson."

Inventory taken by Mr. Gilbert, Mr. Wakeman and Mr. Crane, the 14th of the 11th moneth 1647. Total £89. 4. Debts. 3 bushells of wheat of old Jacocks of Stratford £0. 12. Mr. Gilbert 15s. John Clarke 30s. Thom: Munson 14s. Mr. Robert Newman 8s. Richard Hull 8s. Phillip Leeke for rent of the house and garden the yeere 1645 £3. for rent of the garden 1646 £3. James Clarke 30s. Phillip Leeke received of several men £3. 13.

* "An inventorie of the estate of John Hill" £24. 19. Mr. Winthrope debtor £7. The estate is debtor, to Peeter Browne £4. 10. to old Goodman Willmot £0. 16. to the treasury £0. 3. 6. to Robert Preston £0. 2. 6. to Ro. Hill for 4 bush. wheat £1. to him for a stuff suit £1. 18. 6. more for a goat £0. 8.

† "An inventorie of the estate of Mr. Francis Brewster," amount £555. 6. 2. In the great ship, cost £50. prised December 30, 1647 by Francis Newman, Richard Miles, John Clarke.—The estate debtor, pd out of the estate as appears by acquittances £57. 10. for a debt which Mr. Brothers demands out of the estate £200. for a debt owing to Mrs. Lamberton £30. 14. Total £288. 4.

inconveniences seeme to be charged on M^ris^ Brewster, now his wife, wch was not proved against her, he was tould there was neither any such charge, nor any penny of the fine imposed vpon any such consideration, that his iniurious cariage hearein is agravated in that full light hath bine tendered hime in the case, no excese was charged against her by ye courte, nor in the originall order was ther any word sounding that waye, it was an errour in the secretarie, who probably had left out a line in ingroseing the order out of the first copie, and Mr. Pery, the secretarie that then was, had sinc bine wth Mr. Pell, had showed hime how the originall ranne and the line left oute, offered hime to rectifye it, but he refused. The governer tould Mr. Pell that the line beinge left out as it stands in his copie, it dothe not rune cleare & in good sence, namely, (and sit drinking all excese in drinking wth other inconveniences following.) Mr. Pell said it was good dialect, no oversight in the secretarie, and he could prove it. The gouerner tould Mr. Pell he conceived he did not vnderstand what dialect is, but the courte considering that Mr. Pells charge is made against the courte of magistrats, whoe imposed that fine, thought fitt and ordered, that his miscariage be reffered to the consideration of the next court of magistrats for the jurisdiction, and ordered Mr. Pell to attend them therin.

Ezechiel Cheveres passeth ouer to John Cooper 5 ac^rs^ 2 thirds of vpland w^th^in the two myle, on halfe of it lying in Mr. Eatton quartr, betwixt the land of M^ris^ Turner & William Tuttill, the other halfe lying by the mill highwaye, at the end of Mr. Eatons pasture, next the land of William Tuttill.

John Lawrencson and his wife, being warned to the court, apeared, they were charged for selling stronge watters by small quanteties, contrarie to a courte order. He said he knew not that it was a breach of order, and she sould it for Mr. Westerhouse.

She saide that haveing broke the order, she dissiered to submit to the courte.

But beside the breach of order, their apeares something of disorder, for William Paine saith that the 3 Duchmen, wch were prissoners, lying at his house, were wonte, before she sould stronge watter, to keepe good houres in coming home at night, but sinc, they haue stayde out long, and some time very late, and one of them seemed by his speech to be somewhat distempred, but he sawe hime not for he was in bed.

Arther Halbich saith he hath gone into the house where Goodwife Lawrencson was, and sawe persons sitt drinking of small quanteties of stronge watter two or 3 times, and that her husband tould hime she had gained 30^{s} in a weeke or a fortnights time by that waye of selling out stronge watters.

The sentenc of the courte is that John Lawrencson paye as a fine to the towne for this breach of order, 20^{s}, but if they goe on in this way it is not twic 20^{s} that will excuse them.

William Paine refused to paye his fine for comeing late one Lords day wth his armes to the meeting, because others came late and were not complained of, but he was told he must paye his fine, and the seriant should be warned to the next courte to answer for his neglect.

The treasurer was ordered to paye William Paine for his halfe days worke in attending the courte aboute John Lawrencsons buesnis.

John Benham informed the courte that he was fined by the courte for neglecting to warne Dauid Atwatter to watch. It is by the secretarie that then was, entred 5^{s}, but it was but 2^{s}: 6^{d}, and seing diuers doe remember it was but 2^{s}: 6^{d}, the courte agreed he should paye no more.

[206] || Richard Beech dissiered of the courte that he might retayne the estate of William Iles in his hand till further order, w^{c}h is as apeares by the inventorie 13^{l}: 17^{s}: 00^{d}: the courte tould hime vpon securetie he mighte; he offered himeselfe and 9^{l} worthe of land, as it was valewed by Anthony Tompson & John Clarke as apeares in a note vnder there hands. The land is 22 ac^{rs} of vpland in the second devission, and 5 ac^{rs} of meddowe in the west meddowe, and 2 ac^{rs} of vpland in the quarter at his house, and for the other 5^{l} John Beech becometh suretie w^{t}h hime, as the said Joh Beech declareth in courte, w^{c}h the courte accepted, w^{t}h this proviso, that if John Beech should dye or leaue the towne, Richard Beech put in other securitye to the courts satisfaction.

John Tompson, atturney for Thomas Allcote in the Baye, requiereth youthes of Francis Halle wch he brought from England long sinc, that is to saye, John Whitehead & Thomas Whitehead, and saith he hath order to send them to the saide Thomas Allcote whoe is ther vnkell.

Francis Halle saith at the desier of their vnkell, Mr. Allcote of Roxberey, since deceased, hee brought these youthes ouer, and was at great charges with them for their passage and other occaisons, wch he saith Mr. Allcote promised to paye to his satisfaction when he came heare, but when he came ther vnkell was deade, and knew not of whome to seeke his money, iff the boyes had dyed he should haue lost it, for ought he knowes, for he knew of no other vnkell they had, but he was blamed that he had not vsed that meanes to finde oute ther vnkell or send to ther mother as he might have done, (thoughe he saith he hath sent,) but he acquainted the courte then wth it, and wth ther approbation one of them was disposed of to Mathias Hitchcoke, the other he kept himeselfe till they might haue further light to dispose of them.

The courte being dissierous that the chilldren might haue no wronge, and allso that the ptyes wch haue brought them vp heitherto, (seeing they were small,) might be justly satisfyed, did seriously consider and weighe the charges and hazards the severall ptyes had bine at wth them, as allso the advantages that the boyes might be vnto them. And after a large debate concerning those accounts, in the issue agreed, that Thomas Whithead wch was wth Mathias Hitchcocke, be at the end of 5 yeares and eight moneths from the time he had hime, sett free, at wch time the said Mathias put the said Thomas to Davide Atwatter for 4 yeares and 4 monethes, thoughe he had no right so to doe, but now the said Thomas declareth himeselfe willing to abide wth his master David Atwatter, till he maye heare from his vnkell, so he maye haue just satisfaction for the time to come, so longe as he stayeth wth hime. They bothe agreed before the courte, that he should haue 3l a yeare, meate, drinke and clothes. And concerning John Whithead, it is ordered that Francis Halle sett hime free from this time, and paye vnto hime 50s.

Mr. William Westerhouse, by Mr. Evanc his interpreter, acquainted the courte that he knew it not to be an offenc to the courte that he imployed any to sell his stronge watter, but seing he had done it, he justifyed the courte in the fine they had laide, and he came to tender the payement. The courte tould hime they looked not vpon it as his fault, but Jno Lawrencsons and his wives that sould it, for they intended not to fine hime, but seeing he would paye it, the court considering how vsefull hee hath bine in the towne by giveing phisicke to many persons, and to some of them freely, the courte agreed not to take the fine but returned it to hime againe.

Phillip Galpine acquainted the courte ther was a certaine some of money, aboute 9 l, given hime by will by Nathaniell Drapr deceased, wch some was due to the said Nathaniel for wages, wch Mr. Leach is to paye, and now Mr. Pell, by order from Mr. Leach, wch Mr. Pell refuseth to paye. Mr. Pell saide he denyed not to paye it only he heard that Nathaniel made another will and gave this wages to Mr. Sellicke, as Mr. Tompson of Verginea, David Evanc and another saide, and that he will require it, therfore if Phillip will give hime securitye that he maye not paye it twice, he will paye hime it. The court thought that but just, and agreed that if Philip can give in securitye, it be payde to hime, if not that then it be payde into the tresurers hand till the matter maye be cleared.

Mr. Goodier and Mr. Evanc were dissiered by the courte to see Robert Persons suger waide, and that or any other goodes of his vallewed, wch is to be put into the treasurers hand.

Mr. Malbon dissiered the courte to appointe some to vallew some goodes wch were attached of Mr. Godferyes for on Strong Fornale, of Boston.

A Generall Courte the 14th of Feburarie, 1647.

The Governer acquainted the courte, that he heard that fences aboute the towne are generally so defective that many are discouraged from the laboure of husbandrie, because their corne, when they haue sowne it, is spoyled, therfore it is of necessitie y[t] some course be taken that corne maye be preserved.

It was propounded by some that their might be certaine men appointed as haywards, w[c]h might looke to such a compase of ground as might be convenient, whoe should take and pound all the catle or hoggs they found their, lookeing ouer the ground on every daye, and that if the see any small defect in any fence they might mend it, or if it be too great a breach for them, that then they acquainte the owner w[t]h it, and each hayward to be payde by the severall quarters w[c]h imploye them, as they shall agree. To this the courte inclined, and it was agreed to meete in the severall quarters to put it in execution. And wheras it is founde and complained of, that when meetings of that nature are warned, severall doe not attend them, therfore it is ordered that when a meeting is appointed, and all they in the quarters haue seasonable warning, if any come not, yett the maior ꝑt maye agree any course for the goode of the quarter, provided it croses no order of courte allreadie made.

[207] || It was dissiered by some that Indian and English corne mighte not be planted in on feilde together, but it was answered by diveres that it could not be avoided, but the quarters themselues were to agree hearin, and not to damadge on another, as allso to agree of the time of putting in catle into the severall quarters where corne is sowne, and allso of takeing them out seasonably, that corne be not spoyled. All the orders abovte fences to stand in full force, and every on to hasten the setting vp the fences that are downe.

Mr. Westerhouse dissiered the towne to save their ashes, and he would give them 4[d] a bushell and fetch them at their houses, or 5[d] a bushell if they carrie them to the watter side, to a place he would appointe there.

Mr. Evanc propounded that some would make a sluce at the creekes mouthe w[c]h comes vp to M[rs] Wilkes house. The court was willing to incouradge it, and wished it might be seriously considered against another courte.

The Gouerner dissiered that men would speedely bring in

their rates to ye treasurer, that so the might prevent a warning to the perticuler courte.

William Andrewes was dissiered to acquaint the courte what he intended to doe aboute the ordinarie, he answered thoughe hime was willing yett he dissiered the courte would provide another, because his wife is at present vnwilling. But he had further time given hime to consider of it and to come to the gouerner and give his answer.

Mr. Evanc propounded to the courte that something might be done concerning the setting a size for the waight of breade wch is made and sould, but it was left to be further inquired into till another courte.

Mr. Newman, the ruleing elder, propounded to the courte that they would grant brother Wiggelsworth a small pec of ground neare the meeting-house, to sett hime a litle house vpon and make hime a garden, because he is so lame that he is not able to come to the meeting, and so is many times deprived of the ordinances, when if he was neare he might inioye them. The courte considering and pittying his case, inclined to doe it & left it to the dispose of them whoe are intrusted to dispose of lotts in the towne.

The courte declared themselues that the leather wch was in mens houses, before the last order for sealing leather was in force, be allso sealed before it be vsed or sould.

Mr. Evanc propounded that ther might be some appointed to ouersee and allso to seale the cooppr ware, that it maye be sufficient bothe for gadge and tightnes, but it was refered to a more private consideration.

Mr. Malbon dissiered the workemen in the towne that the would be forwarde to help the elders vp wth their fenc, (and they should be payde) and especially those whoe are debtor^s to ye treasurie.

Jeremiah Howe hath libertie from the courte to sell strong watter by pints or quarts or other small quanteties, so that he suffer it not be drunke in his house, but sell it to ye townes folke or stranges out of his house, provided allso that he haue due respect to any suspicious persons and vnseasonable times, that all disorder maye be prevented; this to continew till the courte find some inconvenienc.

Henery Morall, William Blayden, Thomas Knowles haue libertie to burne a litle meddowe w[c]h is in ther home lotts, provided the doe it at a fitt time, that no damadge come therby, and if any doe, they must answer it.

Leivtenant Seely dissiered the courte that he might haue 50[s] allowed hime, w[c]h he had bine out of ever sinc the plantation begune, for seekeing a shallope w[c]h was lost, but the courte sawe not cause that the towne should paye it, seeing the shallop belonged to perticular men.

Mathew Camfeild declared himeselfe sorye that he had the last courte presented the names of sundrye men to be behinde in payement of their college corne, before he had spoken againe w[t]h them.

The Gouerner acquainted the courte that the Kinges Armes are cutt by Mr. Mullyner for the towne, w[c]h are to be primed and after sett vp in a publique convenient place.*

It was propounded that a comittee might be chossen to consider and dispose of the absent lotts, that the charge w[c]h comes to the towne by them maye be prevented, and the magistrats, elders and deacons, w[t]h the 4 deputies for the towne were chossen as a comitte for this thing.

John Halle acquainted the courte that the higheways against a lott he bought of Henery Pecke was worne awayc w[t]h the watter that their was no safe passing that waye. He propounded to know wheither the towne will mende it, but the courte declared themselues, that the order was that every man maintayne a sufficient waye 2 rods from his home lott thouroughout the towne; but after much debate, John Halle resigned the lott to Leivtenant Seely, vpon condicion that he mende the waye and maintayne it sufficiently, w[c]h Leivtenant accepted.

Captaine Malbon propounded that ther might be a new clarke chossen for the trayne band for the towne, because the former clarke being otherwise imployde, could not attend it.

* From "New Havens case stated," we learn that the kings arms were set upon a post, in the highway, by the sea-side.

John Clarke was by hime propounded, and by the courte chossen clarke for the trayne bande of the towne in the roome of Mr. Pery.

The towne was dissiered that they would be carefull to attend the order in provideing themselues of ladders.

---

[208] A COURTE AT NEWHAVEN THE 7th DAY OF MARCH, 1647.

Sundry at this courte tooke the oathe of fidelitie whose names are entred amoung ye rest.

Edward Wigglesworth passeth ouer to Adam Nickholes, six acrs of vpland ground lying in the Yorkesheir quarter wthin the two myle; and wheras in the towne booke their is but 22 acrs and a halfe of land placed vpon Ed. Wigglesworths lott, bothe for estate and persons, and yett he had layd oute and hathe sould 24 acrs, he declared that the acr and halfe, wch makes it 24 acrs, was given hime in allowanc for shortnes in his home lott.

Dauid Attwater entred an action against Mathias Hitchcocke, for 10l wch the said Mathias Hitchcocke receaved of Dauid Atwatter, for the servic of Thomas Whitehead for 4 yeares and eighte moneths, wch Mathias Hitchcocke could not performe, he not haueing a full right to dispose of the saide Thomas. Mathias Hitchcocke saith, that being demaunded what assueranc he could give David Atwatter that he should inioye the saide Thomas so longe, seing by the courte order he had no full assueranc of hime, but he might goe awaye or another might take hime from hime, he answered he could give no better then he had, vnlesse the boye would give hime any better, so he agreed wth the boye to make an indenture for so longe time, and gaue hime the saide Mathias Hitchcocke, 10l, but being advised by the courte to agree it betwixt themselues, they bothe consented to it and did wthdrawe, and soone after declared to the courte that they had issued the differenc to bothe ther satisfactions.

Arther Halbich passeth ouer to John Beech his house and home lott wth all his accommodations therto belonging wthin Newhauen.

John Nash being warned to the courte for not payeing his rates, answered that he knewe none due from hime till the land was entred in the towne booke, and that the courte might take ther course, but was reproved for so saying, it being a thing vncomely for hime to saye. So further he obiected his land was not laide oute, but was tould it was not the townes faulte, and if that was the reasson, the courte would send presently and take a distrese, but in the issue he promised to paye.

William Paine was called to make goode the charge wch he laide vpon Seriant Munson last courte, wch was the he presented some for comeing late on the Lords daye wth their armes but not others, thoughe they offended equaly alike. William Paine saide he was loath to doe it, but yett presented sundry names he had in a papr, wch came late the last Saboth in Maye, 1647, and the last Saboth in June; some of them came late, and some brought not their armes. Seriant Munson saide he dissiered Willm Paine might prove, first that the men came late, 2dly that he did not present them. William Paine saide hee hade not his proofe in courte; he was tould if ther was indeede a fayling, he should first have tould his seriant of it in a private waye, and if it had bine reformed, well, if not, then he might have complained, for every souldier should strive in all lawfull wayes to vphold the honour of their officers. Further, Seriant Munson saith that he had the names of sundry in a note to give the marshall that they might be warned to the courte, but he lost it oute of his pockett, he knowes not how. The seriant was advised, and wth hime the other seriants, that they would carefully attend the dischargeing of that trust wch is committed to them, for they maye see that the eyes of many are vpon them.

Mr. Leete and Mr. Jordan, attornyes for the towne of Guilford, entreth an action against Mr. John Ceffinch of Newhauen, for certaine rates due vpon a lott wch the saide John Ceffinch houldeth at Guilford, but refuseth to paye them, thoughe they haue bine demanded of hime. Mr. Ceffinch saithe that he knowes not that he owes the towne of Guilforde any thinge for rates, for they haue had the vse of his lande.

Mr. Leete answered that it is true they vsed some of his land, but that was to satisfye rates towards minesters maintaynanc, according to an order of courte made in Guilford the ^ , wch was, that if any remove, and yett hoold the right of ther land in ther hands, and will not paye towards the minesters maintaynanc, it should bee lawfull for the authoritye of the place to seize the whole or any pt of their accommodations, to rayse that pt of the minesters maintaynanc wch he gave in to paye, and to render the ouerplus to the owner, now for this purpose the land hath bine made vse of, but not for the towne rates.

Mr. Ceffinch saide that he treated wth Mr. Disburowe aboute this matter, and tendred the land for that yeare for defrayeing of charges, and Mr. Disburowe accepted it, and produced Mr. Attwatter for his wittnes, whoe testifyed vpon oath that Mr. Ceffinch tendred to Mr. Disburowe the laying downe all his accommodations in Guilford for that yeare for defrayeing publique charges, and Mr. Disburowe, thoughe he was slowe in it, yett at last saide if yow doe it according to towne order we cannot refuse it.

The plantiffe saide that they dissiered to hould to that, that if it was laide downe according to order they will accept it, but that it was not, as apeares by the order which was read in courte, a copie whereof Mr. Ceffinch had from Guilforde.

The plantiffe and deffendant being demaunded had no more to saye. The court proceeded to sentenc, wch is that the deffendant for want of proofe is cast, and must paye the rates to Guilford wch is due for his lott their.

Mr. Robert Newman presented into the courte the inventorie of the estate of Mris Wilkes deceased.

Mr. Goodyear and Mr. Evanc were dissiered by the courte to prise some goodes wch were attached of Joseph Godferies, and if Mr. Malbon put in securitye, he hath libbertie to sell them.

[209] || Mr. Evanc attornye for Mr. Daniel Peirse, merchant, entreth an action against Thomas Moris for takeing awaye a flote or staye of Mr. Peirses and not returning it againe, but

it is lost. And allso for damadge wch the saide Daniell Peirse hath or maye sustaine for want of it.

Thomas Moris saide that Mr. Pery dissiered hime to fetch the flote, but hee answered hime that he would not, and he might send his owne men for it, for if any damadge came, if he fetched it, it would be laide vpon hime, but Mr. Pery was very importunate wth hime, & tould hime that they would beare hime harmlesse, so by much perswasion, he and John the Duchman fetched it, and when they had done wth it, he tould Mr. Pery they must take care of it, and he and Grenfeild Larebe saide they would doe it as Mr. Chadwell can testifye.

Mr. Chadwell testifyeth vpon oathe that being aboarde the Phenix when the worke was neare done, he heard Thomas Moris aske Mr. Larebe what course they would take wth the staye, for Mr. Peirse would haue need of it, he knew not how soone; Mr. Larebe answered that they would take care to haue it made fast and secure till ye river was cleare, that it might be caried into it place; the like passadges was wth Mr. Pery, and Mr. Perys answer was the same. He asked them why the lighter men tooke it awaye and caried it to the old shipp side, they said that that was the secuerest place it could be laide in, till the river was cleare. This they saide both of them, thoughe apart, two or three times.

The courte considering the premises saw cause to judge that the damadge must fall vpon Thomas Moris, yett Mr. Pery and Mr. Larebe will be lyable to make hime just satisfaction, according to the proofe he can make, and the court advised Thomas Moris to make Mr. Peirse another flote, and the plantiffe declared himselfe willing to accept it, so it might be readye by the midle of the next weeke, and Thomas Moris being incouradged by some help that Mr. Chadwell & Mr. Peirses carpenter, and some matterialls wch Mr. Goodier & Mr. Malbon promised to afford, promised to make one.

A Generall Courte the 8th. day of March, 1647.

The Governer acquainted the courte that the millitarie officers, according to their dissire, had considered how the watch might be caried on for more ease to the towne then formerly it hath bine, and thinke that foure men wthout a master maye serue in a night, (leauing extraordinarie occaisons to other considerations as the courte hath before provided.) These 4 men to carye on the watch in manner as followeth, They are to be all at the watch-house an houre and a halfe after sunn sett, wth their armes compleate, according to the former order for the watch; and the 4 seriants in their course, are to come to the watch-house every night, to sett the watch and give them ther charge; and allso that they come at some other times, to see that the watch doe ther duty faithfully, onc a weeke at the least, leauing the sett time to themselues. These 4 men are to walke the rounds, two one pt of the night & two the other pt of the night. And whille two are walkeing, the other two to keepe sentinell in ther course, leauing other circomstances to be ordered by the discretion of the seriant, as, wheither they shall walke halfe the night at onc or no, and the like; and the seriants for their faithfull discharge of this trust are freed from watching in their owne psons.

After some debate aboute this matter, the courte agreed and ordered that till they see some inconvenienc arise by it, the watch be caryed on in this manner.

It was propounded wheither the men at the farmes should not watch in the towne, allso concerning the deacons and deputies for the courte, and seamen.

For the farmes it was answered, that they are by an order of courte to watch, vnlesse it be in a time of danger, and then they are to keepe watch at home.

For the deacons it was voted that they be wholly freed, and likewise for the deputies for the time being. And for seamen, if they were indeed seamen, and such as had no estate in the towne to be preserved, they be freed, but if they have estate in the towne then they are to find a watchman, thoughe they watch not in ther owne persons. It was further ordered that Mr. Pell, Mr. Westerhouse and Mr. Auger be freed from watching.*

It was propounded wheither psons that are aboue 60 yeares of age should be freed from watching. It was ordered that if they be such as haue estate in ye towne, thoughe they be freed in their owne psons, yett they must find a watchman. All others, not exempted by publique place, to watch.

William Judson and John Brockett propounded that they might be freed from watching, but the courte sawe no cause to grant it.

The Gouerner dissiered the seriants that they would be carefull to looke to their squadrons vpon the Lords dayes, that all they wch transgrese the court order maye be presented, that so all show of parallitie maye be avoyded.

---

[210] Att a Generall Courte the 23th of March, 1647.

The Gouerner acquainted the court that those whome they appointed to consider of the absent lotts had done it, and finde the charge wch is vpon them by fencings & rates, to be very highe; and allso that the lotts are not of an equalle goodnesse, hee therfore dissiered to knowe ther minde, wheither they will expect or require all the rates, or abate any pt, and howe much. And wheither they will grant any of them freely to some psons for publique respects, and wheither they will now consider and dispose of the matter themselues, or chuse a comittee to whome they will refer the wholle matter.

The courte considered the propossition, and agreed to chuse a committe. And the persons chossen are the magistrates, elders and deacons, the treasurer and on oute of each quarter, viz^d.

Francis Newman, for Mr. Eattons quarter.
Richard Myles, for Mr. Goodyears quart.
Henry Lindalle, for Mr. Lambertons qurt.
John Cooppr, for Mr. Newmans quart.

---

* Probably because they practiced medicine. For some account of Mr. Pell who had been a surgeon in the Pequot war, and from whom the town of Pelham takes its name, the reader is referred to Bolton's Hist. Westchester County, i. 521.

John Clarke, for the subverbs.
Mr. Crane, for Mr. Malbons quarter.
Mr. Evanc, for his owne quarter.
Mr. Gibbard, for Mr. Wakemans quart.
Mr. Ceffinch, for his owne quart.
Livetenant Seely, for the subverbs where he dwelleth.

To these or the maior pt of them agreeing, the courte gives full power to dispose of the absent lotts, w^t^h what abatement of rates or fencing or publique respects they shall see cause. Allso to consider and reserve what lott they shall see meette & most commodious for a colledg, w^c^h they dissire maye bee sett vp so soone as their abillitie will reach thervnto.

The Gouerner acquainted the courte that brother Andrewes had bine w^t^h hime aboute keepeing the ordinarie, and is willing to keepe it if he could see a waye howe hee might be able to provide things at the best hand in season. He therfore propounds that the towne woulde buy his house, house lott and land, & make hime such paye as he might buy provissions in season at best hand, and he will live in it & paye them rent by the yeare till he can provide himeselfe of another house, convenient and nearer the watter side for this purpose, and he will reffer the pric to indifferent men to judge. The gouerner asked the courte if they would not chuse some to consider w^t^h bro: Andrewes of this matter, and they agreed to doe it, and chosse Richard Myles, Henry Lendalle, Thomas Munson, Jervic Boykine, Francis Newman and John Cooper as a committe to consider of it and make reporte to the courte as they should finde cause. Further William Andrewes propoundes that he might have some part of the Oystershell feild for a pasture for strangers horses and some medowe ground w^c^h lyes convenient to gett haye for strangers horses in the winter, all which vpon the isue of the former matter, the courte would consider further off.

It is ordred that if any cattle be found in any corne feild or other severall ground where they are not to come, the owner shall paye 5^d^ a heade, (beside damadge,) wherof 1^d^ is to the pounder if they be pounded, and 4^d^ to hime that bringes them forthe, either home or to the pound; and for horses it is 7^{d} a pec, 1^{d} to the pounder & 6^{d} to hime that bringes them forthe.

Henry Lindalle was chossen in the roome of Anthony Tompson to joyne with them that are appoynted to view that land for Mr. Goodyeares and Mr. Wakemans quarters.

It is ordred that every cooper w^{t}hin this plantation shall take care that he make his ware tight and good, and full for gadge, and shall sett his burned marke vpon it that his ware maye bee knowne, and allso the just gadge, howe much it holdeth, w^{c}h is to be as followeth; the hogshead 64 gallons, but not lesse then 62; the halfe hogshead or quarter caske, 32 gallons, but not lesse the 30; and the barrell 48 gallons, but not lesse then ^ . Thesse to bee all marked as they will hold vpon tryall, and no otherwise.

Captaine Malbon acquainted the courte that the watches were made vp, but he finds that sundrye old men and seamen find themselues agreived that they are put into watch, therfore wheither the courte will not spare them, but it was respited.

Mr. Robert Newman propounded to the courte, that ther quartr and the next wher Mr. Ceffinch lives, dissires that they might have on third ꝑt of ther land w^{t}hin the two myle exchanged for so much at heither end of the playnes, because that on the hill is so stony they cannot plant it, and yett is better for pasture then ye plaine. The courte considered of it and chose Mr. Malbon, Mr. Wakeman, Mr. Crane and Leivtenant Seely as a committe to view and consider of what they propound, and howe it may stand w^{t}h the townes conveniency or inconveniency, and to make report backe to ye courte.

It is ordered that every man shall attend the putting his cattle that waye his land lyeth, and if any putt any vpon any common where he hath no land lye, he must take care that they maye so goe vnder keepers as that they maye not come vpon other mens land to doe them damadge; if they doe, they are to be pounded & the owner to answer it at the pertickuler courte.

[211] A Courte the 2th of Maye 1648.

Thomas Hogge was warned to the courte for not comeing to watch on night the last weeke in Aprill, but it apeared he had not sufficient warning, so it was passed by.

Richard Spery was complained of for not comeing to watch, but Mr. Goodier answered for hime that when he was neare comeing from the farme they wanted an oxe, the neager said he was sicke & left in the woods, so he was faine to goe forth to seeke hime least hee should be lost.

Jonathan Marsh was complained of for not comeing to watch, he saith he vnderstoode not the warning, for it was in the night when he was asleepe, but because William Russill, whoe warned hime, was not in courte, it was respited.

Old Goodman Willmote and Samuell Marsh tooke the oathe of fidellitie.

James Byshopp was complained of for not comeing to watch but it appeared he had not warning, thoughe he was carefull to inquire after it, so it was passed by for this time.

Mr. Goodanhouse was complained of, and John Fisher, Mr. Westerhouse man, for not comeing to watch. They made ther severall excuses, wch for this time, seeing they were strangers, the court accepted and passed it by, they promising for time to come to attend the servic more carefully.

William Paine was called to make proofe of the charge he made against Seriant Munson. Hee saide it was not his intent to charge Seriant Munson wth partiallitie. The Governer told hime he charged it so as it must be partiallitie or grose negligenc. He produced William Gibbins, whoe saith that he tooke notice that some came late, as Henry Lindalle, Allen Balle, Goodman Lampson, William Blayden; but it is long sinc, and he cannot tell wheither they were complained of or no. John Halle saith he sawe Goodman Lampson and Henry Lindalle come late, but wheither they payde for it or no he cannot tell. William Paine saith that Thomas Moris came wthout armes, and Edward Campe. William Holt saith so allso. Seriant Munson saith he tooke not notice that they came wthout armes, and wheither it were not vpon some day that he was absent, for he was 2 or 3 dayes justly hindred last summer. And for Henry Lindall and Allen Balle, they were not in his squadron. William Payne was tould he had not carried it well, for he should have told the seriant of it before, and not lett it passe till he was complained of himselfe, and then in this distemper to declare it, it did not savour well, but he said he was sorey for it. Seriant Munson was told y[t] the court judged hime faithfull in his trust, yett it had the appearanc of negligenc, but they hoped this would be a warning, and so passed it by.

Mr. Evanc tendred an account betwixt Henry Gibbines and Mr. Trobridg, wherin it appeared Mr. Trobridg was debtto[r] to the said Henry 20[l] 05[s] 05[d], yett because he is not able so fully to cleare the acc[o] as to make oathe it is so much, some paprs being lost, he is content to accept of 10[l] as full satisfaction, and that, he dares take oath, is due to hime at least.

Mr. Crane allso demaunds 10[l] from the same estate of Mr. Trobridg, w[ch] Henry Gibbins saith was due to hime from his master, but being asked if he could make oathe of it, he was at a stand, but they were wished to prepare accounts more perfectly against the courte of magistrats.

Mr. Robert Newman, as M[ris] Wilkes her executo[r], hath sould and passeth ouer to Robert Bassett the house and home lott of M[ris] Wilkes, w[th] what ground aboute the house was granted by the towne to Mr. Wilkes. The price, 40[l], that is 30[l] for the house and 10[l] for the garden or orchyard. He to take the house w[t]houte repaires, as it was prised by William Andrewes and Thomas Munson; and what repaires hath bine done sinc it was prissed, he to paye it beside the 40[l]. He is to paye the one halfe, that is 20[l], betwixt this and the 29[th] of September next, and the other 20[l] at or before the first daye of Maye next. This paye to be made in corne, cattle or wamppome.

John Halle challengeth something of M[ris] Wilkes estate as a legacy given by Mr. Wilkes to his wife, but it was respited.

An inventorie of the estate of William Balle deceased was delivered into the courte, and ordered to be recorded.*

Mr. Samuell Goodanhouse complained of ^ , a Duchman w^c^h is servant to Mr. Henry ^ and was prepareing to rune awaye from hime, for he had gathered many things together for that purpose as himeselfe confeseth. Onc before he did run awaye as farr as Farefeild but was stayde and sent backe by Mr. Ludlowe, and was brought before the governer heare and promised amendment, but yett returnes to the same course againe. He leaues it w^t^h the courte, dissiering them to showe what favoure they maye. The courte considering this delinquent had had warning before and promised amendment, and yett now returnes to the same euill againe, ordered that he should be whipped, yett w^t^h some moderation, seing he is a stranger, and his governers whoe susteyne the damadge dissire it.

[212] ||The marshall tould the courte William Wooden had neglected his watch, and by hime sent this answer, that that night he was not well and gott another to watch, whome he conceives promised hime, but he deceived hime and the watch was neglected, so he leaues it to the courte. The court agreed that William Wooden be warned to the next courte to give his owne answer.

Joseph Gernsye was complained of for want of armes, but he not being in courte himselfe, but sent his answer by the marshall, it was respited.

Mr. Theophilus Higenson propounded to the courte that Edward Chiperfeild owed hime xx^s^, he dissiered the helpe of the courte, that he might have it; he was told when the estate is setled then the debte muste bee proved, and till then it must be respited.

---

* "An inventorie of the estate of William Ball taken the 30th daye of the 2th moneth 1648. £13. 0. 9." by Joshua Atwater and Thomas Kimberlye.

ATT A GENERALL COURT THE 22th OF MAYE 1648.

William Jeanes was admitted a member of this court and tooke the freemans charge.

Mr. Wakeman and Mr. Crane were chossen deputies for the jurisdiction generall court.

Mr. Gibbard, Mr. Crane, Richard Milles & Francis Newman were chosen deputies for the plantation court of Newhaven for the yeare ensuing.

Mr. William Gibbard was chosen treasurer for Newhaven for the yeare ensuing.

Francis Newman was chosen secretarie for Newhaven for the yeare ensuing.

Thomas Kimberly was chosen marshall for Newhaven for ye yeare ensuing.

The Governer propounded to the court that they would consider something aboute the watches, for it is found that as it was last setled ther is inconvenienc in it, because ye warning of the watch is so late that it makes disturbanc in mens families when they are in bed. The court considered of it, and for prevention ordred, that the foure watchmen wch are to watch, come to that sariants house wher they shall be appointed, halfe an houer after sunn sett, vnder the penalltie formerly setled; and the first two that come, the sariant is, (haveing given ther charge,) to send prsently forth to warne the next watch, and so to walke the rounds in ther course as before ordred. The other two haueing ther charge from the sariant, are to march to the watch-house, keeping the court of gaurde, and takeing ther turne to walke the roundes as beefore ordred. And if it fall out that one or more be absent at the time appointed, the sariant hath power from this court to goe and take, to supply his prsent watch, out of that watch wch should watch the night following, and they wch should haue watched shall paye halfe the fine for late comeing to them that watch in ther roome, and thoughe they come after, yett shall returne home againe and watch for them the night following.

John Meges is freed from trayning because he is lame, and

from watching in his owne person, provided that he hire a man to watch, that the sariants shall approve of.

Thomas Moris because of his occaisions aboute watterworke, w^ch, by reason of the tide, is sometimes late at night, (vpon his desire,) is allowed to hire a man to watch wch the sariants shall approve of.

It is ordred that those farmers and their covenant servants wch have no estate in the towne, are for the p^rsent, till the court see cause to alter it, freed from watching.

Mr. Goodyeare, because his farme is allone and farr from the towne, hath two men freed from watching.

David Atwater, Richard Mansfeild, is to finde each of them a man to watch at the towne in regarde of ther house lotts heare.

Mr. Goodanhouse farme is respited till the court more fully vnderstand from him wheither it is lett or no, and how, but his men are to watch in the meane time.

It is ordred that the Necke be driven this afternoone, and what catle are found that transgrese the order, are to be pounded or driven to some yard, and the names of the owners and the number of the catle given to the governer.

John Meges was chosen clarke for ye trayne band of Newhauen.

The officers for the artillary chosen this yeare was p^rsented to the court, viz^d. Robert Seely, Captaine, William Andrewes, Leivtenant, Mr. Chittendine of Guilford, John Nash, William Fowler, Richard Beckly, Sariants. Henry Lendalle, Ensigne. Richard Myles, Clarke.

Samuell Whithead is chosen collecto^r for the colledge corne for this yeare, in the rome of Anthony Tompson deceased.

The Governer propounded to the court to know wheither they thought it convenient and would allow, that two or three house lotts in the towne should be laide into one, by wch meanes the number of planters is deminished and the towne weakened, and many other considerations; also wheither they thinke it not meete, that every house lott in the towne finde a watchman, thoughe ther be no house or no bodey dwell vpon it. The court thought it worthy of consideration and refered it to the magistrats, elders and deacons, and the deputies for the court, as a committee to consider and determine of it.

It was propounded wheither seamen should watch, but after much debate and yett no issue, the governer was desired to wright to the governer in the Baye to know what they did ther aboute it, and then the court will consider of it againe.

[213] || The Governer acquainted the court the heares ther is some families in the towne want releife, as widdow Knowles, widdow Halbich; the ordred that M' Gilbert & Mr. Wakeman joyne wth the treasurer to consider of their state, that they be not put to extremity.

Lancelot Fuller desired the court that they would grant him a pec of land to sett a house vpon, vpon the banke side by the creeke, betwixt M^ris Lambertons house and Sariant Jefferyes. The court chose Mr. Goodyeare, Leivtenant Seely, Jasper Crane & Francis Newman to veiw & consider of it, & report backe to the court how they finde it.

It is ordred that order for killing old wolues and foxes wch allowed 15^s for a woolfe, and 2^s 6^d for a fox be againe in forc; but for younge woolues or younge foxes it is but halfe the price.

Mr. Malbon acquainted the court that those whoe were appointed to veiwe Mr. Newmans quarter haue don it, and find not but the towne might grant the exchange, if ther could be a convenient way found to that they would part w^th, but that not yett appearing, it was respited. Allso that those that were appointed to veiwe one the west side for Mr. Goodyeares and Mr. Wakemans quarters, beyonde Mr. Malbons meddowe, haue done it, and finde nothing but, if they desire their land their, the towne maye grant it w^thout inconvenienc to themselues.

[There was a General Court for the Jurisdiction held on the 31st of May, 1648, as we learn from the MS. Records of the United Colonies, (Hazard erroneously gives the date as May 3d.) The time for the election of officers for the jurisdiction had been changed from October to the last Wednesday in May, probably at the preceding session. At this time Theophilus Eaton and John Astwood were chosen commissioners.]

A COURT HELD AT NEWHAVEN THE 6th OF JUNE 1648.

John Moss passeth ouer to Richard Beech 1 acr, 1 quarter & 14 rod of meddowe, lying in the west meddowe, one end abutting on the West River, the other end runing into a cove in the vpland, betwixt the meddowe of Richard Beech & James Russell.

William Blayden was complained of for not appearing at the last generall court, he sayd he heard not the drume nor knew that their was a court, and sayd he could take his oath of it. The court, seing they could not prove it, past it by.

Mr. Cheffinch declared in court that he approved of his brother Thomas Ceffinch his will, and accepted of the executorship, and prsented an inventorie of the estate of the sayd Thomas Ceffinch in court, amount to 343l 00 : 00. prised by Josua Atwater & Samuel Ceffinch, the 6th of June 1648.*

Joseph Gernsey was warned to the court and appeared, and was complained of for want of armes. He made his excuse that he was poore when he came out of his time, & sinc he hath intended to goe to sea, so hath neglected it, but was tould that these excuses would not serve, for though he was poore or went to sea he must have armes. For this neglect he was fined 5s, & if he be not provided in a moneth, it will bring a greater fine vpon him.

Leivtenant Seely, as sealler of leather for the towne, complained that he saw some leather a dressing that was not sealled nor fitt to be sealed; he inquired whose it was, the currier sayd some of it was Abraham Dowlitles, some John Chidseys, some Jno Gregoryes. Jno Megs had none their, but he saw a pare of shooes wch came from him wch was made of leather gren and horney, neither sealed nor fitt to be sealed, wch was but of the threes, yett the pric 2s 8d or 2s 10d.

John Gregory answered that his leather was sealed as much as he thought necessary, before this last order was made; he was told it was not sealed at all, but onely cutt for tryall; and

* In the margin, "At a court ye 4th Septm. 1649, ye inventorie was proved bye oath of ye prisors for ye vallew & by ye oath of ye executor for ye quantitie."

by that cutting it appeared not fully tanned, so not fitt to be sealed, and that before this last order he sealed or marked other mens hides w^t^h **N. H.** w^t^h a knife, besides cutting them for tryall; that if he had thus sealed or marked this leather, it had bine a double fault, in makeing faultie leather into shooes, and in falsifying an office trust, sealing that w^c^h should not be sealed. But he was further told that this leather was not sealed, and the last order reached all vnsealed leather in any mans house or custody, then he sayd he thought the sealer should have come to his house to inquire after vnsealed leather; he was told it was no part of the sealers worke, they that had vnsealed leather ought to speake or send for them, and so it was generally vnderstood, and others did send for him, & Mr. Malbon was instanced in; then he sayd it was his ignoranc, but that satisfyed not. Lastly it was conceived that from Abraham Dowlitle or John Chidsey he vnderstood that Leivtenant Seely had found fault w^t^h his leather, as neither sealed nor fitt to be sealed, and yett he had wrought it out, or pt of it, into shooes, w^c^h beside the injurye to the buyers, seemed a contempt of ye authority by w^c^h the order was made, this he acknowledged not, whervpon his miscariage was respited till Abraham Dowlitle and Jno Chidsey, (now abroade,) come home.

John Meges being questioned for the shooes he made of faultie vnsealed leather, and perticulerly for a pare sould to Moses Wheeler, pretended ignoranc that leather in mens houses should be sealed. He acknowledged himselfe had curryed a pec of leather which he had in the house, thoughe he knew it was both vnsealed and horney, not tanned. He acknowledged that vpon Moses Wheelers importunity he had made him a small pare of shooes of that leather; what pric he tooke for them he remembers not, but hee intended if Moses Wheeler should after complaine of the shooes, to make satisfaction. The court remembering what had formerly passed betwixt Goodman Megs and old Goodman Gregory, and that at another court sinc, Goodman Meges of his owne
[214] accord had acknowledged || his sinnfull miscariage, in makeing and selling deceitfull shooes, w^t^h such appearanc off

an inward conviction, and suitable sorrowe, that all or most that heard him inclined to satisfaction, was deeply offended at this passage. How many shooes John Meges hath since made and sould of such faultie vnsealed leather they know not, but in this one paire severall evills appeare. First contempt of authority in breaking an order wherin himselfe w^t^h others had bine advised w^t^h and had approved it. Secondly, continewed vnrighteousnes in selling a small paire of shooes made both vpper leathers & soales of faulty leather at so highe a price, not acquainting the buyer w^t^h any defect, or purpose of any restetution if the shooes proved bad. Thirdly much appearanc of guile in his late repentanc, returning so soone to the same sinn for w^c^h he had volluntaryly and publiquely judged himselfe. Wherfore reserving libbertie to themselues to heare and consider any other mans complaint against Goodman Megges for selling such faultie shooes, when any such shall be brought, the court, for this miscariage, agravated by the forenamed circumstances, ordered Goodman Meggs to paye twenty shillings to the towne as a fine, beside due satisfaction to Moses Wheeler when it shall be required.

John Jackson, Beniamen Willmot & Thomas Yale were complained of for not comeing to watch, but it appeared they had not seasonable warning, and it was before the watches were setled in their course, therfore the court for this time past it by.

Francis Hall was warned to the court and appeared, and was complained of for refusing to watch himselfe, and for counselling others to refuse it allso, w^c^h cariage holds forth contempt and a riseing vp against the authority of the place.

Francis Hall sayd he spake some words to Seriant Fowler, but he intended no such thinge. Seriant Fowler sayd he sent Francis Hall word to come to watch one the third day at night, but he came not, nor any for him, so he hired a man to watch in his roome; the next day he mett w^t^h Francis Hall at Mr. Evanc his house, and told him he should have attended his watch, but he hired one to watch for him, and bid him either paye him or watch for him againe, but he answered he would doe neither of them, and was verey stiffe & peremptory, and though Mr. Evanc and Robert Martin both perswaded him, he would not harken.

Mr. Ling sayd that John Jones his farmer told him that Francis Hall dishartened him from watching, saying they should all fare ye better if he, the sd Jno Jones, went not to watch. Francis Hall seemed to fall vnder it, & saide he rather beleived Seriant Fowler then himselfe, and doth allso beleive what Jno Jones saith, and submitts to the courte.

The court considered the cariage of Francis Hall, and saw it contempt of authority wth a disrepective cariage to the seriant in his place, and such counsell gave to others wch as in the nature of it tendes to disturbanc in the commonwealth, therfore ordered that Francis Hall paye as a fine to the towne, twenty shillings.

Richard Myles and Rogger Allen were appoynted to prise the estate of William Ives deceased.

Richard Myles, William Tompson & Mathew Camfeild were appointed to prise and vallew the estate of Anthoney Tompson deceased.

A Generall Court the 3th of July, 1648.

Thomas Moris was admitted a member of this court and received the freemans charge.

Mr. Gibbard being chosen the last court, Treasurer for Newhaven for a yeare, did now desire the court to make choise of another, for he was not fitted wth abillities to carie one that worke to the townes satisfaction nor his owne, but would rather submitt to a fine and be spared from the place. It was propounded to the court wheither they would free Mr. Gibbard according to his desire, but the court did againe confirme ther former choise, judging him a man meete and fitt for that place, and voted that Mr. Gibbard be treasurer for Newhaven for the ensuing yeare.

The Governer acquainted the court that the heardmen have complained to him that ye dry catle, as oxen and steeres, do so trouble their heards that they know not what to doe wth them. It was therfore propounded wheither the court would not make some order to p[r]vent it, w[c]h the court considered how to doe, and ordered that if any dry catle or oxen be found in the cowes walke to trouble the heards, the owner of them paye 3[d] a head, beside poundage if they be pounded; and if any quarter or quarters shall agree together to drive out their catle or hire a keeper, and any refuse, they haueing had seasonable notice therof, the pticuler court shall judg of their miscariage, & order them to paye and beare charges w[t]h their neighbours, according to their proportion.

The planters one the west side of the towne desired they might haue libbertie to fence in the oxe pasture laid out neare the towne, to keepe their oxen in, and some ppounded that that pt next the towne might be lett out to be planted for some yeares. The court considered of the propossition and ordered, that some be appointed to speake w[t]h the planters in the towne, to see if their may be such an exchange made betwixt those one the east side of the towne, & those one the west; the one pt relinquishing their right in the Necke & takeing it whollye in the Oxe pasture, the other leaveing their right in the Oxe pasture, and takeing it wholly in the Necke, and then, if their be a considerable number that will plant, they maye, as they shall agree, fence in some for that purpose, provided that they abridge themselues of keepeing ther. Mr. Gibbard & Richard Milles were appoynted for that side of the towne, and Mr. Ling & Mr. Ceffinch for the other side; that is Mr. Eatons qr., Mr. Malbons, Mr. Newmans, Mr. Ceffinch & the subverbs on the other sid the east creeke, that so the matter might be prepared for another court.

[215] || William Andrewes and Thomas Munson were desired to veiw the pillars of y[e] meeting-house, that any decaye in them maye bee timely discovered and p[r]vented. And the like was allso desired of William Andrewes for *fo* the Necke bridge and the West bridge.

It was propounded to the court wheither they would have George Laremore the millar watch. The court considered of it, and seeing it falls out so that some time he is faine to sitt vp at mill to supply the towne w[t]h meale, therfore ordered that he should be freed from watching.

It was allso propounded to the court wheither they would free Robert Bassett the drumer, from watching, but the court ordered that he be not freed, but that hee watch as other planters doe.

Captaine Malbon propounded to the court that the cullers bought by the artillary company, wch have bine allso vsed in the towne traynings and received some damage therin, might be payde for out of the towne stocke and be the townes cullers, and lett the artillary have the vse of them in their traynings, seeing the townes good is promoved therby. And it was ordered that they be so payde for and vsed.

Veiwers chosen for the fences for the yeare ensuing are as followeth,

Mr. Gilbert and John Walker for Mr. Eatons & Mr. Malbons quarters.

Mr. Ling and Robert Hill for Mr. Newmans & Mr. Ceffinches quarters.

William Fowler & Henry Glouer for Mr. Gibbards quarter.

Henry Lendall, Thomas Mitchell for Mr. Goodyeares quarter.

Phillip Leek, Thomas Lampson for Mr. Lambertons quarter.

John Moss, Mathias Hitchcocke for ye subverbes.

Thomas Beament, Henry Pecke for the playnes.

Francis Browne, Mathew Moulthrop for Oyster-shell-feild till ye corne be out.

Thomas Beament was chosen sealler of leather in the roome of Robert Preston deceased, and tooke oath that he should deale faithfully to seale all leather according to the order wch hath bine made, according to the best of his light.

William Andrewes desired the court to provide some other to keepe the ordinary for he was not able to carie it one, wch they tooke into consideration.

Thomas Moris propounded to the court that himselfe and others imployed aboute vessells as carpenters might be spared from trayning, because some time many mariners wch are vnder paye attend vpon them, wherby the pric of commodities is raysed. The court saw no waight in the argument & therfore granted it not. But what workemen are imployed as carpenters aboute the great ship, when it is in hand, are spared from trayning for that time till she be ready to goe forth.

Jonathan Marsh desired he might have libbertie to sett vp a shop to worke in on his trade, vnder the banke side next the watter before his house. The court reffered it to be veiwed by Leivtenant Seely, Jasper Crane, Thomas Munson, and Francis Newman, and to report to the governer how they finde it, who is to graunt or deney as he shall see cause.

A COURT HELD ATT NEWHAVEN THE 4th OF JULY, 1648.

Samuell Whithead, John Moss, Rogger Allen and Thomas Lampson were complaind of for being absent at the generall court when the names were read, they made their excuse that their cowes were lost the Saboth day before, and they were faine to goe looke them, haueing no other to doe it, and Jno Moss further saith that they had loaded goods aboard the lighter wch he apprhended to be in some danger, because the winde was high that morning, and thought it his duty to goe and looke after them. The court considering that the case of them all is extreordinary, & could not be prvented before, past it wthout a fine for this time.

John Hall was complained of for absenc at a generall court, he sayd he had no warning, & went out in the morning before the drum beate, & knew of no court. William Holt was complained of for the like & gave the same answer, for he was wth John Hall. For both the court past it wthout a fine.

William Bassett was complained of for not bringing his armes to ye meeting on the Saboth day wch was his squadron. He answered that he was changed from one squadron to another, and knew not that it was his day, and when he saw it was, he brought them in the afternoone; but he was told it was his neglect who should knowe, but the court findeing it was no willfull neglect, agreed that he paye halfe the fine, wch is 2s: 6d.

Thomas Wheeler was complained of for defect in his armes,

want of gunsticke, some powder, defective scabbard, w^c^h he confeseth, though for his po^r^ he conceiveth ther was inoughe. For these he was fined 18^d^, and for late coming to trayning w^c^h he acknowledgeth, 12^d^. He was complained of for absenc at a squadron trayning, but he answered he was put into a new squadron & had no warning, that was past by. He was complained of for comeing late w^t^h his armes on Lords day, but it could not be fully proved, wherfore if he can make it appeare he cam before the last drum left beating, as he conceives he did, the court will consider of it againe, but for p^r^sent it is respited.

[216] || John Whithead, servant to Mr. Crane, was complained of for want of a pine in the locke of his pec. His master saith it was no other defect then hath passed ths 8 yeares, and could not be mended w^t^hout a new stocke, and the gunsmith sayd it was sufficient. The court for this time past it w^t^hout a fine, but agreed that it should be mended.

James Clarke was complained of for coming late to a squadron trayning, & late one Saboth day w^t^h his armes. Hee answered the true reason was because his wife was sicke, w^c^h the court accepted and past it w^t^hout a fine, but is fined 12^d^ for late comeing in the afternoone one trayning day as himselfe acknowledgeth.

James Clarke was further complained of for absenc vpon a trayning day when they showed armes. He sayd Sariant Munson tooke him away and he thought he would haue bine at court to have cleared him, but it was respited, and the marshall ordered to warn Seriant Munson to the next court.

John Hall having at a court in July last, 1647, demaunded out of the estate of Mr. Wilkes 10^l^ as a portion promised by Mr. Wilkes to his wife, whoe was his servant, as he then proved by two witnesses, w^c^h proceeding were now reade, and further to confeirme the thinge, he now presenteth Jonathan Marsh, whoe testifyeth vpon oath that Mr. Wilkes a litle before he went to England declared to him that he had promised his maide Jeane Woolen, (now Jean Hall,) a portion, and made a motion of marriage to him concerning her, and if he accepted it he would paye it downe; but he cannot remember distinctly wheither he sayd it was five pounds or tenn pounds. The court considered that it is a case that concerneth the estate of the deade, and that Goodwife Hall herselfe is not now in court to answer to any question might be propounded, and being desierous that the indenture wherin she was bound to Mr. Wilkes might be searched for and showen in court, therfore it was respited till the next court.

Mr. Gibbard was fined for defecte in the cocke of his mans gunn 6^d, and for want of at least 1^l of bullits 2^s.

John Wakefeild was complained of for not bringing his armes to the meeting on Lords day when his turne was. He saith it was one day when his wife was sicke & hindred him, or elc one day when he kept cowes, but he leaves himselfe wth the court.

John Thomas was too late wth his armes one Lords day, the reason he saith, was because he had a child sicke and was faine to goe to Mr. Pell for something for it. The court judging it a worke of mercy and necessary to be done, past it by.

A Court at Newhaven the first of August, 1648.

Mr. Crane and Francis Newman informed the court, that wheras ther have bine and still are certaine questions and differences betwixt Mr. Davenport and Henry Byshop his late farmour, wch Mr. Davenport would have issued by a private arbitration, and for that end hath desired them, one his behalfe to consider the perticulars wth Goodman Byshop in a friendly way & to propound refferenc, but Henry Byshop hath euer refused it, saying he would issue his owne matteres himselfe, wch cariage of his, after three monethes of forbearance, constreyned Mr. Davenport to thinke of other meanes; yett after a warrant was written, Mr. Davenport, vnwilling to commence a suit, stayed it, and vpon his request the Governer sent for Goodman Bishop and indeavoured to ꝑswade him to a refferenc, but could not prevayle, whervpon the warrant was served and Goodman Byshop appearing, the court would have proceeded, but Goodman Byshop desired respite, because some of his witnesses living out of towne were absent, and himselfe at p^rsent vnprepared for triall. He was told that his witnesses were not so farr out of towne but they might have bine sent for & ready since the warrant was served. Mr. Crane and Francis Newman one Mr. Davenports behalfe, desired that since Goodman Byshop is no setled planter, but maye remove at pleasure, he maye put in security to the vallew of 60^l to satisfye and paye what shall be found due from him to Mr. Davenport, wheither by sentence of court or arbitration, and that if it be by arbitration, Goodman Byshope chuse men free from just exception. The court aproving the motion, propounded it to Goodman Byshop. Goodman Byshop desired y^t Mr. Davenport might allso putt in security to him, and that he might have libbertie to except against Mr. Davenports arbitrators. The court told him it was not reasonable that the plantiff, being a man of place and esteeme, and haveing a good vissible estate fixed in the plantation, after such meanes vsed to bringe the cause to an issue, should putt in security to ye defendant whoe is like to be found the debto^r; but if he could make any just exceptions against Mr. Davenports arbitrators, it should be considered. Whervpon Goodman Byshop ingaged all the corne vpon Mr. Davenports farme, wheither in ye barne or abroade, and one mare belonging to him of Mr. Davenports breede, 5 steeres & two heyfers aboute three yeares old, and 5 cowes; all w^ch, both corne and catle, hee affirmed to be free and vningaged at p^rsent, and did now in court ingage them to Mr. Davenport, by way of security to satisfye and paye whatever shall be found due vnto him by arbitrators indifferently chosen betwixt them, betwixte this and the next court, or by arbitrators chosen for them by the court, or by sentenc, or any other waye the court shall order and appointe.

Robert Bassett a planter in Newhaven, ^ Badger boatswaine, Charles Higenson marriner in ye ship Susan, whoe had bine comitted to prison for a late disorder, released vpon baile and bound to answer at this court, appeared wth Thomas Toby and foure others whoe came lately from Boston to worke vpon the ship hear built. The court was informed that vpon the sixt day last weeke, after sunn sett, their was a disorderly meetting and drinking at the house of Robert Basset, wch continewed, as was conceived, till betwixt tenn and eleven of the clocke, wherin ther was severall miscariages, to the great provocation of God, the disturbance of ye peace, and to such a height of disorder that strangers wondered at it, and Robert Basset himselfe confesed he had not seene the like since he came. The manner and ꝑticulars were as followeth,

[217] || Some of the Susans company, after their dayes worke was finished, comeing on shore mett wth the master and owner of a pinnace lately come in from Boston, and foure of the workemen for the ship builte heare, and John Griffen. They went into Robert Bassets and called for sacke. He told them he might not draw less then three quarts, wch was a most ꝑverse interpretation and abuse of an order, as if the court would further drunkennes, forceing men to drinke more then they desired, wheras he should have drawne none at all in that waye; the order being expressly made and penned to suppress such disorderly meetings and drinkings. No man wthout speciall licence being ꝑmitted to sell wine or stronge liquours by retayle in small quantities, much less to vse his house or cellar as a taverne for company to come in and spend their money in drinking wine or stronge liquours; onely if a merchant will drawe out a pipe or pec, he might sell either to neighbour plantations or to the inhabitants of Newhaven a runlet, case of glases, or by the gallon for his private vse, but this company, being in number tenn, (besids Robert Basset himselfe,) Robert Basset drew them three quarts, and after in severall ꝑcells, three quarts more at that sitting, by wch means some of the company, (as appeareth,) dranke to excess and distemper, and brake into quarrelling and other sinfull miscariages. The owner of the pinnace, in their cupps, calling the boatswaine of the Susan, Brother Loggerhead, the boatswaine returns threatening language, thenc they grew to sideing, ꝑt takeing and chalenging, then the master of the pinnace and the boatswaine goeing out of ye house, fall first to wrestling, then to blowes, and theirin grew to that feircnes

that the master of the pinnace thought the boatswaine would have pulled out his eies, and the markes of the blowes appeared some dayes after vpon his face; and in this rage and distempr they toumbled on the ground, downe the hill into the creeke and mire, shamfully wallowing therin; and had they not bine ꝑted, they might have proceeded to further mischeife, for Charles Higenson, distempered as it seemes wth drinke, in a way of sideing wth the boatswaine, grew quarrelsome, wherw^th the owner of the pinnace, being affrighted, rann aboute ye streete crying, Hoe, the watch, Hoe, the watch, and the watch being then in that ꝑt of ye towne walking the rounds, made hast and for ye p^rsent stopped the course of ye disorder, but in this rage and distemper the boatswaine fell a swearing, wounds & hart, as if he were not onely angry wth men, but would provoake the highe & blessed God. After they were thus ꝑted, the master of the pinnace went to ye watter side, but the season not serving to goe on board, he returned to Robert Bassets house, and their the boatswaine fell vpon him againe and theirby frighted Robert Bassets wife & child. Robert Basset moved therw^th, thrust the owner of the pinnace out of dores & told him (as himselfe confesseth,) that if he had him in place where he would beate out his teeth, or as Thomas Toby, (Robert Bassets witnes,) relates it, he would make him sucke as longe as he lived; which words argue distemper, and are vsed by drunken companions, so that the disorder was verey great and verey offensive, both to ye neighbours, the noyse & oathes being heard to the other side of the creeke, and to others who coming theither observed onely some ꝑt of their miscariage. And though it be not fully proved that Thomas Toby was distempered wth drinke, & himselfe denyes it, yett he had a share in the disorderly drinking, and furthered it by drawing, (as himselfe acknowledgeth,) one quart of the wine when they had had two much before, wch was the worse in him, haveing bine onc before fined in this court for miscariage in drinking, wch in himselfe and others should have made him more watchfull against such disorder.

This sinfull miscariage being thus opened, and the ꝑticulars in substanc acknowledged by the pties therin concerned, the court proceeded to sentenc, and first finding Robert Basset guiltie of the breach of a knowne express order of ye generall court, in such selling wine and suffering company to com in, spend their money and sitt drinking at such vnseasonable howers, all agravated both by the warning himselfe had in John Lawrenson & his wifes case, whoe were fined for a less miscariage in strong liquours comitted in his house, and by the sinfull efects wch followed vpon this disorderly drinking, as quarreling and fighting wth disturbanc of the peace as before expressed, swearing in such a fearfull manner as might justly have brought downe the wrath of God vpon the swearer & that whole company, frighting his owne wife and child, and his owne quarreling & threatening, wth the spirit and in ye phrase of a man distempered wth rage or drinke, the court ordered him to paye five pounds as a fine to the towne. And that ^ Badyard, the boatswaine of the Susan, for his distemper in drinking, his quarreling, fighting, and swearing, thoughe Mr. Evanc and Robert Martin testifyed for him that his course and cariage hath bine faire & free from swearing to their best observance sinc his first coming heither till this prsent miscariage, wch did mittigate the censure, yett the court ordred that he paye to the towne forty shillings as a fine, and that Charles Higenson paye 10s, and Thomas Toby 5s. And for ye foure strangers wch came to worke vpon the ship hear built, their being neither proofe nor charge against them for excess in drinking, quarreling, or any other miscariage, save their beeing in company in this disorderly meetting, the court onely advised them to take it as a warning against all future disorder.

Adam Nickholls was complained of for not comeing to watch, he answered that he had lett his watch for ye whole yeare, and he that he hired fayled him. He was told that he must answer for his man & require remedy of him againe, for wch neglect he is fined 5s. He was complained of for comeing late wth his armes one Lords day, he sayd that his wife & child was sicke; he was told that if could say that was ye reason at this time, ther might be something in it, but he could not afirme that, whervpon it was reffered to another court.

Henry Pecke & Joseph Pecke were complained of for comeing two late wth their armes on Lords day in ye morning; they answered that ye night before they watched & had no rest, & when they came home they went to take a litle rest, that so they might be ye fitter for ye ordinances & not sleepe, vpon wch consideration, for this time, ye court past it by.

M^ris Plume and Samuell Plume p^rsented in court an inventory of the estate of Mr. John Plume of Totoket, deceased, but because it was not vnder oath of ye appraisers according to ye generall courts order, the court accepted it not, but onely kept ye copie, inioyning them to bring in one according to order ye next court, or elc to show just cause why not.

[218] ||John Hall having formerly pleaded for a portion for his wife of 10^l out of the estate of Mr. Wilkes, due to her by promise, as did appeare by the testimony of William Paine and Bridget Wilkes vpon oath, and at the last court renewed his plea, and produced another witnes, viz^d, Jonathan Marsh, whoe was allso heard and examined vpon oath, but the cause for some reasons then showen, was not issued, therfore he did now renew his desire that the court would be pleased to put an issue to it, and Goodey Hall being present was asked why her master Wilkes promised her 10^l if she served out her time. She sayd because he knew she deserved it. The indenture wherin Goodwife Hall was bound to Mr. Wilkes was called for and allso read in court, wherin it appeared that she was to serve him for 5 yeares and to have 3^l a yeare, wch the court judged competent wages, her passage being allso payde for by Mr. Wilkes, so that the act was alltogether free one Mr. Wilkes his pt. But he haveing promised and ingadged himselfe to doe it, as appeares fully by testimony of ye witnesses vpon oath, therfore it becomes a due debte to her. Therfore the sentenc of the court is that Mr. Robert Newman, executo^r of ye estate of Mr. Wilkes, paye to John Hall as a debte due from Mr. Wilkes to his wife, 10^l.

James Hayward haveing at a court, December ye 7th 1647,

entred an action of defamation against William Wooden, w^c^h was opened and witnesses heard and examined, but then was respited by ye court, whoe waitted for some further light out of ye Baye concerning this thing, w^c^h now being come, James Hayward desired that their might be an issue put to it, whervpon the proceedings of that former court was read and a further testimony of Beniamin Hill vpon oath, taken before Mr. Malbon the 25th of Maye 1648, wherin Beniamin Hill testifyeth that he heard William Wooden saye, James Hayward was hollowe harted, and if ye church knew that he heard, he would not be received againe, and that he would be banished if all was true he heard (or they knewe as much as he,) and that he dealt basely w^t^h him at Captaine Turners, haveing put a pece of leather of Captaine Turners into his knap-sacke in way of spite, James and William being fallen oute, and that James charged William Wooden that he had stole ye leather, therfore he conceives he put it in, because he was so readie to charge him w^t^h it. Likewise the testimonyes w^c^h came from the Baye were read, wherin it appeared that the things charged by William Wooden and witnessed by John Mascall were true in ye substanc, thoughe William Wooden had spread them in a defameing slanderous waye, and taken vpon him to saye that he would be banished, which was none of his worke nor place to doe. Likewise James Hayward his owne letter now produced, showes that he hath brought an ill report vpon ye place, reporting things of it that were not true. And by Goodman Pery and his wives testimoney vpon oath appeares that he dealt not truely in his promises, but was false harted towards their daughter, and that he was given to disorderly drinking in ye Baye. And by Mr. Noris his wrighting it appeares that he had not caried things fairely w^t^h him. And Goodman Pery and his wives testimoney speakes to that purpose allso. James was now asked what he had further to saye, and why he denyed that to ye court w^c^h he had written in his letter. He sayd he knew not when he answered in court that he had so written, w^c^h the court knewe not how to beleive. James confessed ther was more discovered by the providenc of God then he did expecte, w^c^h yett did not excuse

William Wooden in his slanderous course, wch the court admitted, and as formerly, so now witnessed against him for it. And William Wooden himselfe did acknowledge that the manner of his reporting was scandalous, and that he was out of his way when he sayd he would be banished, but he left himselfe wth the court.

Both ꝑtyes haveing spoken what they would in the case, the court proceeded to sentence, and ordered that William Wooden, for his miscariage in spreding the things in a slanderous way and determining banishment, wch was none of his worke, paye the charges of ye court; and that James Hayward, for his owne sinn, beare his owne shame and charge he hath bine at in sending and goeing into the Baye, wch falls justly vpon him.

William Pecke, one of those intrusted to ouersee the estate of Robert Preston deceased, desired to knowe if they might not paye some debtes that are due out of the estate. The court told him, so they paye nothing but what is justly due, and what Robert Prestons estate maye beare, they maye.

A Court held at Newhaven the 5th of September 1648.

John Vincon was complained of for want of aboute three quartrs of a pound of bullitts, he sd he knew it not, and seeing he is now provided the court past it by wth 6^d fine.

Mr. Ceffinch was complained of for comeing late one Lords day wth his armes, & Jno Downe his man allso. For his man he saith he was necessarily hindred from ye meetting. For himself, he came in before Mr. Davenport, and others was late allso, and instanced in Thom: Meekes, but for himselfe he was fined 12^d.

John Downe, Mr. Ceffinch his man, for absenc at a squadron trayning was fined 2^s 6^d.

John Herreman was complained of for not bringing his armes one Lords day. He said it was because he hath two chilldren, and either his wife or he must staye from ye ordinances at home wth them, or elc he must bringe one of them and then cannot bring his armes, but ye court judged that this was but a common excuse that many might make, and if it should be attended the service would be neglected, therfore agreed the he paye ye fine, wch is 5^s.

Martin Tichener was complained of for comeing late wth his armes one Lords day, & allso for want of suitable bullits for his pec one viewing day; but because ye sariants note is somewhat imperfect wch complaineth of these defects, it was respited till next court.

Henry Gibbons was fined for late comeing one generall trayning day (as himself confesseth,) 12^d. And for late comeing one squadron trayning 6^d. And for not bringing his armes to be viewed one morning to the sariants house as he had warning to doe, 12^d. In all 2^s, 6^d.

Henry Byshopp for want of some bullits & not being yett provided, was fined 12^d.

Peeter Browne for ye like was fined 12^d.

[219] || The court was informed that Adam Nickholls came late wth his armes one Lords day, but because it depended somewhat vpon the corporalls witnes and he is not in court, it was respited till the next court.

Thomas Meekes was complained of for comeing late wth his armes one Lords day, he saith hee thinkes he was their before exercise begane, but leaves himselfe wth the court, was find 12^d. He was complained of for absenc at the generall trayning yesterday, he said he was not well, but it was said in court that he was at worke, wch others tooke notice of and was offended at it, for wch he was fined 5^s.

Job Hall for want of some match & a worme was fined 12^d.

Jeremiah Watts for want of some po^r & bullits was fined 2^s.

Thomas Lampson being warned to this court for some defect in his armes, appeared not, wch hath a show of contempt, & therfore is to answer it at next court.

The marshall informed the court that he had demanded the fine of Robert Basset wch was laid vpon him for his disorder, he refussed to paye & said he would have the matter scanned ouer againe in ye court. The court ordered that he paye his fine betwixt this and y^e next court, or elc make his appearanc then & their to show the reason why he payes it not.

M^{ris} Plume of Totokett and her sonn Samuell Plume brought into y^e court an inventorie of the estate of Mr. John Plume deceased, amounting to $366^l : 09^s : 01^d$, prised by Robert Rose, Robert Abut & Lawranc Ward vpon oath the 4th of Septembr, 1648.

Samuell Plume pleaded for a portion out of the estate, but because the witnesses were not readie, it was respited, onely M^{ris} Plume said it was her husbands will that he should have 100^l & a note from Mr. Swaine signifyed as much.

Henry Bishop informed the court that he had, according to the courts order y^e last court, indeavored to gitt $arbitrato^rs$ to issue the matter in differenc betwixt him & Mr. Davenport, butt could gitt none. He was asked whoe he spake wth to doe it, he named Mr. Wakeman, Mr. Tuttill & Richard Milles. The court thought they were fitt men & sent for Mr. Wakeman to desire him to take this vpon him, but he was not at home. Richard Milles being in court declared himselfe vnwilling, but the court agreed that they must chuse some to doe it, and appointed Mr. Wakeman & Richard Milles, two wch Henry Bishop chose himselfe, and Mr. Crane & Francis Newman chosen by Mr. Davenport. But Henry Bishop excepted against Mr. Crane to be an arbitrator in this buisenes; he was asked the reason why; he said he told Mr. Davenport that he should except against one of his men that he had chosen, whervpon the marshall was sent to Mr. Davenport to acquaint him wth it, whoe brought word againe that he wondered Henry Bishop should make exception against Mr. Crane, seeing he hath bine in all the buisnes from the begining and not excepted against, but Henry Bishop was still called vpon to show the cause of his exception, whoe answered if he must needs show it he would, provided that what he speakes might not be taken ill, for he was loath to speake it in open court; he was told if it was such a private thing as might not be spoken of, he might conceale it and onely declare it to Mr. Davenport, whervpon the marshall & Henry Bishop were sent to Mr. Davenport to declare his reason, whervpon Mr. Davenport came to the court and informed the court that the objection Henry Bishop makes hath not the forc of a just exception in it, for it doth not show any thing of vnfaithfullnes or partiallitie, for the thing was this. Mr. Crane gave his apprehension in a case in question vpon the farme, what he thought the doeing such a thing was worth, and now Henry Bishop saith he can have it done by a workeman for a great deale less, and yett he spake but his judgment and if an arbitrator may not doe soe, to what end is their any? 2dly, Mr. Crane and Francis Newman have stood arbitrators for him above a quarter of a yeare, and he accepted them but then would not joyne others w^{t}h them, and for that he said he told Mr. Davenport he would excepte against one of his men, it was not a possetive exception, but vpon occaision of Mr. Davenports words to him that he ye sd Henry Bishop must chuse men w^{t}hout exception, he answered by way of retort saying it may be he should except against one of his men, and in ye issue it appeared that ye exception was in prising the stubbing of the ground, in w^{c}h Francis Newman had a hand as well and equall w^{t}h Mr. Crane, and therfore the exception must lye against them both alike, nor doth it yett appeare that the thing will be done as it ought to be to fullfill ye covenant for so litle as Henry Bishop thinkes it will. It was propounded to the court wheither they judge the exception just w^{c}h Henry Bishop makes, but the court declared themselues that it is not just, & therfore Mr. Crane must stand an arbitrator for Mr. Davenport. And the court ordered that these foure men, viz^{d}, Mr. Wakeman, Mr. Crane, Richard Milles & Francis Newman doe take the case into their hands and consider of it, and, if they can to the satisfaction of Mr. Davenport and Henry Bishop, issue it, if not then to informe themselues so fully that they maye be able to informe ye court how it stands, that they maye have what light they can further to proceede.

Mr. Pell was warned to this court and appeared; he was told it was for two reasons, first to take the oath of fidellitie, 2dly, to paye in ye fine of 10^{l} laid vpon him ye last court of magistrats. He said for ye oath, he had taken it in England and should not doe it heare; he was told no more is required of him then others doe, yett if he had any grounds against it he might propound them, or elc if he would considr of it he might. He said he desired to considr of it. For his fine of 10l he was asked if he had taken any order to paye it, he said no. Mr. Goodyear said he hoped he would. Mr. Pell said he knew not. He was asked ye reason, he said he should be silent for he had given offenc heartofore wth speaking, but ye court desired an answer, wheither he would paye or no, but his answer was that he desired to be silent.

[220] || William Judson informed the court that aboute this time twelue moneth he hired John Knight to be his servant whoe was then wth Francis Hall, haveing three weekes to serve as he the sd Knight said; and he gave him earnest that he should come to him aboute 14 dayes after Michelltide, and he expected him accordingly but he came not. He asked Francis Hall why he came not, he said because he owed him money. William Judson told Francis Hall that he would paye his debte, yett Hall would not lett him come, wherfore he desires the justice of the court.

John Knight saith that he agreed wth William Judson & tooke earnest to serve him so soone as he was free from Francis Hall.

Mr. Ling saith that he heard Jno Knight saye that if Goodman Judson would paye the money hee owed Francis Hall, he was free from him.

Francis saith that he could prove that John Knight was to doe him servic for the money he owed him, but his witnes was not heare.

William Judson saith that Knight told him that he owed Francis Hall something, but not service. Francis Hall was asked how much Knight owed him now, he said he could not tell justly, but he thought five or six pounds. The case standing as it doth, the court advised them to agree it themselues, and in conclusion they both agreed that Francis Hall shall keepe Knight a moneth longer, & that then he come to Goodman Judson, and that William Judson paye to Francis Hall for Jno Knight what shall appeare to be justly due to him, in a convenient time according as the same shall appeare to be, & that the charge of this p[r]sent court be borne betwixt them.

The court declared themselues that whoesoeuer hath Jn[o] Knight must put in securitie that he shall be forthcomeing when the court calls for him, & Francis Hall promised he should be ready at y[e] courts call, elc he would answer for him & be lyable to what sentenc the court should inflict vpon him if he fayled hearof.

A Generall Court the 9th of October, 1648.

Jervic Boykin was admitted a member of this court and rec y[e] freemans charge.

The Governer propounded to y[e] court to know what corse they would take to prevent the damadge that is done in corne & meddowes, for he heares great complaints; their are orders in force, but wheither it was not necessarie to make some stricter order aboute swine and fences, or that some other course might be taken that these damadges might be prevented, and wheither they will debate the matter now or chuse a committee to prepare the matter against another court; but every one might now propound what way he thinkes of, that if they chuse a comittee they maye consider it. The court agreed & voted to chuse a committe to consider and prepare the matter aginst another court. The committe chosen are, the court, Mr. Tuttill, Mr. Gilbert, Mr. Robrt Newman, John Copr, Jeremiah Whitnell, Henry Lendall, Mr. Wakeman, Jn[o] Gibbs, Thomas Powell, Robert Johnson, Leivtenant Seely, Mathew Camfeild, Sam: Whithead, Jervic Boykin, Jn[o] Tompson, William Davis, Jn[o] Vincon, Mr. Gilbert, David Atwatter for y[e] farmes. The towne was desired to informe those whom they have chosen that all things maye be fully considered & debated when the committee meets.

The court chose the Magistrats and deputies as a committe to dispose of Oyster shell feild for common & publique advantage. Leivtenant Seely propounded for 5 or 6 ac[rs] for a place to shott at a marke vpon, w[c]h is allso refered to y[e] same committe.

William Andrewes whoe keepes the ordinary, propounded to ye court that he might have some helpe afforded him for the better carying of it one. He was wished to acquainte ye court wth what he desired; he said, first a convenient house neare the watter side. 2dly, 100^l of provission laid in and he would returne it againe to ye towne so soone as it pleased God to inable him, wch was taken into consideration to be prepared against another court.

The Governer acquainted the court that the commissioners have ordered to commend it to ye severall generall courts, that wampome should not be forced vpon any man for payment wch is not ^t in some measure suitably stringed, & if any stone wampom be p^rsented, it be broken.

A GENERALL COURT THE 18th OF OCTOBER, 1648.

Ephrahim Penington and John Walker were admitted members of this court and received the freemans charge.

Edward Parker & Jno Walker had libbertie to depart ye court.

The Gouerner acquainted the court that the committee they appointed the last court to consider aboute swine & fences have mett & considered of them, wth the issue of wch consideration the court was acquainted, and after much debate it was ꝑpounded that to prevent damadge by swine & fences, a publique pounder would be the best way, whoe should be vnder oath to looke to all ye corne feilds in ye towne, to pound hoggs & catle, & view ye fences, & warne men of their defective fences onc a weeke, & the man most fitt for this trust and imployment the court conceived was Jno Coꝑr; but ye things being divers and weightie, and lecture time drawing one & ye court of magistrats sitting in ye afternoone, it is reffered to another court.

[221] A GENERALL COURT THE 30th OF OCTOBER, 1648.

John Cooppr was desired to acquainte the court wheither he be willing to be a generall pounder for the towne. He answered yea, so that the towne would sett him in a way what to doe & how he might be payde. He was desired to acquainte the court what he desired, he sd iff he made it his whole implployment he could not doe it vnder 30l a yeare, but the court thought not meete to laye forth so much yearly vpon this worke, therfore it was propounded that he might spend two dayes in a weeke to view all ye fences, & pound catle & swine, & that for his paye he might have 2d vpon every acr of land that is improved for corne wthin ye two mile, and that he gitts for pounding catle beside, wch was propounded to Jno Coppr and he accepted it. Whervpon the court ordered that for ye yeare to come John Coppr be publique pownder for ye towne, to be vnder oath to view the fences aboute the corne feilds belonging to ye towne wthin the two mile, onc every weeke, if no extraordinary providenc hinder. The time for his view is left to himselfe, so as maye be most for ye benifite of the severall quarters, and to tell every man whose fenc is defective onc every weeke, but if any man hath had warning of his fenc to be defective, & it is not mended before the next weeke he view againe, (their being a weekes time betwixt his view,) the fine to be 12d for every post & length of rayles that is defective or downe, & 6d a time for Jno Cooppr's comeing to tell them, and if yet it be neglected it is counted a contempt and they must answer it at the court; and what damadge comes by it to be pd by ye owner of the fenc beside. And for his paye the court ordered & he accepted, that he have 2d for every acr of land wthin the two mile that is improved for corne, house lotts or other, and what swine or catle he pounds according to order, to have the poundage beside, wch is ordered to be 4d a beast as ox, steere, cow or calfe, & 12d a horse, & for swine according to the order following; and thoughe the swine or catle of any sort wch transgrese the order be not pownded, but the owner told of them, they must paye as if they were pounded.

It was propounded and desired by divers that no swine might be kept but what men will keepe vp in their yards, or elc if they keepe them abroad, then at such a distanc as they maye not doe damadge to cornefeilds or meddowes, and then to goe vnder keepers; and that both at towne & at y[e] farmes; and after much debate of the matter the court ordered, that whosoever keepes swine in the woods must have keepers and keepe them 8, 10, or 12 mile distanc from y[e] towne, that they come not to doe damadge in cornefeilds or meddowes; and they w[c]h keepe swine in y[e] towne, or at the farmes, shall keepe them vp in their yards, that they goe not forth to doe damadge, vnder the penaltie of 12[d] apec for each default, & the damadge beside. But if hoggs straye out into y[e] woods, or gitt out of a mans yard into the street accidentally & against his will, then the penaltie to be but 3[d] apec, to goe to him that pounds them or brings them home. This order to take place a moneth henc, till w[c]h time the former order stands in force.

The putting in catle into y[e] severall quarters is left to themselues to order.

It is ordered that if any man in his owne yard or ground make a penn or yard to keepe swine in, if it be against his neighbours fenc, he shall maintayne the fenc so farr as that yard or penn reacheth, that his neighbour be not damnifyed therby.

Jn[o] Coppr desired that the pound might be removed to a place neare his owne house, that it might be more convenient for him to pound swine or catle. The towne was rather willing to make a new pound neare his house and he, the said John Coppr, offered to sett vp one as bige as that w[c]h is allreadie vp, (substantially & strong,) for 50s, w[c]h the court agreed to & was willing to allowe him.

The Governer propounded to the court that seeing what had bine done concerning the absent lotts to dispose of them doth not issue the thing, for though they was willing to abate part of the rates past & to vallew the fenc as it is now worth, yett men accepte not of them, wheither theirfore the will not thinke of some other waye, either by themselues or by a comittee, to dispose of them. The court considered of it and chose the magistrats, elders and deacons, and one out of each quarter in the towne, viz[d]. Francis Newman, Mr. Crane, William Andrewes, Jervic Boykine, John Ponderson, Mr. Gibbard, Richar Milles, Leivtenant Seely, Mathew Camfeild, as a committee to whome the court gives full power to consider & dispose of the absent lotts as they shall see cause.

Mr. Evanc propounded to the court that he might have libbertie to make a wharfe aboute the pointe against Phillip Leekes, and a bridg ouer the creekes mouth their, so as they might come to vnloade a boate at halfe tide.

Leivtenant Seely propounded allso that he might have libbertie to make a wharfe theraboute wher the shipp was built, that they might vnloade a vessell at any time of y[e] tide. It was allso propounded that a sluc might be made at the creekes mouth against Phillip Leekes to keepe vp the watter, that so they might wear a channel, and a wharfe built ther to vnloade goods vpon drye at any time of y[e] tide. It was desired that a comittee might be chosen to whom they would reffer the consideration of these matters, to whome any that propound to doe any such worke might repaire for resolution, and the court chose the magistrats and deputies, Mr. Evanc, Leivtenant Seely, Mr. Rudderford, Robert Martin, and they have libbertie to call in any others y[t] they thinke may give y[m] light in these matters.

The towne was desired to bring in their rates to y[e] treasurer w[t]h speed, elc they must looke to be warned to the court.

William Andrewes desired the court that they would provide some other to keepe the ordinary, elc furnish him w[t]h 100[l] and a convenient house. Mr. Evanc said that himselfe & foure more would lend him 5[l] apec for three yeares freely, w[c]h was looked vpon as a kind offer, but that would not answer, and some proposition was made concerning John Herrimans keeping of it, and aboute the house was M' Lambertons, vpon w[c]h occaision it was reffered till Mr. Goodyeare came home.

They which are to have land on y[e] east side were desired

to bring in ther names whoe they are that they maye have it laid out.

[222] || Mr. Robert Newman againe propounded to know wheither the court was willing to exchange one third part of the land belonging to ther quarters w^t^hin the 2 mile. The court desired the committee before chosen to view that land to view it againe, that they maye be fully informed & be able to give light to the court whoe will considr it.

John Coppr is to begine to view & looke to the fences p^r^sently, and when he gives warning to any quarter that hee will view the first time, they are to goe w^t^h him, to show him every man his fenc, & if they shall neglect, they shall paye 12^d^ a man.

It is ordered that this day fortnight waights & measures & stillyards are to be viewed and tryed by those whoe are appointed for that purpose, at the meeting-house, by 8 a clocke in the morning. And betwixt this & then the marshall is to goe aboute the towne to mens houses & take notice whoe have waights & measures, & what, and give a noat to those appointed to view.

AT A COURT HELD AT NEWHAUEN THE 7th OF NOUEMBER, 1648.

Sariant Fowler complained that his squadron came not to trayne according to ye court order. Hee was asked if the drume beate, he said no, thoughe the drumer knew his duty and ought to attend the townes order, the court said it was true, for he is a towne officer & vnder paye.

Robert Basset the drumer being in court answered, that he was about the shipp worke, but was told that was no excuse, he said the shipp worke freed other men and why not him, but was told their was no ground for it, for he is an officer vnder paye, and ought to have attended his worke, and if his occaisons had called him from home he should have gone to the sariant & intreated him to have gott another to drume. He said he thought he should have had warning from the sariant, but was told it is not the sariants worke, but he should doe his owne worke and attend it. The court witnessed

52

against this his neglect but past it by for this time, w[t]hout a fine, & allso freed the squadron.

Robert Basset was complained of for absenc at two generall courts, he answered that y[e] reason was because he was imployed in druming to call the court together, & went but home to breakefast & came againe presently, but the names were called before he came. The court considered his excuse & freed him. He was advised that one squadron dayes he beate the drume aboute those squadrons that are to trayne that day.

The will of William Ives deceased was presented in court, made the 3th of Aprill, 1648, witnessed and vnderwritten by Richard Milles & Rogger Allen, whoe now in court testify that the said William Ives was in a state fitt to make this will & did make it.*

Allso the inventorie of the estate of the said William Ives amounting to 98[l]: 04: 00[d], prised by Richard Milles & Rogger Allen vpon their oath, the 22th of September, 1648.†

William Basset whoe is neare the mariage, (they being contracted,) of y[e] widdowe, was called to put in securitie to y[e] court for the estate, that the chilldren of William Ives maye have their portions duely pd, according to y[e] generall courts order, but he desired respite till y[e] next court w[c]h the court granted.

William Basset was complained of for absenc at the generall trayning yesterday, he sd it was because he had some haye w[c]h did lye vpon the stroye, ther being many catle lying at it, that if he had not fetched it that day it would have bine eaten vp & spoyled, & he had indeavored to fetch it the weeke be-

---

* Will of William Ives, made April 3d, 1648.

He makes his wife sole executrix and gives her the use of all his goods, house and land for the bringing up of his small children—gives to his son John the house and land at 21 years of age, to his three other children when they come to 20 years of age one cow apiece or its value, to his wife the rest of his estate.

If the Lord should take away any of the daughters, then that portion shall fall to the youngest son, and if the Lord should take away the eldest son, then it shall fall to the youngest son at 21 years of age.

The mark of William Ives, witnessed by Richard Miles, Roger Allen.

† In the margin, "y[e] 4[th] Septem. 1649. Rich. Miles & Roger Allen confirmed vpon oath what they before testifyed concerning William Ives his will, and y[e] 6[th] of Novm. 1649, the executrix tooke oath y[t] to y[e] best of her light y[e] inventorie p[r]sented is a true invent. of her deceased husbands estate."

fore, but it was so wett that he could not; the haye was scarse worth the fetching, but his necessitie required it for preserving his catle, wch things the court considering, past it by w^t^hout fine.

John Nash was complained of for absenc at a generall court the 9th of October, he sd he had lost a cow vpon the last day before, and was faine to goe seeke her, & as soone as he came home he came to ye court, wch ye court accepted & past it by.

Mr. Ling was fined 12d for absenc at a generall court.

Mr. Ling, Mathias Hitchcocke, Jno Wakefeild, Henry Carter, Joseph Nash, Mathew Row, Edward Keely, Joseph Pecke, Nickholas Elsy, all was too late in comeing to trayning yesterday in the afternoone, but they said they was their before the bodye moved, wch as the capt' said was longer before it moved then it vsed to be, yett because it hath bine ye vsiall course to count no man late till ye bodey hath bine removed, the court past it by for this time.

Sariant Andrewes was complained of for absenc at trayning yesterday, he answered he was constrayned by his occaisions to goe to Milford to end a buisines wch should elc have come to this court, wch was waightie as the governer knowes. Mr. Evanc should have gone the sixt day last to have ended it for him but was prevented, so that he had no day but yesterday to goe. The governer said he knew the buisines and it was waightie. The court considered the case & past it by, but advised Sariant Andrewes to attend trayning carefully for time to come.

William Gibbons was complained of for absenc at two generall courts, for the first of them he saith he will paye the fine, for the other he was not well & could not come, wherfore the court past it by.

The will of Anthony Tompson* deceased was presented in

---

* "A wrighting presented in court, for the last Will and Testament of Anthony Tompson deceased, made March 23d, 1647."

Gives to his eldest son his inheritance, house and land and meadow he had given him by the Town, (only the house, his wife is to have during her life,) and ten pounds when he comes to eighteen years of age. To his second son, Anthony, the land and meadow he bought of brother Clarke, and ten pounds to be paid him when he comes to the age of twenty-one years. To his daughter Bridget, what he had by his former wife and fifteen pounds, to be paid her at the age of eighteen years, provided that she court, made the 23th of March, 1647, witnessed and vnderwritten by Mr. John Davenport, pastor, & Mr. Robrt Newman, ruling elder of the church of Newhaven.

Likewise the inventorie of the estate of the said Anthony Tompson, amounting to 236l: 18s: 10d, prised the 26th of September, 1648, by Richard Milles, Mathew Camfeild & William Tompson vpon ther oath. And ^ Tompson the widdowe of the deceased called to put in securitie for the chilldrens portions, but because ye court would not put her vpon it suddenly, they reffered it to ye next court.

William Basset paseth ouer to Mathew Camfeild two acrs of meddow, one acr of it lying in the west meddow one this side the river betweene the meddowe of Richard Osborne & Thomas Knowles, and the other acr lying in sollatarie cove, & 8½ acrs of vpland in the subverbes quarter, on this sid ye West River.

Henry Loyne was complained of for absenc at a generall trayning, but Mr. Crane desired that it might be respited till next court, wch was granted.

[223] || John Benham was complained of for being absenc two generall trayning dayes. Hee answered that the first of them he was their in the morning, and after he had answered to his name, newes came that ther was many oxen in his corne, he went to Mr. Goodyeare and desired to be excused but he refussed, so he was forced to goe to save his corne; he was asked if he came againe, he said no because vpon the last day before he left a cart wth haye wch stoode aboute the necke hill in hazard & he went to looke after that; for the other day,

---

dispose of herself in marriage with the consent and approbation of her mother and the elders of the church then being.

The remainder of his estate to his wife; if she marry again his other daughters to be provided for with equal portions as his other daughter hath, with the advice of the elders then being.

To his brothers William and John Tompson, each ten shillings as a testimony of his brotherly love.

His wife is made sole executrix.

John Davenport and Robert Newman certified that this writing was his nuncupative will. Presented to the court of Magistrates the 27th of May, 1650, not allowed as a legal will, but it was ordered that the wife of the said Anthony Tompson should administer upon the estate, according to the particulars in this writing contained, per Francis Newman, Secret.

his corn was gathered & laye in hazard of being eaten vp & he was faine to goe gett it home, the weeke before being wett that he could not, yett he went to ye captaine & company to giv him libbertie, but they left it to ye court. For ye former day the court past it by wholly, and for ye latter ordered that he paye halfe ye fine for absenc w^c^h is 2^s^ : 6^d^.

Beniamen Willmott was complained of for absenc one trayning day and for late comeing another trayning day. He said his absenc was because he had haye that laye vpon the spoyle, ptly by the tide & ptly by the raine, & if ther had come more wett before it was stirred, it might haue bine quite spoyled, & that day being faire he went to looke to it. For his late comeing he knowes not, but if it was too late it was very litle, but he submitts to the court. The court told him it was many mens case then to have haye lye vpon spoyle by wett, w^c^h attended the trayning; the court for his late comeing ordered him to paye the fine w^c^h is 12^d^, & for his absenc that he paye halfe ye fine w^c^h is 2^s^ : 6^d^.

Mr. Goodanhousen & Mr. Westerhousen by Mr. Evanc made a request to the court that the bond wherin they stand bound to the court in 1000 gilders for the three prisoners that runn awaye to the Dutch, might be remitted, but was told that because it was done, thoughe in this court, yett w^t^h the assistanc of two other magistrats, it must be reffered till a court of magistrats, or till two magistrats sitt heare w^t^h this court.

James Till was warned to this court to attend aboute an action to be tryed betwixt Richard Pery & Jno Megs, but appeared not, w^c^h the court looked vpon as a contempt w^c^h he is to answer for the next court.

The court ordered an attachment vpon Jno Meggs his corn, viz^d^, 10 bushell of wheat, and that it be not removed out of Mr. Perys barne till ye differenc w^c^h is betwixt them concerning the barne be ended, and what Mr. Pery owes Jno Meges he must paye.

A Generall Court the 20th of Nouember, 1648.

The Governer acquainted the court w^t^h & read a letter w^c^h he had received from ye committee of both houses of parliment.*

The Governer informed the court that the committee appointed to dispose of the absent lotts have mett twice and considered of them, & thinke meete that the rates past be forborne, & the fenc pd for as it is now worth, & the first survaye, and that if any to whom any part of them is disposed of shall w^t^hin five yeares remove out of the towne, then they shall returne the land backe againe to the towne, therfore those that find themselues straitened maye give in their names, that so men maye be accommodated so farr as the land will beare.

Mr. Evanc, Mr. Yale, Mr. Atwater had libbertie to depart the court, & Robrt Basset & Mr. Auger.

Mathew Camfeild came late, but the court past it by because he was forced to goe looke after some catle.

The court was informed that the order made last court concerning keeping vp swine was much objected against & taken ill by divers in the towne, whervpon it was againe propounded to the court if they would alter it, but the court would not but confirmed it for a yeare.

The marshall complained that Goodwife Lampson was very troubelsom to his family, and she had bine long at his house, and sees litle amendment & desired he might be freed from this trouble, whervpon the court wished Thomas Lampson to take her home or elc gitt another place wher she might be kept & looked too.

It is ordered that every quarter, or quarters that lye together, shall, w^t^hin the compase of a weeke after this court,

* This letter is referred to in "New Haven case stated," and was "for freeing the several distinct colonies of New England from molestation by the appealing of troublesome spirits unto England, whereby they declared that they had dismissed all causes depending before them from New England, and that they advised all inhabitants to submit to their respective governments there established, and to acquiesce when their causes shall be there heard and determined." The letter was signed by Pembroke, W. Say and Seale, Manchester, Fr. Dacre, &c., Warwick, Denbigh.

meete together and setle & marke the fenc so that the viewer maye know every mans fenc w^t^hout further trouble, and for neglecte hearof, the quarter or quartrs shall paye 20^s^, vnless they can laye it vpon some ꝑticular man or men, for his or their stubbornnese or refractaryness, w^c^h the ꝑticular court shall judge of.

John Hall, William Paine, William Holt, Nathaniel Meriman, Henry Morrell, desire to have their land on ye east sid, betwixt the red rocke & Mr. Davenports farme, & the court ordred that it should be laid out together that they maye plant.

John Coppr tooke oath to be faithfull in the trust committed to him in viewing fences and pounding catle, according to ye courts order, w^t^hout partialitie or respect of ꝑsons.

A Court held at Newhaven the 5th of December, 1648.

Henry Peck was complained of for absenc at a generall court, he said his wife was sick and that was the cause, vpon w^c^h consideration he was excused.

Robert Pigg was complained of for absenc at a generall court, he sayd that it was a wett morning that the drume could not beat aboute towne & he heard it not, but he came as soone as he thought it was time, whervpon he was excused.

Richard Pery declareth that wheras the last court their was an attachment laide vpon tenn bushells of the wheat of Jno Megs w^c^h laye in his, the said Richard Perys barne, and not to be removed out of the barne till ye rent of ye barne was satisfyed for to the sd Richard Pery, yett contrarie to this he, ye sd Jno Megs, hath removed and disposed of the wheate.

[224] || John Meggs answered that he thought their should have bine an actuall attachment laid vpon the corne, therfore he fetched some of it home and thought their would have bine twenty bushels more, & so disposed of three bushells more, that when they came to winowe, their proved but aboute 7 bushells, and he hath indeavored to gett corne to make it vp but could not. The court told him they wondered at his excuse and it offended them much, to saye their was not an

actuall attachment when the court layd it themselues and needed not to send any officer to doe it. Further the governer informed the court that Jn° Megs was wth him and complained that the hoggs came into the barne and spoyled his corne, & it would not be safe to leave so much corne their threshed. The governer told him that he might therfore leave it at Mr. Perys house as he threshed it, but he objected against that, therfore was told he might leave it wth the treasurer, but he did neither, but contrarie to all order caryes the corne away & disposeth of pt of it, which cariage the court looked vpon as contemptuous in John Megs against the court, and should after deale wth him for it.

Further the plantiffe declares that their was an agreement betwixt his wife & James Till, servant to John Meggs, for one pt of his barne, for ye rent of wch he was to have wheat, and for the vallew they both reffered it to his father, Mr. Malbon. James Till was called, whoe saith that hee being servant to Goodman Meggs, went to Mris Pery & desired she would lett him her barne, she saide not all, he sayd then halfe, she sayd yea, she said she must have corne for it, he sayd she should, she said not rye, he said no but wheat and good wheat, she said she knew not the pric but would reffere it to her father, to wch he agreed, so he hired halfe the barne & half ye leantoo on ye side; notwthstanding this agreement, the plant pleads that the defendant will not paye him corne but saith though he promised to satisfy, yett not in corne.

John Meggs answered that his man tooke it before *before* he knew of it, but after Mris Pery came to him (vnderstanding James was his man,) and asked him if he would see the rent for the barn payd, he asked her what it was, she said she could not tell, he asked what it was lett for last yeare, she sayd she could not tell, he sayd what she had last yeare he would give her this yeare, wth wch she was satisfyed. After this Mris Pery came for shooes, both to make & mend, and had what she desired, she said she had no wampom, he said it was no matter, it should goe towards the rent of the barne & she was satisfyed, and Mr. Pery, after he came home, came for a paire of shooes & had them, but said he had no wampom; he, ye sd Jn° Megs, answered it was no matter, it should goe towards the rent of the barne, and he objected not against it, and they neuer spake of corne but one time when they was dressing, Mris Pery said, Goodman Megs, can yow spare me any wheat, he said no, she sayd James promised corne for the barne, he said he had none to spare.

Mris Pery said she knew not of any such bargaine betwixt Goodman Meggs & her, either for the rent or for the paye.

Wherfore Jn° Megs was called to make proofe of these things, first that the rent was to be as it was lett the last yeare, secondly that they was content to take other paye yn corn.

Goodwife Meggs testifyeth vpon oath that her husband asked Mris Pery what the rent of the barne was, she said she could not tell, he said to her, looke what others pd last yeare he was willing to give, & Mris Pery said well, well, seeming to be satisfyed. Further this deponent saith that Mris Pery was willing to take the shooes she had in ꝑt of payement for the rent of the barne, and that Mr. Pery had afterward a paire of shooes for himselfe & was willing, to her apprehension, to take them vpon ye barne acc°.

John Hall servant to Jn° Megs testifyeth vpon oath that Mris Pery had a paire of shooes of his master & said she had no money at that time aboute her. Jn° Megs said it should goe in ꝑt of payement for the barne, she said well, well, seeming to be willing that it should be so.

William Hooke testifyeth vpon oath that Mr. Pery came to Goodman Meges for a paire of shooes, he said he had no wampome to paye at prsent, Goodman Megs said lett them goe in ꝑt of the barne, Mr. Pery said well, well, & went away seeming to be content & yeilding a full consent, in his apprehension.

John Megs was called to show what the barne was lett for the last yeare, but could not, whervpon the court was informed that Thomas Wheeler senior, whoe hired that part the last yeare, could informe, whoe was sent for & cam, & testifyed to ye court that he hired that ꝑt of the barne last yeare wch John Megs hath this yeare & agreed wth Mr. Pery and pd him for it seaven bushells of wheat.

Richard Pery saith further that the shooes he had of Jno Megs is prised too deare, he asked 4^{s} 6^{d} for shooes that he had better of another for 3^{s} 6^{d}.

The sentenc of the court is that the shooes Mr. Pery hath had of Jno Megs, being duely vallewed by Leivtenant Seely & Thomas Beament, be deducted, the rest to be pd to Mr. Pery in wheat, after the rate of seaven bushell for the whole, and that the charges of the court be borne equally betwixt them.

And for the contemptuous cariage of John Meggs to the court in refussing to fullfill their order in the attachment laid vpon the corne the court fined him xx^{s}.

Widdow Tompson was called to put in securitie for her childrens portions, but she not being fit it was respited.

William Pecke was complained of for absenc at a generall court, he answered he was not well to come, whervpon the court past it by.

William Baset was called to put in securitie for ye portions of his wives chilldren, but it was respited.

James Till was warned to this court to answer for his contempt in not appearing the last court; he saith that he acknowledges he was served w^{t}h a warrant to appeare at the last court but did not, but haveing a lighter load of haye to empty went about that, w^{t}hout asking leave of any magistrate.

Thomas Barnes informed the court that he served a warrant vpon James Till two or three monethes sinc, but he could not gitt him to appeare, but hath allway shifted him of one way or other, but this he hath to inform the court against
[225] ||him, that he, the said James, stole a sithe w^{c}h he left in the feild, taking it of from the snath and vseing it as his owne, w^{c}h charge James Till owneth & acknowledgeth it to be true, and that he had slandered Thomas Barnes by reporting that he did but take his sithe as he, ye said Barnes, had taken a grubbing axe of his, whenas Thomas Barnes had borrowed the axe of James Till as he now confesseth. Allso Mr. Gibbard, the treasurer, informed the court that James Till found a dead woolfe in the woodes, & cut of the head and brought it to him to be payde for it, saying he had killed it by

setting a gunn, and gott a noate of him to receive 15^s for it & therin by lying deceived the towne whose order is that those that kill woolfes, (& not find them dead,) should be pd for them, w^{c}h lying and cheatting James Till could not denye.

The sentenc of the court is that for his contempt of the court in not obeying the warrants served, he paye 40^s fine to the towne, for the sith that he make double restetution, ye sith being vallewed at 4^s, for his lying, cheatting and slandering that he be severly whipped, and the he acknowledg the wronge he hath done to Thomas Barnes in slandering of him, & that he sitt in ye stockes as long as the weather will pmitt w^{t}h respecte of mercy to him, thall that pass by maye see what manner of pson he is.

Jno Coppr informed the court that their is a great deale of fenc lye downe about Mr. Evanc hs farme, belonging to divers men w^{c}h have hired the land. The court ordred that it be made vp w^{t}h speed.

Jno Coppr complained that having pounded 3 mares of Robert Pigs, he could not gitt his paye because the fenc is downe. The court ordered that Robert Pig paye John Coppr, and after seeke his remedy of the fenc that is downe.

Mr. Malbon desired the help of the court in a differenc betwixt Mr. Evanc, Mr. Goodanhousen and himselfe, concerning a horse that he, the sd Mr. Malbon, bought and after sold to Mr. Goodanhousen. The case was this: Mr. Malbon bought a horse of Goodman Ford of Windsore, to be pd in merchantable wampome vpon demand, but if in his jurney from Connecticote to Newhaven he liked not the horse, he was to paye Goodman Ford 6^s 8^d for his jurney & send ye horse againe. After Mr. Malbon came home he liked the horse & intended to send him to the Barbadoes, but he was too bigg to goe in ye vessell; Mr. Evanc desired to haue the horse, Mr. Malbon was willing and told him the termes of payement, he said he would paye it, but after a litle consideration refussed him, so then the horse was sold to Mr. Goodanhousen for such paye, to be pd to Goodman Ford vpon demand. Goodman Ford sent onc and had it not, after sent againe by Goodman Meggott; Mr. Goodanhousen proffered him beavo^r

but they could not agree vpon termes, so he went away vnpayde. Mr. Westerhousen sayd that vpon Mr. Goodanhousen desire he offered to paye Goodman Ford at Connecticote in commodities, but he refussed them, (this was in August last.) Mr. Westerhousen then told him that if he went to Newhaven his man should paye him in wampome according to agreement, so he came to Newhaven in the midle of Septem̃ next to the faire, but never called for the wampom though it laye readie. After Mr. Westerhousen asked him the reason, he answered because now he required damages for want of his money.

The court considered the p^r^mises, and ordered that Mr. Westerhousen paye to Mr. Malbon for Goodman Ford, eleaven pounds in merchantable wampom, and for the damadges it is reffered to be considered afterward, the charges of the court to be borne by Mr. Westerhousen or Mr. Goodanhousen.

Mr. Pell being ordered by the last court of magistrats to attend this court, & being a fine of twenty shillings then laid vpon him, appeared not, but Mr. Leach being in court said he was ordered by Mr. Pell to informe the court that it was against his judgment to take an oath, therfore could not doe it; he was asked if Mr. Pell sent the fine of twenty shillings by him, he said no, therfore it was looked vpon as a contempt in Mr. Pell.

William Judson desired libbertie to send John Knight out of the jurisdiction, the court told him he might if he would vndertake to have him heare by tomorrow senit, but y^t, he said, would not suit his occaisions, therfore he would not send him.

John Meggs became suertie for James Till, & binds himselfe in 10^l to deliver him at the prison to the marshall tomorrowe morning.

Sariant Munson informed the court that he was aboute 3 or 4 monthes sinc accused in this court by Captaine Malbon that he had vpon a trayning day come to the company & taken awaye some men & said he would answer it, but the thing was not true. But the thing was this, Mr. Davenports sellar was to be stoned, & the massons had appoynted to come to worke on the second day from Guilford, wch was trayning day hear,

Mr. Davenport spake to him to gitt helpe, & come & vndersett the house, & prepare it so that the men might goe to worke when they came. He told Mr. Davenport it was trayning day, therfore would have done it vpon the last day before, but Mr. Davenport was not willing to haue his house lye open vpon the Saboth day, but said, lett him gett men and he would freely paye the fines if the towne required it, so he spake to two or three before whoe helped him in the worke, but he came not at the company that morning.

Mr. Malbon answered that he cannot name the ꝑticular ꝑson that told him, but he was sure he was told so, & when the company came to his house for the cullars, their was much stirr in the company about it & they was offended at it, insomuch as some said if this was put vp they would trayne no more. That their was a great stirr in the company aboute it, Leivtenant Seely, Ensign Newman & the clarke & others do witnes, but that Sariant Munson was at the company that morning they cannot saye.

The court told Sariant Munson that it seemes their was some mistake in the buisenes, but had he caried it so highly as to take men away and saye he would answer it, they should have bine much offended at it.

Mr. Evanc, atturney for Phillip Galpin, informed the court that aboute a yeare agoe Mr. Pell, as Mr. Leach his agent, was ordered by this court to paye to Phillip Galpine, or elc to the treasurer, a certayne some of money due from Mr. Leach to Nathaniell Draꝑr for wages in his servic, and given by will by Nathaniel Draꝑr to the said Phillip Galpine, w^c^h is not payde, & now Mr. Leach himselfe being p^r^sent refuseth.

Mr. Leach was called to show the reason he pd it not, he answered that he had payde it allreadie to Mr. Sellicke in the Baye, & it was given him by another will of Nathaniel Draꝑrs made after this will wherin it is given to Phillip Galpine, as appeares by the oath of one Goodwife Tillson of Vergenia, now p^r^sented in court.

Mr. Evanc saith that this Goodwife Tillson whoe is the witnes is a ꝑtye, & had a part of Nathaniel Drapꝑrs estate, 5^l^ at least, as Mr. Sellicke acknowledgeth, and he desired libbertie of the court till Aprill next to bring in oath of the trueth of it, wch was granted:

[226] || The court required that the money be pd according to order. Mr. Leach desired that he might not pt wth any more, seeing he had paide it allreadie, wch the court was willing to forbeare, provided he put in securitie, and he ingageth himselfe, the house & home lott, and six acrs of land he bought of Thomas Kimberly, for the money, wch is aboute eleven pounds.

Mr. Evanc declared to the court that according to the court of magistrats order and his ingagment, he now prsented Jeremiah How to the court & hoped he should be freed from his ingagment.

The Governer told Jeremiah How that he heard sinc the court of magistrats that he went to Mr. Goodyeare to have the irons taken of, but he refused, and that he told the marshall beforehand that if the prisoner* escaped it was not his best way to deliver the letter, so that it seemes he thought beforehand what to doe. Jeremiah How answered that Mr. Goodyeer being at watter-side, he asked him if the irons might not be taken of, & for the not delivering the letter, those words was occaisioned by the marshall, for when he brought the letter, Mr. Kitchell of Guilford was by, and Jeremiah How said that the letter might be a snare to him, to deliver it if the prisoner should escape, and the marshall said againe he hoped he had more witt. The marshall acknowledgeth that he spake words to that purpose, for wch he was reproofed, but saith that they was first occaisioned by Jeremiah How, but Jeremiah acknowledgeth that in his hart, out of a foolish pitty to ye man, he was willing to his escape. The governer told Jeremiah How that he had deneyed this, he answered that he remembers it not, he desired to have favour showne him in his fine, but for that the court reffered it to ye court of magistrats.

John Moss atturney for John Charles declared to the court that aboute three yeares sinc or more, Jno Charles sold vnto

* The prisoner, James Turner, was a fugitive from the Dutch. See appendix Q. R.

Jn° Megs a certaine quantitie of hides, to the vallew of aboute fourty pounds, to be paide for them the next Michellmas following, but cannot gett his paye for them to this day, therfore desires the justic of the court.

John Meggs answered that he bought 26 or 27 hides of John Charles, and he was to paye for them when they were tanned, wch hath not bine till now, & now he intends to paye. The plantiffe replyed that the tanner saith that some of Jn° Charles his hides, & y^t the best of them, hath bine tanned long sinc & fetched awaye by Jn° Megs, and that these wch now Jn° Megs saith are Jn° Charles his hides are the last of a 100 hides wch were a tanning, of wch Jn° Charles his hides were but a part; but it appeared that the matter was not readie for tryall, the plant' wanting some witnes wch maye give light in the case, and the defendant deneying what is alleadged. The court refered it, but in the meane time ordered that if Jn° Megs can put in securitie in leather for 40^l, wch is to be laid at M. Gilberts, & pd for to Jn° Charles as it is fetched away, and damage beside for the time it hath bine due sinc Jn° Charles went into the Baye, or if he have not leather inoughe, if M. Gilbert, whom Jn° Megs propounds will be bound for ye rest so that the debt may be secured, that then Jn° Megs have the leather in question, if not, that then the leather be attached & not medled wth till Jn° Charles come home, which his wife thinkes will be next weeke.

Mr. Malbon informed the court that aboute 3 yeeres sinc Edmund Tooley showed him a note vnder Jn° Dillinghams hand, wherin Jn° Dillingham testifyeth that Lawranc Watts told him that if he dyed before Edmund Tooley he would give the sd Edmund his estate.

A Generall Court the 3th of January, 1648.

The Gouerner informed the court that the deputies whom they appointed to looke to their publique workes for the towne have called workemen together & considered this meeting-house & find that three of the pillars are rotten & should be supplyed w^t^h new ones, allso ye groundsells are rotten & needes new ons, beside the raine beates in at the sides and needes to be clapboarded; they have allso considered w^t^h them of the charge, & find, as by a noate given in by the workemen appeares, that it will be above 80^l^, beside some other charges of ropes, vnderpining the groundsells, & worke aboute the seates, & what elc they cannot foresee. Now the charge being so great, they were willing to advise w^t^h the towne aboute it, to know wheither they will have these things done, and how they can pvide paye to discharge it.

It was propounded by some wheither it might not be forborne another yeare, the workmen were desired to speake & informe the court. William Andrewes said that he thought it was not safe to defer it another yeare, and Thomas Munson said that he durst not give counsell to deffer the repairing of it. Jno Basset propounded some other way how it might be done and not take awaye these pillares to put new in, & allso for less charge, whervpon the court ordered that the workemen doe againe meete, viz^d^, William Andrewes, Thomas Munson, Jervic Boykin, Jno Bassett, Robert Bassett & George Laremore, Jonathan Marsh & Thomas Moris, & that Jno Wakefeild keepe the mill till Geo: Laremore attend this meeting & be pd by ye towne for it. The workemen are to consider wheither the house maye staye safely another yeare w^t^hout repaires, if not then how it maye be best done for most safty to the towne and least charge, allso wheither the tower & turrett maye safely stand and will not in a short time decaye the house, and if taken downe, then what will be the charge of that and to make the roofe tight & comely againe, and when these things are prepared ther maye be another court.

It was desired that if any in the court knew of any place wher their was good trees for clapboards, they would informe that they might be for the townes vse. Sariant Fowler a Phillip Leeke spake of some they knew of, and Sariant Andrewes was ordered to goe along w^t^h them or any other that knowes of any, & sett the townes marke vpon such trees as are fitt for the townes vse, that no bodey elc may medle w^t^h them.

It is ordered that the court wth Mr. Evanc & M. Wakeman audit the treasurers acco for ye yeere past.

The governer informed the court that a while sinc the pticular court was informed of a miscariage of Sariant Munsons, that hee came to the company & tooke awaye some men vpon a trayning day morning to goe to worke to Mr. Davenports & said he would answer it, but he saith the thing was not so, therfore if any in the towne can charge it vpon him they are desired to speake, if not that then he maye be cleared & men be more warey how they expresse themselues, but none spake to charge him but rather to cleare him & so it was past by.

It was desired that all that have a desire to have any of ye absent lotts would give in their names to ye secretarie & what they doe desire & where.

[227] || It was propounded that some course might be setled about an ordinarie, William Andrewes said he was vnprovided & vnless the towne afforded him help he could not keepe it. It was then said that Jno Herriman hath bine propounded and is willing, whervpon the court ordered that Jno Herriman and his wife keepe the ordinary for this towne till the court see cause to alter it.

William Andrewes was asked if he desired any time to keepe it still to clear things of his hand, he said no, but onely libbertie to drawe a pipe of wine wch he is to have of Mr. Westerhousen, wch the court granted.

John Harriman was asked if he had not drawne wine wthout order. Mr. Goodyeare said that they had for him drawne wine for the seamen wthout order, but he submitts to the court.

The towne was informed that next second day it is appointed that armes shall be viewed heare at the meeting-house, therfor the was wished to make their appearanc.

A Generall Court the 8th of January, 1648.

The workemen that were desired last court to view the meeting-house & consider of the best way how it might be repaired for ye supporting of it, William Andrewes spake for himselfe and the rest & said, that they conceived that the best way was to put in some halfe pillars, wth a crose beam and braces wch should vphold the roofe and strengthen the house, and so lett the old pillars stand still. It was propounded by some whether the putting in of new pillars would not be as cheape and better, whervpon the workemen considered of it againe, and againe delivered ther judgments that the best way to doe it was wth halfe pillars and lett these as be vp stand, whervpon the court ordered that it should be so done. The court desired to know what the charge would be, William Andrewes said they had considered of it & thought that beside the stoning vnder the old pillars, they stoning vnder the new worke they now sett vp, the charge would be 20l.

The treasurer propounded that Aprill rate might be paid beforehand, but the court was not willing till the former treasurers accots was audited.

William Jeanes was freed from the court to goe to mill for the townes ocasions.

Robert Hill propounded to the court that he might be freed from trayning, but the court thought it not meete, but ordered that he attend traynings as others doe till some further weakness appeare vpon him.

It was propounded that wampome wch is not goode might goe at 7 a penny and that wch is good tradeing wampome at 6 a penny, but it was respited to further consideration.

John Cooppr acquainted the court that he finds great difficultie in viewing fences, because some are gone out of towne & others a goeing, & leave none to take order aboute their fences, (and the treasurer added, nor aboute payeing rates,) wherby great damadge comes, and he knowes not whether to goe to have it helped; ther was mentioned Thomas Fugills lott, Job Hall, John Gregory, Samuell Willson, Thomas James & some of Millford. The court thought it worthy of consideration, and ordered the marshall to warne Jobe Hall & Samuell Willson to come before the governer that some order might be taken wth them before they goe, and the secretarie had order to wright to Thom: James & Jno Gregory & those of Milford that haue lotts heare, to come & take order aboute ther fences & rates. William Bradley was to be warned to come & speake wth the governer aboute Abraham Smiths lott, and Allen Ball being prsent said for Thomas Fugills lott Mr. Evanc had order about that.

A GENERALL COURT THE 31th OF JANUARY, 1648.

The Governer acquainted the court that the comitte they appointed to dispose of the absent lotts have done it, and now (though they left it wholly to the comitte,) they thought good to acquaint the towne wth what was done, that it might be entred vpon their heads whoe accept it & rates pd accordingly, & that for the outland of the second devission & the meddow of M. Roes lott & Mris Eldreds, it is not disposed of, but the comitte thinkes to dispose of it to men fitt for farmes to gett corne and breed catle for the publique goode. A note how the land was disposed of was read to the court and approved, & ye termes it is granted vpon is in fo: 223.

Phillip Leeke said he accepted not of the six acrs allotted to him out of Mris Eldreds lott, and Joseph Nash refussed three acrs granted to him ther. Andrew Loe desired the 6 acrs Phillip Leeke refused, and Jno Vincon the three acrs Joseph Nash refussed, and the court granted them ther desire in it.

The Governer acquainted the court that he heares notwthstanding the order aboute fences, men take not care to doe what they might to keepe them vp so as to keepe catle out of the corne, whervpon the court ordred as a confirmation of their former order, that those wch haue had ther fence defective before this time be warned to the next court, & if it be not sufficiently mended before ye next court following, that then they be againe warned to ye court & a more severe fine laid vpon them for such neglect.

Mathew Camfeild desired the court would grant him a small pec of meddow wch lyes at heither end of the west meddow, ouer against the oyster bankes, aboute two or three acrs.

Richard Beech desired a small pec of meddow in a cove on

ye west side next his owne, but it was said in ye court that it is lotted out allreadie.

Thomas Munson, Jno Basset, Robert Basset, William Peck, Thomas Mitchell desired they might have some meddow granted them out of a pec wch lyes by Livtenant Seelyes, neare ye blacke rocke.

Richard Milles desired that he might have his meddowe wch lyes in sollatary cove exchanged for so much in Oyster River.

Leivtenant Seely and Jno Brocket were desired to view these severall pcells of meddow and report to the court how they find them; they are to be pd for their paines by them wch shall haue the meddow granted to them.

[228] || Mr. Crane desired the court would consider some course that good bulls might be bred and they wch breed them might have just consideration for them; the towne was desired to consider & prepare it against next court.

John Livermore acquainted the court that he desired to exchange his land at the west bridge for that granted him out of Mr. Roes lott, but was told that the land in M. Roes lott is granted to him vpon the condition as other lands are granted out of the absent lotts; that is, if he remove in five yeeres out of the towne it returnes to the towne againe, but for that at the west bridge, if he would exchange it he should haue as much granted to him as neare and convenient. He desired to consider of it & he would tell ye governer.

The towne was desired to see they be provided of ladders, elc they will fall vnder the fine.

Samuell Whithead is appointed to goe wth Jno Coppr to view and judge of fences, wch are good & wch not, and to vallew & prise the fenc belonging to ye absent lots what it is worth at prsent.

The governer acquainted the court that the comittee they appointed to dispose of the absent lotts (vpon William Andrewes & Jno Cooopprs request,) desired Mr. Crane, Richard Milles and Francis Newman to viewe some meddowe one the east side wch they desire, it lying neare ther vpland, they intending and Sariant Beckly to goe to live ther. And the said viewers informed the court that ther is some meddow neare ther land and some further of, maye be to ye quantity of 40 or 50 ac^rs^; allso some vpland grase, two or three mile of from them, wher it maye be some haye maye be cutt, w^c^h they thinke the court maye grant w^t^hout prejudice to them. But because the court would not grant they knew not what, they appointed Jno Brockett to goe w^t^h some of y^m^ w^c^h could show him what they desire, and take notice both of the manner of lying & place & quantity & report it to ye court.

Leivtenant Seely propounded to the court that he might haue libbertie to goe abroade if oppertunity p^r^sents, for some time to provide for his family, though it should for the p^r^sent take him of from performing his place as he is leivtennant, but it was respited to another court.

A Court held at Newhaven the 6th of Feburary, 1648.

John Herriman was called to answer for drawing wine by retayle, before he kept the ordinary, w^t^hout order. He answered he did it for Mr. Goodyere, but wherin he hath done any thing contrary to order he leaves himselfe w^t^h the court; he was asked if he did not owne the thing, he said ther came severall that pleaded necessitie, and said they could not be supplyed elc wher, w^c^h had some, & he did lett the seamen w^c^h worked aboute the shipp have some betwixt meales, but he was told if he would confess no more, it might be proved that he sold out of ye house, out of cases of necessitie, for Robert Bassett sent and had wine two or three times, he said he knew not that Robert Basset had any but vpon M. Goodyers acc^o^, but was told yes for he sent his money for it. He said he left himselfe w^t^h the court, but because Mr. Goodyere, whoe is somewhat concerned in the thing, is not now in court, it was respited.

The court declared themselues that Jno Herriman paye his fine of 5^s^ laid vpon him before by this court for not bringing his armes to ye meeting one Lords day.

John Walker, Jno Harriman, William Andrewes, Christipher Todd, Mr. Goodanhouse, Mr. Evanc, Mr. Westerhousen,

Robert Hill, Samuell Willson, Mr. Attwatter, James Russell, Thomas Wheeler, William Davis, M[ris] Gregson, Mr. Gilbert, William Pecke, Richard Mansfeild & Edward Parker (18 in all) each of them fined 12[d] for not bringing their waights & measures to be tryed vpon the day appoynted.

Samuell Willson passeth ouer to Thomas Powell his house, home lott and barne, and all the commonadge w[c]h belonged to him by buying that house of Edward Wigelsworth, w[c]h was all but a quarter pt, w[c]h he sould to Jeremiah Whitnel before.

Samuell Willson passeth ouer to James Bishop 6 ac[rs] of land lying in the Yorkesheire quarter, betwixt the land of Thomas Powell and Thomas Wheeler.

Christipher Tood passeth ouer to John Tompson the house & home lott, w[t]h all y[e] meddow & vpland he bought of Mr. Higginson, excepting 9 ac[rs] in y[e] 3[d] devission w[t]hin y[e] two mile and the comonadge. The severall pcells he passeth is 24 ac[rs] in the necke,* 1 pec of meddow of 5 ac[rs], be it more or less, & 20 ac[rs] in the 2[d] devission.

Francis Browne passeth ouer to Henry Glover 10 ac[rs] of land at the plaines, lying betwixt the land of Ralph Dayton & the common.

Edward Wiggelsworth passeth ouer to Christopher Todd 16½ ac[rs] of meddow lying in y[e] east meddow, on this side the river, betwixt the meddow of Mr. Goodanhousen eastward, & Thom: Fugill westward; and 26 ac[rs] of vpland lying against it, and foure ac[rs] and a halfe in the necke.

Luke Atkinson passeth ouer to Richard Beech all his meddow in the west meddow beyond y[e] river, betwixt Hartfordsheire quarter & Richard Beeches wives lott, w[c]h was Andrew Hulls, one end butting vpon the river, y[e] other end runnning into the further cove.

John Moss passeth ouer to Mathew Moulthrop 3½ ac[rs] of vpland on y[e] west sid.

Richard Beech passeth ouer to Mathew Moulthrop one ac[r] & a halfe of meddow lying, 1 ac[r] of it in y[e] west meddow on this sid y[e] river, fronts vpon Mr. Lambertons vpland, y[e] reare

---

* In the margin. "This 24 ac[r] is pt of y[e] 2th devision & is but 3[d] an ac rats."

to ye river, a highway through ye meddow to ye north, Mathew Molthrop on ye south, ½ ac^r^ in Sollatary Cove not laid out.

Mathew Moulthrop passeth ouer to Henry Glover on ac^r^ of the same meddow.

Mathew Molthrop passeth ouer to Richard Osborne his house, home lott and barne, before the governer the 27th of January 1648.

[229] Widdow Halbich delivered into the court an inventorie of the estate left by her husband, Arther Halbich, deceased, amounting to 43^l^ 14^s^ 10^d^, prised by Rogger Allen and Samuell Whithead vpon oath, the 31th of January 1648.

Widdow Tompson, the late wife of Anthony Tompson, deceased, being called to give in securitie for the portions given to ye chilldren by her husbands will, doth in court ingage the house, land & whole estate left by him, for securitie.

William Basset whoe hath married the widdow of William Ives deceased, being called to give in securitie for ye portions of the chilldren, according to the will of William Ives, doth in court ingadge the whole estate w^c^h was left by him ye sd William Ives, & will not alter any of it till he acquaint the court w^t^h it & put in as good an estate as he shall dispose of.

Francis Browne was complained of for absenc at a generall court. He said he conceives it was aboute the fery w^c^h ocasioned it, whervpon the court past it by.

Jno Cooppr informed the court that Mr. Malbons quarter had not marked ther fenc, whervpon they was fined 20^s^, w^c^h was after remitted by ye generall court.

William Russells was complained of for absenc at a generall court. He said he was at worke at ye shipp, vpon w^c^h ground he was freed, by a generall courts order.

Mr. Leete & Mr. Jordan, atturneyes for ye towne of Guilford, informed the court that allmost a yeere agoe ther was a sentenc past in this court against Mr. Jno Cefinch, for a som̃e of money due to ye towne of Guilford for certayne rates, w^c^h som̃e hath bine sinc severall times demanded, but Mr. Cefinch refusseth to paye, whervpon the proceedings of that court was reade, wherin it appeared that Mr. Cefinch for want of proofe was cast in his suit, but now saith that he can prove that that order made at Guilford, (mentioned in ye former court,) was, that if any went away, his accomodations should be left in the townes hand to paye all rates, and for that purpose produced a letter from Henry Goldham of Guilford, whoe testifyeth therin that the order was that if any man was called to remove out of the towne, not disposing of his accomodations, it should remaine in the plantations hand to ye payement of all rates in generall, till the owner dispose of it other wayes. Further Mr. Cefinch saith he hath other proofe, but produceth none.

Mr. Leete & Mr. Jordan replyed that it was not so, but onely for ministers mayntainanc & that they can prove abundantly by the planters in the towne whoe did make the order, none w^t hout two or three desenting, wherof Mr. Cefinch was one. And the ocasion of that meeting makes it appeare, w^c h was not aboute towne rates but ministers maintaynanc, for it was when Mr. Higginson was vpon comeing to Guilford, he desired to know what certainty he should be at for his maintaynanc, and desired the towne might meete & consider of it, so they did, and after men had vnderwritten what they would give, it was propounded how this they had vnderwritten should be paide, in case any did remove out of the plantation. Mr. Leete answered for his p̱t he was willing, in case he did remove out of the towne, to leave his accomodations vnder the power of the place to make vse of as they shall see cause, to secure that w^c h he had vnderwritten; and after, the towne generally spake that they was willing to doe so. Mr. Cefinch objected that the order was not penned in ye meeting. Mr. Leete answered that it is longe agoe & he cannot fully saye it was, but the issue and result of the meeting was drawne vp and the plantation acquainted w^t h it afterward and approved it. Mr. Cafinch was told that for want of proofe he was cast in the last court and had warning to provide it against this court, & yett it is not done, therfore the court agreed & ordred as before, that Mr. Cefinch paye to the towne of Guilford the rates that appeare to be justly due to them, & that he paye 20^s for charges w^c h the plantiffe hath bine at in following the suit.

Henry Bishop was called, to know whether he had not disposed of some pt of the corne wch was ingadged to Mr. Davenport by the court of magistrats, he said when he had threshed about 20 bushells of rye he came for sackes to bring it home but could not haue them, wherby he suffered much loss, for the farmers hoggs & henns got into ye barne & made great spoyle of it. But he was told if the farmers haue done him wrong they must answer it, but Mr. Davenport, thoughe he hath bine willing to provide what sackes he could, yett he is not tyed to find sackes, as appeared by the covenant wch was read.

Farther, Mr. Crane, one the behalfe of Mr. Davenport, informed the court that ther is 4l 14s 8d due to Mr. Davenport from Hen: Bishop vpon accot for corne, wch Mr. Davenport requireth in corne according to his covenant, but Hen: Bishope refuseth.

Henry Bishop saith that he had offered wampome and that was refused, after he was to paye in catle & Mr. Crane and Goodman Milles came to his house to prise a steere for it, but they agreed not in ye price, then they questioned him aboute two calues if he was willing to part wth them, he said he was, but Mr. Crane for Mr. Davenport was willing if he brought good wampome in three weekes it should be accepted, if not, yn he was to have the calues. Mr. Crane replyed it was not so; it is true indeed that they went to prise a younge beast for this money but could not agree, and allso that he said if he brought good merchantable wampome in three weekes it should be accepted, but that if he fayled Mr. Davenport should take the calues he denyes; but because Hen: Bishop was to drive awaye certayne catle to Fairfeild to wintering, wch stood ingadged to Mr. Davenport, out of favour to Hen: Bishop he was willing the two calues should stand as ingadged to Mr. Davenport for securitie, but Henry Bishop failing in bringing the wampom to this day, & now the necessites of Mr. Davenports family requiring it, he demandeth it in corne, as justly he maye, the covenant bindeing the farmer to paye to Mr. Davenport what shall be due to him at the end of his time, out of the stocke of catle & out of the corne, & of 21l: 4: 8d, (twelue pounds of w^c^h was for corne,) Mr. Davenport hath taken 16^l 10^s in catle and requires the rest in corne, w^c^h he conceives is a great favour to the farmer.

[230] Richard Milles saith that the two calues was to stand ingadged for securitie, but was not prised to satisfye the debte.

Henry Bishop was asked if he had any witnes, he produced his brother James Bishop, whoe saith that he app^r^hended if his brother pd not the wampome in ye time appointed, that then the calues was to goe for satisfaction so farr as they would reach, but he could not take oath of it. Hen. Bishop was asked if he had any other proofe, he said no. The court, because 3 of the deputies was some way interested in the case, and Mr. Gibbard was not cleare in some thing, respited it till they might have more help.

Henry Bishop declareth that he hired a cannow of James Russell for his ocasions, & Jno Moss and Isacke Whithead tooke it awaye & brought it not againe, but broke it, wherby he was damnifyed. John Moss saith it is true they tooke the cannow away, but it was a mistake, for they had spake to Allen Ball for his cannow, and he told them that if Mr. Gilbert had done w^t^h it they might have it; they inquired and Mr. Gilbert had done w^t^h it, so as they was goeing vp the river w^t^h the lighter, Isacke Whithead knowing wher Allens cannow laye, went to fetch it, and when he came to the place ther was two, and it being in the night, and darke, mistooke, & did take the wronge cannow; so when morning came they saw they had mistaken; the wind blew pretty fresh, & the cannow w^t^h shering gott betwixt the banke and the lighter, & the lighter fell foule on it and brake it; so when they saw what was done they made inquirie whose it was, resoluing to paye for it, and hearing it was James Russells, spake w^t^h him and offered him satisfaction; he required that the cannow should be made as good as she was, and they did mend her, but after vnderstanding that Hen: Bishop had hired the cannow, they spake w^t^h him and offered to paye for the cannow & allso for what damadge he had suffered, but he would not accept it, but said he would haue it in ye court, & yesterday, after he was warned to ye court, Isacke & he tooke Thomas Meekes and went to Henry Bishop and offered him as much, but he demanded 3^d a weeke ever sinc ye cannow was taken away, and that the cannow be pd for, and 10^s for takeing it away as a breach of order.

Thomas Meekes testifyeth that he heard Jno Moss and Isacke Whithead offer Henry Bishop to satisfye Mr. Russell for the cannow and give him 3^d a weeke for his damadge, and for ye 10^s for breach of order, they see no ground for it. Thomas Meekes asked Henry Bishop why he would have it to the court, he said onely for the 10^s. Henry Bishop was told by the governer that ther is no ground that they should paye the 10^s, for it was against their wills they tooke it, the law of God requires no more in higher cases, even in case of blood, if the will be not in it he shall not dye. The sentenc of the court is that the defendants make good the cannow & paye just damadge to Henry Bishop, but that Henry Bishop beare the charge of the court himselfe.

Peeter Mallery and his wife was called before the court & was charged wth the sinn of vncleanness or fornication, a sinn wch they was told shutts out of the kingdome of heaven, w^thout repentanc, and a sinn wch layes them open to shame and punishment in this court. It is that wch the Holy Ghost brands wth the name of folly, it is that wherin men show their brutishness, therfore as a whip is for the horse and asse, so a rod is for ye fooles backe. They confessed ther sinn, and desired the court to show them mercy in respect of ther bodies, she being weakely, & for ought is knowne, wth child, and he subject to distraction, haueing sometime bine distempered that way. W^ch things the court considering, thought it most meete to punish by fine and not by corporall punishment, and therfore ordred that they paye 5^l as a fine to the towne, and that they be imprisoned during the courts pleasure, & that they be brought forth to the place of correction that they maye be ashamed and that it maye appeare the corporall punishment is remitted in respect of mercy to ther bodies, but wth the same hatred of the sinn as if the correction was laide onn.

Mr. Crane haueing had an attachment vpon ye corne & catle of Francis Hall to the vallew of 24^l, declared in court that 18^l of it was due vpon acc^{ot} by arbitration, and 40^s was due to Jno Whithead his servant, wch was ordred by this court for Fran: Hall to paye, wch is 20^l, the other is for securitie till Francis Hall have done sundry repaires vpon the farme, aboute houses and fences, & cut and made some haye wch he hath ingadged himselfe to doe next haye time, therfore desired that some might be appointed by the court to prise the catle for his satisfaction. Francis Hall desired it might be forborne till he had threshed out his corne, and what he makes not paye of then to his satisfaction, in corne or porke, or other good paye, he is content it should goe this waye. It was propounded to Mr. Crane & Francis Hall if they were both willing that the catle should be prised to the vallew of 20^l, and if in a monthes time Francis Hall doe paye in corne or wampom or porke wch is currant & merchantable, such as maye be pd to other men, then the catle to be released, Francis Hall payeing for the keepeing of them if he redeeme them, and for the rest of the attachment, that it stand till other things be cleared. And they both declared themselues willing, and the court appoynted Richard Milles & Francis Newman to prise the catle & that to ye vallew of 21^l, for 20^s wch Francis Hall was fined to the towne was by both ther consents added, & Mr. Crane is to paye it to ye towne againe.

John Livermore, Hen: Gibbons, & M^{ris} Rotherford, Addam Nickholes, the Yorkesheire quarter & divers wch rent ground in Mr. Evanc his lott, were fined for neglect of ther fences, but it was remitted by the generall court afterwards.

Mr. Crane and Francis Newman were desired to call some workemen to them, and they together to view Robert Parsons house what repaires it wants to make it tennantable, and what it is worth a yeere to lett, that William Pecke, if they can agree, maye hire it, the repaires being pd out of the rent.

Mr. Evanc being called to answer concerning Thomas Fugills lott, whose fenc is downe, answered that he had nothing to doe wth it in that kind, for Mr. Cockerill gave Mr. Leach a letter of atturney to receive it into his hand, & he hath delivered it vp, wrightings and all, to him.

[231] ||Mr. Pell was warned to this court & Mr. Powell appeared for him, and said that his vrgent ocasions fell out so that he could not appeare himselfe, but he submitts to the court. He was told that this cariage hath bine full of highe contempt, (on Mr. Pells pt,) against the court, wch he must answer. For he hath neither brought in his fine nor appeared, thoughe he hath bine warned to doe it.

Richard Mansfeild, John Tompson, Andrew Loe was complained of for ther fenc lying downe the most pt of the last sumer, & yett it is not vp, 20 post, Rich. Mansfeild, 12 post, Andrew Loe, 6 post, Jno Tompson, as Jno Cooppr informes. They answered that it was a midle fenc, & some of the quarter was in demurr for some time wheither to haue it maintayned or taken awaye, vpon wch consideration the court ordered that they paye but 12d a post for ye whole time past.

John Meggs desired the court to forbeare his two fines of 20s apece he hath bine fined by this court. The court told hime they would give him 6 monthes time if he could put in securitie.

James Till allso being warned to show cause why he pd not his fine of 40s laid vpon him for sundry miscarriadges, specially for contempt of the court, desired the court to forbeare it six monthes. He was told if he put in securitie it should, elc the marshall must attach for it, but for securitie Jno Tompson ingadgeth himselfe for 45s to see it pd in that time; the five shillings is for another fine now laid vpon James for leauing open a length of rayles into a corne feild.

An inventorie of the estate of Lawranc Watts* deceased was

---

* "An Inventory of the goodes of Lawrance Watts taken and apprised the 31th of January, 1644."

Sum £8, 1, 11.

A debt of Addam Nickholes £0, 4, a debte of Srjant Becklyes £0, 2.

Debtes pd for him out of this estate. To Thom Gregson £0, 11, 6. To John Dillingham £1, 12, 6. To Goodman Hitchcocke £0, 4. To Luke Atkinson, £0, 18, 7. To Goddman Budd £0, 10. To Allen Ball £0, 2, 6,

Goodman Tharp had of theise goods £0, 5, 6. Goodman Kimberly, Browne & Tharp had of theise goods £2, 6, 1. The rest which £1, 11, 3,—23d was lost in the goods; the rest which is 29s 4d, I am to paye. Thomas Gregson.

p^r^sented in court, amounting to ^ vnder the hand of Mr. Thomas Gregson.

Edmund Tooly whoe layes some claime to ye estate, p^r^sented Samuell Hodgkines for a witnes, whoe testifyes that he heard Lawranc Watts saye that if Edmund Tooly caried himselfe well, he thought to leave what estate he had w^t^h him, if ye Lord tooke him awaye before Edmund.

Mr. Theophilus Eaton one behalfe of his brother Mr. Samuell Eaton, passeth ouer to Francis Newman the houses, home lote w^t^h all accomodations & fences belonging to it w^c^h was M. Samuell Eatons lott, given him by the towne at first.

Mr. Evanc propounded to ye court that the fine of 40^s^ laid vpon William Badgard for his disorder might be remitted, for thoughe he vndertooke to paye it, yett he is now runn awaye in his and the rest of the owners debts, but the court did nothing in it.

A Court held at Newhauen the 6th of March, 1648.

Mr. Crane and Francis Newman informed the court that they had according to the courts desire called in William Andrewes to them, & that they together have considered of Robert Parsons house, and find that ther wants divers repaires, but thinke that a yeers rent maye make it tennantable for a while; they thinke the rent maye be 50^s^ a yeere. William Pecke whoe was to hire it said it was too deare, but yett was willing to take it & did, vpon condition that he repaire it out of ye rent, & keepe acc^ot^, that if he expend it not all, he maye then make it vp, but hath not libbertie to goe beyonde the rent, & if the court hears of none in ye compass of this yeere that layes claime to the estate, they will then consider of it againe.

William Andrewes was desired to joyne w^t^h Thom: Munson & Jervice Boykine to prise the house and lott of Robert Preston.

Debts owing to Lawrance Watts. George Ward £1, 12, 6. Edmund Tooly £2, 19, 2. Goodman Booth, Mr. Fugill, Mr. Ling £0, 2, 6. Goodman Mansfield, Goodman Chapman £0, 2.

"Mr. Evance had the originall inventory and saith he cannot finde it."

Mary Preston widdow delivered into the court the will and inventorie of John Hunter deceased;* the will made the 15th of Maye, 1648, witnessed by his owne hand and seale, and Ezekiel Chever and Robert Pigg; the inventorie amounting to 16l: 04s: 08d, prised by Thomas Munson & Thom: Kimberly vpon oath for ye valew of ye goods, and by ye oath of Mary Preston ye executrix for ye quanteite.†

Mr. Newmans quarters was fined 20s for not markeing their fences in time, but after remitted by ye generall court.

Mr. Leach desired of the court that an end and issue might be put to a cause depending in this court betwixt the estate of Robert Parsons and himselfe, wch it seemes for want of full proofe could not then be issued. The proceedings of that former court were read, and Mr. Leach now delivered into ye court a bill vnder Robert Parsons hand, wherin it appeareth that Robert Parsons received of Mr. Leach goods to the vallew of 61l to carie to the Barbadoes & sell & to returne halfe the profitt & the principall to Mr. Leach, and to have the other halfe of the profitt himselfe, and what he cannot sell, to returne to M. Leach againe. Mr. Leach said that he had received so much of the goods backe againe as came to 26l: 10s, and 752l of cotton woole at 10d p l, wch comes to 31l: 06s: 08d, out of wch he pd 5l for fraight of the cotton woole from Barbadoes heither. And he conceives that by his bill he is to have his principall made good heare, wthout payeing fraight. Mr. Leach was told that ther is 8l worth of this goods, as a handkercher, cuffe & brest pec, wch Robert Parsons was to sell as he saw meete, & is not tyed to make the principall good, and possibly he sold not that for so much by

---

* Last will of John Hunter, made May 15, 1648.

He gives to Sarah, wife of William Meaker, twenty shillings; to Peter Mallory, his best jacket; all the rest of his estate to Mary Preston, widdow, late wife of William Preston, deceased, and makes her sole executrix. "Sealed and declared to be the last will and testament of John Hunter, in the presence of Ezekiel Cheever, Robert Pigg.

Inventory taken by Thomas Munson and Thomas Kimberly; amount, £19, 11, 1. Estate Dr. to Mr. Peirse 10s, to Mathew Gunnill 3s, to Richard Beckly 8s, to Mr. Pell £1, charges in his sickness, coffin and burying £1, to Thom. Powell £0, 1, 4, to Adam Nickhols £0, 1, 3, to Richard Mansfeild £0, 1, 2, to Mr. Goodanhouse 3s.

† In the margin. "Ezekiell Chever and Ro: Pig tooke oath ye 4th Septem. 1649, that ye will now prsented is ye last will and testament of Jno Hunter."

a good deale, so that if that be rated at 5^l, he hath his principall allreadie, all but $3^s : 4^d$.

The court considered the case, as it hath bine p^{r}sented to them now and before, & ordred that Mr. Leach haue out of Robert Parsons estate 5^l, wch he pd for fraight of the woole, and allso the charges of the court, and if he can heareafter prove that Parsons sold the handkercher, cuffe, & brest pece, for more then 5^l, it should be made good out of Ro: Parsons estate. Mr. Leach moved for execution, but the court was not willing to grant it so sudenly, but told him ye estate should not be disposed of to his loss.

Thomas Fugill, as appeares by a noate vnder his hand, passeth ouer to Francis Hall 7 ac^{rs} & a halfe of land, lying w^{t}hout side of the Yorkesheire quarter, next the West River, the meddow being on y^e on side of it.

Francis Hall passeth ouer to Jno Meggs the same 7 ac^{rs} & a halfe of land, be it more or less.

Mr. Crane haueing before the last court had an attachment vpon y^e corne and catle of Francis Hall for a debt of 24^l, wherof $21^l : 1 : 11^d$ appeared then cleare to y^e court, for wch catle was prised by men appointed, and is now condemned in court, onely Francis Hall excepts against 6^s in Jno Knights acc^{ot}, wch Mr. Crane promiseth to allow backe, and the rest of the attachment stands till other differences be cleared betwixt them.

[232] || Mr. Goodyere declared to the court that that wch Jno Herriman was questioned for last court, in drawing wine w^{t}hout order, was occasioned by him, for when the ship carpenters came from the Baye to worke vpon the shipp, they required wine to ther diet, wch he was faine to pvide at his greate charge. Towards the latter end of ther being ther, William Andrewes prest to leave the ordinary, and propositions was made to Jno Herriman in the court to keepe it, and then William Andrewes being w^{t}hout wine, some did come to Jno Herrimans & prest to haue some, pleading necessitie, vpon wch he spake to the governer, telling him how people pressed for wine for ther necessitie, he said why doth he not lett them have it, intending to have him take vpon him the ordinary &

so lett them haue it in an orderly waye, but he vnderstood it not so, but that was his error, for he told them what the governer said, and after they did lett some folkes haue some, but for any disorder, he hopes none can saye ther was any.

The gouerner said that it is a breach of order is cleare, and for his pt, he neuer intended any thing but that he should lett people haue wine orderly, but for any disorder he heard of none.

The court considering that it is a breach of order & that for wch others haue bine fined, could not pass it by, but ordred that Mr. Goodyere paye to the towne as a fine fo this breach of order 40s.

William Basset was complained of for absenc at two generall courts, he said for the one, he was keeping cowes, for the other, his wife was not well & he was faine to staye wth her. For both the court past it wthout a fine, but ordred him to paye a fine of 2s: 6d, laid by this court for not bringing his armes to meeting one Lords day.

Mr. Leach declareth that he sold to Mr. Joshua Atwater in July last, goods to the vallew of 20l, to be paide in good wampome, wch Mr. Atwater hath not yett done, therfore desires the justice of this court.

Mr. Atwater answered that it is true, he bought 20l worth of goods of Mr. Leach, and promised to paye him in good wampome, and propounded 6 monethes time, but intended to paye in three, and when he went into the Baye in August, he mett Mr. Leach as he was goeing aboard and told him that so soone as he returned frome the Baye he would paye hime, against wch he objected not but seemed to be satisfyed, and so soone as he came home he applyed himselfe to it, but Mr. Leach was not at home, but in ye meane time Mr. Gilbert, Mr. Powell & Jno Walker came to him for severall goods, Mr. Powell 4 or 5l worth, Mr. Gilbert 12l worth, Jno Walker foure pounds worth, and they all said they were to receive good wampome of M. Leach, and they would sett it of wth him when he came home, so they had the goods, & when Mr. Leach came home, he went to him & told him that there was so much as would paye him in such mens hands, wch said he owed it them, so he might take it so and save a telling ye wampom, but he refussed and said he would paye his owne debts and he should paye his, so he returned to them againe and told them how it was, at wch they marveled and after demanded ther wampome of M. Leach, wch was not all pd till wthin this tenn dayes. And as they received it in paprs readie told they brought it to him & so he carried it to Mr. Leach prsently, but he refussed to receive it. Now this he conceives is not just, that he should paye yt for good wamppome wch he will not receive for good wamppome againe, when as the partyes told hime that they was to paye it him ye sd M. Atwater, & that he would bring it to him againe. And Mr. Gilbert, Mr. Powell & Jno Walker offered to take oath that ye wamppone they received of Mr. Leach they carried to Mr. Attwater, and Mr. Attwater offered to take oathe that the wampome he received of them he carried to Mr. Leach & he refussed it, but M. Leach desired it not, but said he was satisfyed wthout oath.

Mr. Leach replyed, he gave not 6 monethes time nor three monethes neither for payement, but his paye was due prsently, yett did not stand vpon it for 5 or 6 weekes time, therfore he conceives he should haue damadge for being wthout his money so longe.

The court told Mr. Leach that till Mr. Attwater returned from the Baye he was willing to staye, (he said he had rather haue had it,) and if he demands damadge since, by the same reason they wch he owed it too maye require damadge of him, & it is but 4 months time at most. Mr. Atwater said he had offered Mr. Leach his paye & what just damadge he could require, & Mris Pell could testifye it.

Both ptyes haveing spoken what they desired, the court proceeded to sentenc, & ordered yt seeing Mr. Leach pd the wamppome for good, he should so receive it againe, and that Mr. Attwater paye Mr. Leach for damadge for 20l for 4 monthes, after 10l in the 100l, wch is 13s : 4d, and the charges of the court, vnless he can prove that he offered just damadge before, & then Mr. Leach is to beare it, because he had as much offered wthout the court as he could in reason require.

Jno Meggs informed the court that Daniell Turner came to hime for a paire of shooes & had them, and promised him a bushell of corne wch Richard Webb owed him, he required a noate vnder Richard Webbs hand, Daniell brought him one & told him the corne was at mill, so he sent for it and had it; the day after Richard Webb came to him to know by what right he fetched his corne from the mill, he said by his owne order as appeared by his owne hand, he asked to see it & he showed it him, he said it was not his noate, he gave him a bill indeed for widdow Allen but this was a counterfit, so he required paye for his corne & had it, & left him to recover it of Daniell as he could. Further Jno Meggs saith that Daniell hath writt 3 or 4 severall bills for this corne wch was p^{r}sented & showne in court.

Daniell said he had a noate of Richard Webb to fetch a bushell of corne at mill, wch bushell of meale he gave to Goodwife Allen & the noate to fetch it, but she could not gett any bodie to fetch it & gave him ye noate againe, & he lost it, & after thought to dispose of the corne to Jno Meggs and writt another noate & gave him, and sent Goodwife Allen word she could not haue the corne, but was told that it was not in his power to dispose of, haueing given it awaye; and it is true she gave him ye noate againe, but it was to fetch the meale for her & to be pd for fetching it, and therfore after to dispose of it againe by a false & counterfit note seemed to be a cheating cousining way.

Farther Jno Megs said that Daniell Turner charged Richard Webb for wrighting a noate and then deneying his hand, and Goodwife Allen that she found the note & demanded the corne, which are both vntrue & vnjust charges.

[233] || The court considered the case as it hath bine p^{r}sented to them, & thoughe they see a stronge appearanc of a cheating cousening carriage in Daniell Turner, yett not being fully proved, past it by, but for wrighting false notes & vnjust charges vpon Richard Webb & Goodwife Allen, & much lying in this buisenes, & even now before the court, did order that hee paye as a fine to ye towne twenty shillings, and 8^{s} to Jno Megs for costs & charges, & 3^{s} wch he p^{d} Richard Webb for ye bushell of meale, and 3^{s} to Richard Webb for two dayes time he hath spent now at the court, and that he put in securitie for it all before he goe out of ye marshalls hand. Accordingly

Jeremiah Judson of Stratford became suretie for the payement of it all, wch is 34s.

Jno Livermore, widdow Tompson, Mr. Jeanes, Mr. Cefinch, Jno Walker, William Holt, Jno Wakefeild, William Gibbons, Jeremiah How, was complained of for ther fenc being downe, they was all ordered to mend ym vp & paye to Jno Cooppr what is due to him, & for ye fines to ye towne the court respits that.

William Jeanes passeth ouer to Jno Meggs, his house & home lott, lying at the corner ouer against Mr. Gregsons, betwixt the house lott of John Budd & the higheway e.

Mr. Goodyere being called by the court to give in securitie for the portions of his wiues chilldren, desired libbertie till the next court, wch was granted.

Allen Balle was warned to the court aboute Thomas Fugills fenc & rates, for Mr. Leach whoe had a letter of atturney from Mr. Cockerill would not medle wth it, as appeared by a note vnder his hand now prsented in court. It was propounded to Allen Ball if he would not be willing to take the house and land & improve them for defraying charges of rates and fencings; he said that the house was vncomfortable to live in because of the chimney and the sellar is falling downe, that workemen saye it will cost 20l to sett it in repaire, therfore he thinkes it is the best way to take downe the ptitions wthin & make a barne of it, & if ther be cause, it maye be removed of the sellar. For the land he is willing vpon equall termes as things goe, to take some of it. The court desired Mr. Wakeman & Richard Milles to call in William Andrewes and Jervic Boykine, & view and consider of the house, what had best to be done wth it, and that they consider of the land what rent it may yeild, as things are ordinarily lett, that so both house and land if it may be, may be disposed of.

Mr. Crane & Jno Cooppr were allso desired to view & consider of Jeremiah Dicksons lott, and if it maye be, lett it out for payeing rates & vpholding fences.

A Generall Court the 10th of March, 1648.

The Gouerner acquainted the court that he heares ther is great remisnes & neglect in setting vp fences according to the order made in Nouember last, so that Jno Cooppr wch they appointed to view fences hath done it, but wthout any success that is considerable, & so it will be vnless ther be some stricter order made, wherby the fines laid by the pticuler court maye be pd wthout delaye, and that Jno Cooppr maye be surely pd for his time of warning men of ther fences, & for his attendanc at the court, for men make excuses & so necesarily occasion his being ther.

The court considered of what was propounded, as allso of what orders they formerly made, both concerning swine and fences, and see no cause at prsent to alter them, but to confirme them wth this addition, that when catle are found in corne or elcwher, doeing damadge, the owner of the catle shall paye both poundage & damadge, and to looke out the fenc wher they might come in, & the first he finds, to laye it ther and looke no further, but he that oweth that first defective fenc to search out for more if ther be any, wch is all to beare pt, equally alike.

It was propounded wheither the court would not remitt the fines wch have bine laid vpon psons whose fenc hath fallen downe this winter & so could not be sett vp againe because of the frost, and allso the fines for not markeing fences. The court considered it and ordred that what fines have bine laid vpon any man for his fenc being downe, if it hath fallen downe since the 20th of Nouember last, it should be remitted, as allso the fines for fence not being marked, provided that just damadge be pd to them that have suffered by it, and that Jno Cooppr be duely pd what is his right to have, and that from this day the order be strictly attended, both in markeing & mending fences.

It is ordred that if any man be fined for breach of order & doe not paye the fine, (it being demanded,) before the next court after the fine is laid, or bring his money to the court and laye it downe, he must looke for no more warning, but that then execution prsently goe forth to seaze pt of his estate for it; and for what belongs to Jn° Cooppr, either for poundage or warning about fences, if it be not pd at first demand, or before the next court following, that then the marshall warne them to the court, & to have 4d for warning ym, wch is to goe, 2d to Jn° Cooppr & 2d to himselfe, and that the court increase the some to Jn° Coopprs advantage as they shall judge meete, and thoughe they should paye the marshall when he goes to warne them, yett they must paye the 4d for warning because they delayed so longe.

It is ordred that for what blacke birds Jn° Brocket or others kill, he or they applying themselues therto, shall receive from the treasurer after ye rate of 10s a thousand.

It is ordred that whosoever shall sell nailes in this towne shall sell six score to ye hundred.

The order made at the jurisdiction generall court for markeing catle was reade.

It is ordered that whatsoeuer dry catle, as oxen, steeres, or younger catle, shall be found wthin the cowes walke, or amounge the heards, the owner of them shall paye 3d a head to him yt pounds them, or complaines to the owner of them, or bringeth them home.

[234] ||William Andrewes, Jn° Cooppr, Richard Beckly, Nathaniel Merriman & Isacke Whithead desired that they might haue some land & meddowe to sett vp farmes one the east side, next the sea, beyond the Cove River. Mr. Crane and the farmers ther objected against it, whervpon the court appointed Leivtennant Seely, Henry Lendall & Francis Newman, as a comittee to view and consider wheither it would prejudice the farmes ther allreadie or no, & so to make report to the court, & if any of the farmers will goe to make ther objections they maye.

It was ordred that the pec of meddowe on ye further side of ye necke bridge towards the sea, should be for the ordinary to put in strangers horses in the summer, Jn° Herriman, whoe now keepes the ordinary, fencing it at his owne charge, and that a pec of meddow lying by the blacke rocke, next Leivtennant Seelys meddow, being supposed to be 6 or 7 acrs, should be for the ordinary to provide haye for strangers horses in winter, and this to stand till the court see cause to alter it,

& if any horses doe staye longe, as 4 or 5 dayes, or a weeke or more, he hath libbertie to put them in the necke, provided he put none in but strangers horses.

The towne was desired to see that they be provided wth ladders according to the order, and that they keepe ther chimneyes cleane, for Jn° Cooppr whoe hath bine vsed to sweepe them finds it inconvenient for him and layes it downe, onely he said that till another was provided, if any man desired him to come, he would take some time onc w^thin the weeke to doe it if he was well.

It is ordered that if any man goe awaye out of the towne, or sell awaye his best & convenient land, and take no course how the rates of the rest should be pd & the fences vpheld, the pticuler court have power to seize vpon the lott or stopp any such allination, till some order be taken for defrayeing all publique charges, vnless he that buyes the land will put in securitie for the same for time to come, provided that if any more shall be made of such lotts or lands then doth defraye publique charges, it doe returne to the owner of them.

It is ordred that the planters against the banke side to seaward shall haue 4 rodd of ground the breadth of ther lotts backward into oystershellfeild, because the sea & water washeth downe ye banke that ther is no good highe waye, & then according to an order allready in force, they must maintayne a good highe waye at the front of ther lotts next the sea.

It is ordered that a place be left for shooting at a marke in oystershell feild, vpon that 7 ac^{rs} Mr. Gilbert had, wch maye be ye most fitt for that vse.

The Gouerner acquainted the court that the comittee they appointed for oystershellfeild haue disposed of it for 7 yeeres more, for three shillings an ac^r, if they fenc it, then to haue the last yeares rent for fencing, but if they doe not, but by runing a fenc into ye sea as some speake of, they shall doe it at ther owne charge, & that then the last yeers rent be pd to the towne allso, & that such fenc as they make, they leave it standing at ye end of ther time.

Livtennant Seely was desired to take care that the watches might be made vp.

It is ordred that all men that vse measures wth strikes, shall gitt strikes well made, and ye next time measures be viewed they shall bringe their strikes to be viewed and sealed also, & so from time to time, vnder the same penaltie that the measures are.

Leivtennant Seely propounded that the court would consider of some other waye of rateing men then is setled by lands, for divers men w^c^h had good estates at first & land answerable, whose estates are sunke and they not able to paye as they did, & divers psons whoe had land for their heads, whose estates are smalle, yett paye great rates, & others whose estates are increased, haveing but litle land paye but a small matter to publique charges. Divers others in the court concurred w^t^h him, whervpon the court chose a comittee to consider of it and prepare it for another court. The comittee are the pticuler court, (calling in the elders for any helpe or light they want,) & one out of each quarter in the towne, viz^d^, Mr. Gilbert, Henry Lendall, Mr. Wakeman, William Davis, Mr. Attwatter, Jervic Boykin, Mr. Ling, Mr. Tuttill, Mathew Camfeild, Francis Browne.

Leivtennant Seely and Jno Brockett informed the court that ther is of that meddowe Mathew Camfeild desires, on ye other side the West River by ye oyster banke, about 4 ac^rs^ very badd and boggy, & they thinke the towne may grant it him w^t^hout hurt to themselues, vpon w^c^h report the court granted it to him.

John Moss propounded for 6 ac^rs^ of meddow at Oyster River. Richard Osborne & Geo : Smith propounded for some ther allso, but it was reffered to the viewers w^c^h are appointed to view some their allready, viz^d^ Leivtennant Seely & Jno Brockett.

It was ordered that all men w^c^h allinate lands in this plantation, shall come to the secretary before the court, & bring a note vnder the hand of buyer and seller of the quantity of the land, w^t^h the bounds of it, that the secretarie maye search the booke to see wheither such lands be in the sellers power to dispose of.

It is ordered that the gouerner haue three men beside Jno Thomas to goe w^t^h him to Stamford, & they to be pd by ye jurisdiction treasurer, his journey being vpon ye jurisdiction occasions.

A COURT HELD AT NEWHAUEN THE 3th OF APRILL 1649.

Mr. Goodyeare propounded to the court to knowe what securitie they did require of him for ye portions of his wives chilldren, for he was willing that the securitie should be out of the estate; the court declared themselues that they was willing to accept of ye fixed estate for securitie so farr as ther part goeth, the house & fences being kept in due repaire, and so much of ye moveable estate as to make it sufficient securitie, wch moveable estate should be determined of, that if any of it comes to be disposed of, other estate as good maye bee put in ye roome, and that wheras ther was 50l in the shipp Fellowship put into ye inventorie & vallewed at 50l wch now comes to be worth but 15l, the chilldren must beare ther part of the loss in proportion.

[235] ||William Andrewes junior was called to answer to a miscarriage of his by drunkenness wch had bine formerly heard by ye court in a private waye. What the court did then was read & testimoney called for of William Andrewes his good behaviour & sober cariage sinc, and Robert Martin, master of the Susan, a vessell wherin William Andrewes hath gone some voyages sinc, testifyeth that he can vpon his oath saye that for ought he hath seene sinc or heard by others, William Andrewes cariage hath bine well & according to the rules of sobrietie, and Mr. Evanc saith that Mr. Higginson, whoe went masters mate of that vessell, told him that William Andrewes hath carried it well in ye voyage; the court declared themselues by way of sentenc, that, vpon the testimoney given, they remitt the corpporall punishment he then deserved, and wheras 5l was deposited as a fine laid vpon him for which Mr. Evanc was suertie, they take of that allso, and onely ordered that William Andrewes paye as a fine to the towne for that, his miscariage, 20s.

John Vincon, Joseph Allsop & Andrew Low was complained of for ther fenc being downe, they said it was burned downe, & they could not gett help to sett it vp againe, they were told that it is 10 dayes sinc it was burned, & they haue had warning of it by the viewer, & they haue not done what they might haue done to keepe catle out of the corne; therfore the court ordered that the generall courts order be attended in ther payeing 12d a post for those that be downe, wch is 20 post as Jno Coppr saith, & that the viewer be pd what is his due, & what damadge beside hath come by it if it be required, & Andrew Low is further fined 12d a post for 12 post that hath bine downe longer, betwixt the two quarters.

Andrew Low informed the court that he was willing to part wth the land the towne gaue him & Thomas Wheeler was willing to accept it. Thomas Wheeler sd he was willing to take it, that is that wch was given Andrew Low at the first, & that 6 acrs he after had of Phillip Leekes, wth 2 acrs of meddow & 9 acrs of vpland on ye other sid the East River out of the elders lott, & he vndertooke to mend vp the fenc, paye rates & to beare the damadges wch lyes vpon it in regard of its being burnt and not sett vp.

Joseph Allsop informed the court that he desired to leave the 6 acrs of land the towne gaue him and Christopher Todd was willing to have it, as he said himselfe in ye court, and the court was willing he should, onely reserved libbertie to acquainte the comittee wth it, whoe as they conceived would grant ye thing.

Mr. Leach desired that the suit depending betwixt Phillip Galpin & himselfe concerning Nathaniell Drapprs wages, might be issued, whervpon Phillip Gallpin prsented in court the testimoney of Henry Rotherford & Michaell Taintor vpon oath, as foll,

Henry Rotherford testifyeth vpon oath, taken before the gouerner at Newhaven the 7th of January, 1648, that he being at Goodwife Tillsons house in Vergenia, last yeare, and speaking to her aboute Nathaniell Drappr, asked her how long he lived after he was caried ashore, she said he dyed the next day at night, before day he was dead. He asked what he spake concerning his meanes, she said that he gave her his beavor that he had, & for his wages he gave that to Mr. Sellicke, but it did appeare by her words to be vpon this ground, Mr. Sellicke comeing to vissit him told him that he would speake to a surgion to come to looke to him, but Mr. Sellicke said to Nath, yow have made yor will allreadie & given awaye all yow have & what shall I have to secure me. Nathaniell answered, (as Goodwife Tillson said,) that he would give him his wages to secure him & the last will must stand. Further he asked her if ther was any will writt, she said none in p^r^senc of Nathaniell while he lived.

Henry Rotherford.

Michaell Tayntor testifyeth vpon oath, taken before ye gouerner at Newhaven, the 9th of January 1648, that he being at Vergenia when Nathaniell Drapr dyed, went to Goodwife Tillsons house, & falling into speech w^t^h her concerning Nathaniell Drapr, she said that he brought some beavor ashore w^t^h him & some deares skines, w^c^h beavor and deare skines he gave to her, the said Goodwife Tillson, when he dyed, w^c^h was ye next night but one after he came ashore, & that he, ye said Michaell, saw the beavor which was a pretty bigg bundell. Further this deponent saith that Goodwife Tillson said that Nathaniell Drappr had made no will in wrighting sinc he came ashore, but that he expressed himselfe by word of mouth & she was a witnes to it, that what Nathaniell had he gave it to Mr. Sellicke, but remembers not that he heard her saye anythinge of Nathaniells giveing his wages to Mr. Sellicke.

Michaell Taintor.

Mr. Leach allso presented in court the copie of an afidavit of goodwife Tillsons, taken in Vergenia, wherin she testifyeth that Nathaniell Drapr gave to Mr. Sellicke his wages, by vertue wherof Mr. Leach said Mr. Sellicke claimes the wages of him; this last will by word of moueth being made a day after that written will wherin he gives the wages to Phillip Gallpin.

Phillip Galpin pleaded that Goodwife Tillson is not a competent witnes, she being a party & possesing pt of Nathaniel Draprs estate, as appeares by ye testimoney of Mr. Rotherford & Michaell Taintor, but the will wherin it is given to Phillip Galpin is written & witnessed by one not interested, viz^d^, Arthur Branch.

[236] ||The Gouerner informed the court and told Mr. Leach that the case is perplexed, for heare is but one witnes of either side, & if any of Nathaniell kindered should come to claime the estate, it might cause a new trouble, & be questionable wheither any of them should inioye it or no, but takeing the case as it is, wheither a will by word of moueth, witnessed but by one witnes w^c^h is a ptye, haueing a considerable part of the deceaseds estate, as appeares, (thoughe she mentioneth it not

in her owne testimoney,) shall ouerthrow a will written and witnessed by one vpon oath wch is not interested.

The court declared themselues that as the case stands, they conceive that Phillip Galpin hath the best right to the wages, & therfore order Mr. Leach to paye it to him, but with condition that Phillip give in securitie to Mr. Leach to beare him harmless against all future claimes.

Mr. Leach desired that he might be paide that wch the court ordered him to have out of Robert Parsons estate. Mr. Attwater, to whome ye estate was comitted, was ordered to make vp that accot, that Mr. Leach might be paide at or before ye next court.

John Coopr informed the court that ther is sundry catle haue bine pounded, wch is to be paid by divers men whoe owned the fence was then downe, a prsented 3 notes, wherin it appeared that ther was 12 cowes & 5 horses to be paid by Mr. Leach, Mr. Malbon & Thom: Kimberly & the quarter gate; & 29 cowes vpon Thom: Munson, Mr. Gilbert & Jeremiah How; & 25 cowes vpon Mr. Malbon, Mr. Leach & ye qrt' gate. The court ordred that the poundage be pd by these men, it being equally devided, according to the generall courts order, & what damadge is done they whoe haue received it may require it beside.

Richard Platt declareth that he sold a pcell of land to Ralph Dayton, pt of his first devission, & all his second, & 4 acrs of meddow, & would haue passed it ouer to him in ye court, but he would not haue it passed ouer to him, because it would, (he said,) be some prejudice to him, but said he would take order wth the treasurer to see ye rates should be paide. Ralph Dayton saith that he acknowledges he bought the land & they differ not aboute the paye, but he would haue ye land laid out & passed ouer to him, butted & bounded wher it lyes. The plant' said he told him it was not laid out, but he must take it wher it falles, but for the first devission, he ptly knew wher it was, on ye other side of ye West River. For ye meddow, it was pt in Mr. Malbons meddow and pt in Sollatarie Cove, and the second devident he thought might fall aboute ye sheppards penn, & produced Mr. Wakeman for a witnes, whoe saith that he cannot speake to ye bargaine, but Goodman Dayton spake to him asking him wher it was, showing therby that Goodman Platt did not determine the place, but mentioned the sheppards penn, as if Goodman Platt informed him that it might fall ther.

The court told Goodman Dayton that it appeares by this testimoney that he bought Goodman Platts interest in this land, hopeing the 2d devident would fall aboute ye shepards penn, for if he bought land wch he knew was not laid out, how could he looke to haue it butted & bounded. He was asked if he had any witnes to cleare his case any more. Hee said no, whervpon the court ordered that Ralph Dayton take ye land sold him by Richard Platt & haue it entred in the court & paye rates for it to the towne.

Mr. Leach was fined 12d for absenc at a generall court.

Henry Pecke, Robert Basset & Thomas Barnes was fined each of them 5s, because they are not provided wth each man a ladder for his house, to stand by his chimny, thoughe they haue had warning oft times in ye generall court, & pticulerly by ye marshall.

Mr. Malbon, Mr. Pery, Ed. Wigglesworth was allso wthout ladders & must answer it.

Edward Campe & Henry Bishop was allso complained of for want of ladders, but the court saw cause to pase it by, because Ed. Campe said he had one, but it was not in sight when ye marshall was ther, & Hen. Bishop hath lived at farme, & hath hired a house for a litle while, & is now goeing forthe of the towne.

Mr. Goodanhousen was called to put in securitie for the portiones of his wives chilldren, but vpon his desire the court gave him libbertie to consider of it till next court.

At a Court helde at Newhauen the first of Maye 1649.

Mr. Evanc informed the court that their is some lands he hath formerly passed ouer in this court to divers men whoe paye rates for them, yet he is not discharged of it in the treasurers booke. It was said some of the allinations was not cleare, whervpon search was made and it was onely in $16\frac{1}{2}$ ac[rs] passed to Anthony Tompson, w[c]h was sold to foure men & so should have bine entred, w[c]h Mr. Evanc was desired to cleare before the rates for that can bee altered, for y[e] rest they are cleare & must be charged accordingly.

Mr. Evanc passeth ouer to Mr. Goodyeare 110 ac[rs] of land, w[c]h is all the second devission w[c]h belonged to Mr. Trobridge his lott, lying on y[e] west side.

Mr. Newmans and Mr. Chefinches quarters was fined 5[s] for letting the gate of their quarter lye downe and not keeping it vp according to order.

[237] ||John Cooppr informed the court that he was ordered by them the last court to receive of Mr. Malbons quarter 5[s] for poundage of catle w[c]h came in at the quarter gate; and sinc ther is 5[s] 4[d] more for poundage of catle w[c]h cam in ther allso, but he cannot get it, nor knowes he of whome to require it, whervpon Mr. Gilbert and Mr. Crane were desired to take some order to get the quarter to meete and setle some course howe damadges may be paid when they come that waye, & how Jn[o] Cooppr may be pd this 10[s] 4[d] due at p[r]sent, for the court is vnwilling to take distresses, w[c]h they must doe if they cannot prevent disorder other wayes.

Mr. John Cefinch and Samuell Cefinch were complained of for their fenc being defective. It was answered Mr. Cefinch is not well, therfore not in court, but Samuell said hee had bine carefull to keepe his vp and had taken order to haue *haue* his made sufficient, but because Mr. Jn[o] Cefinch is not heare, the court respited it till next court, & wished Samuell Cefinch to tell his brother.

John Cooppr was advised to view all the fences well, and wher he sees them failing & not likely to keepe catle out of the corne, that he warne the owner of them, & if they be not mended sufficiently betwixt this and the next court, that they then be warned to answer it.

James Till was called to answer for a contempt against the court, for being warned to appeare the last court, as himselfe confeseth & owneth, he said he knew no busines he had their

& would not come, but now confeseth it was his ignoranc and foolishnes, but was told it was his stubborne disorderly spirit, wch he must be punished for.

Hee was further charged wth suspition of doeing some worke aboute mending his fenc vpon the Saboth day, wch appeared probable vpon this ground, first by his telling lyes, saying to Thomas Wheeler senio^r he had sett some of it vp vpon the last day at night, wch was not true, as he now confeseth, and then saying he was at it vpon the second day morning by that time it was day light, and yett it was proved to his face and he could not deney it, that he was in the towne and not gone to his fenc when the sunn was halfe an houre highe, and Thomas Wheeler affirmes he came to him & said the worke was done on ye second day morning by that time the sunn was two houres high at most, and he conceives that the worke done would take vp a man halfe a day, and Jno Cooppr said three houres at least, so that it is probable, but not cleare, that pt of it was done vpon the Saboth, but the court, leaving that, for his lying and contempt of the court, sentenced James Till to bee severly whipped.

Thomas Jeffery informed the court that ther was some goodes taken vp by John Griffen of Mr. Pell, for ye vse of the boate wherin Jno Griffen and himselfe were ptners, comeing to 54^s, and he pd his pt wch was 16^s, to Jno Griffen, as his wife can testifye, and Jno Griffen should have discharged it to Mr. Pell but hath not, and now Mr. Pell requires it of him. Mr. Pell said ther was so much due, but he hath received of Jno Griffen, by fraight of goods, 1^l 11^s 10^d, and the rest he requires of Thomas Jeffery as the survivinge man. It was asked Thomas Jeffery if ther was any thing in wrighting to make this appeare, he said he knew not, but ther was many paprs & bookes wch maye be looked vpon, and the treasurer and secretarie were desired to search those bookes & paprs, to see what they can find out aboute his estate, and about this matter in pticular, & then the court will order how Mr. Pell shall be paide.

Mr. Pell informed the court that ther was some things in Robert Parsons house which he was to take awaye, and to cleare it showed the award or arbitration betwixt John Budd and himselfe, vnder the hand of Mr. William Wells and Thom: Munson, wherby it appeared he was to take away a bedsted in ye leantooe of the said house and one in ye chamber, & two lockes, some bages of woole, & some hopp-roots & hoppooles, but is tyed so to take these things away that he deface not the freehold, and Richard Miles was desired to tell William Pecke, whoe is now in ye house, that Mr. Pell hath libbertie to take awaye these things, not defaceing the house, and if William Pecke will buy them of Mr. Pell for his owne conveniency he maye.

Mr. Pell was told he hath bine sundrye times warned to this court aboute a fine laide vpon him by the court of magistrats for ye jurisdiction, but he hath neither appeared at any monthly court hear till this, nor brought his fine, nor sent it by Thomas Powell whoe onc appeared for him, and thoughe at one court it was said he was w^thout, yett he made not his appearanc before the court, and so from time to time hath bine warned but hath not appeared, he was asked if he had now brought his fines, he said no. The court required that hee now give his answer to these miscariages and contempts. Hee desired that seeing the court of magistrats was so neare he might have libbertie to give his answer then, wch the court granted, and wished him to take this as a sufficient warning then & ther to make his appearanc, w^thout fayle.

John Bishop & Sam Hodgkines were complained of for sleeping in ther watch, but their occaisions being such as at p^rsent they cannot be heare now, it was respited till the next court.

---

[238] A Generall Court the 14th of Maye 1649.

Samuell Ceffinch and Joseph Pecke were admitted members of this court, and received the freemans charge.

Mr. Crane and Francis Newman were chossen deputies for ye next jurisdiction generall court.

Mr. Gibbard, Mr. Crane, Richard Miles and Francis Newman were chosen deputies for ye towne court of Newhaven for ye yeare ensuing.

Mr. Gibbard was chosen treasurer for ye towne of Newhaven for ye yeare ensuing.

Francis Newman was chossen secretarie } for ye yeere
Thomas Kimberly was chosen marshall } ensuing.

The millitary officers, wth Mr. Gibbard & Mr. Atwater, were desired & appoynted by ye court to treate wth ye drumer about his druming and maintayning ye towne drumes, viewing them in what case they are, and reporte to the court how they finde things.

Leivtennant Seely made a motion to ye court that they would be pleased to accept off ye service he had done in ye towne in ye place of a leivtennant for the time past, and that they would be pleased to chuse some other to supply the place for the time to come, for he findes it not comfortable for his family, nor pleaseing to his owne spirit to hold it as the case standes. Hee doth not desire to put the towne vpon charge in point of any sollary, yett leaves it to themselues to doe as they shall see cause, proffessing it is an affliction to him to w^t^hdrawe from this societie, but their is a waye open for him, and he desires to attend providenc in it, if he cannot see a waye of comfortable subsistanc here. After much debate, it was agreed that it should be respited till the jurisdiction generall court and bee propounded to them to see if they will doe any thing in it, that he maye not goe out off the jurisdiction.

It was ordred that Mr. Theophilus Eaton, gouerner, be for ye time to come freed from payeing his yearly rates to ye towne.

It was ordred that Mr. Robert Newman, ruling elder, be for the time to come, freed from payeing his yearly rates to the towne.

The pticular court were chosen as a comittee to issue the matter concerning seamen & ship carpenters, wheither they should watch & trayne or noe.

The comittee formerly chosen to consider aboute makeing of wharfes, & a bridge ouer ye moueth of ye creeke against Phillip Leekes, were desired to issue it. Allso it was reffered to them to order some course to be taken for clearing the flats of some loggs & pyles & stons, w^c^h the court was informed lye vp & downe, wherby vessells that come in ar in danger of being hurt.

Mr. Evanc made a motion to the court that Sariant Andrewes might have libbertie to keepe a timber yard, to provide timber for shipping & repairing of vessells, and that he might have libbertie to cut timber vpon the towne common for that purpose. The court was willing to incouradge the thing, yett not willing to make a full grant at p^r^sent, but for his incouradgment gave him libbertie to take what trees are vpon the towne common which the tanners have falled & barked that maye be for that vse, and libbertie to cut six or tenn trees more for that purpose, provided it be w^t^hout the two mile & in no mans ppríetie.

The Governer informed the court that he heares that William Davis & those two that was his men, viz^d^ Henry Bristow & Jno Winston haue falled a great deale of timber w^t^hout leave, w^c^h was by an order to be marked & reserved for the townes vse. William Andrewes said that he heard it spoken of in ye towne as an offenc against William Davis, that he w^c^h helpes to make the order presently goes and breakes it; and he conceives that the damadge to the towne is very great by his falling those trees, for he doth not know where a man can goe w^t^hin five miles of ye towne to finde so much such timber, but it was reffered to the pticular court. Much debate their was wheither it would not suit that the cooprs should fall their timber at that time of the yeare when the barke will peele of & be good for the tanners. Phillip Leeke said the wormes would eat it so as it would be vnservicable for makeing of liquid vessell. Nickholas Elsy said he thought not, & so said some others in ye court. But in regard the season is now allmost past for tanners, the court thought fitt to reffer it to further consideration, provided that all orders concerning falling of timber now in being, stand in full force.

William Paine, Jno Gibbs, Thom: Wheeler, & Francis Browne had libbertie to depart ye court.

It was propounded that something might be pd to the towne towards bearing publique charge, for each tree that is falled vpon the townes land, but it was respited for p^r^sent.

Henry Pecke had libbertie to take of that timber wch the tanners have falled, for his vse in his trade.

[239] ||Henry Morrell had libbertie to inlarge his home lott [into oystershellfeild] the length of his lott.

Jno Coopr is ordered to drive ye necke, & to pound those catell wch are not orderly put in.

The court remitted a fine of 20s laid vpon Jno Vincon, Joseph Allsop & Andrew Low.

They wch were behinde in ther rates were desired to bring them in to the treasurer.

William Andrewes desired the court that they would put an issue to ye matter concerning the land wch was viewed on behalfe of himselfe & John Cooppr, Sariant Beckly, Isacke Whithead & Nathanil Merriman on ye Indian side beyond Sollitary Cove. Those that were appointed to view were desired to informe the court how they found things. Leivtenant Seely said he thought the towne might grant it them, & so said Henry Lendall & Francis Newman, so yt the farmers meddowes might be secured from their cattell spoyling them. Mr. Crane, & Mr. Ling & Mr. Tuttill opposed it & said it would spoyle their farmes, yett if they might have common in ye necke wth them & haue ther medow secured, they were willing, but they wch propounded for it were not willing to take it vpon those termes. After much debate, the matter was left that they might speake privatly together aboute it, but the farmers were told that if they hinder the towne from disposing of the land for them to make vse of, the towne will expect the same rates from them that these offer to paye, that is, for all ye medow and 50 or 60 acrs of vpland, or more if it be taken in for planting land.

Sariant Munson informed the court that James Russells, being a watchman, pleads to be excused, because, by reason of some lameness in one of his hands, he cannot discharge his gunn. Hee was answered and James Russell told the he must hire, or else ye sariant must hire for him whatever he gives & he must paye it, and therfore he had better agree wth some one himselfe to doe it for him who maye bee approved by the sariant.

John Cefinch passeth ouer to Samuell Ceffinch the home lot he had of ye towne, being two acers; 36 ac^rs^ 6 rod of land of ye first devision w^t^hin ye 2 mile; all his land in ye necke being 13 ac^rs^ & ½; 14 ac^rs^ ½ 20 rod of medow; and 36 ac^rs^ & ½ of his second devision.

Edward Banister paseth ouer to William Basset ye 7th of Nouembr, 1648, 12 ac^rs^ of land in ye subverbs qrt' on this sid ye West River, & 7 ac^rs^ of land of ye first devision on ye other sid ye West River, and three acc^rs^ of medow in ye West medow & 24 ac^rs^ of ye second devision in ye subverbs qrt'.

The 7th of December, 1647, John Chapman passeth ouer to Mr. Leach his house, home lott & common, w^t^h 27 ac^rs^ ½ of vpland w^t^hin ye 2 mile, & 11 ac^rs^ of medow lying in ye mill medow, butting on end vpon ye vpland ground, ye other end vpon ye river betwixt ye medow of Mr. Gilbert & that w^c^h was laid out to an elders lot.

Mr. Leach paseth ouer to Thomas Kimberly the same pcell of land, both vpland and medowe, being 27½ ac^rs^, & 11 ac^rs^ of medow.

[There was a general court of election for the Jurisdiction held on the 30th of May, 1649, and also, as we learn from the records of the town of Guilford, a court of Magistrates, upon the same day. The certificate of the appointment of Theophilus Eaton and John Astwood as commissioners, signed by Francis Newman, Secretarie, is preserved in the archives of Massachusetts.

For some of the proceedings of this General Court see *post*, p. 463, note.]

A GENERALL COURT THE 11th OF JUNE, 1649.

Mr. Evanc desired libbertie for Thomas Moris & Nathaniell Merriman to depart ye court, to goe to doe a litle worke to a vessell w^c^h laye loaden & was ready to goe awaye, and they had libbertie.

Robert Martin and Jno Benham desired libbertie to dept ye court & had it.

Jno Thomas allso to goe cary some phisicke to one that was sicke.

The Governer acquainted the court that the principall ocaision of this court was aboute Nehemiah Smith the sheppard, whoe is willing if he maye be accommodated heare to come hither & bring ye flocke of sheep wth him, both them yt belonge to ye towne and his owne allso, thoughe not willing to keepe the townes sheepe because of some weakeness he finds vpon himselfe, but he shall sell some of his owne & keepe aboute 20 or 30 himselfe, and therfore propounds that he might have land wher he formerly propounded for it; that is, twenty acrs of vpland at ye sheppards penn & 10 acrs of meddow in Oyster River meddow.

Affter much debate it was voted that he should have 20 acrs of vpland vpon sheppards hill, & 10 acrs of meddowe in Oyster River meddow for his proprietie, and for the rest of his commonage he must fall vnder ye rules of a planter as other planters doe.*

And order made by this court the 5th of July, 1647, concerning the necke was reade and confeirmed, and ye comittee then chosen to consider of clearing ye necke for ye sheepe was desired to meete and consider what is needfull to be done for ye prsent against the sheepe come, and wheras William Preston, one of ye former comittee, is dead, Henry Lendall was chosen in his roome.

Leivtenante Seely desired the court that they would chuse another leivtenant for he finds it inconvenient to his family to hold ye place. Jno Moss propounded to the court to knowe if ye sallary given by the Jurisdiction for attending the gunns [240] cannot bee || [*given to*] Leivtenant Seely, he was told that the sallary [was offered Leiut] Seely before it was disposed of other wayes, but now this court cannot alter the generall courts order. Leivtenant Seely was desired to consider of it for a fortnight when their would be another generall court; in ye meane time it was propounded that the men in ye towne would vnderwright what they would give towards ye maintaynanc of Leivtenant Seely in his place, wch satisfyed him for ye prsent.

---

* In the margin, "At a towne meeting ye 13th of May, 1650, it was voted yt yt clause in this order of keeping 20 or 30 sheepe should be of no force, but that he keepe what sheep he sees meete selling some to ye towne, and when ye towne sees cause to stint themselues in other catle, that then he be stinted also as others planters."

Nehemiah Smith removed to New London about 1652.

Mr. Robert Newman desired that he might have 12 plankes that are the townes at ye west bridge, and he would either paye the towne for them, or give them 12 as good againe. The court being informed by William Andrewes that the towne might spare them for the present, agreed he should have them according to his proposition.

It was propounded that the necke bridge and west bridge might be mended, William Andrewes said vnles workemen can have corne, they cannot worke, Mr. Evanc said rather then the worke should cease to ye indangering of ye bridges he would lend ye towne fifty shillings worth or 3^l^ worth of corne, so it was agreed that the worke should goe one.

Thomas Kimberly acknowledge a sinnfull miscariage of his aboute a prisoner sent by the governer to the Duch governer by Jeremiah How, first that he said of his owne head to Jeremiah How, that it would be a deed of charitie if he let ye prisoner escape so no hurt might come to ye jurisdiction, secondly y^t^ concerning a letter sent by the governer to the Duch governer, he said to Jeremiah How that if ye prisoner escaped, he hoped he would have more witt then to deliver the letter. And wheras it is said that he should express something as if ye governer was content ye prisoner should escape, which was no such thing, nor doth he remember that he spake so, but he falls vnder testimoney. These things he acknowledgeth was a breach of ye 6th & 9th commandements, and great vnfaithfullness in ye trust comitted to him. The governer declared himselfe satisfyed, hopeing it will bee a warning for time to come, and no other objected against it.

It was desired that the collecto^rs^ for ye colledge corne ye yeare last past & ye yeare before that would cleare matters wth Mr. Evanc and bring to him ye corne they have that it maye now be sent, and what wampome they have allso and he will send provissions for it.

A Generall Courte the 25th of June, 1649.

Thomas Wheeler senio^{r} was admitted a member of this court and received ye freemans charge.

The orders of the last generall court for ye jurisdiction was read, in which it app^{r}ed that the plantation of Southold vpon Long Island are to have that plantation made ouer to them, and seeing it was purchased by this towne, it is by this towne to be made ouer to them, whervpon it being propounded, it was voted by this court that they doe relinquish all their right and desire it maye bee made ouer to them, either by deed or otherwise by act of court, provided that it be still kept w^{t}hin this jurisdiction.*

The Gouerner informed the court that ye comittee they appointed to consider of cleering the necke have mett, and thinke that it would be profitable for ye towne that it should bee cleared for oxen and sheepe, but because it is now neare harvest, and mens ocasions will not give waye to doe it all now, that therfore every planter in the towne would goe or send a man a day, w^{c}h they thinke maye doe inough for ye p^{r}sent, and

---

* "At a general court held at New Haven for the jurisdiction, the 30th May, 1649. The freemen of Southold desired that the purchase of their plantation might be made over to them. The court told them that they are free to make over to them what right they have, either by a deed or an act in court, that it might stand upon to free them from all future claymes from themselves, or any under them, as themselves upon consideration shall propound or desire. Mr. Wells being questioned about some land he had received of some Indians in Long Island by way of gift, in which Mr. Odell of Southampton hath a part, and himself did draw a deed, wherein the land was passed over from the Indians to them, which is contrary to an order made in this jurisdiction. Against which carriage the court showed their dislike. But Mr. Wells doth now before the court fully resign up all his interest in that land to the jurisdiction, and will be ready to give a deed to declare it when it shall be demanded of him. Mr. Youngs informed the court that they at Southold had, according to order, purchased a plantation westward from the Southold, about eight miles, of the Indians, which, by the best information they can get, are known to be the right owners of that land, called by the name of *Mattatuck* and *Aquabouke*, and this for the jurisdiction of New Haven and Connecticut; which purchase comes to, in the whole, six pounds six shillings; the particulars how it arises, being expressed in the deed, which they desired might be repayd; and accordingly the treasurer had an order from the court, and did pay it to them. Likewise Lieutenant Budd spoke of another purchase that was made, but did not give full information, nor a perfect account thereof."

The above note is taken from Thompson's History of Long Island, 2d ed. vol. i. p. 378, but Mr. Thompson gives us no indication of the source whence he derived the citation, and the editor has not hitherto succeeded in discovering it.

the comittee that they might incouradge ye worke, have allready all gon themselues or sent a man a day, except one whose ocasions would not then pmitt, but is now ready. It was desired that those whoe was willing to goe would now give in ther names, whervpon sundery did, a note wherof is in ye secretaries hand.

The Gouerner acquainted the court that the comittee they appointed to consider of seamen and shippcarpenters watching and trayning have done it, whervpon a note vnder Mr. Winthrops hand, then governer in ye Baye, sent for by order of this court to know what ther order is ther aboute these things, wch was read being as followeth,

Persons exempt from trayning & watching & warding by ye Massachusetts law, as Mr. Winthrope certifyed July ye 14th, 1648.

Magistrats, deputies, elders of churches, deacons, the president, fellowes, students and officers of Harvard Colledg, all proffessed schoolemasters allowed by two magistrats, the treasurer, the audito^r generall, the surveyour generall, publique notaries, phisitians & surgeons allowed by two magistrats, masters of shipps and other vessells aboue 20 tunne, millers and such other as shall be discharged by any court for bodily infirmity or other reasonable cause. But ther sonns and servants are not freed, except on servant allowed to every magistrate & teaching elder. Such as keepe familyes at remote farmes shall not bee compellable to send ther servants to watch or ward in ye townes. But all psons exempt &c, shall have compleate armes &c. in ther houses, except magistrats and teaching elders. Wee had a law for seamen & shipcarpenters & fishermen, to trayne onely twice a yeare, (& so is our practise) but I finde it not in our new booke of lawes, so that I feare it is om̄itted through some ouersight. The officers of our courts are allso exempted.

Jno Winthrop.

wth which the court closed, wth some little alteration, first wheras mention is made of remote farmes, the court thinks it should be limited to those w^thout ye two mile, and for masters of vessells of 20 tunne, they thinke for incouraging seamen it maye be limited to 15 tunn and vpward here.

[241] || For other seamen and all shipp carpenters, [that] they watch as others doe and trayne twice a yeere. And to

distinguish whoe are seamen & ship-carpenters, it is left to the ꝑticular court to judge.

The court considered of what was propounded and written, and ordered that, wth the alterations before exprest, it should be here practised as is before expressed in ye note from Mr. Winthrop.

Vpon Robert Bassets desire to be freed from watching because he is drumer to ye towne & to attend his place as drumer if ther should be an allarum in ye night, wch if he be vpon the watch he cannot doe, Leivtenant Seely said it is not vsall for drumers to watch vpon any court of gaurd as common watchmen, but to attend ther place as drumer if their be ocasion. The court for ye prsent saw cause to free him, wishing him yt if at any time he doth goe forth of towne he provide another drumer to supply his place and attend his worke as drumer to ye towne, yt they be not left destitute.

It was propounded to know what armes is proper for every officer of the millitary company to have, which was left to the officers themselues to consider & informe ye court.

William Judson desired that he might be freed from watching, but nothing was done, but he reffered to ye order formerly made.

It was propounded that the oxe pasture might be fenced at the townes charge, and whither it would not be profitable to ye towne that it should be planted three or 4 yeares & after laid againe for an ox pasture, and it was reffered to the consideration of ye comittee chosen for rates the 10th of March, 1648, (the ꝑticular court excepted,) vizd Mr. Gilbert, Mr. Wakeman, Henry Lendall, William Davis, Mr. Atwatter, Jervic Boykin, Mr. Ling, Mr. Tuttill, Mathew Camfeild, Francis Browne, & yt they informe ye court what they judge of it.

Andrew Low desired the court to consider of severall fines, amounting to 44s, for his fenc being downe, but nothing was done in it at prsent.

It was refered to the ꝑticular court to consider of some that might take the estates of any which dye in ye towne and leaves no order aboute ther estates. Instanc was given in ye estate of Robert ꝑsons, William Ball, Lawranc Watts, & what other maye bee, the treasurer desired that he might not be troubled wth them.

The Gouerner informed the court that he hath heard some complaints aboute the smallness of bread that is made and sold in ye towne, and therfore thinkes that some course must be taken that it maye be sized, that the baker maye have a due profit & the buyer not wronged. It was inquired whoe had any booke that might give any light concerning the sizing of bread. Jno Brockett said he had one, and was desired to cary it to the governer whoe was desired to prepare this matter against ye pticular court.

Leivtenant Seely desired the court that they would chuse another leivtenant for his occasions require hime to laye it downe. The court told him they saw no cause nor should chuse any other so long as he remained in ye towne amonge them, and the foure sarjants were desired to take some paines to see what men would vnderwright as it was spoken ye last court.

John Walker & Thomas Mitchell were chosen veiwers for ye fenc at plaines for ye yeare ensuing.

John Cooppr desired that ther might be a man appointed in each quarter to know what quantity of corne every man hath sowen or planted this yeere, that he is to be pd for. And Jno Cooppr propounded, and the court appoynted Francis Newman for Mr. Eatons quarter, Mr. Ling for Mr. Newmans quarter, Jervic Boykine for Mr. Ceffinch his quarter, Robert Johnson for Mr. Evanc his quart', Jno Meggs for Mr. Evanc his lott, Mr. Wakeman for that quat', Richard Miles for yt quart', Henry Lendall for that quart', Mathew Camfeild for ye subverbs on ye other side the creeke, Sam: Whithead for those on this side, Thomas Nash for Mr. Davenports quart', Thom Munson for Oystershell feild & those that live by the east creeke & on the banke side. To wch men every on wch lives in the quarter is to bring in ye number of acrs of corne planted or sowen by them or for them in any feild wthin the two mile, betwixt this and this day senit, vpon ye penaltie for each acr so neglected 4d. And if any shall deale falsly, bringing in less then he hath, wth a purpose to deceive, he shall be vnder such punishment as the ꝑticular court shall judge meete.

A COURT AT NEWHAVEN THE 3th OF JULY, 1649. Capt. Astwood and Mr. Disbrowe being p^rsent wth this courte.

Mr. Evanc declareth in an action of debte for 255^l sterling, disbursed upon the shipp Swallow, which is now possessed by Mr. Westerhousen, for which some Daniell Peirse, merchant and ꝑt owner of ye said shipp, binds himselfe and owners, wth the shipp & all the furniture to her belonging, for securitie, to be paide at Barbadoes in cotton woole, as appeares by a bill subscribed by Daniell Peirse m^rchant and Steeven Reekes master of ye saide vessell, witnessed by Mr. Theophilus Eaton, & Mr. John Davenport, by which bill he conceives he is to be paide the money by the shipp, for the money was expended vpon the shipp, w^thout which she was not fitt to proceede vpon any voyage, and vpon this ground he demandeth the vessell. [242] || Mr. Westerhousen in answer delivered [in]to ye court certayne of the proceedings of the court in Vergenia, wth an inv[oyc]e of shipp & goods, and a testimoney from ye shreiffe wch seized the shipp and delivered it to ye marriners, wch was now reade in court, by which it appeared that the marriners seized the shipp for wages, and by a legall tryall recovered it, and had it delivered to them by ye shriffe.

After which the marriners being possessed of the shipp sold to Mr. Westerhousen, & now stand to pleade their right in the shipp by vertue of ye order of ye court at Vergenia. The marriners were told that here is nothing in ye wrightings from Vergenia mentioning Mr. Evanc, nor doth it appeare that any pleaded for Mr. Evanc nor any copie of it. They said that Mr. Benit, Mr. Evanc his atturney, pleaded for him and was in court when the cause was cast, but they had nothing to doe to bring other mens wrightings.

Mr. Evanc replyed that he conceives he hath proved that the shipp Swallow was made ouer to him by master, merchant & purser, and that this was done, (they saye themselues,) the purser told them, & w^thout this money the shipp could not have proceeded vpon any voyage. Likewise it is cleare that the mens wages, which is the onely plea, was pd out of the moneys disbursed by Mr. Evanc & cleered when they went henc, for they themselues demand but 249[l], and they have bine out from henc 13 monthes, and ther wages is but 20[l] a month, so that the wages must be cleared when they depted. And seing they knew that the shipp was made ouer, they might have chosen whither they would have gone or no, and that so much was disbursed vpon her appeared by a note p[r]sented in court.

The Governer propounded to y[e] marriners, put case a shipp is vpon a voyage, and puting in at a port by the way, throughe some stress of weather, wants a new suit of sayles, or a cable & anchor, the marriners buy them and ingage to make payement at her port of discharge, if ther the ship shall come to be sold for mens wages, shall these sayles paye them ther wages, which they could not have earned w[t]hout them, or suppose a shipp comes into a harboure, wants repaire, a workeman workes vpon the shipp, earnes 20[l], but before the shipp goes awaye, ther falls a differenc & men call for wages & the shipp comes to be sold, shall not the carpenter be paide for his worke. They could not saye but it is equall he should, but yett they saide that the shipp is theirs by order of y[e] court of Vergenia.

The plantiffe and defendant having no more to say, the court proceeded to sentenc, and they find that had the shipp arived in due season at Barbadoes, Mr. Evanc might have required his debte from the owners, & the shipp, w[t]h her furniture, was ingaged for it, yett wheither the shipp be considered as belonging to y[e] former owners, or as new morgaged or sould to Mr. Evanc, and by his consent & w[t]h some goods of his goeing forth towards Barbadoes, God, by an afflicting providenc, keeping her at sea & from her port at Barbadoes till marriners wages have eatton out her vallew, she putting in at Vergenia, giving over her voyage and being arrested vpon other acc[ots] & ingagements, the marriners had, (as the case stood,) y[e] first & cheife right to their wages, and y[e] rather in this case, because the tennour & import of Mr.

Evanc his deede is to secure his debte from ye owners by the shipp & her furniture, not from the marriners out of ye wages which should grow due from henc to the Barbadoes or any other port. They saw not therfore how they could justly dispossess the marriners, (or Mr. Westerhousen claiming from or vnder them,) of the shipp granted them by sentenc of court in Virginea.

Robert Newman, plant' }
[Rob]ert Basset, defendt' } Mr. Newman declareth that he being intrusted to dispose of M^ris Wilkes estate, sold Robert Basset her house for 40^l and past it ouer to him in this court, to be paide halfe of it the 29th of September last past, and ye other halfe ye first of May last, but none is paide but 5^l a litle while agoe, and now Robert Basset would have him take ye house againe, wch he cannot doe but wth wronge to others, being but a trustee in the buisnes.

Robert Basset said he was disabled by some loss he hath had, and if he should ingage himselfe for further security, he might bring further trouble, and he doubts wheither he shall ever be able to paye for it or no, but is willing to submitt to any loss the court shall thinke meete, for he acknowledgeth the bargaine, and so leaves it.

The court declared that they neither made nor can breake the bargaine, and therfore if betwixt this and ye next court satisfaction be not given, execution must goe forth if it be desired.

Thomas Meekes and Rebecka Turner was called before ye court to answer to their sinfull miscariag in matter of fornication, wth sundry lyes added therto by them both in a grose and hainiouse manner. The matter hauing bine formerly [heard before the] gouerner in a private way, wch was now de-
[243] clared to ye court ||in ther p^rsenc, and they called to answer. Thomas Meekes said he could say nothing against whath bine declared but it is true, and he desires to judge and condeme himselfe for it in ye sight of God and his people. And for Rebecka Turner, she acknowledg the things ye charged was true, and though she had saide Thomas Meekes

had had to doe w^t^h her but once, yett it was oftener, as she now saith.

The Gouerner further declared to ye court, that he hath heard of sundry passages w^c^h render Mr. Westerhousen suspicious in this buisnes, first that Rebecka should say that she could not love Mr. Goodanhousen, but she could love Mr. Westerhousen. Mr. Westerhousen answered that she said not so to him, she said allso that it was not to him but to some body in ye house. Secondly that Mr. Westerhousen should say to her that if his wife was deade, he would make her his wife. Mr. Westerhousen answered that he said not so. She said it is true that she said so, but cannot tell but she might be mistaken, w^c^h ye court witnessed against in her.

Thirdly that he gaue her sundry gifts to a considerable vallew, insomuch that Mr. Goodanhousen, her father, was troubled at it, and told Mr. Westerhousen that he could maintayne his daughter w^t^hout his gifts. Mr. Westerhouse said it was at ye faire, and then Mr. Peirse gaue her lace for a handkercher, and he gaue he cloth.

Fourthly that he caried her behinde him to ye farme; he said that on night she was goeing to ye farme very late, her mother pittyed her, he bid them sett her behinde him & he would cary her, and so did.

Fiftly that he mette William Wooden & Henry Humerstone, he coming from ye farme, they goeing theither, they asked him if he was not at ther farme, or wheither he had not called at ther farme, to both w^c^h he answered no, yett when they came home asking Rebecka, she said he was their and she knew not that he had bine any wher else. Mr. Westerhouse denyed it, whervpon ther oathes were required. Mr. Westerhouse desired the one might be put forth whilst ye other tooke oath, and it was so.

William Wooden testifyeth vpon oath, that he and Henry Humerston being together, mett Mr. Westerhousen w^t^hin ye necke gate, against David Atwaters, he asked him wher he had bine, he said at further farmes. William asked him, was yow not at o^r^ farme, he said no. William said, did yow not call ther, he said no, when he came at farme he asked Rebecka if Mr. Westerhouse was not ther, she said yes, & whether he were any wher else, she said not that she knew of.

Henry Humerstone testifyeth vpon oath, that vpon ye highway as William Wooden & hee was goeing home to ye farme, they mett Mr. Westerhousen and asked him wher he had bine, he said at ye other farmes beyonde, this deponent said was yow not at o^r^ farme, he said no, did yow not call ther, he said no, at wch they wondered; when they came at farme William Wooden asked Rebecka if Mr. Westerhousen was not ther y^t^ day, she said yes, he asked her if he was any wher else, she said no, he asked her what he did ther, but what her answer was he cannot tell.

Sixtly that he hath line at ye farme in ye same roome wth her, as Hen: Humerston & Wiłł Wooden say.

The Gouerner told ye court that they haue heard ye severall passages of ye buisnes concerning Thomas Meekes and Rebecka Turner, wherin beside ye fornication ther hath bine much impudenc in lying, espicially one his ꝑte, calling God to witness ye truth of a thing wch himselfe knew to be false, as he now professeth. Allso ye passages concerning Mr. Westerhousen, and what is proved vpon oath, yett not owned by him, wch leaves ye court much vnsatisfyed.

Matters being thus prepared, before ye court proceeded to sentenc Mr. Goodanhouse desired to speake, and desired the court to consider that Rebecka is weake and hath sore breasts & a froward child, that therfore, if it may be, they would spare corporall punishment, and if they laid a fine he would see it paide.

The court having heard and weighed what was spoken proceeded, and ordered that Thomas Meekes be severely whipped for this folly of sinnfull vncleanness, and for his lying and miscariages that way y^t^ he fined 5^l^.

For Rebecka Turner that she allso be whipped, if in refferenc to herselfe and child it may stand wth due mercy, but vpon a veiw & search & a report made by the midwife and sister Kimberly, the court saw cause to forbeare that, and ordered her to paye a fine of 10^l^, wch Mr. Goodanhousen promised to paye for her.

Beniamine Wright, of Guilford, hauing bine, at a court of magistrats held at Newhauen in May last, charged w^t^h and proved guilty of sundry grose miscariages, for w^c^h he deserved seveere correction, but ye court seeing some showe of remorse, and hoping for better fruit then now they see, vpon Mr. Disburow request, past it by, vpon condition that he should make a full acknowledgment at Guilford of his severall miscariages, as he had done in court and promised to doe ther, as appeared [244] || by the proceedings of that court w^c^h was now read, but when he came at Guilford and should have made his acknowledgm^t^, he refused, and in a stubborne and bold way said he must fall vnder many things because he wanted proofe, as appeares by a note vnder ye hand of Mr. Leete, Secretary at Guilford, and said that he had acknowledged he went aboute to delude the townes order because the gouerner did so threaten him, as is testifyed by Mr. Leete, Mr. Chittendine & Mr. Jordan, vpon oath taken before Mr. Disbrowe, July 2th, 1649.

Wright was asked what threatening was vsed, but he answered not. Hee was told that he had bine brought to corporall punishm^t^ before but y^t^ he made that acknowledgment he did, and gave hopes of better fruit then appeares, for instead of doing what he promised, he returnes to his former pride and stubbornness againe, and when he was bound to appeare at this court, and put in baile to doe it, he came to ye magistrate and told him plainly he would not come ther, as Mr. Disbrowe affirmed before him and he denyed it not. Hee was therfore desired to speake if he could show any reason why he should not now have sharp punishm^t^ inflicted. Hee said he can say nothing against it but it is just, for though he had thoughts when he went from ye court to doe as he had saide, yett God left him and he returned to his former course againe, because he was not faithfull to those purposes that God had put into his heart.

The sentenc of the court concerning Benjamin Wright is that he bee seveerly whipped heare at Newhauen, and a month henc at Guilford, and that he paye as a fine to ye jurisdiction, 10^l^, for ye charge & trouble he hath put them too.

Mr. Goodanhousen p^r^sented in court a wrighting by w^c^h it appeared that ther is sundry accounts betwixt Mr. Westerhousen and himselfe wch hee desires may be cleared, and allso a bill of Mr. Westerhousens of 90^{l}, wch he is to paye to Major Gibbons for him ye said Sam: Goodanhousen.

Mr. Westerhouse said that Mr. Goodanhouse owes him money allso, whervpon for the matter of accounts, the gouerner propounded to them that they would put it to arbytration, that acc^{ots} might be issued betwixt them, and the matters ended in a louing way, to wch they both consented, and before the court chose Mr. Goodyeare, Mr. Evanc, and Mr. Gilbert for a third man, and they, the said Sam: Goodanhousen & William Westerhousen, binde themselues in 100^{l} a pec to stand to ye arbytration of these three men chosen by themselues shall make, this to begine one ye sixth day of ye weeke next, and to be issued by ye last day at night following, and for ye bill to Major Gibbons, the sentenc of ye court is, that Mr. Westerhousen paye it according to ye bill & ye charges of this court beside.

Lancelot Fuller, plant',
Fra: Newman and his wife, defendants.

Lancelot Fuller declared that Mrs. Newman had wronged his wife, saying she had interteined young men or a young man, (Mr. Stone by name,) in her husbands absenc & made a feast or breakefast for him, & that his wife having heard of it abroad, went to Mrs. Newman & desired nothing but due satisfaction in private, according to ye nature of ye case. Mrs. Newman said she was sorrey for it, his wife thought that not sufficient except she clered her where it had bine spoken, and to her husband when he comes home. M^{ris} Newman said she knew not how to doe y^{t}, his wife said she must then learne, whervpon Mrs. Newman told her she were best hold her tongue & say no more in it, for if she did not put vp that, it would bring out worse. Lancelot Fuller therfore desired to knowe what that worse is wch it would bring out.

The court calling for proofe, Mrs. Higenson vpon oath testified that she heard M^{ris} Newman say that Goodwife Fuller intertayned a young man in her husbands absenc, & made a diner or a breakfast for him, (Mr. Stone by name.) Being asked how this came to be published, she answered the elders wife was p^rsent when Mrs. Newman spake it, but it came thus, (as she conceiveth,) to be published; she asked her brother, Charles Higenson, why he staid out so late and came not home in seasonable time, he, (as she remembers,) named some places wher he had bine, as at Mr. Goodanhouse at ye ordinary, & said as he was coming home he went into goodwife Fullers to take a pipe of tobacco & stayed some time ther, whervpon she, this deponent, asked him why he did so & did not come home, she said it would be taken notice of & give occasion of speech, and thervpon told him what she heard, and ye next Saboth day on asked Charles Higenson to goe take a pipe of tobaco at Goodwife Fullers, & he would not, but told him what he had heard. Goodwife Fuller to this replyed, that Charles Higenson came in wth her brother, Sam: Marsh, they having bine together at ye gouerners. She was asked what was ye reason William Andrewes came theither. She answered he never came late, nor did she let any come but aboute buisnes, & when ther buisnes was don she bid them be gone, and would not let them come in if it were late.

[245] ||Lancelot Fuller saith further that Mrs. Newman coming after to his wife, told her she were best hold her tongue or else it would bring out worse, for proofe Hanah Gregson testified that M^ris Newman said she was sorrey for what she had spoken and she could doe no more, if Goodwife Fuller were not satisfied she must goe w^thout satisfaction, adding that would bring out worse. For farther proofe, Abraham Kimberly vpon oathe testified, that goeing to Goodwife Fullers for a band, he heard some body talking, and standing still he saw M^ris Newman & heard her saye she was sorrey she had given such an offenc, or to that purpose. Goodwife Fuller said that would not serve. Mrs. Newman replyed if she would not take that for satisfaction she must goe w^thout satisfaction, & said yow were best let this dye, for feare least it bring out more. Lancelot Fuller further declared that when Francis Newman came to his wife to heale ye buisnes, (as probably he intended,) he made it worse, charging his wife wth things he cannot prove, first that she had made a proverb

& song of ye satisfaction his wife had given, wch his wife denyeth, & secondly Mr. Newman told Goodwife Fuller that she was onc brought to ye court for her tongue, and in a thretning manner said he would tame her tongue, for he knew well inough what she was, and for proofe brought Rebecka Gregson, who testified that Francis Newman coming to Goodwife Fullers told her she had made a proverbe & songe of his wives satisfaction. She said she had not. Mr. Newman affirmed she had, & said she was onc brought into ye court for her tongue and he would tame her tongue. Goody Fuller denyed that she was brought into ye court for her tongue, and told him she should haue scorned to haue told any lyes of them. Mr. Newman asked if he had told any lyes of her, she said his wife had, & he and his wife were one. Mr. Newman asked goodwife Fuller what satisfaction she would haue, she answered she desired to be cleared where she was wronged, and if any man of wisdome and judgment would say that was satisfaction wch was tendered, she would fall vnder all, she said she would have put vp that, if his wife, before others, had not spoken as if ther were some worse thing against her.

Francis Newman declared in court that vnderstanding from Mr. Higenson that Goodwife Fuller made a proverb of his wives satisfaction, he went to cleare it, told her what he had heard, that vpon her denyall it ended wth him, but she fell into high words. Rebecka Gregson testified that Mr. Newman bid Goodwife Fuller doe her worst & she bid him doe his worst, that Goodwife Fuller was high, but not so high as he.

Francis Newman complained that Goodwife Fuller said his wife was a lyar, and that she would scorne to goe vp & downe to cary lyes as they did, & when he asked what lyes he caryed vp & downe, she answered he and his wife were all one, wher-vpon he told her she was onc in ye court for her tongue, & if she would not rule her tongue he must haue it ruled, he now added that he apprhended her tongue was ye cause of he being brought into ye court. Goodwife Fuller declared what had passed betwixt Fra: Newman and her, & Mr. Newman answered, but both to ye same purpose, as is before expressed.

Lancelot Fuller to clere his wife aboute ye forementioned invitation, informed ye court y^t^ it was hmselfe (and not his wife) that invited Mr. Stone and M. Westerhouse wth him to breckfast, and it was by way of returne for intertainment & kindnes he received from Mr. Stone in ye Bay, and M. Westerhouse being p^r^sent testified in court, that Lanclot Fuller did invite Mr. Stone & himselfe to his house.

Vpon due consideration of ye p^r^mises, the court tooke notice of that passage wher Goodwife Fuller saith she would haue scorned to goe vp & downe wth lyes, &c. and that she would haue wrapt vp Mr. Newman in ye guilt, they told her it was from her pride and selfe confidenc, and that vsually leaues such to miscary, but in refferenc to the action as it hath bine opened & proved, they find that Mrs Newman was out of her way & breake rule in receiving a reproach against a neighbour from Mary Pery a girle, that ye spreading of it increased ye sinn, and tended to ye defamation of Goodwife Fuller, & that the satisfaction tendered was short of what the case required, not reaching to ye healing of her name so farr as she might [246] haue gone, || and that those after passages, if Goodwife Fuller were not satisfied she must goe w^t^hout satisfaction, and that she were best let this dye for feare it should bring out more or worse, were full of provocation and did increase ye offence. And for Mr. Newman, the court also found that he fell short of his duty, both in not pressing ye rule vpon his wife, that by due satisfaction the matter might have bine ended in private, and that himselfe instead of speaking healing words did vnnecessaryly provoake, in saying Goodwife was onc brought into ye court for her tongue, & that he would tame her tongue or must haue it ruled; ye court remembred ye passage aimed at, and that Goody Fuller, (then maid servant to M. Evanc) was plantife, they caused ye tryall of that action to be read, and found M. Newman was out of his way in making such vse of that suit in this case, when he should rather haue aplyed himselfe to make vp what was defective in his wives satisfaction, they therfore thought fitt and ordered, that Mr. Newman paye 5^l^ to Launclot Fuller & his wife, to repaire her in poynt of injury.

AT A COURT HELD AT NEWHAVEN THE 7th OF AUGUST, 1649.

Rogger Allen & John Brocket being both warned to watch neglected and came not. Rogger Allen being in court answered that it is true he had warning but forgott to tell ye man that he hired to watch for him. For Jno Brocket Mr. Evanc said he was wth him and sent this answer to the court, that he conceives he is exempted from watching by the court order, but Jno Brocket not being prsent and ye last order made aboute that not being in court, it was refferred till ye gouerner come home. For Rogger Allen the court ordered that he paye ye fine wch is 5s.

Nickholas Slooper for being found asleepe in ye meeting-house when hee should have bine vpon his watch was fined 2s 6d.

William Judson was fined because his man Jno Knight came not to trayne one squadron day, 2s 6d, for when his man would haue gone and told him it was time he wthheld him. He saith himselfe because he went to trayne ye day before when they trayned not because it rained, yet his man staied out till night, but was told he must looke to his man for that.

Mr. Rudderford & Phillip Galpin were appoynted to prise ye estate of Addam Beere a Duchman that dyed at William Andrewes, & yt an inventorie be brought in court.

Mr. Evanc hath sold to Mathew Moulthrop 4 acrs 26 rod of Mr. Trobridges first devission of land lying on ye west side.

Mr. Evanc hath sold to Mathias Hitchcocke 4 acrs 26 rod of Mr. Trobridges first devission of land lying on ye west side.

Mr. Evanc hath sold to William Ives, now possessed by William Basset, 4 acrs 26 rod of Mr. Trobridges first devission of land lying on ye west side.

William Basset passeth ouer to Robert Emry one house and barne somtime Edward Banisters, wth 6 acrs & ½ of vpland on this side ye West River in ye subverbes quarter, the front to ye west lane, ye reare to ye midle of ye quarter. And 3 acrs of meddowe in ye west meddow betweene Jno Clarke & Anthony Tompson, on end butting vpon ye West River, ye other end vpon ye quarter; and 30 ac^rs^ of vpland on ye other side of ye West River.

Jeremiah Osborne informed the court that Henry Pecke reported that their maide (Sarah Ollard,) was wth child by him ye said Jeremiah. Henry Pecke answered that such a report of ye maid was brought into his house as he tooke it vp, but vpon examination it proved to be but a supposition, and he reported that it was so, but he sees that it was his mistake and his sinn & is sorrey that he was so foolish to speake so, and for Jeremiah being the father of it, it was his mistake also, for he hearing some a talking of Jeremiah and the maide, tooke it vp that they spake of that matter and him to be ye father, but vpon examination it appeared they spake of no such thing, but that Jeremiah was to haue her, but vpon this mistake he reported it. He was asked whoe brought it to his house, he said goodwife Bunill. Goodwife Bunill said that she had said to goodwife Pecke that goodwife Charles wished ther was no more in ye towne in Rebecka Turners case, for ther was a maide that satt neere her at meeting that did bar-
[247] nish apace, || but she named nobody, nor could she tell who it was, and she said to goodwife Charles, if that be yor thoughts yow were best speake of it wher yow best may. Goodwife Charles, that she and Thomas Marshall (whoe was at worke at her house,) being speaking aboute Rebecka Turner, what a sad thing it was, she said it is well if ther be no more in her case, she remembers no more that she saide. Henry Pecke was asked if he had any witnes that could cleare it that either of these women was ye auther of this report, he said he had none. The plantifs hauing also spoken what they would in ye case, the court proceeded to sentence, and ordered that Henry Pecke paye to Jeremiah Osborne & Sarah Ollard for ye wrong he hath done them 5^l^, wch is to be devided betwixt them.

Mr. Crane complained of Samuell Whithead for leaving open ther quarter gate, he owned the thing, but said ye fenc was downe aboute it. Mr. Crane sd true, and was fined for it, and ye gate also because catle came in at it. The court declared themselues that they could not alter the generall courts order, and therfore Samuel Whithead must paye for this miscariag 5[s].

AT A COURT HELD AT NEWHAVEN THE 4[th] OF SEPTEMBER, 1649.

The last will and Testament of Edward Banister (deceased) was p[r]sented in court,* made the 8[th] of May, 1649, confirmed by his owne hand and witnessed by Richard Miles, William Andrewes & Jn[o] Nash, whoe now in court tooke oath that the said Edward Banister being in good vnderstanding and memory as farr as they could judg, did make this wrighting now p[r]sented in court to w[c]h their hands are subscribed, his last will and testament. Also the inventory of y[e] estate of the said Edward Banister was p[r]sented in court, amounting to 66[l]: 04: 00, made the 21[th] of May, 1649, prised by Richard Miles, William Andrewes and John Nash, vpon oath for y[e] valew of the goodes, and Ellen Banister widdow and executrix of y[e] last will & testament of her deceased husband, tooke oath that his whole estate, to y[e] best of her light and knowledg is conteyned in y[e] ꝑcells and ꝑticulars mentioned & prised in the said inventorie.

The court granted to William Davis administration vpon y[e] estate of James Hayward deceased, and he accepted it and delivered into y[e] court an inventorie of the estate of the said James Hayward, amounting to 00: 4: 7[d], beside 59: 0: 0 in y[e] ship Fellowship, prised by William Andrewes, Thomas Munson, Thomas Kimberly and Thomas Wheeler jun[r], vpon oath for y[e] vallew of it. And William Davis y[e] administrator tooke oath that y[e] whole estate of James Hayward, to the best

---

* The last will and testament of Edward Banister late of New Haven deceased, made 8th of May, 1649.

He gives his daughter ten pounds more than his wife, his daughter to receive her portion when she is sixteen years of age—makes his wife executrix, and elder Newman and Francis Newman overseers of his will.

Goodman Miles is to have his daughter to bring her up till she is sixteen years of age—his wife and the overseers to have the dispose of her marriage—if his daughter die before she come to sixteen years of age, her portion to return to her mother; if they both die without a lawful heir, then it shall go to the churches use. The mark of Edward Banister, witnesses, Richard Miles, William Andrewes, John Nash, the mark of Thomas Wheeler.

of his light and knowledg, is conteyned in ye pcells & pticulars mentioned and prised in the said inventory.*

Mr. Samuel Goodanhousen was called to give in security for the portions of his wives chilldren. Hee said he had paide Mr. Yale 35l, wch he accepted for full satisfaction for his wives portion, and for Thomas Meekes he is willing to accept of the house and 19 acrs of land next the towne (lying by ye necke highway) for ye portion of Rebecka Turner, now his wife, and Thomas Meekes declared in court that he is willing to accept of ye said 19 acrs of land, be it more or less & ye house & home lott & barne at towne, in full satisfaction for his wives portion, and Mr. Goodanhouse did now in court pass the house, home lot & barne, and the said 19 acrs of land, be it more or less, wch was Capt. Turners, and Thom Meekes accepted it for full satisfaction.

For the rest of the chilldrens portions, the court refferred Mr. Goodanhousen till ye next court, that he might consider wth his wife aboute it, for the portions of ye chilldren doe come to more then 35l a pec, according to ye order, the estate being as it is, and then the court will consider of it againe.

The portions of Mris Goodyeares chilldren were allso considered of, but some difficulty appearing, it was respited to ye next court, and in ye meane time Mr. Goodyeare was desired to confere wth the gouerner & Mr. Evanc to prepare it for ye next court, yt the estate may be equally devided, that the

---

* Date of the inventory not given.

Carpenters tools and lumber, prised by Thomas Munson, William Andrewes, sum £57, 18, 7.

Debts due to the estate—From Derrecke Johnson £10, 10, from Mr. Goodyear £16, 19, from William Holt £1, 8, 4, from Jeremiah Osborne £0, 7, from Ephraim Penington £0, 3, from Richard Beech £0, 16, from John Beech £0, 5, 11, from Thomas Moris £0, 16, 8, besides his part in the ship Fellowship £59.

The Estate of James Hayward is Debtor—To Mr. Evans £4, 11, 10, to John Jackman £0, 10, to John Gibbs £0, 18, to Jeremiah Whitnel £0, 18, to Thomas Johnson £0, 4, to Henry Glover £3, 13, 7, to the smith at Stratford £0, 3, to Robert Usher £3, to Phillip Leeke £5, to John Tompson £1, 18, to widow Preston £0, 5, to John Harriman £0, 10, 6, to Richard Williams £0, 12, to Richard Webb £0, 5, 3, to John Tompson, farmer £0, 1, to William Fowler £0, 9, 6, to Ralph Dayton £0, 5, 6, to William Davis £2, 3, to John Moss of Boston £4 to Mr. Ting of Boston, for a but of wine £12, 10, to Edward Fletcher of Boston £4, 15, 9, to Thomas Munson £0, 2, 6, to William Pecke £0, 4, 6, to the ferryman £0, 1, 4, to Thomas Osborne £2, 2, to Henry Bristow £0, 6, to Benjamin Willmot £0, 3, to Mr. Gibbard £0, 14, 7, to Mr. Crane £0, 4, to Mr. Hooke £0, 5, 3, to Mr. Atwater £6, 7, 8, to John Basset £0, 2. Court charges £0, 6. Total £57, 12, 9.

mother and the chilldren may haue ther due proportions, both in the better & more hazardous pts of the estate.

Mr. Gibbard & Richard Miles, calling Thom Moris to them, were desired to prise the estate of Adam Beere a Duchman w^c^h dyed at William Andrewes, and to bring the inventorie of it into the court, according to order.

Thomas Munson tooke oath that ye apprism^t^ he made of Robert Prestons goods or estate was justly done.

AT A GENERALL COURT HELD AT NEWHAUEN THE 10th OF SEPTEMBER, 1649.

The Governer acquainted the court w^t^h the rumores he heares concerning the Indians and allso w^t^h what Thomas Stanton brought in way of returne from them, in w^c^h answers and cariages ther pride and insolencie appeared, so that he conceives it is not safe for the towne to goe on in ther watch as it was last ordered, but that some other manner of watch be setled for ye p^r^sent, and likewise that ye gaurd be doubled on ye Lords dayes and lecture dayes, and that men whose turne it is not to bring armes, yet bring ther swords.

The court considered of the things propounded, and refferred the whole ordering of these matters and what else is necessary to ye pticular court and ye sarjants joyned w^t^h them.

[248] || The Gouerner also informed the court that ther is need that a generall court be called for ye jurisdiction & therfore deputies must be chosen for this towne, and accordingly Mr. Crane and Francis Newman were chosen deputies for ye next generall jurisdiction court, and to continew as deputies for that service vpon any ocasion, till ye chusing of deputies for the generall jurisdiction court to be held in May next.

The Gouerner further informed the court that Sarjant Munson is aboute goeing to Connecticote, to staye their this winter, therfore the court maye consider whether it be safe for ye towne to lett him goe, seeing Sarjant Andrewes is not at home. The court thought it not fitt that he should now goe, but desired the gouerner to informe them at Connecticote whom it concernes, that it is not his neglect but the towne hinders him for publique respects.

It is ordered that next fourth day ther be a view of armes in ye morning before lecture, and trayning in ye afternoone if it be faire, and if not, that then the trayning be the next second day following.

AT A GENERALL COURT FOR NEWHAVEN THE 24th OF SEPTEMBER, 1649.

Jno Ponderson, Jno Moss & Nickholas Elsy had libbertie to depart the court.

The Governer acquainted the court that the generall jurisdiction court have thought meete that provission be made and in a readines for our defenc against the Indians,* and for a goeing forth of men, if ther be ocasion, though they know not what will be don till they haue advised wth other colonies, for wch purpose letters are sent to them, but for ye better makeing provission for ourselues, they haue laid a rate vpon the jurisdiction, of 200l, of which Newhaven is to paye 93l: 16s: 00d, beside ther pte of ther former rate, wch was 70l: 07s: 00d, both wch are to be paide now prsently, vizd: one halfe by the first of October next, the other halfe by the first of November next following, to be paid either in money, beavour, good wampom, or in wheat at 4s, 6d, pease or rye at 3s: 6d, Indian corne at 2s: 6d, beefe or porke as they can agree wth the treasurer. The court considered of what is propounded, and ordered that 1 year and a halfe rate be paide forthwth, beside the ordinary rate due in October next.

---

* The general court of Connecticut, Sept. 13, 1649, taking into serious consideration what might be done according to God in way of revenge of the blood of John Whittmore late of Stamford, and well weighing all circumstances together with the cariage of the Indians bordering thereupon, in and about the premises, declared themselves that they judged it lawful, and according to God, to make war upon them, they therefore desired the deputy governor, Mr. Ludlow and Mr. Talcott to ride the next day to New Haven, and confer with Mr. Eaton and the rest of the magistrates there about sending out against the Indians, and on Sept. 18th they sent out 45 men to assist the colony of New Haven. These spirited measures appear to have had the desired effect. The Indians at Stamford it seems soon became peaceable.

Trumb. Col. Rec. Conn. i. 197. Trumb. Conn. i. 192.

Further the gouerner informed the court that those whom they appointed to order the watch and other things of that nature, haue done it, and for the prsent while these dangers of ye Indians continew, they thinke that the watch must consist of 9 men, that is 8 and a watch master, all wch are to be at ye place appointed halfe an hower of sunsett at furthest, and ye watch to be sett an hower after sunsett, and that 4 be sent to walke the rounds on pte of ye night, and ye other at ye court of gaurd keepe sentinell in ther course, and the other 4 walke ye other pt of ye night, and them that first walked keepe sentinell. The other orders of ye watch, when it consisted of 7 men, standing still in force. They also thinke that two squadrons com wth ther armes vpon ye Saboth and other meeting dayes, and that those whose turne it is not to bring armes, yett bring ther swords, and for neglect of bringing ther swords should paye 12d a time. They haue further ordered that 20 cotton quilted coates, and 20 boxes for cartrages, and 20 knapsackes, at ye townes charge. Care also is taken to gett lead that bullits may be made for ye townes service.

The drumer was ordered to beate the drum every morning, halfe an hower before day, wthin ye square of ye markit place and in some of ye streetes, and that the last watch call him an hower before day and walke wth him as a gaurd while he continewes beating.

The drumer was ordered not to beate the drum in ye day time vpon his owne ocasions, that men that are abroade may not be disturbed wth feares of an alarum when ther is none, onely tomorrow and the day following he hath libbertie to beate, to fitt vp a drum for Stamford.

It is ordered that hencforward, during the troubles and dangers wth and from ye Indians, if any pson or psons (hauing ocasion to be abroade in or aboute the towne after the watch is sett, wch shall be at furthest wthin an hower after the sunn is sett every night,) being required by ye sentinell or any of ye watchmen wch shall be appointed to walke ye rounds to stand, and shall refuse so to doe, but shall vpon the first call runn away or indeavour to hide themselues or shifte from the watch, or vpon the second or third call of any of ye watchmen, sentinel or other, shall not stand & speake w^t^h the watch, that he or they may bee knowne and examined if ther be cause, but shall afront the watch and make from them, the sentinell or watchmen in such case, to secure the towne from danger, and ꝑticularly from Indian stratagems and mischeife, are to shoote at him or them that so stubbornly and suspitiously cary themselues, and if they receive any hurt, they haue brought it vpon themselues, and the watchmen in such cases shall be accounted innocent, hauing done nothing but what ther trust and duty calls for.

It is further ordered that if those that walke the rounds shall discover any danger by Indians or fire, & shoote of
[249] though but one gunn, it shall be answered ||by the sentinel, and ye drum to beate, w^c^h is to lye at the prison, and Nathaniel Kimberly to beate it vpon such ocasion. The watch is also to cry arme, arme, or fire, fire, as the danger is, this to be taken by the towne as an alarum, or if ye watch should be hindered of shooting and yett cry as before, the sentinel is to shoote & another pec at ye court of gaurd, & ye drum beate, that ye towne may be raysed to secure themselues.

The Gouerner informed the court that the jurisdiction had ordered that the matters to be caryed on by a counsell of warr, they left to himselfe and ye magistrats and whome else he should call into them, w^c^h the court approved and confirmed.

It is ordered that 20 of ye pikes that may be most fitt for it, should be cut to make 20 halfe pikes of.

It is desired that the farmers aboute this towne would consider how to provide for ther owne safety in this time of danger, and that neither they nor any other leave armes in ther houses vnless they hide them, least ye Indians breake in and steale them; and that men would be carfull not to leave their armes carelesly in ye meeting house or elswhere.

It was propounded that some wood might be provided for ye watch. The sarjants were desired to inquire who hath not wrought in ye markit place, that they might cut some wood out, and in ye meane time ye treasurer was to provide a loade.

It was propounded that some pannels or packsadles might be provided.

It was desired that men would be spareing in shooting of gunns in the towne, least they should make those abroade thinke ther was an alarum.

The watch was desired in ther walking ye rounds not to talke as they goe.

It is ordered that a man being put into ye watch, if he hire another to watch for him, it shall be such a one as ye master of the watch shall alowe of, and that he give the watchmaster notice beforehand, that if he like not ye man he may haue time to provide another, wch if ye master of ye watch is put to doe, it must be at ye watchmans charge, thoughe he give double paye and ye fine of totall absenc beside, if he neglect to send a sufficient man or to give due notice, and ye watchmasters were desired to see that they send not out two youthes together, but that one be a man in whom they may repose trust.

It is ordered that vpon ye dayes of publique meeting, a sentinel should stand vpon the meeting house to discover any danger that may be, and that every night on of ye watchmen be sent vp ther two or three times to looke aboute and make discovery of any danger by fire or Indians, or other danger that may be espied. And Thomas Munson & Jervice Boykin were desired to mend ye ladder that they goe vp vpon and ye floure, both goeing to it and landing from it.

It was thought fitt that when men shall goe forth against the Indians, y^t^ our Indians be sent for and warned not to come to or aboute ye towne but vpon their perill.

It was propounded and debated that some course might be taken that fences might be made better, that swine might goe abroade; that some feild might be onely for planting Indian corne, and not plant Indian and English together; that ye fenc might be brought to a less quantity, that men might ye better maintayne them. The court considered of the things, and thought they were weightie and of great concernmt to the towne, therfore ordered to chuse a comittee to consider and debate these things privatly and prepare it against another court. The comittee chosen is the pticular court, and one out of each quarter, viz[d], Mr. Tuttill, John Coopr, William Judson, Robert Johnson, Mr. Wakeman, William Davis, Samuel Whithead, Henry Lindall, Thomas Nash & Francis Browne.

---

[250] AT A COURT HELD AT NEWHAUEN THE 2th OF OCTOBER, 1649.

Mathew Camfeild was fined for want of some powder last viewing day 12[d], and for not bringing his armes to meeting one lecture day, 2[s] 6[d].

Henry Pecke and Thomas Marshall for not bringing ther armes to y[e] meeting on day when it was their turne, was fined each man, 2[s] 6[d].

Widdow Tompson tooke oath that the inventory she formerly delivered in to the court, of her late husband, Anthony Tompsons estate, was a just and true inventorie, to y[e] best of her light and knowledge.

Richard Miles, William Tompson and Mathew Camfeild tooke oath that they prised the goods conteyned in y[e] same inventorie justly, according to the best of ther light and knowledge.

William Basset for coming late to his watch was fined 12[d].

Luke Atkinson being hired to watch for William Tompson, and hauing seasonable warning, yet came to late, was fined 12[d].

Robert Meaker for refusing to watch when he was warned was fined 5[s].

Sarjant Munson was complained of for neglecting to give out the bills of y[e] watches in his squadron in season, wherby the watch could not be full one night, and he seeing and confessing it was his mistake, told y[e] master of y[e] watch he would come downe & see y[e] watch made vp, but did not, nor can tell any reason w[ch] might justly hinder his coming. The court considered of his miscariage herein, and ordered that he paye as a fine to y[e] towne, 6[s] 8[d].

John Bud passeth ouer to William Tompson a pcell of land

lying in ye quarter called Mr. Lambertons quarter, w^thin the two mile, conteyning 35 ac^{rs}, be it more or less, bounded on ye east wth the sea, the subverbes quarter on ye west, betwixt of William Jeanes and Thomas Lampson. Also 17 ac^{rs} of meddow lying on ye Indian side, bounded by the sea on ye west & north, Thomas Lamsons meddow on ye east, and ye Indians land on ye south.

Thomas James passeth ouer to Richard Hull 6 ac^{rs} 1 quarter of meddow lying at y^e bottom of y^e necke next y^e East River, and 5 acres, a halfe & 20 rod of vpland lying in y^e Yorksheir quarter by the towne side, y^e other side lying next Mr. Yales lott, the one end butting vpon Robert Johnsons lott; and 5 ac^{rs} $\frac{1}{2}$ 20 rod on y^e other side the West River, w^thin y^e two mile; and halfe his proprietie in his second devission, not yet laid out.

Thomas James allso passeth ouer to Robert Johnson the same proportion of meddow and vpland as before exprest to Richard Hull, butted & bounded as y^t is.

Robert Johnson, because he wanted some match, was fined 12^d.

John Knight, because his wrest was broake and his gunn rusty, so that they were both vnservicable, was fined 5^s.

James Russell, because he wanted some match, was fined 12^d.

John Walker, because his mans wrest was too short, was fined 12^d.

Henry Bristow, because the scabbard of his sword was broke so that the point came out, wch is dangerous, was fined 12^d.

Richard Hull, because his sonn Jeremiah wanted worme & scourer, fined 12^d.

Edward Granest, for want of worme, scourer & flints, was fined 18^d.

Benjamin Willmot, for want of some bullits, fined 12^d.

Jeremiah Watts, for want of flints & a socket for his gunnsticke, fined 12^d.

James Clements, for want of 2^l of bullits & a scourer, fined 2^s 6^d.

Samuel Hodgkins, for goeing into ye watch-house and lying downe by the fire and sleeping, when he should have stood sentinel, was fined 5s, and is not to watch for any man but himselfe.

John Bishop & Joseph Watters, for sleeping in ther watch, was fined each of them 2s 6d, and John Bishop, for sleeping at another time in ye watch, fined 2s 6d.

Jeremiah Osborn was fined 2s because he wanted 7 yards of match, & is injoyned to provide himselfe forthwth.

Thomas Osborn senior, because the scabbard of his owne sword & of his sonn Johns allso, was fined 2s.

Richard Perey passeth ouer to Thomas Kimberly his house & barne, & home lott, conteyning 2 acrs ½, and 18 acrs ½ of land in ye necke, and Thomas Kimberly is to haue 20s out of ye rent Mr. Malbon is to paye for that pte of the barne wch he hires this yeare.

[251] James Clements & Nickholas Slooper were complained of for vnfaithfullnes in the watch, and for plotting and contriving to make & maintayne a lye to hide & cover this ther willfull miscariage, for Richard Hull being mr of ye watch, would not haue had them two goe forth together, but they seemed not satisfied vnless they might goe together, hauing, as he conceiveth, bine plotting the former part of ye night, (when he observed them buisie in private talke,) what to doe, so he resolved to lett them goe together & watch them to see what they would doe, and aboute 12 a clocke in ye night he sent them forth; they said they would goe downe Mr. Eatons streete, he himselfe followed them and saw them goe directly downe the other streete to Thomas Meekes his house, and went in at ye gate; afterward he returned to ye court of gaurd and called Robert Tamadge, and they two walked aboute ye towne and mett aboute Robert Bassets but saw them not. After they cam in againe and sent forth Robert Tamadge & Jno Bishop towards morning, for ye day starr was pretty high, and they goeing downe the same streete, when they came neere aboute Richard Becklyes house they saw them coming, and heard James Clements say that they would make them beleeve they had walked the rounds two or three times, and accordingly when they came to ye watch-

house, James began to speake discontentedly that they were put to walke so long, as if he would haue outfaced the master and watchmen also, but they being caled to answer before ye court to this charged vpon them, James Clements at first denyed ye charge and said they did goe downe Mr. Eatons street and walked the rounds, but Slooper being examined said they went to Thomas Meekes his yard to eat peaches, and after they both confessed they staide vnder ye barne side because it was warme, thoughe they both say they walked onc vp to Thomas Wheelers and staide a while vnder ye pailes. They was asked why they agreed together to make and tell such a lye, to hide and cover ther vnfaithfullnese in such a trust comitted to them, and that in this time of danger.

Slooper said he did not first move it, and James at first said he remembers not that he spake such words, but it being testifyed by Robert Tamadge & John Bishop, he owned ye thing, and sd he confeseth it was his fault, and it was from ye guilt of his conscienc and working of Sathan, and he desires to be humbled before God for it.

The sentenc of ye court is, that for this miscariage of theirs they be both whipped.

Mr. Eaton informed the court that he sometime lett his farme to Robert Emry and Richard Webb, but Robert Emry grewe weary and Richard Webb was very earnest to haue it himselfe, and did take it vpon ye former termes, but he kept not ye covenants, wherevpon Mr. Eaton told Richard Webb, if he would not put in securitie to keepe his covenants, he must leave the farme. Richard Webb at first was vnwilling, but after consented to leave the farme, and they both agreed to refferre matters of differenc to Jasper Crane and Richard Miles. After Richard Webb desired Henry *Henry* Lendall might be added, and the gouerner was content; but beside ther is a clear debte of 14l 16s 07d, due from Richard Webb to Mr. Eaton, as appeares vpon accounts made vp betwixt them, but when those three before mentioned had considered things and drawne vp ye result of ther thoughts, Richard Webb was vnsatisfied & said it should come to the court.

Richard Webb said he ownes the debte of 14l 16s 07d, but

his cattle are attached that he cannot sell them to paye the debte. Hee was told that if w^t^hin 10 dayes he can procure a chapman to buy so many of his catle as will paye this debt to the gouerner, he shall haue his libbertie to make the best of so many of them, for ye rest the attachment is to stand till other differences be issued. Richard Webb declared himselfe freely willing to it, and said it should be done.

Hee was further told that if it was not don in ye time appointed, Mr. Crane and Richard Miles are ordered by this court to haue ye catle looked vp at his charge, and prise so many of them as will paye this debt, to w^c^h he agreed also.

Richard Webb further said that for ye other differences he doubted not but if the arbytrators would meete once againe they should issue all matters, wherupon the court desired them that they would take a litle more paines in it. They were very vnwilling, yett were perswaded, desiring that Mr. Evanc might be p^r^sent, whoe being a magistrate, might if ther was cause give oath to the witnesses. To this the gouerner agreed and desired it might be so, and Richard Webb promised before the court to stand to what issue these arbytrators should put to it, as the gouerner had declared himselfe sundry times before. This Richard Webb promised should be done betwixt this & the next court, at his care and charge, else it must come to the court againe whoe will then issue it.

---

[252] AT A GENERALL COURT HELD AT NEWHAUEN THE 8th OF OCTOBER, 1649.

The Gouerner acquainted the court that the comittee they appointed to consider aboute fences and swine have mett twice, and doe thinke that swine may have libbertie to goe abroade for a month or 6 weekes, now while akehornes last, being well and sufficiently ringed and approved of by one whome the court may appointe for that service. They thinke also that fences may be reduced to a less quantitie, and that that w^c^h is vpheld should be maintayned substantiall & sufficient against hoggs or any other catle. They thinke that every mans swine should be marked and the marke of them brought into a place $w^{c}h$ the court shall appointe, $w^{t}h$ every mans name to his marke, vnder such a fine as y^{e} court shall thinke fitt.

The court considered of the severall things propounded, and ordered that for 6 weekes from this day all swine, whether belonging to farmes or towne, shall haue libbertie to goe abroade, being well and sufficiently ringed, $w^{t}h$ on ringe in y^{e} midle of y^{e} nose, $w^{c}h$ shall either be done by Jno Coopr, or approved of by him, whoe is to be vnder oath to doe faithfully therein. And whatever swine shall be found abroade, aboue 12 weekes old after this day vnringed, or not sufficiently ringed, the owner shall pay for every swine 12^{d} for each default, and for them that are vnder 12 weekes old, the damage that they doe, if it be required. They further order that every man marke his swine and bring in his marke, $w^{t}h$ his name, to Jno Coopr. And if after this day any mans swine be found abroade vnmarked, to pay 3^{s} 4^{d}, according to y^{e} jurisdiction court order, and if not brought in to Jno Coopr, 12^{d} a swine, and whatever swine shall doe damage in meddowes, the owner of y^{e} swine shall paye the damage, because it is supposed if they were well ringed they could doe none ther.

And it is further ordered, that if after 6 weekes time swine shall goe abroade and doe damage, (thoughe ringed) the owner of y^{e} swine shall paye it, vnless he can prove the fence was downe wher they went in, then y^{e} owner of y^{e} fenc to beare it.

It is ordered that all the fences $w^{c}h$ the severall quarters shall agree to vphold and maintayne, shall betwixt this and y^{e} first of May next, be made substantial and stronge, both against swine and other catle, and if after swine (though ringed,) shall be found in any quarter or corne feild, the owner of y^{e} swine must beare all damage, and if he can finde any fenc downe where they did or might come in, he may releive himselfe from y^{e} fence, as in case of other catle formerly ordered, but if no fenc be found downe it is supposed they swime y^{e} rivers ($w^{c}h$ must be at y^{e} owners perill,) $w^{c}h$ are supposed and alowed for a fenc in this case.

It is ordered that after on yeere no man shall plant Indian

corne in any quartr by small spotts or pcells to y^e^ prejudice of y^e^ quarter vnless it be by joynt consent.

It is ordered that when ther shall be a meeting warned by any quarter or quarters, the severall proprietors therin haueing had 24 howers warning, if any of them shall neglect to come to such meeting, the major pte of ye quarter being together, may & haue power from this court to conclude of any thing wch is for the publique good of ye quarters, proprietie of land or other pticular interest of that nature excepted. And for the more orderly carying on of such meetings it is thought fitt and ordered, that when any of ye Yorksheire quarter, Mr. Wakemans quarter or Mr. Goodyears quarter, shall see cause of a meeting, they shall repaire to Mr. Goodyeare and inform him of ye cause of such meeting, and if Mr. Goodyeare see cause, he shall give order to haue a meeting warned. The same is for ye subverbes quarter and Mr. Lambertons quarter, and if any of Mr. Eatons quarter, Mr. Dauenports quarter or Oyster shell feild, thinke ther is neede of a meeting, they shall repaire to ye gouerner and informe him, and if he see cause he shall order a meeting to be warned. And for Mr. Ro: Newmans quarter & that next wher Mr. Ceffinch lives, they shall repaire to Mr. Robert Newman, and if he thinkes ther is cause of a meeting he shall order one to be warned. But it is desired that care may be taken that not any two of these meetings be warned vpon on day, because some men haue land in severall quarters.

The court granted to Lancelot Fuller the land lately granted to Jonathan Marsh, out of Mr. Roes lot, vpon ye same conditions he had it, provided that they agree together that ye rates for the time past be pd w^t^hout trouble to ye treasurer.

The Gouerner acquainted the court that ther is a differenc betwixt this towne & Totoket in ye bounds of ye lands betwixt vs & them, wch is to be reffered to arbytration. They haue chosen Mr. Disbrowe and Mr. Leete of Guilford, and this towne must chuse two out of another towne. The court agreed and chose Capt. Astwood & Mr. Tapp of Milford, & doe desire y^m^ for this service.

Leivtenant Seely was desired to remember when ye magistrats come to ye court, to speake that the bounds betwixt Milford and vs may be sett forth w^t^hout delaye.

The comittee chosen the 10th of March last to consider aboute rates were ordered to meete vpon the fourth day next, at three a clocke, that the buisnes aboute rates comitted to them may be forthw^t^h issued.

[253] ‖ At a meeting of the pticular court in a private way the 6th of October, 1649, Thomas Whitway of Totoket charged 3 men, viz. the two Bartlets & on Hegbe, a young man, that they lying at Totoket or nere theraboute w^t^h ther boate to mend it as they said, did shoote at and kill on of his the sd Thom Whitwayes swine, w^c^h came downe to feed at ye watter side. They confessed they had so done, but said they was in want of provission and did it to supply ther neede, though that appeared not, because they had Indian corne aboarde & some chese. They said also that they intended to paye him for it, but though they had time they did not any way acquainte him w^t^h it, till Thomas Whitway mising one of his hoggs & inquiring after it was told by Mr. Swaines sonn Samuell, that he suspected these men had killed it, whervpon he went to search the boate, & hauing first inquired of them for his swine, they said they saw none that day, but the day before they saw some w^c^h went that way, but said not a word that they had killed on of them till he told them he suspected they had killed on of them & he was come to search for it; then they said he need not search, they had it.

The court considered of the miscariag and it appeared very foule, and they could not judg it any less then plaine theft, & therfore ordered that the two Bartlets & this Hegbe pay to Thomas Whitway double for his hogg, (w^c^h was by him, & they owned it, vallewd at 23^s^,) that they allso pay Thomas Whitwayes charges, w^c^h he saith is 5^s^, and y^t^ they pay to ye marshall for his time & trouble aboute ye buisnes 3^s^ : 4^d^, & if Thomas Whitway should refuse to take the other 23 for himselfe, yet he must take it and give it to ye poore of that towne, and so be accountable for it.

At a Generall Court held at Newhauen the 15th of October, 1649.

The Gouerner acquainted the court that the comittee they appointed to consider aboute rates haue mett twice and considered of it, and in debate it was inquired how rates are caried one in other places, and to give light in the case, the law for carying one publique rates in ye Massachusets, wch is now in print, was read & considered, (wch was now also read in court,) and the comittee therin also advising wth the elders thought the way just and that it might suit vs and be followed here, onely they leave it to ye courts consideration whether houses and houshold goods should be rated, and for tradesmen they thinke something should be done that may be equall in waye of rateing them for their trades.

The court considered and debated sundry things in ye order, and in ye issue concluded and ordered, that the order of ye Massachusets for publique rates should be an order heare in this towne, except in case of houses and household goodes, wch the court orders shall be forborne and not rated for this next yeare, but if any man haue a house that he letts for rent, it is to be vallewed at a moderate price, and if any servant come oute of England at lowe wages, it is left to the comittee to consider wheither his master or he shall paye his polle money. And seeing that labourers and handycrafe trades & seamen are of divers sorts & conditions, some live more comfortably, some less, some follow ther trades more & some less, ther time being taken vp more aboute husbandry wch payes another way, that therfore a due consideration be had, and every man justly rated as neere as the comittee can judge, and that other men whoe trade in way of merchandizing bee duely rated according to ther trades and stockes they improve, as neere as they can judge. And for makeing the matter the more easie to the comittee, the court further ordered, that seing the prise of catle are already sett in ye Massachusets order and now confirmed by this court, so allso they now set the price of all lands belonging to this towne for ye yeare ensuing, vizd, 1d an acer for all vpland fenced in, the necke also included, and 1d an ac^{r} for all meddowes that any man hath a proprietie in. And that betwixt, and ye fourth day at night next, every man, both at towne and farmes, shall bring in to ye men appointed for ye quarter wher they live, or to w^{c}h they belong, how many catle they have of every sort aboue 1 yeare old, swine & other. Allso what catle they haue killed already this yeare, and how many ac^{rs} of land they haue fenced in in any place belonging to this towne, house lott or other, w^{t}h the quarter where it lyes, also what meddow & what in ye necke, vpon ye penaltie of 2^{s} : 6^{d} for each default. And to hasten the buisnes, (because ye yeares rate ordered to be pd the first of Nouember next is now ordered to be pd by men as they shall be vallewd this way,) the court chose a comittee w^{c}h are hereafter mentioned, whoe are to meete vpon the 6th day next at 4 a clocke in ye afternoone, to consider & drawe vp ye severall rates w^{c}h they thinke every man should paye, and then to p^{r}sent it to ye gouerner and magistrats, whoe are to consider of it, and, if they finde it just, pass it, but if neede be, vpon any mans just complainte, they haue power to releive him.

The comittee chosen for this worke of rateing are two men out of each quarter, viz^{d}, Mr. Tuttill, Francis Newman, Mr. Gilbert, Mr. Crane, Leivtenant Seely, Henry Lendall, Richard Miles, William Davis, Mr. Wakeman, William Fowler, Mr. Atwater, Mr. Powell, William Judson, Mr. Ceffinch, Mr. Ling, William Andrewes, William Tompson, Samuell Whithead, Thomas Munson, Francis Browne.

John Basset was spared from watching for ye p^{r}sent because he is lame by a fall that he had, so that he cannot watch himselfe nor worke to inable him to hire, but promiseth if God inable him to his laboure he shall hire a man.

[254] || The Gouerner read to ye court the order made in ye Baye aboute baker, w^{c}h the court approved of and ye bakers were desired to consider of it against another court.

The order made ther concerning customs sett on wines was allso read, but respited.

Mr. Evanc desired that Jeremiah How might haue libbertie to brew beare to sell.

It was desired by some that ye watches might be lessened, but the court voted that they should continew as they are.

At a Court held at Newhauen the 6th of Nouember, 1649.

Mathias Hitchcocke for refusing to watch when he was sent for by the sarjant to supplye another mans place, according to order, was fined 5^s.

Thomas Osborn $senio^r$ for absenc at two generall courts as himselfe saith, was fined two shillings.

John Cooꝑr complained of Thomas Osborne for letting 4 hoggs of his goe abroad in y^e summer for the most ꝑt, contrary to order. Thom Osborne could not deney it. The court ordered that he paye to John Cooꝑr 12^d a hogg, wch is 4^s. Further John Cooꝑr complained of him for not carying in to ye man appointed for ther quarter, the number of ye ac^{rs} of land he planted or sowed last yeere, as it was ordered he should. The court ordered that he paye to John Cooꝑr the double as it was ordered in that case, wch is 4^d ꝑ ac^r.

John Cooꝑr complained of David Atwatter and William Wooden that their hoggs went abroad in ye summer contrary to order, and that they haue not bine ringed, according to ye last order, *till* now w^thin this two or three dayes. The court witnessed against their disorderly walking, and they are to paye to John Cooꝑr for each swine wch he found abroade of theirs, 12^d, and for each swine not ringed & marked according to order 12^d.

John Tompson was complained of for suffering his hoggs to goe abroad in the summer contrary to order, and that they haue not bine ringed according to the last order. John Tompson said it was before he had charge of them that Jno Cooꝑr tooke them, and offered his owne, his wives & Jno Wakefeilds and his wives oathes to cleere it. The governer said if they would all testifie that vpon oath he would paye it, so that that ꝑte was refferred as not cleere. But the court ordered that what hoggs John Cooꝑr hath taken of John Tomꝑsons abroad contrary to order, at other times, or not ringed & marked according to the last order, he should paye to John Coopr 12d a pece.

Edward Parker desired that he might be freed from his ingagment concerning the house & lott, and land wch was John Potteres and is securitie for the chilldrens portions, for he is willing to leave it to the court to dispose of otherwise. He was wished to call vpon ye secretary to search for ye agreement concerning that matter, and come to ye gouerner to prepare it for the court.

Mr. Leete and Mr. Jordan atturneyes for ye towne of Guilford, declareth against Thomas Standish of Wethersfeild for certaine rates due to the towne of Guilford from ye said Thom Standish for a lott he possesseth their, wch rates, beside what is due towardes ministers maintaynanc, is aboute 57s. Thomas Standish said he had nothing to doe wth the rates, he changed his lott away, and hee that had it vndertooke to paye the rates, and he tendered them and they would not be received.

Mr. Leete replyed that the court hath bine acquainted wth the nature of ye exchange in Wrights case of Guilford, and haue judged it a nullitie. They were asked if Thom Standish was admitted a planter that he might know ther was such an order in ye towne that lotts should be sold to none but such as ye towne approved of. They answered that he desired not to be a planter, but if he had they had nothing against it but he might, but for his knowing of ye order, Mr. Jordan testefied that he acquainted him wth it, and that the towne would not accept of Wright to possesse such accomodations as a lott of 500l, for he was not able to paye the rates of a 50l lott, much less would he of one of 500l, this Mr. Jordan would haue taken oath of, but Thomas Standish deneyed it not, but said they required rates yett improved ye land. Mr. Leete said no, but ye case was this, that ther being a pece of meddowe of Thom Standishes wch laye amonge other meddowe, and none appearing for Thom Standish to devide, the other made vse of some of it, but yett Thom Standish cannot saye wch pte is his.

The court hauing heard what both pties haue or would say, ordered that Thomas Standish paye to ye towne of Guilford the rates due to them for ye lott he hath ther, beside ye charges of this court, & to doe it p^r^sently or give security to doe it, that ye court be not further troubled aboute it.

[255] || John Budd paseth ouer to Richard Hull 7½ ac^rs^ of land in ye necke, and 1¾ ac^rs^ at Oyster poynt.

Richard Hull paseth ouer to John Budd 11¾ ac^rs^ 4 rod of land in ye second devission on ye west sid betwixt the land of John Budd & William Jeanes.

Richard Webb was called & asked if he had attended the last courts order and his owne promise in looking vp the catle & issuing the buisnes depending betwixt the gouerner and him, he said he had not done it because of some hinderancs; ꝑtely by Mr. Evanc being from home, ꝑtely by the court of magistrats, & ꝑtely because of some occasions Goodman Miles had, but if ye court please, he shall now apply himselfe to it, and if it be faire weather, will goe tomorrowe to seeke ye catle, and will indeavour to gett Kester Lupton who knowes them best to come & help to distinguish them one from ye other, and will call vpon the arbytrators to issue the buisnes.

Vpon condition this might be done the court were willing to forbeare any sentenc, and agreed to haue the arbytration issued the next second day.

It is ordered that the outside fenc of ye feild first fenced in at Stoney River should be measured and ye number of ac^rs^ inclosed cast vp, and so every man to beare equally according to ye land he hath fenced in, wch the court desires John Brockett may doe, & to be pd by ye owners of ye land in proportion.

Isacke Beecher was warned to this court about the defect of Samuel Farnes his armes, (his servant,) but appeared not. He is to be warned to ye next court to show reason why he came not now, for ther is appearanc of contempt in it.

Thomas Moris was complained of for neglecting his watch. Answer was made he was not well. It was replyed that he was aboute his occasions the day before, and went to Connecticote the day following, and it was strange he could not watch. James Bishop the master of ye watch said he knew not of it till w^t^hin night, and then he could not gett one to supply his place, but some of ye other watchmen wch caried on ꝑt of his worke expect to be paide. It was said that Thom Moris would haue hired thoughe he had given double paye, but could gitt none.

The court ordered that Thomas Moris paye for this neglect 2s 6d, wch is to goe 12d to ye men wch supplyed pt of his watch and 18d to ye towne.

Henry Morrell, for want of a scoverer & some powder, was fined 12d.

Henry Humerston, for want of a sword & a wrest, was fined 2s 6d.

[A General Court for the Jurisdiction was held at New Haven on the 7th of November, 1649, at which sundry "capital and other lawes and orders" were made, as we learn from the records of the town of Guilford.]

At a Generall Court for Newhauen ye 12th of November 1649.

The orderes of the last generall court for ye jurisdiction were reade.

Mr. Thomas Yale and John Beech had libbertie to deppte the court.

The severall notes drawne vp by the comittee appointed for assesing of rates were read, in wch notes some things were considered; first whether the shipp Fellowshipp should be rated, and ye court ordered that she should be freed for this time; in wch notes also are sundry men rated for trades & merchandizing, but some objected against what was sett downe by the comittee, as Mr. Evanc, Mr. Atwatter, Mr. Goodanhousen, & some for Mr. Westerhousen & Mr. Allerton.

The court considered of what they said, and wth ther consent that were prsent, ordered that Mr. Evanc paye for trade, beside what he payes for other estate, for on single rate, after ye rate of 550l, Mr. Atwatter for 400l, Mr. Goodanhousen for 300l, Mr. Westerhousen for 500l, Mr. Allerton 20s for a single rate.

It was voted that the land wthin ye fence, on this side ye

East River paye, till by agreement the fence is laid downe & the land be laid common.

John Bassett propounded that the court would free him from payeing his poll money, because he is lame by a fall & cannot worke, the court inclined to doe it for the p^r^sent, till God shall inable him to his labour againe.

The Gouerner propounded to the court that Leivtenant Seely might haue some help from ye towne to buy Robert Bassetts house, for he is now resolved to staye here & to follow his trade of shooemakeing, and shall not remove vnless ye towne be satisfyed that God by his providence calls him away.

It was propounded to know what the sarjants haue done in ye buisnes com̃itted to them concerning Leivtenant Seely, but they hauing done little in it, it was propounded by some that [256] those of ye towne that ||were p^r^sent would speake what they would give freely, and sundry did speake, w^c^h amount to a som̃e of 16 or 17^l^, a note of ye pticulars wherof was given by the secretary to Leivtenant Seely, and the sarjants were desired to speake w^t^h those that are not p^r^sent, to see what they will doe.

The court was acquainted by the deputies for the jurisdiction generall court, that ther is a certaine quantity of powder & lead, match & gunns to be provided, according to the jurisdiction court order, w^c^h will amount to neare 50^l^, and some course must be taken to provide them, the furthest time being the 24th of June next. It was thought best that they might be sent for to England, and Mr. Evanc offered that if the towne would delr in pease to him, at ye rate sett by the jurisdiction, inough in quantity, as neere as they can gess, to procure them, and that w^t^hin three weekes or a month, he will vndertake to provide them for the towne by the time appointed, and they shall haue the things as they cost in England, the towne beareing the adventure too & froo.

The court considered of ye proposition & accepted it, and ordered that every man in ye towne paye two thirds of this single rate in pease to Mr. Evanc, 3^s^ 6^d^ p bushell, and to cary them in to Mr. Evanc his warehouse vpon some lecture day, the last of w^c^h lecture dayes being the 12th of December next, each man for neglect to paye the double, and seizure p[r]sently to be made, that the worke be not hindered; no man carying any od measure less then a pecke.

William Paine propounded to y[e] court that he might be freed from bringing his armes one y[e] Lords day and lecture dayes, because he lives farr of and hath three small children, and his wife is lame and cannot help to bring y[e] children.

The court voted that so long as his wife continewes lame he be freed.

It is ordered that the planters w[c]h hire Oystershellfeild doe laye it into common w[t]h the quarters next it, and fence in proportion w[t]h them, by the ac[r], and that they from time to time maintayne their severall proportions of fence substantially, and so leave it to the towne when ther time is out, and vpon that ground the court allowes them to take awaye the fence allready made, w[c]h is propr to that land they hold, and free them from payeing the last yeeres rent to y[e] towne, and that Francis Browne haue that pece of meddowe beyonde the ferry house, to make and maintayne a good sufficient fenc from y[e] corner of widdow Knowles his fenc, downe into y[e] flatts, so farr as catle may not goe aboute to doe damage.

Jeremiah How desired & were licenced to drawe stronge watter, vpon y[e] termes of y[e] jurisdictions order in that case, and was wished to be carfull to keepe good order.

Mr. Ling & Jervic Boykin were chosen collectors for the colledg corne for 1 yeere.

The Gouerner informed y[e] court that Sarjant Munson doth expect the towne should allowe him something, because they kept him from goeing to Connecticote to worke, w[c]h was a hinderanc to him. The court considered it, and in regard he attended his owne occasions at home, and what he did for y[e] towne was pd for it, they voted to allow him nothing.

At a Gen'all Court for Newhaven the 29th of November 1649.

The Gouerner acquainted the court that he heares rates are not pd according to order and expectation, nor the pease caried in to Mr. Evanc as it was thought they would; also he heares that ther is some vnsatisfiednes in some men because that houses are not rated, and therfore the polle money will come the oftener, therfore the court might consider what to doe. After much debate, the court ordered that all houses belonging to this towne shall be rated after ye rate of 10 yeeres purchase, being vallewed at a moderate rent by the comittee.

The court was informed that sundry of the comittee for rates haue neglected to meete when they haue had due warning, for wch the court blamed ym, and now ordered that when a comittee is appointed for publique buisnes, and shall haue due warning, that is, 24 howers, or ye evening before the comittee is to meete, and shall not come, but be absent, shall paye to the towne 3s for each default & 18d for late coming, that is if they staye aboue halfe an hower after the time appointed, and ye major pt being mett are to conclude the buisnes in hand.

[257] ||Nathaniel Meriman and William Russell are chosen for this comittee for rates, in ye roome of Thomas Munson & Francis Browne, because the one is not at home, and the other cannot attend it because of the ferry.

It was propounded whether that Mr. Hitchcockes & Mr. Hawkins lotts should not paye as absent lotts, that is, as they did before. It was considered and voted that for this yeere they paye after the new way of rateing, that the owners may be informed, and then the court will consider it againe.

It is also ordered that John Brocket, Thomas Barnes, & those that haue Mris Eldreds lott at farme, and those that had land granted them at towne and farmes out of ye absent lotts, should paye as others doe after this new way of rateing.

George Smith propounded for a small pece of meddowe, 2 or 3 acrs, wch lyes where Mr. Lambertons meddowe lyes, and is aboue his proportion. The court granted that if after

Mr. Lambertons is laide forth ther be so much left wch belongs to no other, he should haue it.

William Andrewes propounded that himselfe & John Cooper wth some others wch formerly propounded for the necke of land and meddowe adjoyning to it next the sea, wch is on ye east side at ye harbours mouth, might be granted to them. He was asked vpon what termes they desire it. He said that they might haue the necke pecular to themselues, & the meddowe, and they would paye as others did for it. He was told that if they had it as ther propr right, that none may common wth them, then they must paye for the whole necke as inclosed land, but that they were not willing to doe. Further they were told that the towne expected that it should be improved for ye getting of corne, that ye towne may haue a benefit by it that way, he said they did intend it, but cannot doe it suddenly. After much debate spent, the farmers already at Stoney River plead ing what needethey had of it, it was refferred to further consideration, that William Andrewes might speake wth ye rest aboute it.

It is ordered that the 16 muskits to be provided for the towne, are to be procured heare by turning match-lockes into fire-lockes, wch the gunnsmithes offer to doe vpon reasonable termes, and now this being taken of and houses added, the towne is to paye into Mr. Evanc in pease, but one third pte of a single rate, wch is to be done vpon ye same termes as was before ordered.

Henry Morrell desired that he might be freed from trayning wth a muskit, because of some defect in his arme, the court left it to Leivtenant Seely, but injoyned him to keepe his armes.

Robert Johnson desired that he might haue libbertie to make a well in ye streete, neere his house. The court fearing some danger might come by it, propounded that he and his neighbours joyning wth him would put a pumpe in it, wher-vpon he tooke time to speake wth them & consider of it.

It is ordered that every souldiour in ye towne shall provide himselfe of a goode horne wch will hold 1l of powder and fitted to weare for service, and a bagg for bullitts, and every souldiour comeing to show armes w^t^hout such a horne & bagg fitted, shall paye as in case of othe defect of armes, this to be done by the next showing day, and so to continew furnished from time to time.

It is ordered that swine, after a weekes time, be kept vp as before ordered, vnder ye same penalty.

Thomas Lampson being called to answer to something ye court had to say to him, was not p^r^sent, whervpon ye m^r^shall was ordered to call for his fine.

John Coopr ꝑpounded for a small pece of meddow in ye mill river meddow, but nothing was don.

In the monthes of December and January ther was no courts, because no buisnes was p^r^sented, though the court attended ther some time.

F. N. 1649.

FINIS.

ERRATA.

Page 20, line 16, *for* church esof, *read* churches of.
Page 140, line 20, *for* Sam: Farres, *read* Sam: Farnes.
Page 168, line 15, *for* page 194, *read* page [194.]
Page 360, line 27, *for* Robret, *read* Robert.

State of Connecticut, ss.

Secretary's Office.

I hereby certify, that I have caused the printed matter contained in the foregoing pages of this volume to be carefully compared with the original Record, and that the same is a true, full and literal copy thereof.

In testimony whereof, I have hereunto set my hand and the seal of the State, at Hartford, this 9th day of April, A. D. 1857.

L. S.

N. D. SPERRY,

Secretary of State.

APPENDIX.

The following letters, with one exception, are from a volume in the office of the Secretary of the State of New York, endorsed, "New York Colonial MSS. (New Netherland,) vol. XI. The letter marked I, is from the files of the Commonwealth of Massachusetts, at Boston.

A.

GOVERNOR EATON TO GOVERNOR STUYVESANT.

The first letter of Mr. Eaton, being supscribed,

To the Right Wors^ll^ his much honoured friend Tho: Steuenson Esqr, Generall of the forces for the West Indie Company, & Gouernour of the Dutch Collonye att Manhatans.

Right Wor^ll^ & much honoured S^r^

Yours of the 20th of June new stile, I haue receiued, & congratulate yor saufe arriuall att the Manhatans, with your accesse vnto, & settlement in that weighty trust of gouerm^t^. I readilie close with your equall proposition of a neighbourlie correspondencie, that justice may haue a full & free passage in all occasions betwixt vs; & particularlie, that if any either breake prison or flie from one of these iurisdictions to the other, wheather to defraude creditours, or to escape deserued punnishment, hee or they, vppon due notice & demand, may be apprehended, deteined, & retourned, wth due allowance of charges, as the cause may require, & accordinglie haue by our Marshall haue made serious enquirie after Michaell Piket, the malefactour yow mention but cannot yett heare of him. If in such causes hereafter yow please to describe the pson, by his natiō: his age, stature, apparell, or by any other obseruable markes, the discouerie may be more easie and certaine, such guiltie fugitiues (fearing a pursuit) being apt through a guilefull subtiltie to change & denye theyre names, & the place from whence they came, but if any suspected stranger come heather, I shall indeauour by examination to plucke of the disguise, & if it may bee to retourne yor prisoner. With my due respects to your selfe & Mouns^r^ Kieft I rest,

Yours in all seruice of loue,

Theophilus Eaton.

Newhauen, June the 19th, 1647, St: Angl:

B.

Governor Eaton to Governor Stuyvesant.

2 letter, To the Right Wor[ll] Peter Styvesant Esq: Gouern[r] of the Dutch plantation att Manhatans.

S[r]

By yo[r] agent Mr. Gouert I rec[d] two paps from yow, the one sealed, the other open, but neither of them written either in Lattin, as yo[r] predecessour vsed, or in English as your selfe haue formerlie done, both to me, & to the other Collonys, but in Low Dutch, whereof I vnderstand little, nor would yo[r] messenger though desired interpret any thing in them, soe that in pte att least they must lye by mee, till I meete with an interpreter.

In the meane tyme, as formerlie wee were sensible of sundrie wrongs, & protested against yo[r] predecess[r] Mouns[r] Will: Kieft, soe I hereby witnes against your vnneighbourlie & iniurious course, in seuerall writings which I haue seene. Without groun[d] you pretend title to the land in these ptes, one while from Deleware, to Connecticut Riuer, & another while you extend yo[r] limits further, euen to Cape Cod, from whence drawing any line landward North or West, yow wholy take in, or trench farre in to the limits of all the Vnited English Collonies, who by lycence & auntient pattent from King James, of famous memorie, since confirmed by his Maiestie that now is, first came into these ptes, & vppon due purchase from the Indians, who were the true proprietours of the land (for we fownd it not a vacuum) haue built, planted, & for many yeares quietlie, & without any claime or disturbance, from the Dutch or others, posessed the same.

And now latelie in a ship belonging to Newhauen, as bought by Mr. Goodyeare, yow haue sent armed men, & (without lycence, not soemuch as first acquainting any of the magistrates of this Jurisdiction with the cause or grownds thereof) ceised a shipp within our harbour, and though Wiłł: Westerhowse, the Dutch merchant, & without our knowledge, before treated with yow, & then offered the recognition, which in a former writing to him, yow seemed to accept, yett your agent refused it, & protested hee would carrie away the ship. Whereuppon I did first protest against him, & the Generall Court considering how highlie they were considered in the premises, though they would not meddle in a controuersie which belongs not to them, much lesse defend any knowne vnrighteousnes, & though they desire to keepe peace (as farre as may bee) with all men & particularlie with theyre neighbours of the Dutch plantatiō, yet they fownd it necessarie, & resolued by all iust meanes, to asist & vindicate theyre right, in Newhauens lands & harbour, & theyre iurisdiction of both, that themselues & posteritie be not, (through theyre neglect,) inthralled & brought vnder a forreigne gouerment, by a ceisure made in theyre harbour vppon such an vnjust claime, the court conceuing it free for them, according to the laws of God & nations, to entertaine trade brought vnto them, wheather by land or sea, without enquiring into the priuilidges of forraigne companies, or examining wheather recognitiō be due, or paid in another countrie, nor is propable that your selfe, if an English ship or vessell bring necessarie prouisions to the Manhatans, will be sollicitous wheather custom be p[d] in England.

Wherefore, wee haue protested, and by these presents doe protest, against yow Peter Styvesant, Gouern[r] of the Dutch att Manhataes &c: for disturbing the peace betwixt the Engl: & Dutch in these ꝑtes, which hath bynne soe long & so hapilie maintained betwixt the two nations in Europe, for obstructing & hindering those passages of justice & neighbourlie correspondencie, which yo[r] selfe haue propownded & desired betwixt the Engl: Collonies & y[e] Dutch plantations, by making vniust claimes to our lands & plantations, to our hauens & riuers, and by taking a ship oute of our harbour, without our licence, by yo[r] agents & comission, & wee hereby professe that what further inconuenience may hereafter growe, yow are the cause and author of it, as we hope to cleere, & proue before our superiours in Europe.

Dated in Newhauen in New England this 8th day of Octob[r], 1647. stil: vet: Theophilus Eaton.

C.

Governor Eaton to Governor Stuyvesant.

Mr. Eatons 3[d] letter, in answere of those in Dutch & one in English sent with the predecent.

Sr

Since the two former papers mentioned in the inclosed, I haue by yo[r] fiskall rec[d] yo[r] letter dated Octob[r] the 16th new stile, though I doe not fullie & particularlie vnderstand the contents of the former, yet the sownd & sense of them are offensiue. In the former ꝑte of yor letter I could close, & as a reall friend of righteousnes & peace, (vppon your ingagem^{t} of doeing like offices of loue and justice as opportunitie serueth to all the English Collonies) could willinglie giue an example of neighbourlye correspondence and respect in returning your fugitiues, but protests & threatnings are ill arguments to drawe on performances which are free & of courtesie; when therefore yow interpret your meaning, that it may passe and be receiued as a neighbourlie office of loue, without expectation or implication of any authoritie on your ꝑte or subordinate in ours, I shall readilie deliuer the prisoners, to any yow shall appoint to receiue and discharge them, in the meane tyme yow were misinformed when yow heard they walked free in our plantaciō, yor agent was present when I first sawe & committed them.

Concerning the latter parte of yor letter, I know that princes and states in amitie haue somtymes by power ceised ships in each others harbours, the English (yow say) ceised some of the French in yor ꝑtes, and the Hollanders haue probablie seised some of the Spaniards in the English harbours, but this reacheth not the question, an iniurie against the which, I did & still doe protest, that without any iust grownde, yow should first pretend title to the lands, streames, riuers, etc: truly belonging to the English Collonys, & by them many yeares quietlie, & without any question, claime, or intimation of title from others, lawfullie posessed & planted, & then giue com̄ission vnder that respect & consideration, to seise a ship in one of theyre harbours, without lycence, this, thus done would haue giuen offence in any ꝑte of Europe, or of the world, and were this iustlie cleered, I hope all other questions betwixt vs might issue to mutuall satisfaction, in expectatiō whereof I rest as formerlie. Yo^{r} lo: friend

Theoph: Eaton.

Newhauen in New Engl: this 15th of Octob^{r},
1647, st: vet:

D.

DEPUTY GOVERNOR GOODYEAR TO GOVERNOR STUYVESANT.

This followeing was sent by Mr. Goodyeare, Deputy Gouernr of Newhauen, & directed to the Right Worll P. Styvesant Esq:, Gouernr for the West Indie Company.

these present att Manhatans.

Sr

Yors of the 16th present is come to hand, wherein yow take notice of fauour to yow in taking the thre fugitiues, & promise as opportunitie shall present, to doe the like for vs, but I suppose yow would better consider it, then to send vs any pson of ours (with yow) wee claiming him or them, as from our owne Jurisdiction, but I haue what may bee spoken in that poynt to further information from our Gouernr.

I further pceiue yow are informed of our discontent in taking awaye the ship oute of our harbour, yor Captt knowes wee carried it with loue & respect to him, & without any appearance of discontent, when hee shewed yor comission; and Sr, if wee had bynne greived or offended, we had a full opportunitie to haue righted ourselues, yea, if we would haue giuen libertie, & ourselues not haue acted, yow had failed of your purpose.

But that which moved vs, (and doth offend vs att this present,) is that yow, in a letter to Mr. William the merchant, write that he was in your harbour, the whole towne taking notice of that claime did forthwith resolue to stay the ship, and accordinglie attempted it, but to late, for allthough neighbourlie correspondencye is desired and will euer be indeauored, yett the English in these partes will not easilie be brought vnder any forraigne nation, nor loose theyre lawfull rights, and priuilidges not only purchased of the true proprietours, the Indians, but allsoe by pattent from the King of England many yeares since, yea, allsoe our Gouernr, Mr. Eaton, is allsoe a pattentee of that graunte to the Bay of Boston; & it is well knowne to most that or friendship with the state of England, & theyre fauour to vs, is as free & as full any in New England, & we came with theyre full consent & approbatiō, & more then ordinary incouragement; wee purpose, neither haue we any thing in our hearts but loue & neighbourlie correspondencie with yow; & in nothing are, nor I hope shall bee iniurious to yow, or any of yours, but if we shall be requited with the contrary, I doubt not but through Gods asistance, yow will finde vs able to maintaine o[r] iust rights, and not in the least to feare the sword or threats of any adversarie, but if yow still desire any neighbourlie correspondence, (as you desired it when I was with yow,) yow shall finde us ready to our vtmost. I am in haste, your seruant calling for my lett[r]; only one word to desire yow to send me 50 or 100 skipples of salte, and to fetch your beefe and porke ; I doubt I must presentlie kill the beefe, for it will fall dayly. I cannot yett gett or procure men to thresh corne, but I shall further it soe farre as I may ; your fiskall hath only receiued 25 gild[rs]. I profferred him what euer hee desired, but it was what hee would accept for his present occasion, soe in greate haste, desiring yow to excuse my scribling, I rest,

Yours in what I may,
Stephen Goodyeare.

Not dated, but it came with the fiskall
with the other two of Mr. Eaton.

E.

Governor Stuyvesant to Governor Eaton.

The answere to Mr. Eatons letter, being directed to the Right Worsh[ll] Theoph : Eaton, Gouernour of Newhauen.

S[r]

Yours of the 15th of Octob[r] st : vet : I receiuied ; the obstacle is yo[r] misenterpreting of some passages in myne to yow, for the cleering of which & remouall of all doubtes & iealousies, I hereby declare, I doe not in any measure desire either to usurpe vppon your right, or assume vnto my selfe any power or gouerm[t] ouer the English there ; but as I haue formerlie writt to yourselfe, and others, I am, (and hope shall soe continue,) as studious for the preservation and encreasing of loue and amitie betwixt your nation and ours in these ptes as any, of the which I suppose you cannot be ignorant, in my propositions to my worthy friend, Gouernour Winthrop, the which I shall on my parte be ready to make good and giue pregnant testimonie to the world of my readines & willingnes of a faire and neighbourlie composure of any difference betweene vs, (God blessing) our ioynt meeting with the comissions[rs] when the tyme shall be appointed.

For what have I either written or done, that may seeme offensive to your self, or any other impartiall wise man, I as yett am ignorant, for I suppose they cannot but knowe, that (as I am deputied by authoritie from my souereigne Lords and masters, the High & Mighty, the Estates Generall of the Vnited Belgicke Provinces, soe to them must I giue accompte, and by them be adiudged in whatsoeuer shall appeare amisse in any action or passage of myne; and should I, in the least measure, transgresse in the observation of theyre commands, yow well know my lyfe, estate and reputation lyes att stake and must answere, and therefore for whatsoeuer I haue done concerning my countriemen in my supprising theyre ship there, they may haue recourse to the Justice of theyre natiue land, and I shall not only deliuer them theyre comission, but the coppie allsoe of all our proceedings heere against them, and for my threatning of any belonging to your Jurisdiction, I suppose yow are either misenformed or mistaken; therefore I shall entreate your deliuerie of the fugituies to this bearer, our commissaries, your charitable opinion both of my actions and intentions, your compliance, & correspondent neighbourlie respect from one to the other, a leauing of all altercation on either side, but a ioynt indeavour in vs both for the full effecting of all mutuall offices of loue, and composing all differences, att our ioynt meeting in the spring with our worthy friends, the Gouernours of Boston & Plimouth, I shall rest

Yo[rs] in any office of Christian loue

P. Styvesant.

Fort New Amsterdam in New Netherlands,
Nouemb[r] 13th, 1647. st: no:

F.

Governor Stuyvesant to Deputy Governor Goodyeare.

The answere to Mr. Goodyears letter.

S[r]

Yours I receiued wherein yow are pleased to write concerning my supprising the vessell there, and of your townsmens discontent att some passages in my letter to Will: Westerhowse; what he hath diuulged I know not, yett sure I am, I was desirous to carrie it as inoffensiuelie to my neighbours there as I could, howeuer they may apprehend, yett you and yours shall reallie finde mee as cordiallie willing, att all tymes and all occasions, to indeauour a continuance of all friendlie and neighbourlie amitie betwene vs, allthough haplie many vaine rumours may arise whereby iealousies & discontents may be fomented.

I haue sent according to your desires for the receiuing the prouisions. For whatsoeuer yow shall please to deliuer to our comissarie, his note shall be a sufficient discharge. Sr, I thanke yow for your supplieing our fiscall and for your further tender to him, and your respects to my selfe, the which I shall indeauour to requite, and remaine,

Your assured louing friend

P. Styvesant.

Fort New Amsterdam, in New Netherlands,
Nouembr the 13th, 1647. St: Nouo:

G.

Governor Eaton to Governor Stuyvesant.

Mr. Eatons 4th letter.

Sr:

By yor comissarie I haue latelie receiued yors dated Nouembr the 15th, new stile, but finde not that satisfaction therein which I expected. My former, Octobr the 8th, (though it came to your hands in that of the 15th, delivered by yor fiscall,) yow mention not, & your expressions in this, (considered with the questions betwixt vs,) are att best darke and need explanatiõ: how you can saye you desire not, in any measure, to vsurp vppon our right, when yow lay claime to the land, riuers, streames, &c. wch iustlie belongs to the English collonies, I vnderstand not. It is well knowne, both in Europe & heere, that by auntient pattent, the Kings of Engl: haue graunted (all that pte of America called New England, lyeing & being in breadth from 40 to 48 degr. of northerlie latitude) vnto his subjects for theyre incouragemt to settle & plant abroad; and accordinglie, vppon due purchase from the natiues, the true pprietours of the land, (for we found it not a vacuũ,) we haue built, fenced & setled our selues heere, nor hearing soemuch as of any the least pretence the Dutch did or could make to any of this land, in many yeares after; it is true that aboute fiue yeares since, yor predecessr, Mounsr Will: Kieft, grew iniurious to vs, both att Deleware and else where, wee then witnessed & protested against his course, & required satisfaction, which we still expect, & in due tyme shall offer the particulars to consideration.

From your selfe, according to the tennour of yor first lett^{rs}, wee hoped for a more neighbourlie correspondence, but yow haue not only trod in his steps, but in a short tyme since your entrance, haue allready, in some respects, gone beyond him, as may appeare in this briefe account of particulars.

In yo^{rs} of the 25th of June, to the Gouern^{r} of the Massachusets collony, wch yow now mention, yow pretend an indubiate right to all the land betwixt Conneticut & Deleware; in yor protest dated Octob^{r} the 12th, yow grow in your demands, extending yor limmits from Cape Codd, within Plim̄outh collonye, to Cape Hinlopen towards the sowth, (a place or name to me yett vnknowne;) yow charge Newhauen in particular, as vsurping your grownds, land, riuers, streames, & are offended for theyre trading first with Simson Johnson, since with Wiłł: Westerhowse and other Dutch men; yow ceise a ship in our harbour without licence, pretending title to the place, & complaine of a purpose & iust resolutiō in vs to vindicate our owne right in a lawfull waye; yow require vs to send the Dutch merch^{ts} & theyre goods, with a recognitiō, &c., to the Manhataes, and if wee attend not your directions, yow threaten hostilitie to Newhauen, pretending to keepe peace with the other collonies, & in yor letter which came & beareth date with the forementioned ꝑtest, you vniustlie charge vs concerning yor fugitiues, & in a com̄anding, threatning stile, require them from vs, & att or aboute the same tyme, in a letter to Wiłł: Westerhowse, (as I am informed,) you threaten to fetch his goods oute of Newhauen by force; you haue imposed or taken an excessiue high custom, excise or recognitiō for all goods sould within your jurisdiction, with ceisures for om̄issions or misentries; our vessells must anchor vnder your erected hand, a place very inconvenient, and as if you ment to shut vp the passage by the Manhataes, or by vnsufferable burthens to wearie the English oute of trade, you beginne to take recognition, &c. vppon goods traded else where, & in theyre retourne passing only by the Manhataes; I heare allsoe you threaten to burne or beate downe our trading howse, built vppon our owne purchased land, within our owne lim̄its, and farre from any trading howse of yours or any ꝑte of Hudsons riuer, and which is yett worse, it is reported to vs by seuerall ꝑsons & from seuerall places, that your secretarie hath indeauoured by a slanderous report to incense the Long Isl: Indians, and your selfe, att Aurania fort, haue attempted to trye other companies of Indians against the English. If this agree with rules of Christianitie or good neighbourhood, I doubt not but we may retaliate and when wee see cause turne the edge and point of those weapons vppon your selues. I enquire not after your grownds in sending Captaine Forrester to Holland, the English collonys may haue occasion to write after the same coppie hereafter.

In the meane tyme, the scope and tendencye of the premises doth directlie crosse & contradict your profession of peac and amitie, & will in each particular afford matter of serious consideration to the English collonies, and vnlesse things be cleered speedilie to satisfaction, yow will constreine vs either to require and receiue recognition in proportion to what wee paye, or to prohibit all comerce betwixt the English and Dutch jurisdictions in these partes; for our selues we accompt and with good warrant call our title to the land, riuers and streames wee posesse, an indubiate right. Wee know wee have as full libertie to trade with Dutch merchants within our harbours & to admit Dutch inhabitants into our plantacions as yow the English, in either case; yett wee readilie close with your propositions to considder, examine and issue all differences, and though it be not vsuall for one ptye to choose both arbitratours, I shall for this once consent to the choice your selfe haue made. The Gouernours of the Massachusets and Plimmouth collonies are men approued for wisdom and integritie, nor shall I differ from yow in those circumstances of tyme and place, supposing yow will haue due respect to conueniencye, only by way of preparatiō it would be considered and agreed what shall be put to referrence, wheather the title of land, riuers, streames, &c., or any pte of the forementioned tract from 40 to 48, including the Manhataes and Newhauen, or only other questions and iniuries which haue bynne formerlie or more latelie greiuous and are not yett satisfied. If yow please herein to expresse your meaning fullye & cleerlie you shall finde mee reall and readye to meet you in any peaceable & iust waye. In expectation of your speedy answere that occasions may be ordered accordinglie, I rest,

Yor louing friend,
Theoph: Eaton.

Newhauen in New Engl:
Nouembr 16th, 1649. st: vete:

H.

Deputy Governor Goodyear to Governor Stuyvesant.

Much Honoured S^{r},

Yo^{r} beefe according to couenant is deliuered. Mr. Keisar yor Commissarie, his late comeing being very pr[ ] (cattle being fallen in theire flesh) & yett nothing to yor aduantage, I was necessitated to furnish a greate ꝑte out [of what] I had ꝑuided for the Barbadaes, but my indeauours are, & shall be to my vtmost to ꝑforme my couenants in all thi[ngs. I] desire wee may attend peace & neighbourlie loue, & correspondencie one with another; and if in any thing wee may pleasu [ ] I shall be ready to my vtmost to shew it in any friendlie & neighbourlie waye to doe it. I reioyce to heare of the late blessing in the little one giuen you, & of yor wifes strength, soe com̄itting yow, & your weighty affaires to Gods goodnes, I rest.

Yours in any office of loue to my power,
Stephen Goodyeare.

Newhauen, Nouemb^{r} the 22th, 1647.

I.

Governor Eaton to Governor Winthrop, of Massachusetts.

S^{r},

Yours of the 9th came to my hand the 24th of Nov: wth one inclosed to the Duch Govern^{r}. I am much ingaged to you, for your labour of love, and should gladly improve any opportunity, in a way of thankfull returne.

In all afflicting providences I desire to looke higher then the instrument, I can also readily confess wth you, that our holy & righteous father hath just cause of controversye wth all the colonyes & churches in these ꝑts, for abating, if not declining, from their first love, zeale, workes, &c. And could heartily wish that besides prayers, &c. the magistrates and elders would joyne heads & hearts, fill up their places & improve their interests (as Esay & Hezekiah, whom you mention to another purpose, Ezra and Nehemiah,) for a thorough reformation, that our wise & gracious God might finde & see many making up the hedg and standing in the gapp, &c.

Concerning the Duch, and our exercises & intercourses with them, I must be a litle more large, but would premise that the high esteeme & respect, I have & doe justly beare you, makes me consider and seriously question my owne way when ever (though but in circumstantialls) I dissent & differ. It suites my judgment certainly and I hope my practise also, that (putting in what weight I can into argument,) I steere a midle course, betwixt provoking an adversary by unnecessary invectives, or uncomely language, and giving undue titles, whereof he may make ill use, and I may after repent.

What hath passed betwixt Monsr Kieft, and us of Newhaven, you have formerly heard at large, and what passed betwixt the com̄issionrs for the colonyes and him, in refference both to Connecticutt & Newhaven, will appeare by those records. In all wch I doe not yet know that we gaue any just cause of offence, but that euer any advice of yours was rejected, as proceeding from weakenes, or that euer you did advise to more mildenes & moderation then we used, I cannot yet call to mind.

For the present governr, I know the place he holds under the West India company putts an honour upon him wch upon all occasions I would shew due respect, and concerning his psonall abilities and indowments, I would suppose his principalls may know that, to wch I am yet a stranger and I doubt shalbe, but either his actions speake more of his justice & prudence, or those that come from thence, less of his passions & exactions, but what euer the man be, I suppose I may safely say some stepps in his way have bin to us causelesly injurious. What passed formerly, you fully understood by my letter, Octobr 20th, and the copies inclosed, since wch it is brought to us from seuerall places, that he and his agents haue bin working with the Indians to incense & hire them against the English. It is true we haue but Indian testimony for this, nor are we like to haue more in such a buisnes, but it comes with the greater euidence because one of the Sagamors reporteth, that as a motiue he told the Mohawkes, the English would fight with him for selling them peeces, powder and shott, wch (though streyned) may refferr to the com̄issionrs letter to him from Boston, yet in a letter sent by the com̄issary, dated Nov. 15th new stile, he pretends to be studious of preserving love & amity, suposeth I am mistaken or misinformed, when I speake of his threatning any in our jurisdiction, he desires a charitable opinion of his actions & intentions, and that all differences may be composed at our meeting in the spring wth your self and the governour of Plimouth, which compared wth his forementioned letter & protest dated Octob[r] 12th, with his actions and report of other proceedings, w[ch] best shew his intentions, seeme (that I say no more) very stronge, I desired the comissary, before Mr. Atherton, to read and reconcile them; he read but could put no other interpretation upon them then I had done, hereupon I returned answer, as by the inclosed copie may appeare.

Since w[ch] I am informed from Captayne Mason, that David Provost (late agent for the Duch at their house by Hartford) tells the Indians at Saybrooke, that the Duch will shortly fight wth the English, and that they have ingaged all Indians to them except the Moheages. These reports can hardly be imagined to grow without roote or cause, but how ever, they are inconvenient and chargable to us. Connecticut hereupon will hasten the finishing of their fort, and Newhaven at their great charge have made some slight workes or platformes to plant a few gunns, to secure the towne as they may from smaller vessells.

So that when I consider how things stand betwixt the Colonyes & the Duch in these pts, what heavy burdens they lay upon trade, even to discouragment, what claimes to our land, &c., what attempts & threatnings of hostility they make, I see no better way to preserve our owne liberty & peace, and to suppress such injurious, insolent courses of unneighbourly neighbours, then that all the colonyes prohibitt all trade with them till trade & peace (by some meeting) may be freed and better settled.

For the Duch fugitives, upon occasion of some delinquents lately fledd from these pts, I wrote to the Govern[r] by Mr. Atherton, Nov. 19th, before yours came to hand, that upon any reasonable satisfaction in the questions betwixt us, they shalbe delivered to any he shall appointe to receive them, and that none of theirs of suspicious quality shall hereafter (wth our knowledg & consent) pass through these pts, unless they bring something under his hand for their warrant; to conclude, though I have sealed your letter to the Duch Govern[r] wth a purpose to send it forward by the next opportunity, yet upon further consideration I thought fitt first to advise w[th] you whether (in refference to the premises) some thing may not be altered, & some thing added according to later occurrents and as may best prepare for the meeting propounded, if your self and the comission[r]s see cause & please to write another letter (wherein I suppose you would not vary any thing from the sense & ayme of your Generall Court,) I shall send that or this according to direction.

Wth my due respects to your self, Mr. Cotton, & other friends, I rest

Yrs many wayes ingaged to all service of love,

Nov. 26, 1647. T. E.

[Endorsed in the hand-writing of Mr. Joseph Hills, "No 26, 1647, Mr. Eaton touching the Dutch."]

K.

Governor Stuyvesant to Deputy Governor Goodyear.

This vnderwritten was in answere of Mr. Eatons, being directed to the Deputy Gouernr Mr. Goodyeare, the E: H:* thinking it inconuenient to answere Mr. Eaton in respect of his vniust charges.

Worthy Sr,

By or Comissaries Keisar I recd one letter from yor selfe, & another from yor Gouernr, & latelie one from both by Mr. Allerton; you complaine of our commissarie's breach of promise concerning some salte, his pretences are, the windproueing faire hee would not loose the opportunitie, that he was longer deteined there, for the receiuing of what was pd him, then hee expected; soe small a quantitie will not be worth the sending a vessell purposelie theather, therefore for the future I shall accept the paymt of wt is due from Mr. Allerton: In myne to yor Gouernr I had thought I had giuen him sufficient satisfactiō: & expected the like from him, but contrarie to my expectatiō: & opinniō: of his wisdom, his letter was full of complaints and pretended iniuries.

And whereas he writes my lettr was at best darke, & neede explanatiō: thus farre I will expound myselfe: that claimes to pretended rights are noe iniuries & giues me noe lawfull ꝑprietie to what I claime, vnlesse lawfullie adiudged, (in which neither hee nor I can be competent judges) and I suppose yow and he well knowes, that many protests and passages in this nature are only pro formâ, and therefore for whatsoeuer I haue done in that kinde, I haue not as I conceiue, wronged him, or the right of his countriemen there, vnlesse I had

* An abbreviation for "Edele Heer," two Dutch words signifying "Honorable Gentleman."

sought to make good my claime by force of armes, the which I haue not as yett soe much as thought of: although he semes to adiudge the cause on his owne side, by vertue of the graunte of his Matie of England his pattent to his subiects of England, likewise blaming my predecess^{r} for some passages att Deleware who I hope is nowe in his natiue countrie, & if he, or any one else, haue any thing to laye to his charge, they may there question him, and I doubt hee will answere what soeuer they can obiect against him.

For myne owne pte I canne noe ways interpret his, but as an aggrauating of former passages, to the worse sense, laying many things to my charge, ripping vp (as he conceiues) all my faultes, as if I were a schole boy, & not as one of like degree with himselfe, and they are soe vaine, and by me soe sufficientlie answered that I shall be silent, and only instance in 2 or 3 of the cheifest of them.

First concerning my receiuing recognition heere, that it is soe excessiue high, &c: I only answere, Euery State hath power to make what lawes, and impose what customs in theyre owne precincts they shall thinke conuenient, without being regulated or prescribed by others, yet notwithstanding wee haue bynne soe fauourable to your countriemen trading heere, that they pay 8st p cent. lesse then our owne, and I am confident all things considered not 4 p cent.

Hee likewise obiects against me (his heare say) of my threatning to burne or beate downe yor trading howse, & of report from seuerall places & psons, concerning my selfe, & secretarie's indeauouring to raise the Indians against the English, threatning a retaliation and turning the edge and point of those weapons vppon vs heere, I had thougth he had had more noble worth being a gouern^{r}, or charitie as he was a Christian, (hearing such reports of one of like qualitie as himselfe) not to haue giuen credit to them, but rather imprisoned the reporters vnlesse they could haue sufficientlie proued it; and I take it to be as greate an iniurie to me, (to haue such reportes raised and beleued) as possible may bee.

Concerning my sending Capt. Forester for Holland, and that the English collonies may haue occasiō to write after the same coppie (I vnderstand him very well) and I doubt not but theyre wisdoms will doe that which they may well answere to theyre principalls, as I to myne, and therefore neede not giue him, or any one else heere, an accompt, yett for yor satisfactiō, he claimed the gouerm^{t} of all Long Isl: Dutch & English, and produced a comissiō wheather counterfeit or noe, I know not, for it was sealed but not signed.

His conclusion is indifferent faire, but I shall not begg it from him. If I meete in the spring with the gouern[r] of Boston & Plimmouth I hope we shall doe our best for the reconciling of all differences; to put any thing to them as arbitratours I am not yett resolued, but shall willinglie complie with them in what they shall thinke conuenient, and whereas he is soe full of his retaliatiō, according to his owne words and practise, hee must giue vs leaue to giue libertie to any that shall flye from your jurisdiction to remaine vnder our protection vntill our fugitiues are deliuered, which assone as done I shall indeauour to send theyres backe, soe S[r] with my loueing respects I take leaue, and rest,

Yo[r] assured lo: friend,

P. Styvesant.

Fort New Amsterdam in New Netherlands,
Decemb[r] the 16th, 1647. st: no:

L.

Governor Stuyvesant to Governor Eaton.

This following letter was sent to Mr. Eaton by the Secret: Teinoh.

To Mr. Eaton.

Worthy S[r],

Certaine reportes comeing to my eares that, some of my countriemen & others vsing to trade with natiues of yo[r] ptes, doe indirectlie sell vnto the s[d] natiues powder, gunnes & lead, & that in particular one Gouert Lockoman had done it, & withall had indeauoured to instigate the Indians there against the English, I could doe noe lesse then in discharge of my duty to God & my neighbour, but seriouslie to enquire into it, and haue vsed my best indeauour for the fineding oute the truth, it being of soe high a concernement as to arme the Indians against the Christians, vppon all occasions, & making debate & iealousies betwixt the two nations in these ptes, that haue soe long & happilie liued in vnion in our natiue countries. I haue therefore thought good to send our secretarie vnto yow aboute it, togeather with such information as I haue receiued vnder the hands of Mr. Throckemorton, Mr. Willet, & Mr. Hart, & humblie entreate yow, yow would be pleased to vse yo[r] indeauours to the magistrates of Sowthampton & other places, that the truth may be knowne in the premises, concerning the s[d] Gouert or any other that haue relation vnto our jurisdiction, & if proued against him or others, yow shall apparrentlie finde that I will not countenance any of ours in such wayes of vnrighteousnes, but cause such examplarie punnishment to be inflicted vppon them, as shall deterre others from doeing or attempting the like in both respects, either in indirect trading or instigating the Indians against o[r] Christian brethren of the English nation.

I very well know such practises & speeches by any of o[rs] is & may be cause, (& that iustlie,) of iealousies and discontents between vs, but I doe hereby protest, before God & the world, my innocencie in either respects, & doe reallie & heartilie desire a continuation, growth & encrease of neighbourlie loue & correspondencie betwene vs in these ptes, and for the effecting of which I haue latelie written to the Gouern[rs] of Boston & Plimmouth, that if they, with yo[r] selfe, will please to giue me a meeting att Conneticut att any tyme you shall appoint, this summer, I doubt but through the blessing of God wee shall giue that mutuall satisfaction to one another, in euery respect, that past differences may be forgot, future preuented, & a happie union betwixt our nations in these ptes firmelie knit. Desiring yow will please to giue me an answer to each particular by o[r] secret. I shall take my leaue & rest,

Yo[rs] to my power in any office of loue,

Pet. Styvesant.

May the 28th (48) 1648.

M.

Governor Eaton to Governor Stuyvesant.

The answere.

Honoured S[r]

Yo[rs] of the 28th May, 1648, st. no., I rec[d] by yo[r] secret., in the former pte whereof yow expresse a due sense of y[e] miscarriage of some of yo[r] traders, who neglecting y[e] publique saftie & peace, for priuate gayne & respects, not only dispose & arme the Indians for warre in generall, but incense them against the English in particular. Yo[r] secret. to this purpose hath shewed me the testimonies Mr. Willet, Mr. Throckemorton & Mr. Heart hath giuen against Gouert Lockoman. Yow may please to remember both what the comission[rs] for the vnited English Collonies wrot from Boston, August 17, 1647, concerning this dangerous trade, (of selling gunnes, powder, shot, &c., to the Indians,) driuen by some of yo^{rs} att Aurania fort, at Long Island, within the riuer of Conneticut, att Narrowgansett, & other places within the English jurisdictions; but how to discouer & suppresse it, (the ꝑticular traders then vnknowne to the comission^{rs},) they left to yor wisdom & iudgem^{t}, & what information I gaue, Nouemb^{r} 16, 1647, concerning that vnchristiā & neighbourlie course of incensing the Indians att Long Isl: & else where against christian neighbours. It is true we had but Indian testimonie, nor may it be expected that they which are exercised in such crooked & vndermining workes should blowe a trumpet & call in witnesses of more credit. Soone after I heard from Saybrook that Dauid Prouost, (somtimes agent at yor howse neere Hartford,) tould the Indians aboute Conneticut riuers mouth that the Dutch would shortlie fight with the Indians, & that they had ingaged all the Indians in these ꝑtes, (the Moheags excepted,) vnto them. Janu. the 3^{d}, 1647, a complaint was brought from the English att Sowthampton, that Gouert Lockoman had bynne latelie trading with the Indians of those ꝑtes, who reported that after he had sould them some coates he declared that if they would buye more, with euerie coate hee would giue a pownd of powder, which ꝑcured him a quicke markett & soe furnishes the Indians with powder that they could sell to the English.; & the same Indians further testified that Gouert wisht them to cutt of the English, and the Dutch, (to such a worke,) would furnish them with peeces, powder & shott enough, wch soe prouokes the Engl: att Sowthampton, that had they had order they would haue staide Gouert & his vessell; since wch I vnderstand that Dauid Prouoost in that ꝑte of Long Isl: hath indeauored to take, (as it were,) the ground from vnder the feet of the English, purchasing lands wch the Indians haue long since passed ouer & vnto which the Eng^{ls} for many yeares haue had a knowne & vnquestioned right, & had giuen a price for the same, till the Indians, (convinced by the English of theyre vnrighteousnes,) retourned his pay.

These concerne the Engl. collonies more generallie & are as soe many sparkes fitt to kindle a fire of contention, but I should allsoe haue added yor late proclamatiō, which is a reall inuitatiō to discontented ꝑsons & delinquents to become fugitiues, with seuerall other greiuances which more directlie concerne Newhauen, to those mentioned No^{r} 16, 1647, but that by yor lett^{rs} to Mr. Goodyeare, Decemb^{r} the 13th, to the Gouern^{r} of the Massachusets, Febr^{ry} the 8th, it appeareth yow tooke offence att my open dealing, tending only to prepare for a meeting wherein all questions & iniuries might be duly considered, satisfied and remoued, & a iust wholesom peace setled & confirmed betwixt the Engl: & Dutch in these ptes. To conclude, I soe fully close with the contents of this yor last lett^{r} that I haue allready written to the Gouern^{rs} of the Massachusets to further the meeting, & to the Gouern^{r} of Conneticut to enquire if further light might be had from Sowthampton, (which is in that jurisdictiō,) concerning Gouert Lockoman crooked & puerse waye. In the meane tyme, our owne iust rights duly preserued in retourning of fugitiues, & in all other offices of neibourly correspondencie, I shall walke with yow passib. æquis, I rest,

Yo^{r} louing friend,
Theophilus Eaton.

Newhauen in New Engl:,
May the 31th, 1648. st. vet.

N.

Governor Eaton to Governor Stuyvesant.

Mr. Eaton's 2^{d} letter.

Honoured S^{r}

In my last, by yor secret., May the 31th, (48,) I exprest my full closing with the contents of yo^{rs} dated May 28th, new stile. By letters from the Gouern^{r} of the Massachusets, I am since informed that he had rec^{d} yo^{rs} of Aprill the 3^{d} & May the 24th, that with much content he intertaines yor motion for a meeting & treaty att Conneticut, & vppon a retourne from the Gouern^{r} of Plimmouth will more fully satisfie. In the meane tyme, I shall offer to yor consideration wheather by waye of preparation it may not conduce to a more speedy & comfortable setling of things, if you thinke fitt to admit Mr. Wiłł. Westerhowse to open his cause & speake in his owne defence. Heatherto I suppose all intercourse hath bynne by messengers or letters, wherein there may be somthing mistaken or somthing omitted wch might cleere or mittigate the offence or censure; if, therefore, yow please to graunte him, by yor lett^{r} to mee, or otherwise, as shall seeme best to yor selfe, a warrant or safe conduct to come to the Manhataes, to stay there a conuenient tyme, & againe thence to retourne in safetie, without molestatiō, either by land or watter, that hee may expresse & open the grownds of his former proceedings & present hopes to receiue a milder issue, (in a cause soe weighty & neerelie concerning him,) then the former sentence & executiō importe, I shall aduise him in that waye to attend yow with his first conueniencie. I desire yo[r] answere, but to preuent mistakes shall assure yow, that though vppon different apprehensions yow for the present refuse to heare or treate in this matter, yet on my ꝑte it shall neither hinder nor cast any new difficulties vppon the meeting ꝑpounded. I rest,

Yo[rs] in all offices of neighbourlie correspondence,

Theo: Eaton.

Newhauen in New Engl. June the
20th, 1648. st. vet.

O.

Governor Stuyvesant to Governor Eaton.

The answere.

Honoured S[r]

Yo[rs] of June the 20th, st. vet., I rec[d], & ꝑceiue that my ꝑpositions for a meeting att Conneticut are well accepted both by yo[r] selfe & the worthy Gouern[r] Winthrop. In his to me I vnderstand the tyme will be aboute the middle of Sept[r]. I shall further entreate yow if it may stand any waye with yo[r] conueniencie, that the s[d] meeting may be aboute the 20th of Aug[st], ould stile, in respect o[r] shipping will presentlie after be ready to goe for o[r] natiue countrie, and I should be very glad by the first opportunitie to giue accompt to my Lords the Estates Generall of my ꝑceedings with yow, & shall then haue opportunitie of sending one expresse to my s[d] Lords, otherwise I shall haue noe opportunitie till the next summer. And whereas yow are pleased to write concerning my countrieman, Wiłł. Westerhowse, that he may haue free admissiō heere, without molestatiō, either by land or watter, I shall desire yow will please to excuse me therein, in respect I cannot ꝑmit to come heere without questioning him for his contempt of the souereigne justice of o[r] natiue land in his disobeying theyre established orders; but if hee hath any thing to speake to me, I doubt not but with the ꝑmissiō of God to make him an answere att Conneticut, & soe S[r], for present I shall take my leaue & rest,

Yo[rs] in all reall offices of loue,

Pet: Styvesant.

Fort New Amsterdam in New Netherlands,
July the 8th, 1648. st. no.

P.

Governor Eaton to Governor Stuyvesant.

Mr. Eaton's answere concerning the Comissioners being sent ouer land by one expresse.

Honoured S[r]

I vnderstand from the Gouern[r] of the Massachusets that he hath written by a vessell bownd to Vir[ginia] and that lett[r] may possible be with yow before this came to my hands, yett considering the conueyance by s[ea] is vncertaine & somtymes slowe, I thought fitting to send an expresse that yow may order occasions accordinglie. I haue with my vtmost indeauor recommended yo[r] ppositiō that there might be a meeting, to settle peace vppon due considerations & vppon a firme bottome, & did desire that the place & tyme might suit yo[r] conueniencie, the Gouern[r] of Conneticut did in all respects fullie concurre, but it seemes Mr. Bradforde & the comission[rs] for the Massachusets haue other pressing occasions, w[ch] they cannot breake through, for that the meeting must necessarilie be deferred till the Spring or till the middle of June, but wheather sooner or then, (if the Lord will,) I shall readilie attend it. In the meane tyme, (referring former questions to a due consideratiō in the fittest seasō,) I shall walke with yow in all wayes of righteousnes, peace & neighbourlie respect, & shall rest,

Yo[r] lo: friend,

Theo: Eaton.

Newhauen, Aug. 4th, (48) st. vet.

Q.

Governor Stuyvesant to Governor Eaton.

Honoured S[r]

Yo[rs] of the 4th of August, by yo[r] messenger, I rec[d], togeather with 2 from Mr. Winthrop, of one by Mr. Pebles, the other by the man yow sent, wherein I vnderstand of the differring the meeting vntill the next yeare, through some indisposition in Mr. Bradforde. I shall therefore recommend vnto yow that in the interim there may be all neighbourlie & mutuall intercourse of friendship between vs, & noe incroaching vppone one anothers pretended right, vpon any pretences whatsoeuer, but that things may remaine in the same state as they are, vntill wee shall come to a friendlie, iust and faire agitation. I shall likewise informe yow that yor intertainement of my countrieman, Will. Westerhowse, amongst yow is not only dangerous, but may proue destructiue to yo^r^selues & the other plantations in his vnderhand selling of gunnes & powder, for I haue sufficient testimonie of one of ours that bought 50 gunnes oute of his ship & being questioned, (by our court heere,) for it, confessed it, & that he sawe 8 or 9 chests more of gunnes aborde; and, as I am likewise in pte informed, sould one of yor towne (who vseth to trade) some 50 more, so that by computatiō there was aboute some fiue or six hundred gunnes aborde the ship purposelie for that damnable trade with the Indians. This I am sure of; there was taken oute of the ship, (after she was heere,) some 500li of powder in brandwine caske, besides his ships store. Soe much I thought good to giue yow a touch of, that yow may doe therein as yow in yor wisdom shall thinke conuenient. Gouert intends to come amongst yow to purge himselfe of those things obiected against him. Whereas of late there are two fled from our ptes, the one of them by name James Turner, a squint eyde fellowe aboute 35 or 40 yeares of age, the other likewise a well sett fellow by name James Hallet, aboute the same age, I shall request your asistance in apprehending them if in yor ptes, & that they may be sent heather; I shall paye all charges, & be ready to doe the like vppon any like occasion, & rest

Yo^r^ assured friend,

Pet: Styvesant.

August the 20th, 1648. st. no.

R.

Governor Eaton to Governor Stuyvesant.

Honoured S^r^

Vppon the receipt of yo^rs^ I sent o^r^ marshall to search for & apprehend all suspected strangers, particularlie such as yow had described. Two were brought; the one vppon certificate from Stamforde was presentlie cleered, the other pued to be James Turner, an Englishman and squint eyed; him I sent by sea in a pinnace whereof Jeremy How, mentioned in my letter dated August 28th, st. vet. I desired further light with due proofe, concerning Mr. Westerhowse his trade for gunnes, powder, to whom both of yo[rs] & ours he sould those 100 gunnes in 2 pcells, & wheather they be come into the Indians hands & by what meanes, that I may call him to an accompte for what is past & stop the waye of a trade soe mischeiuous for the future. I haue entreated your Secret[ry] that the proofe may be the more full & conuincing, because Mr. Westerhowse being questioned by the comission[rs] doth denye that he brought any considerable number of gunnes with him, much more that he hath sould according to the importe of the charge.

By yo[rs] of the 7th of Octob[r], 1648, st. no., which vppon my retourne from Plimmouth I rec[d] by yo[r] secret., I perceiue that neither my letter nor the prisoner were deliuered att the Manhataes, for which I shall call Jeremy Howe to accompte. In the meane tyme yow may rest assured that I was as reall & carefull in apprehending & retourning the fugitiue as I could haue bynne had any of the English collonies bynne interressed. Concerning Gouert Lookomans trading with the Indians & carriage towards the English, I haue to himself exprest my thoughts before yo[r] secret., & shall leaue him to yo[r] justice: If Samuell Goodenhowsen proue reallie indebted att the Manhataes, and that through his defaulte Gouert Lookoman as suertie susteine damage, I shall without referrence to other questions afforde him iust asistance; but if it be only a question aboute goods brought to Newhauen, &c., it will fall vnder due consideratiō att the meeting ppownded, w[ch] meeting the comission[rs] desire to prepare & further, according to the tennour of theyre letter heere inclosed, w[ch] they haue entreated me to conuey, & from me they will expect a retourne. If therefore yow please, either by this messenger whom I purposelie send to attend yow therein, or by some other conueyance, with yo[r] first to retourne answere to the pticulars, I shall imparte the same to the other collonies.

As one that desireth by all just meanes to follow peace with all men but especiallie with a Christ: natiō, both yow and mee, (though all questions be fairelie composed) may haue exercise enough with the wilde natiues, who being ouer plentifullie furnished with gunnes, powder and shott, are apt to be iniurious, but if they finde vs diuided and att difference, they will growe insolent & full of puocations, but I shall not inlarge. I haue rec[d] a testimonie of yo[r] loue & respect which with due thankefulnes I accept, and shall improue the first opportunitie to make a more reall retourne, in the meane tyme I rest,

Yo[rs] in all offices of loue,

Theo: Eaton.

Newhauen in New Engl: this 9th of Octob[r], 1648. st: vet:

Vppon the opportunitie of soe safe & speedie conueiance, as by this gentelman Ensigne Baxter, I thought I might spare the sending of an expresse messenger, but I still desire yow will be pleased with your first conuenience to retourne me an answere to the particulars in the comission^{rs} lett^{r}, soe I take leaue, resting,

Yo^{rs}, T. E.

S.

Governor Eaton to Governor Stuyvesant.

Honoured S^{r},

I long since acquainted the rest of the com̃iss^{rs} for the vnited English collonies with yor answere to [ ] but the winter season hath so shut up all passages that till now of late could not retourne theire thoughts. In theyre names I am now desired to certifie that your answere in diuerse particular be not to theire satisfaction, yett the [y are] not only willing but desirous of a meeting that all differences and grieuances may be heard, considered & satisfied, accord[ing] to righteousnes, & a iust wholesome peace, by all due meanes setled & confirmed, betwixt these English collonies & the neighbour plantacions vnder the Dutch gouerm^{t}, only whereas yow desired the presence & helpe of the gouernours of the Massachusets and Plimmouth, to weigh and arbitrate &^{c}: (they being both aged & vnfit for long land journeys, the com̃issioners, (in referrence to them) thought Boston would be the fittest place, & for the tyme they are willing to the vtmost, to suit your occasions, and doe therefore consent that the meeting be the last weeke in June, or first weeke in July, according to the English accompt, as yourselfe shall please to appoint, declaring yor mynde in due season, that I may certifie the com̃issioners thereof; sooner it cannot bee, in referrence to other publique occasions of the collonies, & they would not vnnecessarilie deferr it as hoping (through Gods blessing) wee may all reap the comfortable fruites of such a meeting & treaty, yett if the last weeke in July will better answere yor occasions, vppon notice I conceiue the com̃ission^{rs} will agree & order according. In the meane tyme the com̃ission^{rs} desire me to informe yow that they cannot submit to the taxes, recognitions & other burdens imposed att the Manhataes; if they be not speedilie taken of, yow may not blame them if they prouide due remedy against them; this is all I haue from them to ꝑpound, but since I hearde from the com̃ission^{rs} by other conueiance I haue rec^{d}

informatiõ of the death of our worthy & much honoured friend Mr. Jo: Winthrop, late gouernr of the Massachusets collonye; he departed this lyfe the 26th of March. I am assured he is a rich gainer by his remoue, the losse is ours, and accordinglie I beleue his death will be lamented through all the collonies. In referrence to this vnexpected & afflicting prouidence, I desire to vnderstand yor mynde, whom you will choose in his roome to compose & arbitrate differences, or how the meeting may be carried on to answere our ioynt aymes & hopes, thus with my due respects I rest, Yors in all

Theo: Eaton.

Newhauen in New Engl: the 11th of Ap:
1649. st: veter.

T.

Governor Stuyvesant to Governor Eaton.

Worthy Sr,

I hope yow have receiued myne in answere to yors of the 17th of Febr: & whereas yow are pleased to write concerning the answere of the comissioners to myne, first that they are vnsatisfied in diuerse pticulars, yett willing & desirous of a meeting, that all things may be composed in a neighbourlie & iust waye, I hope I haue giuen yow and them sufficient satisfactiõ of my readines therein, & shall willinglie attend all due meanes for the accomplishing it, wch they & myselfe conceiue may be effected by our ioynt meeting; and vppon some considerations is intended att Boston. I suppose my inabilitie to trauaile soe farre by land is well knowne to yow & them; and vnderstanding by the latter pte of yor letter of the death of that euer honoured & worthy gent: Mr. Winthrop, I doe reallie condole with yow, we being all of vs in these ptes participants in the sad losse of one whose wisdom and integritie might haue done much in composing matters betweene vs, & shall therefore referre to yow and theyre considerations wheather or noe the meeting may not as well be att Conneticut, according to the tyme appointed (& vppon notice thereof shall willinglie attend it,) if not I shall neuerthelesse giue yow a visit att Newhauen, where wee may haue some speech betwene vs indeauouring to remoue all mistakes or misapprehensions betwene vs, Sr, I rest, Yor assured friend,

Pet: Styvesant.

Fort New Amsterdam in New Netherlands,
May the 4th, 1649.

U.

Governor Eaton to Governor Stuyvesant.

Honoured S^r,

Yours of the May the 4th by Mr. Allerton I receiued; in both yow expresse att least a purpose to call Joseph Scot to an accompte aboute the cowe, &c. I hope yow will prouide that the man at Stamforde, who bought the cowe after she had bynne condemned in that courte, may haue speedy & iust satisfactiō, with due allowance for dammage, but what place Toby Feekes held vnder you att Greenwich, what order he had first to deteine and then to send awaye the cowe, after judgement in the English jurisdictiō, without satisfaction to the pty interressed, & how justice may haue a due course hereafter in these neighbour jurisdictions, without disturbance & offence, is of higher consideratiō then the vallew of the debt or price of the cowe.

Your answere to the commissioners letter from Plimouth, in diuerse pticulars did not satisfie them, I therein gaue yow there owne words, yet they were willing & desirous of a meeting, that all differences being considered & duly satisfied, a just peace betwixt the English collonies and neighbour plantations vnder the Dutch gouerment, might be continued & confirmed, only in referrence to Mr. Winthrop & Mr. Bradforde, whose presence & helpe to heare & compose your selfe propounded and desired, the commissioners thought Boston would be the fittest place for meeting, not att all questioning yor abilitie to trauell att least by sea, to soe neere a port, but I haue sent the contents of yor last letter to the Massachusets, & shall retourne theyre answere with my first conueniencie. I haue spoken to Mr. Allerton to whose informatiō yow referred me, aboute the customs or recognitions, with other burthens imposed att the Manhataes; from him I vnderstand they are all taken of, & the hand taken downe, att least that all in the English collonies may anchor where they themselues see good, in referrence to theyre safetie and conuenience, whence I conceiue that in all respects they shall finde the Manhataes, both in theyre trade there, & in theyre passage to and froe, as open & free as the English harbours haue hitherto bynne to the Dutch, but whether Mr. Allertons informatiō or my apprehension be free from errour and mistake I knowe not, & may hereafter possiblie be questioned, if therefore your selfe had been pleased in a matter of this weight to haue certified what is concluded & setled in the former pticulars, vnder yor owne hand, that all the English collonies might fully vnderstand theyre libertie, or what will be expected from them, it would certainelie byn more to satisfactiō.

Lastley whereas yow are pleased to offer a visit att Newhauen for conferrence, & to remoue mistakes, &c. though in referrence to ꝑsonall respects, I am free for all friendlie offices, wheather att Manhataes or Newhauen, yet remembring what hath passed not only formerlie in Mounsʳ Kiefts tyme, but more latelie since yoʳ selfe haue managed that publique trust, I shall offer it to yoʳ consideratiō wheather after a publique treatye hath bin soe often ꝑpounded by yow, and by vs accepted, to compose differences wherein other collonies are interressed, it be on your ꝑte conuenient, or comly on myne, to resolue it (without theyre satisfactiō or consent) into a priuate visit & conference att Newhauen, and in referrence to offences heere, whether you be prepared, (according to what shall appeare & be proued just) to giue satisfaction to the questions yow know in discharge of my duty to the crowne of England, my ingagement to this jurisdiction, & in answere to the complaints of some ꝑticular ꝑsons, I shall be necessitated to propownd & presse, or wheather without such satisfaction we may propablie expect that our meeting att Newhauen should ꝑduce any comfortable fruites or effects. I hope yow will neither misconsture nor censure this open and plaine dealing, wherein I still ꝑfesse my only aime is to further a due setling of peace & amitie, and soe I shall rest,

Yours in all offices of loue,

The: Eaton.

Newhauen in New Engl:
Aprˡˡ the 30ᵗʰ, 1649, st. vet.

V.

Governor Stuyvesant to Governor Eaton.

To Mr. Eaton.

Sʳ,

Yours of the 30ᵗʰ of Aprˡˡ, stil: vetere, I receiued & receiuing a lettʳ from Heemstate after the vpsealing of my last vnto yow, I sent it yow by Mr. Allerton, togeather with a discharge to Joseph Scot from the atturney of the man att Stamford.

And whereas yow are pleased to write againe concerning the commissioners being vnsatisfied in diuerse particulars in myne to them, I hope they will neither expect or require more from me then what I may well answere to the state I serue.

Concerning Mr. Allertons informing yow of the taking of the recognitiõ of goods imported heere (from New England) by your countriemen, yow may please to vnderstand that the ten ꝑ centum formerlie demanded and paid, it is for present suspended & not to be demanded or paid till further order, and allthough vppon very good considerations there was a signe erected for to anchor within, yet being now blowne downe by accident shall be no more sett vp, allthough vppon request I neuer denyde any of yor countriemen libertie to anchor where they pleased after they had shewne theyre obedience to the said order.

Concerning my writing vnto yow aboute my intentions of giueing yow a visit att Newhauen in case that the commissioners did not meete at Conneticut, and that in reference to ꝑsonall respects yow were free for all friendlie offices, wheather att Manhataes or Newhauen, yet remembring things past in the tyme of my predecess^r^, & what hath bynne done by my order, yow referre to my consideratiõ the inconueniences that may thereby arise, S^r^, I haue no reason to miscontrue or censure your open & plaine dealing therein, but to embrace it with a friendlie acknowledgem^t^ of yor wisdom, for I suppose it is well knowne vnto yow that in relation of my duty to the state I serue, I cannot answere those ends you may be necessitated to vrge & presse, and shall therefore further attend yor answere from the comissioners, in the interim shall rest,

Yo^r^ lo: friend,

May the 26th, (49.) Pet: Styvesant.

W.

Governor Eaton to Governor Stuyvesant.

Honoured S^r^,

Yours of the 26th May, 1649, st: no: I haue rec^d^ & since that another dated June concerning fugitiues, of whose arriuall in these ꝑtes I yett heare nothing, but haue g[iven] order to our marshall to enquire and apprehend them.

The comission^rs^ cannot but conceiue & conclude, that the states you serue will approue & commend a just carriage and correspondencie towards all the English collonies, & certainelie in such passes of righteousnes the state of England will direct & walke with them; we haue formerlie protested against Mouns^r^ Kiefts iniurious course att Deleware & else where, as yow haue bin informed; our right there is well knowne (not only to the English but) to the Duch & Sweeds & Indians. Wee neuer claimed, nor doe we desire to posesse a foote of land to which yow can shew any iust title, but we may neither lose nor let fall the English interest & claime in and to what we haue purchased & paid for in those ptes; had yow bin pleased to haue met the comission[rs] att Boston, these & other greiuances which (I need not mynde yow of) might haue bin dulie debated, & by such a referrence as your selfe haue ppounded, justice issued. The comission[rs] for the Massachusets haue latelie certified me that with conueniencie they cannot meet at Conneticut, besides Mr. Bradford his indisposition to trauaile, of w[ch] I wrote formerlie; Mr. Dudley, one of the present comissioners, is aboue 70 yeares of age, and vnfit for such a iourney.

By yo[rs] of the 26th of May, I vnderstand that the 10 p cent. formerlie required & taken for good[s] imported, is only for the present suspended, it may then be reimposed or increased att pleasure, which yow know cannot satisfie; that the hand erected for anchoring is downe by accident, and shall be sett vp noe more, but I desire if yow please to be further certified, wheather the English in theyre trading att the Manhataes, and in theyre passing by to and from Deleware, Virginia, &c. may expect a full freedome from all recognition, imposition or charge, by what name soeuer called, both for goods imported and exported, or what duties, restraints or confiscations they must paye and submit vnto, & vppon what grownds, that the merchant seing his waye, may walke safelie, and the comission[rs] may order theyre counsells and courses accordinglie, as they wrote to yow from Plimouth, Septemb[r] 16th, 1648. So S[r], I take leaue & rest,

Yo[rs] in all offices of loue,
Theo: Eaton.

Newhauen in New Engl: June the 7th, 1649, st: vet:

X.

Governor Stuyvesant to Governor Eaton.

The answere.

S[r],

Yo[rs] of the 7th of June I rec[d] and wonder much att Mr. Allertons neglect in shewing yow the letter and discharge concerning the cowe; assone as he retournes I shall speake with him aboute it, & then write to yow againe.

Concerning yo[r] ꝑtest against my predecessour, Mouns[r] Kieft, aboute some passages att the Sowth riuer, called Deleware, I doubt not but what he did was vppon warrantable grownds, and made yow a sufficient answere, but concerning our right there, and of my intentions of maintaining it, I haue allready written to the gouernours of the Massachusets & Plimmouth, who I suppose will acquaint the comissioners with it.

Whereas yow write to me concerning yo[r] countriemens trading heere, and passing to and from Virginia and Deleware, &c. I haue allready written & graunted as much as I can or dare doe, vntill I haue further order from my souereignes and masters, and am not to be responsible to any but them, nor regulated by any but them.

Your assured friend,

Pet: Styvesant.

July the 2[d], (1649,) st: no:

INDEX.

www.ingramcontent.com/pod-product-compliance
Lightning Source LLC
LaVergne TN
LVHW021243110826
845150LV00002B/395

* 9 7 8 1 4 2 5 5 6 1 2 3 9 *